THE ROUGH GUIDE TO
WALES

ROUGH GUIDES

This ninth edition updated by
Tim Burford, Norm Longley and James Stewart

P9-EGM-569

Contents

INTRODUCTION 4

Where to go	8	Things not to miss	12
When to go	10	Itineraries	22
Author picks	11		

BASICS 24

Getting there	25	Festivals and events	38
Getting around	27	Sports and outdoor activities	39
Accommodation	31	Alternative, New Age and green Wales	45
Food and drink	34	Travel essentials	46
The media	36		

THE GUIDE 52

1 Cardiff and southeast Wales	52	5 The Dee Valley and around	302
2 Southwest Wales	134	6 Snowdonia and the Llŷn	330
3 The Brecon Beacons and Powys	194	7 The north coast and Anglesey	386
4 The Cambrian coast	250		

CONTEXTS 428

History	429	Film	457
Modern Welsh nationalism	442	Books	459
Natural history of Wales	445	Welsh	463
Music in Wales	451		

SMALL PRINT & INDEX 468

Introduction to
Wales

Wales, a small country on the rocky fringe of western Europe, punches well above its weight when it comes to looks, attractions and visitor appeal. Barack Obama praised its "extraordinary beauty, wonderful people and great hospitality", while *National Geographic* magazine named Pembrokeshire the world's second-best coastal destination, and its coastal path second among the world's top ten long-distance paths. Even the national football team enjoyed success (and won hearts) at the Euro 2016 championships. This is a country that remains utterly authentic in an increasingly homogenized world, and while it's happy to keep up with the best new trends – witness an ever more sophisticated hotel scene and a raft of gourmet restaurants displaying real creativity – Wales stays always true to itself.

It's not all about the **landscapes**, either: the solid little market towns and ancient castles reward repeated visits as much as the stirring mountains, gorgeous valleys and rugged coastline. The **culture**, too, is compelling, whether Welsh- or English-language, Celtic or industrial, ancient or coolly contemporary. Even its low-key profile serves it well: while the tourist pound has reduced parts of Ireland and Scotland to Celtic pastiche, Wales remains gritty enough to be authentic, and diverse enough to remain endlessly fascinating.

Recent years have seen a huge and dizzying upsurge in Welsh **self-confidence**, a commodity no longer so dependent on comparison with its big and powerful neighbour England. Popular culture – especially music and film – has contributed to this, as did the creation in 1999 of the National Assembly, the first all-Wales tier of government for six hundred years. After centuries of subjugation, the national spirit is undergoing a remarkable renaissance. The ancient symbol of the country, *y ddraig goch* or the **red dragon**, seen fluttering on flags everywhere you go, is waking up from what seems like a very long slumber.

As soon as you cross the border from England, the differences in appearance, attitude and culture between the two countries are obvious. Wales shares many physical and

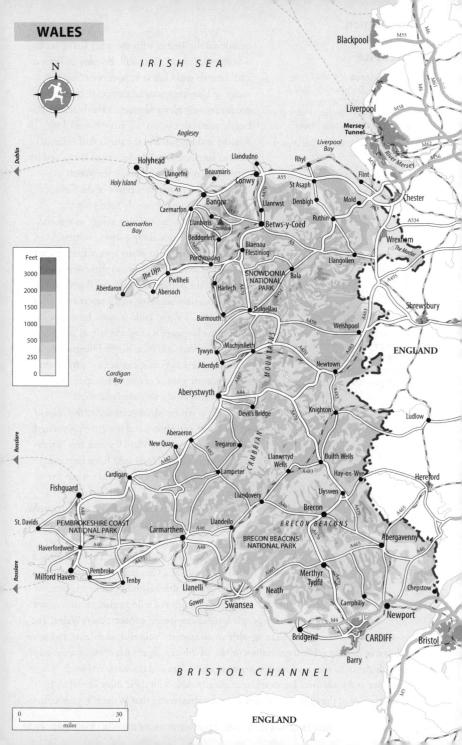

FACT FILE

• With an **area** of 8000 square miles (20,800 square km), Wales is less than a sixth the size of England and a little larger than the American state of New Jersey.

• While Wales is part of the United Kingdom and – for now – a member state of the European Union, it also has its own devolved **Welsh Government**, responsible for certain local affairs.

• The **population** of Wales is just over three million, sixty percent of whom live in the southeastern corner of the country. One quarter of the population was born outside the country, the vast majority being migrants from England. Cardiff, the capital city, has a population of 358,000.

• As well as being the second-longest place name in the world, **Llanfairpwllgwyngyllgogery-chwyrndrobwllllantysi-liogogoch** was used in the cult 1968 sci-fi movie *Barbarella* starring Jane Fonda – it's the password to enter a secret resistance headquarters.

· **Lawn tennis** has its roots in Wales. Apparently, one Major Walter Clopton Wingfield was playing with a new-fangled India rubber ball in the gardens of Nantclwyd Hall, near Ruthin, in 1873. It bounced on grass, the major had a lightbulb moment and in 1874 patented the rules of a game he called "sphairistrike", ancient Greek for "the art of playing ball".

emotional similarities with the other Celtic lands – Scotland, Ireland, Cornwall, Brittany in France, and Asturias and Galicia in northwest Spain. A rocky and mountainous landscape, in hues of predominantly grey and green, a thinly scattered, largely rural population, a culture rooted deeply in folklore and legend, and the survival of a distinct, ancient language are all hallmarks of Wales and its sister countries. To visitors, it is the **Welsh language**, the strongest survivor of the Celtic tongues, that most obviously marks out the country, with tongue-twisting village names and bilingual signposts making a strong cultural statement. Everyone in Wales speaks English, but a 2016 government survey found that twenty percent of the population were also fluent in Welsh, that number rising to 25 percent for 16- to 25-year-olds. TV and radio stations broadcast in Welsh, the language is taught at school and restaurant menus are increasingly bilingual. As a visitor, any attempts to speak at least a fragment of the rich, earthy tones of one of Europe's oldest living languages will be warmly received.

Despite seven hundred years under the yoke of its far larger neighbour, and the growing strength of independence party Plaid Cymru, few Welsh nationalists call for a total split from England. Nevertheless, it causes great offence when the distinct nationality of Wales is blatantly disregarded or patronized. As a visitor you should avoid referring to England when you really mean Britain or the United Kingdom, and never say English when you mean Welsh: it is like calling a Kiwi an Aussie or a Canadian an American.

Although it is the wealth of prehistoric sites, crumbling castles and wild landscapes that draws visitors here in the first place, many people leave championing **contemporary Wales**. The cities and university towns are buzzing with an understated youthful confidence and sense of cultural optimism, while a generation or two of urban escapees has brought a curious cosmopolitanism to the small market towns of mid-Wales and the west. Although conservative and traditional forces still sporadically clash with these more liberal and anarchic strands of thought, there's an unquestionable feeling that Wales is big enough,

both physically and emotionally, to embrace a number of diverse influences. Perhaps most importantly, Welsh culture is underpinned by an iconoclastic democracy that contrasts starkly with the establishment-obsessed class divisions of England. The Welsh character is famously endowed with a **musicality**, lyricism, introspection and sentimentality that produces far better bards and singers than it does lords and masters. And Welsh culture is undeniably inclusive: anything from a sing-song in the pub to the grandiose theatricality of an **eisteddfod** involves everyone – including any visitor eager to learn and join in.

Where to go

Just 160 miles from north to south and 50 miles from east to west, Wales is smaller than Massachusetts and only half the size of the Netherlands. Most of its inhabitants are packed into the south – if you're after wide empty spaces, head for north or mid-Wales.

PREHISTORIC AND LEGENDARY WALES

Whether walking through a dew-soaked field to some mysteriously inscribed **standing stone**, or catching the afternoon sun as it illuminates the entrance to a cliff-top **burial chamber**, exploring Wales' prehistoric sites is thoroughly rewarding. At all but a few of the most popular, the bleating of sheep will be the only sound to break the contemplative silence of these spiritual places.

Prehistoric sites litter the country. **Hut circles** defensively set atop windswept hills attest to a rugged hand-to-mouth pre-Celtic existence dating back four or five thousand years, while stone circles, intricately carved **monoliths** and finely balanced capstones set at crucial points on **ancient pathways** suggest the more spiritual life led by the priestly druids. Britain's greatest **druidic** centre was Anglesey, and the island is still home to many of Wales' best prehistoric sites, including the splendid chambers of Barclodiad y Gawres and Bryn Celli Ddu. Elsewhere, numerous standing stones and circles can be found on the mysterious slopes of the Mynydd Preseli in Pembrokeshire and in the area around Harlech in north Wales. Many sites take their names from great figures in Celtic history and folklore, such as Arthur and Merlin (Myrddin in Welsh); legends abound to connect much of the landscape with ancient tales.

Like most capital cities, **Cardiff** is atypical of the rest of the country. The majority of the national institutions are based here, not least the National Assembly, housed amid the massive regeneration projects of **Cardiff Bay**. The city is also home to the National Museum and St Fagans National History Museum – both excellent introductions to the character of the rest of Wales – and the superb Principality Stadium, which stages huge sporting events and blockbuster gigs. The only other centres of appreciable size are loud-and-lairy **Newport** and breezy, resurgent **Swansea**, lying respectively to the east and west of the capital. All three cities grew as ports, mainly exporting millions of tons of coal and iron from the **Valleys**, where fiercely proud industrial communities were built up in the thin strips of land between the mountains.

Much of Wales' appeal lies outside the larger towns, where there is ample evidence of the conflict that has shaped the country's development. There are more castles per mile than anywhere else in Europe, from the hard little stone keeps of the early Welsh princes to Edward I's incomparable series of thirteenth-century fortresses at **Rhuddlan**, **Conwy**, **Beaumaris**, **Caernarfon** and **Harlech**, and grandiose Victorian piles where grouse were the only enemy. Fortified residences served as the foundation for a number of the stately homes that dot the country, but many castles were deserted and remain dramatically isolated on rocky knolls, most likely on spots previously occupied by prehistoric communities. Passage graves and **stone circles** offer a more tangible link to the pre-Roman era, when the priestly order of druids ruled over early Celtic peoples, and later religious monuments such as the great ruined abbeys of **Valle Crucis**, **Tintern** and **Strata Florida** lend a gaunt grandeur to their surroundings.

Yet for all the appeal of its castles, megaliths or cultural highpoints – Dylan Thomas' home at **Laugharne**, for example – many people find that the human monuments of Wales are upstaged by the beauty of the countryside. From the green lowland meadows and river valleys to the inhospitable heights of the moors and mountains, Wales is a spectacular place. The rigid backbone of the **Cambrian mountains** terminates in the peaks of **Snowdonia** – rapidly transforming into the adventure capital of Britain – and the

LAND OF SONG

"Praise the Lord! We are a musical nation," intones the Rev. Eli Jenkins in Dylan Thomas' masterpiece, *Under Milk Wood*. It's a reputation of which the Welsh feel deservedly proud. Although the image of plucky miners singing their way to the pithead was largely a dewy-eyed, Hollywood-born fabrication, Wales does make a great deal more noise, and makes it a great deal more tunefully, than most other small countries.

The **male voice choirs**, many struggling to survive in the aftermath of the decimation of the coal industry that spawned them, are the best-known exemplars of Welsh singing, but traditions go back much further, to the bards and minstrels of the Celtic age. Wales continues to produce wonderful **musical talent**; from big-lunged legends Sir Tom Jones and Dame Shirley Bassey to experimental musicians like The Velvet Underground's John Cale and more recent champions of Welsh culture including Manic Street Preachers, Cerys Matthews and Super Furry Animals.

angular ridges of the **Brecon Beacons**. Both are national parks, and both offer superb walking country. A third national park follows the **Pembrokeshire Coast**, with its golden strands separated by rocky bluffs. Much of the rest of the coast remains unspoilt, with long sweeps of fine sand and the occasional traditional British seaside resort; highlights include the often-overlooked **Cambrian coast** and the glorious **Gower peninsula**, the first region in Britain designated an Area of Outstanding Natural Beauty. The entire coast is now linked by the 870-mile **Wales Coast Path**; be sure to spend some time wandering its length.

When to go

The **climate** (see p.47) in Wales is **temperate**, with summers rarely getting hot and nowhere but the tops of mountain ranges ever getting very cold, even in midwinter. Temperatures vary little, unless you're near the mountains, that is; Llanberis, at the foot of Snowdon, is always a few degrees cooler than Caernarfon, seven miles away, and gets doused with more than twice as much rainfall. For much of the summer, Wales – particularly the coast – can be bathed in sun, and between June and September the Pembrokeshire coast, washed by the Gulf Stream, can be as warm as anywhere in Britain. That said, the bottom line, year-round, is that the weather is predictably unpredictable. May might be wet and grey one year and gloriously sunny the next, and the same goes for the autumn months – November stands just as much chance of being crisp and clear as being foggy and grim. However, if you're planning to lie on a beach, or want to camp in the dry, you'll need to go in **summer** (between June and September); book your accommodation as far in advance as possible for late July and August. For a chance of reasonably good weather with fewer **crowds** go in April, May, September or October. When it comes to **outdoor pursuits** you'll find June to October the warmest and driest for walking and climbing.

Author picks

Our authors have explored every corner of Wales over several editions of this guide in order to uncover the very best the country has to offer. Here are some of their favourite things to see and do.

Finest scramble Snowdon is splendid, but the north ridge of Tryfan (see p.346) gives wonderful exposure and views, and the scramble up borders on rock-climbing.

Better slate than never Genuine and gritty among its verdant surroundings, Blaenau Ffestiniog (see p.364) has put its slate-mining past to brilliant use, offering thrilling biking, zip wires and underground trampolines.

Sublime views Head to Beaumaris (see p.415) and settle down with a coffee to admire the superb view across the Menai Strait to the Snowdonian mountains.

Skeletal grandeur Ride Newport's Transporter Bridge (see p.89), "A giant with the might of Hercules and the grace of Apollo", as it was described when it opened in 1906.

Magnificent birdlife Watch red kites swoop for their daily feed at Gigrin Farm near Rhayader (see p.230).

Buy a pint from Bessie Spend an evening at the quirky *Dyffryn Arms* (see p.193) in bucolic Cwm Gwaun.

End of the world The Llŷn peninsula excels in escapism, be it the panorama from the summit of Tre'r Ceiri (see p.384) or the lovely seaside village of Aberdaron (see p.380).

Coastal wonder Savour the glorious views of Worms Head (see p.131) and Rhossili Bay (see p.131) from the head of the Gower peninsula.

Proud heritage Learn about Wales' industrial past at evocative sites from the Llechwedd Slate Caverns in Blaenau Ffestiniog (see p.365) to the Rhondda Heritage Park in Trehafod (see p.114).

Our author recommendations don't end here. We've flagged up our favourite places – a perfectly sited hotel, an atmospheric café, a special restaurant – throughout the Guide, highlighted with the ★ symbol.

FROM TOP MENAI SUSPENSION BRIDGE; HIKER DESCENDING GLYDER FACH TOWARDS TRYFAN

27

things not to miss

It's not possible to see everything that Wales has to offer in one trip – and we don't suggest you try. What follows, in no particular order, is a selective taste of the country's highlights, including beautiful beaches, outstanding national parks, thrilling outdoor activities and unforgettable urban experiences. All highlights are colour-coded by chapter and have a page reference to take you straight into the Guide, where you can find out more.

1

1 CONWY
Page 403

One of north Wales' finest walled medieval towns, with more than two hundred listed buildings and a superb castle, Conwy also exudes small-town charm.

2 CADAIR IDRIS
Page 281

The dominant mountain of southern Snowdonia, the magnificent Cadair Idris is chock-full of classic glacial features.

3 THE GOWER PENINSULA
Page 126

Beautiful beaches, open moorland, pretty villages and even a castle or two: there's a reason why this gorgeous stretch was designated Britain's first Area of Outstanding Natural Beauty.

4

5

6

7

 4 SURF SNOWDONIA
Page 409

What do you do with a disused HEP plant lying in a beautiful valley? If you're Welsh, you create the world's first man-made surfing point-break, naturally.

 5 WACKY LLANWRTYD WELLS
Page 225

Bog snorkelling, the Man versus Horse Marathon and the Real Ale Wobble bring a wonderful sense of fun to this quiet corner of mid-Wales.

 6 FFESTINIOG RAILWAY
Page 370

Of Wales' many "great little trains", the Ffestiniog Railway, winding down through the Snowdonia mountains, is one of the very best.

 7 ST DAVIDS CATHEDRAL
Page 179

The heart of Welsh spirituality, St Davids Cathedral is at Wales' westernmost extremity and has drawn pilgrims for a millennium and a half.

 8 MAWDDACH TRAIL
Page 294

Ride or walk this easy trail beside Wales' finest estuary, the Mawddach, crossed by the 2253ft rail and foot bridge into Barmouth.

9 CARREG CENNEN CASTLE
Page 148

The most romantic ruin in Wales, Carreg Cennen Castle sits in glorious isolation amid pastures grazed by Welsh longhorns.

10 PEMBROKESHIRE COAST PATH
Page 159

If you don't want to tackle the full 187 miles in one big push, break it up into a series of day-walks and enjoy some of Wales' wildest coastal scenery.

11 SNOWDON
Page 354

Hike one of half a dozen demanding tracks to the top of Wales' highest mountain – or take the train and sup a beer at the summit café.

12 TRYFAN
Page 346

Fabulous views along the Ogwen Valley in the wilds of Snowdonia are just one of the rewards for making the arduous ascent of Tryfan.

13 EDWARD I'S IRON RING
Page 405

The might of the thirteenth-century English monarchy found its fullest expression in this chain of virtually impregnable fortresses, now evocative hollow shells.

14 CARDIFF
Page 57

With its brilliant mishmash of old and new architecture, rugby, rollicking nightlife – and, of course, a castle – the capital couldn't be more Welsh.

15 PORTMEIRION
Page 373

The most audacious folly in Britain is even more eccentric during its annual arts extravaganza, Festival No. 6.

10

11

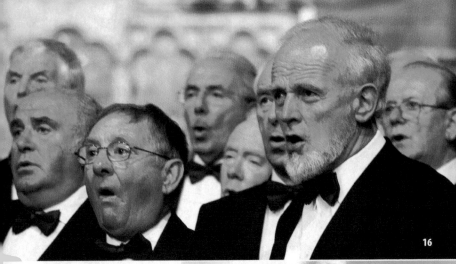

16 MALE VOICE CHOIRS
Page 116

Burly miners singing their hearts out at eisteddfodau may be a thing of the past, but Welsh male voice choirs still provide a poignant insight into this most musical of nations.

17 THE WYE VALLEY
Page 77

Soak up the pastoral beauty of this wonderful valley and the spectacular ruins of Tintern Abbey.

18 INDUSTRIAL HERITAGE
Page 106

The Valleys are the very heart of Wales' proud coal-mining past, nowhere seen better than at Blaenavon's Big Pit.

19 LLŶN PENINSULA
Page 375

A place of brilliant beaches, stirring walks and profound mysticism, the wellspring of the Welsh language offers pure escapism.

20 ABERGAVENNY'S FOOD
Page 218

Sample some of the best dishes Wales has to offer in this gastronomic hotspot or, better still, time your visit to coincide with September's food festival, among the best in Britain.

21 ZIP-WIRE MADNESS
Page 348

Europe's fastest zip wire, the world's longest zip wire and a crazy underground course for kids, all in Snowdonia.

17

18

22 ABERGLASNEY
Page 146

Rescued from near-terminal decay, these formal gardens in the Tywi Valley are a perfect counterpoint to the nearby National Botanic Garden of Wales.

23 MOUNTAIN BIKING
Page 42

Whether for pros or families, Wales now has some of Britain's finest single-track riding.

24 PRINCIPALITY STADIUM
Page 60

Although Wales' standing in international rugby fluctuates wildly, the game remains practically a religion here, never more so than when the national team is playing at Cardiff's awesome Principality Stadium.

25 LLANDUDNO
Page 396

North Wales' most genteel seaside resort, Llandudno spreads languidly around the bay beneath the ancient rock plug of the Great Orme.

26 BRECON BEACONS
Page 199

The rambling moors of the Brecon Beacons are perfect for wild, lonely walks with thundering waterfalls and limestone caverns as destinations.

27 HAY-ON-WYE
Page 221

Rub shoulders with the literati at the famed festival or just come along to enjoy superb secondhand-book shopping in this pretty riverside border town.

26

27

HARDBACKS 50ᴾ
PAPERBACKS 30ᴾ

Itineraries

Our Grand Tour is ideal for a first visit to Wales, sampling the best cities and towns, the country's industrial heritage and its breathtaking mountain and coastal scenery. Fans of Neolithic cromlechs, ruined abbeys and stately homes should follow our Historic Buildings itinerary, while the Active Wales options point you to a thrilling range of outdoor pursuits.

THE GRAND TOUR

If you've got the luxury of a fortnight and want to tick off Wales' acknowledged highlights, hit these.

❶ **Cardiff** Ground-breaking architecture, top-notch culture and blistering nightlife in the cool Welsh capital. **See p.57**

❷ **Blaenavon** South Wales' industrial heritage: the powerful Big Pit mining museum and the evocative ruins of the Ironworks. **See p.104**

❸ **Gower** Welsh natural splendour at its most stunning, the Gower peninsula boasts wide-open beaches, rocky bays and steep cliffs. **See p.126**

❹ **St Davids peninsula** Sample some of the finest sections of the Pembrokeshire Coast Path, and stay in delightful St Davids. **See p.179**

❺ **Cadair Idris** The folds of this fine mountain harbour old castles, churches and a steam railway, the Centre for Alternative Technology and the sublime Mawddach estuary. **See p.281**

❻ **Snowdonia** Hard-working narrow-gauge railways, slate-mining heritage and nuggety villages in inspiring mountain scenery. **See p.332**

❼ **Portmeirion** Enjoy the whimsical Italianate beauty of Clough Williams-Ellis' "home for fallen buildings". **See p.373**

❽ **Conwy and Llandudno** A domineering castle and ancient houses within an intact ring of walls make Conwy an essential stop, best

visited from Llandudno, with its grand seaside architecture and blustery walks on the Great Orme. **See p.403 & p.396**

❾ **Llangollen** Head inland to find a canal aqueduct, a heritage railway, a hilltop castle, an abbey ruin and the home of the Ladies of Llangollen all wedged into a bucolic valley. **See p.312**

HISTORIC BUILDINGS

Edward I's massive castles and the wonderful St Davids Cathedral are well known and widely covered; these equally fascinating monuments can be enjoyed in a visit of ten days or so.

❶ **Tintern Abbey** Admire the beautiful roofless ruin that inspired Wordsworth's poetry, by the placid River Wye. **See p.81**

❷ **Soar-y-Mynydd chapel** Wales' most remote chapel, in the wild countryside of Mynydd Eppynt. **See p.227**

❸ **Carreg Cennen** The most wonderfully located of all the native Welsh castles, high on a cliff. **See p.148**

❹ **Pentre Ifan** Wales' largest burial stone, with its 16ft-long top-stone precariously balanced on stocky legs. **See p.192**

❺ **Penrhyn Castle, Bangor** Old masters in a grandiose Victorian mansion that loves to show off its slate-mining wealth. **See p.411**

ABOVE FROM LEFT MAWDDACH RAIL BRIDGE; SOAR-Y-MYNYDD CHAPEL, NEAR LLANDOVERY

❻ Plas Mawr, Conwy A superb example of an Elizabethan townhouse. **See p.406**

❼ Plas Newydd, Llangollen Fascinating mock-Tudor bolt hole, once home to two aristocratic Anglo–Irish ladies. **See p.420**

❽ Erddig Hall, Wrexham This seventeenth-century pile is perhaps Wales' most intriguing stately home. **See p.309**

ACTIVE WALES

You'll enjoy that slice of bara brith or pint of Purple Moose all the more if you've earned it hiking, biking or surfing. Set aside around two weeks for a full-on activity holiday – longer if you want to tackle Offa's Dyke.

❶ Whitewater rafting: Cardiff Abundant thrills and spills on these superb man-made rapids. **See p.67**

❷ Surfing: Gower Suit up and surf some of the UK's finest waves among the bays and beaches of the glorious peninsula. **See p.130**

❸ Walking: Pembrokeshire Coast Path Spend a few hours or a few weeks exploring the gorgeous coves, windswept headlands and long beaches of this magical coastal walk. **See p.159**

❹ Coasteering: St Davids peninsula Jump off rocks into the sea, swim across bays and explore dramatic caves. **See p.181**

❺ Mine exploring: Corris Get kitted out with harness and headlamp and listen to real tales of mining life in an abandoned slate mine. **See p.286**

❻ Mountain biking: Coed y Brenin Among the very best of many fine places to ride off-road in Wales. **See p.293**

❼ Rock climbing: Llanberis Pass The ultimate mountain challenge in the home of Welsh rock climbing; some climbers engage guides from the nearby Plas y Brenin mountain centre. **See p.352 & p.345**

❽ Walking: Offa's Dyke Path It takes a couple of weeks to walk the whole of this classic 177-mile long-distance path, which largely follows the ancient earthwork along the English border. **See p.237**

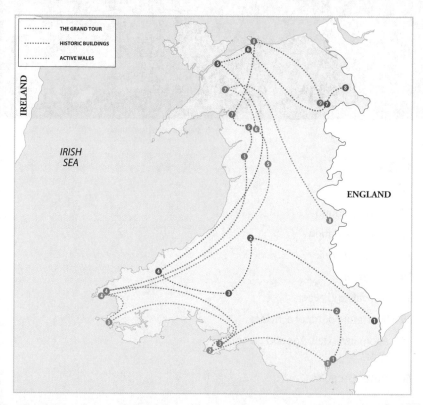

SNOWDON MOUNTAIN RAILWAY

Basics

25 Getting there

27 Getting around

31 Accommodation

34 Food and drink

36 The media

38 Festivals and events

39 Sports and outdoor activities

45 Alternative, New Age and green Wales

46 Travel essentials

Getting there

Coming to Wales from elsewhere in Britain, or from Ireland, is easy enough by train, bus or ferry, though it may not necessarily work out cheaper than flying. Crossing the border from England into Wales is straightforward, with train and bus services forming part of the British national network. The two roads providing the quickest access into the heart of the country are the M4 motorway in the south and the A55 expressway in the north. Both are fast and busy; minor routes are more appealing if you aren't in too much of a hurry.

Flights to Wales from Ireland and continental Europe are few and far between, and non-existent from outside Europe, in which case you're best off flying to England and continuing overland from there. Manchester is well placed for north Wales and you might consider Birmingham for direct access to mid-Wales. With most airlines nowadays, how much you pay depends on how far in advance you book and how much demand there is during that period – generally speaking, the earlier you book, the cheaper the prices.

Visas and red tape

Citizens of all European countries – other than Albania, Bosnia Herzegovina, Macedonia, Montenegro, Serbia and most republics of the former Soviet Union – can enter Britain with just a passport for up to three months. US, Canadian, Australian and New Zealand citizens can travel in Britain for up to six months with a passport. All other nationalities require a **visa**, available from the British consular office in the country of application. Note though, that given Britain's 2016 vote to leave the EU, visa regulations will almost certainly change in the future, so it's always wise to contact the nearest British embassy or high commission before you travel. Check ⓦgov.uk /browse/visas-immigration for all the latest information.

Flights from England, Scotland and Ireland

The only airport of any size in Wales is **Cardiff Airport** (ⓦcardiff-airport.com), twelve miles southwest of the capital. There are very limited flights from the rest of the UK; from Aberdeen and Newcastle with Eastern Airways (ⓦeasternairways .com) and from Belfast, Edinburgh and Glasgow with flybe (ⓦflybe.com). Note that many of these routes mostly run business flights, timed and priced accordingly, and often don't operate at weekends.

From Ireland, there are flights from Dublin and Cork with flybe, though the frequent ferries (see p.27) may be more convenient.

Flights from mainland Europe

Cardiff Airport is also poorly served with flights **from mainland Europe**; presently, flybe operates services from a handful of cities, including Berlin, Milan, Munich, Paris and Rome, while KLM (ⓦklm .com) flies from Amsterdam. The best bet for travellers from Europe is to fly into Bristol airport (ⓦbristolairport.co.uk) just across the border, which has some excellent connections with mainland Europe, or Birmingham, Liverpool and Manchester airports, which are handily placed for onward travel into mid- and north Wales. Alternatives to air travel are the traditional cross-Channel ferry services or the Channel Tunnel (see p.26).

Flights from the US and Canada

Numerous airlines, including British Airways (ⓦbritish airways.com) and United Airlines (ⓦunited.com), fly from both the **eastern and western US seaboards** to London, the principal gateway for visitors to Wales, and also offer direct flights to both Manchester and Birmingham; flight time from the east coast is around seven hours, ten hours from the west. Low-season round-trip **fares** from New York to London range from US$650 to US$800, and in summer you can expect to pay more than US$1000 (add US$100–200 from other eastern cities). Low-season fares from the west coast start at a little under US$1000, rising to around US$1400 in summer and around Christmas.

From **Canada**, you'll get the best deal flying to London from Toronto or Montreal, for example with Air Canada (ⓦaircanada.com), where fares are around Can$1000–1200 return. From the west, fares range from Can$1200 to Can$1650.

Flights from Australia, New Zealand and South Africa

To get to Wales **from Australia**, **New Zealand** or **South Africa** you'll need to fly through London, or possibly Manchester in northern England. Flights via Southeast Asia or the Middle East are generally the cheapest options, with the likes of Etihad (ⓦetihad.com) and Emirates (ⓦemirates.com). Average return fares from eastern Australian cities to London are Aus$1500–2500 depending on the season; from Perth or Darwin you'll pay around Aus$200 less. Return fares from Auckland, for example with Air New Zealand (ⓦairnewzealand .com), range from NZ$2000 to NZ$3000.

There are direct flights from **South Africa** to London Heathrow with South African Airways (Jo'burg; ⓦflysaa.com), British Airways (Jo'burg and Cape Town) and Virgin Atlantic (Jo'burg; ⓦvirgin -atlantic.com). It is sometimes possible to find cheaper deals on indirect routes with Emirates (from Cape Town, Durban and Jo'burg), KLM (from Jo'burg) and Lufthansa (from Jo'burg; ⓦlufthansa .com). Return fares are generally around ZAR7000– 8000, depending on the season.

By car

The **M4 motorway** (from London to Cardiff and Swansea) makes the most dramatic entry into Wales, across the graceful Second Severn Crossing bridge (no footpath or cycle lane). A few miles north, the **M48** links England and Wales over the smaller, but original Severn Bridge (footpath and cycle lane available); the hitherto expensive **tolls** for both bridges were due to be abolished by the end of 2018. High winds can sometimes lead to bridge closures, so if in doubt check ⓦsevernbridge.co.uk. The only other fast road into Wales is the **A55 expressway** running along the north Wales coast to the Ireland-bound ferries at Holyhead.

By train

Britain's trains are run by a myriad of **operators**, but all are required to work as a single network with integrated ticketing. Travelling to Wales from the rest of the UK, most people use the fast, frequent service from London Paddington to **Newport** (1hr 45min), **Cardiff** (2hr) and **Swansea** (3hr), operated by Great Western Railway (ⓦgwr.com). Very few direct trains from England go beyond Swansea, although connections at Newport, Cardiff and Swansea link up with services to Carmarthen and stations in Pembrokeshire.

The **north coast service** from London Euston to Holyhead (4hr), via Chester, also stops at Prestatyn, Rhyl, Colwyn Bay, Llandudno Junction and Bangor, and is operated by a combination of Virgin Trains (ⓦvirgintrains.co.uk) and Arriva Trains

(ⓦarrivatrainswales.co.uk). From other cities in England and Scotland, you'll probably need to change en route – at Bristol for the south coast line, at Crewe for the north coast.

We've listed some useful **train contacts** in our "Getting around" section (see p.29).

From Europe

England has direct, high-speed passenger trains from France and Belgium via the Channel Tunnel with **Eurostar** (☎03432 186186, ⓦeurostar.com), which runs hourly between Paris, Lille and Brussels and London (St Pancras). The cheapest return fares from Paris or Brussels to London start at around €85, though there are frequent promotional deals, particularly for advance bookings, so it's always worth checking the website.

Drivers travelling between Calais and Folkestone can use **Le Shuttle** (from the UK ☎08443 353535, from France ☎+33 (0)810 630304, ⓦeurotunnel .com), a vehicle-carrying train that whisks through the Channel Tunnel in just 35 minutes. You can just turn up on the day you want to travel, but booking is advised and usually cheaper, especially at weekends. Return fares start from as little as €55 for a car and up to nine passengers.

By bus

Throughout Britain, long-distance bus (aka coach) services are almost all run by **National Express**, (ⓦnationalexpress.com) which serves most parts of Wales. The **chief routes** are from London to Cardiff; London to Milford Haven via Chepstow, Swansea and Pembroke Dock; London to Wrexham via Birmingham and Llangollen; London to Aberystwyth via Birmingham and Welshpool; from London along the north Welsh coast to Holyhead and Pwllheli, both via Birmingham; Birmingham to Cardiff, Swansea and Haverfordwest; from Chester along the north coast to Llandudno, Bangor, Caernarfon and Pwllheli and Holyhead; and Chester direct to Holyhead.

Fares vary enormously, with the cheapest tickets sold early. One-way London–Cardiff fares can be as little as £5. There are also numerous discount cards available (see box, p.28), while children under 3 travel free.

Low-cost intercity services are also operated by **Megabus** (ⓦuk.megabus.com), with coaches running from a handful of UK cities to Carmarthen, Cardiff, Newport, Swansea and Pembroke Dock; fares can be obtained from as low as £1 if you book well in advance.

SEA CONNECTIONS FROM IRELAND

Route	Company	Frequency	Duration
Dublin–Holyhead (ferry)	Stena	4 daily	3hr 15min
Dublin–Holyhead (ferry)	Irish	3 daily	3hr 25min
Dublin–Holyhead (catamaran)	Irish	2 daily	2hr
Rosslare–Fishguard (ferry)	Stena	2 daily	3hr 30min
Rosslare–Pembroke Dock (ferry)	Irish	2 daily	4hr

By ferry

Travellers from **Ireland** have the choice of three **Welsh ferry ports**, which are variously served by Irish Ferries (ⓦ irishferries.com) and Stena Line (ⓦ stenaline.co.uk). Passenger fares are very competitive, with diverse special deals and midweek and advance purchase offers. The busiest port is **Holyhead**, on the northwest tip of Wales, with ferries and fast catamarans from Dublin, though the fast cats often only run in the busiest summer months. Both **Fishguard** and **Pembroke Dock** are served by ferries from Rosslare (just outside Wexford).

From Europe

From mainland Europe, ferries arrive at various **ports in England**. The shortest, most convenient route is the crossing from Calais to Dover with P&O ferries (ⓦ poferries.com). Other useful crossings are Zeebrugge and Rotterdam to Hull, the Hook of Holland to Harwich, and Le Havre to Portsmouth.

For ferry **routes** and prices, contact the ferry companies direct or visit Seaview Ferries (ⓦ seaview.co.uk/ferries) and Direct Ferries (ⓦ direct ferries.co.uk).

Package deals and tours

Hundreds of **tour operators** specialize in travel to the British Isles. Most can do packages of the standard highlights, but of greater interest are the outfits that help you explore Britain's unique points: walking (see p.41) or cycling trips (see p.43), say, and any number of themed tours based around, for example, literary heritage, history, pubs, gardens, theatre or golf. A few of the possibilities for Wales are listed below.

AGENTS AND OPERATORS

North South Travel UK ☎ 01245 608 291, ⓦ northsouthtravel. co.uk. Friendly, competitive travel agency, offering discounted fares worldwide. Profits are used to support projects in the developing world, especially the promotion of sustainable tourism.

STA Travel UK ☎ 0333 321 0099, US ☎ 1800 781 4040, Australia ☎ 134 782, New Zealand ☎ 0800 474 400, South Africa ☎ 0861

781 781; ⓦ statravel.co.uk. Worldwide specialists in independent travel; also student IDs, travel insurance, car rental, rail passes and more. Good discounts for students and under-26s.

Trailfinders UK ☎ 020 7368 1200, Ireland ☎ 021 464 8800; ⓦ trailfinders.com. One of the best-informed and most efficient agents for independent travellers.

Travel CUTS Canada ☎ 1800 667 2887, ⓦ travelcuts.com. Canadian youth and student travel firm.

USIT Ireland ☎ 01 602 1906, Australia ☎ 1800 092 499; ⓦ usit.ie. Ireland's main student and youth travel specialists.

WALES SPECIALISTS

Busy Bus ⓦ busybus.co.uk. Excellent outfit offering adventure day-trips (£39) from Chester, Liverpool and Manchester to north Wales, taking in Conwy Castle and Snowdonia National Park, among other places. They also operate cruise excursions from Holyhead (£49).

Dragon Tours ☎ 01874 658102, ⓦ dragon-tours.com. Tailor-made day-trips (historic, cultural, sporting) from any location in the UK, alongside six-, ten- and fourteen-day tours across Wales, with prices determined by your choice of accommodation (from hostels to five-star hotels).

Shaggy Sheep Tours ☎ 07919 244549, ⓦ shaggysheep.com. Great fun and hugely enthusiastic, the booziest backpacker tours around leave weekly from London. Choose between the Merlin weekend trip (£118) or the four-day All-Wales Dragon trip (£148); adventure activities cost £40 extra. For independent travellers, there's also a handy jump-on, jump-off return bus service from London (£79) stopping at key destinations in Wales.

Getting around

The large cities and densely populated valleys of south Wales support comprehensive train and bus networks, but the more thinly populated areas of mid- and north Wales have to make do with skeletal services. Getting about by car is easy and, outside the cities, sheep and vehicles with agricultural equipment are likely to be a more persistent problem than other road users. Take the more scenic backroads unless you're in a real hurry. Information for cyclists is listed in the outdoor activities section (see p.39).

By train

The train is one of the best ways to get around Wales; the views are superb and the engineering often impressive. In addition to the mainline network, there are more than a dozen **narrow-gauge trains** (see box, p.30).

Services in Wales cover all the main cities and a seemingly random selection of rural towns and wayside halts. As well as the two major lines – which also have several slower services – detailed in our "Getting there" section (see p.26), there is the **Cambrian Coast line** from Birmingham and Shrewsbury through Welshpool, Newtown and Machynlleth. Beyond Machynlleth it divides at Dyfi Junction; the southern spur goes a few miles to Borth and Aberystwyth, the northern one crawls up the coast through Tywyn, Barmouth, Harlech and

Porthmadog to Pwllheli. Even slower (but very picturesque) is the second route from Shrewsbury, the **Heart of Wales line**, which runs through Knighton, Llandrindod Wells, Llanwrtyd Wells, Llandovery, Llandeilo and a host of tiny halts on the way to Llanelli and Swansea.

Apart from the major intercity services from England, all services are run by **Arriva Trains Wales** (Ⓦ arrivatrainswales.co.uk) with timetables covered in detail on **Traveline Cymru** (Ⓦ traveline.cymru) and on the useful "See Wales by Bus and Train" map, free from tourist offices.

Services on all but the main north- and south-coast train lines are infrequent, and are occasionally replaced by buses on Sunday. At many smaller stations, **ticket offices** close at weekends and in a lot of minor towns they've shut for good. In these instances, either use the vending machine on the

---

TRAIN AND BUS PASSES AND DISCOUNTS

Ordinary standard-class fares on UK trains are high and **first-class** costs an extra 33 percent, but there are various ways to save money. Off-peak and **advance-purchase** fares are much cheaper, **railcards** can save you a third off the price and there's a huge array of **rail passes** that cover all of Britain, just Wales or smaller regions.

TRAIN TICKET TYPES

Up to two children under 5 travel free with each adult-fare-paying passenger, while those aged 5–15 inclusive pay half the adult fare on most journeys. Bicycles are generally carried free with restrictions (see p.42). As a guide to **prices**, a standard-class one-way ticket on the London–Cardiff route might cost £22 (Advance), £60 (Off-Peak) or £110 (Anytime).

Anytime Fully flexible ticket allowing travel on any train at any time within a month after purchase. Expensive.

Off-peak Return off-peak fares cost about a third of the price of Anytime fares, though one-way fares are seldom much cheaper than returns (if you're doing a lot of travelling on one-way journeys, rail passes make a lot of sense). You generally cannot travel during weekday peak hours (these vary by route and company) and must complete outbound travel on the date shown on the ticket: the return portion is more flexible with the possibility of breaking the journey. At any station outside the morning rush hour, you'll routinely be sold an off-peak ticket.

Advance Advance-purchase tickets are the cheapest available, with no refunds and generally only valid on the train(s) you've booked. They must be bought at least the day before you travel and they're generally cheaper the further in advance you book. These are usually sold as single tickets, making planning a series of one-way journeys realistic if you are prepared to book ahead.

RAILCARDS

You can save a third on fares with one of several **railcards**, all of which cost £30 for a year (Ⓦ railcard.co.uk): the 16–25 Railcard; the Senior Railcard, for travellers over 60; the Family and Friends Railcard, for use by up to four adults travelling with up to four children (aged 5–15); and the Two Together Railcard, for two named people travelling together. Children under 5 travel free at all times. Railcards also give a third off Explore Wales passes (see opposite).

NATIONAL EXPRESS COACHCARDS

You can save a third on fares with one of three **coachcards**, all of which cost £10 (Ⓦ nationalexpress.com): the 16–26 Coachcard; the Senior Railcard, for people over 60; and the Disabled Coachcard.

platform, or if there isn't one, buy your ticket on board – but if you've boarded at a station with a machine or ticket office and haven't bought a ticket, you're liable for an on-the-spot fine. Note that a number of money-saving **rail passes** are available (see box below).

RAIL CONTACTS

The Man in Seat Sixty-One Ⓦ seat61.com. Superb site covering all aspects of British and European train travel.

National Rail Enquiries Ⓣ 08457 484950, Ⓦ nationalrail.co.uk. Primary contact for all train timetables and booking.

Trainline Ⓦ thetrainline.com. Independent UK-wide online ticket retailer.

Traveline Cymru Ⓣ 0800 464 0000, Ⓦ traveline.cymru. Comprehensive train and bus info on all of Wales, particularly useful for planning integrated journeys.

By bus

Intertown **bus services** in Wales duplicate a few of the major rail routes, often at half the price of the train or less, but take considerably longer. Buses are reasonably comfortable and on longer journeys there are refreshment stops.

Much bus travel is provided by local services run by a bewildering array of companies: consult Traveline Cymru (see opposite) for details or visit Ⓦ showbus .co.uk/timetables/wales.htm, which has links to all the major companies. Though buses are more expensive and less frequent in rural areas, there are very few places without any service, even if it's only a private minibus on market day. All regions have their own detailed local **timetables**, easily obtained from tourist offices, libraries and bus and/or train stations. For occasional bus journeys, it's easy enough to simply

---

RAIL AND BUS PASSES: BRITAIN AND WALES

All-Line Rail Rover Ⓦ nationalrail.co.uk. Unlimited travel on almost the entire network throughout England, Scotland and Wales (including the Ffestiniog Railway) for seven consecutive days (£492). Available within Britain from larger train stations.

BritRail Pass Ⓦ britrail.net. Overseas visitors planning several long-distance trips through other parts of Britain in addition to Wales might consider purchasing a BritRail Pass online – these must be bought before you enter the country. A range of passes is available for unlimited travel in England, Scotland and Wales over various combinations of consecutive days or a certain number of days over

two months; one child can travel free on each adult pass (other children travel half-price).

Explore Wales Pass Ⓣ 0870 900 0773, Ⓦ arrivatrainswales /ExploreWalesPass.co.uk. Eight consecutive days' bus travel and four days' rail travel within the same period (£99). Covers all of Wales and extends to Crewe, Shrewsbury and Hereford in England. Includes a fifty-percent discount on the Ffestiniog narrow-gauge railway (see p.370), twenty-percent discounts on many other narrow-gauge railways and reduced entry to CADW and National Trust properties. The pass can be bought at most staffed train stations.

RAIL AND BUS PASSES: NORTH AND MID-WALES

Explore North & Mid Wales Pass The same deal as the Explore Wales Pass but only covering the northern half of Wales (£69). The pass can be bought at most staffed train stations.

North Wales Rover All-day pass on all trains and most buses in north Wales and down the Cambrian coast to Aberystwyth. The area is divided into seven zones; you can choose to travel within two

zones (£13), three zones (£22) or all zones (£38). Buy at the stations.

Red Rover All-day bus travel throughout northwest Wales for £6.80 (though not valid east of Llandudno). Buy on the bus.

Snowdon Sherpa Day Ticket All-day travel on the routes immediately surrounding Snowdon (see p.337) for £5. Buy on the bus.

RAIL AND BUS PASSES: WEST AND MID-WALES

Explore Cambrian One day's train travel between Aberystwyth and Pwllheli (£12), valid after 9.15am and all weekend. Buy at the stations.

Heart of Wales Line Circular Day Ranger One day's unlimited train travel on the route Shrewsbury–Llandrindod Wells–Swansea–

Cardiff–Hereford–Shrewsbury with as many breaks as the timetable will allow (£39). You can buy the pass at most staffed train stations.

Explore West Wales All-day train travel in Pembrokeshire, west of Carmarthen (£12.50). Valid after 8.45am on weekdays and all weekend. Buy at the stations.

RAIL AND BUS PASSES: SOUTH WALES

Explore South Wales Pass Same deal as the Explore Wales Pass but only covers the southern half of Wales (£69). The pass can be bought at most staffed train stations.

First Bus & Rail Card Ⓦ firstgroup.com/south-west-wales. Unlimited one-day travel (£10), after 9.30am and all weekend, on all Great Western Railway trains and First company buses between

Newport and Carmarthen. Buy from any bus driver or any train station between Newport and Carmarthen.

Explore Cardiff and Valleys One day's Cardiff and Valleys bus and train travel. The Day Explorer (£12) is valid after 9.30am weekdays and all weekend; the Valleys Night Rider (£6.50) is only available after 6.30pm. The pass is sold at most staffed train stations.

WALES' STEAM RAILWAYS: SIX OF THE BEST

With the rising demand for quarried stone in the nineteenth century, quarry and mine owners had to find more economical means of transport than packhorses to get their products to market, but in the steep, tortuous valleys of Snowdonia, standard-gauge train tracks proved too unwieldy. The solution was rails, usually about 2ft apart, plied by steam engines and dinky rolling stock. The charm of these **steam railways** was recognized by train enthusiasts, and long after the decline of the quarries, they banded together to restore abandoned lines and locos. Most lines are still largely run by volunteers, who have also started up new services along unused sections of standard-gauge bed.

Tickets are generally sold separately, but eleven railways (including all those listed here) operate as **The Great Little Trains of Wales** (GLT: ⓦ greatlittletrainsofwales.co.uk) and offer a Discount Card (£10; valid one year), giving you twenty percent off the cost of the return journey on each of the GLT railways.

The railways below are listed north to south:

Snowdon Mountain Railway Llanberis. See p.349.
Welsh Highland Railway Porthmadog. See p.371.
Ffestiniog Railway Porthmadog. See p.370.
Llangollen Railway Llangollen. See p.314.
Talyllyn Railway Tywyn. See p.288
Vale of Rheidol Railway Aberystwyth. See p.276.

---

pay as you board, but good savings can be made with one of the various **bus passes** and combined bus and rail passes (see box, p.28).

In the **northern** half of Wales, Arriva Buses Wales (ⓦ arrivabus.co.uk/wales) runs the majority of local services. Further south the system is far less unified, though most buses west of Cardiff and south of Carmarthen are run by the Swansea-based First Bus (ⓦ firstgroup.com).

Cardiff Bus (ⓦ cardiffbus.com) is the major company serving **Cardiff** and the Vale of Glamorgan. Various day, weekly and monthly passes are available, all of which can be bought aboard the bus (see p.69).

Traws Cymru (ⓦ trawscymru.info) operates seven excellent **medium- to long-range services**: #T1 from Aberystwyth to Carmarthen; #T1C from Carmarthen to Cardiff; #T2 from Bangor to Aberystwyth via Porthmadog; #T3 from Wrexham to Barmouth; #T4 from Cardiff to Newtown, calling at Merthyr, Brecon and Llandrindod Wells; #T5 from Aberystwyth to Haverford West via Cardigan; and #T6 from Brecon to Swansea. In a remarkable initiative, travel is free on all these buses at weekends.

By car

If you want to cover a lot of the countryside in a short time, or just want more flexibility, you'll need your own transport. An extensive network of dual carriageways and good-quality roads links all major centres, including the **A5** through Llangollen into Snowdonia and the **A40** into the Brecon Beacons. In rural areas you'll often find yourself on winding, sometimes hair-raisingly narrow, single-track lanes with slightly broader **passing places** where two vehicles can squeeze by – with this in mind, you might want to select a compact rental car.

As in the rest of the UK, you **drive on the left** in Wales. **Speed limits** are 30–40mph (50–65km/h) in

---

PAY AND DISPLAY

You often have to pay for **parking** in towns and at popular beaches, many of which are tucked into folds in the mountains or wedged below cliffs, giving little space for parking on the road. At most pay-and-display car parks, tickets are issued by machine (you may have to type in your car registration number). Some shopping centres may require you to pay for parking, though you usually get your parking costs redeemed at the check-out if you make a purchase.

Parking prices are typically 50p to £1 an hour, though some places charge a flat fee of up to £5. It's definitely an incentive to use public transport – some eco-oriented attractions even give discounted entry to visitors arriving without a car. Note that members of NT/CADW (see p.46) do not have to pay for parking at their respective properties – where parking charges apply, that is.

WALES' BEST DRIVES

You can't go far in Wales without experiencing great views, but if you're set on seeking out some of the very finest scenery, try these drives:

Abergwesyn Pass Follow the ancient drovers' road through the spectacularly remote moorland of the Cambrian Mountains from Llanwrtyd Wells to Tregaron. See p.226.

Elan Valley and Cwmystwyth From Rhayader take the mountain road past the reservoirs of the Elan Valley up to the blasted landscapes around Cwmystwyth and down past Devil's Bridge into the Vale of Rheidol. See p.232 & p.276.

Gospel Pass Take the narrow road over the roof of the Black Mountains from Abergavenny past Llanthony Priory to Hay-on-Wye. See p.221.

Marine Drive A short but wonderfully scenic loop around Great Orme. See p.399.

Wye Valley Savour the wooded gorge of the River Wye on a journey from Monmouth past Tintern Abbey to Chepstow. See p.77.

built-up areas, 70mph (110km/h) on motorways (freeways) and dual carriageways, and 60mph (97km/h) on most other roads. Be alert to posted signs as **speed cameras** are everywhere.

Road signs are pretty much international ("Give Way" means "Yield"), and road rules are largely common sense. Many road signs give instructions in English and in Welsh. You are not permitted to make a kerbside turn against a red light and must always give way to traffic (circulating clockwise) on a **roundabout**. This applies even for mini-roundabouts, which may be no more than a white circle painted on the road.

Petrol (gas) is sold in litres (a UK gallon = 4.56 litres, a US gallon = 3.8 litres), and at the time of writing, was around £1.20 per litre – diesel costs only fractionally more. The Automobile Association (AA; breakdowns ☎0800 887766, ⓦtheaa.com), the Royal Automobile Club (RAC; breakdowns ☎0800 828282, ⓦrac.co.uk) and Green Flag (breakdowns ☎0800 0510636, ⓦgreenflag.com) all offer 24-hour emergency **breakdown** services. You may be entitled to free assistance through a reciprocal arrangement with a motor organization in your own country – check the situation before setting out. You can call the breakdown numbers even if you are not a member, although you'll be charged a substantial fee.

Most foreign nationals can get by with their **driving licence** from home, but if you're in any doubt, obtain an **international driving permit** from a national motoring organization. All foreign vehicles should carry vehicle registration, ownership documents and **insurance**, so be sure to check your existing policy.

Hitchhiking and lift-sharing

Hitchhiking is rare nowadays, for obvious reasons. A safer and more reliable alternative is **lift-sharing**, whereby you share the travel costs with someone already going in your direction. The best way to do this is through online agencies such as BlaBlaCar (ⓦblablacar.co.uk) and Freewheelers (ⓦfreewheelers.co.uk), where you register (free) and enter your desired route so that the database can come up with suitable matches. You then contact the resulting matches by email and make arrangements.

Car rental

Car rental in Wales is cheaper than it used to be thanks to online advance deals with comparison websites like ⓦholidayautos.co.uk. Expect to pay around £110 a week for the most economical cars. **Automatic transmissions** are rare at the lower end of the price scale – if you want one, you should book well ahead and expect to pay at least £170 a week for a slightly bigger model. Damage Liability Waiver (aka Collision Damage Waiver) is often included but still leaves you liable for the first several hundred pounds; this can be eliminated by paying roughly £10 a day. Most agencies offer vehicles with **diesel** engines, which give better overall economy.

Few companies will rent cars to drivers with less than one year's experience, and most will only rent to people between 21 and 70 years of age. Some charge an additional fee for under-25s.

Accommodation

Tourist accommodation in Wales is constantly improving, with a good selection across the board, from top-rank hotels via restaurants-with-rooms and ubiquitous B&Bs to simple bunkhouses. The growing array of farmhouse B&Bs

and country houses typically offer a genuinely warm welcome, informal hospitality and high-quality home cooking; at the lower end of the scale are plenty of hostels and bunkhouses, and a great spread of campsites, many of which are in fantastically scenic spots.

For hotels and guesthouses, good online resources include **Great Little Places** (🕸little -places.co.uk), which features around fifty of the best small hotels, country inns and farmhouse B&Bs in Wales, and **Welsh Rarebits** (🕸rarebits .co.uk), a similarly select listing of more substantial hotels and country mansions. Both sites give full coverage of all listed establishments; you can pick up hard-copy booklets at most tourist offices. It's also worth consulting Visit Wales' website (🕸visit wales.com), which lists other types of accommodation too.

Guesthouses and B&Bs

Places calling themselves **bed and breakfasts** (B&Bs; in Welsh Gwely a Brecwast) run the gamut from private houses with a couple of bedrooms set aside for paying guests to small, stylish boutique establishments. **Guesthouses** tend to be larger, usually with around half a dozen rooms plus a guests' lounge, and can vary from homely to very flash. In the countryside you'll find similar establishments described as a **farm** (essentially a B&B on a working farm) or an **inn** (usually a village pub with rooms above). **Breakfast** is almost always included in the price – we indicate in our reviews throughout the Guide where breakfast costs extra or isn't available.

Staying in any of these places you can usually expect a double room with TV, tea- and coffee-making facilities and, usually, your own en-suite bathroom, for anywhere between £50 and £90 (sometimes a little less out of season or in less popular areas). However, as visitor expectations and the demand for weekend breaks increase, establishments in all the above categories are ramping up the standards, with sumptuous furnishings, better food and little touches which make your stay special – and you will pay considerably more for such pampering. Free **wi-fi** is commonplace everywhere. Most places accept credit cards, but at lower-end B&Bs you might have to **pay in cash**.

Hotels

Hotels come in all shapes and sizes. At the upper end of the scale, and offering most character, are Wales' country houses and mansions (and occasionally castles), many of which are beautifully located; most will also offer dinner, too, often as part of a package. **Boutique hotels** are very much in fashion, though you'll generally (not exclusively) find these in the larger towns. Budget hotels, typically run by national (and international) chains, are largely confined to Cardiff, though you may find a smattering elsewhere. Free Wi-fi is commonplace everywhere.

If you arrive without having made a reservation, it can be worth asking the local **tourist office** to book you a room (£3 fee); note, though, that they will only provide information on "verified" accommodation (see opposite), and can sometimes be reluctant to divulge details of places that don't advertise in the official local guide. If you don't see something suitable in their guide, don't be afraid to ask if there's anywhere else that matches your requirements for price and location.

ACCOMMODATION PRICES

Throughout this Guide, hotel and B&B **accommodation prices** have been quoted based on the lowest price you would expect to pay per night in that establishment for a **double room in high season**, but not absolute peak rates (such as at certain bank holidays). The accommodation reviews in this Guide always mention if a place has rooms without a private bathroom (though usually with a sink in the room) for which you'll pay slightly less. **Single occupancy** rates vary widely: though typically around three-quarters of the price of a double, some places charge almost the full double rate and others charge only a little over half that. Many establishments offer **discounts** for multiple-night stays, and/or drop their rates considerably (or offer special deals) outside the late May to early September summer season.

For hostels and bunkhouses we've listed the price of a **dorm bed**, plus the price for any double or twin rooms. For YHA hostels, prices quoted are for members – non-members pay an extra £3 a night (£1.50 for under-18s). Unless otherwise stated, **campsite** prices are quoted per pitch, based on two people in one tent.

TOP 5 COUNTRY HOTELS

The Grove Narberth. See p.156
Llangoed Hall Bronllys. See p.212
Plas Dinas Caernarfon. See p.361
Tyddyn Llan Llandrillo. See p.321
Ynyshir Hall Machynlleth. See p.281

Star ratings

Visit Wales (Ⓦvisitwales.com), the country's tourist board, operates a **grading system** for accommodation, assigning them a minimum of one star (seldom used) to a maximum of five stars (of which there are few), largely based on amenities rather than subjective impressions such as the general atmosphere of the place or the friendliness of its owners. However, for various reasons not every establishment participates, so the absence of a rating alone needn't be a deterrent.

Hostels and bunkhouses

Wales has around 35 **YHA hostels** (Ⓦyha.org.uk), ranging from remote, simple barns in the wilds of mid-Wales and Snowdonia to relatively swanky centres in places such as Cardiff and Conwy. The greatest concentration of hostels is in Snowdonia, with smaller clusters around the Pembrokeshire coast and in the Brecon Beacons.

Prices vary according to demand, but in summer dorm beds typically range from £14 to £20 per night per person; most also have double rooms available (sometimes en suite), which usually go for around £40–45. Bed prices quoted in this book are for **members** (see box opposite). One year's membership of the England and Wales YHA, which is open only to residents of the EU, costs £15 per year (£5 for under-26s; £25 for two adults living at the same address), and can be obtained online or in person at any YHA hostel. Members gain automatic membership of the hostelling associations of the ninety countries affiliated to Hostelling International (HI).

Most YHA hostels have self-catering **facilities** and many also serve breakfast (around £5.50); some, too, will offer a three-course dinner (around £12), as well as packed lunches (around £6). **Wi-fi** is free. Note that most receptions close from 10am to 5pm and have an 11pm **curfew**.

It's always best to **book ahead**, particularly at Easter, Christmas and from May to August. If you're tempted to turn up on the spur of the moment,

bear in mind that few hostels are open year-round and several have periods during which they take only group bookings.

Independent hostels and bunkhouses

YHA hostels still outnumber **independent hostels**, though there are a growing number of non-affiliated places offering similar facilities to YHAs, often with a less regimented regime and no curfews or lockouts. We've reviewed the best of the independent hostels in the Guide but it's also worth consulting Ⓦindependenthostels.co.uk.

There are also a number of **bunkhouses**, more primitive affairs designed for hikers, climbers, mountain bikers and the like. The flashest are up to hostel standards, but many are little more than barns with toilet, shower and basic cooking facilities; prices start from around £12 per person. Bunkhouses may give preference to group bookings, and some purely cater to groups. We've reviewed a selection in this Guide; check out, too, Ⓦbunkhousesinwales.co.uk.

You'll find free **wi-fi** in most hostels and bunkhouses, except perhaps in the most remote places.

Camping, caravanning and self-catering

Wales has hundreds of **campsites**, charging from around £3 per person per night for a spot in a field with a tap and a toilet, to upwards of £20 for a two-person tent at the plushest sites, where you'll find amenities such as laundries, shops and sports facilities; such places are typically used both by campers and **caravans**. As in many other parts of Britain, **glamping** has caught on in a big way, and a good number of campsites now also boast yurts, shepherd's huts, gypsy caravans and the like.

Some **hostels** have small campsites on their property, for which you'll pay roughly half the dorm fee. Farmers without a reserved camping area may let you pitch in a field if you ask, and may charge

TOP 5 CAMPSITES

Cae Du Llangelynin. See p.292
Caerfai Farm St Davids. See p.185
Gwern Gôf Uchaf Ogwen Valley.
See p.348
Rynys Farm Betws-y-Coed. See p.342
Three Cliffs Caravan Park Gower.
See p.129

you nothing for the privilege; setting up a tent without asking is an act of trespass and won't be well received. Note that **wild camping** is illegal in national parks and nature reserves.

As a hangover from the days when thousands of holidaymakers from northern England and the Midlands decamped to the Welsh coast for a fortnight, many of the traditional seaside resorts are enveloped by camp upon camp of **permanently sited caravans**, rented out for self-catering holidays. Although these can certainly be cost-effective, with facilities such as bars, shops and discos thrown in, many people prefer self-catering holidays in self-contained **cottages**, **farms**, **townhouses** or **apartments**. The usual minimum rental period is a week, though long-weekend breaks can often be arranged out of season. In midsummer or over Christmas and New Year, **prices** start at around £400 for a place sleeping four, although in winter, spring or autumn they can dip towards £250 for the same property. A few companies specializing in Welsh holiday cottages are detailed below; tourist offices throughout Wales also have lists of self-catering holiday options.

The best of the detailed annual **directories** of Wales' camping and caravan sites are: the AA's *Caravan & Camping: Britain & Ireland*, which lists their inspected and graded sites, and *Cade's Camping, Touring and Motor Caravan Site Guide* (Ⓦ cades.co.uk). More niche alternatives include Rough Guides' *Camping in Britain* and *Cool Camping: Wales* (Ⓦ coolcamping.com), both of which offer in-depth reviews of superbly situated tent-oriented campsites. Many campsites now have **free wi-fi**, except perhaps in the most remote places.

SELF-CATERING ACCOMMODATION

Brecon Beacons Holiday Cottages ☎ 01874 676446, Ⓦ breconcottages.com. More than three hundred cottages and other buildings, some decidedly quirky, in the Brecon Beacons National Park and Wye Valley.

Coastal Cottages of Pembrokeshire ☎ 01437 765765, Ⓦ coastalcottages.co.uk. Dozens of cottages, chalets, flats and houses – some with impressive leisure and activity facilities – around or near the Pembrokeshire coast.

Landmark Trust ☎ 01628 825925, Ⓦ landmarktrust.org.uk. Some fifteen self-catering properties around Wales, from a seventeenth-century rural farmhouse sleeping two to a tower in Caernarfon's town walls (sleeps five).

National Trust Holiday Cottages ☎ 0344 800 2070, Ⓦ nationaltrust.org.uk/holidays. Around sixty beautiful cottages all over Wales, usually with a three-night minimum stay.

North Wales Holiday Cottages & Farmhouses ☎ 01492 582492, Ⓦ northwalesholidaycottages.co.uk. Extensive array of cottages in the Snowdonia National Park and throughout the northern half of Wales, both on the coast and in the countryside.

Powell's Cottage Holidays ☎ 01834 812791, Ⓦ powells.co.uk. Concentrates on properties in Pembrokeshire and the Gower.

Quality Cottages ☎ 01348 837871, Ⓦ qualitycottages.co.uk. More than three hundred cottages throughout Wales, mostly coastal.

Under the Thatch ☎ 0844 500 5101, Ⓦ underthethatch.co.uk. A select choice of cottages and cabins, many beautifully restored. Most are traditional Ceredigion thatched cottages, but there are also Romany caravans and yurts. Lets are generally weekly or half-weekly with most in Snowdonia and Pembrokeshire or the southern Cambrian coast.

Wales Cottage Holidays ☎ 01686 628200, Ⓦ walescottage holidays.co.uk. A varied selection of more than five hundred properties all over Wales.

Food and drink

Wales' culinary landscape has changed beyond all recognition in recent years, and while there are still many cafés, restaurants and pubs where you can get chips with everything, the overall standard of dining has improved dramatically. The country today is home to some truly world-class food festivals, restaurants, farmers' markets and producers – part of the general renaissance of British cuisine and an increasing focus on fresh local produce. Wales' natural larder includes freshly caught fish, tender local lamb and a fabulous array of cheeses. These staple ingredients are used in everything from traditional dishes to fusion creations in restaurants throughout the land.

Native **Welsh cuisine** is traditionally rooted in economical ingredients, but many menus today do wonderful things with salt-marsh lamb (best served with mint, thyme or rosemary), Welsh black beef,

---

TOP 5 FARMERS' MARKETS AND FOOD SHOPS

Bodnant Welsh Food Centre Conwy. See p.409
Leonardo's Deli Ruthin. See p.328
Riverside Market Cardiff. See p.72
Swansea Indoor Market Swansea. See p.121
Ultracomida Aberystwyth and Narberth. See p.276 & p.157

TOP 5 RESTAURANTS
The Checkers Montgomery. See p.243
Cwtch St Davids. See p.182
James Sommerin Penarth. See p.96
Plas Bodegroes Pwllheli. See p.378
Tyddyn Llan Llandrillo. See p.321

fresh salmon and sewin (sea trout), frequently combined with the national vegetable, the leek. **Specialities** include **laverbread** (bara lawr; edible seaweed frequently served for breakfast with sausages, egg and bacon), **Glamorgan sausages** (a spiced vegetarian combination of Caerphilly cheese, breadcrumbs and leeks), cawl (a chunky mutton broth) and cockles, trawled from the estuary north of the Gower.

The best-known of Wales' famed **cheeses** is Caerphilly, a soft, crumbly, white cheese that forms the basis of a true Welsh rarebit when mixed with beer and toasted on bread. Creamy goat's cheeses can be found all over the country, such as the superb Cothi Valley goat's cheese, as well as delicacies like organic Perl Las blue cheese and Collier's mature cheddar. Other dairy products include ice cream, which, despite the climate, is exceptionally popular, with numerous companies creating home-made ices, such as the Swansea area's Joe's Ice Cream or north Wales' Cadwaladr's.

Two traditional **cakes** are almost universal. Welsh cakes are flat, crumbling pancakes of sugared dough (a little like a flattened scone), while bara brith, a popular accompaniment to afternoon tea, literally translates as "speckled (with dried fruit) bread".

Breakfast

In most hotels, guesthouses and B&Bs, you'll be offered juices, cereal, toast and tea or coffee, alongside a full **Welsh breakfast**, typically comprising eggs, bacon, sausage, mushrooms, tomatoes and possibly black pudding and laverbread. In fancier places there'll also be a choice of fresh fruit, yogurt and smoked fish, fresh pastries and perhaps Welsh dishes such as Glamorgan sausages (see above).

Cafés and tearooms

Cafés and **tearooms** (the terms are used pretty much interchangeably) can be found everywhere, and are generally the cheapest places to eat, providing hearty, cholesterol-laden breakfasts, a solid range of snacks and full meals for lunch (and occasionally, evening meals). Wales' steady influx of New Agers has seen the cheap and usually vegetarian **wholefood café** become a standard feature of many mid- and west Welsh towns. Cafés are also increasingly equipped with espresso machines, though that doesn't necessarily always equate to great coffee; that said, there are now some excellent artisan **coffee shops** around the country, and while these are mainly the preserve of larger cities like Cardiff and Swansea, you will occasionally find them elsewhere.

Restaurants and gastropubs

Inevitably, standards in **restaurants** vary enormously, but there are some exceptional independent establishments across the length and breadth of Wales, seven of which (at the time of writing) have a coveted Michelin star. A number of places sport menus that rely extensively on fresh local produce – they can often tell you which farm the beef came from, and in coastal areas the chef may even know the fisherman. Decent **ethnic restaurants** are still difficult to find, even in the bigger centres, though there are a clutch of outstanding Indian and Italian places in Cardiff and Swansea. Food in **pubs** varies as much as the establishments themselves, and while relatively few Welsh hostelries have done the full **gastropub** conversion, the standards in some pubs can now be very high. In many towns, the local pub is the most economical place (and, in smaller towns, sometimes the only place) to grab a filling evening meal.

Drink

Welsh **pubs** vary as much as the landscape, from opulent Edwardian palaces of smoked glass, gleaming brass and polished mahogany in the larger towns and cities, to thick-set stone barns in wild, remote countryside. Where the church has faltered as a community focal point, the pub often still holds sway, with those in smaller towns and villages, in particular, functioning as community centres as much as places in which to drink alcohol.

TOP 5 FOOD PUBS
The Bell Skenfrith. See p.85
Felin Fach Griffin Brecon. See p.208
Ty Gwyn Rowen. See p.409
The White Eagle Rhoscolyn. See p.424
Y Polyn Nantgaredig. See p.144

Live music – and, this being Wales, singing – frequently round off an evening. The legal drinking age is 18, though an adult can order alcohol for someone aged 16 or 17 who is dining.

Beer

Beer, sold by the pint (generally £3–4.50) and half pint (half the price), is the staple drink in Wales, as it is throughout the British Isles. Traditionalists drink **real ale**, an uncarbonated beer, usually hand-pumped from the cellar but sometimes served straight from the cask; it comes in many varieties (some seasonal), including the almost ubiquitous deep-flavoured **bitter**, but sometimes mild, or **dark** as it is often known in Wales. **Lager**, which corresponds with European and American ideas of beer, is also stocked everywhere. Also quite common is the sweeter and darker **porter**. Irish **stout** (Guinness, Murphy's or Beamish) is widely available.

There's been a renaissance in the Welsh brewing industry in recent years, and you can now find superb independent **breweries** across the country. The most widely known is Cardiff-based **Brains** (Ⓦsabrain.com), whose heady brews include SA and Dark; also in the south, there's Llanelli-based **Felinfoel** (Ⓦfelinfoel.com), with Double Dragon Premium bitter the aromatic ace in their pack. Others worth looking out for include the Tomos Watkin brewery (Ⓦtomoswatkin.com) in Swansea, Evan Evans from Llandeilo (Ⓦevanevansbrewery .com), Otley (Ⓦotleybrewing.com) from Pontypridd and Tiny Rebel (Ⓦtinyrebel.co.uk) from Newport. There's no shortage of great breweries in mid- and north Wales either, with Monty's (Ⓦmontysbrewery .com) from Montgomery and Purple Moose (Ⓦpurplemoose.co.uk) from Porthmadog currently going great guns.

Many pubs are owned by large, UK-wide breweries, which sell only their own products, so if you are interested in seeking out distinctive brews, choose your pub carefully. The best resource for any serious hophead is the annual *Good Beer Guide* produced by **CAMRA** (the Campaign for Real Ale; Ⓦcamra.org.uk): if you see a recent CAMRA sticker in a pub window, chances are the beer will be well worth sampling. As in other Celtic regions, **cider** has a huge following; look out for Orchard Gold (a traditional farmhouse apple cider) and Perry Vale (pear cider), both made by the Welsh Cider and Perry Company (Gwynt y Ddraig; Ⓦgwyntcidershop.com).

Whiskey, wine and gin

Welsh **whiskey** is represented by the Penderyn distillery (Ⓦpenderyn.wales) on the southern edge

TOP 5 INDUSTRIAL HERITAGE SITES

Ironworks and the Big Pit Blaenavon. See p.104 & p.106

Llechwedd Slate Caverns Blaenau Ffestiniog. See p.365

National Slate Museum Llanberis. See p.350

National Wool Museum Dre-fach Felindre. See p.266

Rhondda Heritage Park Trehafod. See p.114

of the Brecon Beacons National Park, which produces signature single malt whiskies as well as Merlyn (cream liquor), Five (vodka) and Brecon gin. As elsewhere in the UK, there has been an upsurge in **gin** distilleries in recent years, with around half a dozen now in production; look out for Eccentric Gin in Llantrisant (Ⓦeccentricgin.com), the Dyfi Distillery (Ⓦdyfidistillery.com) in Corris, near Machynlleth and the Snowdonia Distillery (Ⓦsnowdoniadistillery .co.uk) in Conwy.

Surprisingly perhaps, there are also a number of creditable Welsh **wines** available – the Llanerch Vineyard (Ⓦllanerch-vineyard.co.uk) near Barry (see p.98) being the most prominent producer – though you rarely see these offered on restaurant wine lists. Wines sold in pubs have improved considerably in recent years, although the best world selections tend to be found in the places serving good food, in effect the better restaurants.

The media

The media that you will encounter in Wales is a hybrid of Welsh and Britain-wide information. Although the London-based UK media attempts to cover life in the other corners of Britain, few people would agree that Wales receives a fair share of coverage in any medium. Of all the solely Welsh media, newspapers are probably the weakest area, and periodicals and TV coverage the strongest and most interesting.

Newspapers

The **British daily newspapers** are all available in Wales, but news of Wales is not terribly well covered – even the goings-on at the Welsh Assembly in

Cardiff are rarely analyzed, let alone any other area of Welsh life. The only quality **Welsh daily** is the *Western Mail* (Ⓦ walesonline.co.uk), a sometimes uneasy mix of Welsh Assembly news, wider Welsh and British news and a token smattering of international affairs coupled with lifestyle and celebrity features. From the same stable comes Wales' national **Sunday paper**, *Wales on Sunday*. What the *Western Mail* is to south Wales, the *Daily Post* (Ⓦ dailypost.co.uk) is to the north of the country, with a fairly decent spectrum of news and features that marks it out from other local dailies. All areas have their own long-standing **weekly papers**, generally an entertaining mix of local news, parish gossip and events listings.

Magazines

Go into any bookshop in Wales, and you may be surprised by the profusion of Welsh **magazines**, in both English and Welsh. For a broad overview of the arts, history and politics, it's hard to beat *Planet* (Ⓦ planetmagazine.org.uk), an English-language bimonthly that takes a politically irreverent line, combining Welsh interest with a wider cultural and international outlook. The more serious English-language quarterly *New Welsh Review* (Ⓦ newwelshreview.com) is steeped in Wales' political, literary and economic developments, while *Poetry Wales* (Ⓦ poetrywales.co.uk) is an excellent publication of new writing. For a wider view of Welsh social issues, with insights into "alternative" culture and news, pick up the weekly *Big Issue Cymru*, sold by homeless vendors on the streets of major towns and cities.

Television

In marked contrast to the London-centric print media, **TV** is wholeheartedly moving out of southeast England. Cardiff is home to the Welsh branches of devolved broadcasting organizations including the BBC and ITV, and indigenous Welsh operators such as S4C. The state-funded BBC (Ⓦ bbc.co.uk/wales) operates two **TV** channels in

the country – the mainstream **BBC One Wales** and the more esoteric **BBC Two Wales**. They may sound avowedly Welsh, but the vast majority of programming is UK-wide, with Welsh programmes, principally news and sport, but also features, political and education programmes, slotted into the regular schedules. This is even more the case with the determinedly populist **ITV Wales** (Ⓦ itv.com/wales).

The principal **Welsh channel** is **S4C** (*Sianel Pedwar Cymru*, verbally *"ess pedwar eck"*; Ⓦ s4c .cymru), which has grown from shaky beginnings (see box, p.443) to become a major player, sponsoring diverse projects including Welsh animation and feature films. These include the Oscar-nominated films *Hedd Wyn* and *Solomon a Gaenor* and the terrifically tasteless prehistoric cartoon *Gogs*. It now broadcasts solely in Welsh and each weeknight includes a dose of the BBC's longest-running TV soap, *Pobol y Cwm* (*People of the Valley*). The sister English-language Channel 4 is also available throughout Wales.

Radio

The **BBC radio** network broadcasts five FM stations in Wales: Radio 1 (youth focused, playing pop and dance music; FM 97.7–99.8), Radio 2 (mainstream pop, rock and light music; FM 88.1–90.2), Radio 3 (classical music; FM 90.2–92.4), Radio 4 (current affairs, drama, arts and highbrow quizzes; FM 92–95) and Radio 5 Live (sport and news; MW 693/909). The BBC also operates two stations in Wales alone: **BBC Radio Wales** (FM 103.9), a competent, if gentle, English-language service of news, features and music, and **BBC Radio Cymru** (FM 93–104.9), a similarly easy-going mix in the Welsh language. Both can often be more entertaining in the evening and at weekends, away from the daytime tyranny of rolling news, sport, weather and traffic reports.

Of the commercial stations, the brashest is Radio One soundalike **Capital FM** (FM 97.4), serving Cardiff, Newport and around, together with **Capital Gold**, its twin for news, features and the greatest hits and oldies music. Also in the capital and along the south coast is **Heart Radio** (FM 105.4) with its twin station, **Heart North Wales** (FM 88), operating out of Wrexham; both are good for music, sport and phone-ins. **Kiss 101** (FM 101), meanwhile, provides dance, hip hop and drum n' bass. **Swansea Sound** (FM 96.4), whose reception extends west towards Pembrokeshire, is solid and frequently interesting. There are bilingual services from **Radio Ceredigion**

TOP 5 CASTLES

Beaumaris See p.416
Caernarfon See p.357
Caerphilly See p.108
Carreg Cennen Llandeilo. See p.148
Conwy See p.404

(FM 103.3) and **Radio Pembrokeshire** (FM 102.5) on the west coast, and **Radio Carmarthenshire** (FM 97.1) inland.

Festivals and events

Ranging from the epic to the absurd, Wales' wealth of festivals sees all walks of life partying in muddy fields across the country. Many of the events on the nation's annual calendar are uniquely Welsh with an ancient pedigree, notably the eisteddfodau – age-old competitions in poetry and music – that still form the backbone of national culture.

Many towns and cities now have annual **arts festivals** of some kind, mentioned throughout the Guide and, in the case of the major events, in the list below. Numerous other events display a distinctly surreal edge – the Cilgerran **coracle races** (see p.266), for example, along with bizarre happenings (peat-bog snorkelling, anyone?) in Llanwrtyd (see box, p.225) and Llangynwyd village (see p.117) where locals parade with a horse's skull to welcome in the new year (the Mari Lwyd).

Wales is also host to some of the UK's best summer **rock and pop music festivals**, in addition to some excellent **DJ-led events** and New Age **fairs**; these are usually publicized by handbills, posters in wholefood shops and cafés, and word of mouth.

A festival calendar

Visit Wales maintains a fairly comprehensive events list at ⓦ visitwales.com, and we've covered folk festivals in Contexts (see box, p.454).

JANUARY–APRIL

Mari Lwyd Llangynwyd, near Maesteg, Jan 1; ⓦ folkwales.org.uk/mari.html. Ringing in the new year, this is the most authentic survivor of the ancient Welsh custom of parading a horse's skull through the village streets to guard against evil spirits. See p.117.

Crickhowell Walking Festival End Feb; ⓦ crickhowellfestival.com. Hugely enjoyable nine-day series of guided walks and events around town and throughout the nearby Black Mountains. See box, p.214.

Six Nations rugby championship Cardiff, Feb–March; ⓦ sixnationsrugby.com. Wales plays five matches, two or three of which are hosted by the Principality Stadium.

St David's Day March 1. Wales' national day, with *hwyrnos* (late nights) and celebrations nationwide.

Wonderwool Wales Builth Wells, late April; ⓦ wonderwoolwales.co.uk. Held at the Royal Welsh Showground, this two-day gathering showcases the best of Welsh wool and wool products, from raw materials to designer fashion – with plenty of sheep on show, too.

MAY

Tredegar House Folk Festival Early May; ⓦ tredegarhousefestival.org.uk. A weekend of international dance, music and song at this grand seventeenth-century mansion.

Hay Festival Hay-on-Wye, late May to early June; ⓦ hayfestival.com. One of the most feted literary festivals in the world; this huge ten-day gathering has also spawned a dedicated festival for children and HowTheLightGetsIn, a unique celebration of philosophy and music. See box, p.223.

Urdd National Eisteddfod Last week of May; ⓦ urdd.cymru. Vast and enjoyable youth eisteddfod – one of the largest youth festivals in Europe – held in a different part of the country each year.

St Davids Cathedral Festival End of May to first week in June; ⓦ stdavidscathedralfestival.co.uk. Superb setting for ten days of classical and contemporary concerts and recitals.

JUNE

Cardiff Singer of the World competition Mid-June; ⓦ bbc.co.uk/cardiffsinger. Huge, and very prestigious, week-long festival of music and song held in odd-numbered years, with a star-studded list of international opera and classical singers.

Man Versus Horse Marathon Llanwrtyd Wells, mid-June; ⓦ www.green-events.co.uk. The best known of Llanwrtyd Wells' many infamous madcap events, this endurance race sees runners take on horses over 22 miles. See box, p.225.

Criccieth Festival Third week June; ⓦ cricciethfestival.co.uk. Week-long festival of music, theatre and art around this Llŷn resort town. See p.376.

Gregynog Festival Newtown, last half of June; ⓦ gwylgregynogfestival.org. Ten-day classical music festival in the superb surroundings of Gregynog Hall. See p.241.

Pembrokeshire Fish Week End June; ⓦ pembrokeshirefishweek.co.uk. Guided beach walks, boat trips, snorkel safaris and learn-to-fish sessions, alongside all manner of other coastal jollity at this week-long festival celebrated throughout the region.

JULY

Beyond the Border St Donat's Castle, early July; ⓦ beyondtheborder.com. Three-day international storytelling festival at the fairy-tale setting of St Donat's Castle, Vale of Glamorgan, held every even-numbered year. See p.99.

Cardigan Bay Seafood Festival Aberaeron, first or second Sun in July; ⓦ aberaeronfishfest.com. Some of Wales' best chefs whip up delicious morsels. See p.263.

Gower Festival First half of July; ⓦ gowerfestival.org. Two weeks of mostly classical music in churches around the Gower.

Llangollen International Eisteddfod First week July; ⓦ international-eisteddfod.co.uk. More than twelve thousand participants from all over the world attend this week-long happening, including choirs, dancers, folk singers, groups and instrumentalists. See p.312.

Royal Welsh Show Builth Wells, late July; Ⓦ rwas.co.uk. Europe's largest agricultural show and sales fair is a Welsh institution and a top day out. Watch the ultra-serious judging of prize farm animals, competitive sheep-shearing or wood chopping, witness displays of falconry and craftsmanship, or simply feast on farm-fresh produce. Hundreds of stallholders sell everything from artisan products to agricultural equipment. See p.227.

Snowdon Race Late July; Ⓦ snowdonrace.co.uk. A ten-mile race from Llanberis to the summit of Snowdon and back down again, attracting masochists from across the world. The best runners record times of just over an hour.

The Big Cheese Caerphilly, late July; Ⓦ caerphilly.gov.uk /bigcheese. Tasting aside, this massive three-day festival – taking place mostly within the grounds of Caerphilly Castle – features re-enactments, craft stalls, a traditional fun fair and a Big Cheese Race. See p.107.

AUGUST

World Alternative Games Llanwrtyd Wells, Aug; Ⓦ worldalternativegames.co.uk. Set up in response to the London Olympics in 2012, this two-week event (every even-numbered year) features utterly bonkers events like gravy wrestling, synchronized bath-tubbing and wife carrying. See box, p.225

National Eisteddfod First week Aug; Ⓦ eisteddfod.org.uk. The centrepiece of Welsh culture (originally meaning "a meeting of bards"), this ten-day festival is very much a Welsh affair (largely conducted in Cymraeg) and the country's biggest single annual event. The vast maes (field) hosts art, craft, literature, rock music, Welsh-language lessons, theatre and major music and poetry competitions. Venues alternate each year; in 2018 it's in Cardiff and in 2019 it's in Conwy. See box, p.452.

Green Man Crickhowell, mid-Aug; Ⓦ greenman.net. One of the UK's premier music and arts festivals, featuring a sparkling line-up of indie, folk, dance and Americana, alongside film, theatre and drama and loads of stuff for kids, over four days. See box, p.214.

Pride Cymru Cardiff, late Aug; Ⓦ pridecymru.co.uk. Cardiff's one-day LGBT festival takes over Coopers Field with live music, market stalls and bars.

Gŵyl Machynlleth Machynlleth, late Aug; Ⓦ momawales.org.uk. Wide-ranging, week-long arts festival, with a solid programme of chamber music at its core.

Llandrindod Wells Victorian Festival Late Aug; Ⓦ victorian-festival.co.uk. A week of family fun, street entertainment and Victorian costumes rounded off with a fireworks display.

World Bog Snorkelling Championships Llanwrtyd Wells, Aug Bank Holiday Sun; Ⓦ www.green-events.co.uk. Muddy swim-off along a 180ft-long bog course. See box, p.225.

SEPTEMBER

Festival No. 6 Portmeirion, beginning Sept; Ⓦ festivalnumber6 .com. Superb, sophisticated four-day festival set in atmospheric Portmeirion, with a wide-ranging selection of music, from big-name rock bands to Welsh male voice choirs. DJs, comedy, film and poetry, too. See box, p.373.

Great Welsh Beer & Cider Festival Cardiff, mid-Sept; Ⓦ gwbcf .info. Three days to sample from nearly two hundred ales and sixty ciders (the majority from Welsh breweries).

The Good Life Experience Hawarden Estate, Flintshire, mid-Sept; Ⓦ thegoodlifeexperience.co.uk. Founded and curated by celebrated Welsh singer Cerys Matthews, this three-day festival incorporates a fabulous mix of alternative music, literature, crafts workshops, campfire cooking sessions and much more.

Abergavenny Food Festival Mid-Sept; Ⓦ abergavenny foodfestival.com. This weekend chow-down is Wales' premier gastronomic event, with a smorgasbord of fresh food showcased by celebrity chefs. See p.218.

Sŵn Festival Cardiff, mid-Sept to mid-Oct; Ⓦ swnfest.com. Superb month-long happening showcasing the best in new music in Wales; takes place at various venues in the city.

Tenby Arts Festival Last week Sept; Ⓦ tenbyartsfest.co.uk. Well-established week-long arts romp, with a high-spirited Fringe festival attached. See box, p.163.

OCTOBER–DECEMBER

Swansea International Festival First two weeks Oct; Ⓦ swanseafestival.org. Two weeks of stellar music, theatre, dance and art throughout the city. See box, p.125.

Brecon Baroque Festival End Oct; Ⓦ breconbaroquefestival.com. A wonderful five-day celebration of Baroque music and dance plus loads of other good stuff including guided walks and a pop-up café. See box, p.208.

Dylan Thomas Festival Swansea, late Oct to early Nov; Ⓦ dylan thomas.com. Celebrating their hometown son, this two-week gathering comprises talks, performances, exhibitions, readings and music throughout the city. See box, p.125.

Bonfire Night and Lantern Parade Machynlleth, early Nov. Superb procession culminating in a spectacular fireworks display.

Real Ale Wobble Llanwrtyd Wells, mid-Nov; Ⓦ www.green -events.co.uk. Non-competitive mountain biking and real-ale drinking over a course of 15, 25 or 35 miles. See box, p.225.

Sports and outdoor activities

With craggy mountains, large areas of moorland, a deeply indented coastline, wide beaches and fast-flowing rivers, Wales makes a fabulous outdoor playground – you're never far from a stretch of countryside where you can lose the crowds on a brief walk or cycle ride. From short day-hikes to some of Britain's most epic long-distance paths, there are opportunities galore for keen walkers. Cyclists have the option of many wonderfully scenic, and little-frequented, back roads, while mountain

TOP 5 WALKS
North Ridge Tryfan. See p.346
Pen y Fan/Corn Du Brecon Beacons. See p.204
Pony Path Cadair Idris. See p.294
Port Eynon to Rhossili via Worms Head Gower. See p.130
Snowdon Horseshoe Snowdon. See p.354

bikers can course around Wales' many excellent forest bike parks. Elsewhere, the mountains and cliffs provide scope for fabulous rock climbing and thrilling coasteering trips. Along the coasts, watersports prevail, notably surfing, but also kiteboarding, wakeboarding and stand-up paddleboarding. And, of course, there are plenty of fine beaches for less active fresh-air fun.

Walking and trekking

There isn't a built-up area in Wales that's more than half an hour away from decent walking country, but three areas are so outstanding they have been designated **national parks**. Most of Wales' north-western corner is taken up with the **Snowdonia National Park**, comprising a dozen of the country's highest peaks separated by dramatic glaciated valleys, and laced with hundreds of miles of ridge and moorland paths. From Snowdonia, the Cambrian mountains stretch south to the **Brecon Beacons National Park**, with its striking sandstone scarp at the head of the south Wales coalfield and lush, cave-riddled limestone valleys to the south. Some 170 miles of Wales' southwestern peninsula make up the **Pembrokeshire Coast National Park**, best explored along the **Pembrokeshire Coast Path**, just one of Wales' wonderful designated **long-distance paths** (see box opposite).

Many of the best one-day walks in the country are detailed in this Guide, but for more arduous

mountain treks you'll benefit from bringing a specialist walking guidebook (see p.462). You can also get information from The **Ramblers' Association** (ⓦramblers.org.uk/wales), Britain's main countryside campaigning organization and self-appointed guardian of the nation's footpaths and rights of way. Take a look, too, at the **National Mountain Sports Centre** (ⓦpyb.co.uk; see p.345) at Plas y Brenin; among their many excellent courses they offer a navigation skills course for hill-walkers.

Rights of access

Although they are managed by committees of local and state officials, all three Welsh national parks are predominantly privately owned. Until recently it was the goodwill of landowners that gave access to much of the land, but the 2005 **Countryside and Rights of Way Act** (CRoW) gives open access on foot (but not generally by bike or horse) to "all land that is predominantly mountain, moor, heath or down" across Wales. Such areas (almost a fifth of the country) are marked on all Ordnance Survey maps, and at boundaries you'll see a brown "walking man" sign. Landowners are, however, allowed to restrict access for a number of reasons and signs to that effect are posted locally.

Access to other land is restricted to **public rights of way**: **footpaths** (pedestrians only; yellow waymarkers), **bridleways** (pedestrians, horses and bicycles; blue waymarkers) and **byways** (open to all traffic, but generally unsurfaced; red waymarkers) that have seen continued use over the centuries. Historically, these are often over narrow mountain passes between two hamlets, or linking villages to mines or summer pastureland. Rights of way are marked on Ordnance Survey maps (see p.48) and are indicated from roads with signposts, and intermittently waymarked across the countryside; any stiles and gates on the path have to be maintained by the landowner. Some less scrupulous owners have been known to block rights of way by destroying stiles – and with some walkers wilfully straying from official rights of way, some resentment is perhaps understandable. Disputes are

SAFETY IN THE WELSH HILLS
Welsh **mountains** are not high by world standards, but they should still be treated with respect. The fickle weather makes them more dangerous than you might expect, and you can easily find yourself disoriented in the low cloud and soaked by unexpected rain. If the weather looks like it's closing in, start descending fast. It is essential that you are properly equipped – even for what appears to be an easy expedition in apparently settled weather – with proper warm and waterproof layered clothing, supportive footwear, adequate maps, a compass, food and water. Before you set off, always tell someone your route and expected time of return.

HEROIC HIKES AND LENGTHY RAMBLES

Wales is traced by a spider's web of more than a dozen wonderful **long-distance paths** (LDPs). Three of these – the Pembrokeshire Coast Path, Offa's Dyke Path and Glyndŵr's Way – are additionally designated National Trails, waymarked at frequent intervals by an acorn symbol. The following is a brief rundown of the most popular LDPs.

Cambrian Way (291 miles; ⓦcambrianway.org.uk). The longest, wildest and most arduous of the Welsh LDPs, cutting north–south over the remote Cambrian mountains.

Glyndŵr's Way (135 miles; ⓦnationaltrail.co.uk/glyndwrsway). A lengthy meander among the remote mountains and lakes of mid-Wales, visiting sites associated with the great fifteenth-century Welsh hero. See box, p.235.

Landsker Borderlands Trail (60 miles; ⓦldwa.org.uk). Gentle waterways, quiet villages and easy trails characterize this slightly contrived circular walk around the Landsker region in Pembrokeshire.

Offa's Dyke Path (177 miles; ⓦnationaltrail.co.uk/offas-dyke-path). The classic Welsh LDP, running from Prestatyn in the north to Chepstow in south Wales, tracing the line of the eighth-century earthwork along the English border for a third of the way. A blend of wooded lowland walking and higher hilltops, with exhilarating open territory through the Black Mountains. See box, p.237.

Pembrokeshire Coast Path (186 miles; ⓦnt.pcnpa.org.uk). Almost all within the Pembrokeshire National Park, this hugely rewarding coastal trail dips into quiet coves and climbs over headlands, with sweeping ocean views and plenty of birdlife on the cliffs and offshore islands. See box, p.159.

Wales Coast Path (870 miles; ⓦwalescoastpath.gov.uk). Opened in 2012, the Coast Path links Chepstow (Severn estuary) in the south with Queensferry in the north; it's split into eight geographical areas, and incorporates many already established paths including the Pembrokeshire Coast Path, the Llŷn Coastal Path and the Anglesey Coastal Path.

Wye Valley Walk (136 miles; ⓦwyevalleywalk.org). A lovely, sylvan, sea-to-source trek following the River Wye from Chepstow to Plynlimon, beginning with a long section through a dramatic wooded gorge. The English section visits Ross-on-Wye and Hereford. See box, p.80.

uncommon, but your surest way of avoiding trouble is to meticulously follow the right of way on an up-to-date map.

Ordnance Survey maps also indicate routes with **concessionary path** or **courtesy path** status, where access is given over private land at the goodwill of the owner; though these are usually open for public use they can be closed at any time.

WALKING HOLIDAY OPERATORS

Celtic Trails ⓦ celtictrailswalkingholidays.co.uk. Guided walks of most of the country's classic paths, from Offa's Dyke (around £585 for seven nights) to the Beacons Way (£765 for six nights).

Contours Walking Holidays ⓦ contours.co.uk. Walks covering all Wales' long-distance footpaths, such as Glyndŵr's Way (£855 for ten nights) and the Pembrokeshire Coast Path (£1055 for thirteen nights).

Drover Holidays ⓦ droverholidays.co.uk. Offers walks all over the country but with an emphasis on the area around Hay, for example a fifteen-day Wye Valley Walk (£965).

Footpath Holidays ⓦ footpath-holidays.com. Guided walks of the northern section of Offa's Dyke (£425 for eight days) and sections of the Wales Coast Path (£330 for six days).

Walkalongway ⓦ walkalongway.com. Walking holidays focusing on Pembrokeshire (£499 for six nights) and Ceredigion (£480 for six nights).

Rock climbing and scrambling

As well as being superb walking country, Snowdonia offers some of Britain's best **rock climbing** and several challenging **scrambles** – ascents that fall somewhere between walks and climbs, requiring the use of your hands. One or two of the tougher walks included in the Guide have sections of scrambling, but for the most part this is a specialist discipline, well covered in books available locally.

The scale may not be huge (the highest route only takes you up 800ft), but the quality is excellent, and there's an astonishing variety of routes in a small area. In fact, the term "cragging" comes from *craig*, Welsh for cliff. **Llanberis**, at the foot of Snowdon, is the home of Welsh climbing, with routes ranging from easy hands-on scrambles up mountain ridges to impossibly difficult ascents only achievable by the world's best climbers.

Further south, the pick of the crags are the limestone sea cliffs along the **Pembrokeshire coast**: the bulk of the action happens near Bosherston. The military ordnance testing areas of

Range East and Range West here mean that parts of the coast are off limits, but there are plenty of areas with much freer access. Further east, the Gower peninsula is also ringed by tempting sea cliffs.

If you're interested in increasing your rock-climbing skills, it's worth checking out the **National Mountain Sports Centre** (ⓦ pyb.co.uk; see p.345) at Plas y Brenin. An internationally recognized outdoor training centre, it runs a huge range of residential courses and samplers at all levels, plus expedition training. Typical options include a weekend introduction to rock climbing, an advanced scrambling week and a multi-activity weekend; it also offers qualification courses for all levels of instructors. The **British Mountaineering Council** (ⓦ thebmc.co.uk) can also put you in touch with climbing guides and people running courses.

Cycling

Wales ranks as one of Britain's premier **cycling** destinations, with a complex web of traffic-free bike paths, off-road tracks and low-traffic cycle routes, plus some excellent **mountain bike parks**. Back-road routes along river valleys and over mountain passes have a sufficient density of pubs and B&Bs to keep the days manageable, and while steep gradients can be a problem, ascents are never long, with Wales' highest pass barely reaching 1500ft. Note, however, that in **urban areas** cyclists face the same dangers and difficulties as in any other British town. If you plan to ride in built-up areas, be sure to use a **helmet** and a secure **lock**.

Transporting your bike by **train** is a good way of getting to the interesting parts of Wales without a lot of stressful pedalling. Bikes are generally carried free on suburban trains outside the weekday rush hours of 7.30 to 9.30am and 4 to 6pm. On most routes within Wales there is only space for two bikes and you are expected to make a reservation (Arriva Trains; ☎0870 9000 773), though they'll accept unreserved bikes if there is space. Note that **folding cycles** can be carried free on all services without a reservation. For more information, check Arriva's free *Cycling by Train* brochure (downloadable from ⓦ arrivatrainswales.co.uk/Bicycles) and ⓦ national rail.co.uk/stations_destinations/cyclists.aspx.

Bike rental is available in some large towns (we've listed options throughout the Guide) and many resorts. Expect to pay in the region of £20–25 per day, more for specialist off-road machines with suspension.

Britain's biggest **cycling organization**, Cycling UK (ⓦ cyclinguk.org), supplies members with touring and technical advice as well as insurance. Its website has a wealth of information, including dozens of routes through Wales.

Cycle touring routes

The best of Wales' narrow lanes, disused railway lines and forest paths have been linked to form 1200 miles of **cycle routes** – three hundred miles of which are traffic-free – as part of the National Cycle Network created by **Sustrans** (ⓦ sustrans.org.uk) to promote sustainable transport.

In addition to numerous local routes, three major cycling routes cross Wales. The main north–south **Lôn Las Cymru** (the Welsh National Route; Route 8) covers 250 hilly miles from Anglesey through Snowdonia, the Brecon Beacons and the industrial valleys of the south, to the Severn Bridge. Sustrans publishes two maps of the route, one covering Holyhead to Llanidloes and the other from Llanidloes to Chepstow and Cardiff. **Lôn Geltaidd** (Celtic Trail; Routes 4 and 47) traverses 220 miles across the south of the country (seventy percent of it traffic-free) from Fishguard to Chepstow, while along the north coast the busy roads are avoided on the 105-mile long **North Wales Coast Route** (Route 5) – again, Sustrans produces maps for both these routes.

Shorter **local routes** sometimes follow dedicated traffic-free paths but are often directed along quiet lanes; free leaflets available locally are easy to follow. Areas worth considering are the Gower peninsula, Pembrokeshire, Anglesey, the Llŷn and the supremely unspoilt and fairly challenging three-day **Radnor Ring**, near Llandrindod Wells.

Mountain biking

Since the 1990s, the forests of Wales have gained an enviable reputation for top-class **mountain biking**. Every weekend mud-splattered bikers weave along miles of single-track at more than a dozen dedicated **bike parks** dotted along the mountainous spine of the country – from the Gwydyr Forest just outside Betws-y-Coed to Cwm Carn in the Valleys northwest of Newport. There's something to suit everyone, from beginners to hardened speed freaks. There's no charge for using the parks (though there may be a small parking fee) and most have bike rental facilities.

Elsewhere, off-road cycling is allowed along designated bridleways (waymarked with blue arrows), including the Snowdon Ranger, Rhyd Ddu and Llanberis paths up Snowdon (see box, p.352), but conflict between hikers and bikers has led to the creation of the **Snowdon Voluntary Cycling Agreement**, which limits the hours riders can use them. Anytime in winter (Oct–April) is OK and you can ride before 10am and after 5pm throughout the summer: slog up in the pre-dawn cool for that summit sunrise, or head up for sunset and a nerve-wracking dusk descent. If you really fancy a challenge, make for **Sarn Helen**, an epic route across the country through Snowdonia and the Brecon Beacons, loosely following an old Roman route. At 270 miles long – running from Conwy to Gower – it's reckoned to be the most ambitious off-road ride in Britain and is likely to take over a week.

Footpaths, unless otherwise marked, are for pedestrian use only, and even on bridleways you should always pass walkers at a considerate speed and with a courteous warning of your presence. For more **information** check out Ⓦ mbwales.com, which concentrates on the main bike parks, or Ⓦ mtbtrails.info, which has excellent articles on routes along with forums where you can hook up with other riders.

CYCLE TOUR OPERATORS

Bicycle Beano ☎ 01962 867699, Ⓦ bicycle-beano.co.uk. Book well ahead to join the four-day Brecon Beacons Beano (£440) and the week-long Snowdonia Beano (£750–850). Guides pedal along with you and trips include accommodation and all meals (except lunch), which are usually vegetarian. Good value and great fun.

Crwydro Môn ☎ 01248 713611, Ⓦ angleseywalkingholidays .com/awh/cycling. Tailored, five- and seven-day self-guided packages (from £360) around Anglesey with bike, B&B and luggage transfer included.

Drover Holidays ☎ 07501 495868, Ⓦ droverholidays.co.uk. More than a dozen guided and self-guided bike tours all over Wales with everything organized and even the option of an electrically assisted bike to help with the nastier hills.

Wheely Wonderful Cycling ☎ 01568 770755, Ⓦ wheelywonderfulcycling.co.uk. Several self-guided tours around wonderfully rural sections of mid-Wales and the borders, from a weekend to a week (£165–720).

Water-based activites

Wales is ringed by fine **beaches** and **bays**, many of which are readily accessible by public transport – though some get very busy in high summer. With most of the Welsh coast influenced by the currents of the North Atlantic Drift, **water temperatures** are higher than you might expect for this latitude, but only the truly hardy should consider swimming outside summer. For tuition, contact the **National Outdoor Centre** near Caernarfon (Ⓦ plasmenai.co.uk), which offers all manner of predominantly two- and five-day

---

TOP 5 BEACHES
Barafundle Bay Pembrokeshire.
See p.169
Porth Oer (Whistling Sands) The Llŷn.
See p.382
Rhossili Bay Gower. See p.126
Tresaith Near New Quay. See p.259
Ynyslas Near Borth. See p.280

---

courses covering dinghy sailing, windsurfing, kayaking and powerboating in a beautiful location on the Menai Strait.

Swimming

For **swimming** and sunbathing, the best areas to head for are the Gower peninsula, the Pembrokeshire coast, the Llŷn and the southwest coast of Anglesey. Though it has more resorts than any other section of Wales' coastline, the north coast certainly hasn't got the most attractive beaches, nor is it a particularly alluring place to swim. **Wild swimming** is popular all over Wales, the country's many wonderful lakes and rivers providing ample opportunities for a refreshing dip.

Surfing, windsurfing, kiteboarding and paddleboarding

Wales' southwest-facing beaches offer the best conditions for **surfing**, **windsurfing** and **kiteboarding**. The water may not be that warm, but great sweeping beaches lashed by strong, steady winds off the Atlantic make for some excellent spots. Key surfing centres are Rhosneigr on Anglesey, Aberdyfi along the Cambrian coast, Rest Bay in Porthcawl, Whitesands Bay (Porth Mawr) near St Davids, and Langland Bay and Llangennith, both on the Gower peninsula. All these places have shops selling gear and offering lessons. For surfing information, contact the **Welsh Surfing Federation Surf School** (Ⓦ surfschool.wsf.wales) on the Gower peninsula. Kiteboarding isn't exactly an easy sport to learn, but a class can get you body-dragging (more fun than it sounds) inside a day, and actually riding a board in a couple of days. Easier to learn is **stand-up paddleboarding**, which has taken wing in Wales recently; there are dozens of great spots all over the country to try this, from Cardiff Bay to the Mawddach estuary near Barmouth.

Coasteering

Wales has led the way with **coasteering**, an exhilarating combination of hiking, coastal scrambling, swimming and cliff-jumping. Clad in a wetsuit, helmet and buoyancy aid, you aim to make your way as a group along the rugged, wave-lashed coastline. It was pioneered by St Davids-based **TYF** (see box, p.181), which runs a range of trips from the relatively tame (many are suitable for families) to full-on blasts along the coast.

Kayaking and rafting

Board riders constantly have to compete for waves with the surf ski riders and **kayakers** who frequent the same beaches. Paddlers, however, have the additional run of miles of superb coastline, particularly around Anglesey, the Llŷn and the Pembrokeshire coast. The best general **guide** is the encyclopaedic *Welsh Sea Kayaking* by Jim Krawiecki and Andy Biggs.

Inland, short, steep bedrock **rivers** come alive after rain. As equipment improves, paddlers have become more daring, and Victorian tourist attractions such as Swallow and Conwy falls, both near Betws-y-Coed, are now fair game for a descent. Most of the kayaking is non-competitive, but on summer weekends you might catch a slalom or freestyle kayaking event at the **National White Water Centre** (see box, p.323) outside Bala, or at the **Cardiff International White Water centre** (see p.67). In both places you can ride the rapids in **rafts**.

Pony trekking

Wales' scattered population and large tracts of open land are ideal for **pony trekking**. Don't expect too much cantering over unfenced land: rides tend to be geared towards unhurried appreciation of the scenery from horseback and are often combined with a night in farm accommodation. Rates are typically around £20 for the first hour and £10–15 for each subsequent hour. Mid-Wales has the greatest concentration of stables, but there are places all over the country, amply detailed on the Wales Trekking and Riding Association website (Ⓦ ridingwales.com).

Rugby

Rugby (the "Union" variety) is a Welsh passion and their national game. Support is strongest in the working-class valleys of south Wales, where the fanaticism has traditionally been fuelled by the national side's success. The sport saw its glory days in the 1970s, when the scarlet jerseys regularly dominated the annual **Five Nations Championship**

(now the Six Nations), winning six out of the ten tournaments – three of them **Grand Slams** (where every match is won). This formidable side included fearless fullback J.P.R. Williams, the elusive and magical outside-halves Barry John and Phil Bennett, and the dynamic scrum-half Gareth Edwards.

The 1980s and most of the 1990s were barren times, but when rugby turned professional in 1995, it was able to coax back players who had defected to the rival code, rugby league. The recruitment of New Zealander Graham Henry in 1998, and the building of the 72,500-seater **Millennium Stadium** (now the Principality Stadium) in Cardiff, coincided with a gradual reversal in the national side's fortunes. In 2005, Wales lifted the **Six Nations trophy** with a Grand Slam, and, after a poor World Cup in 2007, the team secured another Grand Slam in 2008, this time under another Kiwi coach, Warren Gatland. Following a superb 2011 World Cup campaign, when they reached the semi-finals, they completed yet another Grand Slam in 2012. The 2015 World Cup was a disappointment, Wales being defeated at the quarter-final stage by South Africa. As ever though, optimism runs high among the natives, with many hoping that the 2019 World Cup in New Zealand will finally be their year.

To see an **international game**, you'll have to be affiliated to one of the Rugby Union clubs or be prepared to pay well over the odds at one of the ticket agencies. Most tickets are allocated months before a match and touts are often found selling tickets for hundreds of pounds outside the gates on the day.

Away from the international arena, a thriving rugby scene exists at **club level**, with upwards of a hundred clubs and forty thousand players taking to the field most Saturdays throughout the season (from September to just after Easter). The upper tier is known as the Pro 14, with four Welsh teams – Cardiff Blues, (Llanelli) Scarlets, Newport Gwent Dragons and (Swansea) Ospreys – playing against the top teams from Ireland, Scotland, Italy and South Africa. Of the Welsh sides, Scarlets were the most recent winners of the league, in 2017. It's often worth going to a match purely for the light-hearted crowd banter – if you can understand the accents. Check with individual clubs for fixtures and ticket prices, which start at around £20.

Football

Though **Welsh football** (soccer) is seen as a minority sport, it has just as many participants as rugby. Following years in the doldrums, the national team's stock has risen dramatically. Under manager Chris Coleman and their talismanic winger Gareth Bale (currently playing for Real Madrid), not only did they qualify for the 2016 European Championships – their first major tournament since 1958 – but the team's incredible run to the semi-finals captured the imagination of football fans throughout Wales and beyond. The next target is qualification for the World Cup.

At club level, the game is in pretty rude health too, thanks largely to the recent success of Swansea City, who were promoted to the Premier League in 2011 and have remained there ever since (Cardiff City did manage one season in the Premier League in 2013–14). Both sides have also fared well in the cups, with Swansea winning the League Cup in 2013 – its first major piece of silverware – and Cardiff reaching the FA Cup Final in 2008, the first Welsh club to achieve this since doing so itself in 1927. Traditionally, Wrexham is the third team in Wales, though its 87-year stay in the Football League came to an end in 2008 and it has remained a non-league team since. The rest of the clubs play in the lacklustre **Welsh Premier League** (Ⓦ welshpremier.co.uk). For more on the Welsh game, check the website of the Football Association of Wales (Ⓦ faw.cymru).

Alternative, New Age and green Wales

Possibly more than any other part of Britain, Wales – the mid and west in particular – has become a haven for people searching for alternative lifestyles. Permanent testimonials to this include the Centre for Alternative Technology (CAT), near Machynlleth, now one of the area's most visited attractions, and Tipi Valley, near Talley, a permanent community living in Native American tepees who run a regular public sweat lodge. Both institutions were founded in the idealistic mid-1970s and have prospered through less happy times. For the most part, it's been a fairly smooth process, although antagonism between New Agers and local, established families does break out on occasion.

For visitors, the legacy of this "green" influx is evident throughout Wales. Even in the smallest rural towns, you'll often find a health-food shop, wholefood café, a little boutique flogging esoteric ephemera or an alternative resource centre. Any of these will give you further ideas and contacts for local happenings, places, groups and individuals.

There's also a plethora of good **festivals** from spring to autumn, ranging from big folk and blues bashes to smaller gatherings in remote fields with little more than a couple of banging sound systems. Information travels best by word of mouth, so keep your eyes peeled and your ears open and don't hesitate to ask around. For ecologically minded tourists, there are now numerous package deals that include walking, cycling, dancing and healing holidays, and **retreats** in remote centres, usually with vegetarian and vegan food as part of the deal. Some of these are static, many are in temporary sites, while others keep you on the move.

RETREATS AND WORKSHOPS

Buckland Hall Bwlch, near Brecon Ⓣ 01874 730330, Ⓦ bucklandhall.co.uk. Beautiful hall and gardens hosting holistic lifestyle courses and workshops.

Cae Mabon near Llanberis, Gwynedd Ⓣ 01286 871542, Ⓦ caemabon.co.uk. Stunning Snowdonia setting for residential courses, storytelling and arts events, with accommodation in roundhouses and a Navajo-style hogan.

Centre for Alternative Technology Llwyngwern, near Machynlleth, Powys Ⓣ 01654 705982, Ⓦ cat.org.uk. Residential courses on green themes such as building your own home and organic gardening.

Dance Camp Wales Pembrokeshire Ⓦ dancecampwales.org. Ten-day participatory dance festival held at the end of July and into August in a beautiful location, with about five hundred participants.

Healing Tao Britain Conwy Ⓣ 01492 515776, Ⓦ healingtaobritain.com. Residential weekend workshops on meditation and Qi Gong, most of which take place in Colwyn.

Spirit Horse Near Llanidloes Ⓣ 07882 522878, Ⓦ spirithorse .co.uk. Camps to celebrate ancient ceremonial and cultural traditions in a stunning, secluded Powys setting.

Vajraloka Buddhist Meditation Centre Corwen, Denbighshire Ⓣ 01490 460406, Ⓦ vajraloka.org. Regular retreats, either men-only or mixed.

TOP 5 GARDENS
Bodnant Conwy. See p.409
Colby Woodland Gardens Amroth. See p.158
Dyffryn Gardens Barry. See p.96
National Botanic Garden Tywi Valley. See p.145
Powis Castle Welshpool. See p.244

Travel essentials

Costs

Wales is by no means a cheap destination, but prices are generally lower than in many parts of England. However, given the UK's unstable political and economic climate in the wake of Brexit, costs are likely to fluctuate for the foreseeable future. The **minimum expenditure**, if you are travelling by public transport, self-catering and camping, would be in the region of £20–25 per day, rising to £35–40 per day if you're using the hostelling network and grabbing the occasional meal out. Couples staying at budget B&Bs, eating at unpretentious restaurants and visiting the odd tourist attractions are looking at £65–75 each per day – if you're renting a car, staying in comfortable B&Bs or hotels and eating well, reckon on at least £90–100 a day per person.

Inevitably, entry prices for attractions vary considerably, but you can expect to pay £3–5 for your average museum, and anywhere between £5 and £10 for a visit to a National Trust property or any CADW property that charges (see box below). Many other old buildings are owned by the local authorities, and admission is often cheaper, or free. Municipal **art galleries** and **museums** are usually free, as are seven major sites run by National Museum Wales (Ⓦ museum.wales), including the St Fagans National Museum of History in Cardiff and Big Pit in Blaenavon. Although a donation is sometimes requested, **cathedrals** tend to be free, except for perhaps the tower or crypt for which a small charge is made. Increasingly, **churches** are kept locked except during services, in which case you'll normally be able to find a notice in the porch or on a board telling you where to get a key; when they are open, entry is free.

Entry charges given in the Guide are the full adult rates, but the majority of the fee-charging attractions have good **reductions** for senior citizens, full-time students and people under 16 – under-5s are admitted free almost everywhere. Family tickets are also common, usually priced just under the rate for two adults and a child and include up to three kids.

Discount cards

The various official and quasi-official **youth/ student ID cards** are of relatively minor use in Wales, saving only a few pence for entry to some sites. If you already have one, then bring it, but if you don't, it's barely worth making a special effort to get one.

Full-time students are eligible for the International Student Identity Card (ISIC; Ⓦ isic.org), while anyone under 26 can apply for an International Youth Travel Card, which carries the same benefits; both cost £12. A university photo ID might open some doors, but is not as easily recognizable as the ISIC cards.

Crime and personal safety

As in any other country, Wales' major towns have their dangerous spots, but these tend to be around inner-city housing estates where you're unlikely to find yourself. The chief risk on the streets – though still minimal – is **pickpocketing**, so carry only as much money as you need, and keep all bags and pockets fastened. For the most part, Welsh **police** are approachable and helpful to visitors; should you

---

NATIONAL TRUST AND CADW

Many of Wales' most treasured sites – from castles, abbeys and great houses to tracts of protected landscape – come under the control of the privately run UK-wide **National Trust** or the state-run **CADW** (a Welsh verb meaning "to keep" or "to protect") whose properties we denote in this Guide by "NT" and "CADW". The National Trust charges an entry fee for most places, which can be quite high, especially for the more grandiose estates; CADW admission charges are usually a little lower and often free. If you think you'll be visiting more than half a dozen NT places or a similar number of major CADW sites, it's worth buying an annual pass.

Membership of the National Trust (Ⓦ nationaltrust.org.uk; £64.80, under-26s £32.40, family £114.60) allows free entry and parking at its properties throughout Britain. Sites operated by CADW (Ⓦ cadw.gov.wales; £44, seniors £29, ages 16–20 £24, under-16s £18, family £73) are restricted to Wales, but membership also grants you half-price entry to sites owned by English Heritage and Historic Scotland. CADW also offers the Explorer Pass, which allows free entry into all CADW sites on three days in seven (adult £21, family £44), or seven days in fourteen (£32/£62). Entry to CADW sites is free for Welsh residents over 60.

AVERAGE MONTHLY TEMPERATURES AND RAINFALL

	Jan	Feb	Mar	Apr	May	Jun	Jul	Aug	Sep	Oct	Nov	Dec
CARDIFF												
Max/min (°C)	8/2	8/2	11/4	13/5	17/8	19/11	21/3	21/13	18/10	15/7	11/4	9/3
Max/min (°F)	47/36	47/36	51/40	55/41	62/47	67/51	71/55	71/55	65/50	58/45	51/40	48/38
Rainfall (mm)	119	91	89	65	65	66	61	90	104	117	117	128
DOLGELLAU												
Max/min (°C)	6/1	6/1	8/2	11/4	14/6	16/9	18/11	18/11	16/9	12/7	9/4	6/2
Max/min (°F)	43/34	43/34	47/36	51/40	57/43	61/48	65/51	65/51	61/48	54/45	48/40	43/34
Rainfall (mm)	172	156	116	96	104	83	90	81	99	187	147	184

have anything stolen or be involved in an incident that requires reporting, go to the local police station.

Electricity

In Britain, the **current** is 240V AC at 50Hz. North American appliances will need a transformer, though most laptops, phone and MP3 player chargers are designed to automatically detect and adapt to the electricity supply and don't need any modification. Almost all foreign appliances will require an adapter for the chunky British three-pin electrical sockets.

Emergencies

For **police**, **fire** and **ambulance** services phone ☎999 (British) or ☎112 (pan-European). There is also a non-emergency number for the police ☎101 (10p/call).

Health

No vaccinations are required for entry into Britain. Citizens of all EU countries are currently entitled to free **medical treatment** at National Health Service hospitals, though this may change depending on what happens as a result of Brexit; citizens of other countries are charged for all medical services except those administered by accident and emergency units at National Health Service hospitals. Health insurance is therefore strongly advised for all non-EU nationals.

Pharmacies (known generally as chemists in Britain) can dispense only a limited range of drugs without a doctor's prescription. Most pharmacies are open during standard shop hours, though you'll find late-night branches in larger cities and 24-hour supermarkets. For anything that requires immediate attention, head to the casualty department of the local hospital. In a real **emergency**, call for an ambulance on ☎999 or ☎112.

Insurance

Even though EU health-care privileges apply in the UK, it's a good idea to take out **travel insurance** before travelling to cover against theft, loss and illness and injury; again, the situation could well change once the UK leaves the EU. For non-EU citizens, it's worth checking whether you are already covered before you buy a new policy. If you need to take out insurance, you might want to consider the travel insurance deal offered by Rough Guides (see box below).

ROUGH GUIDES TRAVEL INSURANCE

Rough Guides has teamed up with WorldNomads.com to offer great travel insurance deals. Policies are available to residents of over 150 countries, with cover for a wide range of adventure sports, 24hr emergency assistance, high levels of medical and evacuation cover and a stream of travel safety information. Roughguides.com users can take advantage of their policies online 24/7, from anywhere in the world – even if you're already travelling. And since plans often change when you're on the road, you can extend your policy and even claim online. Roughguides.com users who buy travel insurance with WorldNomads.com can also leave a positive footprint and donate to a community development project. For more information, go to ⓦroughguides.com/travel-insurance.

A typical travel insurance policy usually provides cover for the loss of baggage, tickets and – up to a certain limit – money, as well as cancellation or curtailment of your journey. Most of them exclude so-called dangerous sports unless an extra premium is paid; in Wales this can mean whitewater rafting, windsurfing and coasteering, though probably not ordinary hiking. If you take medical coverage, ascertain whether benefits will be paid as treatment proceeds or only after return home, and whether there is a 24-hour medical emergency number. When securing baggage cover, make sure that the per-article limit – typically under £500 – will cover your most valuable possession. If you need to make a claim, you should keep receipts for medicines and medical treatment, and in the event you have anything stolen, you must obtain an official statement from the **police**.

Internet

Just about every hotel, guesthouse/B&B and hostel, as well as many campsites, will have free **wi-fi**, though it may be fairly patchy in the more remote areas. Most cafés and bars, too, have free wi-fi, though you will of course be required to pay to eat or drink something to use it. An increasing number of town and city centre spaces offer free public wi-fi, too, even if it is only for an hour or two. Failing that, you could always head to the local tourist office or try a public library, most of which will have wi-fi and computers for use – some libraries may require you to be a member, however.

LGBT travellers

Homosexual acts between consenting males were legalized in Britain in 1967, but it wasn't until 2000 that the age of consent for gay men was made equal to that of straight men, at 16. Lesbianism has never specifically been outlawed, apocryphally owing to the fact that Queen Victoria refused to believe it existed. In December 2005, civil partnerships between same-sex couples were legalized – marriage in all but name. The most significant step, however, came in 2014, when **same-sex marriage** was finally legalized.

With such a rural culture, it's perhaps not surprising that Wales is less used to the LGBT lifestyle than its more cosmopolitan English neighbour. That said, there's little real hostility, and the traditional Welsh "live and let live" attitude applies as much in this area as any other. Several Welsh celebrities have come out in recent years, notably former Wales rugby captain Gareth Thomas, and it's barely caused a stir.

The organized LGBT scene in Wales is fairly muted, even in the main cities, Cardiff and Swansea, though there are a number of pubs and clubs; Cardiff, too, stages the annual Pride Cymru Festival each August (see p.39). The best resource for LGBT events in the capital is Ⓦcardiff.gaycities.com. Beyond the two big cities, LGBT life becomes distinctly discreet, although university towns such as Lampeter, Bangor and Wrexham manage support groups and the odd weekly night in a local bar, while Aberystwyth is a significantly friendly milieu. **Border Women** (Ⓦborderwomen.net) is a well-organized lesbian network for mid-Wales and the Marches.

Maps

Most bookshops have a good selection of **maps** of Wales and Britain, though the best can be found in specialist travel bookshops. Virtually every petrol station in Britain stocks large-format **road atlases** produced by the AA, RAC, Collins, Ordnance Survey (OS) and others, which cover all of Britain at a scale of around three miles to one inch and include larger-scale plans of major towns. The best of these is the OS road atlas, which handily uses the same grid reference system as their accurate and detailed folding maps.

When hiking, you should go for the widely available maps by **OS** (Ⓦordnancesurvey.co.uk), renowned for their accuracy and clarity. The maps in its 1:50,000 (a little over one inch: one mile) Landranger series cover the whole of Britain, while the more detailed 1:25,000 Explorer series has field boundaries to aid navigation, and is at an ideal scale for walkers. The site also offers an OS MapFinder app, whereby you can download (for a fee) high-resolution maps to your smartphone or tablet.

Money

The unit of **currency** in the UK is the pound sterling (£; *punt* in Welsh, and informally referred to as "quid"), divided into 100 pence (p; in Welsh, c for *ceiniogau*). Coins come in denominations of 1p, 2p, 5p, 10p, 20p, 50p, £1 and £2. Notes come in denominations of £5, £10, £20 and £50. Shopkeepers carefully scrutinize any £20 and £50 notes tendered, as forgeries are not uncommon. At the time of writing, £1 was worth around €1.10, US$1.30, Can$1.60, Aus$1.60 and NZ$1.75. For the latest exchange rates, check ⓦxe.com.

Contactless payment is widely available and most hotels, shops and restaurants accept the major **credit**, **charge** and **debit cards**, particularly Access/MasterCard and Visa/Barclaycard. American Express and Diners' Club are less widely accepted. Cards are accepted at most B&Bs, though you should check beforehand. Most Welsh towns will have a branch of at least one of the major **banks**: NatWest, Halifax, HSBC, Barclays and Lloyds TSB. General banking hours are Monday to Friday 9 or 9.30am to 4.30 or 5pm, and branches in larger towns are often open on Saturday from 9am to 1pm. **Post offices** charge no commission and have longer opening hours, and are therefore often a good place to change currency.

Opening hours and public holidays

General **shop hours** are Monday to Saturday 9am to 5.30/6pm, although there's an increasing amount of Sunday and late-night shopping in the larger towns, with Thursday or Friday being the favoured evenings. The larger shopping malls tend to stay open until 8 or 9pm from Monday to Saturday, and from 11am to 5pm on Sunday, as do many of the big supermarkets. Note that not all **petrol stations** are open 24 hours, although you can usually get fuel around the clock in the larger towns and cities. When it comes to **tourist attractions**, most fee-charging sites are open on bank holidays, when Sunday hours usually apply.

PUBLIC HOLIDAYS

New Year's Day January 1.
Good Friday late March to mid-April.
Easter Monday late March to mid-April.
Early May Bank Holiday first Monday in May.
Spring Bank Holiday (sometimes referred to as Whitsun) last Monday in May.
Late summer Bank Holiday Last Monday in August.
Christmas Day December 25.
Boxing Day December 26.
Note that if January 1, December 25 or December 26 falls on a Saturday or Sunday, the next weekday becomes a public holiday.

Phones

Public **payphones** are still to be found in some places, but the ubiquity of mobile phones means they are seldom used. In general **call costs** vary greatly depending on whether you are calling from a private landline, a public payphone or a mobile. If you're bringing your own **mobile phone/cellphone** with you to Wales from overseas, check with your service provider whether your phone will work abroad and what the call charges are. The cost of calls within the EU has decreased significantly within recent years – indeed, roaming charges were finally abolished in 2017. As with so many things, though, the Brexit vote means that the future is uncertain with regard to how this will affect the UK. Calls to destinations further afield are still unregulated and can be prohibitively expensive.

The **GSM system** used in Britain is compatible with European and Australasian systems, though most North American single-band phones don't work. A better bet might be to bring your phone and buy a new prepaid SIM card (under £5, available from any phone provider); with no contract you can then simply top up your account as you need to. If your phone doesn't work on UK frequency bands you may need one that does; these are available from numerous high-street outlets such as Carphone Warehouse from as little as £15.

To **call Wales** from outside the UK, dial the international access code (☎011 from the US and Canada, ☎0011 from Australia and ☎00 from New Zealand), followed in all cases by 44, then the area code minus its initial zero, and finally the number. Beware of **premium-rate numbers**, which are common for pre-recorded information services – and usually have the prefix ☎09. Numbers starting with ☎0800 are **free** to call.

Post

Virtually all **post offices** (*swyddfa'r post*) are open Monday to Friday 9am to 5.30pm, Saturday 9am to 12.30pm. In small communities, you'll find sub-post offices operating out of a shop, but these work to the same hours even if the shop itself is open for longer. Stamps can be bought at post office counters and from a large number of newsagents and other shops, although often these sell only books of four or ten stamps. A first-class letter to anywhere in Britain (up to 100g) costs 65p and should arrive the next day; second-class letters cost

56p, taking two to three days to arrive, in theory. Prices to Europe and the rest of the world vary depending on the size of the item and how quickly you would like it delivered. For parcel rates visit W royalmail.com.

Shopping

The quintessential Welsh memento is a **lovespoon** – an intricately carved wooden spoon that in centuries gone by was offered by suitors when courting. The meanings of the various designs range from a Celtic cross (faith/marriage) to vines (growing love) and a double spoon (commitment), with dozens of others available. Prices range from a few pounds for a small version to several hundred pounds for a large, elaborate spoon by a well-known carver. You'll find them in craft shops all over the country, including some dedicated solely to these ornaments.

Other unique items include paintings, jewellery, leatherwork and screen-printing from **arts and crafts** galleries throughout Wales. Some are run by the artists themselves, and you can often watch them at work. Given that the country has an estimated three to four times as many sheep as humans, it's not surprising that there are some wonderful **woollen products** (notably blankets) available. Elsewhere, you'll find products made from **slate**, including a large number of coasters, while **food and drink** – whiskey from Penderyn, gin from one of Wales' many distilleries, local cheeses – are all sure to go down a treat, literally.

Studying

Numerous places around Wales offer full-day or multiday courses (residential or otherwise) where you can pursue interests in, for example, the Welsh language or the country's unique landscape. In addition to the following, Plas y Brenin, the National Mountain Sports Centre (see p.345) and Plas Menai, the National Outdoor Centre (see p.43) run a varied range of **outdoor activity courses**.

COURSES IN WALES

Nant Gwrtheyrn Ten miles north of Pwllheli ☎ 01758 750334, W nantgwrtheyrn.org. Extensive range of Welsh-language courses run for everyone from complete beginners to near-fluent speakers.

Plas Tan y Bwlch Near Porthmadog ☎ 01766 772600, W eryri-npa.gov.uk. The Snowdonia National Park Study Centre runs residential courses focusing mainly on the environment and appreciation of the countryside. They extend to landscape photography, botanical painting and the study of mushrooms and toadstools, drovers and drovers'

roads, heritage railways and much more. Many are taught in Welsh or bilingually, and are suitable for Welsh-language beginners.

Time

Greenwich Mean Time (GMT) is in force from late October to late March, when the clocks go forward an hour for British Summer Time (BST). GMT is five hours ahead of New York, ten hours behind Sydney and twelve hours behind New Zealand.

Tipping

There are no fixed rules for **tipping** in Britain, but if you think you've received good service, then a ten-percent tip should suffice (unless service has already been included, which it sometimes is). Taxi drivers will also expect a tip of around ten percent. You do not generally tip bar staff.

Tourist information

Wales promotes itself enthusiastically through **Visit Wales** (Croeso Cymru: W visitwales.com). Their central information service is excellent for pre-trip planning, with a detailed website and plenty of free downloadable brochures which can also be sent by mail. By way of contrast, many of the country's **tourist offices** (often called Tourist Information Centres or TICs) have been closed in recent years. Where they do exist, they are usually very well stocked with information on the local area and elsewhere throughout the country – you'll find contact details and opening hours of all tourist offices throughout the Guide. Note that opening hours are generally shorter in winter, and in more remote areas they may well be closed altogether off season. All offices offer information on accommodation (which they can often book; see p.32), local public transport, attractions and restaurants, as well as town and regional maps.

Areas designated as national parks (the Brecon Beacons, Pembrokeshire Coast and Snowdonia) also have a fair sprinkling of **National Park Information Centres**, which are generally more expert in giving guidance on local walks and outdoor pursuits.

Travellers with disabilities

Visitors with **disabilities** generally fare pretty well travelling in Wales, though many older buildings (and especially cheaper places to stay) are difficult or impossible to adapt – it always pays to call ahead to check the situation. Disabled parking spaces are common; new buildings (including accommodation) are required to make appropriate provision; and a fair number of existing hotels, B&Bs and restaurants are retrofitting accessible bathrooms and ramps. Many hostels now also have disabled facilities.

Public transport companies are making more of an effort to accommodate passengers with mobility problems. Most rail services now cater for wheelchair users, and assistance is usually available at stations if you call at least 24 hours in advance; call National Rail Enquiries (see p.29) to get the number of the appropriate rail company. You may be eligible for the Disabled Persons Railcard (£20/year; ⓦ disabledpersons-railcard.co.uk), which gives a third off most tickets for you and a companion. The link for "Passengers with disabilities" at ⓦ national rail.co.uk has information for journey planning, including maps identifying stations that have access to platforms without steps. There are no bus discounts for disabled passengers who are not Welsh citizens. Rental cars with hand controls are rare and expensive.

Access to **monuments and museums** is improving all the time. The National Trust (see box, p.46) produces a downloadable sheet detailing accessibility to NT properties in Wales; disabled visitors must pay entry fees, but they can bring a friend or carer in to assist them free of charge. CADW (see box, p.46) allows wheelchair users and the visually handicapped, along with their assisting companion, free entry to all monuments. You can download a booklet with detailed site access details from their website (ⓦ cadw.gov.wales).

Some **public toilets** are kept locked, but some local authorities have joined the National Key System (NKS) in which disabled people can gain access to facilities via a standard key – contact RADAR (see below). Some tourist offices also hold a key that you can borrow.

RESOURCES FOR DISABLED TRAVELLERS

Disability Rights ⓦ disabilityrightsuk.org. Campaigning organization that's a good source of advice on holidays and travel in the UK.

Disability Wales ⓦ disabilitywales.org. Welsh equivalent of Disability Rights (see above).

Mobility International USA ⓦ miusa.org. Information and referral services, access guides, tours and exchange programmes.

Open Britain ⓦ openbritain.net. Excellent online resource listing a whole range of accessible travel-related information, from accommodation to attractions.

Society for Accessible Travel and Hospitality (SATH) ⓦ sath. org. Long-standing nonprofit educational organization with useful travel tips and access information on its website.

Tourism For All ⓦ tourismforall.org.uk. Offers various guides and advice for access throughout Britain.

Wales Council for the Blind ⓦ wcb-ccd.org.uk. Though not specifically set up with visitors in mind, it does provide a good contact point.

Wales Council for the Deaf ⓦ wcdeaf.org.uk. Also not specifically set up with visitors in mind, but another good contact.

Cardiff and southeast Wales

57 Cardiff and around

77 Wye Valley

86 Mid-Monmouthshire

88 Newport and around

94 Vale of Glamorgan

102 The Valleys

119 Swansea

126 Gower

KAYAKERS ON RHOSSILI BEACH

1

Cardiff and southeast Wales

Home to some sixty percent of the country's population, the southeastern corner of Wales is one of Britain's most industrialized regions. People and industry are most heavily concentrated around the sea ports and former mining valleys, though quiet hills and beaches are only ever a few miles away. Once the world's busiest coal port, Cardiff is today the country's commercial, cultural and political powerhouse, an upbeat capital offering stellar museums, a storybook castle and invigorating nightlife. Beyond Cardiff, Wales unfolds from the English border in a beguilingly rural manner.

The River Wye flows forth from its mouth at the fortress town of **Chepstow**, where you'll find one of the most impressive castles in a land where few towns are without one. In the Wye's beautiful valley lie the spectacularly placed ruins of **Tintern Abbey**, downstream from the old county town of **Monmouth**. Industrialization intensifies as you travel west to the River Usk, which spills out into the Bristol Channel at **Newport**, Wales' third-largest conurbation, and home to the remains of an extensive Roman settlement in adjacent **Caerleon**.

To the west and north are the world-famous **Valleys**, once the coal- and iron-rich powerhouse of the British Empire. This is the Wales of popular imagination: hemmed-in valley floors packed with seemingly never-ending lines of slate-roofed terraced houses, slanted towards the pithead. Although all the deep mines have closed, the area is still one of tight-knit towns, with a rich working-class heritage displayed in some gutsy museums and colliery tours, such as the **Big Pit** at Blaenavon and the **Rhondda Heritage Park** in Trehafod.

Immediately west of Cardiff, and a world away from the industrial hangover of the Valleys, is the lush **Vale of Glamorgan** and **Glamorgan Heritage Coast**, which stretches westwards to include the neighbouring county of Bridgend. The entire area is dotted with stoic little market towns and chirpy seaside resorts – notably **Barry** in the east and **Porthcawl** in the west.

West again is Wales' second city, **Swansea**. Bright, breezy and brash, Swansea is renowned for its nightlife and is undergoing rapid development, particularly along its historic waterfront. Like Cardiff, the city grew principally on the strength of its now revitalized docks, from where the coast arcs round from the **Port Talbot** steelworks in the east to the elegant holiday town of **Mumbles** on the jaw of the magnificent **Gower peninsula** in the west. Gower was Britain's first-ever designated Area of Outstanding Natural Beauty, and remains a microcosm of rural Wales, with its grand beaches, rocky headlands, ruined castles and bracken heaths roamed by wild horses.

Cardiff tours and trips p.69
Cardiff farmers' markets p.72
Spectator sport in Cardiff p.76
Walks from Chepstow p.80
The Chartists p.90
King Arthur p.93
Porthcawl activities p.100
All shook up p.101

The Welsh coal industry p.105
The Big Cheese p.107
The Merthyr radicals p.112
Male voice choirs p.116
Swansea festivals p.125
Surfing on Gower p.130
Arthur's Stone p.133

SIX BELLS, ABERTILLERY

Highlights

❶ **Cardiff** Dazzling architecture, a city-centre castle and cracking nightlife mark the Welsh capital out as a must-visit destination. **See p.57**

❷ **Tintern Abbey** Get your poetic juices flowing at Tintern's towering ruins, romantically situated in the Wye Valley. **See p.81**

❸ **Transporter Bridge, Newport** Check out this remarkable feat of engineering by climbing up to the walkway – you'll need a head for heights. **See p.89**

❹ **Caerleon** Contemplate whether Wales' best-preserved Roman remains were indeed the site of King Arthur's fabled court, Camelot. See p.92

❺ **Blaenavon** Strap on a hardhat and headlamp and follow ex-coal miners into the Big Pit – one of the country's most poignant and powerful museums. **See p.104**

❻ **Mining memorials** From the colossal Six Bells monument in Abertillery to the Senghenydd gardens, the Valleys are littered with moving memorials commemorating the many disasters that have befallen the old mining communities. **See p.106 & p.109**

❼ **Rhossili beach** Surf some of Britain's best waves, where the Gower peninsula ends in a flourish. **See p.131**

HIGHLIGHTS ARE MARKED ON THE MAP ON P.56

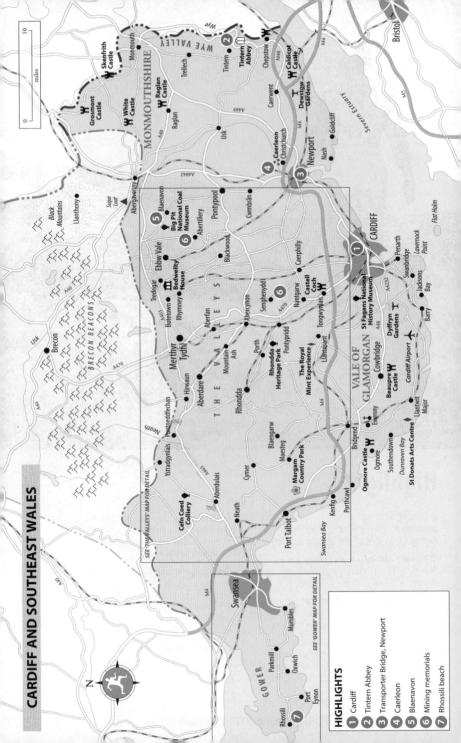

CARDIFF AND SOUTHEAST WALES

N

0 miles 10

Bristol

WYE VALLEY

Wye

Monmouth

Skenfrith Castle

Grosmont Castle

White Castle

Raglan Castle

MONMOUTHSHIRE

Trellech

Tintern

Tintern Abbey

Chepstow

M48

Caldicot Castle

M4

Raglan

Usk

Dewstow Gardens

Caerwent

M4

Newport

Nash

Goldcliff

Severn Estuary

Llanthony

Black Mountains

Sugar Loaf

Abergavenny

Blaenavon

Big Pit National Coal Museum

Abertillery

Pontypool

Cwmbrân

Caerleon

Christchurch

Flat Holm

Brecon

Usk

BRECON BEACONS

A40

A470

Pontneddfechan

Neath

Hirwaun

Ebbw Vale

Tredegar

Rhymney

Butetown

Bedwellty House

Merthyr Tydfil

Aberfan

Abercynon

Blackwood

Senghenydd

Caerphilly

Nantgarw

Castell Coch

St Fagans National History Museum

CARDIFF

Penarth

Lavernock Point

Swanbridge

Cefn Coed Colliery

Ystradgynlais

Aberdulais

Aberdare

Mountain Ash

Porth

Pontypridd

Rhondda Heritage Park

The Royal Mint Experience

Llantrisant

THE VALLEYS

Rhondda

Tongwynlais

Dyffryn Gardens

Cardiff Airport

Jacksons Bay

Barry

Swansea

Mumbles

GOWER

Parkmill

Oxwich

Port Eynon

Rhossili

Swansea Bay

Porthcawl

Kenfig

Port Talbot

Neath

Cymer

Maesteg

Blaengarw

Margam Country Park

Bridgend

Ogmore

Ogmore Castle

Ewenny

Southerndown

Dunraven Bay

St Donats Arts Centre

Llantwit Major

Cowbridge

VALE OF GLAMORGAN

Beaupre Castle

M4

SEE 'THE VALLEYS' MAP FOR DETAIL

SEE 'GOWER' MAP FOR DETAIL

HIGHLIGHTS

1 Cardiff
2 Tintern Abbey
3 Transporter Bridge, Newport
4 Caerleon
5 Blaenavon
6 Mining memorials
7 Rhossili beach

By car Southeast Wales is by far the easiest part of the country to travel around. Swift dual carriageways connect with the M4, bringing all corners of the region into close proximity.

By bus and train This is the only region of Wales with a half-decent train service, and most suburban and rural services interconnect with Cardiff, Newport or Swansea. Bus services fill in virtually all of the gaps, though often rather slowly, while Sunday services are often dramatically reduced.

Cardiff and around

Official capital of Wales only since 1955, the buoyant city of **CARDIFF** (Caerdydd) has, since the turn of the millennium, witnessed a remarkable evolution from a large town to a truly international city, with massive developments in the centre as well as on the rejuvenated waterfront. With a reputation as a party town, allied to lots of top-class sport and a cultural attractions, it is one of the UK's most enticing destinations.

The sights are clustered around fairly small, distinct districts. Easily navigable on foot, the **commercial centre** is bounded by the River Taff on the western side. The Taff flows past the high stone walls of Cardiff's **castle** and the **Principality Stadium**, the city's two defining landmarks. Near the southeastern tip of the castle walls is Cardiff's main crossroads, where the great Edwardian shopping boulevards, Queen Street and High Street, conceal a world of arcades, great stores and run-of-the-mill malls. North of the castle, a series of white Edwardian buildings is home to the **National Museum and Gallery**, **City Hall** and **Cardiff University**.

Northwest of the centre, the well-heeled suburb of **Pontcanna** is home to the city's best restaurants; beyond is the village-like suburb of **Llandaff**, built around the city's patchwork **cathedral**. A mile south of the commercial centre lies **Cardiff Bay**, revitalized since the construction of a barrage to form a vast freshwater lake. Home to the **National Assembly** and **Wales Millennium Centre**, among many other attractions, it's a bona fide destination in its own right.

Brief history

Cardiff's origins date back to **Roman** times, when tribes from Isca settled here, building a small village alongside the Roman military fort. The fort was largely uninhabited from the Romans' departure until the Norman invasion, when William the Conqueror offered Welsh land to his knights if they could subdue the local tribes. In 1093, Robert FitzHamon built a simple fort on a moated hillock that still stands today in the grounds of the castle. A town grew up in the lee of the fortress, developing into a small fishing and farming community that remained a quiet backwater until the end of the eighteenth century.

Industrial expansion

The **Bute family**, lords of the manor of Cardiff, instigated new developments on their land, starting with the construction of a canal from Merthyr Tydfil (then Wales' largest town) to Cardiff in 1794. The second Marquess of Bute built the first **dock** in 1839, opening others in swift succession. The Butes, who owned massive swathes of the rapidly industrializing south Wales valleys, insisted that all coal and iron exports use the family docks in Cardiff, and it subsequently became one of the busiest ports in the world. By the beginning of the twentieth century, Cardiff's population had soared to 170,000 from its 1801 figure of around one thousand, and the ambitious new **Civic Centre** in Cathays Park was well under way.

Changing fortunes

The **twentieth century** saw the city's fortunes rise, plummet and rise again. The dock trade slumped in the 1930s, and the city suffered heavy bombing in World War II, but

1

CARDIFF

■ ACCOMMODATION

Cardiff Caravan Park	1
Cardiff University	2
Cathedral 73	5
Jolyon's at No. 10	6
Lincoln House	3
Town House	4
YHA Cardiff Central	7

M4 Junction 32 ◀

M4, Merthyr (23 miles) & Brecon (41 miles) ◀

ROATH

WATERLOO GARDEN
COLCHESTER AVENUE
WATERLOO ROAD
KIMBERLEY ROAD
MARLBOROUGH ROAD
PEN-Y-LAN RD
PEN-Y-LAN ROAD
ROATH COURT ROAD
ALBANY ROAD
BROADWAY
CLIFTON STREET
RAILWAY STREET
CARLISLE STREET
CONSTELLATION ST
NEWPORT ROAD
MOIRA PLACE

Royal Infirmary

EASTERN AVENUE
TY-DRAW ROAD
Roath Park
NINIAN ROAD
MACKINTOSH PLACE
RICHMOND ROAD
CITY ROAD
SALISBURY RD
College of Art
Queen Street Station
QUEEN STREET

SHIRLEY ROAD
FAIROAK ROAD
ALLENSBANK ROAD
COBURN ST
CRWYS ROAD
WOODVILLE ROAD
WYEVERNE RD
SENGHENNYDD RD
Cathays Station
Sherman Theatre
National Museum
STUTTGARTER STRASSE
BOULEVARD DE NANTES
New Theatre

WHITCHURCH ROAD
CATHAYS TERRACE
MAENDY ROAD
PARK PLACE
Cardiff University
CATHAYS PARK
MUSEUM AVE
Alexandra Gardens
KING EDWARD VII AVE
City Hall
County Hall
Cardiff Castle

COLUM ROAD
NORTH ROAD
Temple of Peace
National War Memorial
Sophia Gardens
Welsh Institute of Sport
SEE "CENTRAL CARDIFF" MAP FOR DETAIL
Bus stop (National Express buses)

University Concert Hall

Bute Park

River Taff

Swalec Cricket Stadium
SOPHIA WALK
CATHEDRAL ROAD
TALBOT ST
HAMILTON ST
PONTCANNA
KINGS ROAD
WYNDHAM CRESCENT
PONTCANNA STREET
SEVERN GROVE
ROMILLY CRESCENT
LLANDAFF ROAD
Chapter Arts Centre

Pontcanna Fields

N

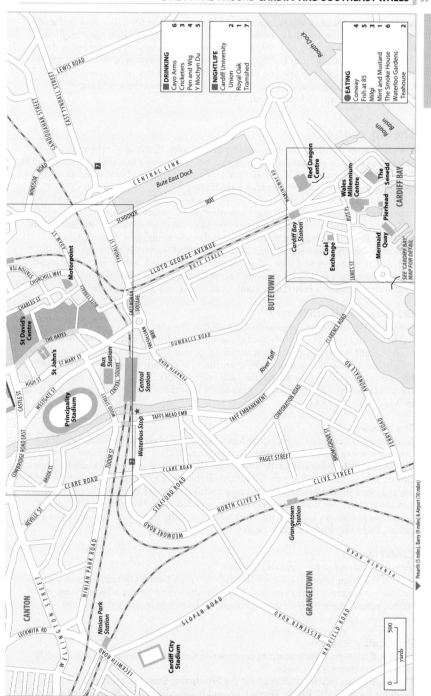

DRINKING
Cayo Arms 6
Cricketers 3
Pen and Wig 4
Y Mochyn Du 5

NIGHTLIFE
Cardiff University
Union 2
Royal Oak 1
Tramshed 7

EATING
Conway 4
Fish at 85 5
Milgi 3
Mint and Mustard 1
The Smoke House 6
Waterloo Gardens
Teahouse 2

1

its elevation to status of **Wales' capital** in 1955 suffused Cardiff with a renewed sense of purpose. This optimism and confidence blossomed further still after the inauguration of the National Assembly in 1999, which coincided with many government and media institutions relocating from London and elsewhere; the creation of the BBC Drama Village, in 2011, and the opening of Pinewood Studios a few years later was proof of Cardiff's burgeoning appeal. Then, in 2017, Cardiff entered the world stage in style, hosting the Champion's League final.

The city centre

The city's main north–south thoroughfare is the **Hayes**, dominated on one side by the **St David's Centre**, a gargantuan complex that holds some two hundred shops and the **St David's Hall** concert venue. The major point of interest in the Hayes, however, is the **Old Library**, home to the enlightening **Cardiff Story**.

On the north side of the St David's Centre, pedestrianized **Queen Street** is Cardiff's most impressive shopping street, with many fine nineteenth-century buildings (and a good few typical chain-store frontages). At the western end of the street, a statue of **Aneurin Bevan**, postwar Labour politician and classic Welsh firebrand, stands aloof from the bustle.

Hidden away between the Hayes and **St Mary Street** – another thoroughfare lined with ornate Victorian and Edwardian shop frontages – are Cardiff's wonderful **arcades**. Beyond here, the High Street presages **Cardiff Castle**, the city's premier tourist hangout, while the magnificent **Principality Stadium** nearby is well worth a guided tour.

Old Library and Cardiff Story

The Hayes, CF10 1BH • Mon–Sat 10am–4pm • Free • ☎ 029 2034 6214, ⦿ cardiffstory.com

At the top of the Hayes is the beautifully colonnaded frontage of the **Old Library**, home to the **Cardiff Story**. Using artefacts, hands-on gizmos and audiovisual displays, it's an enlightening romp through the city's colourful history, with emphasis on how Cardiff has been shaped by the docks and the local coal industry. Don't miss the stunning **tiled corridor**; this was the original library entrance, its ornate floor-to-ceiling tiles produced by Maw & Co in 1882.

The arcades

Secreted away between the Hayes, St Mary Street and High Street, Cardiff's half a dozen renovated Edwardian **arcades** conceal some of the city centre's most interesting shops. The **High Street** and **Castle arcades** are the most rewarding, packed with great clothes shops, quirky gift stores, fab little coffeehouses and a range of esoteric emporia, but the glorious **Morgan Arcade** is a beauty, with original 1896 detailing and Venetian windows. Here, you'll find **Spillers Records**, founded in 1894 and the world's oldest record shop; you can easily spend a few hours browsing its hard-to-find tracks of all genres, including loads of local releases.

Cardiff Market

St Mary St, CF10 1AU • Mon–Sat 8am–5.30pm • ☎ 029 2078 5470

Just off the High Street, the Grade II-listed Victorian **Cardiff Market** has been a fixture on this site for more than a century. While livestock is no longer a feature here, this indoor market is great for all manner of goods, including fresh food, specialist bric-a-brac stalls and music.

Principality Stadium

Westgate St, CF10 1NS • Hourly guided tours only (1hr; starting from the WRU store): Mon–Sat 10am–5pm, Sun 10am–4pm • £12.50 • ☎ 029 2082 2432, ⦿ principalitystadium.wales

Dominating the city from all angles is the **Principality Stadium**, built as the Millennium Stadium for the 1999 Rugby World Cup and renamed in 2016. Shoehorned so tightly

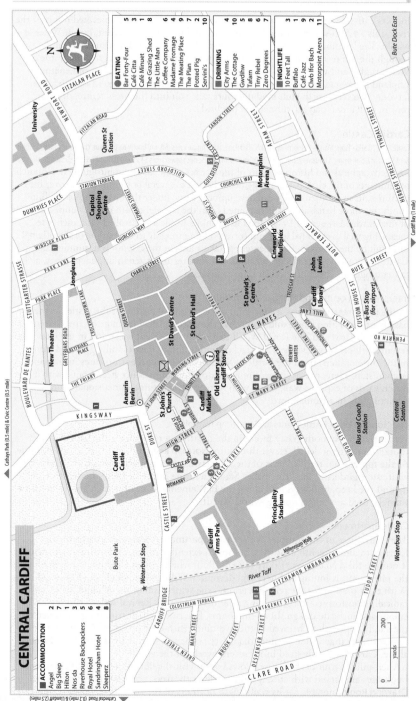

CENTRAL CARDIFF

ACCOMMODATION

Angel	2
Big Sleep	7
Hilton	1
Nos da	3
Riverhouse Backpackers	5
Royal Hotel	6
Sandringham Hotel	4
Sleeperz	8

EATING

Bar Forty-Four	5
Café Citta	3
Café Minuet	1
The Grazing Shed	8
The Little Man	
Coffee Company	6
Madame Fromage	4
The Meating Place	9
The Plan	7
Potted Pig	2
Servini's	10

DRINKING

City Arms	4
The Cottage	10
Gwdihw	5
Tafarn	8
Tiny Rebel	6
Zero Degrees	7

NIGHTLIFE

10 Feet Tall	3
Buffalo	1
Café Jazz	9
Clwb Ifor Bach	2
Motorpoint Arena	11

1

into its Taff-side site that the surrounding walkways had to be cantilevered out over the river, this 74,500-seat giant has become a symbol not only of Cardiff, but of Wales as a whole. The location was once occupied by the legendary Cardiff Arms Park, and though the old terraces and the famous name have gone, the turf is still the home of Welsh rugby, and when Wales has a home match – particularly against old enemy England – the stadium and surrounding streets are charged with good-natured, beery fervour. The very worthwhile **stadium tours** take you into the press centre, dressing rooms, VIP areas, players' tunnel and pitchside.

Cardiff Castle

Castle St, CF10 3RB • Daily: March–Oct 9am–6pm; Nov–Feb 9am–5pm; house tours (50min) hourly on the hour; clock tower tours (30min) April–Oct Sat & Sun hourly 11.30am–2.30pm • £12.50; house tours £3.25; clock tower tours £4.25 • ☏ 029 2087 8100, ⓦ cardiffcastle.com

The geographical and historical heart of the city is **Cardiff Castle**, an intriguing hotchpotch of remnants of the city's past. Having been the seat of several powerful families over the centuries, its most intense phase of development came under the ownership of the Bute family, in whose hands the castle remained from the late eighteenth century until the death of the fourth Marquess in 1947. The fortress hides inside a vast walled yard, each side measuring well over 200yd long and corresponding roughly to the outline of the original fort built by the Romans. Before entering, take a look at the exterior wall running along Castle Street to the river bridge, where stone creatures are frozen in impudent poses, a rather tongue-in-cheek nineteenth-century creation.

Interpretation centre and Firing Line exhibition

In the **interpretation centre** a short film offers a concise history of the castle. In the basement, the **Firing Line exhibition** relays the distinguished heritage of The Queen's Dragoon Guards and The Royal Welsh Regiment since their inception in the late seventeenth century. Cabinets are stacked with military memorabilia garnered from numerous conflicts, from the Battle of Waterloo to more recent ventures in Iraq and Afghanistan. Here, too, is the sole reminder of Roman presence hereabouts, with a few dozen yards of exposed **wall**, along with some excellent three-dimensional murals depicting life in a Roman fort.

The Norman keep, battlements and wartime tunnels

Perched atop a smooth grassy motte in the northwestern corner is the handsome, though much remodelled, eleventh-century **Norman keep**, built of Blue Lias limestone. At the top you get terrific views of the silky lawns spread out below and the gleaming white steel girders of the Principality Stadium in the distance. From the North Gate behind the keep, walkways lead along the **battlements**, beneath which are the **wartime tunnels**, used as shelters during World War II.

Castle apartments

The centrepiece of the complex is the **castle apartments**, dating in part from the fourteenth and fifteenth centuries, but much extended in late Tudor times. Ultimately, it was the third Marquess of Bute (1847–1900) who lavished a fortune on upgrading the pile, commissioning architect and decorator William Burges (1827–81) to aid him. With their passion for the religious art and the symbolism of the Middle Ages, they radically transformed the crumbling interiors in Gothic-Revival style, a riot of vivid colour and intricate design. In all the rooms, fantastically rich trimmings complement the gaudy approach so beloved of the two nineteenth-century eccentrics; it's worth remembering that as one of more than sixty residences owned by the Butes in Britain alone, Cardiff was only lived in for several weeks of the year.

A self-guided tour of the house allows you to visit the **library**, whose richly stocked bookcases are carved with cheeky animal friezes (beavers, possums, platypuses), the **Drawing Room**, notable for its wall-length portraits of the Butes and, upstairs, the grand **Banqueting Hall**, originally from 1428, which was transformed by Bute and Burges with a riotously kitsch fireplace and a church-like ceiling.

Paying a little extra gives you a **guided tour** of all the above plus access to the fabulous **Winter Smoking Room**, run through with elaborate gold leaf and with stained-glass windows illustrating the zodiac; admire, too, the walnut buffet estimated to be worth a cool half a million pounds. You'll also get to see the **Nursery**, with hand-painted tiles and silhouette lanterns depicting contemporary nursery rhymes and, in the Bute Tower, **Lord Bute's bedroom**, with a mirrored ceiling, and the **Roof Garden**, awash with Sicilian marble.

The **clock tower tour** (also extra) takes in the **Clock Chamber**, the **Bachelor's Bedroom** – complete with a remarkable sarcophagus-like marble bath inlaid with brass animals – and, above that, the **Summer Smoking Room**, decorated in rich gold, maroon and cobalt, with images culled from medieval myths and beliefs; there are superlative city-wide views from the balcony.

Bute Park to Pontcanna Fields

Immediately west of Cardiff Castle lies **Bute Park**, once the private estate of the castle, and now containing an **arboretum**, superb flowerbeds, a stone circle, the remains of an old priory and some pleasant walks along the Taff banks. The main road crosses over the river at Cardiff Bridge, with a right turn leading up into the coolly formal **Sophia Gardens**. A quarter of a mile along the river is the multipurpose **Welsh Institute of Sport** (the national sports centre), and the Swalec cricket stadium, home to Glamorgan and, since 2009 when it staged the first England versus Australia Ashes match (reprised in 2015), a test arena. Beyond the gardens lie the less formal open spaces of **Pontcanna Fields**, which lead along the Taff for a couple of miles to the suburb of Llandaff.

Cathays Park and the Civic Centre

On the north side of the city centre, just a hundred yards from the northeastern wall of the castle precinct, is the area known as **Cathays Park**. The "park" itself forms the centrepiece for the impressive Edwardian buildings of the **Civic Centre** – containing the County Hall, **City Hall**, **National Museum** and Cardiff University – although the name Cathays Park is generally used for the whole complex. Dating from the first couple of decades of the twentieth century, the gleaming white buildings arranged with Edwardian precision speak volumes about Cardiff's self-confidence a full half-century before it was officially declared capital of Wales.

City Hall
Cathays Park, CF10 3ND • Mon–Fri 9am–5pm

The centrepiece of the Civic Centre is the magnificent, domed, dragon-topped **City Hall** (1905), an exercise in ostentatious civic self-glory. Note the Peace sculpture in the main entrance lobby: it depicts one of the women who marched from Cardiff in 1981 to establish the Greenham Common peace camp. The ornate interior is a riot of finery that reaches a peak in the showy first-floor **Marble Hall**: all Sienese marble columns and statues of Welsh heroes. Among the figures are twelfth-century chronicler Giraldus Cambrensis, thirteenth-century native prince of Wales, Llywelyn ap Gruffydd, fifteenth-century national insurgent and perpetual hero, Owain Glyndŵr, Welsh king Henry Tudor and tenth-century architect of Wales' progressive codified laws, Hywel Dda (Howell the Good). Overseeing them all is the figure of Dewi Sant himself – the national patron saint, St David.

Alexandra Gardens and around

Behind City Hall, two ruler-straight boulevards, designed with ceremonial splendour in mind, run through the rest of the Civic Centre, arranged in symmetrical precision around **Alexandra Gardens** in the middle. At the very centre of the park is the colonnaded circular **National War Memorial** (1928), a popular and surprisingly quiet place to sit and contemplate the rush of civic and governmental duty all around. At the north end of the western boulevard, **King Edward VII Avenue**, is the **Temple of Peace** (1938), dedicated just before the outbreak of World War II to Welsh men and women the world over who were fighting for peace and relief of poverty. The eastern road, **Museum Avenue**, runs past an assortment of buildings belonging to Cardiff University.

National Museum

Cathays Park, CF10 3NP • Tues–Sun 10am–5pm • Free • ☎ 0300 111 2333, ⓦ museum.wales/cardiff

Housed in a massive domed Portland-stone building, the exceptional **National Museum** attempts to tell the story of Wales and reflect the nation's place in the international sphere.

Evolution of Wales and Natural History galleries

The museum's most obvious crowd-pleaser is the epic **Evolution of Wales** gallery, a natural-history exhibition packed with high-tech gizmos and spectacular big-screen visuals. The slow beginnings of life on earth are brought to life through fossils, rocks and footage of volcanoes, earthquakes and the galaxies. Dinosaurs and the early mammals get a look-in too, the most intriguing exhibit being the fossilized remains of a Jurassic-era dinosaur discovered at Lavernock Point near Penarth in 2014 following a rock fall; this remarkable specimen – parts recovered included the skull, claws, teeth and feet bone – was subsequently given the title *Dracoraptor hanigani* – the first part translating as "Dragon Robber", the second part named in honour of the brothers who found the dinosaur.

The adjacent **Natural History** galleries have a magnificent collection of sparkling crystals, re-creations of assorted environments – mountain, wetland, seashore, dunes – and some great interactive technology. Its "Man and the Environment" display features numerous animals and their habitats, including the world's largest leatherback turtle, caught off Harlech in 1988.

Galleries 1 to 10: historic art

The principal focus of **galleries 1 to 10** is Wales' artistic heritage, with a particularly strong collection from the **eighteenth century**, perhaps the heyday of Welsh art, with its three main protagonists – Richard Wilson, William E. Parry and Thomas Jones – well represented. Unsurprisingly, the Welsh landscape is to the fore. Among the enlightening **Welsh Landscapes** in Gallery 7, Wilson's skill in capturing Wales' light can be seen to lustrous effect in his studies of castles at Caernarfon and Dolbadarn. There's a nod to Wales' mining heritage too, courtesy of Lowry's evocative *Six Bells Abertillery*. While the prolific Jones also dealt in landscapes – look out for *A View in Radnorshire* and his evocative images of Naples, both in Gallery 8 – his most notable offering is *The Bard* (Gallery 9), a dramatic historical piece based on Thomas Gray's tale of Edward I's massacre of the Welsh bards. The **Faces from Wales** in Gallery 5 features an intriguing collection of portraits of various esteemed natives, such as Cedric Morris, painted by his former pupil Lucian Freud – look out, too, for the wonderfully expressive *A Welsh Collier* by Evan Walters. There's also a superb collection of **ceramics**, one of Wales' most prolific areas of applied art.

Galleries 11 to 15: Impressionists and Modern Art

The real action lies in **galleries 11 to 15**. Gallery 11 is dominated by **nineteenth-century French art**, featuring the likes of Millet (the haunting, unfinished *Peasant Family* and lovely, pastoral *Goose Girl at Gruchy*), Rodin (*Head of Victor Hugo*), Boudin (watery landscapes) and Manet (numerous works, including the intricately observed *Effect of Snow at Petit Montrouge*). Concentrating on **Art in Britain after 1930**, Gallery 12 offers highlights from stunning, wild pieces by Welsh supremo Ceri Richards to a typically raw and bizarre *Study for Self Portrait* by Francis Bacon. Sculpted pieces here include fine works by Henry Moore, among them *Upright Motif*, and Barbara Hepworth's haunting *Oval Sculpture*. Gallery 14, **Art in Europe after 1900**, features *Nature Morte au Poron* by Picasso and Magritte's *The Empty Mask*, as well as sculptures by Matisse and Epstein, while in Gallery 15, the emphasis is very much on **British art around 1900**, with the likes of Walter Sickert, Sylvia Gosse and Gwen John, and Harold Gilman's colourful London scenes (*Café Royal* and *Mornington Crescent*).

Gallery 16: Impressionists and Post-Impressionists

Gallery 16 is unquestionably the star, owing to its fabulous **Impressionists and Post-Impressionist** collection. Dominating the room are several pieces by Monet, including a smog-bound *Charing Cross Bridge*; these sit alongside artists such as Cézanne, Sisley (including his views of Penarth and Langland Bay), Carnière, Degas, Pissarro and Renoir, whose coquettish *La Parisienne* is a standout. The centrepiece, though, is Van Gogh's stunning *Rain at Auvers* – angry slashes of rain run right across the otherwise harmonious canvas – which was painted just weeks before his suicide. Mesmerizing pieces by Rodin also pepper the gallery, including a version of *The Kiss* and his original *Eve*.

Welsh sculpture

In the rotunda beyond Gallery 15, a fabulous collection of **Welsh sculpture** is dominated by the one-man Welsh Victorian statue factory, Goscombe John (1860–1952). Far better here than on the dreary municipal plinths they usually adorn, his male studies verge on the homoerotic (*Morpheus*), while his female forms (*Thirteen*) are exquisite. Look out for the moving *Parting* and, inevitably, the nod to Celtic mythology in the playful, Rodin-esque *Merlin and Arthur*.

Cardiff Bay

Although the bay is an easy 30min stroll from the city centre, the most relaxing way to reach it is by waterbus (see box, p.69), train (every 15min from Queen Street station; 5min) or the #6 Baycar bus from outside Central station (every 10–15min; 5min)

The recent regeneration of **Cardiff Bay** has resulted in a remarkable transformation of the derelict old docks into a bona fide tourist attraction. In times gone by, when the docks were some of the busiest in the world, the area was better known by its evocative name of **Tiger Bay** – immortalized by locally born chanteuse Shirley Bassey in her hit *Girl from Tiger Bay*.

Ever-expanding, the Bay area now comprises four distinct parts, situated either side of **Roald Dahl's Plass**, the main square, named after the Cardiff-born children's author: on the eastern side lie the swanky civic precincts around the glorious **Wales Millennium Centre**, while to the west is **Mermaid Quay**, an airy jumble of shops, bars and restaurants. North of here is the **BBC Drama Village** – where *Doctor Who* and *Casualty* are shot – and finally, set back from the water's edge, the somewhat down-at-heel, but increasingly gentrified, Taff-side suburb of **Butetown**.

Wales Millennium Centre

Bute Place, CF10 5AL · ☎ 029 2063 6464, ⓦ wmc.org.uk

Dominating Cardiff Bay is the mesmerizing **Wales Millennium Centre**, a vibrant performance space for theatre and music, and home to many of Wales' premier arts organizations. Likened by critics to a copper-plated armadillo or aardvark, the WMC soars over the rooftops, its exterior swathed in Welsh building materials, including different slates, wood and stone, topped with a stainless-steel shell tinted with a bronze oxide to resist salty air.

Writ large across the frontage in 7ft-high letter windows, the inspirational bilingual **inscription** was crafted by poet Gwyneth Lewis; the phrases read downwards – in English "In these stones, horizons sing" and in Welsh "Creu gwir fel gwydr, o ffwrnais awen" ("Creating truth like glass, from the furnace of inspiration") – but, ingeniously,

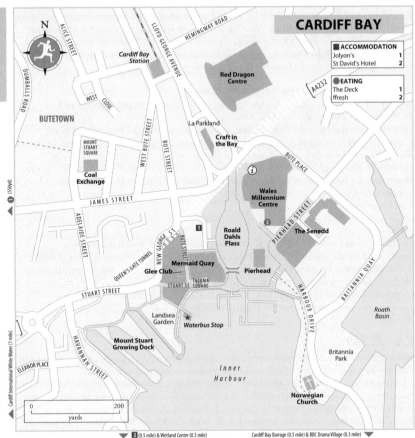

CARDIFF BAY

■ ACCOMMODATION	
Jolyon's	1
St David's Hotel	2

● EATING	
The Deck	1
ffresh	2

they also read across each line, in two languages, and still make crystal-clear poetry. The grace and style continue throughout the interior, fashioned from materials that hark back to Wales' mineral-extracting past, from the native oak, ash, beech, sycamore, alder, birch, chestnut and cherry woods to the riveted steel and coal-like pillars. The ground floor houses the main box office, music shop, souvenir shop, tourist office and excellent bar and brasserie *ffresh* (see p.72).

The Pierhead

CF10 4BZ • Daily 10.30am–4.30pm • Free • ☎ 0300 200 6565, ⊛ pierhead.org

The most obvious, and evocative, reminder of the bay's shipping heritage is the magnificent red-brick **Pierhead**, which has beckoned vessels into Cardiff port since its construction in 1897. A typically ornate neo-Gothic terracotta pile, it was built for the Cardiff Railway Company – formerly the Bute Dock Company, which burnt down in 1892 – and perfectly embodies the wealth and optimism of the Bute family and their docks; the building became the administrative centre for the Port of Cardiff in 1947, and the last shipment of coal left here in 1964. It now houses a surprisingly enjoyable **exhibition** documenting the rise and fall of the coal-exporting industry hereabouts, although its most striking exhibit is the binnacle from the *Terra Nova*, which set sail from the bay in June 1910 ahead of Captain Scott's ill-fated polar expedition.

The Senedd

CF10 4BZ • Mon–Fri 9.30am–4.30pm, Sat & Sun 10.30am–4.30pm; free guided tours (1hr) daily 11am, 2pm & 3pm; plenary sessions in the debating chamber Tues & Wed 1.30pm • Free • ☎ 0300 200 6565, ⓦ assembly.wales

The **Senedd**, designed by Richard Rogers and opened in 2006, is among the bay's landmark buildings. Although on nowhere near the scale of the neighbouring Wales Millennium Centre, the home of the Welsh National Assembly, distinguished by its wraparound glass facade and soaring wooden roof, was also constructed using traditional Welsh materials, notably slate and Welsh oak. Daily guided tours explain more about the building, and the public can attend plenary sessions in the debating chamber; it's possible to book ahead for these, but not essential. Otherwise, you can always pop in to the perky **café**, which affords marvellous views of the bay; note that all visitors have to undergo a brief security check.

Norwegian Church

Harbour Drive, CF10 4PA • Daily 10.30am–4pm; hours can vary depending on events • ☎ 029 2087 7959, ⓦ norwegianchurchcardiff.com

Now a prominent arts and performance centre, the **Norwegian Church**, an old seamen's chapel, was built in 1868 on land donated by the Marquess of Bute; it was moved here in 1992 from its original location on the site of the Wales Millennium Centre. Once one of the most important Scandinavian missions in Britain – it regularly served up to seventy thousand sailors per year – the gleaming white building is better known for being where **Roald Dahl**, whose parents were Norwegian, was christened. Inside you'll see a pair of crossed oars (symbolizing good luck), discovered under the floorboards when the church was moved. There's a charming little **café**.

Cardiff Bay Barrage and Bay Trail

CF10 4PA • Daily 7am–10pm • Free • ☎ 029 2087 7900, ⓦ cardiffharbour.com • Waterbuses run between the waterfront and the southern end of the barrage daily 10.30am–4.30pm (£4 return)

Central to the whole Cardiff Bay project is the half-mile-long **Cardiff Bay Barrage**, built right across the Ely and Taff estuaries, which transformed a vast mud flat into a freshwater lake and created eight miles of useful waterfront. Despite its controversies, including the destruction of certain bird habitats, the barrage is a phenomenal bit of engineering, and it's well worth having a wander along the beautifully landscaped embankment to see the lock gates, sluices, fish path and stunning views; there's a good kids' play area and skate park too. You could also tackle the 6.2-mile-long **Bay Trail**, a circular path for walkers and cyclists that wends its way around the bay and across to Penarth. Note, too, that **waterbuses** shuttle between the waterfront and the southern end of the barrage at Penarth.

Wetland Centre

Jutting out over the water like an ocean liner, the **St David's Hotel**, south of Mermaid Quay, acts as a stylish full stop to the sweep of the bay. From its car park, a path leads a couple of hundred yards to the twenty-acre **Wetland Centre**, created partly to help offset the loss of wading-bird habitats when the barrage was built and the bay flooded. There are more than fifty species here at any one time, including resident grey herons, coots and kingfishers; migratory birds include swifts, warblers and in winter, starlings – it's a great spot to observe murmurations.

Cardiff International White Water

Watkiss Way, CF11 0SY • Mon, Tues, Thurs, Sat & Sun 9am–5pm, Wed & Fri 9am–8.15pm • ☎ 029 2082 9970, ⓦ ciww.com • Bus #7 (every 30min; 10min) from Canal St in the centre, via Cardiff Bay

Rounding off the waterfront's varied attractions is **Cardiff International White Water**, within the International Sports Village down by the mouth of the River Ely. The main attraction is the indoor **simulated surf machine**, but the rapids course is hugely popular too, accommodating adrenaline-fuelled watersports from rafting and canoeing to

1

kayaking and stand-up paddleboarding. The variable river flows make it suitable for everyone, including beginners.

Butetown

Immediately inland from the bay is the salty old district of **Butetown**, whose inner-city dereliction is still evident despite the rampant gentrification that has taken place here and the surrounding area over the past couple of decades. James Street is the main commercial focus, while to its north the cleaned-up old buildings around **Mount Stuart Square** now mostly accommodate offices and the occasional art studio.

Butetown's most distinguished structure, however, is the mammoth **Coal Exchange** building. Built in the 1880s as Britain's central Coal Exchange, the building was used as a base for trade negotiations in the south Wales coal mining industries; it also saw the world's first £1 million cheque, signed in 1908. After years of neglect, it reopened in 2017 as a luxury hotel.

Craft in the Bay

The Flourish, CF10 4QH • Daily 10.30am–5.30pm • Free • ☎ 029 2048 4611, ⓦ makersguildinwales.org.uk

Set out rather stylishly at the southern end of Lloyd George Avenue, **Craft in the Bay** occupies the "D Shed", an old maritime warehouse. In this fabulous glazed building you can see a range of contemporary applied arts and crafts from the length and breadth of Wales, including ceramics, jewellery, weaving and woodturning. Many of the products are for sale, but they're not cheap.

Llandaff Cathedral

Cathedral Rd, Llandaff, 2 miles northwest of the city centre, CF5 2LA • Cathedral: Mon–Sat 9am–7pm, Sun 7am–7pm; walled garden open access • Free • ☎ 029 2056 4554, ⓦ llandaffcathedral.org.uk • Bus #33 or #33A from Cardiff bus station (15min)

A small, quiet ecclesiastical village, **Llandaff** lies northwest of the centre. The church that has now grown up to become the city's **cathedral** is believed to have been founded in the sixth century by St Teilo, but was rebuilt in Norman style from 1120 well into the thirteenth century. From the late fourteenth century, the cathedral fell into disrepair, hurried along by the adverse attention of Cromwell's soldiers during the Civil War. In the early eighteenth century, one of the twin towers and the nave roof collapsed. Restoration only began in earnest in the early 1840s, and Pre-Raphaelite artists such as Edward Burne-Jones, Dante Gabriel Rossetti and the stained-glass firm of William Morris were commissioned to provide colourful new windows and decorative panels. In January 1941, a German landmine destroyed whole sections of the cathedral, but faithful restoration was finally completed in 1960.

The fusion of different styles and eras is evident from outside, especially in the mismatched western **towers**. The northwest tower is by Jasper Tudor, a largely fifteenth-century work with modern embellishments, while the adjoining tower and spire were rebuilt from nineteenth-century designs.

The interior

Inside, Jacob Epstein's overwhelming *Christ in Majesty* sculpture, a concrete parabola topped with a circular organ case on which sits a soaring Christ figure, was the only new feature added in the postwar reconstruction, and dominates the nave today. At the west end of the north aisle, the **St Illtyd Chapel** features Rossetti's cloying triptych *The Seed of David*, whose figures – David the shepherd boy, David the King and the Virgin Mary – are modelled on Rossetti's Pre-Raphaelite friends. A little further on, in the south presbytery, the tenth-century Celtic cross is the cathedral's only pre-Norman survivor. At the far end of the cathedral is the elegantly vaulted and beautifully painted **Lady Chapel**, notable for its gaudy fifteenth-century reredos on the back wall that contains, surrounded by golden twigs and blackthorn in each niche, bronze panels with named flowers (in Welsh) in honour of Our Lady – more than two dozen flowers take their Welsh names from the Virgin.

The walled garden

Take a quick look at the medieval **walled garden** of the Llandaff Bishops' Palace on the Cathedral Green. With herbaceous plants arranged according to medieval patterns, it makes a pleasant – and fragrant – place to sit for a few minutes.

ARRIVAL AND INFORMATION	CARDIFF

By plane Cardiff Airport (☎ 01446 711111, ⓦ cardiff -airport.com) is 10 miles southwest of the city on the other side of Barry. The most direct way to reach the city centre is by Express bus #T9 (every 20–30min; 30min; £5). A taxi from the airport to Cardiff Central will cost around £30. Travelling to the airport, buses currently leave from Custom House St; they also call in at Cardiff Bay, by the Red Dragon Centre.

By train Cardiff Central train station, south of Principality Stadium, handles all intercity services, as well as many suburban and Valley Line services. Queen Street station, at the eastern edge of the centre, is for local services only, including those to Cardiff Bay.

Destinations Abergavenny (every 45min; 40min); Barry Island (every 20–30min; 30min); Bristol (every 30min; 50min); Caerphilly (every 15min; 20min); Carmarthen (hourly; 1hr 45min); Chepstow (every 30min–1hr; 40min); Haverfordwest (9 daily; 2hr 30min); Holyhead (7 daily; 5hr); Llanelli (every 30min–1hr; 1hr 15min); Llantwit Major (hourly; 40min); London (every 30min; 2hr); Merthyr Tydfil (every 30min; 1hr 5min); Neath (every 30–45min; 40min); Newport (every 15–30min; 15min); Penarth (every 15min; 15min); Pontypridd (every 15min; 30min); Swansea (every

30–45min; 1hr); Trehafod (every 30min; 35min).

By bus Pending the (much delayed) construction of a new bus station in front of Cardiff Central train station, buses currently depart from all over the city – check ⓦ cardiffbus .com for up-to-date details. For the time being, National Express buses leave from Bute Park.

Destinations Abergavenny (Mon–Sat hourly; 1hr 45min); Barry Island (every 30min; 1hr); Brecon (Mon–Sat 8 daily; 1hr 35min); Bristol (8 daily; 1hr 20min); Caerphilly (every 20min; 40min); Chepstow (Mon–Sat every 30min–1hr, Sun 5, 1 change; 1hr 20min); Cowbridge (every 30min– 1hr; 50min); Llantwit Major (hourly–every 2hr; 1hr 15min); Merthyr Tydfil (Mon–Sat every 20min, Sun hourly; 1hr); Newport (Mon–Sat every 20min, Sun hourly; 40min); Penarth (every 30min; 20min); Pontypridd (every 15min; 35min); Senghenydd (hourly; 55min); Swansea (hourly; 1hr 20min).

Tourist information There's no tourist office in the city centre, but you can get lots of information, both on Cardiff and further afield, at the Wales Millennium Centre in Cardiff Bay (Mon–Sat 10am–6pm, Sun 10am–4pm; ☎ 029 2087 3573, ⓦ visitcardiff.com). *Buzz*, a free monthly guide to arts and events in the city, is worth seeking out.

GETTING AROUND	

On foot Cardiff is an easy, flat and compact city to walk around; even Cardiff Bay is within a 30min stroll of Central station.

By bus Cardiff Bus (Bws Caerdydd; ⓦ cardiffbus.com) runs an extensive and reliable bus network, with buses

generally operating between 5.30am and 11.30pm. A one-way fare anywhere in the city costs £1.80 (payable on the bus, exact money only). Various travel passes offer good savings: a "Day to Go" ticket (£3.60) gives unlimited bus travel around Cardiff and Penarth for a day, which can be

---

CARDIFF TOURS AND TRIPS

Open-top hop-on, hop-off **sightseeing bus tours** (daily every 30min: April–Oct 10am–5pm; Nov–March 10am–3.30pm; 24hr ticket £12.50) start from outside the castle and carve a circuit around the city and Cardiff Bay. A little more energetic, **Cardiff Walking Tours** offers a guided tour from in front of the castle; booking is required (daily 11am; 2hr; £10; ☎ 029 2022 7227, ⓦ cardiffwalkingtours.com).

A scenic **waterbus service** (hourly 10am–5pm; £4 one-way; ☎ 029 2034 5163, ⓦ aquabus .co.uk) operates between Bute Park, near Cardiff Castle, to Mermaid Quay in the bay, though occasionally (depending on the river flow), the service will only run as far as Taff's Mead Embankment, diagonally across from the Principality Stadium; they also offer **cruises** down to the barrage (see p.67). **Bay Island Voyages** (☎ 029 2078 2733, ⓦ bayislandvoyages.co.uk) offers high-octane trips in a rigid-hulled inflatable boat around Cardiff Bay (£7.50 for 15min), as well as boat trips out to Flat Holm island (see p.95).

1

extended to Barry and the Vale of Glamorgan with the "Day to Go Plus" ticket (£4.90). The Network Dayrider ticket (£8) covers all the above plus much of the rest of southeast Wales. All are available from the customer service centre in the library on the Hayes (Mon–Fri 10am–6pm, Sat 9am–4.30pm; ☎ 029 2066 6444), at Paypoint outlets throughout the city, or on board buses themselves; you can also buy the "Day to Go" tickets from the tourist office.

By taxi There are ranks at Central station, Queen Street station, Duke St by the castle and St Mary's St; try Capital Cabs (☎ 029 2077 7777) or Dragon Taxis (☎ 029 2033 3333).
By bike Pedal Power offers an excellent bike-rental scheme with outlets at *Cardiff Caravan Park* (see opposite) and at a kiosk just beyond the Norwegian Church in Cardiff Bay (£16/3hr, £24/day; ☎ 029 2039 0713, ⓦ cardiffpedalpower.org).

ACCOMMODATION

Cardiff has a reasonable, though by no means extensive, stock of **accommodation**. The centre, in particular, is surprisingly lacking in good-quality establishments, while the more interesting places, including a couple of outstanding boutique hotels and a well-established belt of Victorian guesthouses, are a 15min walk northwest of the centre along leafy Cathedral Rd, towards the suburb of Pontcanna. There's a decent spread of hostels, most of which are central. **Prices** for all forms of accommodation are ramped up hugely during rugby weekends.

HOTELS AND GUESTHOUSES

CITY CENTRE

Angel Castle St, CF10 1SZ ☎ 029 2064 9200, ⓦ thecairncollection.co.uk; map p.61. Much-restored Victorian bauble occupying a prime city-centre location between the castle and the Principality Stadium; although the building looks slightly tired from the outside, the rooms are large and modern enough; some have castle views. **£75**
Big Sleep Bute Terrace, CF10 2FE ☎ 029 2063 6363, ⓦ thebigsleephotel.com; map p.61. Snazzy, if somewhat soulless, budget(ish) option occupying a former 1960s office block turned retro designer hotel. The colourful rooms – doubles, triples and family – are well furnished, their dual-aspect windows affording panoramic city views. Breakfast £7.95. **£70**
Hilton Kingsway, CF10 3HH ☎ 029 2064 6300, ⓦ 3hilton .com; map p.61. Cardiff's most agreeable high-end hotel, offering warmly decorated, generous rooms and sparkling bathrooms with large walk-in showers; those on the upper floors have wonderful views into the castle grounds. First-rate facilities include a heated lap pool, spa and gym. **£110**
Royal Hotel 88 St Mary St, CF10 1DW ☎ 029 2055 0750, ⓦ royalhotelcardiff.com; map p.61. Despite its air of faded grandeur, this Victorian building – where Scott and his team has their last banquet before setting off for the Antarctic – conceals a modern interior; the bold red-and-black furnished rooms and limestone-finished bathrooms are well appointed, if somewhat devoid of charm. Given that it's on one of the city's busiest streets, it's surprisingly quiet. Some good advance rates available. Breakfast £9. **£60**
Sandringham Hotel 21 St Mary St, CF10 1PL ☎ 029 2023 2161, ⓦ sandringham-hotel.com; map p.61. Pleasantly old-fashioned, family-run hotel – rooms may be careworn and bathrooms antiquated, but it is friendly, convenient and very cheap. Better still, it's just a short stumble up the stairs from the excellent *Café Jazz* (see p.74). **£40**
★**Sleeperz** Station Approach, CF10 1RH ☎ 029 2047 8747, ⓦ sleeperz.com; map p.61. Cleverly utilizing the architectural space in between the train line and two roads, this funky hotel has light-filled rooms (all doubles) in breezy white/orange and black/grey colour schemes. The corner cabin bunk rooms are particularly neat. Terrific value. Breakfast £9.45. **£55**

CATHEDRAL ROAD

★**Cathedral 73** 73 Cathedral Rd, CF11 9HE ☎ 029 2023 5005, ⓦ cathedral73.com; map p.58. The yellow Rolls-Royce sitting outside this immaculately restored Victorian property is the giveaway; glamour and luxury are the watchwords here. The nine sparkling rooms, spread over two floors, are awash with bespoke design furnishings, while the Porcelanosa stone bathrooms feature capacious walk-in showers. Rates include a sumptuous breakfast to see you on your way. **£125**
Jolyon's at No. 10 10 Cathedral Rd, CF11 9LJ ☎ 029 2009 1900, ⓦ jolyons10.com; map p.58. There's no scrimping on style at this gorgeous boutique hotel, with 21 handsome rooms (eight are larger suites; £129) with Italian-/French-inspired furnishings. Ask for a room overlooking Bute Park. **£99**
Lincoln House 118 Cathedral Rd, CF11 9LQ ☎ 029 2039 5558, ⓦ lincolnhotel.co.uk; map p.58. The most upmarket accommodation in the upper reaches of the road, this small but graceful Victorian hotel has six impeccable rooms furnished with button-leather couches and heavy brocade. There's a comfortable lounge bar for guests. **£125**
Town House 70 Cathedral Rd, CF11 9LL ☎ 029 2023 9399, ⓦ thetownhousecardiff.co.uk; map p.58. One of the more modern guesthouses along Cathedral Rd, this restored Victorian house offers eight en-suite rooms, a guest lounge and better-than-average facilities. **£65**

CARDIFF BAY

Jolyon's 5 Bute Crescent, CF10 5AN ☎ 029 2048 8775, ⓦ jolyons.co.uk; map p.66. Sister hotel to *Jolyon's* on Cathedral Rd, this exquisite boutique hotel in a former

seaman's house has seven beautifully conceived rooms, each unique, perhaps with a wrought-iron or antique carved wooden bed, Indian teak fittings or slate-tiled bathroom walls; one even has its own roof terrace. **£75**
St David's Hotel Havannah St, CF10 5SD ☎029 2045 4045, ⓦwww.thestdavidshotel.co.uk; map p.66. An air of cool sophistication pervades the super-swish *St David's*, whose waterfront location is unmatched in the city; encircling the vast, sunny atrium are a choice of rooms, nearly all with floor-to-ceiling windows and balconies from which to take in the views. Top-notch spa facilities to boot. **£100**

HOSTELS, SELF-CATERING AND CAMPING
Cardiff Caravan Park Pontcanna Fields, CF11 9XR ☎029 2039 8362, ⓦcardiffcaravanpark.co.uk; map p.58. Very good council-run caravan park, an easy 25min walk from the city centre, with limited tent pitches, two service blocks, laundry and dishwashing facilities; usefully, Pedal Power bike rental is on site (see opposite). The entrance is from Pontcanna Fields or at the end of Dogo St, off Cathedral Rd. Open all year. **£27**
Cardiff University Cathays Park, CF10 3AT ☎029 2087 4616, ⓦcardiff.ac.uk/conferences; map p.58. Thousands of en-suite single (£33) and double student

rooms near the city centre are available from late June to mid-Sept on a B&B or self-catering basis. A good, cheap option. Breakfast Mon–Fri only. **£55**
Nos da 53–59 Despenser St, CF11 6AG ☎029 2037 8866, ⓦnosda.co.uk; map p.61. Hip hostel/budget hotel on the riverbank opposite the Principality Stadium with singles, doubles (some en suite) and four- to ten-bed dorms, some with flip-down beds. There's a kitchen and comfy lounge, though most folk just decamp to the popular *Tafarn* bar (see p.73). Dorms **£12.50**, doubles **£32**
★**Riverhouse Backpackers** 59 Fitzhamon Embankment, CF11 6AN ☎029 2039 9810, ⓦriverhousebackpackers.com; map p.61. Cosy, contemporary backpackers' hostel in a 120-year-old Victorian villa with mixed and female-only dorms and twin rooms, as well as a self-catering kitchen, a welcoming dining/lounge area and a sunny wraparound garden terrace. Dorms **£18**, twins **£40**
YHA Cardiff Central East Tyndall St, CF10 4BB ☎0345 371 9311, ⓦyha.org.uk/hostel/cardiff-central; map p.58. Enormous, spanking-new hostel in a former four-star hotel east of the city centre towards the bay; rooms, all en suite, are either doubles or quads. There's a restaurant, bar, lounge, laundry and self-catering kitchen. Breakfast £6.25. Dorms **£10**, doubles **£40**

EATING

The city's long-standing internationalism, particularly its Italian influence, has paid handsome dividends in its range of **restaurants** and **cafés**. That said, there's a lack of top-drawer restaurants in the centre itself, and you'll have to head a little further out to sample the best of Cardiff's food, in particular to **Pontcanna** to the northwest. Mermaid Quay in Cardiff Bay is home to a staggering number of restaurants, many of them chains.

CITY CENTRE
CAFÉS
★**The Little Man Coffee Company** Ivor House, Bridge St, CF10 2EE ☎07933 844234, ⓦlittlemancoffee .co.uk; map p.61. This erstwhile post office and bank has been superbly repurposed into one of the city's most stylish coffeehouses, whose easy-going retro vibe owes much to the stripped-back wooden flooring, 70s armchairs and pew-style seating – it's the kind of place you could quite happily laze around in all afternoon. The staff really do know their beans and the beautifully crafted coffee (there are typically two espressos on the go each day) tastes superb, particularly with a slice of sticky home-made ginger cake. Mon–Fri 7am–9pm, Sat & Sun 8am–5pm.
Madame Fromage 21–25 Castle Arcade, CF10 1BU ☎029 2064 4888, ⓦmadamefromage.co.uk; map p.61. A small slice of Paris at this delightful corner café-cum-deli where cheese is king – the menu offers a lot more besides, from tartlets and quiche to lamb cawl and charcuterie platters. Check out, too, the shop's tempting stock of jams, pickles and chutneys. Mon–Fri 10am–5.30pm, Sat 9.30am–5.30pm.

★**The Plan** 28–29 Morgan Arcade, CF10 1AF ☎029 2039 8764, ⓦtheplancafecardiff.co.uk; map p.61. This great-looking, two-storey artisan coffee bar has been around for ages and remains *the* place in Cardiff to come for a caffeine shot; it also offers a super range of light meals, including breakfasts, home-made burgers and quiches (£7–8), all created using locally sourced organic produce. Mon–Sat 8.45am–5pm, Sun 9.45am–5pm.
Servini's 6–10 Wyndham Arcade, CF10 1FJ ☎029 2039 4054, ⓦserviniscardiff.co.uk; map p.61. Secreted away down an arcade, this cheery family-run local serves a wide variety of filling sandwiches and baguettes, with some great veggie choices; there's a cracking all-day breakfast (£5.95), too. Eat in or take away. Mon–Fri 8am–4pm, Sat 8am–6pm, Sun 9am–4pm.

RESTAURANTS
Bar Forty-Four 15–23 Westgate St, CF10 1DD ☎03333 444049, ⓦbar44.co.uk; map p.61. From the colourful tiled entrance to the low-brick-vaulted ceiling, there's an understated elegance about this glamorous tapas bar. Perch yourself on a high stool and peruse a lengthy menu

1

CARDIFF FARMERS' MARKETS

For picnic staples, you could do a lot worse than head to one of Cardiff's terrific **farmers' markets** (w riversidemarket.org.uk), where you can pick up great local produce. The biggest and best is the Sunday **Riverside Market**, opposite the Principality Stadium on Fitzhammon Embankment (10am–2pm). On Saturdays (9.30am–1pm) the **Roath Market**, at the Mackintosh Sports Club on Keppoch St, in Roath, also has an arts and craft bazaar.

featuring the likes of *fabada Asturiana* (white bean stew with chorizo and smoked *morcilla*), *pulpo* (octopus with capers and red wine) and exclusively Spanish wines. The express weekday lunch menu (three courses £11) is a good deal. Mon–Thurs & Sun 11.30am–11pm, Fri & Sat 11.30am–midnight.

Café Citta 4 Church St, CF10 1BG ☎ 029 2022 4040, w cafecitta.com; map p.61. A friendly, laidback pizzeria straight out of Italy, with a fine little wood-burning oven knocking out freshly cooked pizzas (£9–10) using dough and sauces made on the premises from locally sourced ingredients. Ideal for a quick lunch or a quiet evening meal. Mon 4–11pm, Tues–Sat noon–11pm.

Café Minuet 42 Castle Arcade, CF10 1BW ☎ 029 2034 1794, w restaurantminuet.co.uk; map p.61. Cheap, cosy and delightfully odd restaurant, whose hearty, authentic Italian regional cooking has been attracting a loyal band of locals for years. Park yourself at one of the check-clothed tables or out in the arcade itself, where there's a tiny hatch for takeaway snacks. Mains £8–10. Tues–Sat 11am–4.30pm.

The Grazing Shed 37 St Mary St, CF10 1AD ☎ 07599 882363, w thegrazingshed.com; map p.61. The gourmet burger phenomenon is alive and kicking in Cardiff, as is the fashion for industrial-style decor, hence the bare-brick walls, ceiling pipes and communal wooden tables. Burgers like the Bunga Bunga (beef with gorgonzola, smoky bacon and Cajun mayo) and Daisy Duke (chicken with cheddar, red onion confit and rocket) go for around £7–9. Mon–Thurs 11am–10pm, Fri & Sat 11am–11pm, Sun 11am–9pm.

The Meating Place 40 St Mary St, CF10 1AD ☎ 029 2022 4757, w themeatingplace.co.uk; map p.61. The clue is in the name at this sparkling grill house where you can choose from a concise menu of gut-busting meat dishes; it's the signature hanging skewers (£16–18), marinated and cooked on an open charcoal barbecue, that really pull in the punters. Mon–Wed 5.30–10.30pm, Thurs–Sat noon–10.30pm, Sun noon–4.30pm.

★ **Potted Pig** 27 High St, CF10 1PU ☎ 029 2022 4817, w thepottedpig.com; map p.61. A terrific spot – in the reconditioned vaults of a former bank – to tuck into all things piggy, from crispy pig's ear with black pudding salad to roast belly of pork with pomme purée (£18). There's much more besides, including crab, rabbit and duck. The wine list complements the food brilliantly. Just the place for a romantic liaison. Tues–Sat noon–2pm & 7–10pm, Sun noon–2.30pm.

CARDIFF BAY
CAFÉ

The Deck 20 Harrowby St, CF10 5GA ☎ 029 2115 0385, w thedeckcoffeehouse.co.uk; map p.66. Outstanding neighbourhood coffeehouse and cake shop whose genial staff delight in serving some of the best coffee in the city, alongside baked goodies – the cupcakes are the showstealers – sandwiches and breakfasts. The Vintage High Tea (£18) is filling and fun. Mon, Tues & Sun 11am–3pm, Wed–Sat 9.30am–5.30pm.

RESTAURANT

ffresh Wales Millennium Centre, CF10 5AL ☎ 029 2063 6465, w wmc.org.uk; map p.66. Deservedly a big hit with pre-show diners, this is as fresh as its name suggests, its nicely crafted lunch and dinner menus featuring the likes of pan-fried bream with sautéed potatoes, samphire and leeks (three-course pre-theatre menu £23.50). The crisp, minimalist lounge bar serves scrumptious burgers with onion marmalade and potato chips. Restaurant Tues–Sat noon–2.30pm & 5–9.30pm, Sun noon–3.30pm; bar Tues–Sat 10am–11.30pm, Sun & Mon 10am–5pm.

OUT FROM THE CENTRE
CAFÉS

★ **Milgi** 213 City Rd, CF24 3JD ☎ 029 2047 3150, w milgicardiff.com; map p.58. Quirky, boho-chic café where (veggie) food, art and music all have equal sway. Weekly and monthly events include the supper club, the art and curry club and the Northcote Lane vintage market (every third Sun). The Sun veggie roast is superb and the yurt out back is a perfect spot for a cool drink. Mon–Fri noon–12.30am, Sat 9am–12.30am, Sun 9am–6pm.

Waterloo Gardens Teahouse 5 Waterloo Gardens, CF23 5AA ☎ 029 2045 6073, w waterlootea.com; map p.58. Upmarket teahouse, a 20min walk north of the centre in Roath, whose reputation for artisan teas and home-made cakes (including gluten-free options) is unrivalled in the city. Sample one of fifty or so loose-leaf teas alongside a slice of courgette and lime cake. Well worth the short trek. Mon–Sat 8am–6pm, Sun 9am–6pm.

RESTAURANTS

Conway 58 Conway Rd, CF11 9NW ☎ 029 2022 4373, w knifeandforkfood.co.uk; map p.58. Fine gastropub with a daily blackboard menu offering a mix of upmarket pub classics (beer-battered cod with chips and pea purée; £13) alongside more polished dishes (lobster ravioli in a prosecco sauce; £18). The living-room-style dining area, surrounding a central fireplace and shelves of books, is delightful. Daily noon–11pm.

★ **Fish at 85** 85 Pontcanna St CF11 9HS ☎ 029 2023 5666, ⓦ fishat85.co.uk; map p.58. Wholesalers, fishmongers and restaurant all in one, and quite brilliant it is too. The "catch menu" allows customers to pick something from the counter – brill, snapper or red mullet, for example – along with an accompanying sauce, and then it'll be cooked just the way you like it. Alternatively, select something from the menu, perhaps roast monkfish with *boulangére* potatoes and creamy curried mussels (£22.50). Tues–Sat noon–2.30pm & 6–9pm.

Mint and Mustard 134 Whitchurch Rd, CF14 3LZ ☎ 029 2060 0333, ⓦ mintandmustard.com; map p.58. Don't let the dull, rather distant location put you off: this is the city's finest Indian restaurant, with a menu as brilliant as it is bold. Try the pan-fried sea bass on a bed of curry mashed potato (£15.25) or one of the many exceptional vegetarian dishes – the melt-in-the-mouth Bombay chaat is sensational. Daily noon–2pm & 5–11pm.

The Smoke House 77 Pontcanna St, CF11 9HS ☎ 029 2034 4628; map p.58. Lunchtime deli foods are laid out in crates on the counter (check out the pig pie) in this rustic spot, then, in the evening, the American barbecue – dry rubbed using naturally smoked spices and seasoning – takes over. A sizzling array of meats (ribs, patties, steaks) are served on heavy wooden boards with hand-cut chips, pickled gherkins and red cabbage slaw. Wash it all down with a Honker's craft beer. Mains £15–18. Deli Mon–Fri 11am–2.30pm; restaurant Tues–Fri 6.30–10.30pm, Sat noon–2.30pm & 6.30–10.30pm, Sun noon–2.30pm.

DRINKING

Cardiff's **pub life** has expanded exponentially in recent years, with chic cosmopolitan bars jostling for space alongside the more traditional Edwardian palaces of etched smoky glass and gleaming wood. You'll find plenty of both in the **centre**, particularly along Mill Lane, Greyfriars Rd and Westgate St – weekend nights are legendarily raucous, during which time the city centre is not for anyone of a nervous disposition. The most agreeable pubs are out on the margins, notably along **Cathedral Road** in the direction of Pontcanna, with more out towards the student quarter around **Cathays**.

CITY CENTRE

City Arms 10 Quay St, CF10 1EA ☎ 029 2064 1913; map p.61. Opposite the Principality Stadium, this no-nonsense boozer is always popular, especially on international match days and before gigs at *Clwb Ifor Bach* just around the corner. Brains beers and choice guest ales. Mon–Thurs 11am–11pm, Fri & Sat 11am–2.30am, Sun noon–10.30pm.

The Cottage 25 St Mary St, CF10 1AA ☎ 029 2033 7195; map p.61. Traditional Edwardian pub with cheerful staff serving some of the best Brains beers in the city centre, alongside good cask options and decent home-made pies. Mon–Thurs & Sun 11am–11pm, Fri & Sat 11am–midnight.

★ **Gwdihw** 6 Guildford Crescent, CF10 2HJ ☎ 029 2039 7933, ⓦ gwdihw.co.uk; map p.61. Pronounced "goody-hoo", this is a wonderful little corner café/bar, its exterior painted bright orange and the interior decked out with stripped wood flooring, odd bits of furniture and retro-style accoutrements. Daily happenings include alternative film, poetry recitals, micro-festivals and regular bouts of live music on the dinky stage. Mon–Wed 3pm–midnight, Thurs–Sat noon–2am, Sun 4pm–midnight.

Pen and Wig 1 Park Grove, CF10 3BJ ☎ 029 2037 1217; map p.61. Large boozer in a quiet residential street, with an unspoilt flagstone-floored interior and a decent beer garden. It's popular with local professionals and students for the fine selection of reasonably priced guest ales. Mon–Thurs 11.30am–midnight, Fri & Sat 11.30am–1am, Sun noon–11.30pm.

Tafarn 53–59 Despenser St, Riverside, CF11 6AG ☎ 029 2037 8866; map p.61. Part of the hostel *Nos da*, with a heated outdoor deck overlooking the Taff, serving an impressive range of Welsh beers, ciders and spirits plus locally sourced meals and bar snacks. Occasional live music. Daily noon–11.30pm.

★ **Tiny Rebel** 25 Westgate St, CF10 1DD ☎ 029 2039 9557, ⓦ tinyrebel.co.uk; map p.61. Cool craft beer bar owned by the Newport-based brewery of the same name. There's a bewildering choice of cask and keg beers – mostly their own – so if deciding is too onerous, try a flight of thirds. Brilliant themed nights include Americana, Bring Your Own Vinyl and, on Mon, board games. Daily noon–2am.

Zero Degrees 27 Westgate St, CF10 1DD ☎ 029 2022 9494, ⓦ zerodegrees.co.uk; map p.61. Shiny micro-brewery in a lino-clad converted garage with friezes made from heat-compressed Wellington boots and discarded mobile phones. The five house brews, which include a black lager, a wheat beer and a mango-infused beer, are complemented by a raft of speciality ales. Great gourmet pizzas, too. Daily noon–midnight.

OUT FROM THE CENTRE

Cayo Arms 36 Cathedral Rd, CF11 9LL ☎ 029 2023 5211, ⓦ cayopub.co.uk; map p.58. Within a six of the cricket ground, this large, busy and proudly Welsh pub,

1

in two conjoined Victorian townhouses, offers Tomos Watkin beers and decent food. Mon–Sat noon–11pm, Sun noon–10.30pm.

Cricketers 66 Cathedral Rd, CF11 9LL ☎029 2034 5102, ⓦcricketerscardiff.co.uk; map p.58. Set in a gorgeous Victorian townhouse, this combines a sunny interior – big sofas from which to admire the cricket memorabilia – with lively beer gardens front and back. The Welsh cask-conditioned beers from the Evan-Evans brewery in

Llandeilo are some of the best in Cardiff, and the food is creditable, too. Daily noon–11pm.

★**Y Mochyn Du** Sophia Close, off Cathedral Rd, CF11 9HW ☎029 2037 1599, ⓦymochyndu.com; map p.58. Right in the shadow of the cricket ground, this old gatekeeper's lodge is a fine place to sup a pint of Welsh brewed beer, either in the conservatory or outside among the greenery. Popular with Welsh-speakers. Mon–Fri noon–11pm, Sat noon–midnight, Sun noon–10.30pm.

NIGHTLIFE

There's plenty of choice when it comes to **nightlife** in Cardiff, whether your tastes run to banging clubs, sweaty rock gigs (in English or Welsh) or a night of soothing jazz. That said, despite the healthy state of Welsh music, there is a surprising dearth of small- to mid-sized **music** venues. In addition to the places listed here, Cardiff Castle (see p.62) and the Principality Stadium (see p.60) stage major events.

CLUBS

Buffalo 11 Windsor Place, CF10 3BY ☎029 2031 0312, ⓦbuffalocardiff.co.uk; map p.61. Upbeat, retro bistro-cum-cocktail bar/club with fabulously quirky decor and a cool vibe from lunchtime until the wee hours. Electronica is *Buffalo's* forte, but there's plenty else happenning, including experimental art and fashion parties. Daily noon–4am.

Cardiff University Union Park Place, CF10 3QN ☎029 2078 1400, ⓦcardiffstudents.com; map p.58. With four venues under one roof, there's a lot going on here, from assorted dance nights to big-name live bands. Open to non-students. Days and times vary.

Clwb Ifor Bach 11 Womanby St, CF10 1BR ☎029 2023 2199, ⓦclwb.net; map p.61. Widely known as the "Welsh club", due to the prevalence of Welsh-language acts and punters, this is a sweaty and massively fun live music venue and dance club on three floors with nightly gigs, sessions or DJs, including 70s and funk nights. Mon–Wed & Sun 7–10.30pm, Thurs–Sat 7pm–4am.

LIVE MUSIC VENUES

10 Feet Tall 11a Church St, CF10 1BG ☎029 2022 8883, ⓦ10feettall.co.uk; map p.61. Perennially popular tapas-cum-cocktail bar that rocks hard most nights of the week. The vibe is ramped up even further when the basement club *Undertone* – hosting gigs and themed

nights – clicks into gear. Mon–Wed 3pm–midnight, Thurs, Fri & Sun 3pm–3am, Sat noon–3am.

Café Jazz 21 St Mary St, CF10 1PL ☎029 2038 7026, ⓦcafejazzcardiff.com; map p.61. Unassuming, popular venue, below the *Sandringham Hotel*, hosting a diverse range of concerts – electric blues, funk, swing, gypsy jazz and the like – nightly from Tues to Fri, with the house band on Sat. Entrance typically £4–6. Tues–Sat times vary.

Motorpoint Arena Mary Ann St, CF10 2EQ ☎029 2022 4488, ⓦmotorpointarenacardiff.co.uk; map p.61. Large concrete venue rising high over the city centre's southern streets and playing host to major rock and pop gigs, comedy and all manner of sporting events. Days and times vary.

Royal Oak 200 Broadway, Newport Rd, Roath, CF24 1QJ ☎029 2049 6628; map p.58. Renowned music pub with acoustic and electric jam sessions on Wed, starting from 9pm (free), and occasional bands on other nights. Days and times vary.

Tramshed Clare Rd, Grangetown, CF11 6QP ☎029 2023 5555, ⓦtramshedcardiff.com; map p.58. Occupying Cardiff's old red-brick tram depot in the southern suburb of Grangetown, this atmospheric one-thousand-capacity space fills the gap between the city's smaller, niche venues and the behemoth that is the Motorpoint. Expect a top quality roster of gigs. Days and times vary.

ENTERTAINMENT

Cardiff's **theatre** scene encompasses everything from the radical and alternative at the smaller venues to big, blowsy productions and West End spectaculars at the Wales Millennium Centre, home of Welsh National Opera (ⓦwno.org.uk). The WMC and St David's Hall are the main venues for **classical music**.

THEATRE AND COMEDY

Chapter Arts Centre Market Rd, Canton, CF5 1QE ☎029 2030 4400, ⓦchapter.org; map p.58. Although best known for its arthouse movies, this superb multidisciplinary arts complex also hosts comedy, local and

touring theatre and dance companies, and art exhibitions; invariably there's a strong Welsh theme.

Glee Club Mermaid Quay, Cardiff Bay, CF10 5BZ ☎029 2023 0130, ⓦglee.co.uk/comedy/cardiff; map p.66. Cardiff's best comedy club, with appearances by some of

OPPOSITE PUB SIGN IN THE RHONDDA (P.114) >

The
Colliers

1

SPECTATOR SPORT IN CARDIFF

With a strong sporting pedigree, Cardiff boasts several world-class sporting arenas. Inevitably, **rugby** takes centre stage, and there are few more atmospheric places to be than Cardiff on international match day at the magnificent Principality Stadium. The city's club side, **Cardiff Blues** (☎029 2030 2030, ⓦcardiffblues.com), plays in the Pro 12 league at Cardiff Arms Park, adjoining the Principality Stadium.

Despite playing second fiddle to rugby, **football** remains popular, thanks to the (relatively) recent success of **Cardiff City** (☎0845 365 1115, ⓦcardiffcityfc.co.uk), who were promoted to the Premier League for the first time in 2013, though they were relegated the following season; they play at the Cardiff City Stadium a mile or so west of the centre on Leckwith Road. Cardiff's **cricketing** profile has increased massively in recent years, thanks to the staging of test matches at the Swalec Stadium in Sophia Gardens, including two England versus Australia Ashes tests, in 2009 and 2015. Sophia Gardens is also the home of **Glamorgan**, Wales' one and only first-class cricket team (☎029 2040 9380, ⓦglamorgancricket.com).

the biggest names on the British stand-up circuit, mostly on Fri and Sat evenings. Occasional live music, too, with some well-established artists.

Jongleurs Corner Park Place, Greyfriars Rd, CF10 3DP ☎0870 0111 960, ⓦjongleurs.com; map p.61. More corporate than the *Glee*, but dependable for decent comedy; shows on Fri and Sat, with four acts each night.

New Theatre Park Place, CF10 3LN ☎029 2087 8889, ⓦnewtheatrecardiff.co.uk; map p.61. Splendid Edwardian city-centre theatre staging big shows, musicals and pantos.

Sherman Theatre Senghennydd Rd, Cathays, CF24 4YE ☎029 2064 6900, ⓦshermantheatre.co.uk; map p.61. An excellent two-auditorium rep theatre known for its strong line-up of plays in Welsh and English. New and translated classic Welsh-language pieces, stand-up comedy, children's entertainment, drama, music and dance.

CONCERT HALLS

Norwegian Church Harbour Drive, CF10 4PA ☎029 2045 4899, ⓦnorwegianchurchcardiff.com; map p.66.

Venue for all kinds of musical events and performances, typically classical or operatic. Days and times vary.

St David's Hall The Hayes, CF10 1AH ☎029 2087 8444, ⓦstdavidshallcardiff.co.uk; map p.61. Part of the huge St David's shopping centre, this venue is home to visiting orchestras and musicians in genres from jazz to opera, and is frequently used by the excellent BBC National Orchestra of Wales. The 1pm lunchtime concerts are well worth attending and run on a pay-what-you-will basis.

University Concert Hall Corbett Rd, Cathays Park ☎029 2087 4816, ⓦcardiff.ac.uk/music; map p.58. Between Oct and May, this impressive performance space hosts public concerts by university and local orchestras, jazz groups and easy-listening ensembles.

Wales Millennium Centre Roald Dahls Plass, Cardiff Bay, CF10 5AL ☎029 2063 6464, ⓦwmc.org.uk; map p.66. Stunning performance space that's home to Welsh National Opera, along with other music and dance companies. Also used for touring West End and other mega-productions.

Castell Coch

Tongwynlais, 6.5 miles northwest of Cardiff, CF15 7JS • March–Oct daily 9.30am–5pm; July & Aug daily 9.30am–6pm; Nov–Feb Mon–Sat 10am–4pm, Sun 11am–4pm • £6.50, including audio guide • ☎029 2081 0101, ⓦcadw.gov.wales/daysout/castell-coch • Bus #26 from Westgate St in Cardiff (every 30min; 25min)

The coned turrets of **Castell Coch** rise mysteriously out of a steep wooded hillside above the village of **Tongwynlais**. A ruined thirteenth-century fortress, Castell Coch was rebuilt into a fantasy castle in the late 1870s by William Burges for the third Marquess of Bute, complete with a working portcullis and drawbridge. Numerous similarities with Cardiff Castle include the lavish decor, culled from religious and moral fables, that dazzles in each room. An excellent audio guide leads you around, beginning in the banqueting hall, with its striking painted timber ceiling and Burges-designed furnishings. From here you enter the octagonal drawing room, its walls and domed ceiling decorated with murals depicting Aesop's Fables; a Three Fates sculpture on the chimney piece illustrates the the three stages of life. Above the winch room is Lord Bute's bedroom, with a typically ostentatious bronze-plated bed; this is relatively staid compared to Lady Bute's bedroom, incorporating a mirrored, double-dome ceiling around which 28 panels depict frolicking monkeys – some of these were considered lascivious in their day. Despite the extravagance, however, the castle was hardly ever lived in and sees more life today, especially the **tearoom**, in what was once the valet's room.

St Fagans National History Museum

St Fagans, 4 miles west of Cardiff city centre, CF5 6XB • Daily 10am–5pm • Free • ☎ 0300 111 2333, ⓦ museum.wales/stfagans • Bus #32A (every 25min; 20min) from Westgate St in Cardiff takes you to the museum car park

Separated from Cardiff by a sliver of greenery, the village of **St Fagans** (Sain Ffagan) has a rural ambience only partly marred by the busloads of tourists that regularly roll in to visit the unmissable **St Fagans National History Museum**. Note that parts of the site are currently being renovated.

St Fagans Castle

The museum is constructed on grounds near **St Fagans Castle**, a country house built in 1580 on the site of a ruined Norman castle and furnished in early nineteenth-century style. Surrounding the castle are the formal gardens, from where grassy terraces slope down to a chain of eighteenth-century fishponds, which have also been restored to something akin to their original design. It's a lovely spot for a picnic.

Open-air museum

Beyond the parkland area is the **open-air museum**, an outstanding collection of period buildings – houses, shops, dwellings, churches – garnered from all corners of Wales and faithfully rebuilt here. There's much to see, and many of the structures can be entered, so give yourself a good couple of hours to take it all in.

Many of the domestic structures are farmhouses of different ages and styles – compare, for example, the grandeur of the seventeenth-century red-painted **Kennixton Farmhouse** from Gower or the homely Edwardian comforts of **Llwyn-yr-Eos Farm** with the threadbare simplicity of the Gwynedd farmworkers' **Llainfadyn Cottage**, which, incredibly, slept ten people. The best demonstration of how life changed over the years for a section of the Welsh population comes in the superlative **Rhyd-y-car** ironworkers' cottages from Merthyr Tydfil. Built originally around 1800, each of the six houses, with their accompanying strip of garden, has been furnished in the style of a different era from 1805 to 1985. Even the frontages and roofs are true to their age, and each garden still harvests heritage varieties. A short walk further along are the Victorian **Gwalia Stores** from the mining community of Ogmore Vale; owned by the Llewelyn family, the store closed in 1973, having succumbed to the march of the superstores – the aroma of polished mahogany is as evocative as the jars of boiled sweets that the starch-aproned assistants sell. In between the cottages and the store, take a quick look at the ornate Victorian **urinal**.

Other buildings to look out for include the diminutive whitewashed 1777 **Pen-Rhiw Chapel** from Dyfed, which is still used by a small Unitarian community; the pristine and evocative Victorian **St Mary's Board School** from Lampeter, which closed in 1916; and the ordered mini-fortress of a 1772 **Tollhouse** that once guarded the southern approach to Aberystwyth.

Elsewhere, an interesting variety of workplaces includes a **tannery**, a **pottery**, three **mills** and a **smithy**. In most of them you'll see people demonstrating the original working methods; you can even buy goodies from the early twentieth-century **bakehouse**.

Wye Valley

Only after the local government reorganization of 1974 was the **Wye Valley** finally recognized as part of Wales; before this, the area was officially included as part of neither England nor Wales, so that maps were frequently headlined "Wales and

Monmouthshire" (the county name). In this easterly corner, the two main towns are decidedly English in flavour: **Chepstow**, at the mouth of the Wye, with its massive castle radiating an awesome strength; and **Monmouth**, sixteen miles upstream, a spruce, old-fashioned town with the lingering air of an ancient seat of authority.

Six miles north of Chepstow, on the banks of the Wye, stand the inspirational ruins of the Cistercian **Tintern Abbey**, while across the river the southern segments of the **Offa's Dyke** earthworks are shadowed by a long-distance footpath (see box, p.237).

Chepstow

Of all the places that call themselves "the gateway to Wales", **CHEPSTOW** (Cas-Gwent) – the first Welsh town on the main road into the country – has probably the strongest claim. Situated on the western bank of the River Wye, just over a mile from where its tidal waters recede into the Severn estuary, Chepstow is an easy-going and engaging place, and worth a stop to visit its ancient **castle**.

Chepstow's position as a former river port is evident in the thirteenth-century **Port Wall**, encasing the castle precincts and the town centre in their loop of the river. The fifteenth-century **West Gate** marks the southern end of the **High Street**, a handsome thoroughfare sided by Georgian and Victorian buildings and sloping down from the gate towards the river. Here, the elegant five-arch cast-iron **Old Wye Bridge**, built in 1816, is still in use for cross-border traffic into England. This section of the Wye is tremendously tidal, with a mighty 49ft difference in the water level between high and low tides – one of the world's highest tidal drops. A short street with a riverside esplanade, The Back, runs southeast from the bridge; a plaque on the wall of the *Riverside Wine Bar* commemorates the quay as the site from which the three leaders of Newport's Chartist March of 1839 were dispatched to Van Diemen's Land (now Tasmania), in Australia.

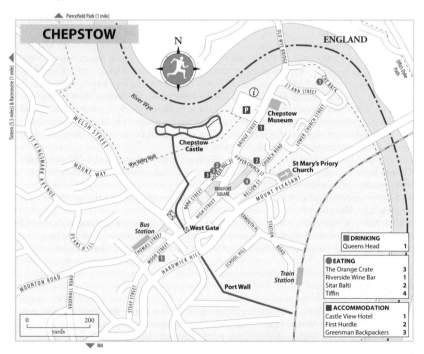

CHEPSTOW

ENGLAND

DRINKING
Queens Head 1

EATING
The Orange Crate 3
Riverside Wine Bar 1
Sitar Balti 2
Tiffin 4

ACCOMMODATION
Castle View Hotel 1
First Hurdle 2
Greenman Backpackers 3

A five-minute walk up the hill from The Back, **St Mary's Priory church** was founded at the same time as the castle, in around 1072, as a Benedictine priory. Much of what survived has been modernized over the centuries, but Norman features do remain, including an intricate arched eleventh-century doorway.

Chepstow Castle

Bridge St, NP16 5EY • March–June, Sept & Oct daily 9.30am–5pm; July & Aug daily 9.30am–6pm; Nov–Feb Mon–Sat 10am–4pm, Sun 11am–4pm • £6.50; CADW • ☎ 01291 624065, ⓦ cadw.gov.wales/daysout/chepstow-castle

Tight in a loop of the River Wye, the strategic location of **Chepstow Castle** could scarcely be bettered, guarding as it does one of the most important routes into Wales. Chepstow was the first stone castle to be built in Britain, with its first Norman incarnation, the Great Tower keep, rising in 1067, just one year after William the Conqueror's victory at Hastings. William had realized the importance of subduing the restless Welsh, creating borderland Marcher Lordships and encouraging the title holders to expand into Welsh territory: a succession of Chepstow's lords attempted this, necessitating the renewed and increasingly powerful fortification of their castles over the next two hundred years.

The castle enclosures

The walled castle comprises three separate enclosures, the largest of which is the **Lower Ward**, dating mainly from the thirteenth century. Here, you'll find the modest **Great Hall** and the colourful Earl's chamber; the latter is currently off limits pending extensive renovation. Standing in the hall porch (though originally located in the main gatehouse), the iconic wood-latticed **castle doors** date from around 1190, making them the oldest in Europe. Underneath the Great Hall is the fine – if now somewhat weather-beaten – vaulted **cellar**; wine would be hauled from the river below via its arched windows.

Twelfth-century defences separate the Lower Ward from the **Middle Ward**, which is dominated by the imposing ruins of the **Great Tower**, an immense hall-like structure that still bears some fantastic ornamentation. Beyond the Great Tower the far narrower **Upper Ward** leads up to the Barbican **watchtower** from where there are superlative views back over the castle and down the cliff to the mud flats of the river estuary.

Chepstow Museum

Bridge St, NP15 5EZ • Daily 11am–4pm • Free • ☎ 01291 625981

Opposite the castle, a cream-painted Georgian townhouse contains the **Chepstow Museum**. Staid but comprehensive displays cover pretty much every aspect of local life over the years, with nostalgic photographs and paintings of the trades supported in the past by the River Wye, including records of Chepstow's brief spell as a shipbuilding centre in the early part of the twentieth century. The mock-up hospital ward, meanwhile, harks back to the days when the house functioned as a Red Cross hospital during World War I, and then the district hospital until 1976. Take a look upstairs, too, at the rather fine eighteenth-century topographical prints of Chepstow Castle.

ARRIVAL AND INFORMATION   **CHEPSTOW**

By train Trains between Cardiff and Birmingham stop at Chepstow's train station, 5min walk south of the High St. Destinations Cardiff (every 30min–1hr; 40min); Gloucester (every 30min–1hr; 30min); Newport (every 30min–1hr; 25min).

By bus The bus station is on Thomas St, near the West Gate. Destinations Bristol (Mon–Sat hourly, Sun 5; 50min); Caerwent (Mon–Sat hourly; 15min); Cardiff (Mon–Sat every 30min–1hr, Sun 5, 1 change; 1hr 20min); Monmouth (Mon–Sat hourly, Sun 5; 50min); Newport (Mon–Sat every 30min, Sun 5; 25min–1hr); Penhow (hourly; 20min); Tintern (Mon–Sat hourly, Sun 5; 20min); Usk (Mon–Sat 5 daily; 35min).

Tourist office In the castle car park, off Bridge St (daily: July & Aug 10am–5pm; Sept–June 10am–3pm; ☎ 01291 623772, ⓦ visitmonmouthshire.com); it's well stocked with maps and local walking guides, and staff can book local accommodation.

1

WALKS FROM CHEPSTOW

The OS 1:25,000 Explorer map OL14 (Wye Valley & Forest of Dean) is recommended.
Chepstow is the starting point for three of Wales' most popular **long-distance walks**.
Offa's Dyke Path This well-known trail (see box, p.237) starts (or ends) at Sedbury Cliffs – a mile or so east of town on the English side of the border.

Wye Valley walk Established in 1975, but extended over the years, this route heads northwest to Plynlimon, near Aberystwyth, a total distance of 136 miles. The first section to Tintern (6 miles) is especially lovely, if challenging, though a return trek can easily be accomplished in a day: starting from the castle car park, the walk brushes past the picturesque old estate of Piercefield Park, a mile north of town, part of which has metamorphosed into Chepstow Racecourse, Wales' premier racing venue. From here the path tucks and meanders around and above the twisting Wye. You'd do well to arm yourself with a map – or Cicerone's official route guide (£12.95) – both available from the tourist office.

Wales Coast Path Chepstow is the official, if unlikely, starting point for this path. It begins in Riverside Gardens near the Old Wye Bridge, before cutting inland across fields and then meeting up with the Severn estuary; 13.5 miles of the path are covered within Monmouthshire.

ACCOMMODATION

Castle View Hotel 16 Bridge St, NP16 5EZ • 01291 620349, ⍟ wyevalleyaccommodation.com. Bags of charm in this seventeenth-century building, with a grand oak spiral staircase leading off to thirteen cosy rooms featuring crooked floors, thick oak beams and exposed stone walls; some have Nespresso machines and castle views. Good value. **£80**

First Hurdle 9–10 Upper Church St, NP16 5EX • 01291 622189, ⍟ thefirsthurdle.co.uk. This sweet little guesthouse – popular with cyclists and walkers – offers twelve pleasingly spare, warm rooms (including an attic room for four) in two conjoined townhouses. **£75**

Greenman Backpackers 13 Beaufort St, NP16 5EP • 01291 626773, ⍟ chepstowbackpackers.com. A cut above your average hostel, this lovingly restored building on the main square has a handful of single-sex dorms (sleeping four or six) with wide bunks and chunky mattresses (the bottom bunks have curtains too), plus en-suite twins. Guests gather around the farmyard-like table for continental breakfast (included in the rates), and there's also a rather smart lounge bar (not open to non-guests). Dorms **£22**, twins **£55**

EATING

The Orange Crate 9 Beaufort Square, NP16 5EP • 01291 630153, ⍟ theorangecrate.co.uk. Breezy juice bar and health-food café whose jolly staff whizz up all manner of fresh fruit and veg drinks, which you can enhance with a shot of garlic, beetroot or ginger. Soups, salads and wraps (banana, apple and peanut butter, anyone?) too, with gluten-free options. Mon–Sat 8.30am–4.30pm.

Riverside Wine Bar 18a The Back, NP16 5HH • 01291 628300, ⍟ theriversidewinebar.co.uk. With a great location, this riverside restaurant offers super tapas (green lip mussels, salt'n'pepper squid, stilton mushrooms, all around £4.95) and modern Mediterranean cuisine, such as paella (£12.95). Good gin menu, too. Mon–Thurs & Sun

noon–11pm, Fri & Sat noon–midnight.

Sitar Balti The Cellar, Beaufort Square, NP16 5EP • 01291 627351, ⍟ sitarbalti.co.uk. Well-regarded Indian restaurant in a townhouse basement. They specialize in balti lamb and chicken, but the fish specials (tandoori trout or the sardine *bortha*) are well worth a punt, too. Mains £8–10. Daily 6pm–midnight.

Tiffin 8 St Mary's St, NP15 5EW. This engaging vintage tearoom, with the requisite mix'n'match furnishings, floral formica tablecloths and bunting, is loved above all for its griddled crumpets, whether with lashings of butter or smoked salmon and cream cheese. Spanish omelettes, home-made cakes and much more are also on offer. Mon–Sat 10am–4pm.

DRINKING

★**Queens Head** 12 Moor St, NP16 5DD • 07793 889613. You wouldn't give this place a second glance from the outside, but step inside and you'll find a minute single-room pub with a bar culled from an old church altar, locals chatting merrily on pew seating, and no TV,

music or wi-fi in sight. Not only that, but the microbrewed ales and ciders are terrific; a flight of three thirds costs £3.20. Tues–Fri 5–11pm, Sat noon–11pm, Sun 2–8pm.

Tintern Abbey and around

Six miles north of Chepstow, NP16 6SE • March–June, Sept & Oct daily 9.30am–5pm; July & Aug daily 9.30am–6pm; Nov–Feb Mon–Sat 10am–4pm, Sun 11am–4pm • £6.50; CADW • ☎ 01291 689251, ⓦ cadw.gov.wales/daysout/tinternabbey

The roofless ruins of **Tintern Abbey** are spectacularly located on one of the most scenic stretches of the River Wye. The abbey and its valley have inspired writers and painters ever since the Reverend William Gilpin published a book in 1782 extolling their picturesque qualities, and the "tall rock/The mountain, and the deep and gloomy wood" written about by Wordsworth are still visible today. It can get murderously busy, so it's best to go out of season or at the beginning or end of the day when the crowds are thinner.

The best way to appreciate the scale and splendour of the ruins is by walking along the opposite bank of the Wye. Just upstream from the abbey, a bridge crosses the river, from where a path climbs a wooded hillside. Views along the way and from the top are magnificent.

Brief history

The abbey lasted as a monastic settlement from its foundation by the **Cistercian** order in 1131 until its dissolution in 1536, and the original order of monks was brought wholesale from Normandy, its members establishing themselves as major local landholders and agriculturalists. This increased the power and wealth of the abbey, attracting more monks and necessitating a massive rebuilding and **expansion** plan in the fourteenth century, when Tintern was at its mightiest. Most of the remaining buildings date from this time, after which the influence of the abbey and its order began to wane. Upon dissolution, many of the buildings were plundered and stripped, leaving the complex to crumble. The fact that the ruins have survived at all is largely thanks to their remoteness, as there were no nearby villages to use the stone for rebuilding.

The church

The centrepiece of the complex is the magnificent Gothic **church**, built at the turn of the fourteenth century to encase its more modest predecessor. At more than 230ft long, it retains an extraordinary sense of grandeur, despite, or perhaps because of, being completely roofless. Much of the rest of the building remains intact, including the remarkable tracery in the west window and intricate stonework of the capitals and columns. On the neat grass floor, meanwhile, lie pieces of the former pulpitum, an enormous decorative screen that once ran across the width of the nave.

The monks' quarters

Around the church are the less substantial ruins of the **monks' quarters**, mostly reduced to one-storey rubble. Rooms are easily distinguishable, however, including an intact serving hatch in the kitchen and the square of the monks' **cloister**. The course of the abbey's waste disposal system can be seen in the **Great Drain**, an irregular channel that links kitchens, toilets and the infirmary with the nearby Wye. The **Novices' Hall** lies close to the Warming House, which, together with the kitchen and infirmary, would have been the only heated parts of the abbey, suggesting that novices might have gained a falsely favourable impression of monastic life before taking their final vows. In the dining hall, you can still see the **pulpit door** that would once have led to the wall-mounted pulpit, from which a monk would read the scriptures throughout each meal.

Tintern

Now cluttered with teashops and overpriced hotels, the tiny village of **TINTERN** (Tyndyrn), immediately north of the abbey, is strung along a mile or so of the A466 around a loop of the river. Some 200yd along the road, by the small stone arch bridge, the **Abbey Mill** centre (daily 10.30am–5.30pm) houses a restored nineteenth-century water wheel – which springs into action at half past each hour – as well as craft shops and a coffeehouse. Further along Monmouth Road, bibliophiles will want to browse

1

through the collectable and out-of-print titles – including some particularly rare children's titles – at Tintern's wonderful **bookshop**, Stella Books (Mon–Fri 10am–5.30pm, Sat & Sun 9.30am–5.30pm; **☎**01291 689755, **🖥**stellabooks.com).

ARRIVAL AND INFORMATION   TINTERN

By bus The #69 bus between Chepstow and Monmouth stops at the abbey, the Abbey Mill, the visitor centre and several other points along the main village road.

Destinations Chepstow (Mon–Fri hourly, Sat 6, Sun 4; 20min); Monmouth (Mon–Fri hourly, Sat 6, Sun 4; 35min).

Tourist information The excellent Old Station visitor centre (daily: April–Sept 10.30am–5.30pm; Oct

10am–4pm; **☎**01291 689566) is in the former Tintern station; two refurbished carriages house an exhibition on the Wye Valley, while you can pick up leaflets on local walks, including the surrounding wild-flower meadows and cliff rambles above the river. For kids, there's a play area and a miniature railway (generally Sat; £1). There's a good café, too, plus some camping space (see below).

ACCOMMODATION AND EATING

Kingstone Brewery Opposite the visitor centre, NP16 7NX **☎**01291 680111, **🖥**kingstonebrewery.co.uk. Small microbrewery currently producing around twelve ales, the pick of which is the Kingstone Gold; you can sample some on a brewery tour (£5), for which you should book. Mon–Sat 10am–4pm.

Old Station Behind the visitor centre, NP16 7NX **☎**01291 689566. The former waiting room of the old Tintern station is now a quaint Victorian-era tearoom; the grassy lawn in front is a delightful spot for a picnic. Tents can be pitched in the paddock behind the old station (booking essential; closed Nov–March); the only facilities are toilets and washbasins. April–Oct daily 9.30am–5.30pm. Per person <u>£4.20</u>

Parva Farmhouse North of the abbey off the main road, NP16 6SQ **☎**01291 689411, **🖥**parvafarmhouse .co.uk. Restful B&B accommodation in this pretty seventeenth-century farmhouse, with en-suite, mostly river-view rooms. Downstairs there's an honesty bar and a cosy restaurant warmed by a beamed fireplace and serving a three-course dinner menu for £21. <u>**£88**</u>

Royal George Monmouth Rd, NP16 7SF **☎**01291 689205, **🖥**bestwestern.co.uk. Opposite the Abbey Mill, this neat, if slightly old-fashioned, hotel has fourteen modern rooms in a chalet-style building facing a large, willow-fringed garden. <u>**£85**</u>

Monmouth

Bordered on three sides by the rivers Wye and Monnow, elegant **MONMOUTH** (Trefynwy) retains the quiet charm of its days as an important border post and one-time county town. At its centre is cobbled **Agincourt Square**, a large and handsome open space dominated by old coaching inns; from here the wide, shop-lined Monnow Street gently descends to the distinctive thirteenth-century **bridge** over the River Monnow.

Monnow Bridge and gate

Monnow St, NP25 3EG • Free guided tours of the gate summer Sats (times and duration vary; book in advance); at other times by prior arrangement • Free • **☎**01600 775257, **🖥**shirehallmonmouth.org.uk

At the bottom of Monnow Street, the road narrows to squeeze into the confines of the fortified **Monnow Bridge** and its hulking stone **gate**, dating from 1262. Having served both as a means of defence for the town and a toll collection point, this is now the sole remaining medieval fortified river bridge in Britain in which the gate tower actually stands on the bridge. Look up at the medieval garderobe (toilet), which originally emptied straight into the river below.

Shire Hall

3 Agincourt Square, NP25 3DY • April–Sept daily 10am–4pm; Oct–March Mon–Sat 10am–4pm • Free • **☎**01600 775257, **🖥**shirehallmonmouth.org.uk

The arched **Shire Hall** was built in 1724 as a Court of Assize. Its facade includes an eighteenth-century statue of the Monmouth-born King Henry V, victor at the 1415 Battle of Agincourt, which brought Normandy (and soon afterwards France) under the rule of the English Crown. In front is John Goscombe's florid statue of another local, the Honourable Charles Stewart Rolls, co-founder of Rolls-Royce.

1

It was here, in 1840, that the Chartists' trial was held, which resulted in the death penalty for its three ringleaders – Frost, Williams and Jones – though this was later commuted to transportation (see box, p.90). The hall continued to function as a court until 2002, and you can still see the original courtrooms, as well as the holding cells below. In the foyer, the exhibition *Dig Monmouth* is worth a peek for its small but intriguing archeological finds, in particular the medieval comb, flute and oddly shaped bone dice.

The castle and Regimental Museum

Regimental Museum Castle Hill, NP25 3BS • April–Oct daily 2–5pm • Free • ☎ 01600 772175, ⚙ monmouthcastlemuseum.org.uk

The **castle**, founded in 1068, was rebuilt in stone in the twelfth century and almost annihilated in the Civil War. The only notable remains are the Great Hall and Great Tower, the former little more than several chunks of wall, the latter featuring a fine traceried window; it was here, too, that Henry V is thought to have been born in 1387. Adjacent, the gracious seventeenth-century **Great Castle House**, built from castle bricks from the old Round Tower, has variously served as an Assize court, judges' lodging and a girls' school. These days it serves as the headquarters of the Royal Monmouthshire Royal Engineers, whose distinguished history is celebrated in the **Regimental Museum**. Formed in 1539, the regiment is the most senior in the British Army Reserve (Territorial Army), and unique for having the word "Royal" in its title twice.

Nelson Museum and Local History Centre

Priory St, NP25 3XA • March–Oct daily 11am–4pm; Nov–Feb Mon, Tues & Thurs–Sun 11am–4pm • Free • ☎ 01600 710630

The market hall complex is home to the **Nelson Museum and Local History Centre**, containing a voluminous display of Nelson memorabilia accumulated by Lady Llangattock (Charles Rolls' mother), who was an ardent admirer of the admiral. Among the many personal artefacts are letters and medals, and his epaulette, book and bible; here, too, is the logbook from HMS *Boreas*, which he captained between 1784 and 1787, and the breakfast table that he dined at when visiting Kymin (see below).

The Kymin and Round House

Just over a mile east of Monmouth, NP25 3SF • **Kymin** Daily dawn–dusk • Free • ☎ 01600 719241 • **Round House** Easter–Oct Mon, Sat & Sun 11am–4pm • £3; NT • ☎ 01600 719241, ⚙ nationaltrust.org.uk/the-kymin

East of Monmouth, a steep road climbs up to **The Kymin**, a fine viewpoint over the town and the Wye Valley. It's crowned by the crenellated Georgian **Round House**, built as a banqueting hall, and a Neoclassical **Naval Temple**, constructed in 1801 to cheer Britain's victories at sea. Fittingly, Nelson, and his wife Lady Hamilton, visited the temple a year later.

ARRIVAL AND DEPARTURE

MONMOUTH

By bus The bus station is at the bottom of Monnow St. **Destinations** Abergavenny (Mon–Sat 7 daily, Sun 4; 1hr); Chepstow (Mon–Sat hourly, Sun 5; 50min); Newport (Mon–Sat 8 daily, Sun 3; 1hr); Raglan (Mon–Sat hourly, Sun 7; 25min); Ross-on-Wye (Mon–Sat 10 daily; 40min); Tintern (Mon–Fri hourly, Sat 6, Sun 4; 35min); Usk (Mon–Sat 7 daily, Sun 3; 40min).

INFORMATION AND ACTIVITIES

Tourist office In the foyer of the Shire Hall (Mon–Sat 10am–4pm; ☎ 01600 775257, ⚙ visitmonmouthshire.com). **Canoeing** The Monmouth Canoe and Activity Centre (☎ 01600 716083, ⚙ monmouthcanoe.co.uk), right by the Wye in Castle Yard, offers canoe and kayak rental (two-person canoes £40/£55/day; single and double kayaks from £25/half-day, £50/day), plus instruction if needed, and guided river trips. Advance booking required.

ACCOMMODATION

#7 Church Street 7 Church St, NP25 3BX ☎ 01600 712600, ⚙ numbersevenchurchstreet.co.uk. Eight individual, tightly packed rooms in a cosy B&B above the town's finest restaurant; Scandinavian wood furnishings, pastel-painted walls and anglepoise lamps are all standard, and there's a residents' lounge. **£90**

1

Monnow Bridge Campsite Drybridge St, NP25 5AD ☎01600 714004. Simple, clean and convenient town-centre site with no facilities but for toilets and showers. To get there, cross Monnow Bridge and turn right; it's behind the *Three Horseshoes* pub. **£11**

Punch House 4 Agincourt Square, NP25 3BT ☎01600 713855, ⍟sabrain.com/punchhouse. The refurbished, generous rooms above this popular tavern look the part, all grey-painted timber beams, contemporary furnishings and mirrored walls, while the uneven floors and doors lend old-fashioned character. **£70**

EATING AND DRINKING

#7 Church Street 7 Church St, NP25 3BX ☎01600 712600, ⍟numbersevenchurchstreet.co.uk. The best place to eat in town, this sprightly bistro offers different lunch and dinner menus, utilizing fantastic local produce in plates like Wye Valley asparagus with black pudding and poached egg, and pan-seared salmon fillet with ginger and chilli risotto (£19). Daily noon–2.30pm & 6.30–9.30pm.

Gate House 125 Monnow St, NP25 3EG ☎01600 713890, ⍟the-gate-house.co.com. In an enviable location by the medieval bridge, and with a veranda perched over the water, *Gate House* is one of the most agreeable spots in town for a pint on a warm summer's day. Excellent draught beer from the Wye Valley and a creditable gin menu. Mon–Fri 11am–11pm, Sat & Sun 11am–midnight.

Punch House 4 Agincourt Square, NP25 3BT ☎01600 713855. Adjacent to the Shire Hall, the Tudor-looking *Punch House* is the town's most popular hostelry, a rambling, reputedly haunted inn serving mainly Brain's beers; popular with the breakfast and mid-morning coffee crowd. Mon–Fri 8.30am–11pm, Fri & Sat 8.30am–midnight.

Robin Hood 126 Monnow St, NP25 3EQ ☎01600 713240. Diagonally across from *Gate House*, but a far more traditional boozer, this centuries-old inn – with bowed wooden beams and a thick-set stone fireplace – is where Shakespeare is believed to have once drunk; decent beers and a fun, relaxed atmosphere. Mon–Fri 10am–11pm, Sat & Sun 10am–midnight.

Stonemill Just beyond Rockfield, 2 miles west on the B4233, NP25 5SW ☎01600 716273, ⍟thestonemill .co.uk. Fine dining with seasonal menus using locally sourced ingredients, most gathered from the surrounding woodland; treats include Carmarthenshire goat's cheese with toasted honey walnuts and beetroot carpaccio, and roasted loin of venison with parsnip purée and chocolate *jus*. The restaurant itself, in a sixteenth-century barn with thick brick walls and chunky oak beams, looks gorgeous. Set menus £22.95–27. Tues–Sat noon–3pm & 6–11pm, Sun noon–2.30pm.

The Three Castles

The fertile, low-lying land north of Monmouth, between the Monnow and the River Usk, was important as an easy access route into the agricultural lands of south Wales, and in the eleventh century the Norman invaders built a trio of strongholds here – **Skenfrith**, **Grosmont** and **White castles** – within an eight-mile radius of each other.

The castles' size and splendour demonstrate their significance in protecting the borderlands from the restless English, as well as the disgruntled Welsh, who first attacked nearby Abergavenny Castle in 1182, prompting King Ralph of Grosmont to rebuild the three castles in stone. In July 1201, all three were presented by King John to Hubert de Burgh, who fought extensively on the Continent and brought back sophisticated new ideas on castle design to replace earlier models with square keeps. He rebuilt Skenfrith and Grosmont, and his successor as overlord, Walerund Teutonicus ("the German"), worked on White Castle. In 1260, the advancing army of Llewelyn ap Gruffydd threatened the king's supremacy in south Wales, and the three castles were refortified in readiness.

Gradually, as the Welsh began to adapt to English rule, the castles were used more as living quarters and royal administrative centres than as military bases. The only return to military usage came in 1404–05, when Owain Glyndŵr's army pressed down to Grosmont, only to be defeated by the future King Henry V. The castles fell into disrepair, and were finally sold by the Duchy of Lancaster to the Duke of Beaufort in 1825. The Beauforts sold the castles off separately in 1902, the first time since 1138 that the three had fallen out of single ownership.

White Castle

Eight miles west of Monmouth, near Llanvetherine, NP7 8UD • April–Oct daily 10am–5pm; Nov–March generally free access • April–Oct £3; Nov–March free; CADW • ☎ 01600 780380, ⓦ cadw.gov.wales/daysout/whitecastle

Named for its white rendering (a few patches remain on the exterior walls), **White Castle** (Castell Gwyn) is the most dramatic of the three castles, situated in open, rolling countryside with superb views over to The Skirrid mountain (see p.220). From the grassy Outer Ward, a bridge leads over the moat into the dual-towered Inner Gatehouse, where the western tower, on the right, can be climbed for its vantage point. Here, you can appreciate the scale of the tall twelfth-century curtain walls in the Inner Ward. Of the domestic buildings within the walls, only the foundations and a few inches of wall remain. At the back of the ward, there are massive foundations of the Norman keep, demolished in about 1260 and unearthed in the early part of the twentieth century. The southern wall that took the place of the keep was once the main entrance to the castle, as can be seen in the postern gate in the centre, on the other side of which a bridge leads over to the Hornwork, one of the castle's three original enclosures, although now no more than a grass-covered mound.

Skenfrith Castle

Skenfrith, 8 miles north of Monmouth, NP7 8UH • Open access • Free; NT • ☎ 01874 625515, ⓦ nationaltrust.org.uk/skenfrith-castle

Serenely located alongside the River Monnow in the pretty border village of **SKENFRITH** (Ynysgynwraidd), the thirteenth-century **Skenfrith Castle** is dominated by the circular keep that replaced an earlier Norman incarnation. Behind the walls, built of sturdy red sandstone in an irregular rectangle, the 21ft-high, roofless round keep stands in the centre of the ward, raised slightly on an earth mound to give archers a greater firing range; below lie the vestiges of the great hall and private quarters. Domestic buildings include an intact thirteenth-century window, complete with its original iron bars.

Grosmont Castle

Grosmont, 5 miles northwest of Skenfrith, NP7 8EP • Open access • Free; CADW • ☎ 01443 336000, ⓦ cadw.gov.wales/daysout /grosmontcastle

Upstream of Skenfrith, on the English border, the most dilapidated of the Three Castles, **Grosmont Castle** (Castell y Grysmwnt), sits on a small hill above the village of **GROSMONT**. Entering over the wooden bridge above the dry moat, you pass through the ruins of the two-stage gatehouse. This leads into the small central courtyard, dominated on the right-hand side by the ruins of a large Great Hall, dating from the first decade of the thirteenth century. The village **church** is also worth a look, its impressive Norman features including nave arches and the font. A memorial in the nave is popularly believed to be of John Kent, a fifteenth-century bard and magician thought by some to have been Owain Glyndŵr in hiding.

GETTING AROUND   THE THREE CASTLES

By bike You can drive around all three castles in a couple of hours, though it's much more enjoyable to cycle or hike the nineteen-mile circuit of paths, which are detailed in a booklet available from the Abergavenny and Monmouth tourist offices (see p.217 & p.83).

ACCOMMODATION AND EATING

★**The Bell** Skenfrith, NP7 8UH ☎ 01600 750235, ⓦ skenfrith.co.uk. Opposite the castle, this sumptuous sixteenth-century riverbank inn accommodates eleven thoughtfully styled rooms, with pure-wool Welsh blankets, gorgeous linens and rolltop baths; most look out either over the hills or the river. The Bell's well-regarded restaurant sources ingredients from its organic kitchen garden, creating fresh, elegant dishes such as wild mushroom, spinach and crème fraiche risotto; Tues is steak night (£20–25). The cosy Dog and Boot Bar, meanwhile, is, as you'd expect, well geared up for walkers and their pooches. Pub & kitchen daily noon–2.30pm & 6.30–10pm. **£150**

Hunter's Moon Inn Llangattock Lingoed, NP7 8RR ☎ 01873 821499, ⓦ hunters-moon-inn.co.uk. Four

1

floral (but not too floral) en-suite rooms are complemented by the intimate thirteenth-century pub (stone-flag flooring, bare brick walls and low ceilings) serving good food and superb ales, many from the Wye Valley. Daily noon–11pm; kitchen noon–9pm. **£85**

Mid-Monmouthshire

The disputed past of **mid-Monmouthshire**, between Chepstow and Newport, is obvious from the yet more castles that dot the landscape, such as that at **CALDICOT**, just off the M4 near the southern Severn Bridge – the once great Roman town of **Caerwent**, meanwhile, is now a quiet village.

To the north is an undulating land of forests and tiny villages, crisscrossed by winding lanes that offer unexpectedly delightful views – and quaint pubs – around each corner. The contours shelve down in the west to the valley of the **River Usk**, the former border of Wales as decreed in the sixteenth century by Henry VIII. Today, the A449 roars through the valley, bypassing lanes, villages and the peaceful small town of **Usk** before joining the A40 near the spectacular ruins of **Raglan** castle.

Caldicot Castle

Church Rd, Caldicot, NP26 4HU • April–Oct Tues–Sun 11am–4pm • Free • ☎ 01291 420241 ⓦ visitmonmouthshire.com • Bus #74 (every 2hr; 30min) from Chepstow and Newport (every 2hr; 50min) stops at the cross in the village, from where it's a 5min walk

Wedged between the M4 and the railway, **CALDICOT** (Cil-y-coed) is the first sight of Wales for train travellers using the main line from London and drivers using the second Severn bridge crossing from Bristol. Contained within a densely wooded country park on the eastern side of the village, the heavily restored **castle** dates from the twelfth century – one of the Norman Marcher castles built to keep a wary eye on the Welsh. The castle crumbled in the years leading up to the 1800s, before being rebuilt by a wealthy Victorian barrister, Joseph Cobb. The only original parts are a large fourteenth-century round tower and elaborate gatehouse, either side of a grassy courtyard, whose centrepiece is one of Nelson's battle cannons from his flagship *Foudroyant*. The tower contains a smattering of furniture and an intriguing collection of Cobb family photos. The castle grounds have become a popular venue for all manner of events, not least a raft of summer pop concerts and food festivals.

Dewstow Gardens

Dewstow House, Caldicot, NP26 5AH • April–Oct daily 10am–3.30pm • £7 • ☎ 01291 431020, ⓦ dewstowgardens.co.uk • Bus #X74 from Chepstow (hourly; 25min) and Newport (hourly; 45min) stop at the cross in the village, from where it's a 10min walk over the M48 to the gardens

Designed in the late nineteenth century by renowned London landscapers Pulham & Son (whose work includes gardens at Buckingham Palace), **Dewstow Gardens** remained almost totally forgotten for some sixty years following the death of the last landowner during World War II. In 2000, the Harris family bought the property and set about reviving its fortunes; the result is delightful. One of very few Pulhamite creations still in existence, at least on this scale, the Grade I-listed gardens' chief attraction is its **labyrinth** of subterranean grottoes and sunken ferneries – a miniature fantasyland. From this sequence of grottoes you emerge into the old Tropical House, whose rusting, ornately crafted iron columns still look fantastic. Beyond the house itself (not open to the public), perfectly clipped lawns slope down to abundant gardens pockmarked with fountains, waterfalls, lily-strewn ponds and delicate stone bridges. Once you've absorbed all that, grab a coffee or a bite to eat in the charming café-cum-visitor centre.

Caerwent

Two miles northwest of Caldicot lies the historic village of **CAERWENT**. Almost two thousand years ago, the village was known by the Romans as Venta Silurum, the "market town of the Silures", a local tribe forcibly relocated here from a nearby hillfort by the conquering Romans in around 75 AD, after 25 years of battle.

The most notable remnants of the Roman town are the crumbling **walls** that form a large rectangle around the modern village. Access is easiest from the steps in front of the *Coach and Horses* pub, leading you up onto stone ramparts that command melancholic views around the quiet valley – a leisurely stroll around the walls should take no more than forty minutes. The South Wall is the most complete, still maintaining its fourth-century bastions; follow it as it continues around to the old West Gate. Halfway along, a lane cuts up towards the village **church**: maps and diagrams in the porch explain the site of the village, and you can also see two inscribed stones, one a dedication from the Siluri tribe to their Roman overlord, Paulinus, and another, dedicated to Ocelus Mars, demonstrating the odd merging of Roman and Celtic gods for worship. Opposite the church, on the village's main street, the shin-high, rectangular outline of a Roman temple has been excavated.

Usk

Bypassed by the main A449, the quaint town of **USK** (Brynbuga) straddles the river of the same name. The town's hub is **Twyn Square**, where pastel-painted houses, flower boxes, shops and pubs make an exceptionally pretty picture. At the top of the square – beyond the handsome clock tower – is a thirteenth-century **gatehouse**, once part of a Benedictine convent, and now guarding the passage to the impressive twelfth- and thirteenth-century church. The nave and tower survive from its days as a nunnery.

Usk Castle

Castle House, NP15 1SD • Daily dawn–dusk • Free; donation requested • ☎ 01291 672563, ⓦ uskcastle.com

Looming up on a hilltop five minutes' walk from the centre of town stand the ivy-clad ruins of **Usk Castle**. Central to this eccentric little twelfth-century structure, which formed the backdrop to the Battle of Usk in 1405, are three impressive towers: the Great Keep, with two fine intact Norman windows; the Dovecote Tower, with niches set inside for nesting birds; and, best of all, the circular, French-influenced Garrison Tower, built around 1200 and still almost intact. Ranged across the northern side of the inner ward is the roofless shell of the old banqueting hall. Geese and chickens roam freely among the vegetable, herb and flower gardens; a great spot for a picnic.

Usk Rural Life Museum

New Market St, NP15 1AU (enter by the car park on Maryport St) • March–Oct Tues–Sat 10.30am–4.30pm, Sun 11am–3pm • Free • ☎ 01291 673777, ⓦ uskmuseum.org

Housed in a converted eighteenth-century malt barn, the illuminating **Usk Rural Life Museum** packs everything from animal-castrating implements to re-creations of domestic and farming interiors (including ironmonger's and blacksmith's workshops and stables) into every available corner; you'll find much more besides, including a superb cider press and coracles (see p.265). Adjoining covered barns continue the exhibition with a vintage collection of tractors, ploughs and stagecoaches.

ARRIVAL AND INFORMATION

USK

By bus Buses pull in at the top of Twyn Square.
Destinations Monmouth (Mon–Sat 6 daily, Sun 3; 40min); Newport (Mon–Sat 9 daily, Sun 4; 30min).
Tourist office Located inside the same building as the

Rural Life Museum, with plenty of information on the town and region (March–Oct Tues–Sat 8.30am–5pm, Sun 10am–4pm; Nov–Feb Tues–Sat 8.30am–4pm, Sun 10am–4pm; ☎ 01291 673777).

1

ACCOMMODATION AND EATING

Glen-yr-Afon House Pontypool Rd ☎01291 672302, ⓦglen-yr-afon.co.uk. An elegant and gracious – if pricey – country house, a 5min walk west of town across the river. Rooms all differ, design-wise, but each is furnished to a high standard and has appealing garden views. **£140**

Mad Platter 7–9 Bridge St, NP15 1BQ ☎01291 760630, ⓦthemadplatterusk.co.uk. Bringing a welcome dollop of fun to Usk is this creatively designed microbar, sporting retro fittings and Alice in Wonderland-themed accoutrements. Food-wise, and as the name suggests, it's all about the platters (typically meat, fish or cheese) and other nibbles, which are a great match for the extensive gin and ccocktail menus. There's also a terrific selection of locally sourced ales and ciders. Tues–Fri 11am–11pm, Sat & Sun 11am–midnight.

Nag's Head Twyn Square, NP15 1BH ☎01291 672820, ⓦnagsheadusk.co.uk. Usk's most enjoyable pub: an engagingly cluttered space with local memorabilia and brass plates scattered around the bar. Dishes such as home-made rabbit pie (£10.50) complement the terrific real-ale selection. Daily 9.30am–2.30pm & 5–11pm.

Three Salmons Bridge St, NP15 1RY ☎01291 672133, ⓦthreesalmons.co.uk. A hotel of sorts for some four hundred years, this striking listed building conceals the most contemporary rooms in town, each with fabulous beds, smart flatscreen TV/DVD players and sparkling bathrooms, though it's perhaps a little overpriced even so. The handsome restaurant serves a lot of fish – halibut fillet with squid ink linguini and pernod sauce, for example (£17.50) – though locally sourced game is never far from the menu. Excellent wine match-ups, too. Daily noon–2.30pm & 6.30–11pm. **£100**

Raglan Castle

Castle Rd, Raglan, 7 miles north of Usk, NP15 2BT • March–June, Sept & Oct daily 9.30am–5pm; July & Aug 9.30am–6pm; Nov–Feb Mon–Sat 10am–4pm, Sun 11am–4pm • £6.50; CADW • ☎01291 690228, ⓦcadw.gov.wales/daysout/raglancastle • Bus #60 (every 45min; 20min) from Monmouth to Newport, via Usk

The village of **RAGLAN** (Rhaglan) is lorded over by its glorious **castle**, whose ornate style and comparative intactness set it apart from other more crumbling Welsh fortresses. The late medieval castle was constructed on the site of a Norman motte in 1435 by Sir William ap Thomas. Various descendants added to the complex after his death, and building carried on into the late sixteenth century.

The **gatehouse** is still used as the main entrance; the finest examples of the castle's showy decoration appear in its heraldic shields, intricate stonework edging and gargoyles. Inside, stonemasons' marks, used to identify how much work each man had done, can be seen on the walls. Ap Thomas' grandson, William Herbert II, was responsible for the two inner courts, built in the mid-fifteenth century around his grandfather's original gatehouse, hall and keep. The first is the cobbled **Pitched Stone Court**, designed to house the kitchen and servants' quarters.

To the left is the grass-covered **Fountain Court**, once surrounded by opulent residences that included grand apartments and state rooms. Separating the two are the original 1435 **hall**, the **buttery**, the remains of the **chapel** and the **cellars** below. The most impressive element, though, is the moated yellow ashlar **Great Tower** (aka the Yellow Tower of Gwent), which displays Continental influences and appears surprisingly contemporary. Two sides of the hexagonal tower were blown up by Cromwell's henchman, Fairfax, after an eleven-week onslaught against the Royalist castle in 1646. Climbing its five floors gives you some marvellous views of the complex and the three peaks of Blorenge, Skirrid Fawr and Sugar Loaf away in the distance. Just below the Great Tower is the pristine **bowling green**, standing on 12ft-high walls above the Moat Walk, and reached by a flight of stone steps from the green.

Newport and around

Wales' third-largest urban area, lively, gritty **NEWPORT** (Casnewydd-ar-Wysg) grew up around the docks at the mouth of the Usk. Long existing in the shadow of Cardiff, just up the road – its rich history was largely erased by unfortunate twentieth-century development – things are changing: a massive **regeneration project** is making its mark, while the staging of the Ryder Cup golf tournament at nearby Celtic Manor in 2010 and the NATO summit in 2014 helped raise Newport's profile massively. Its **sporting links** have helped, too; its rugby team, the Newport Gwent Dragons, are the source of much local pride, while the national velodrome is located here.

Scything the city in two is the River Usk, whose tidal waters flow to the Severn estuary, three miles away. Between the rail and main road bridges are the risible remains of the town's **castle**, first built in 1191, rebuilt in the fourteenth century, sacked by Owain Glyndŵr in 1402 and refortified later in the same century. The heart of the city, though, is **Westgate Square**, overlooked by the now defunct Westgate Hotel, an ornate Victorian successor to the hotel where soldiers sprayed a crowd of Chartist protesters with gunfire in 1839, killing nearly two dozen – the hotel's original pillars still show bullet marks. At the bottom of Commercial Street, **John Frost Square** (named after a former mayor and one of the 1839 Chartist leaders) is home to a vast new shopping and entertainment complex called **Friar's Walk**, and the **library**, which incorporates the superb **city museum**.

Transporter Bridge

Stephenson St, NP20 2JG • April–Sept Wed–Sun 10am–5pm (last crossing west to east is 4.30pm) • Car toll £1, free for cyclists and pedestrians; walkway £3; visitor centre free • ☏ 01633 656656, ⓦ newport.gov.uk/heritage

Dominating the Newport skyline, the magnificent **Transporter Bridge** was built by French engineer Ferdinand Arnodin in 1906 to enable cars and people to cross the river without disturbing shipping, by hoisting them high above the Usk on a dangling blue gondola. One of only six such bridges still in operation in the world (there is another in

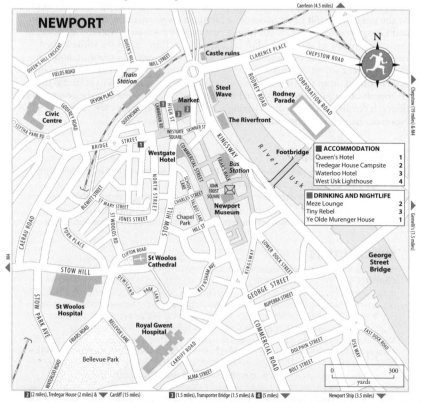

1

Middlesbrough), its comical, spidery legs flare out to the ground, connecting Brunel Street on the west bank and Stephenson Street opposite; it's a smooth, two-minute ride. If you've got a head for heights, it's also possible to climb the 177ft (or 270 steps) up to the walkway, though this is very weather-dependent. Needless to say, the views are spectacular. A small **visitor centre** on the river's west bank elaborates on the bridge's history.

Newport Museum

John Frost Square, NP20 1PA • Tues–Fri 9.30am–5pm, Sat 9.30am–4pm • Free • ☎ 01633 656656, ⓦ newport.gov.uk/heritage

The enlightening **Newport Museum** documents the city's spectacular growth from a small Uskside dock in 1801 to, a century later, a grimy port town of seventy thousand people. The Chartists (see box below) are given due prominence – the star exhibit a pistol belonging to John Frost himself – while other notable objects include bronze finds from Caerwent (the so-called "Chi Rho" hoard) and the remains of a Roman mosaic ("The Four Seasons"), as well as items retrieved from the Newport Ship (see below).

Upstairs are some wonderful exhibits pertaining to the Transporter Bridge: large wicker baskets used to winch workmen up and down, the trowel used to lay the foundation stone and rare footage of assembled dignitaries at the bridge's opening in 1906. The top-floor art gallery contains the **Wait Collection** of Edwardian kitsch, including three-hundred-plus teapots – strictly one for fanatics, this.

St Woolos Cathedral

103 Stow Hill, NP20 4EA • Mon–Fri 7.45am–5.40pm, Sat 9am–4pm, Sun 10am–8pm • Free • ☎ 01633 212077, ⓦ newportcathedral.org.uk

At the top of **Stow Hill** you'll find one of Newport's few remaining rows of Victorian and Georgian townhouses. A ten-minute walk uphill leads to **St Woolos Cathedral**, a fascinating jigsaw of architectural styles and periods. Entry is via the whitewashed twelfth-century St Mary's Chapel, notable for its pre-Conquest stonework and font. Beyond here, a superb Norman arched doorway – supported by columns reputedly of Roman origin, from Caerleon – leads into the Norman nave, with its splendid timber ceiling, thick-set pillars with rounded arches and clerestory windows; the two aisles are fifteenth century. The cathedral's jarringly modern chancel harks back to these original Norman features, sporting a circular marble east window.

The Newport Ship

Unit 20, Estuary Rd, Queensway Meadows Industrial Estate, NP19 4SP • Mid-Feb to Easter & Nov Sat 10.30am–4pm; Easter–Oct Fri & Sat 10.30am–4pm • Free • ☎ 01633 274167, ⓦ newportship.org

In June 2002, during construction of the Riverfront Theatre, a remarkable discovery was made: the remains of a fifteenth-century clinker-built ship buried deep in the riverbank. The oldest and most complete vessel of its kind to have been recovered along

---

THE CHARTISTS

In an era when wealthy landowners bought votes from the enfranchised few, the struggles of the **Chartists** were a historical inevitability. Thousands gathered around the 1838 People's Charter that called for universal male franchise, a secret (and annual) ballot for Parliament and the abolition of property qualifications for the vote. Demonstrations in support of these principles were held all over the country, with some of the most vociferous and bloodiest taking place in the radical heartlands of industrial south Wales. On November 4, 1839, Chartists from throughout Monmouthshire marched on Newport and descended Stow Hill, whereupon they were fired at by soldiers hiding in the *Westgate Hotel*; around 22 protesters were killed. The leaders of the rebellion were sentenced to death, which was commuted to transportation, by the wealthy leaders of the town. Queen Victoria even knighted the mayor who ordered the arbitrary shooting.

these shores, believed to have originated in the Basque country, the **Newport Ship** is one of the most significant marine archeological projects in Britain.

You can see what all the fuss is about at the Newport Ship Centre, an undistinguished little unit on an industrial estate 3.5 miles south of the city. The ship is not here *in situ*; rather, it has been systematically dismantled with each one of its 2300 pieces undergoing painstaking restoration – the most optimistic estimate is that the ship won't be reassembled much before 2021, at the earliest, and even then it's unclear as to where it will be located. For now, you can view those parts of it that are in storage, alongside an exhibition on the vessel and its recovery. The enthusiastic volunteers will talk as long as you allow them to on every aspect of the ship and the latest developments.

Tredegar House

Pencarn Way, 2 miles southwest of Newport, just off M4 junction 28, NP10 8YW • **House** Easter–Sept daily 11am–5pm • £8.35; NT • **Park** Daily dawn–dusk • Free; NT • ☏ 01633 815880, ⓦ nationaltrust.org.uk/tredegar-house • Buses #30 and #36 from Newport stop within a 5min walk of the house

The red-brick **Tredegar House**, built in 1674, was the latest in a line of homes built for the Morgan family, who lived on this site from 1402 until 1951. Its interior is far more lavish than its unassuming exterior suggests, and of the thirty or so rooms variously open to the public – the house is currently undergoing a long-term restoration – most memorable is the ground-floor **Gilt Room**, an explosion of glittering fruit bosses, intricate gilded marble fireplace, mock-walnut panelling and elaborately painted gold stucco ceiling. This is the only original ceiling left in the house, the others having been extensively damaged many years ago when a Vulcan bomber flew too close overhead and shattered the plasterwork. Architecturally more impressive is the adjacent stable block, dating from the same time as the house, which still retains its original loose boxes.

The trio of formal walled **gardens** have been relaid in patterns culled from eighteenth-century designs: the gorgeous Orchard Garden, the immaculate, parterre Orangery Garden and the Cedar Garden, where a stone obelisk marks the burial spot of Godfrey Morgan's horse, Sir Briggs, who survived the Charge of the Light Brigade. Elsewhere, you can take a circular walk of the park, complete with boating and fishing lake, and watch craftspeople in their workshops. The **tearoom**, meanwhile, is an inviting spot.

ARRIVAL AND INFORMATION
NEWPORT

By train The train station is on Queensway at the top of the High St.
Destinations Abergavenny (every 30min–1hr; 25min); Bristol (every 30min; 35min); Caldicot (hourly; 15min); Cardiff (every 15–30min; 15min); Chepstow (every 30min–1hr; 20min); London (every 30min–1hr; 1hr 50min); Swansea (every 30min–1hr; 1hr 20min).
By bus The bus station is underneath John Frost Square, on the Kingsway.

Destinations Abertillery (hourly; 1hr 5min); Blaenavon (Mon–Sat every 15min, Sun hourly; 50min); Cardiff (Mon–Sat every 30min, Sun hourly; 40min); Chepstow (Mon–Sat every 30min, Sun 5; 30min–1hr); Monmouth (Mon–Sat 7 daily, Sun 3; 1hr); Raglan (Mon–Sat 7 daily, Sun 4; 40min); Usk (Mon–Sat 7 daily, Sun 4; 30min).
Tourist information You can get information at the library/ Newport Museum reception (Tues–Fri 9.30am–5.30pm, Sat 9am–4pm; ☏ 01633 656656, ⓦ newport.gov.uk/visiting).

ACCOMMODATION

Queen's Hotel 19 Bridge St, NP20 4AN ☏ 01633 844900, ⓦ jdwetherspoon.com. This Wetherspoon hotel, above a busy, youthful pub, is a very good-value central option, with modern, appealing guestrooms. Breakfast £5. **£50**
Tredegar House Campsite 2 miles southwest, NP10 8TW ☏ 01633 815600, ⓦ caravanclub.co.uk. Picturesque, well-equipped and family-friendly campsite within the grounds of Tredegar House. Open all year. **£25**
Waterloo Hotel 113 Alexandra Rd, NP20 2JG ☏ 01633

264266, ⓦ thewaterloohotel.co.uk. Opposite the Transporter Bridge, this landmark turreted red-brick building has been a hotel/hostelry of sorts since 1870, when it functioned as a docks pub (and brothel). It's slightly more refined these days, with mod cons including underfloor heating in the bathrooms. Most rooms have dramatic views of the floodlit bridge by night; for something a little special, take one of the two tower rooms, which have four-poster beds (£100). **£80**

1

★**West Usk Lighthouse** Lighthouse Rd, 5 miles south, NP10 8SF ☎ 01633 810126, ⓦ westusklighthouse.co.uk. Beyond the suburb of Duffryn, this place is set inside an 1821 lighthouse (decommissioned in 1922) at the mouth of the Usk on its western bank. There are four exquisite nautical-style rooms, a rooftop hot tub, holistic therapies (fee charged) and a life-size Dalek at the entrance signed by the third Doctor Who, Jon Pertwee. A bit special. **£150**

EATING

Gemelli's Tesco, Newport Retail Park, Spytty Rd, NP19 4TX ☎ 01633 270210, ⓦ gemellinewport.co.uk. Curious and inconvenient location aside, this artfully decorated restaurant is by some distance Newport's best, run by chirpy Italian brothers Pasquale and Sergio. Dishes, inviting and authentic, might include ravioli of sea bass or rigatoni with *guanciale* (cured pork cheek) and smoked black garlic (£13.95). A gluten-free menu is also available. Mon noon–11pm, Tues–Sat 9.30am–11pm.

DRINKING AND NIGHTLIFE

Meze Lounge 6 Market St, NP20 1FX ☎ 01633 211432. Newport is a centre of the buoyant Welsh rock and dance scene. This hip venue stages the city's best live music, with a roster of indie-rock bands and premier DJs.

★**Tiny Rebel** 22–23 High St ☎ 01633 252538, ⓦ tinyrebel.co.uk. Dedicated, and quite brilliant, craft beer bar (sister to the one in Cardiff; see p.73) with a superb range of real ales and keg beers on tap – most of them *Rebel*'s own creations, including *Cwtch* (a former champion beer of Britain). They also serve inviting comfort food, such as cider-braised ham with bubble-and-squeak fritters (£9.95). There's a punk ethos about the place that gives it considerable charm. Mon–Thurs & Sun noon–11pm, Fri & Sat noon–midnight; kitchen Mon–Wed noon–8pm, Thurs–Sat noon–9pm, Sun noon–4pm.

Ye Olde Murenger House 53 High St, NP20 1GA ☎ 01633 263977. Dating from 1530 and featuring a beautiful Tudor frontage and inviting lamplit interior, this great old place offers Sam Smith's beers and good guest ales. Local photos, as well as many of Dylan Thomas, look down from the walls. Mon–Sat 11am–11pm, Sun noon–2.30pm & 7–10.30pm.

ENTERTAINMENT

The Riverfront Kingsway, NP20 1HG ☎ 01633 656757, ⓦ newportlive.co.uk/riverfront. The city's principal venue, staging everything from theatre, dance and comedy to contemporary and classical music and cinema – watch out, too, for unplugged sets by local artists in the café.

Caerleon

Predating Newport by at least a thousand years, **CAERLEON** (Caerllion) lies northwest of the town bridge over the River Usk (Wysg), which gave Caerleon its old Roman name of Isca. Its well-preserved remains constitute one of the most important **Roman** military stations in Britain, but it's best known for its reputed association with **King Arthur**.

Brief history

This was a major administrative and legionary centre, built by the **Romans** to provide ancillary and military services for smaller, outlying camps in the rest of south Wales. An enormous **garrison** housed up to five thousand members of the Second Augustan Legion in a neat, rectangular walled town. Its only near equivalents in Roman Britain were Chester, servicing north Wales and northwest England, and York, dealing with the Roman outposts up towards Hadrian's Wall and beyond.

Although the settlement gradually decayed after the Romans left, there were still some massive remains standing when itinerant churchman **Giraldus Cambrensis** visited in 1188, chronicling the "immense palaces, which, with the gilded gables of their roofs, once rivalled the magnificence of ancient Rome". Today, the remnants of the Roman town lie scattered throughout the centre.

The fortress baths

High St, NP18 1AE • April–Oct daily 9.30am–5pm; Nov–March Mon–Sat 9.30am–5pm, Sun 11am–4pm • Free; CADW • ☎ 01633 422518, ⓦ cadw.gov.wales/daysout/Caerleon-roman-fortress-baths

Atmospheric and cleverly presented, the superb Roman **fortress baths** date from

KING ARTHUR

The name **King Arthur** is ubiquitous in Wales – in history, folklore and dozens of place names (only the Devil has more places named after him across Britain). He has become one of the greatest Celtic allegories, a figure to be invoked for all manner of causes and one claimed by almost every part of the British Isles, but the earliest and strongest evidence for the reality of Arthur comes indisputably from Wales.

The first mention of King Arthur was around 800 AD in the *Historia Britonum* (History ofthe British), by the Welsh monk Nennius. Three centuries later, his compatriot Geoffrey of Monmouth used this work, among others, as the source material for his magisterial twelve-volume *Historia Regum Britanniae* (History of the Kings of Britain), in which he asserted that Arthur was a sixth-century Celtic British king who defeated the invading Saxon army in the turbulent decades after the departure of the Romans. From sparse, semi-factual beginnings, epic stories developed. Arthur became an idealized medieval European knight, a totem of Celtic resistance.

Caerleon is widely believed to be the location of Arthur's court, **Camelot**, although other claims place Camelot near Llangollen (see p.312), at Glastonbury and in Cornwall in England, and in Brittany in France. Wales, however, remains perhaps the strongest contender; dozens of areas throughout the country have Arthurian associations, and there is a plethora of books on the subject. Laurence Main's *In the Footsteps of King Arthur*, for example, has some great walks to get you to remote spots of Arthurian significance.

around 85 AD. Used by soldiers and their families as a place to unwind, the baths were the most important social spaces of the time; men bathed separately from women and children. The greater part of the excavations uncovered a wonderfully intact communal pool, which is where people would go after visiting the cold hall baths (frigidarium). Sections of the frigidarium adjoin the main pool, but the warm and hot hall baths are believed to be still buried under the town.

Also clearly visible are the foundations of the heated changing rooms and the drain, in which a hoard of gemstones (see below), as well as teeth, buttons and food remnants, were found. Judging by the splendid mosaic fragments on display, it would seem that the baths were richly decorated.

National Roman Legion Museum

High St, NP18 1AE • Mon–Sat 10am–5pm, Sun 2–5pm • Free • ☎ 0300 111 2333, ⓦ museum.wales/roman

A Victorian Neoclassical portico is the sole survivor of the original **National Roman Legion Museum**, now housed in the modern building behind. There are hundreds of artefacts dug from the remains of Isca and a smaller fortress at nearby Burrium (Usk): coinage, tools, pottery and glassware, military fittings and, best of all, some ninety beautifully carved gemstones retrieved from the fortress bath drain. No less impressive is a collection of chunky funerary and dedication stones, though perhaps the most curious exhibit is a sandy-coloured stone coffin with bone fragments, discovered in 1995 when ground was being dug for the University of Newport.

Caerleon amphitheatre

Broadway Lane, NP18 1AY • April–Oct daily 9.30am–5pm; Nov–March Mon–Sat 9.30am–4pm, Sun 11am–4pm • Free; CADW • ☎ 01443 336000, ⓦ cadw.gov.wales/daysout/caerleonamphitheatre

Opposite the National Roman Legion Museum, Broadway Lane leads down to the Roman **Caerleon amphitheatre**, one of the best preserved in Britain, which was hidden under a grassy mound called King Arthur's Round Table until excavation brought it to light in the 1920s. The amphitheatre was built around 80 AD, the same time as the Colosseum in Rome; legions of up to six thousand would sit tightly packed on the grassy stepped walls to watch the gory combat of gladiators, animal baiting or military exercises. Although sadly under-utilized these days, the arena is the venue for the **Gladiators Festival** in July of every even-numbered year, comprising a number of riotous events and re-enactments. Over the road, alongside the school playing fields,

1

are the extensive foundations of the legion's **barracks** (also called the Prysg Field), the only Roman barrack blocks still visible in Europe; you can easily make out the circular ovens and latrines.

Ffwrwm Centre

High St, NP18 1AG • Most shops daily 9.30am–5.30pm • ☎ 01633 430777, ⓦ ffwrwm.co.uk

The **Ffwrwm Centre** is home to several crafts workshops, an art gallery and a fine bistro. Scattered around the cobbled courtyard – where, it is alleged, Tennyson came to investigate rumours that Caerleon was the seat of King Arthur's court (see box, p.93) – are dozens of sculptures inspired by ancient Celtic and Arthurian lore. You can clasp the gold horns of a Welsh fertility bull, an act that is supposed to lend you untold powers of procreation. The centre is also home to the largest-ever Welsh lovespoon (see p.50), carved from a 44ft cedar trunk.

ARRIVAL AND DEPARTURE   CAERLEON

By bus From Newport, take bus #28 or #60 and get off by the post office on the High St. Returning to Newport, catch the bus from the same spot or from the *Hanbury Arms*.

ACCOMMODATION AND EATING

Hanbury Arms Uskside, NP18 1AA ☎ 01633 420361. At the bottom of the High St, by the River Usk, the whitewashed *Hanbury* dates from the sixteenth century. Tennyson spent several weeks here in 1856 writing *Idylls of the King* – seek out the plaque. It's a Brains pub, with a selection of guest ales, plus live jazz most Sun evenings. Mon–Thurs & Sun 11.30am–11.30pm, Fri & Sat 11.30am–midnight.

Pendragon House 18 Cross St, NP18 1AF ☎ 01633 430871, ⓦ pendragonhouse.co.uk. Formerly a house for Basque refugees during the Spanish Civil War, this listed Georgian residence near the baths offers three fresh en-suite rooms, with super beds, cool linens and flatscreen TV/DVD players. The friendly proprietors will be only too happy to show you a section of the Roman drains that run under the floorboards through the centre of the house. **£70**

Priory Hall High St, NP18 1AG ☎ 01633 421241, ⓦ thepriorycaerleon.co.uk. A long, low stone-built twelfth-century building opposite the baths, this quiet, rambling place has reasonably decent, restful rooms in the hotel itself and the adjoining Priory Cottage. **£85**

The Snug Ffwrwm courtyard, NP18 1AG ☎ 01633 430238, ⓦ thesnugcaerleon.co.uk. This warm, friendly café serves full meals – typically of an Italian bent, such as wild boar ragout with *casarecce*, or pork Tuscan sausage *crostini* – on Fri and Sat evenings, and a popular Sun lunch (three courses £19). There's outdoor seating in summer and a roaring log fire in winter. Mon–Thurs 8.30am–4pm, Fri & Sat 8.30am–4pm & 7.30pm–late, Sun 8.30am–11am & noon–4pm.

Vale of Glamorgan

South and west of Cardiff, the **Vale of Glamorgan**'s rich pastoral landscapes and cliff-fringed coastline, broken by long, sandy beaches, are worth at least a couple of days' exploration. Lively seaside resorts at **Porthcawl** in the west and **Barry** in the east contrast with the more refined atmosphere of **Penarth**, clinging to the coat-tails of the capital. In between lie yawning wide bays and tumbledown castles, linked by bracing coastal walks along spectacularly stratified cliffs. Inland, the lower parts of the Vale's urban features – such as Wales' international **airport** at Rhoose and occasional looming factories – are set against rolling green pastureland sprinkled with charming, low-key market towns including **Cowbridge**, **Llantrisant** and **Llantwit Major**.

GETTING AROUND   VALE OF GLAMORGAN

By train and bus The Vale's proximity to Cardiff makes it easy to explore using public transport. The mainline train route has a stop at Bridgend, a handy interchange for bus services to the coast and some of the larger inland settlements, while the Vale of Glamorgan line, an alternative route from Cardiff to Bridgend, stops at Rhoose and Llantwit Major. Barry and Penarth, practically suburbs of Cardiff, are easily reached by bus and train.

Penarth and around

An easy and enjoyable day out from Cardiff, the upmarket Victorian seaside town **PENARTH** lies just across the Barrage from Cardiff Bay. Upon arrival, most people make a beeline for the tidy esplanade, presided over by its smart **pier**, while the town centre has plenty of fine Edwardian and Victorian architecture.

Ffotogallery and around

Plymouth Rd, CF64 3DH • Tues–Sat 11am–5pm • Free • ☎ 029 2070 8870, ⓦ ffotogallery.org

The fine red-brick **Turner House**, across the road from the train station, is home to the small but engaging **Ffotogallery**, which stages contemporary photographic and other lens-based media exhibitions, as well as artist talks and multimedia events. Running down the left-hand side of Turner House, the Dingle path leads into showy **Alexandra Park** with its flowerbeds and bandstand.

Pier and pavilion

The Esplanade, CF64 3AU • Daily 10am–6pm • Free • ☎ 029 2071 2100, ⓦ penarthpavilion.co.uk

The charmingly fusty **Esplanade**, a surprisingly short but tidy promenade, has had new life breathed into it courtesy of the newly restored **pier and pavilion**. Built in 1895, the pavilion fell into serious disrepair in the 1990s, but has been brilliantly restored to its original Art Deco condition, and now houses a seventy-seater boutique cinema, café and exhibition space.

Lavernock Point and Flat Holm

Two miles south of Penarth • Boats to Flat Holm are run by MW Marine (☎ 01934 636734 or ☎ 07754 833158, ⓦ mwmarine.org; £30, plus a £5 landing fee; book well in advance); they start from Weston-Super-Mare (across the water in Somerset), and call in at Cardiff fortnightly throughout the year – alternatively, you can hire a commercial boat from Cardiff Bay, though this is expensive

Jutting out into the Bristol Channel, **Lavernock Point** today provides a forlorn setting for assorted campsites and pubs, but is notable as the place in which conversation was first heard by means of radio waves. This – as a plaque on the wall of the Victorian church notes – took place on May 11, 1897, when Guglielmo Marconi sent the immortal words "Are you ready?" to his assistant George Kemp on the island of **Flat Holm** (Ynys Echni), three miles out in the channel, officially Wales' most southerly point.

Over the years, Flat Holm has been used as a Viking anchorage, a cholera hospital and a lookout point. Today it's an interesting and beautifully remote **nature reserve**, the nesting place of thousands of gulls and shelducks. It's possible to visit the island, where you will be met by a warden and given a guided tour (included in the price of the boat trip) of the island's history, flora and fauna.

ARRIVAL AND DEPARTURE · PENARTH

By foot One of the most agreeable ways to reach Penarth from Cardiff is by foot, crossing the Cardiff Bay Barrage (see p.67) and following the signs for the Wales Coast Path; this takes about 30min.

By train Trains from Cardiff (every 15min; 15min) arrive on Station Approach. A path on the right leads up to Stanwell Rd, which continues into the town centre, 5min away.

ACCOMMODATION AND EATING

Beach House Hotel The Esplanade, CF64 3AU ☎ 029 2070 0333, ⓦ beachhousepenarth.co.uk. Although somewhat plain from the outside, this comely little hotel right on the seafront has eight polished rooms; four of them have expansive sea views (£99). The deck is a good spot to kick back with a beer and soak up the rays. **£79**

Fig Tree The Esplanade, CF65 3AU ☎ 029 2070 2512, ⓦ thefigtreepenarth.co.uk. The interior is a bit charmless, but the balcony terrace fronting this ornate

Victorian building is a neat spot to try Gower mussels (£12) or, appropriately enough, baked figs stuffed with Perl Las cheese. In summer, the roof terrace is an even more attractive proposition. Tues–Sat noon–3pm & 6–10pm, Sun noon–3pm.

Foxy's 7 Royal Buildings, CF64 3ED ☎ 029 2025 1666, ⓦ foxysdeli.wales. Opposite the train station, this sunny deli, stacked with great local produce, is also an ideal breakfast or lunch stop; stuffed panini, warm salads,

1

mouthwatering cakes and a great-value afternoon tea (£16 for two). Mon–Fri 8am–5pm, Sat 8.30am–5pm.

★**James Sommerin** The Esplanade, CF65 3AU ☎029 2070 6559, ⓦjamessommerinrestaurant.co.uk. Whether you go à la carte or plump for a six-/nine-course tasting menu (£70/£90), you're in for a treat at James Sommerin's sublime Michelin-starred restaurant. Begin with home-made sourdough with salted seaweed butter (presented on a pebble) followed, perhaps, by pork belly

with octopus, peanut and soy sauce, or wood pigeon with black pudding and raspberry. The space looks fabulous, with an all-glass facade for sea views, spaciously arranged tables, marine-blue crushed velvet chairs and intimate mood lighting; a long window allows diners to view the chef at work. If your wallet stretches to it, retreat upstairs into one of the nine gorgeous guest rooms, each with floor-to-ceiling windows offering unencumbered estuary views. Tues–Sun noon–2pm & 6.30–9.30pm. **£170**

Barry and around

Six miles southwest of Penarth, **Barry** (Barri) is the quintessential Welsh resort of old. Until the 1880s, when it was developed as a rival port to the Bute family's Cardiff, the main centre for activity, **Barry Island** (Ynys y Barri), was indeed an island due to its position on the tidal estuary. The docks' construction saw the river diverted, however, and today, the "island" fronts Whitmore Bay, an expansive Blue Flag **beach**, behind which runs a cheerful promenade. For a bit more solitude, head east around the headland to **Jacksons Bay** or, better still, west beyond **Knap Point** – itself a nice spot for a stroll – to Cold Knap, a deep pebbly beach that you'll have almost all to yourself.

The main features on the island are the **Pleasure Park** (noon–8pm: April–Sept Sat & Sun; school holidays daily), with the usual assortment of faintly grim fairground rides; a crazy golf course on the promenade; and, inevitably, a handful of tacky arcades. One of these, as well as many other attractions hereabouts, trades on the back of the hit TV sitcom *Gavin & Stacey*, which was mostly filmed in Barry.

Dyffryn Gardens

Dyffryn, 7 miles north of Barry, CF5 6SU • **Gardens** Daily: March–Oct 10am–6pm; Nov–Feb 10am–4pm • **House** Daily: March–Oct noon–4.30pm; Nov–Feb noon–3pm • £8.60; NT • ☎029 2059 3328, ⓦnationaltrust.org.uk/dyffryn-gardens

In the hamlet of **DYFFRYN**, the magnificent **Dyffryn Gardens** are set around the Victorian home of local merchant John Cory. You could quite easily spend a couple of hours exploring the grounds, which offer everything from formal lilyponds and billiard-table-smooth lawns to joyous bursts of floral colour and the russets, golds and greens of an arboretum. The glasshouse, holding some spectacular cactuses from south and central America, stands alongside a fragrant walled garden brimming with fruit and vegetables. Seek out, too, the Pompeii Gardens, setting for many a *Doctor Who* scene.

Although the **house** itself is currently undergoing a lengthy restoration project, there's a certain appeal in its slightly dishevelled state. Highlights include the Great Hall, sporting splendid stained-glass windows, and the dining room, which boasts a magnificent carved oak fireplace. You can try your hand at snooker in the oak-panelled billiards room, or if you've got kids, head to the Red Library and park yourself on a sofa with a book or two. Back outside, there's a cool little play area for children, and two excellent **cafés**.

St Lythan Long Cairn and Tinkinswood Long Cairn

St Lythan Long Cairn Just south of Dyffryn Gardens • Open access • Free; CADW • ☎01443 336000, ⓦcadw.gov.wales/daysout /stlythansburialchamber • **Tinkinswood Long Cairn** On the other side of Dyffryn Gardens, beside the wooded lane between Dyffryn and St Nicholas, a village on the A48 2 miles from Cardiff's Culverhouse Cross roundabout • Open access • Free

By the lane junction just south of Dyffryn Gardens, **St Lythan Long Cairn** is more than 4000 years old. It's nowhere near as impressive, however, as its near neighbour, the **Tinkinswood Long Cairn**, a huge, capstoned burial chamber that dates back around 4500 years. Legend has it that anyone who sleeps beneath the fifty-ton monolith for a night will either die, go raving mad or become a poet – a threat commonly ascribed to other megalithic sites in Wales.

1

Llanerch Vineyard

Hensol, 4 miles northwest of St Nicholas and 1 mile south of M4 junction 34, CF72 8GG • **Shop** Mon–Sat 8am–6.30pm, Sun 8am–4pm •
Tours April–Oct Wed–Sun noon & 5pm; 1hr • £12 • **Tastings** Wed–Sun 1.30–4pm • Three wines £7.50 • ☎01443 222716, ⓦllanerch
-vineyard.co.uk

Among rolling hills, **Llanerch Vineyard** is Wales' most successful winery, producing
around ten thousand bottles of white and rosé Cariad wine each year, most of it sold
within Wales. On a **tour**, you can nose around the vines and a patch of ancient woodland
before sitting down to a taste of the finished product; it's also possible to come along and
pay for an informal **tasting** as and when. Also on site is a wine **shop**, restaurant and
bistro/café (see below), accommodation (see below) and a cookery school.

ARRIVAL AND DEPARTURE	**BARRY AND AROUND**

By train Trains from Cardiff Queen Street (every 15min;
35min) rattle through Barry Docks and Barry stations
before terminating at Barry Island.

By bus Buses from Cardiff (every 30min; 1hr) drop
passengers on Friars Rd, just above the promenade.

ACCOMMODATION AND EATING

Cadwaladers 11 Paget Rd, CF62 5TQ ☎01446 736486.
A welcome reprieve from the surrounding tack, this smart
little café, just behind the Pavilion, offers a range of light
bites, but the best reason to pop by is the good strong
coffee and marvellous ice cream. Mon–Thurs 9am–7pm,
Fri–Sun 9am–8pm.

Llanerch Vineyard Hensol, CF72 8GG ☎01443 222716,
ⓦllanerch-vineyard.co.uk. Smart, contemporary
accommodation just outside Barry, with a collection of suites
and studios overlooking the vineyard (see above) and in the
farmhouse. The fabulous-looking *Cariad* restaurant knocks

up home-cooked seasonal food such as rack of Welsh lamb
with minted bonbon and sweet potato (£22), while the
adjoining bistro/café is a lovely spot for coffee or a glass of
wine. Restaurant: Mon–Sat 6.30–9pm, Sun noon–4pm;
bistro/café: Mon–Sat noon–9pm, Sun noon–4pm. £130
New Farm Port Rd West, between Barry and Cardiff
Airport, CF62 3BT ☎01446 735536, ⓦnewfarmbarry
.co.uk. A welcoming early seventeenth-century farmhouse
B&B whose six cosy rooms have nice touches, though not
all are en suite. The farmhouse breakfast will set you up
nicely for the day. £65

Llantwit Major and around

At first glance, **LLANTWIT MAJOR** (Llanilltud Fawr) appears to be all modern housing
estates and rows of shops, but at its heart is a tiny kernel of winding streets fanning out
from a quaint town square. This is where, in around 500 AD, the scholarly **St Illtud**
educated a succession of young men at his monastery, giving the town the chance to
claim the title of Britain's earliest centre of learning. Among Illtud's pupils were
St David and St Patrick, who was abducted from the monastery by Irish pirates to
become the patron saint of Ireland.

St Illtud's church

Burial Lane, CF61 1SG • Daily 8am–6pm • ☎01446 795551, ⓦllanilltud.org.uk

From the main square, Burial Lane winds its way down to the front of the magnificent
St Illtud's church, sheltering in a hollow next to the trickle of the Col Huw River. The first
thing that strikes you about the church is its size: it is, in fact, two churches joined at the
tower. The older **west church**, nearer the stream, dates from around 1100; aisles were added
in the twelfth and thirteenth centuries to transform it into the nave of a new church.
Tagged on to the rear of the west church is the beautifully restored Galilee Chapel, though
the original whitewashed stone walls sit somewhat incongruously with the modern glass
windows and tiled flooring. Prize among the chapel's fine collection of decorative Celtic
crosses and stones is the **Illtud Cross**, an exquisitely carved eighth-century boulder, on which
the letters ILT and half of a U (remains of ILLTUD) can still be seen. Similarly impressive
is the Houelt Cross, one of the finest examples of a wheel cross anywhere in Wales.

The **east church** is notable chiefly for some fresco remains, the most impressive being
that of St Christopher on the north wall, dating from around 1400.

The beach

At the junction at the top of Burial Lane, Colhugh Street descends for a little over a mile along the scrubby valley of the Col Huw River to the rocky **beach**, popular for surfing and a great starting point for wonderful walks along the caves and inlets of the stratified cliffs and back into the rolling countryside. There's a tidy little beach café, too.

St Donats Arts Centre

St Donat's, 2 miles west of Llantwit Major, CF61 1WF • ☎ 01446 799100, ⓦ stdonats.com

From the beach, the clifftop path runs for two miles west to **St Donat's Bay**, dominated by a fourteenth-century castle that was bought and restored in mock-Gothic style by US tycoon William Randolph Hearst in the 1930s. It's now home to the international Atlantic College and multipurpose **St Donats Arts Centre**, at the forefront of Welsh efforts to internationalize local culture. As well as music, theatre, film, dance, exhibitions and community outreach, the centre hosts the excellent **Beyond the Border Storytelling Festival** (ⓦ beyondtheborder.com) in the first weekend of July, which typically features more than one hundred performances. The *Glass Room Café* is a delightful spot to while away an hour or so.

ARRIVAL AND INFORMATION   LLANTWIT MAJOR

By train The train station on the Vale line is just above the bus stop.

By bus Buses drop passengers behind the modern shopping precinct, from where it's a short walk down East St into the town centre.

Destinations Barry (Mon–Sat 6 daily; 30min); Cardiff (Mon–Sat 6 daily; 1hr).

Destinations Barry (hourly; 10min); Bridgend (hourly; 20min); Cardiff (hourly; 40min).

Tourist information The heritage centre in the town hall on Church St (April–Sept Mon–Fri 9.30am–4pm; ☎ 01446 796086, ⓦ visitthevale.com) has loads of information on the town and the Vale.

ACCOMMODATION AND EATING

Acorn Camping Ham Lane South, CF61 1RP ☎ 01446 794024, ⓦ acorncamping.co.uk. Large, well-shaded site a mile or so south of town. Excellent modern amenities include a shop, laundry, indoor games and children's play area. **£17.50**

Café Velo 3 Church St, CF61 1SB ☎ 01446 792564, ⓦ cafevelo.info. Welcoming saddle-sore cyclists, and anyone else who cares for a decent cup of coffee and a slice of home-made cake, this super bike-themed café is run by an ex-pro; posters and jerseys adorn the walls while TV screens relay whatever race happens to be taking place around the world. Good fun. Tues–Fri 9am–5pm, Sat & Sun 9am–3pm.

Illtud's 216 Church St, CF61 1SB ☎ 01446 793800, ⓦ illtuds216.co.uk. Satisfying restaurant offering exceptional meat and seafood dishes, such as honey-glazed poussin with seasonal veg (£13.50). Once beyond the front bar, you enter a seductive, hall-like interior graced by candle-topped tables, drapes hanging from the ceiling and splashy artwork. Tues–Sat noon–2.30pm & 6–10pm, Sun noon–3pm.

The Old Swan Inn Church St, CF61 1SB ☎ 01446 792230, ⓦ knifeandforkfood.co.uk. Dating back to the twelfth century, Llantwit's oldest public house is the most agreeable place for a pint. The sociable bar/dining room offers a better-than-average blackboard menu and a choice selection of largely local beers. Mon–Sat noon–11pm, Sun noon–10.30pm; kitchen daily noon–3pm & 6–9.30pm.

Dunraven Bay

West of Llantwit Major, the coast ducks and dives past remote cliffs and sandy beaches towards **DUNRAVEN BAY**, a beautiful, wide beach backed by jagged cliffs of perfectly defined layers of limestone and shale. Dunraven lies at the western end of a magnificent fifteen-mile **coastal walk**, dipping down into tiny, wooded valleys and up across wide stretches of cliff and sand. Just up from the car park by Dunraven Beach is the **Heritage Coast Centre** (usually Wed–Sun 10am–3/4pm, but erratic; free; ☎ 01656 880157, ⓦ valeofglamorgan.gov.uk), a small information point with an exhibition on the bay and leaflets about great walks along this splendid, yet underrated, section of the south Wales coastline.

Frolics Beach Rd, CF32 0RT ☎01446 880127, Ⓦ frolicsrestaurant.co.uk. Highly rated in these parts, this unassuming-looking restaurant, a 10min walk from the bay, is the real deal when it comes to authentic Italian cuisine; alternatively, you could just opt for a good old-fashioned pizza (£10) – they're exceptional. Tues–Sat noon–2.30pm & 5.30–9.30pm.

Porthcawl

One of Wales' most enduring family resorts, **PORTHCAWL** possesses a quaint village centre, several sandy beaches and some fantastic **surf**. The main pedestrianized thoroughfare, **John Street**, extends down to the **Esplanade**, an extensive seafront promenade. Lined with a typical array of Victorian and Edwardian hotels, the Esplanade stretches the full length of the town and changes its name throughout. Midway along you'll find the domed **Grand Pavilion** (☎01656 815995, Ⓦ grandpavilion.co.uk), which stages seaside entertainment shows and pantomimes.

Eastwards, the Esplanade runs to a lifeboat station at the harbour before veering north along the coast under the name of Eastern Promenade. This is where you'll find the **Coney Beach amusement park**, behind the line of whelk stalls and candy-floss shops looking out over the popular **Sandy Bay** and neighbouring **Trecco Bay**.

Porthcawl Museum

John St, CF36 3DT • Tues–Fri 10am–noon & 2–4pm, Sat 10am–4pm • Free • ☎01656 788853, Ⓦ porthcawlmuseum.com

Housed inside the town's Grade II-listed Old Police Station, the small but engaging **Porthcawl Museum** documents the history and heritage of the town and surrounding area through a series of rotating exhibitions. Beyond the old prisoner's yard to the rear, the three holding cells, which retain their original graffitied metal doors, house temporary exhibitions. Here too is a Victorian washhouse, compete with original (functioning) copper boiler, an old Anderson bomb shelter and the Porthcawl cannon, discovered on a local beach following heavy storms and now re-submerged in water in order to protect it.

PORTHCAWL ACTIVITIES

Porthcawl provides fantastic opportunities to participate in a range of outdoor activities.

SURFING

On the northwest side of town, a twenty-minute walk from the centre, beautiful **Rest Bay** is one of the best **surfing** beaches in Wales. Operating out of a container by the car park just above the beach, the excellent Porthcawl Surf (☎07583 348013, Ⓦ porthcawlsurf.co.uk) offers surfing lessons (£30/2hr) as well as board (£10/day) and wetsuit (£5/day) rental; changing and shower facilities are also available.

FAT BIKING

One of the newest, and most thrilling, activities hereabouts is **fat biking**, riding large-rimmed bikes that can traverse mud, rock and sand. Located next to Coney Beach, Porthcawl Bike Hire (☎07850 684740, Ⓦ porthcawlbikehire.co.uk) rents fat bikes (£20/4hr), but more fun are the tours (£55/4hr), which take in a fabulous stretch of coast from the beach towards the mighty sand dunes of Merthyr Mawr, some of the largest in Europe – it's an absolute blast.

GOLFING

Porthcawl attracts large numbers of **golfers**, here to test themselves on the magnificent Royal Porthcawl course (☎01656 782251, Ⓦ royalporthcawl.com), consistently ranked one of Britain's finest – it's not cheap, though (£130 for eighteen holes).

ALL SHOOK UP

Each year, on the last weekend of September, Porthcawl becomes the unlikely destination for one of Europe's largest **Elvis Presley** celebrations (🌐 elvies.co.uk). This rip-roaring festival sees the town overrun with thousands of Elvis impersonators keen to outdo each other in a host of tribute shows at the Grand Pavilion and other venues. The somewhat more refined **International Jazz Festival** takes place in April (🌐 porthcawl-jazz-festival.com).

ARRIVAL AND INFORMATION PORTHCAWL

By bus Buses set passengers down on John St, from where it's a 2min walk along the pedestrianized section of this same street into the centre.
Destinations Cardiff, via Cowbridge (every 30min; 1hr 35min); Swansea (hourly, 1 change; 1hr 30min).
Tourist information There's no tourist office; 🌐 bridgendbites.com is an excellent resource.

ACCOMMODATION AND EATING

Brodawel Moor Lane, Nottage, CF36 3EJ ☎ 01656 783231, 🌐 brodawelcamping.co.uk. About a 15min walk north of town, this simple field site offers reasonable, well-kept facilities, including showers, laundry, utility room, and a play area for kids. Closed Nov–March. **£17.50**

Foam Edge 9 West Drive, CF36 3LS ☎ 01656 782866, 🌐 foam-edge.co.uk. Despite the nondescript exterior, this is a cheerful, family-run guesthouse with two warm and beautifully decorated rooms. One has an enclosed balcony, and both have sensational sea views; there's a hearty cooked Welsh breakfast, too. **£95**

Olivia House 44 Esplanade Ave, CF36 3YU ☎ 01656 789022, 🌐 oliviahouse.com. On the road running up from the pavilion, this townhouse has been converted into a boutique hotel sporting six lavish, individually styled rooms, with thoughtful touches given to each. Breakfast typically consists of kippers or smoked salmon and scrambled egg. **£85**

Rava 29 Mary St, CF36 3YN ☎ 01656 773888, 🌐 ristoranterava.co.uk. Atmospheric, family-run restaurant dishing up good-value Italian food; there's invariably a cracking catch of the day. The two-course early evening menu (6–7pm) is terrific value (£11.95). Tues–Sat 6–11pm.

The Royal Mint Experience

Pontyclun, 1 mile north of Llantrisant, CF72 8YT • Daily 9.30am–5pm, obligatory tours (1hr) every 15min 10am–4.30pm • £13.50 • ☎ 0333 241 2223, 🌐 royalmint.com • Buses from Cardiff (hourly; 45min) and Pontypridd (every 20min; 20–40min) set down at the Bull Ring in the centre of Llantrisant, from where it's a 15min walk

It may come as a surprise to many to learn that all domestic coinage, as well as coins for some sixty other (mostly Commonwealth) countries, are minted here in south Wales. The **Royal Mint** was founded in 886 AD, operating from the Tower of London, and later Tower Hill, for nearly all of its existence – until 1968, when it relocated to Llantrisant, with Queen Elizabeth II striking the first coin in December of that year.

Visits to the marvellous **Royal Mint Experience** are by guided tour only. These begin with an informative film before heading across to the plant itself; for obvious reasons, access to the factory floor is forbidden, but you do get to view live coin production from behind glass screens – minted around the clock, a remarkable 90 million coins are struck here each week – and at the end you get to strike your own £1 coin. You are then left to your own devices in the superb **museum**, which lucidly relays the history of the Mint. Among the many exhibits are portrait medals, including one of Sir Isaac Newton (a former Master of the Mint); the gold sovereign of Henry VII; and a stack of medals, including samples made for the 2012 Olympic Games in London. Once done, you can have a bite to eat in the excellent **café**.

Cowbridge

High-class boutiques, cafés and restaurants line the long and handsome main street of well-heeled **COWBRIDGE** (Y Bont Faen), Wales' wealthiest town. On the south side of

1

the High Street, **Church Street** leads under the narrow gatehouse that is the sole survivor of the four that once punctuated the town's fourteenth-century walls.

Old Beaupre Castle

1.5 miles south of Cowbridge, CF71 7LT • Daily 10am–4pm • Free; CADW • ☎ 01443 336000, ⓦ cadw.gov.wales/daysout/oldbeauprecastle

A little more than a mile south of town, down St Athan Road, a quiet lane fringed with high hedges, there's a tiny lay-by opposite the Regency finery of Howe Mill. A path opposite leads along the bank of the River Thaw for a quarter of a mile to the gauntly impressive ruins of **Old Beaupre Castle**, largely an Elizabethan manor house. Built by the local noble family, the Bassetts, Beaupre is a huge shell of ruined Italianate doorways and vast mullioned windows in the middle of a quiet Glamorgan field.

ARRIVAL AND DEPARTURE COWBRIDGE

By bus Buses set passengers down by the town hall on the High St.

Destinations Cardiff (every 30min; 50min); Porthcawl (every 30min; 50min).

ACCOMMODATION AND EATING

Bear Hotel 63 High St, CF71 7AF ☎ 01446 774814, ⓦ townandcountrycollective.co.uk. An upgraded, long-established coaching inn with supremely comfortable, individually designed rooms; all are typically furnished in classical style and some have four-poster beds. **£110**

Market Place 66 High St, CF71 7AH ☎ 01446 774800, ⓦ the-marketplace.co.uk. Beautiful restaurant divided into different sections, with the graceful bare-brick interior of the listed seventeenth-century dining room contrasting with the modern garden terrace and mezzanine bar. The exceptional menu features the likes of roasted cod with

feta-and-green-peppercorn crust, spinach and mash. The three-course lunch menu (£19.95) is terrific value. Wed–Sat noon–3pm & 6–10pm, Sun noon–3pm.

★**The Penny Farthing Café** 54 High St, CF71 7AH ☎ 01446 774999, ⓦ townandcountrycollective.co.uk. Park yourself in one of the little brick alcoves of this superb café/wine bar and enjoy a smoked salmon and cream cheese sandwich with a glass of Prosecco. Early birds can tuck into the Quarter Penny Big Breakfast (£7.95). The summery terrace out the back is delightful. Mon–Thurs 8.30am–5pm, Fri & Sat 8.30am–6pm, Sun 9am–5pm.

The Valleys

No other part of Wales is as instantly recognizable as the **Valleys**, a generic name for the string of settlements packed into the narrow cracks in the mountainous terrain north of Newport, Cardiff and Swansea. This section covers the Valleys from Blaenavon in the east to Cwm Afan and Port Talbot in the west. Historically, the region depended almost solely on **coal mining** (see box, p.105) and, as you approach the Valleys from Monmouthshire, the change from rolling countryside to a post-industrial landscape is almost instantaneous. That's not to say the Valleys are devoid of greenery – the mining industry is practically defunct, and the lush hills that you see today are a far cry from the slag heaps and soot-encrusted buildings of a mere twenty to thirty years ago. Nonetheless, the ghost of the industry looms large in the staunchly working-class towns, where row upon row of brightly painted terraced houses, tipped along the slopes at incredible angles, are broken only by austere chapels, the occasional remaining pithead or the miners' old institutes and drinking clubs.

Although not traditional tourist country, this is without doubt one of the most fascinating corners of Wales. Some of the former mines have reopened as hard-hitting museums, notably the absorbing **Big Pit** at Blaenavon and the **Rhondda Heritage Park** at Trehafod. You'll also gain a deeper impression of Valley life from less conventional attractions such as the utopian workers' village at **Butetown** and the iron gravestones of **Blaenavon**, as well as the dignified memorials, found in almost every community, to those who died underground – or, in the heart-rending case of **Aberfan**, while simply going about their daily lives. In addition to the industrial landmarks, older

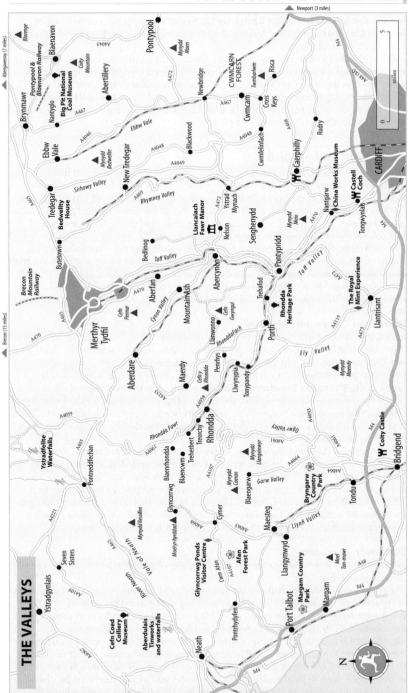

Newport (3 miles)

THE VALLEYS

Blorenge

Blaenavon

Pontypool

Pontypool & Blaenavon Railway

Big Pit National Coal Museum

Mynydd Maen

Abergavenny (7 miles)

Coity Mountain

A4043

A472

Brynmawr

Nantyglo

Abertillery

Newbridge

CWMCARN FOREST

Risca

A467

Twmbarlwm

Cross Keys

Cwmcarn

A467

Ebbw Vale

A4046

Ebbw Vale

Mynydd Bedwellte

Blackwood

A4048

Cwmfelinfach

A468

A4049

Caerphilly

Rudry

A48 (M)

CARDIFF

Tredegar

Bedwellty House

Sirhowy Valley

New Tredegar

A469

Rhymney Valley

Ystrad Mynach

A472

China Works Museum

Nantgarw

Castell Coch

Tongwynlais

Brecon Mountain Railway

Butetown

Bedlinog

Taff Valley

Llancaiach Fawr Manor

Nelson

Senghenydd

Mynydd Meio

A470

M4

Brecon (15 miles)

A465

Cefn Pennar

Abercynon

Pontypridd

Taff Valley

The Royal Mint Experience

A4054

Aberfan

Cynon Valley

Mountain Ash

Trehafod

Rhondda Heritage Park

Merthyr Tydfil

A470

Cefn Gwyngul

Llanwonno

Rhondda Fach

Porth

A4119

Llantrisant

A473

Aberdare

A4233

Maerdy

Cefn Rhondda

Penrhys

Llwynypia

Tonypandy

Ely Valley

Mynydd Maendy

A4059

A4058

Rhondda Fawr

Rhondda

Ogwr Valley

A4093

A4061

A4061

Pontneddfechan

Ystradfellte Waterfalls

A4059

Blaenrhondda

Treorchy

Treherbert

Blaencwm

A4107

Mynydd Llangeinwyr

Garw Valley

A4064

Bryngarw Country Park

A4061

Coity Castle

Bridgend

Seven Sisters

A465

Mynydd Resolven

Glyncorrwg

Cymer

A4107

Blaengarw

Maesteg

Llynfi Valley

Tondu

A48

Ystradgynlais

A4109

Vale of Neath

River Neath

Moel-Hyddgad

A4068

Afan Valley

Glyncorrwg Ponds Visitor Centre

Afan Forest Park

Cwm Afan

A4063

Llangynwyd

Moel Ton-mawr

Margam Country Park

Margam

M4

Cefn Coed Colliery Museum

Aberdulais Tinworks and waterfalls

A4067

Neath

Pontrhydyfen

Port Talbot

M4

N

Swansea (10 miles)

0   5   miles

1

historic sights include the vast **Caerphilly Castle** and the sixteenth-century manor house of **Llancaiach Fawr**. The Valleys also offer unforgettable **walking** holidays; paths are best on the high ridges.

This region has a distinct geography. As a result of the formidable terrain, each valley was almost entirely isolated. Canals, roads and train lines competed for space on the valley floor, petering out as the contours became untameable at the upper end. Connecting roads were built only in the 1920s, and even today **transport** is frequently restricted to the outer reaches, with roads and train lines radiating out through the south Wales coalfield like spokes on a giant wheel.

Blaenavon and around

Situated in the northeastern extremities of the Valleys is the iron and coal town of **BLAENAVON** (Blaenafon). Its lofty hillside position makes it feel less claustrophobic than many Valley towns, but its decline is testified by a population of little more than five thousand, a third of its nineteenth-century size. It remains a spirited and evocative place, however, a fact recognized when the town and surrounding landscape gained UNESCO World Heritage Site status in 2000.

Blaenavon is perhaps best known for its **Big Pit**, an old coal mine-turned-museum, though the former ironworks is no less gripping, and there are vestiges of the industrial past scattered all over town – you could easily be detained here for a day. It's particularly lively during **World Heritage Day** at the end of June, with live music, street entertainers, a Victorian fun fair and a heritage costume parade.

Blaenavon Community Museum

High St, NP4 9PT • Mon, Tues, Thurs & Fri 10am–4pm, Sat 10am–1pm • £2 • ☎ 01495 790991

The town's Victorian boom can be seen in its architecture, most notably the florid **Working Men's Hall**, built in 1895 as a library and recreational centre – miners were obliged to pay a halfpenny a week for the privilege of using its facilities. Today it is home to the **Blaenavon Community Museum**, which proudly documents the roles played by various groups throughout the community. Look out for trophies won by the fabulous Blaenavon Male Voice Choir, and items belonging to Ken Jones, one of Wales' first true rugby superstars (he was also an Olympic sprinter) – there's a fine statue of him at the bottom of Broad Street.

Another room examines the life and works of author **Alexander Cordell** (1914–97), including his jacket, books, typewriter and Tippex-splattered desk. Born in Ceylon (now Sri Lanka), Cordell developed a deep affinity with Wales and its industrial past during the many years he spent living in the area, a theme covered in his renowned 1959 novel, *Rape of the Fair Country*. The main upstairs hall is today used for concerts, including the occasional performance by the male voice choir, and another room downstairs has been converted into a cinema with fairly regular screenings.

Blaenavon Ironworks

North St, NP4 9RQ • April–Oct daily 10am–5pm; Nov–March Thurs–Sat 10am–4pm • Free; CADW • ☎ 01495 792615, ⓦ cadw.gov.wales /daysout/blaenavonironworks

The remarkable **Blaenavon Ironworks** constitute one of the most complete extant sites of its period in the world. Although iron smelting in the area dates back to the sixteenth century, it wasn't until three Midlands businessmen formed these ironworks in 1789 that the industry took off. Limestone, coal and iron ore – ingredients for successful smelting – were locally abundant, and at peak production there were five furnaces here. The Blaenavon works grew to become one of the largest in Britain, finally closing in 1900. The remains of the site offer a thorough picture both of the process used to produce iron – three furnaces and a cast house remain, alongside the hulking water balance tower – and the workers' lifestyles that went with it.

1

Entering the cast house, you're greeted by the clanking and roar of a furnace accompanied by dramatic light and smoke effects in a very well-conceived multisensory experience entitled, appropriately enough, "**Welcome to Hell**".

Across from the water tower are the whitewashed **Stack Square cottages**, Middle Row and Engine Row, built for the foremen and craftsmen between 1789 and 1792 and inhabited until as recently as 1971. Each of these six, four-room abodes remain *in situ*, with another housing an exhibition on the history of iron- and steel-making, and a model of how the site would have once looked. The neighbouring **truck shop** (truck meaning "exchange") was where miners would go to purchase goods, albeit at deeply inflated prices (there were no other shops in town). Given that workers were invariably paid late, and therefore had little or no money, arrears were docked from their pay, ensuring that they were permanently in debt.

Pontypool and Blaenavon Railway

Furnace Sidings, NP4 9SF • Easter–Sept Sat & Sun 11am–4pm, plus Wed in summer school hols, and on selected days • £9 return (ride all day) • ☎ 01495 792263, ⓦ pontypool-and-blaenavon.co.uk

Between Easter and September, steam-train buffs can ride on the **Pontypool and Blaenavon Railway**, which shunts between the Furnace Sidings (signposted just off the B4248 between Blaenavon and Brynmawr) and the *Whistle Inn*, before heading down to the Big Pit halt (near the museum) and Blaenavon High Level station, where there's a small **museum** detailing the history of the line. The five-mile round trip takes about one hour. Railway fanatics may also want to visit the **Railway Shop**, in Brownings bookshop at 33 Broad St (Mon–Fri 10.30am–5pm, Sat 10.30am–4pm), which sells all sorts of model trains and accessories.

THE WELSH COAL INDUSTRY

The land beneath the inhospitable hills of the south Wales valleys had some of the world's most abundant and accessible natural seams of **coal**, as well as iron ore. During the boom years of the nineteenth and early twentieth centuries, wealthy English capitalists came to Wales and ruthlessly stripped the land of its natural assets, while paying paltry amounts to those who risked life and limb in the mines. The mine owners were in a formidably strong position – thousands of Welsh working class, bolstered by their Irish, Scottish and Italian peers, flocked to the Valleys in search of work and some sort of sustainable life. The Valleys – virtually unpopulated at the start of the nineteenth century – became blackened with soot and packed with people, pits and chapels by the beginning of the twentieth.

By 1920, there were 256,000 men working in the 620 mines of the south Wales coalfield, providing one-third of the world's coal resources. Vast **miners' institutes**, paid for by a wages' levy, jostled for position with the Nonconformist chapels, whose muscular brand of Christianity was matched by the zeal of the region's politics, trade-union-led and avowedly left-wing. Great socialist orators rose to national prominence, and even Britain's pioneering **National Health Service**, founded by a radical Labour government in the years following World War II, was based on a Valleys community scheme run by Aneurin Bevan.

More than half of the original pits closed in the harsh economic climate of the 1930s. World War II saw a brief respite in the closure programme, which continued even more swiftly in the years immediately after. As coal seams became less economical (due to the additional distance to reach the coalface from the pitheads), and the political climate shifted, the number of people employed in the industry dipped down into four figures in the aftermath of the 1984–85 miners' strike. No coalfields were as solidly behind the strike as south Wales, whose workers and families responded wholeheartedly to the call to defend the industry, which their trade union, the **National Union of Mineworkers** (NUM), claimed was on the brink of being decimated. The year-long war of attrition between the Thatcher government and Arthur Scargill's NUM was bitter, finally seeing the government victorious as the number of miners returning to work outnumbered those staying out on strike. More than a quarter of a century on, all but a few privately run south Wales pits have now closed.

1

Big Pit National Coal Museum

Signposted on the west side of Blaenavon, off the B4246, NP4 9XP • Feb–Nov daily 9.30am–5pm, hourly tours (1hr) 10am–3.30pm; Jan & Dec call for tour times • Free • ☎ 0300 111 2333, ✆ museum.wales/bigpit • #30 bus from Cwmbran (hourly; 40min) stops outside the entrance

Just west of Blaenavon lies the marvellous **Big Pit National Coal Museum**, occupying a former colliery that opened in 1880 and closed exactly a century later. One of the largest coal-mining sites in the region, it employed some 1300 men at its peak.

The pit

Of all the mining museums in south Wales, Big Pit brings you closest to the experience of a miner's work and life, as you descend 300ft into the **pit**, kitted out with lamp, helmet and heavy battery pack into a labyrinth of shafts and coal faces. The guides are ex-miners, who give you a personal insight into mining life as they lead you through examples of the different types of coal mining, from the old stack-and-pillar operation, where miners would manually hack into the coalface before propping up the ceiling with a wooden beam, to more modern mechanically worked seams. Constant streams of rust-coloured water flow by, adding to the dank and chilly atmosphere that terrified the small children who were once paid twopence for a six-day week (of which one penny was subtracted for the cost of their candles) pulling the coal wagons along the tracks. Just as integral to the working of the mines were the pit ponies, hardy creatures who worked at Blaenavon until 1972; you also get to see the now forlorn stables.

The pithead baths

On the surface the superbly preserved **pithead baths**, dating from 1939, are just about the last surviving anywhere in the country. Beyond the rows of lockers, some of which contain miners' belongings, several rooms offer a compelling and moving insight into the lives and times of the workers and their families. The plight of women is given due prominence, with emphasis on their role during the miners' strikes, when they organized food parcels and soup kitchens, and in many cases joined the men on the picket lines. The exhibition concludes with coverage of the explosive 1984–85 strikes; look out for the series of feisty testimonies from the miners made redundant here.

ARRIVAL AND INFORMATION   BLAENAVON

By bus Buses from Newport (every 15min; 1hr) stop at the top of High St, which runs parallel to Broad St, the main focus of activity (such as it is here) in town.

Tourist information The Blaenavon Heritage Centre, on Church Rd (Tues–Sun 10am–5pm; ☎ 01495 742333, ✆ visitblaenavon.co.uk), has an enlightening exhibition on the history of the town's coal-mining and ironworking industries, as well as a café.

ACCOMMODATION AND EATING

Coffi Bean 76 Broad St, NP4 9NF ☎ 01495 790127. There are very few places to eat or drink in Blaenavon, but this charmingly staffed coffee shop more than compensates; park yourself at a stripped wooden table under the building's original green and cream tiling and enjoy a home-made pastry and a steaming cup of coffee. Tues–Sun 8am–3pm.

Lion Hotel 41 Broad St, NP4 9NH ☎ 01495 792516, ✆ thelionhotelblaenavon.co.uk. The town's one hotel is a bright affair, its twelve deep-burgundy-coloured rooms comprising warm fluffy carpets, cool fabrics and sparkling, marble-tiled bathrooms; perhaps surprisingly, there's a sauna and steam room, too. **£85**

Abertillery

It's worth taking a short detour down the Ebbw Vale Valley to **ABERTILLERY**, ten miles southwest of Blaenavon, where the magnificent **Guardian monument** pays tribute to fallen miners of the Six Bells colliery disaster. In 1960, 45 miners were killed here in an underground explosion, an event commemorated some fifty years later with the unveiling of this, the largest memorial in the Valleys, on the former site of the colliery, now a peaceful landscaped park. Designed by Sebastien Boyesen, the 40ft-high statue of a bare-chested miner with arms outstretched was constructed from some twenty thousand individual slices of steel; the names of the victims are cut into the handsome sandstone plinth on which the miner stands.

Six Bells Heritage Centre

Chapel Rd, NP13 2ND • Mon–Fri 9am–4pm • Free • ☏ 01495 211732

You can learn about the Guardian at the superb little **Six Bells Heritage Centre**, some 500m from the monument near the baptist church. This tiny, one-roomed venue has footage of the monument's construction and installation, alongside detailed history of the mine itself, which opened in 1892 and peaked towards the end of World War I when it employed some 2450 men. Mining at Six Bells continued after the disaster, before eventually closing in 1988, by which time it had merged with the nearby Marine colliery in Cwm. Artefacts donated by ex-miners – mandrels, boots, lamp checks (tags) and carbide lamps among other things – are displayed in battered old lockers, while you can sit in a story chair and listen to miners regale you with stories of life below ground.

Cwmcarn Forest

Crosskeys, 8 miles south of Abertillery, NP11 7FA • **Cwmcarn Forest Drive** March, Sept & Oct daily 11am–5pm; April–Aug daily 11am–7pm; Nov–Feb Sat & Sun 11am–4pm • £5/car • **Visitor centre** Daily 9am–5pm • ☏ 01495 272001, ⊛ your.caerphilly.gov.uk/cwmcarnforest

Offering plentiful opportunities for cycling and walking, the **Cwmcarn Forest** is best seen along the seven-mile figure-of-eight Cwmcarn Forest Drive. This is closed until late 2018 or early 2019 for the removal of infected larch trees, but experienced riders can still use the four mountain-bike trails, which are graded either difficult or severe. In addition to the Forest Drive, half a dozen waymarked **walks** weave through the forest. The longest and most strenuous is the twelve-mile Raven Walk, which circles the Sirhowy and Ebbw valleys, affording terrific views of the Severn estuary and the Brecons; the thirty-minute Bluebell Walk is ideal for families. Information about all the trails can be obtained from the **visitor centre** at the entrance to the forest, which also has walking maps and guides, and a pleasant **café**. Just below the centre, PS Cycles offers **bike rental** (daily except Tues 10am–5.30pm; £32.50/day; ☏ 01495 272279, ⊛ pscycles.co.uk).

ACCOMMODATION   **CWMCARN FOREST**

Forest Drive campsite Next to the visitor centre ☏ 01495 272001. This very small, neat and grassy campsite also has ten wooden pods each sleeping three to four people and a couple of which are dog-friendly; there are cooking and shower facilities for use by all. Camping **£17**, pods **£42**

Caerphilly

Now almost a suburb of Cardiff, just seven miles north of the capital at the foot of the **Rhymney Valley**, the town of **CAERPHILLY** (Caerffili) is wrapped around its staggering moated **castle**, the largest in Wales and the second largest in the UK after Windsor Castle. Caerphilly was also the birthplace of legendary comedian **Tommy Cooper**, a large bronze statue of whom stands opposite the castle.

> ### THE BIG CHEESE
>
> In addition to its castle, Caerphilly is also synonymous with its crumbly white **cheese**, which has inspired the vibrant **Big Cheese festival** (⊛ caerphilly.gov.uk/bigcheese), held over three days in late July in the shadow of the castle. Events include street theatre and concerts, a funfair, falconry, historical re-enactments and a cheese race. There's a craft market and, of course, a food market selling cheese along with all manner of local produce. Throughout the rest of the year, the only place in town to buy actual Welsh Farmhouse Caerphilly cheese (rather than those made elsewhere but still carrying the Caerphilly label) is the tourist office.

1

Caerphilly Castle

Castle St, CF83 1JD • March–June, Sept & Oct daily 9.30am–5pm; July & Aug daily 9.30am–6pm; Nov–Feb Mon–Sat 10am–4pm, Sun 11am–4pm • £7.95; CADW • ☎ 029 2088 3143, ⓦ cadw.gov.wales/daysout/caerphilly-castle

Built on the site of a Roman fort and an earlier Norman fortification, the present **Caerphilly Castle** was begun in 1268 under Gilbert de Clare, who wanted to protect the vulnerable coastal plains around Cardiff from Llywelyn ein Llyw Olaf (Llywelyn the Last). For the next few hundred years, Caerphilly was given at whim by various kings to their favourites – most notably by Edward II to his minion, and some say lover, Hugh le Despenser, in 1317. The Civil War necessitated the building of an armoury, which prompted Cromwell to seize it, drain the moat and blow up the towers. By the early twentieth century, the castle was in a sorry state, sitting amid a growing industrial town that saw fit to build in the moat and the castle precincts. In the late 1920s, under the supervision of the fourth Marquess of Bute, the castle underwent an extensive period of restoration, followed, in 1958, by the demolition of houses and shops so that the moat could be reflooded.

The castle grounds

You enter the castle through the much-restored great **gatehouse** that punctuates the barbican wall by a lake. From here, a bridge crosses the moat, part of the wider lake, to the outer wall of the castle itself, behind which sits the hulking inner ward. Located here is the massive **eastern gatehouse**, which includes an impressive upper hall and oratory and, to its left, the wholly restored and reroofed **Great Hall**, largely built around 1317 by Hugh le Despenser. Running round from the eastern gatehouse, behind the Great Hall and down to the southwestern corner, is an elevated walkway. Strolling along here, you'll pass the iconic southeastern **leaning tower**, with a dramatic cleft in its walls where Cromwell's men are said to have attempted to blow it sky-high (though the tilt is more likely due to simple subsidence). With the exception of the ruined northeastern tower, the other corner turrets have been blandly restored since the Civil War, though the northwestern tower houses a reasonably interesting exhibition on the castle's restoration. A platform behind the barbican wall exhibits medieval war and siege engines, pointing ominously across the lake.

ARRIVAL AND INFORMATION

CAERPHILLY

By train From the station, it's a 5min walk up Cardiff Rd to the centre of town and the castle.
Destinations Cardiff (every 15min; 20min); Rhymney (hourly; 40min).
By bus Buses from Cardiff (every 15min; 25min) stop

alongside the train station.
Tourist office Just along from the castle entrance on Twyn Square (daily 10am–5pm; ☎ 029 2088 0011, ⓦ visitcaerphilly.com). There's an excellent café with splendid views of the castle.

The Rhymney and Sirhowy valleys

Following the traditional border between the former counties of Glamorganshire and Monmouthshire north of Caerphilly, the **Rhymney Valley** is light on worthwhile sights, and becomes increasingly industrialized as it steers past a seamless succession of small towns. That said, there are one or two points of interest, as there are in the similarly low-key **Sirhowy Valley** across to the east.

Winding House

Cross St, off White Rose Way, New Tredegar, NP24 6EG • Mon–Fri 10am–5pm, Sat & Sun 11am–4pm • Free • ☎ 01443 822 666 • A 10min walk south of Tir-phil train station

Ten miles up the valley from Caerphilly is **NEW TREDEGAR**, where the **Winding House**, with its gleaming Victorian-era steam engine that once powered the colliery's high-speed lifts, is worth a visit. The engine usually only runs on the last Saturday of each month and bank holidays, though other dates are sometimes scheduled in. Otherwise, there's an enlightening exhibition on the history of Caerphilly and its surrounds.

Butetown

At the head of the Rhymney Valley, a mile beyond Rhymney town and just short of the A465 Heads of the Valleys road, tiny **BUTETOWN** (Drenewydd) was constructed as a model workers' estate in 1802–03 by the idealistic Marquess of Bute, a member of Wales' richest land- and minerals-owning family, although only the central grid of houses was ever built. An enlightening **heritage trail** ("A walk around Bute Town"; available via app on ⓦbutetownhistory.info) brings to life some of the town's most prominent buildings.

Bedwellty House and park

Morgan St, Tredegar, NP22 3NA • **House** Daily 9am–5pm • **Park** Daily 8.30am–8pm • Free • ☎ 01495 353370, ⓦ bedwelltyhouseandpark.co.uk

A mile east of Butetown, at the head of the Sirhowy Valley, the little town of **TREDEGAR** boasts **Bedwellty House and park**, a Georgian mansion built for the Homfray family, cofounders of the Tredegar ironworks. With major restoration work now complete, it is possible to visit, though there's not an awful lot to see beyond the Great Chamber, which is used principally for weddings. However, there is a lovely **tearoom** (daily 10am–4.30pm) in the old Orchid room. The main reason to stop by is the **park**, laid out in 1818 and now featuring rolling lawns, an arboretum, grotto and ice house – and the world's largest lump of coal, a fifteen-ton block exhibited as part of the 1951 Festival of Britain.

The Taff and Cynon valleys

Like the River Rhymney, the River Taff also empties into the Bristol Channel at Cardiff, after passing through a condensed 25 or so miles of industry and population that obscure the former **china works** at Nantgarw. The first town in the **Taff Valley** is **Pontypridd**, one of the most cheerful in the Valleys, where the Rhondda River hives off west. Continuing north, the river splits again at **Abercynon**, where the Cynon River – at the heart of the **Cynon Valley** – flows in from **Aberdare**. Just outside Abercynon is the enjoyable seventeenth-century **Llancaiach Fawr** manor house, while to the north, the Taff is packed into one of the tightest of all the Valleys, passing **Aberfan** five miles short of the town of **Merthyr Tydfil**.

China Works Museum

Tyla Gwyn, on the A470, CF15 7TB • Wed–Sun 10am–4pm • Free • ☎ 01443 844131, ⓦ nantgarwchinaworksmuseum.co.uk

Barrelling north along the A470, you'd never suspect that the **China Works Museum** is tucked behind a thicket of trees just by the junction for **Nantgarw**. Painter William Billingsley set up the works in 1813 with high ambition, using Valleys coal and Cornish clay, but the extremely difficult "soft paste porcelain" process resulted in just a ten-percent firing success rate and the enterprise lasted only ten years. But during this period the Nantgarw China Works produced some of the finest porcelain in the world, a few examples of which – decorative plates, teapots, cups and saucers – are on display here; there are far more extensive collections in the National Museum in Cardiff (see p.64) and the Glyn Vivian Gallery in Swansea (see p.121). Following the closure of the china works, the building reopened as a pottery in 1833 under William Henry Pardoe (his father, Thomas, was a distinguished ceramic painter), before ceasing to function in 1921; look out for the wonderful collection of clay pipes. Pardoe's descendants lived here until 1974, before the house and buildings were abandoned.

One room now functions as a delightful little **tearoom**, where you can sample delicious home-made cakes alongside a cup of tea or coffee served, naturally, in china cups.

Senghenydd Heritage Museum and around

Gwern Ave, Senghenydd, CF83 4HA • Mon–Sat 11am–2pm • Free • ☎ 029 2083 0445, ⓦ thecentresenghenydd.co.uk

One of the Valleys' lesser-known mining villages, **SENGHENYDD**, six miles north of Nantgarw, has had to contend with its own pit disasters over the years. The stories of the 1901 and 1913 disasters at the village's Universal colliery are relayed in the superb little **heritage museum**. The second of these explosions was particularly catastrophic, resulting in the loss of a staggering 439 men – there was just one survivor, William Harris, a photo of whom is displayed among the commemoration cards and other mementos from that time. Further cabinets display a host of other mining-related memorabilia: tobacco boxes, tommy (lunch) boxes, watches, lamps and such like.

A ten-minute walk away, on the site of the old Universal colliery at the northern end of Commercial Street, the **Welsh National and Universal Mining Memorial** opened in 2013 on the hundredth anniversary of the second disaster. Encircled by a wall of remembrance, with individual plaques for every man that died, is a superb bronze sculpture – *The Rescue* – of a stricken miner being dragged from the pit by a rescue worker. The surrounding landscaped garden bears slate floor plaques denoting every other pit disaster in Wales that resulted in the deaths of five or more miners – more than 150.

Pontypridd

Home town of singer Sir Tom Jones, **PONTYPRIDD** retains its own unique spirit even while rapidly gentrifying as the Cardiff commuters move in. Arriving, you're greeted by the distinctive arched **bridge** of 1775, once the largest single-span stone bridge in Europe. Featuring three holes either side to lessen the bridge's overall weight and allow gusty winds through, it was built by local amateur stonemason William Edwards, whose previous attempts crumbled into the river below. Wednesdays and Saturdays are good days to be here, with the old-fashioned **market** spilling out onto Market Street and the surrounding squares.

Ponty Lido

Ynysangharad Park, CF37 4PE • May–Sept daily 7.30am–7.15pm • £1; children free; booking advised • ☎ 0300 004 0000, ⓦ rctcbc.gov.uk

On the far side of the river from the town centre is **Ynysangharad Park**, established after World War I as a memorial park, but now the town's popular green space. The focal point is the beautifully restored **Ponty Lido**, a Grade II-listed building, constructed in 1927, which closed in 1991. Reopened in 2015, it comprises three heated pools (main, activity and splash pools), heated changing facilities and a superb **café**. It's a brilliant place to spend a few hours on a summer's day, with or without kids; note that thirty percent of the tickets are available at the gate on the day but these get snapped up quickly so booking is advised. There's also an excellent **adventure play** area (free) adjoining the lido.

Pontypridd Museum

Bridge St, CF37 4PE • Mon–Sat 10am–4.30pm • Free • ☎ 01443 490748, ⓦ pontypriddmuseum.cymru

Right next to the bridge, the **Pontypridd Museum** is housed in what was one of the town's great chapels. Built in 1861, it has been lovingly restored, and boasts unusually ornate ceiling bosses, pillars, pulpit, stained-glass window and organ, all of which contribute to the reverential atmosphere. On display are a real treasure-trove of photographs, video, models and exhibits that paint a warm picture of the town and its outlying valleys. Among local heroes celebrated here are singer Tom Jones and boxer Freddie Welsh, who fought an astonishing 166 times, becoming World Lightweight champion in 1913.

World of Groggs

159 Broadway, CF37 1BH • Mon–Fri 9am–5pm, Sat 10am–5pm • ☎ 01443 405001, ⓦ groggs.co.uk

A ten-minute walk southeast of Pontypridd's elegant and impressive train station, the wonderfully quirky **World of Groggs** shop has been producing figurine caricatures of Welsh rugby stars, as well as other sporting and world celebrities, since 1965. Also on display are photos, rugby shirts and memorabilia donated by some of those who've been made into a "Grogg", and an autograph wall signed by various stars.

By train The train station is a 10min walk south of the old bridge on The Graig.

Destinations Abercynon (every 15min; 10min); Aberdare (every 30min; 35min); Cardiff (every 20–30min; 30min); Merthyr Tydfil (every 30min; 35min); Treherbert (every 30min; 40min).

By bus The bus station is directly above the old bridge on the western bank.

Destinations Abercynon (every 15min; 10min); Aberdare (every 15min; 50min); Caerphilly (every 30min; 30min); Cardiff (every 15min; 35min); Merthyr Tydfil (every 15min; 25min).

Tourist office Inside the Pontypridd Museum, Bridge St (Mon–Sat 10am–4.30pm; ☎ 01443 490748).

ACCOMMODATION AND EATING

Blueberry Hotel Market St, CF37 2ST ☎ 01443 485331, ⓦ blueberryinn-pontypridd.co.uk. An appropriately appealing name for this sparkling little hotel, whose nine rooms are fashioned in one of two styles: cool, crisp white-on-white, or classic French. Breakfast £11. **£74**

Bunch of Grapes Ynysangharad Rd, CF37 4DA ☎ 01443 402934, ⓦ bunchofgrapes.org.uk. Curiously located in a residential street beyond the park and A470 flyover, this is nevertheless a terrific combination of restaurant and pub, whose imaginative menu lists such dishes as pan-fried guinea fowl with home-smoked new potato and caramelized pumpkin (£15). There are typically more than half a dozen real ales on at any one time, and many beer events are held here. Daily 11am–11pm; kitchen Mon–Sat noon–9.30pm, Sun noon–2.30pm.

Clwb-y-Bont Off Taff St, CF37 4SL ☎ 01443 491424. Down a narrow lane just behind Boots, this thick-set building is the town's principal club and live music venue, with open mic evenings and acoustic, jazz and blues concerts. Mon–Thurs 6pm–11am, Fri 6pm–1am, Sat noon–1am.

Llanover Arms Bridge St, CF37 4PE ☎ 01443 403215. Retaining a certain worn charm, the stone-fronted *Llanover*, right by the bridge, is one of the town's better watering holes. The beer is good, with a couple of decent guest ales. Daily noon–11pm.

Llancaiach Fawr Manor

Gelligaer Rd, Nelson, 6 miles northeast of Pontypridd, CF46 6ER • Tours (90min) Tues–Sun 10am–5pm (last admission 4pm) • £8.50 • ☎ 01443 412248, ⓦ your.caerphilly.gov.uk/lancaiachfawr • Bus #X38 from Pontypridd (Mon–Sat hourly; 15min)

The river divides at **Abercynon**, four miles up the Taff Valley, with the Cynon River flowing in from Aberdare in the northwest. Two miles east of Abercynon is **Llancaiach Fawr Manor**, a Tudor house built around 1530 which has been transformed into a living-history museum set in 1645, the time of the Civil War, with guides dressed as house servants and speaking seventeenth-century English. Although the whole experience could easily be nightmarishly tacky, it's deftly done, with well-researched authenticity and fascinating anecdotes from the staff.

The three-storey residence was originally built for the Prichard family, erstwhile Sheriff of Glamorgan and Justice of Peace, the latter a position he held throughout the Civil War. Visits are by **guided tour** only, on which you get to view the kitchen and dining room, the Great Hall (which was used as a courtroom), the bed chambers and counting house (an arms store). Special tours are also available, including seventeenth-century-themed evenings, and, between October and March, ghost and candlelit tours.

Aberfan

North of Abercynon, the Taff Valley village of **ABERFAN** contains one sight that's impossible to forget: the two lines of arches that mark the **graves** of the 144 people – including 116 children – killed in October 1966 when an unsecured slag heap slid down a hill and onto the Pantglas Primary School. Official enquiries revealed the sorry inevitability of the disaster, given the cavalier approach to safety so often displayed by the coal bosses. Visible for miles around, the cemetery is located on a steep hillside high above the village; to get there, head along Bronheulog Terrace before veering right and following the winding road upwards. The messages, especially those from parents who lost their children, are unbearably sad. Back down in the village, on the site of the school on Moy Road, is a beautifully tended **memorial garden**.

1

Aberdare

Eight miles northwest of Abercynon, towards the top of the Cynon Valley, is the sprawling town of **ABERDARE** (Aberdâr). The town was built on the local iron, brick and brewing industries, in addition to playing a prominent role in the development of early Welsh-language publishing. Aside from the rows of terraced houses, the centre offers a handful of good shops, **cafés** and **pubs**, such as the lively *Yr Ieuan ap Iago* on the High Street.

Cynon Valley Museum & Gallery

Depot Rd, CF44 8DL • Wed–Sat 11am–4pm • Free • ☎ 01685 886729 ⓦ cynonvalleymuseum.org

A short walk from Aberdare train station brings you to one of the Valleys' best museums, the **Cynon Valley Museum & Gallery**, housed in an old tram depot next to the Tesco superstore. Exhibits convey the social history of the valley, from the appalling conditions of the mid-nineteenth century, when nearly half of all children born here died by the age of 5, to stirring memories of the 1926 General Strike and the 1984–85 miners' strike. Alongside are videos and displays on Victorian lantern slides, teenage life through the ages, the miners' jazz bands and the local publishing industry. To round things off, there's also a bright art gallery and decent **café** on site.

Dare Valley Country Park

Western side of town, CF44 7RG • **Visitor centre** Daily: April–Sept 9am–5.30pm; Oct–March 9am–4pm • ☎ 01685 874672, ⓦ darevalleycountrypark.co.uk

On the western flank of town, the **Dare Valley Country Park** has three waymarked trails ranging from two to four miles. The birdwatching is good, too; there's a platform from where you can view nesting peregrines, and the chain of small lakes harbours moorhen, little grebe and coots. The **visitor centre** has an exhibition on the park's formation, in addition to a café; it's also the starting point of the 32-mile **Glamorgan Forest Way** to Afan Argoed and Margam Country Park (see p.118).

Merthyr Tydfil

On the cusp of the grand, windy heights of the Brecon Beacons to the north and the industrial Valleys to the south, the fortunes of **MERTHYR TYDFIL** (Merthyr Tudful) have risen and fallen more than once. Merthyr's strategic location was first exploited by the Romans as an outpost of their base at Caerleon. In 480 AD, Tydfil, Welsh princess and daughter of Brychan, Prince of Brycheiniog, was captured as she rode through the area, and murdered for her Christian beliefs. She became St Tydfil the Martyr, and her name

---

THE MERTHYR RADICALS

In the seventeenth century, Merthyr became a focal point for the Dissenters and Radicals, movements which, through poverty and oppression, gained momentum in the eighteenth century as the town's four massive ironworks were founded to exploit locally abundant seams of iron ore and limestone. Merthyr became the largest iron-producing town in the world, and by far the most populous settlement in Wales: in 1831, the town had a population of sixty thousand, more than Cardiff, Swansea and Newport combined. Workers flocked from all over Britain and beyond, finding themselves crammed into squalid housing, while the ironmasters built themselves great houses and palaces nearby. Merthyr's **radicalism** bubbled furiously: it was here that the red flag was first raised, when rioters in 1831 gathered around a standard dipped in the blood of a killed calf; another martyr, union organizer Dic Penderyn, was hanged unjustly for his role in the riots. Later, the town saw the election of Britain's first-ever socialist MP, Keir Hardie, in 1900.

Merthyr's precipitous development saw it peak and trough earlier than anywhere else: of its four mighty ironworks, only one was still open at the end of World War I, and that closed in the 1930s. In 1939, a Royal Commission suggested that the town be abandoned and the inhabitants shifted to the coast. The plan was forgotten when war broke out.

was bestowed on the area. Merthyr was at the heart of Wales' industrial might in the early nineteenth century, with Cyfarthfa and Dowlais among the largest **ironworks** in the world at the time. Following their decline, renewed impetus was provided by the steel and coal **mining** industries, though their subsequent demise has seen high unemployment and deprivation ever since. That said, its relatively cheap house prices have made it an attractive proposition for commuters from Cardiff.

Cyfarthfa Castle

Brecon Rd, CF47 8RE • **Castle** April–Sept daily 10am–5.30pm; Oct–March Tues–Fri 10am–4pm, Sat & Sun noon–4pm • £1 • **Miniature railway** April–Sept Sat & Sun noon–5pm, daily during school hols • £1.50 • ☎ 01685 727371, ⓦ cyfarthfa.com

Cyfarthfa Castle, north of the centre, is Merthyr's key site. Built in 1825 as an ostentatious mock-Gothic castle for William Crawshay II, boss of the town's original ironworks, it's set within an attractive, 160-acre **park** that slopes down to the river and once afforded Crawshay a permanent view over his iron empire.

Cyfarthfa's current incarnation, however, is as a **museum**, and although it's all rather random, it's no worse for it. Passing through the café and downstairs into the old wine cellars, you come to a spirited history of the town, with detailed coverage of Merthyr's formidable **industrial and political heritage** – keep an eye out for a model of Trevithick's Pen-y-Darren locomotive, which, when it hauled iron along the tramroad in 1804, became the world's first steam loco on rails. Other exhibits examine the 1984–85 miners' strike, pubs and the temperance movement, as well as the beleaguered 1980s Sinclair C5 car, constructed here at the Hoover plant – "built by Hoover, driven by suckers" as the local phrase memorably had it.

Coverage upstairs starts with the town's **sporting heroes**. The Valleys have produced some notable pugilists over the years, none more so than the "Merthyr Matchstick" Johnny Owen, who, following a world title fight against Lupe Pintor in 1980, fell into a coma and died several weeks later – on display here are the gloves he wore during that fight. Touchingly, Pintor returned to Merthyr in 2002 to unveil a statue of Owen, which stands in the town's main shopping centre.

Unsurprisingly, the Crawshays themselves feature prominently; elsewhere you'll find **Bronze Age and Iron Age** remains (ceramic vessels, jewellery and the like) recovered from the old Penydarren Roman fort (now Penydarren football ground) and Morlais Castle, alongside some beautiful specimens from the **Nantgarw China Works** (see p.109). There's also a very respectable collection of Welsh and international **art**. Highlights include an uncharacteristically gentle study of *The Elf* by monumental sculptor Goscombe John, several oils portraying the Dowlais ironworks, such as *The Tips*, by Cedric Morris, and a mesmerizing double portrait of Salome by Alfred Janes.

The surrounding **park** contains landscaped walks, a plant nursery, café, bowling green, tennis courts and a stage set next to the main lake. Best of all is the **miniature railway**, which runs a loop around the lake, island and castle.

Joseph Parry's Cottage

4 Chapel Row, CF48 1BN • April–Sept Sat & Sun 2–5pm; Oct–March by appointment • Free • ☎ 01685 727371, ⓦ cyfarthfa.com

Tucked among modern houses just off the A4102 (Bethesda St), alongside the River Taff, is **Chapel Row**, a line of cottages built in the 1820s for skilled ironworkers. One of these is **Joseph Parry's Cottage**, where the composer was born, though this mini-museum is most interesting as a social record of slightly better-than-average workers' domestic conditions of the nineteenth century. Parry's music, including the national favourite *Myfanwy*, is piped between rooms, and the upstairs section of the house is given over to a display of his life and music.

ARRIVAL AND DEPARTURE   **MERTHYR TYDFIL**

By train The train station lies east of the town centre, a minute's walk from the High St.

Destinations Cardiff (every 30min; 1hr); Pontypridd (every 30min; 30min).

1

By bus The bus station is right in the centre on Wheatsheaf Lane.

Destinations Brecon (Mon–Sat hourly, Sun 2; 40min); Cardiff (Mon–Sat every 20min, Sun hourly; 50min).

ACCOMMODATION AND EATING

Grawen Farm Cwm Taf, 4 miles north on the A470, CF48 2HS ☎ 01685 723740. This family-run farm campsite is well equipped with modern facilities. Closed Nov–March. **£15**

Redhouse Cafe High St, CF47 8AE ☎ 01685 384111, ⓦ redhousecymru.com. Inside the beautifully renovated Old Town Hall – itself now a fine exhibition and performance space – this bright and breezy café is comfortably the best

place in town for cake and coffee, as well as something a little bit more substantial. Daily 9am–4pm.

Tregenna Hotel Park Terrace, next to Penydarren Park, CF47 8RF ☎ 01685 723627, ⓦ tregennahotel .co.uk. It's far from inspiring, possessing an austere exterior and rather dated rooms, but this low-rise hotel is in a quiet location and is just about the cheapest place in town. Rooms also available in an annexe. Breakfast £6. **£54**

The Rhondda

The twin valleys of the **Rhondda** – Rhondda Fach (Little Rhondda) to the east and Rhondda Fawr (Great Rhondda) to the west – are each sixteen miles long yet less than a mile wide. Between them they once formed the heart of the massive south Wales coal industry. Hollywood romanticized the area in the 1947 Oscar-winning weepie *How Green Was My Valley*, although the story was based on author Richard Llewellyn's early life in nearby Gilfach Goch, outside the valley.

Early records show that in 1841 the Rhondda had a population of less than a thousand, but that exploded with the discovery of coal and, by 1924, 167,000 people had squeezed into the available land in ranks of houses packed around sixty or so pitheads. Poverty and hardship were rife, but so were pride, self-reliance, radical religion and firebrand politics; the Communist Party ran the town of Maerdy (nicknamed "Little Moscow" by Fleet Street in the 1930s) for decades. In addition to the excellent **Rhondda Heritage Park**, there's rewarding hillwalking here, with astounding views over the densely packed houses below.

Rhondda Heritage Park

Coed Cae Rd, Trehafod, CF37 2NP • Tues–Sat 9am–4.30pm; tours (1hr 15min) on the hour 9am–3pm • Free; tours £5.95 • ☎ 01443 682036, ⓦ rctcbc.gov.uk • Bus #130 (every 20–30min; 10min) runs to the Heritage Park from Pontypridd; otherwise, Trehafod train station is a 5min walk from the park

The Rhondda starts just outside **Pontypridd**, winding through the mountains alongside railway, road and river to **Trehafod** and the colliery museum of the **Rhondda Heritage Park**. Although the first pits were sunk here in 1850, it wasn't until William Lewis (later Lord Merthyr) reopened the site in 1880 that the pit began to prosper, and by 1900 some five thousand men were producing in excess of a million tons of coal a year. Production at the Lewis Merthyr colliery ceased in 1983, seven years before the last pit closed in the Rhondda. Wandering around the yard, you can see the 140ft-high chimney stack, which fronts two iconic latticed shafts, named Bertie and Trefor, after Lewis's sons. The best way to get a feel for the site is on a **guided tour**, which are led by retired miners and take you through the engine winding houses, lamp room and fan house.

Upstairs in the main building, the illuminating **Black Gold exhibition** recalls the history of mining in the Rhondda, largely through informative wall panels, but there are some wonderful photos, too, including a handful showing staff and miners working the last days of the Lewis Merthyr colliery. Inevitably, disaster looms large and the sad facts reveal that fatalities from pit explosions were an annual occurrence up until World War II – the worst disaster at the Lewis colliery was in 1956 when nine men perished. What few exhibits there are on display also draw on the theme of mine safety – methanometers, water jacks and self-rescuers – though the most poignant item is the pocket watch belonging to Gildas Jones, one of the victims of the 1956 disaster.

1

MALE VOICE CHOIRS

Although Wales' **male voice choirs** can be found all over the country, it is in the southern, industrial heartland that they are loudest and strongest. The roots of the choirs lie in the Nonconformist religious traditions of the seventeenth and eighteenth centuries, when Methodism in particular swept the country, and singing was a free and potent way of cherishing the frequently persecuted faith. Throughout the breakneck nineteenth-century industrialization in the Valleys, choirs of coal miners came together to praise God in the fervent way that was typical of the packed, poor communities. Classic hymns like *Cwm Rhondda* and the Welsh national anthem, *Hen Wlad Fy Nhadau* (*Land of My Fathers*), are synonymous with the choirs, whose full-blooded interpretations render all other efforts insipid.

Despite the collapse of coal mining in the twentieth century, many Valleys towns have their own choir, and these continue to perform in Wales and abroad. Most will happily allow visitors to sit in on rehearsals – a wonderful chance to hear one of the world's most distinctive choral traditions in full, roof-raising splendour. Perhaps the best known is the **Treorchy Male Choir**, Wales' oldest, formed in 1883 (w treorchymalechoir.com). Rehearsals are usually held at 7pm each Monday and Thursday at Treorchy primary school on Glyncoli Road, in Treorchy; phone ahead to confirm (t 07849 466080). The choir also often performs at the town's splendid Parc and Dare Theatre on Station Road (t 08000 147111). **Pontypridd** also boasts a superb choir, formed in 1949 (w malechoir.com) – rehearsals take place in the basement of the Pontypridd museum on Sunday evenings at 6pm; access is via the stone stairs to the right of the museum entrance (see p.110). Elsewhere, ask at the local tourist office or library.

Rhondda Fach

The Rhondda's two valleys divide at the bustling town of **PORTH** ("Gateway"), a mile beyond the Rhondda Heritage Park, from where the Rhondda Fach (Little Rhondda) River twists its way northwards through the smaller and frequently forgotten valley of the same name, passing endless archetypal Valleys towns like Ynyshir, Pontygwaith, Tylorstown, Ferndale and Maerdy – row after row of tiny houses clinging to sheer valley walls.

Rhondda Fawr

The **Rhondda Fawr** (Great Rhondda), stretching from the outskirts of Pontypridd to Blaenrhondda, is blessed with a train line, a decent road and most of the sights. The first notable settlement is **Tonypandy**, followed a mile later by **Llwynypia**, wedged in between walkable, forested hillsides. From here, a steep two-mile climb leads up to **Mynydd y Gelli**, where the remains of an Iron Age hut settlement and a Bronze Age burial chamber and stone circle can be seen. Further up the valley, spirited **Treorchy** is known, above all, for its marvellous male voice choir (see box above).

ARRIVAL AND GETTING AROUND   THE RHONDDA

By train A train line, punctuated with stops every mile or so, runs the entire length of the Rhondda Fawr from Pontypridd to its terminus at Treherbert.

By bus Buses also cover the route; change in Merthyr Tydfil for connections to the Brecon Beacons.

The Ogwr, Garw and Llynfi valleys

Southwest of the Rhondda, the **Ogwr**, **Garw** and **Llynfi valleys** are different to their bigger, better-known neighbour: the contours are slightly softer, the open spaces wider and the towns less bustling.

Ogwr Valley

South from Treorchy, the **Ogwr Valley** plunges through the Rhondda Fawr to the ancient settlement and now county town of **BRIDGEND** (Pen-y-bont ar Ogwr), a useful transport interchange. Just over a mile northeast of the town are the substantial remains of **Coity Castle** (free access; CADW; ⓦcadw.gov.wales/daysout/coitycastle), built around the end of the twelfth century by one of the earliest Norman knights in the area. Bridgend is also handy for Porthcawl (see p.100).

Garw Valley

The dead-end **Garw Valley** consists of a road, river and the disused railway crammed in on the valley floor, before they all peter out into wooded hillsides. Most of the scars of the mining past have now been levelled and landscaped, leaving it surprisingly pretty, and, as it's well off any tourist track, very rewarding for walks and congenial company in local pubs and shops. At the southern end, the **Bryngarw Country Park** (daily dawn–dusk; free, but charges for special events) is a pleasant diversion, with landscaped gardens, exceptional flower collections and mature woodlands.

Llynfi Valley

Stretching up from Bridgend and Tondu along the A4063 is the broad-bottomed and leafy **Llynfi Valley**. The main settlement here is **MAESTEG**, from where the main road links up with the A4107 at Cymer, for Cwm Afan. On top of the mountain to the south of Maesteg is the beautiful village of **LLANGYNWYD**. Birth- and burial-place of bard Wil Hopcyn, it has an ancient atmosphere in stark contrast to the ex-mining towns below. The splendid pub *Yr Hen Dy* is said to be the oldest inn in south Wales, where revellers traditionally congregate on New Year's Day for the hallowed Welsh custom of the **Mari Lwyd** (Grey Mare), during which a horse's skull is paraded through the village to ward off evil spirits during the forthcoming year.

Cwm Afan

Winding its way between the top of the Llynfi Valley and the coast at Port Talbot, the main attraction in bucolic **CWM AFAN** is the **Afan Forest Park**, whose 9000 acres of hilly forest has become one of the country's premier **mountain biking** destinations.

Afan Forest Park

Cynonville, SA13 3HG • **Park** Open access • Free • ☎ 01639 850564, ⓦ www.afanforestpark.co.uk • **South Wales Miners' Museum** Daily: April–Sept 10am–4pm; Oct–March 10.30am–3.30pm • £3 • ☎ 01639 851833, ⓦ south-wales-miners-museum.co.uk

Three miles west of little **CYMER** is the **Afan Forest Park**, starting point for nine walking trails and five waymarked **mountain bike** trails; Rookie Trail aside, the others are fairly demanding, so not really suited to families or anyone seeking a gentler time of it. Bikes can be rented from **Afan Valley Bike Shed**, in the building just above the car park (daily except Tues 9am–5pm; from £20/3hr, £30/day; ☎01639 851406, ⓦafanvalleybikeshed .co.uk). In the same building you'll also find the small but intriguing **South Wales Miners' Museum**, where a mocked-up miners' tunnel leads through to all manner of mining-related memorabilia including documents, photographs and a fabulous assortment of lamps. The two main progenitors of safety lamps, in the early nineteenth century, were Dr William Clanny and Sir Humphrey Davy, and it's their designs that steal the show here. Refreshments are available at the *Trailhead* **café**.

Glyncorrwg Ponds Visitor Centre

Ynyscorrwg Park, SA13 3EA • May–Oct Mon–Sat 8am–8pm, Sun 8am–6pm; Nov–April daily 9am–4pm • Free • ☎ 01639 851900, ⓦ glyncorrwgpondsvisitorcentre.co.uk

Five miles up the valley from Afan Forest Park, the **Glyncorrwg Ponds Visitor Centre** is a dedicated **biking centre**, and the starting point for half a dozen trails, all rated between difficult and severe; bikes can be rented from Skyline Cycles (daily 9am–5pm; from £30/day; ☎01639 850011, ⓦskylinecycles.co.uk), just below the café. Four walks also fan out from here, the longest a fairly strenuous seven-mile jaunt around Glyncorrwg. Other facilities include a bike park, jet wash, showers and camping.

Afan Forest Park campsite Afan Forest Park, SA13 3HA ☎ 01639 851900. Very basic campsite with shower and toilet facilities; fires are also permitted. Closed Oct–March. Per person **£3.50**

Afan Lodge Duffryn Rhondda, SA13 3ES ☎ 01639 852500, ⓦ afanlodge.com. On the main road between Afan Forest Park and Cymer, this former miners' institute building has been converted into a superb alpine-style chalet dedicated to mountain bikers; many of the bright, cool a/c rooms have fantastic views down towards the lush forest. Bike wash, lock-up and drying room available. **£80**

Glyncorrwg Ponds campsite Glyncorrwg Ponds Visitor Centre, SA13 3HA ☎ 01639 851900. Level pitches look out over a picturesque landscape, though facilities are limited to a shower and toilet block. Open all year. Per person **£7**

Pontrhydyfen

Cwm Afan Valley descends for a couple of miles towards the village of **PONTRHYDYFEN**, picturesquely situated at the confluence of the Afon and Afon Pelenna rivers. Slicing through the village are two monuments that testify to the region's proud industrial heritage: a magnificent four-arch **aqueduct** dating from 1827, and, a little further downstream, an equally impressive nine-arch **viaduct**, built in 1898. The village is best known, however, as the birthplace of actor Richard Burton, who was born in a house (unmarked) at the foot of the aqueduct. From here, roads either side of the river continue south to the industrial sprawl of **PORT TALBOT**, dominated by its massive steelworks.

Margam

A couple of miles southeast of Port Talbot, on the other side of junction 38 of the M4, **MARGAM** was originally a Cistercian settlement and later the home of various industrial magnates. The first left turn after the motorway junction leads to the arcaded twelfth-century **abbey church**, the sole remaining Cistercian house of worship in Wales.

Margam Stones Museum

Abbey Rd, SA13 2TA • April–Sept Wed–Sun 10.30am–4pm • £2.50; CADW • ☎ 01639 871184, ⓦ cadw.gov.wales/daysout /margamstonesmuseum

The little-known **Margam Stones Museum**, occupying a nineteenth-century schoolhouse, is often unjustly bypassed in the rush to get to the neighbouring country park. This outstanding collection of memorial stones, sculptured crosses, grave slabs and tomb covers dates mostly from Celtic and medieval times. The most prized exhibit is the tenth-century Cynfelin (or Conbelin) stone, an intricately carved wheel-headed cross. Take a close look, too, at the figures and gargoyles from destroyed Welsh churches and monasteries.

Margam Country Park

Margam, SA13 2TJ • **Margam Country Park** April–Aug daily 10am–5pm; Sept, Oct & mid-Jan to March daily 10am–4.30pm; Nov to mid-Jan Mon & Tues 1–4.30pm • Free • **Miniature railway** April & Sept Sat & Sun; May–Aug daily • £2 • ☎ 01639 881635, ⓦ margamcountrypark.co.uk • Bus #X1 (hourly; 45min) from Swansea stops outside the entrance

The 850-acre **Margam Country Park** has enough to see and do to keep you occupied for the best part of half a day, longer if the weather is kind. The park is centred around the nineteenth-century Gothic pile of **Margam Castle**, much of which was gutted by fire in 1977. It's essentially off-limits, but you can still wander into the lobby and peer up the octagonal lantern tower and see a few models and photos. One of these is of Eisenhower, taken when he visited American troops stationed here during World War II.

Down from the castle, and tucked in by the abbey church walls, are the impressive remains of the original Cistercian **abbey**, most notable for the vaulting of its twelve-sided chapterhouse, which survived the dissolution of the monasteries only to have its roof collapse under the weight of weeds in 1799. Alongside is Margam's showpiece **orangery**, a splendid Georgian outhouse, built in 1790 and, at 327ft long, reputedly the longest in Britain. There's plenty for kids to do here, including a **miniature railway** (which runs from the entrance up to the castle), a "fairyland" play area, an adventure playground, a farm trail and, for older kids, a Go Ape centre.

Vale of Neath

Although the town of **NEATH** (Castell-Nedd) is not particularly worthy of a visit, the **Vale of Neath**, spearing northeast, boasts several fascinating remnants from both the Industrial Revolution and the coal-mining industry.

Aberdulais Tinworks and waterfalls

Aberdulais, Main Rd, 2 miles northeast of Neath, SA10 8EU • Feb–April, Sept & Oct daily 11am–4pm; May–Aug daily 10.30am–5pm; Nov–Jan Fri–Sun 11am–4pm • £5; NT • ☎ 01639 636674, ⊛ nationaltrust.org.uk/aberdulais-tin-works-and-waterfall • Bus #T6 from Swansea (hourly; 35min) stops outside the tinworks

Aberdulais was once one of the world's largest tinplate manufacturing centres, thanks largely to its position at the confluence of the Dulais and Neath rivers. Indeed its waterfalls have been harnessing hydroelectric power since the sixteenth century – initially for the manufacture of copper – before the tinworks opened in 1831 under the enterprising William Llewellyn. By the end of the nineteenth century, Aberdulais was just one of 205 tin mills in south Wales. Among the impressive extant remains is the tinning house and chimney stack – the water wheel was installed in 1982. The **waterfalls** themselves provide a picturesque backdrop to the site, particularly after heavy rain; artists including Turner and Ruskin frequently used this place as a source of inspiration.

The old stable building accommodates an illuminating exhibition on the industry with, among other things, beer cans from the Felinfoel Brewery in Llanelli (the first brewery in Europe to mass produce beer in tins) and a delightful selection of tin-plated toys. Across the way, the old school room is now a tempting **tearoom**.

Cefn Coed Colliery Museum

Neath Rd, 3 miles north of Aberdulais, SA10 8SN • May–Sept Tues & Thurs–Sun 10.30am–4.30pm • Free • ☎ 01639 750556 • Bus #T6 (hourly; 40min) from Swansea

What was once the world's deepest anthracite mine is now the **Cefn Coed Colliery Museum**. Nicknamed "The Slaughterhouse" – owing to the extreme dangers faced by miners working at depths in excess of 2250ft – the colliery closed in 1968, with workers transferred to the nearby Blaenant drift mine, which subsequently closed in 1990. This is lower-key than many of the Valleys' other heritage sites, and does look a little forlorn these days, but a walk around the mining gallery and boiler house through to the magnificent steam winding engine gives yet another stark reminder of a region's once proud but now lost way of life. Crowning the site are the colliery's iconic latticed steel pithead frames, which are currently being restored to something like their former glory.

Swansea

More than half a century ago, Dylan Thomas dubbed his native **SWANSEA** (Abertawe) an "ugly, lovely town" – a scathing but affectionate epithet that was well deserved. The famous poet probably wouldn't recognize the place these days. Devastated by bombing in World War II, Swansea was hastily rebuilt, but since the turn of the millennium the city has been undergoing a renaissance, with a number of bright, bold new developments.

Swansea's wide seafront overlooks the huge sweep of **Swansea Bay**, the focal point of much of the redevelopment, particularly around the old docks, location for some of the best-funded **museums** in Wales. The seafront arcs around to the **Gower peninsula**, with the elegant but relaxed seaside resort of Mumbles, as well as some of Britain's best **surfing**, on its doorstep.

1

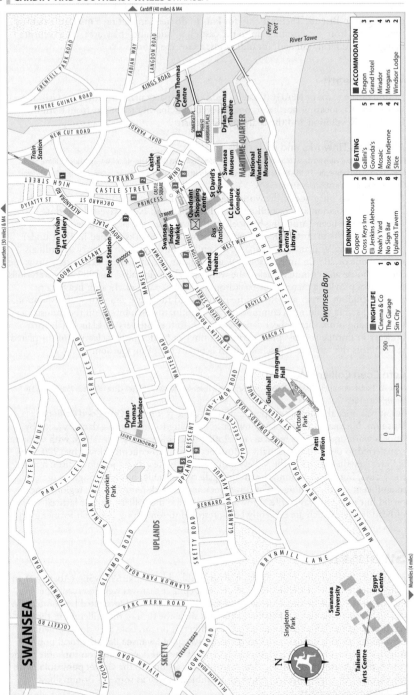

Cardiff (40 miles) & M4

River Tawe

Ferry Port

SWANSEA

MARITIME QUARTER

Swansea Bay

Singleton Park

UPLANDS

SKETY

Train Station

Castle ruins

Dylan Thomas Centre

Dylan Thomas Theatre

Swansea Museum

National Waterfront Museum

Glynn Vivian Art Gallery

Police Station

Swansea Indoor Market

Grand Theatre

Quadrant Shopping Centre

Bus Station

St David's Square

LC Leisure Complex

Swansea Central Library

Dylan Thomas' birthplace

Guildhall

Brangwyn Hall

Victoria Park

Patti Pavilion

Cwmdonkin Park

Swansea University

Egypt Centre

Taliesin Arts Centre

Carmarthen (30 miles) & M4

Gower (5 miles)

Mumbles (4 miles)

0   500   yards

N

■ ACCOMMODATION	
Dragon	3
Grand Hotel	1
Mirador	4
Morgans	5
Windsor Lodge	2

● EATING	
Gallini's	2
Govinda's	3
Mosaic	5
Rose Indienne	8
Slice	4

■ DRINKING	
Copper	2
Cross Keys Inn	3
Eli Jenkins Alehouse	7
Noah's Yard	5
No Sign Bar	8
Uplands Tavern	6

■ NIGHTLIFE	
Cinema & Co	1
The Garage	9
Sin City	6

Brief history

The city's Welsh name, Abertawe, refers to the settlement at the mouth of the River Tawe, now being coaxed back to life as part of Swansea's redeveloped waterfront after centuries of use as a repository for metal trades. The English name derives from Viking sources, suggesting that a pre-Norman settlement existed in the area. The first reliable records of Swansea date back to 1099, when a Norman castle was built here as an outpost of William the Conqueror's empire. A small settlement subsequently grew near the coalfields and the sea, developing into a mining and shipbuilding centre that, by 1700, was the largest coal port in Wales.

Metal-smelting days

Copper-smelting became the area's dominant industry in the eighteenth century, soon attracting other activities to pack out the lower Tawe Valley. Drawn by the town's flourishing activities, a swiftly growing port and the arrival of the Swansea Canal, thousands of emigrants moved to the city from all over Ireland and Britain; by the nineteenth century, the town was one of the world's most prolific metal-bashing centres.

Decline and revival

Smelting was already on the wane by the beginning of the twentieth century, although Swansea's port continued to thrive. Britain's first oil refinery was opened on the edge of the city in 1918, with dock developments growing up in its wake. Civic zeal, best exemplified by the graceful 1930s Guildhall, was reawakened after the establishment of an important branch of the University of Wales here in 1920. Swansea was devastated during World War II, however, when thirty thousand bombs rained down on the city in just three nights in 1941. Initial rebuilding left the city disjointed but now, with a population of around 240,000, Swansea boasts resurgent music, club and surf scenes, and some spirited rebuilding and redevelopment. The recent success of the city's **football club**, now a Premier League regular, has brought even more energy to the city.

Castle Square and around

The heart of the city centre is **Castle Square**, a not entirely lovely concrete amphitheatre centred on a fountain. Standing somewhat incongruously on the east side of the square are the **castle ruins**, the most obvious landmark being the semicircular arcades, built into the wall between 1330 and 1332 by Bishop Gower to replace a Norman predecessor. Running south from the castle is **Wind Street**, nocturnal Swansea's main drag, chock-full of bars, pubs and restaurants; evenings are quite something along here.

Swansea Indoor Market

Oxford St, SA1 3PQ • Mon–Fri 8am–5.30pm, Sat 7.30am–5.30pm • ☎ 01792 654296, Ⓦ swanseaindoormarket.co.uk

There has been a market here or hereabouts since the mid-eighteenth century, though the current glass-roofed **Swansea Indoor Market** – Wales' largest – has been here since 1961. It's a lively bustle of colourful stalls, fresh flowers and freshly baked food, including local delicacies like laverbread (made from laver, aka seaweed), cockles trawled from the nearby Loughor estuary, traditional Welsh cakes, fish and cheeses. You'll also find stalls selling clothing, jewellery and gifts.

Glynn Vivian Art Gallery

Alexandra Rd, SA1 5DZ • Tues–Sun 10am–5pm • Free • ☎ 01792 516900, Ⓦ swansea.gov.uk/glynnvivian

The one, very worthy, site around Castle Square is the **Glynn Vivian Art Gallery**, a delightful Edwardian venue named after the philanthropist. The main exhibition, on Vivian himself, is slated to run until 2019, though it may be extended beyond this date. In 1869 he embarked upon an epic two-year journey to the Far East, during which time he amassed a wealth of extraordinary items, including Chinese vases and Japanese fans. Vivian was also an inveterate collector of European porcelain, though most pieces here are from Swansea and the renowned Nantgarw China Works (see p.109).

The museum also houses an inspiring collection of **Welsh art**, which tends to rotate, but expect works by Gwen John, her brother Augustus (his mesmerizing portrait of Caitlin Thomas, Dylan's wife, is a real highlight), Kyffin Williams and Ceri Richards, Wales' most respected twentieth-century painter.

The Maritime Quarter

The spit of land between Oystermouth Road, the sea and the Tawe estuary has been christened the **Maritime Quarter**, with its vast centrepiece marina surrounded by contemporary apartments, cafés, shops, museums and a leisure centre. Entering the quarter from the east, the main road bridge over the Tawe is guarded by a World War II ack-ack gun, which stands as a memorial to Swansea's decimation by the Luftwaffe.

Swansea Museum

Victoria Rd, SA1 1SN • Tues–Sun 10am–4.30pm • Free • ☎ 01792 653763, ⓦ swanseamuseum.co.uk

Founded in 1835 as the Royal Institution of South Wales, **Swansea Museum** is Wales' oldest public museum. Much of it is still appealingly old-fashioned, with a wizened Egyptian mummy, lots of archeological finds and local porcelain and pottery. More interesting is the Cabinet of Curiosities room, full of glass cases stuffed with oddments including offbeat household items, memento moris – miniature shrines containing photos and models of the deceased – and intriguing local photos, including several of Winston Churchill taken during his visit to Swansea in World War II. There's also a marble bust of Gower-born Edgar Evans, who died with Scott in Antarctica in 1912.

Dylan Thomas Centre

Somerset Place, SA1 1RR • Daily 10am–4.30pm • Free • ☎ 01792 463980, ⓦ dylanthomas.com

In the former nineteenth-century guildhall is the **Dylan Thomas Centre**, where a superb exhibition offers a compelling insight into his life and times. Unique archive material includes a love letter to Caitlin written on a cheque stub, bar tabs, a tweed jacket borrowed from Jorge Fick during a stay at New York's *Chelsea* hotel in 1953, and the last photos of Thomas taken in a New York bar just days before his death. The original sky-blue doors of the shed in which Thomas wrote at Laugharne (see p.153) front a mocked-up version here that contains original manuscripts, doodles and some of the books and poems that inspired him. Meanwhile, another room shows footage of original cast members recalling their experiences of performing *Under Milk Wood* for the first time on BBC radio in January 1954. Look out for the many terrific **literary events** held at the centre throughout the year.

National Waterfront Museum

Oystermouth Rd, SA1 3RD • Daily 10am–5pm • Free • ☎ 0300 111 2333, ⓦ museum.wales/swansea

Carved out of the shell of the old Industrial and Maritime Museum, the fine **National Waterfront Museum** accommodates wide-ranging exhibitions on Wales' history of innovation and industry. It is divided into fifteen zones, each with an interactive take on topics such as energy, metal, coal and the sea.

The Achiever's zone considers the contributions of writers and poets such as Alexander Cordell and Dylan Thomas, the successes of Wales' much loved colliery brass bands, and the influences brought to bear by the trade unions. If music is your thing, make a beeline for the Worker's section, where you can listen to a selection of artists and view awards given to the likes of the Super Furry Animals. Look out too for the many superb heritage pieces, such as the 1907 Robin Goch (Redbreast) monoplane, one of the very few pre-World War I planes still in existence, Mumbles trams and a 1904 Benz Duc motor car.

West Swansea

Aside from being one of the greenest parts of the city, thanks to a generous spread of parks and gardens, **west Swansea** also has a few architectural gems, a couple of fine little museums and **Dylan Thomas' birthplace**, in the well-heeled Uplands area a thirty-minute walk from the centre.

The Guildhall and Brangwyn Hall

Guildhall Rd South, SA1 4PE • ☎ 01792 635432, ⓦ swansea.gov.uk/brangwynhall

St Helen's Road dips down to the seafront near the tall white tower of the **Guildhall** – a soaring piece of 1930s civic architecture. Within, **Brangwyn Hall** takes its name from Sir Frank Brangwyn, who painted the eighteen enormous British Empire panels lining the walls. It functions today as one of the city's premier classical concert venues (see p.125), and really comes into its own during the Swansea International Festival (see box, p.125).

Egypt Centre

Swansea University, Mumbles Rd, SA2 8PZ • Tues–Sat 10am–4pm • Free • ☎ 01792 295960, ⓦ egypt.swan.ac.uk

Along the coast road, the **Swansea University** campus affords a commanding view over the bay stretching to Mumbles Head. On site is an imaginative performance space, the **Taliesin Arts Centre** (see p.125), in addition to the **Egypt Centre**, Wales' pre-eminent Egyptology display. The acquisition of eminent pharmacist Sir Henry Wellcome, the collection is split in two: the House of Death, with its funerary paraphernalia (look out for the beautiful painted coffin of a female musician from Thebes), and the House of Life, covering day-to-day existence, although most of the artefacts come from tombs.

Dylan Thomas' birthplace

5 Cwmdonkin Drive, SA2 0RA • Daily 10.30am–4.30pm • £8 • ☎ 01792 472555, ⓦ dylanthomasbirthplace.com

Roughly half way up the very steep Cwmdonkin Drive, a blue plaque denotes one solid Victorian semi as **Dylan Thomas' birthplace**. Thomas actually lived here until he was 20, and while nothing remains from his time, the house has been sympathetically restored to re-create the atmosphere of early twentieth-century life in Swansea. In-depth **guided tours** of the surprisingly spacious interior take in the many rooms, including the grand lounge, his father's study, the kitchen and Thomas' boxy bedroom. Despite the scheduled opening times, it's always best to call in advance as there isn't always someone in attendance; moreover, the house is available for self-catering lets so it may be occupied. Directly across the road in **Cwmdonkin Park** is a memorial to Dylan Thomas inscribed with lines from *Fern Hill*, one of his best-loved poems.

ARRIVAL AND DEPARTURE SWANSEA

By train Swansea is the main interchange station for services out to the west of Wales and for the slow but scenic line across the middle of the country to Shrewsbury in Shropshire. The train station is at the top end of the High St, a 10min walk from Castle Square.

Destinations Cardiff (every 30min; 55min); Carmarthen (hourly; 50min); Ferryside (11 daily; 40min); Haverfordwest (9 daily; 1hr 30min); Kidwelly (11 daily; 30min); Knighton (4 daily; 3hr); Llandeilo (4 daily; 1hr); Llandovery (4 daily; 1hr 20min); Llandrindod Wells (4 daily; 2hr 20min); Llanelli (hourly; 20min); Llanwrtyd Wells (4 daily; 1hr 45min); London (hourly; 3hr); Milford Haven (9 daily; 1hr 50min);

Newport (every 30min; 1hr 20min); Pembroke (5 daily; 2hr 5min); Tenby (6 daily; 1hr 40min); Whitland (hourly; 1hr 10min).

By bus Swansea's enormous bus station is in the centre of the city next to The Quadrant shopping centre.

Destinations Aberdulais (every 45min–1hr; 45min); Brecon (Mon–Sat 7 daily, Sun 4; 1hr 45min); Cardiff (every 30min; 1hr); Carmarthen (Mon–Sat every 30min; 1hr 45min); Dan-yr-ogof (Mon–Sat 7 daily, Sun 4 daily; 1hr); Mumbles (every 10min; 15min); Oxwich (8 daily, 1 change; 1hr); Pennard (hourly; 35min); Port Eynon (8 daily, 1 change; 1hr 15min); Rhossili (10 daily; 1hr).

1

GETTING AROUND

By bus The bus network is useful for further-flung areas, including the suburbs near the University such as Uplands and Sketty (a bracing 30min walk from the centre) and to get out to Mumbles and Gower.

ACCOMMODATION

For a reasonably large city, Swansea's **accommodation** stock is poor. That said, there are some inexpensive hotels and B&Bs lining the seafront Oystermouth Rd, and it's just a stone's throw to Gower, where there are further, albeit slightly pricier, options (see p.126). There are no **hostels** in Swansea, and the nearest **campsite** is west of the city towards Mumbles (see p.128).

Dragon Kingsway Circle, SA1 5LS ☎01792 657100, ⓦdragon-hotel.co.uk. Despite its officious-looking facade, this landmark central hotel is an elegant and modern establishment with plush, a/c rooms coloured vivid red. Amenities include a gym, indoor pool, lounge and piano bar and restaurant. Book early for good rates. £75

Grand Hotel Ivey Place, High St, SA1 1NX ☎01792 645898, ⓦthegrandhotelswansea.co.uk. Accomplished yet pleasingly informal hotel next to the train station, with softly coloured, a/c rooms with large flatscreen TVs, and sparkling bathrooms with fantastic showers. Convivial café/sports bar downstairs. £60

Mirador 14 Mirador Crescent, Uplands, SA2 0QX ☎01792 466976, ⓦthemirador.co.uk. Swansea's most enjoyable accommodation, a family-run townhouse with seven fun rooms, each furnished around a particular geographical theme (African, Oriental, Egyptian, Roman and so on). £89

★**Morgans** Somerset Place, SA1 1RR ☎01792 484848, ⓦmorganshotel.co.uk. Swansea's showpiece boutique hotel, split between the sumptuously converted old Port Authority HQ and the beautiful Regency terrace townhouse opposite. The superbly appointed rooms boast hardwood flooring, polished wood fittings, Egyptian cotton bed linen and goosedown duvets. £110

Windsor Lodge Mount Pleasant, SA1 6EG ☎01792 642158, ⓦwindsor-lodge.co.uk. This 200-year-old house has nicely decorated, if slightly dated, rooms, and the bathrooms are a little poky, but it's in a good location and provides fair value. £70

EATING

Swansea is no gastronomic paradise, but it does boast a select core of worthwhile **restaurants**; there are few, however, in the city centre itself.

Gallini's 3 Fishmarket Quay, SA1 1UP ☎01792 456285, ⓦgallinisrestaurant.co.uk. This somewhat ordinary-looking but cheery restaurant offers terrific flavour combinations such as venison steak in a gin and cranberry sauce (£15.95). The downstairs coffee shop is a relaxing spot to kick back with a fresh cup of coffee and take in the view across the marina. Great-value two-course lunch menu £9.95. Daily: restaurant noon–2.30pm & 6pm–midnight; coffee shop 10am–5pm.

Govinda's 8 Craddock St, SA1 3EN ☎01792 468469, ⓦgovindas.org.uk. Simple and clean vegetarian restaurant in the Hare Krishna tradition, selling wholesome light bites like chapati wraps and *subji* for as little as £4.50, as well as freshly pressed juices. Mon–Sat noon–6pm.

Mosaic 11 St Helen's Rd, SA1 4AB ☎01792 655225, ⓦmosaicswanseauk.com. Modern industrial design and understated cool mark this café-cum-restaurant out as something a little different from most places in Swansea; the tapas-style menu comprises delicious light bites such as salt cod croquettes or chorizo with fig and goat's cheese

(£7.50) – a great accompaniment to the occasional live music. Wed–Fri 6–11pm, Sat noon–3pm & 6–11pm.

Rose Indienne 73–74 St Helen's Rd, SA1 4BG ☎01792 467000, ⓦrose-indienne.co.uk. Comfortably the best of Swansea's many Indian restaurants, the beautifully appointed *Rose Indienne* offers exciting and unusual dishes such as Goan duck curry (£12.95) and a spicy fish masala, in addition to a dozen or so lentil- and vegetable-based options. Charming staff, too. Mon–Thurs 5.30pm–midnight, Fri & Sat noon–2pm & 5.30pm–1am, Sun noon–midnight.

★**Slice** 73–75 Everley Rd, Sketty, SA2 9DE ☎01792 290929, ⓦsliceswansea.co.uk. Out in the Sketty area, the diminutive *Slice* – so named because of the quirkily shaped building – offers a level of cuisine unmatched anywhere in the city, with confident contemporary dishes such as wild boar loin with pickled red cabbage, celeriac fondant and apple. Two-course lunch menu £29, three-course evening menu £42. Booking essential. Thurs 6.15–10pm, Fri–Sun 12.30–2pm & 6.15–10pm.

DRINKING

There's no shortage of nightlife in Swansea, which has a proliferation of **bars** and **clubs**. While most of the action is overwhelmingly centred on **Wind Street** – not a place for the faint-hearted at the weekend – the **Uplands** area is far more enjoyable, offering a number of independent-minded pubs and live music venues.

SWANSEA FESTIVALS

In mid-June, various venues around the Maritime Quarter (principally the Dylan Thomas Centre) host the terrific **Swansea International Jazz Festival** (Ⓦsijf.co.uk). The highbrow **Swansea International Festival** (Ⓦswanseafestival.org) takes place during the first two weeks of October with concerts in the Brangwyn Hall and several other venues, while the two-week-long **Dylan Thomas Festival** (Ⓦdylanthomas.com/festival) in late October celebrates the city's favourite son with events at the Dylan Thomas Centre.

Copper 38–39 Castle St, SA1 1HZ ☎01792 456689. Groovy artisan coffeehouse-cum-craft-beer bar serving superb locally roasted coffee alongside ales from its own Boss brewery. The decor's great, with tables carved from pallets and stools culled from copper kegs. There's also a free juke box, but if it all gets too raucous upstairs (and it can), head downstairs for a game of ping-pong. Mon–Thurs & Sun 10am–10pm, Fri & Sat 10am–midnight.

Cross Keys Inn 12 St Mary St, SA1 3LH ☎01792 630921, Ⓦoxkeys.com. Dating from the 1700s, Swansea's oldest hostelry is a deceptively large affair, offering good ales, a sunny beer garden (BBQs in summer) and a loyal band of rugby followers. Mon–Sat 11am–11pm, Sun noon–10.30pm.

Eli Jenkins Ale House 24 Oxford St, SA1 3AQ ☎01792 641067. Named after the Dylan Thomas character in *Under Milk Wood*, this pleasant, popular locals' pub sits surprisingly well amid the surrounding shopping precincts. The beer is pretty good, and very cheap (from £2 a pint). Mon–Thurs 8am–11pm, Fri & Sat 8am–midnight, Sun 11am–11pm.

Noah's Yard 38 Uplands Crescent, SA2 0PG ☎01792 447360. Classy wine bar with big bay windows, bare-brick walls, Art Deco lighting, Chesterfield sofas and trunks for tables, as well as lots of contemporary artwork including a piece by Banksy. Live jazz Mon 8.30pm (£3) and an ace pop-up kitchen each Wed at 6.30pm. Daily 2pm–midnight.

No Sign Bar 56 Wind St, SA1 1EG ☎01792 465300, Ⓦnosignwinebar.com. If you deign/dare to visit one place on Wind St, make it *No Sign*, one of the oldest hostelries in town. A narrow frontage leads into a long, warm pub interior with bare-brick walls, pale wood flooring and squishy sofas, while down in the vaulted cellar you'll catch live music most weekends. The meaning of the name is explained in depth in the window. Mon–Thurs 11am–midnight, Fri & Sat 11am–1am, Sun noon–11pm.

Uplands Tavern 42 Uplands Crescent, SA2 0PG ☎01792 458242, Ⓦuplandstavern-uplands.co.uk. Despite looking a little tired these days, this former haunt of Dylan Thomas – the walls of the Dylan snug corner are plastered with fabulous photos – remains a bastion of local live music, especially rock and blues, usually from Thurs to Sat. Open mic on Mon. Mon–Thurs & Sun 11am–11pm, Fri & Sat 11am–midnight.

NIGHTLIFE

★ **Cinema & Co** 17 Castle St, SA1 1JF ☎07982 626959, Ⓦcinemaco.co.uk. Secreted away beyond its cheery chipboard-designed coffee shop/bar is a brilliant cinema, with seating crafted from wheel-mounted pallets that can be removed to accommodate other events, such as live music and art exhibitions. Screenings – typically classics, independent movies and foreign films – are at 8pm and cost £8. Tues–Sun 6pm–midnight.

The Garage 47 Uplands Crescent, SA2 0NP ☎01792 475147, Ⓦwhitez.co.uk. The city's premier live music venue, by virtue of its quality (and wonderfully varied) acts and understatedly cool atmosphere; rock is to the fore, but there's much else besides. It's tricky to find; the entrance is through Whitez pool club. Mon, Tues & Sun 8.30am–8pm, Wed–Sat 8.30am–11pm.

Sin City 14–16 Dillwyn St, SA1 4AQ ☎01792 468892, Ⓦsincityclub.co.uk. A superb live music venue with the emphasis firmly on indie and heavy rock, notably the Fri-night Monsters rock/metal shindig. Riotous club nights too, including Sink (drum'n'bass/dubstep) on Sat. Thurs–Sat 10pm–late.

ENTERTAINMENT

Brangwyn Hall The Guildhall, Guildhall Rd South, SA1 4PE ☎01792 635432, Ⓦswansea.gov.uk/brangwynhall. This vastly impressive music hall in the Art Deco civic centre hosts regular concerts by the BBC National Orchestra of Wales and others.

Dylan Thomas Theatre Dylan Thomas Square, Maritime Quarter, SA1 1TY ☎01792 473238, Ⓦdylanthomastheatre.org.uk. Thriving community operation staging reruns of Thomas's classics, alongside modern works in the Little Theatre.

Grand Theatre Singleton St, SA1 3QJ ☎01792 475715, Ⓦswansea.gov.uk/grandtheatre. One of Britain's best provincial theatres, with a wide-ranging diet of visiting high culture, comedy, panto, farce and music.

Taliesin Arts Centre Swansea University, SA2 8PZ ☎01792 602060, Ⓦtaliesinartscentre.co.uk. Welsh, English and international visiting theatre, film, dance and music (jazz, world), including offbeat and alternative offerings.

1

Gower

Thrusting into the Bristol Channel west of Swansea, the nineteen-mile **GOWER** (Gŵyr) peninsula is fringed by sweeping yellow bays and precipitous cliffs, caves and blowholes to the south, and wide, flat marshes and cockle beds to the north. Inland, brackened heaths are dotted with castle ruins and curious churches, prehistoric remains and tiny villages.

Gower starts in Swansea's western suburbs, along the coast of Swansea Bay, which curves round to a point in the charmingly old-fashioned and increasingly swish resort of **Mumbles** and Mumbles Head, marking the boundary between the sandy sweep of Swansea Bay and the rocky inlets along the southern Gower's serrated coastline. This southern coast is punctuated by sites exploited for their defensive capacities, best seen in the eerie isolation of the sandbound **Pennard Castle**, high above **Three Cliffs Bay**. West, the wide sands of **Oxwich Bay** sit next to inland reedy marshes, beyond which is the picturesque village of **Port Eynon**. West again, the coast becomes a wild, frilly series of inlets and cliffs, capped by a five-mile path that stretches all the way to the peninsula's glorious westernmost point, **Worms Head**.

Rhossili Bay, a breathtaking four-mile span of sand backed by the village of Rhossili, occupies the entire western end of Gower from Worms Head to the islet of **Burry Holms**, and, when conditions are right, provides some of the best **surfing** in Wales. The northern coast merges into the tidal flats of the estuary, running past the salted marsh of **Llanrhidian**, overlooked by the gaunt ruins of **Weobley Castle**, and on to the famous cockle beds at **Penclawdd**. Mumbles aside, there's not a lot of **accommodation** on Gower, so you'd do well to make reservations in advance, including for campsites.

GETTING AROUND   **GOWER**

By bus There are no train services on Gower, but with its proximity to urban Swansea, bus transport is reasonably comprehensive. Buses (services #115 to #118) run regularly from Swansea's bus station to Rhossili, Port Eynon, Parkmill and Oxwich in south Gower; and through north Gower to Llanrhidian, Llangennith and Llanmadoc.

By car Traffic at the height of the summer can be heavy, so take care when driving, especially when rounding blind corners on the narrow – often single-lane – twisting roads.

On foot and by bike Cycling and walking are ideal ways to tour the area, as the peninsula's attractions are all within a short distance of each other and, in many cases, well off-road.

Mumbles

At the westernmost end of Swansea Bay on the cusp of Gower, the lively, upmarket seaside town of **MUMBLES** (Mwmbwls) takes its name from French sailors who dubbed the twin islets off the end of Mumbles Head *mamelles* (French for "breasts"). Today, the name "Mumbles" also refers interchangeably to the entire loose sprawl of **Oystermouth** (Ystumllwynarth), the area between Swansea and Mumbles.

Once known as the "Mumbles Mile", thanks to the stags and hens that used to trawl the pubs here, the seafront is now an uninterrupted curve of stylish hotels and B&Bs, restaurants, cafés and ice-cream parlours leading down to the old-fashioned **pier**, towards rocky Mumbles Head. Behind the promenade, a warren of streets climbs the hills, lined with boutiques, craft shops and galleries and further places to eat and drink; indeed, the town has a reputation as a foodie destination. Around the headland, reached either by the longer coast road or a short walk over the hill, is **Langland Bay**, with a sandy beach popular with **surfers**.

Oystermouth Castle

Castle Ave, SA3 4BA • April–Sept daily 11am–5pm • £3.50 • ⦿ swansea.gov.uk/oystermouthcastle

The hilltop above town is crowned by the ruins of **Oystermouth Castle**. Founded as a Norman watchtower, the castle was strengthened by the Normans to withstand Welsh attacks before being converted into a residence during the fourteenth

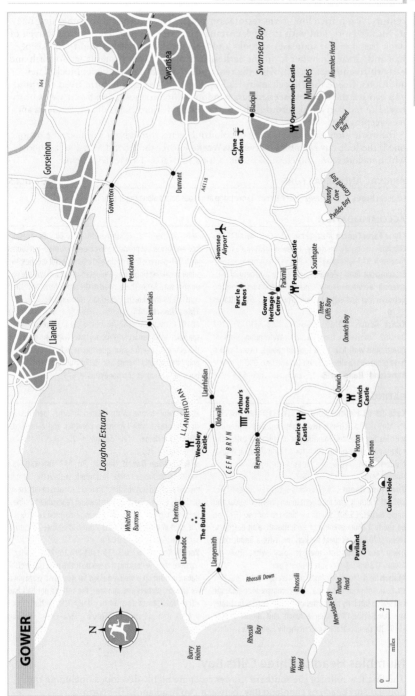

GOWER

N

Swansea Bay

Swansea

M4

Gorseinon

Llanelli

Loughor Estuary

Gowerton

Dunvant

A4118

Penclawdd

Llanmorlais

LLANRHIDIAN

Llanrhidian

Oldwalls

Weobley Castle

CEFN BRYN

Reynoldston

Cheriton

The Bulwark

Llanmadoc

Llangennith

Whitford Burrows

Rhossili Down

Rhossili Bay

Burry Holms

Worms Head

Mewslade Bay

Thurba Head

Paviland Cave

Culver Hole

Port Eynon

Horton

Penrice Castle

Oxwich

Oxwich Castle

Oxwich Bay

Three Cliffs Bay

Pennard Castle

Parkmill

Southgate

Pwlldu Bay

Brandy Cove (Caswell Bay)

Langland Bay

Mumbles Head

Mumbles

Oystermouth Castle

Blackpill

Clyne Gardens

Swansea Airport

Parc le Breos

Gower Heritage Centre

Arthur's Stone

0   miles   2

1

century. A sensitive long-term restoration project has returned it to something like its former glory, and with its thick curtain walls, turreted battlements and warren of dank passages and staircases, it looks and feels just how a castle should. The keep, hall and Great Chamber form the earliest part of the castle (roughly late twelfth and early thirteenth centuries), with the remainder (including the chapel block) later additions. Inside the chapel, stairs lead up to a glass bridge platform from where you can see the superb traceried east window, which frames magnificent views of the bay. The ramparts, too, afford lush vistas over the Mumbles headland, Swansea and its sweeping bay.

The castle grounds stage an array of colourful events throughout summer; the major one is the four-day **Mumbles Marvellous Weekend** over the second May Bank Holiday, which includes jazz and classical music, a food festival and a Medieval fayre.

ARRIVAL AND DEPARTURE   **MUMBLES**

Frequent **buses** from Swansea (every 10min; 15min) stop at various points along the seafront.

ACCOMMODATION

Clyne Farm Centre Westport Ave, just off the A4118 in Blackpill, roughly midway between Mumbles and Swansea, SA3 5AR ☎ 01792 403333, ⓦ clynefarm.com. Ecoconscious farm with a campsite and a variety of self-catering accommodation, including cottages sleeping between four and eight. Camping/person **£7.50**, cottages **£170**

Coast House 708 Mumbles Rd, SA3 4EH ☎ 01792 368702, ⓦ thecoasthouse.co.uk. Welcoming seafront guesthouse with four fresh-looking rooms, two of which have glorious sea views. Closed Jan and Dec. **£80**

Langland Road B&B 17 Langland Rd, SA3 4ND ☎ 01792 361170, ⓦ langlandroad.co.uk. Gay-friendly bed and breakfast providing five cleverly turned-out rooms with DVD players, iPod docks and a few playful touches; the super breakfast (including a vegetarian option) will see you on your way. To get there, head to the top of Newton Rd and turn left by the church. Closed Jan, Nov and Dec. **£85**

Tides Reach 388 Mumbles Rd, SA3 5TN ☎ 01792 404877, ⓦ tidesreachguesthouse.com. There are seven spacious and immaculate rooms (two with sea views) in this elegant, cheerfully run guesthouse, where you can also enjoy the homely lounge and delightful courtyard garden bursting with roses and honeysuckle. **£75**

EATING

Café 93 93 Newton Rd, SA3 5TW ☎ 01792 368793, ⓦ cafe93.co.uk. Cheery, two-storey pink and white café, with leather sofas and woodburner, offering tea, coffee and cakes, plus crisp pizzas (two for £12 on Wed) and juicy burgers. Mon 9am–5pm, Tues 9am–8pm, Wed–Sat 9am–11pm.

The Front Room 618 Mumbles Rd, SA3 4EA ☎ 01792 362140. Homely spot for a light lunch (Welsh cheddar and onion tartlet; £5.20), afternoon high tea for two (£17) or, on the first Thurs evening of each month, a three-course menu (£20.95). It's great for kids too, with a "munchkins" menu and boxes of toys to play with. Tues–Fri 10am–4.30pm, Sat & Sun 10am–5pm.

Munch 650 Mumbles Rd, SA3 4EA ☎ 01792 362244, ⓦ munchofmumbles.co.uk. The inconspicuous frontage conceals a similarly plain interior, but the food is first-rate; the fixed-price three-course lunch and dinner menus (£19–30) demonstrate a determinedly French bias – duck and apricot terrine with toasted brioche, perhaps, or chicken breast with Lyonnaise potatoes and a herb *jus*. BYOB (£1 corkage). Wed–Sat noon–2pm & 6.15–10pm, Sun noon–2.30pm.

★ **P.A.'s Wine Bar** 95 Newton Rd, SA3 4BN ☎ 01792 367723. Mumbles' most rewarding restaurant, whose myriad seafood possibilities (around £20) and meaty treats perfectly complement its outstanding repertoire of wines; there's a big Sun lunch too. The vine-covered terrace is a fine spot in warmer weather. Mon–Sat noon–2.30pm & 6–11pm, Sun noon–2.30pm.

Verdi's Knab Rock, SA3 4EE ☎ 01792 369135, ⓦ verdis -cafe.co.uk. Overlooking the sea near the pier, this Welsh-Italian institution is well regarded for its superb pizzas and ice creams, sorbets and sundaes; the coffee's not half bad either. Mid-March to mid-Oct daily 10am–9pm; mid-Oct to mid-March Mon–Thurs 10am–6pm, Fri–Sun 10am–9pm.

Mumbles Head to Three Cliffs Bay

The first few miles of the southern Gower coast are highly developed, including the popular **surf beach** of **Langland Bay**, between two headlands. The narrow,

1

golden-sanded **Caswell Bay** – another great spot for surfing – comes next, from where you can follow the cliff path to the tiny and remote former smugglers' haunt of **Brandy Cove**, or pebbly **Pwlldu Bay**. The last two are inaccessible by car; park in Bishopston village and walk the last mile or so.

Three miles along, huge **Three Cliffs Bay** is one of Gower's finest beaches, at the end of a silent valley fringed by dunes and the eerie ruins of **Pennard Castle**. The best approach is from the car park at **Southgate**, from where you hike a mile or so west along clifftops to Three Cliffs Bay, where you turn inland and follow the boundary of the golf course to the castle.

Gower Heritage Centre

On the main A4118 in Parkmill, SA23 2EH • Daily 10am–5pm • £6.95 • ☎ 01792 371206, ⊕ gowerheritagecentre.co.uk

Located in the centre of the village of **Parkmill**, the **Gower Heritage Centre** is a large crafts and **rural life museum** arranged around the area's last remaining water mill, whose magnificent wheel is still operating at full tilt. At one time there were around fifty mills in Gower, as well as a similarly robust spinning and weaving industry, whose history is also relayed in the woollen mill, where demonstrations are given.

There are plenty of **kids' attractions**, too, including a puppet theatre with a classic Punch and Judy show, and adventure play area and a farm with geese, goats, sheep and the like; children can also participate in pottery, glassblowing and woodturning activities. Take a peek inside La Charrette, a disused railway carriage that was converted into Wales' smallest cinema, seating just 23 people – today, it shows a film on Gower on a loop. Several useful leaflets outlining **local walks**, including to Three Cliffs Bay, are available at reception.

Parc le Breos

One mile north of Parkmill • Daily 10am–4pm • Free; CADW • ☎ 01443 336000, ⊕ cadw.gov.wales/daysout/parclebreosburialchamber

A mile north of Parkmill (reachable via the lane that heads past the Gower Heritage Centre) is the Neolithic burial chamber (3000–1900 BC) known, in honour of the thirteenth-century lords of Oystermouth Castle, as **Parc le Breos**. Although over-restored, the roofless chamber is impressive for its age and sheer size – 70ft long and divided into four chambers. In 1869, the skeletons of two dozen people were found inside. Just beyond the chamber and to the right, a deep fissure in a limestone outcrop marks the position of the dank and musty **Cathole Rock Cave**, in which flint tools, dating back more than twelve thousand years, have been found.

ACCOMMODATION	**MUMBLES HEAD TO THREE CLIFFS BAY**
Parc-le-Breos House A mile up a lane beside the Gower Heritage Centre, SA3 2HA ☎ 01792 371636, ⊕ parc-le-breos.co.uk. This old shooting lodge was one of the original Gower manor houses, but is now a grand B&B offering tidy, Victorian-era furnished rooms; they've also got a games room with pool table. **£102** **Three Cliffs Caravan Park** North Hills Farm, between Parkmill and Penmaen, SA3 2HB ☎ 01792 371218,	⊕ threecliffsbay.com. Well-appointed site with two fields, one spectacularly positioned overlooking Three Cliff Bay and the other slightly further inland without sea views; the latter also has six yurts sleeping four. The large farm shop has all the provisions you need, including loads of beach equipment, and there's a super little café, too. Closed Oct–March. Camping **£29**, yurts **£140**

Oxwich

One of the most curious landscapes in Gower is the reedy **nature reserve** around **Oxwich Burrows**, a flatland of salt and freshwater marshes reached via the lane that forks left off the A4118 at the ruined gatehouse of the privately owned **Penrice Castle**. Close by on the coast, the scattered village of **OXWICH** is grouped next to the gaping sands of **Oxwich Bay**. The sands and sea around here regularly receive awards, including the coveted Blue Flag, and the **surfing** is terrific.

1

SURFING ON GOWER

Gower has some of the finest surf in Britain, the best of which is to be had around the bays and beaches of **Langland**, **Caswell**, **Oxwich** and **Rhossili**; the most consistent is at **Llangennith**, which is also suitable for beginners. The website ⓦ gowerlive.com has live webcams and tide times.

COURSES AND EQUIPMENT RENTAL

PJ's Surfshop Llangennith, SA3 1HU ☎01792 386669, ⓦpjsurfshop.co.uk. The best place for equipment rental, with a wide range of surfboards (£11/day), boogie boards (£6/day) and wetsuits (£11/day). Daily 9am–5pm.

Sam's Surf Shack Rhossili, SA3 1PL ☎01792 390519, ⊖ rhossilileisure@hotmail.com. Offering equipment rental and lessons (£20/hr). Daily 9am–5pm, though erratic.

Welsh Surfing Federation's Surf School Hillend campsite, just beyond Hillend, SA3 1JD ☎01792 386426, ⓦsurfschool.wsf.wales. The Welsh Surfing Federation's Surf School runs half- and full-day surfing courses (£25/£45). Open all year.

Oxwich Castle

Above Oxwich Bay, SA3 1ND • April–Oct Wed–Sun 10am–5pm • £4; CADW • ☎01792 390359, ⓦ cadw.gov.wales/daysout/oxwichcastle

Crowning a headland above the beach, **Oxwich Castle** is a fine example of early sixteenth-century house gentrification by Sir Rice Mansel, member of a powerful Welsh dynasty. His son Edward added the many-windowed eastern range, a pile of rooms with a highly fashionable long gallery that fell into ruin shortly afterwards. Standing just outside the walls is the substantial ruin of the dovecote, whose nesting holes would have been used for the storage of eggs, meat and other provisions.

ACCOMMODATION   **OXWICH**

Oxwich Bay Hotel Above Oxwich Bay, SA3 1LS ☎01792 390329, ⓦoxwichbayhotel.co.uk. Set in splendid isolation just above the sands, this plain-looking hotel has well-turned-out rooms and six fabulous wood-clad cabins in a "Secret Garden", each of which sleeps two in beds that pull down from the walls and has a private patio (£110). The mirrored restaurant serves exciting dishes

(seafood gnocchi with cockles and samphire £15.95), while the hotel's grassy terrace overlooking the beach is an alluring spot for a beer on a warm day. **£99**

Oxwich Camping Park Penrice road, more than a mile back from the beach, SA3 1LS ☎01792 390777. A large but low-key site with modern washing facilities, a laundry and a small outdoor pool. Closed Oct–March. **£8**

Port Eynon and around

The rocky cliffs from Oxwich Point fade into wide stony bays towards **PORT EYNON** and its deep, sweeping bay, its name allegedly taken from the tenth-century prince, Einion ab Owain. During World War I, the bay was a key training site for American troops in preparation for the D-Day landings.

The village's sands and dunes are sheltered by a prominent **headland**, easily reached by a series of paths that wind their way along the shore from the car park above the bleak ruins of the old shoreline salt house near Port Eynon Point. As well as being a place for salt extraction, the sixteenth-century salt house (now inaccessible) would probably also have been used as a smugglers' retreat. Now owned by the National Trust, the lichen-spattered headland is a wild and windy spot, where tufted grass gives way to sharp limestone crags. There's exceptional flora and fauna along this stretch, with bloody cranesbill, evening primrose and purple orchids, and along the coast it's not uncommon to see grey seals, porpoise and short-beaked common dolphins.

A natural cave at the tip can be seen from above, a great dome-shaped chasm that plunges into the hillside. Around the headland to the west is the remarkable, but fairly hard to find, **Culver Hole**, built into the cliffs. A man-made cave, it may originally have

1

been a stronghold for the long-gone Port Eynon castle, though more prosaically it would certainly have served as a dovecote – given that culver comes from the word "culfre", meaning dove or pigeon.

The **coastal path** west from here is the most spectacular walk on Gower, veering along crags above thundering waves for five miles. The only real beach along this stretch is the secluded **Mewslade Bay**, just short of Rhossili and accessible by the path from Pitton. Along the coast walk, about midway between the two villages, is **Paviland Cave**, the site of an astonishing find in 1823, when the skeleton of a Stone Age hunter, at least 26,000 years old, was unearthed (see p.429). At **Thurba Head**, on the eastern side of Mewslade Bay, there are a few scant remains of an Iron Age hillfort sited magnificently a few hundred feet above the waves.

ACCOMMODATION   PORT EYNON

Carreglwyd Camping and Caravan Park Above the YHA hostel, SA3 1NN ☎01792 390795, ⓦporteynon .com. Backing onto the beach and surrounded by cliffs, this large and picturesque site comprises five hedged-off fields and good facilities (modern showers, laundry, shop). __£22__
Culver House Behind the sand dunes, SA3 1NN ☎01792 720300, ⓦculverhousehotel.co.uk. Nineteenth-century dwelling nicely tucked away, offering eight apartment-style suites, each one comprising one or two bedrooms and an open-plan kitchen/lounge area. Most have sea-facing

balconies. To find it, turn left at the sign for Borfa House, just before the beachfront. __£95__
YHA Port Eynon By the beach, SA3 1NN ☎0845 371 9135, ⓦyha.org.uk/hostel/port-eynon. Occupying a tremendous beachside location, this Victorian-era lifeboat station has been converted into a super hostel, with four- to eight-bedded dorms and double rooms. Shared shower facilities, self-catering kitchen and lounge. Groups only Nov–March. Dorms __£18__, doubles __£40__

Rhossili and around

Heading west, Gower saves the best for last. The sublimely located village of **RHOSSILI** (Rhosili) has wraparound views up into the hills and out to sea. It's a great place for coastal walking, particularly out to **Worms Head**, an isolated string of rocks with the spectacular appearance of a basking Welsh dragon, accessible for only five hours around low tide. Take care in this area: the **tidal currents** are extremely dangerous and people have died here. If you do get cut off, don't attempt to wade back – wait on the promontory until the tide recedes.

Below the village, a great curve of white sand stretches away into the distance, a dazzling coastline vast enough to absorb the crowds, especially if you are prepared to head a little way north towards **Burry Holms**, an islet three miles distant that is cut off at high tide. These coastal waters were notorious for **shipwrecks** in the nineteenth century, and towards the Rhossili end of the beach you can see (at low tide) the black ribs of the hull of the *Helvetia*, which foundered here in 1887. The northern end of the beach can also be reached along the small lane from Reynoldston, in the middle of the peninsula, to **Llangennith**, on the other side of the towering sandstone **Rhossili Down**, rising up to 633ft. This is by far the best spot for **surfing** on the Gower.

Church of St Mary
Rhossili, SA3 1PL • Easter–Oct daily 8am–6pm

Standing in the heart of the village, the thirteenth-century **church of St Mary** is a typical Gower church, a thick-set stone construction with a distinctive saddleback tower. There are some delightful details, notably the late Norman carved door archway, to the left of which you can just about detect a scratch sundial, suggesting that, at one time, the door would have been open to the sky. Inside, take a look at the wall-mounted tablet dedicated to Rhossili son, Edgar Evans, who was the first member of Scott's Antarctic team to perish.

1

INFORMATION

Tourist information The National Trust Centre, at the head of the road beyond Rhossili, stocks plenty of literature, excellent local walking maps and a tide timetable (Jan &

RHOSSILI AND AROUND

Feb Tues–Sun 10.30am–4pm; March–May & Sept–Dec daily 10.30am–4.30pm; June–Aug daily 10.30am–5pm; ☎ 01792 390707, ⓦ nationaltrust.org.uk).

ACCOMMODATION

★**Blas Gwyr** Llangennith, by the roundabout on the lane towards the beach, SA3 1HU ☎ 01792 386472, ⓦ blasgwyr.co.uk. An old farmhouse with four cottagey-style rooms set away from each other around a little courtyard; stripped-back stone walls, colourful Welsh fabrics and large wet rooms are standard, while Dafydd, the affable proprietor, will whip you up a cracking breakfast at the same time as regaling you with entertaining stories. **£115**

Hillend Through Llangennith, just beyond the hamlet of Hillend, SA3 1JD ☎ 01792 386204, ⓦ hillendcamping .com. Enormous, fabulously situated campsite behind the dunes and with direct access to the glorious beach. Two of the four fields are set aside for families and couples. Facilities include a shop and on-site café/bar. Closed Nov–March. There's a surfing school on site (see box, p.130). **£20**

King's Head Llangennith, SA3 1HX ☎ 01792 386212, ⓦ kingsheadgower.co.uk. The most prominent accommodation in the village is in this sixteenth-century pub, offering rooms of a fairly high standard (some with sea views), both in the pub annexe and, better still, in the newer stone building across the car park. It's the only place to eat in the village, and suffices for a dependable meal and a decent pint. **£99**

★**Pitton Cross Caravan and Camping** Rhossili, SA3 1PT ☎ 01792 390593, ⓦ pittoncross.co.uk. The only

campsite in the vicinity of Rhossili is this excellent, compact site with segregated paddocks and magnificent sea views; you can walk directly down to the beach. The four- and five-berth shepherd's huts (two-night minimum stay) are superb. There's a great kite shop here, too. Camping **£14**, huts **£97.50**

Rhossili Bunkhouse A mile or so out of Rhossili, near the village of Middleton, SA2 1PL ☎ 01792 391509, ⓦ rhossilibunkhouse.com. This bunkhouse, attached to the village hall, offers clean and simple two-, three- and four-bedded rooms. There's a kitchen for self-catering use. Note, though, that a minimum two-person, two-night stay is required. **£20**

Western House Llangennith, on the lane towards the beach, SA3 1HU ☎ 01792 386620, ⓦ westernhouse bandb.co.uk. There are four wildly colourful and wonderfully oddball rooms in this red limewashed B&B, whose remarkably chilled-out proprietors will ensure nothing less than a totally relaxing stay. Dogs welcome. **£70**

Worm's Head On the clifftop SA3 1PP ☎ 01792 390512, ⓦ thewormshead.co.uk. Spectacularly located on the clifftop, this small, welcoming hotel has fairly ordinary rooms but sensational views. Even if you're not staying here, take a coffee on the terrace. **£96**

EATING

Bay Bistro Rhossili, SA3 1PP ☎ 01792 390519, ⓦ thebaybistro.co.uk. Easy-going café serving light meals, including terrific burgers (Welsh wagyu; £13.95) and home-made cakes; park yourself inside on one of the

sunken armchairs or out on the windy terrace, although coastal views are not as good as those from *Worm's Head* next door. Daily: June–Sept 10am–5pm & 7–9pm; Oct–May 10am–5pm.

Mid- and north Gower

The great sweep of land that rises to the north of the main Gower road does not attract anything like the number of visitors that the south and west do, due to the lack of comparable coastline. **North Gower** comprises a flattened series of **marshes** and **mud flats** merging indistinguishably with the sands of the Loughor estuary. Wading birds, gulls and bedded cockles, as well as herds of cattle and wild horses, are all found among the flats, dunes and inlets burrowing into the land from the estuary.

The central plateau of **mid-Gower** is a pleasant patchwork of pastoral farmland. Its backbone, the 500ft-high sandstone ridge **Cefn Bryn**, stretches across the centre of the peninsula, with wiry peat and grass dotted with hardy sheep, ancient stone cairns and holy wells. The best views over the peninsula are from the road brushing over its roof.

Reynoldston

The **Cefn Bryn** ridge makes a sublime walk, most easily explored from the quiet village of **REYNOLDSTON**, grouped around a sheep-filled village green and *King Arthur Hotel*.

ARTHUR'S STONE

Gower is littered with more dolmens, standing stones and other prehistoric remains than any other landscape in Wales. The most celebrated of all is **Arthur's Stone** (near Reynoldston and sometimes referred to as King Arthur's Stone), a massive burial chamber topped by a quartz capstone weighing more than 25 tons. The dolmen is thought to be anything up to six thousand years old, while the ruptured capstone (which, before it split sometime around 1693, rested on six supporting stones) is mentioned, often as *Maen Ceti*, in documents dating back a thousand years.

Some believe that it's part of an astronomical alignment along with Lady's Well, a spring deemed holy and now enclosed in a hut, across the road; and Penmaen's ruined chapel and Neolithic burial chamber, three miles southeast. This alignment is allegedly charged with a special energy that has, in fact, shown up in some curious photographs with streaks and dots in otherwise clear skies. Whatever the truth, the views from up here are extraordinary.

From Reynoldston, a dramatic road rises up the slope of Cefn Bryn before skating across its summit in a perfect, straight line. Several tracks lead off from the road giving clear views to both Gower coasts, but you might be best off stopping at the small car park about a mile east of Reynoldston; from here, a path leads about half a mile across the boggy moor to **Arthur's Stone** (see box above).

Weobley Castle

1.5 miles west of Llanrhidian, SA3 1HB • Daily: April–Oct 9.30am–6pm; Nov–March 9.30am–5pm • £4; CADW • ☎ 01792 390012, ⓦ cadw.gov.wales/daysout/weobleycastle

The small village of **LLANRHIDIAN** sits above the largely inaccessible marsh of the same name, which is virtually indistinguishable from the sands of the Loughor estuary. Standing gaunt against the backdrop of the marsh and the estuary, **Weobley Castle** was built as a fortified manor in the latter part of the thirteenth century. Its first residents were the de la Bere family, who remained here until the fifteenth century, after which time it was variously lived in by a succession of wealthy landowners, such as Rhys Thomas and the Mansels, the latter owning Oxwich Castle. The most intact parts of the complex are the north and west portions, formerly the hall, kitchen and accommodation block. The views across the marshes and mud flats are wonderful.

Llanmadoc

West of the village of **Cheriton**, with its charming thirteenth-century church, is **LLANMADOC**, where you can park and venture onto the land spit of **Whitford Burrows**, a soft patch of dunes now open as a nature reserve, with the only sea-washed cast-iron lighthouse in the UK. Steep paths lead from Llanmadoc village up **Llanmadoc Hill** to the south. **The Bulwark**, a lonely and windy hillfort, can be seen at the eastern end of Llanmadoc Hill's summit ridge.

ACCOMMODATION AND EATING   MID- AND NORTH GOWER

Dolphin Inn Llanrhidian, SA3 1EH ☎ 01792 391069. Warmly run eighteenth-century pub with a cosy interior, fine real ales and a half-decent menu. The garden is a great place to kick back, and has a children's play area. Mon–Sat 1–11pm, Sun noon–11.30pm.

King Arthur Hotel Reynoldston, SA3 1AD ☎ 01792 390775, ⓦ kingarthurhotel.co.uk. The village's convivial pub has half a dozen comfortable en-suite rooms, though the annexe offers larger, more attractive options, with French windows and cast-iron beds (£105). Dining-wise, the restaurant is fine, but better is the lovely bar, where you can eat succulent Welsh rump washed down with one of the superb guest ales; in fine weather, do as the locals do and take a drink from the bar out to the green, where you can sup among the sheep. Daily 10am–11pm; kitchen noon–2.30pm & 6–9pm. **£90**

Tallizmand Guesthouse Llanmadoc, SA3 1DE ☎ 01792 386373, ⓦ tallizmand.co.uk. The main accommodation option along Llanmadoc's main road, with three en-suite rooms and a cosy communal lounge warmed by an open fire. **£80**

Southwest Wales

139 Llanelli and around

141 Carmarthen and around

144 Tywi Valley

152 Southern Carmarthenshire

155 Narberth and the Landsker Borderlands

158 South Pembrokeshire coast

165 Mid-Pembrokeshire

174 St Bride's Bay

185 North Pembrokeshire coast

189 Mynydd Preseli

TENBY

Southwest Wales

The most westerly outposts of Wales, the counties of Carmarthenshire (Sir Gar) and, in particular, Pembrokeshire (Sir Benfro) harbour fabulous scenery: bucolic and magical inland, following the Tywi Valley into the heart of Carmarthenshire; rocky, indented and spectacular around the Pembrokeshire Coast National Park and its 186-mile path. Industrial south Wales peters out at Llanelli, before the undistinguished county town of Carmarthen; a glorious road winds along the Tywi Valley, past ruined hilltop forts and the National Botanic Garden of Wales on the way to Wales' most impressively positioned castle, Carreg Cennen, high on a dizzy plug of Black Mountain rock. Further inland, the sparsely populated hill country is broken only by endearing small market towns such as Llandeilo and Llandovery, the gloomy ruins of Talley Abbey and the Roman gold mines at Dolaucothi.

The wide sands of southern Carmarthenshire, just beyond Dylan Thomas' adopted home town of **Laugharne**, merge into the popular south Pembrokeshire seaside resorts of **Tenby** and **Saundersfoot**. These sit at the entrance to the south Pembrokeshire peninsula, its turbulent, rocky coast ruptured by some remote historical sites, including the Norman baronial castle at **Manorbier** and tiny **St Govan's chapel**, wedged into a rocky cliff. At the neck of the peninsula is the old county town of **Pembroke**, dominated by its fearsome castle; to the north, beyond the **Milford Haven estuary**, is the market town and transport hub of **Haverfordwest**, dull but hard to avoid. St Bride's Bay is one of the most glorious parts of the coastal walk, leading north towards the village-sized city of **St Davids**, its exquisite cathedral sheltering in a protective hollow. Close by are opportunities for spectacular coast and hill walks, hair-raising boat crossings to islands, surf galore and numerous other outdoor activities.

The coast turns towards the north at St Davids, becoming the southern stretch of Cardigan Bay. The northernmost section of the Coast Path, from the pretty ferry port of **Fishguard** past the delightful little town of **Newport** to the outskirts of Cardigan, is the most dramatic and remote. Inland are the eerie **Mynydd Preseli**, relic-spattered mountains overlooking windswept plateaus of heathland and isolated villages – none more remote than the leafy valley of **Cwm Gwaun**.

GETTING AROUND   SOUTHWEST WALES

Despite the remoteness of much of southwest Wales, public transport is surprisingly efficient and comprehensive, though you'll have to plan carefully, even in summer. Bus and train **timetables** are widely available locally, and online at ⓦ pembrokeshiregreenways.co.uk and ⓦ carmarthenshire.gov.uk.

Merlin p.144
Dylan Thomas p.154
Little England Beyond Wales p.156
The Pembrokeshire Coast National Park and Coast Path p.159
Tenby festivals p.163
Palmerston's follies p.164
Cleddau Bridge p.168

Water activities around Dale p.174
Skomer, Grassholm and Skokholm boat trips p.176
Activities around St Davids p.181
Walks around St Davids p.182
Cruises to Ramsey Island p.184
The last invasion of Britain p.187
Fishguard's festivals p.188

ST GOVAN'S CHAPEL

Highlights

❶ **Tywi Valley** Castles, follies and the National Botanic Garden set among one of Wales' lushest and most atmospheric valleys. **See p.144**

❷ **Carreg Cennen Castle** The region's most dramatically sited fortress, perched on a vertiginous plug of rock and framed by green hills and glowering mountains. **See p.148**

❸ **Laugharne** A must for all Dylan Thomas devotees, of course, but much more besides, this quirky place is the quintessential small Welsh coastal town. **See p.153**

❹ **St Govan's chapel** This tiny grey chapel is wedged into a fissure in the cliffs, just above the churning sea: a phenomenal statement of faith. **See p.169**

❺ **Skomer, Skokholm and Grassholm** Rough and rugged islands, where squawking colonies of birds rule the roost. **See p.176**

❻ **St Davids** The jewel of Pembrokeshire, Britain's smallest city is surrounded by fabulous scenery and fosters a burgeoning surf scene with superb après-surf. **See p.179**

❼ **Carn Ingli** One of Wales' holiest mountains, with great views over the mysterious Mynydd Preseli and the charming little seaside town of Newport. **See p.190**

HIGHLIGHTS ARE MARKED ON THE MAP ON PP.138–139

By train Direct trains connect Cardiff and Swansea with Llanelli, Carmarthen, Tenby, Pembroke, Haverfordwest, Milford Haven and Fishguard, while the Heart of Wales Line shuffles out of Swansea and Llanelli to Llandeilo and Llandovery before delving into Powys. An Explore West Wales day ticket (£12.50) gives free travel at any time west of Carmarthen.

By bus Most towns and villages are linked by regular and dependable services, especially in high summer. Carmarthen and Haverfordwest are the main hubs, with some services from Tenby, Pembroke and Fishguard. The Pembrokeshire coast is well covered, with various winsomely titled "hail and ride" services – the Coastal Cruiser, the Puffin Shuttle, the Poppit Rocket – operating year-round under the banner of Pembrokeshire Coastal Bus Service (W pembrokeshire.gov.uk/coastbus). A West Wales Rover ticket (£8/day, £30/week) gives unlimited travel on most buses in Carmarthenshire and Pembrokeshire.

By boat Most of the offshore islands are reached by regular (seasonal) boat services, although few allow for overnight stops. Details are given in the relevant sections of this chapter.

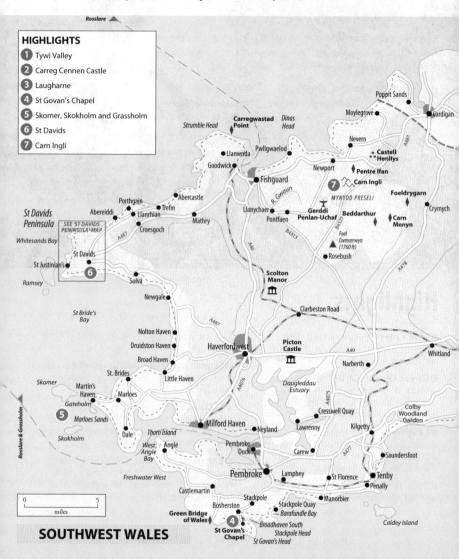

HIGHLIGHTS

1. Tywi Valley
2. Carreg Cennen Castle
3. Laugharne
4. St Govan's Chapel
5. Skomer, Skokholm and Grassholm
6. St Davids
7. Carn Ingli

SOUTHWEST WALES

Llanelli and around

LLANELLI, once a major industrial hub, marks the border between anglicized southeast Wales and the *bro*, Welsh Wales, where the native language is part of everyday life. Rugby remains a local passion, focused on the **Scarlets**, one of Wales' four regional teams.

While the old steelworks have almost all been cleared, replaced with massive retail developments that have sucked the life from the town centre, there are a couple of sights; in addition, the nearby **Llanelli Wetland Centre** makes a rewarding excursion.

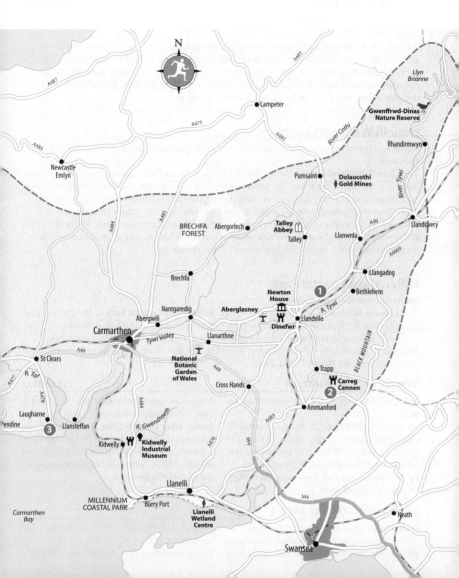

Llanelly House

Cnr of Vaughan St and Bridge St, SA15 3UF • Mon–Sat 10am–5pm; tours (1hr) 11am & 2pm • Great Hall free; tours £7 • ☎ 01544 772857, ⓦ llanelly-house.org.uk

By the parish church in the centre of town, historic **Llanelly House** is a Jacobean manor rebuilt in 1714. Access to the ground-floor café and Great Hall (where you can see an armorial dinner service, imported from China in 1762) is free. Tours of the family's and servants' rooms finish in the attic where an interactive inquest room reveals the truth (or not) behind their resident ghost.

Parc Howard Museum

On the A476, 0.5 mile north of the centre, SA15 3LJ • April–Oct Wed–Sun 10am–5pm; Nov–March Thurs–Sun 11am–4pm • Free • ☎ 01267 228696

To learn something about Llanelli's metal-bashing heyday, when the town was known as Tinopolis, visit the **Parc Howard Museum**, housed in an Italianate mansion in a lovely park. It provides good coverage of the town's industrial boom, from 1800, when its population was three thousand, to 1891, when it reached 33,464. It also displays samples of the famous hand-painted Llanelly pottery.

Llanelli Wetland Centre

Two miles east of town off the B4304, SA14 9SH • Daily 9.30am–5pm; grounds open till 6pm in summer • £8.62 • ☎ 01544 741087, ⓦ wwt.org.uk

The **Llanelli Wetland Centre** overlooks an extensive area of salt marsh where unprofitable farmland has been "returned" to nature, with "natural" ponds and landscaped walkways created around existing hedgerows. Important populations of lapwing, redshank and over-wintering pintail, wigeon and teal draw **birders**, but the centre caters just as well to kids and the curious – there are even sixty Caribbean flamingos here. There are hides and a viewing tower, but the wilder western section is best explored by canoe safaris or on bikes (both free; daily mid-July to early Sept noon–4pm).

Millennium Coastal Park

From Llanelli to Pembrey • Open access • Free

The Llanelli Wetland Centre is linked by the **Millennium Coastal Park** to Burry Port and Pembrey via the Llanelli waterfront and the eight-mile-long Cefn Sidan beach. Formerly industrial land along the Loughor estuary, the coastal park incorporates National Cycle Route 4 from London to St Davids, the three-hundred-mile Celtic Trail (see p.42) and the Welsh Coast Path.

ARRIVAL AND INFORMATION — LLANELLI

By train The train station is a mile south of the town centre.
Destinations Cardiff (20 daily; 1hr 20min); Carmarthen (25 daily; 30min); Llandeilo (5 daily; 40min); Llandovery (5 daily; 1hr); Llandrindod Wells (4 daily; 2hr); Shrewsbury (4 daily; 3hr 30min); Swansea (29 daily; 20min).
By bus Buses arrive and leave from Island Place, immediately east of the centre.

Destinations Carmarthen (every 30min; 1hr); Kidwelly (every 30min; 30min); Swansea (every 15min; 1hr).
Tourist office Discovery Centre, North Dock, 0.5 mile southwest of the town centre beside the Coast Path (daily: mid-May to Sept 10am–8pm; Oct to mid-May 10am–5pm; ☎ 01554 777744, ⓔ DiscoveryCentre@carmarthenshire .gov.uk). They offer bike rental.

ACCOMMODATION AND EATING

Coastal Park 86 Queen Victoria Rd, SA15 2TH ☎ 01554 755357, ⓦ coastalpark.co.uk. Not actually on the coast but not far west from the train station, this large but fairly ordinary B&B also has a grill-bar (Tues–Sat from 5pm). **£60**
Langostinos 1 Murray St, SA15 1AQ ☎ 01554 773711, ⓦ langostinosllanelli.co.uk. A relaxed, unassuming place

serving classy tapas and starters (£5–7), standard mains (all around £16) and steaks (£15–20). Tues & Sun noon–2pm, Wed–Sat noon–2pm & 6–10pm.

Llwyn Hall Llwynhendy, SA14 9LD, 2 miles east off the B4297 ☎01554 777754, ⓦllwynhall.com. The best of the town's guesthouses, with welcoming staff and a good

restaurant; there's also a cottage for groups. **£70**

Sheesh Mahal 53 Stepney St, SA15 3YA ☎01554 773773, ⓦsheeshmahal.net. Some of south Wales' finest curries, with fast and friendly service (starters £3–6, mains £6–10). Mon–Thurs & Sun 5.30–11pm, Fri & Sat 5.30pm–midnight.

Kidwelly

2

KIDWELLY (Cydweli) is a sleepy little town dominated by an imposing **castle**, strategically sited above the River Gwendraeth and a vast tract of coast. Just west, beyond the station, the recently refurbished **Kymer's Quay** was built in 1768 as the start of the first significant industrial canal in Wales; the vast expanse of marshy coast here offers good **birdwatching**.

Kidwelly Castle

Just north of the town centre, SA17 5BQ • March–June, Sept & Oct daily 9.30am–5pm; July & Aug daily 9.30am–6pm; Nov–Feb Mon–Sat 10am–4pm, Sun 11am–4pm • £4; CADW • ☎01554 890104, ⓦcadw.gov.wales/daysout/kidwellycastle

A wooden **castle** was built here around 1106, rebuilt in stone in the 1270s and extended in the fourteenth century. On Castle Street, the main road through Kidwelly, a fourteenth-century town **gate** marks the approach to **Kidwelly Castle**. Continuing through the massive **gatehouse**, which forms the centrepiece of the impressively intact **outer ward walls** (c.1275), you can still see portcullis slots and murder holes, through which noxious substances could be poured onto intruders. Views from the musty solar and hall, packed into the easternmost wall of the inner ward, show the castle's defensive position at its best, with the river directly below.

Kidwelly Industrial Museum

One mile north of town (up Priory St and beyond the bypass), SA17 4LW • Feb half-term & mid-April to Oct Fri–Sun 10am–5pm • Free • ☎01554 891078, ⓦkidwellyindustrialmuseum.co.uk

A 167ft brick chimney marks the modest but informative **Kidwelly Industrial Museum**, housed in a former tinplate works. Many of the works' old features have been preserved, including the rolling mills, where blocks of tin were rolled and spun into wafer-thin slices.

Carmarthen and around

The ancient capital of its region, **CARMARTHEN** (Caerfyrddin) is a lively market town with fifteen thousand inhabitants. Unlike in Llanelli, the town centre has some life to it, and it's the first major settlement in west Wales where the native language is widely heard, but really there's little reason to stay – and fortunately, with so many beautiful and interesting places nearby, there's little need to. Two miles east, **Abergwili** is of interest for the Carmarthen County Museum, and as Merlin's supposed resting place.

Brief history

Founded as a Roman fort, Carmarthen's mythological fame dates from the Dark Ages and the supposed birth of the wizard **Merlin** just outside the town (see box, p.144) – its Roman name, Moridunum, may have given him his Welsh name, Myrddin. The Normans built a castle in 1095, and two priories, and in 1313 Carmarthen was granted a charter by Edward I, helping it flourish as a port and centre of the wool trade. In the early eighteenth century this was the largest town in all Wales, but it then declined as industry developed elsewhere in south Wales.

Carmarthen Castle

The Mount, SA31 1JP • Daily roughly 8am–5.30pm • Free

Across the river from the train station, the stern facade of the 1930s **County Hall** stands within the uninspiring remains of **Carmarthen Castle**, Edward I's reworking of a Norman fortress later destroyed by Owain Glyndŵr in 1405. In an obscure corner of the car park, steps lead to the top of the keep, for lacklustre views over the town. Exit through the gatehouse (1410) to **Nott Square**, beneath which spreads the most picturesque eighteenth- and nineteenth-century part of town, around King Street.

Lammas Street and the market

From Nott Square, broad Darkgate slopes down to **Lammas Street**, a wide Georgian thoroughfare flanked by coaching inns. To the north, Mansel Street leads to the striking **market** (Mon 9.30am–4.30pm, Tues–Sat 9.30am–5pm), a great centre for local produce, secondhand books, antiques and endearingly useless tat. On the main market days – Wednesday and Saturday – stalls spill onto the streets outside.

Carmarthen County Museum

Abergwili, 2 miles east of Carmarthen, SA31 2JG • Tues–Sat 10am–4.30pm • Free • ☎ 01267 228696, Ⓦ carmarthenmuseum.org.uk • Served by Carmarthen–Llandeilo buses (6 daily; 12min from Carmarthen)

The severe grey Bishop's Palace at Abergwili, seat of the Bishop of St Davids between 1542 and 1974, now houses the **Carmarthen County Museum**, a spirited amble through the area's history. Pottery, archeological finds, wooden dressers and a lively history of local castles are well presented, along with material on crime and policing, geology, education, coracles and Carmarthen's role in the development of the eisteddfod tradition. There's also a surprisingly interesting display on the first Welsh translation of the New Testament, produced here in 1567. Upstairs you can see the bishop's chapel and a re-created schoolroom and farmhouse interior. The bishop's gardens, including a pond and walled kitchen gardens, are currently being restored.

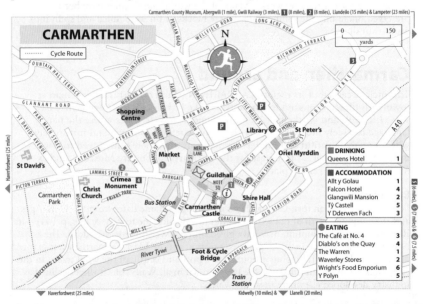

Gwili Railway

Services from Bronwydd Arms train station, 3 miles north, SA33 6HT • Easter, July & Aug daily; May & Oct Wed, Thurs, Sat & Sun; June & Sept Tues–Thurs, Sat & Sun; Dec Sat & Sun • All-day ticket £11 • ☎ 01267 238213, ⓦ gwili-railway.co.uk • Buses #460 (Mon–Sat) and #215 (Mon–Fri) to Bronwydd Arms

South Wales' only standard-gauge tourist railway, with steam and diesel haulage, the **Gwlili Railway** gives a delightful trundle through seven miles of bucolic riverside. It's recently been extended to Abergwili Junction on the edge of Carmarthen, but you have to catch trains at Bronwydd Arms, where there's a small museum, shop and tearoom.

2

ARRIVAL AND DEPARTURE

CARMARTHEN AND AROUND

Frequencies given below are for Monday to Saturday services; on Sunday there are four to six trains on most lines (though the main line east from Carmarthen is served more frequently), and very few buses.

By train Trains between Swansea and Pembrokeshire stop at the station across the river from the town centre.
Destinations Cardiff (20 daily; 1hr 45min–2hr 10min); Fishguard Harbour (4 daily; 1hr); Haverfordwest (11 daily; 40min); Kidwelly (15 daily; 15min); Llanelli (28 daily; 25min); Milford Haven (11 daily; 1hr); Narberth (9 daily; 25min); Pembroke (9 daily; 1hr 10min); Swansea (26 daily; 50min); Tenby (9 daily; 50min).
By bus The bus station is on Blue St, north of the river.
Destinations Aberaeron (hourly; 1hr 45min); Aberystwyth

(hourly; 2hr 20min); Brechfa (2 daily; 30min); Cardigan (hourly; 1hr 25min); Cenarth (hourly; 1hr 10min); Haverfordwest (3 daily; 1hr); Kidwelly (every 30min; 25min); Lampeter (hourly; 1hr); Laugharne (5 daily; 30min); Llandeilo (10 daily; 40min); Llandovery (8 daily; 1hr 20min); Llanelli (every 30min; 1hr); Llansteffan (7 daily; 20min); London (2 daily; 6hr); Narberth (3 daily; 50min); National Botanic Garden of Wales (Mon–Thurs & Sat 1 daily; 25min); Swansea (every 30min; 1hr 20min); Tenby (1 daily; 1hr 10min).

INFORMATION

Tourist office In the Old County Lockup, Castle House, between the castle's ring walls (Mon–Sat 9.30am–4.30pm; ☎ 01267 231557, ⓔ carmarthentic@carmarthenshire.gov .uk). In summer they offer free town tours on Wed and

occasional ghost tours.
Internet There's free wi-fi at the tourist office and at the library (Mon–Sat 9am–5pm) on King St opposite St Peter's church.

ACCOMMODATION

The range of **accommodation** in Carmarthen is limited, and few places are truly notable, so the following reviews include a selection of places in the nearby Tywi Valley.

Allt y Golau Felingwm Uchaf, 8 miles northeast, between Brechfa and the Botanic Garden, SA32 7BB ☎ 01267 290455, ⓦ alltygolau.com. Superb sustainability-aware B&B in a renovated 1812 farmhouse, with three tastefully decorated rooms and sumptuous breakfasts. **£70**
Falcon Hotel 111 Lammas St, SA31 3AP ☎ 01267 234959, ⓦ falconcarmarthen.co.uk. The best town-centre option, this well-established family-run hotel has recently been refurbished, with fresh individually styled rooms, a good restaurant and attentive service. **£75**
Glangwili Mansion Llandllawdog, 7 miles northeast, SA32 7JE ☎ 01267 253735, ⓦ glangwilimansion.co.uk.

A beautiful designer guesthouse, with lots of bright abstract art plus hens, alpacas and an eagle owl; it's near Brechfa Forest, a good place for hiking or biking. **£110**
Tŷ Castell Off Station Rd, Nantgaredig, 5 miles east, SA32 7LQ ☎ 01267 290034, ⓦ ty-castell.co.uk. Wonderful outdoorsy farmhouse B&B by the Tywi, with evening meals available. **£80**
Y Dderwen Fach 98 Priory St, SA31 1NB ☎ 01267 234193, ⓦ ydderwenfach.co.uk. The best of the budget B&Bs in the centre, in a simple seventeenth-century house. Some rooms have bathtubs as well as showers. **£50**

EATING

The Café at No. 4 4 Queen St, SA31 1JR ☎ 01267 220461, ⓦ cafeno4.com. This stylish café offers a three-course set menu (£30) that might start with chèvre and mascarpone mousse or carpaccio of beetroot, pomegranate and hazelnuts, followed by beef daube, Welsh lamb or mushroom, spinach and ricotta gnocchi. Good desserts, too.

It's unlicensed – bring your own wine. Thurs–Sat 6–9pm.
Diablo's on the Quay Coracle Way, SA31 3JP ☎ 01267 223000, ⓦ diablos.co. Lively bar by the river that's ideal for the two-course lunch (£15). Otherwise choose from starters (£6–7) such as goat's cheese pannacotta and beetroot salad; mains from cod and chips to beef pie (£12.50), pan-roasted

2

MERLIN

Merlin (Myrddin) is a difficult character to pin down. A mythic figure throughout Europe's Celtic fringe, he is variously described as a wizard and prophet, though over the centuries he has also been called a half-demon and Antichrist, as well as being credited with building Stonehenge. His most common association is with **King Arthur** (see box, p.133) to whom he was tutor, wizard and advisor. It was Merlin who arranged Arthur's rise to the throne through the sword-in-the-stone contest, who founded the Round Table and who accompanied Arthur to the Isle of Avalon at the end of his life.

This interpretation dates back to **Geoffrey of Monmouth** who, in his *Historia Regum Britanniae* of 1134, drew on all sorts of tales and folklore (plus a fair bit of fabrication) to create the Merlin we know today. He built on stories of very different Merlins under different names – Myrddin Wyllt (Merlin the wild), Merlin Caledonensis (Scottish Merlin), and the most Welsh, Myrddin Emrys (Merlin Ambrosius) – perhaps separate people whose stories have blended, or the same person whose stories diverged over centuries of telling. He is even credited with inventing the Latinized "Merlin" form to avoid any association with "merde", the French for excrement.

According to Geoffrey and, half a century later, Giraldus Cambrensis (see box, p.376), Merlin was born in Carmarthen, and legend has it that, trapped by the enchantress Vivien, he now sleeps under **Merlin's Hill** (Bryn Myrddin; daily 10am–dusk; £3), where he will remain until the country is in great danger and King Arthur and his men rise up. Another story tells of Merlin predicting that "when Merlin's tree shall tumble down, then shall fall Carmarthen town". The oak, which once stood in the town centre, died a few years back, but Carmarthen remains. A piece of the tree can be seen in the Carmarthen County Museum.

Carmarthen celebrates the **Gŵyl Myrddin** (Merlin Festival; ⓦcarmarthenshire.gov.uk) in March, with wizards, magicians and fortune tellers performing in the streets.

---

sea-bass (£16) and steaks (£16–24); and desserts including Eton mess (£5–8). The outside deck is a good place to enjoy cocktails; there's no real ale but the wine list is good. Daily noon–late; kitchen noon–3pm & 6–9pm.

The Warren 11 Mansel St, SA31 1PX ☎01267 236079, ⓦwarrenmanselst.co.uk. This new café-bar promises craft beers and gins, interesting starters (£3.50–7) such as spiced Moroccan carrot dip or courgette and kale fritters, and mains (£11–16) from veggie burgers to lamb moussaka. Live music first Sun of the month. Thurs–Sat 11am–3pm & 6–9.30pm, Sun 11am–3pm.

Waverley Stores 23 Lammas St, SA31 3AL ☎01267 236521, ⓦwaverleyonline.co.uk. A large health-food shop with a vegetarian café and tea garden, serving tasty lunch dishes for around £5. Mon–Sat 10am–3pm (lunch 11.30am–2pm).

★ **Wright's Food Emporium** Llanarthne, 8 miles east, SA32 8JU ☎01558 668929, ⓦwrightsfood.co.uk. This former pub is now a wonderful café-deli, run by food writer Simon Wright. It sells local cheese, meat, beer and cider as well as olive oil and wine (by the glass or bottle or in bulk), its own bread and cakes, and sophisticated versions of simple dishes such as Welsh rarebit, *bruschetta* or poached sewin (sea-trout) tartine. It still feels pubby, with its open fire, and has six en-suite rooms. Mon & Tues 11am–7pm, Wed & Thurs 9am–7pm, Fri & Sat 9am–10pm, Sun 11am–5pm.

★ **Y Polyn** Capel Dewi, on the B4310, 2 miles north of National Botanic Garden, SA32 7LH ☎01267 290000, ⓦypolyn.co.uk. A country pub offering some of the area's best food. The modern British cuisine makes superb use of local ingredients and everything is served with relaxed panache. Set dinners £28 for two courses, £35 for three. Tues–Thurs noon–2pm & 7–9pm, Fri noon–2pm & 6.30–9.30pm, Sat noon–2.30pm & 6.30–9.30pm, Sun noon–2.30pm.

DRINKING

Queens Hotel 10 Queen St, SA31 1JR ☎01267 231800. The best beer in town, in a wood-panelled coaching inn (with beer garden) that also offers pub grub, notably cawl (Welsh broth) as well as sandwiches and jacket potatoes (all around £5). Mon–Thurs 10am–11.30pm, Fri & Sat 10am–midnight, Sun 10.30am–8pm; kitchen daily noon–6pm.

Tywi Valley

The **River Tywi** winds its way east from Carmarthen through some of the most spellbinding scenery in south Wales. It's not hard to see why the Merlin legend has taken such a hold in the **Tywi Valley** – the landscape does seem infused with a kind of eerie magic. The thirty-mile trip from Carmarthen to **Llandovery** is punctuated by gentle, impossibly green hills topped with ruined castles, notably the wonderful **Carreg Cennen** near the appealing town of **Llandeilo**. There are two fine gardens here, each very different: the flagship **National Botanic Garden of Wales** and the faithful restoration of the walled gardens around the long-abandoned house of **Aberglasney**.

Brechfa Forest

2

Ten miles northeast of Carmarthen in the lovely Cothi Valley, **Brechfa Forest** is becoming increasingly renowned for its **mountain biking** trails (Ⓦmbwales.com), but it's a beautiful area for **walking** too. Quiet narrow lanes cut through the sixteen thousand acres of mixed ancient forest and recent plantations, emerging near Talley and Dolaucothi.

ARRIVAL AND DEPARTURE
BRECHFA FOREST

By bus Brechfa and Abergorlech are reached by services from/to Carmarthen (Mon–Sat 2 daily; 30min) and Llandeilo (2 weekly; 1hr).

ACCOMMODATION AND EATING

Black Lion Abergorlech, 5 miles northeast of Brechfa, SA32 7SN Ⓣ01558 685271, Ⓦblion.co.uk. A fine old inn close to the start of the main mountain bike trails, with a flagstone bar, riverside beer garden, restaurant extension and bike-washing facilities. Mains are around £8–14. April–Oct Mon–Fri noon–3pm & 7–10pm, Sat & Sun noon–11pm; Nov–March Tues & Wed 7–11pm, Thurs & Fri noon–3pm & 7–11pm, Sat & Sun noon–11pm; kitchen same days generally noon–2pm & 7–9pm.
Gilfach-Wen Barn 0.5 mile south of Brechfa, SA32 7QL

Ⓣ01267 240077 or Ⓣ07780 476737, Ⓦbrechfa -bunkhouse.com. A short, potholed lane leads to this useful, well-appointed and pleasantly located self-catering bunkhouse. £17.50
Tŷ Mawr Country Hotel Brechfa, SA32 7RA Ⓣ01267 202332, Ⓦwales-country-hotel.co.uk. Upmarket accommodation (with two accessible ground-floor rooms) that's winning a reputation for its menu of (partly organic) seasonal local food on a daily changing menu. Booking required. Daily from 7pm; last orders 8.30pm. £100

National Botanic Garden of Wales

Seven miles east of Carmarthen, 1 mile north of the A48, SA32 8HN • Daily: April–Oct 10am–6pm; Nov–March 10am–4.30pm • April–Oct £9.55; Nov–March £8.86; half-price for visitors arriving by bike • Ⓣ01558 668768, Ⓦgardenofwales.org.uk • Bus #279 runs daily from Carmarthen (25min)

Since its construction in 2000, the great glass "eye" of the **National Botanic Garden of Wales** has become the Tywi Valley's centrepiece. It occupies what's left of the vast estate of the nineteenth-century banker William Paxton, whose house, Middleton Hall, burnt down in 1931. A central walkway leads past sculptures and lakes, with paths down towards planted areas and various wood and wetland habitats. These continue through the **Waun Las National Nature Reserve** all the way to the three-cornered **Paxton's Tower** (built to honour Nelson in 1809) on a hilltop two miles northeast.

Paxton's **double-walled garden** now provides vegetables for the café-restaurant, and has been enhanced by the addition of a small but exquisite Japanese garden, a tropical house, and a bee garden housing a million bees. The entire garden is sustainably managed: the glasshouses are heated by burning wood coppiced on the grounds; waste water is purified through a series of reed beds; rainwater is used for irrigation; and a large tract of surrounding land is being turned over to organic farming using Welsh breeds of cattle and sheep.

The glasshouse and Millennium Square

At the top of the hill is the garden's most audacious feature: the vast oval **glasshouse**, a stunning piece of architecture by Norman Foster. It houses endangered plants from regions with a Mediterranean climate, including South Africa, Australia, Chile and California. The stableyard houses a **café-restaurant** and an excellent exhibition on medicinal plants and the dynasty of Welsh herbalists known as the Physicians of Myddfai (Meddygon Myddfai, supposedly descended from the Lady of the Lake), abutting **Millennium Square**, a venue for open-air performances.

Aberglasney

Five miles northeast of the National Botanic Garden of Wales, 0.5 mile south of the A40, SA32 8QH • Daily: April–Oct 10am–6pm; Nov–March 10.30am–4pm • £8 • ☎ 01558 668998, ⓦ aberglasney.org

A natural twin to the Botanic Garden lies nearby at **Aberglasney**, where a restored seventeenth-century manor house plays second fiddle to its remarkable **gardens**. Much smaller and more intimate than the National Botanic Garden, they are being steadily re-created as living historical documents.

The house

The **entrance hall** shows fortnightly displays by local artists; in a side room you can watch an interesting video history of the estate. The heart of the house has been glassed in to form an **atrium** populated with subtropical plants – tree ferns, cycads, orchids and more. Dubbed a Ninfarium (after gardens at Ninfa, near Rome), it makes a beautiful counterpoint to the outdoor gardens.

The walled gardens

Once massively overgrown, the mostly sixteenth- to eighteenth-century **walled gardens** have regained much of their formal splendour. Especially noteworthy are the replanted **kitchen garden** and what is thought to be Britain's only secular **cloister garden**, dating from the late sixteenth century. Above, the walkway to the (now birdless) Victorian aviaries gives great views over the Jacobean Pool Garden to mature woodlands beyond. On the lawn near the gatehouse (c.1600, but long thought to be a Victorian folly) is a line of five yews planted three centuries ago, and trained over to root on the far side, a feature unique in Britain. Leave time for tea and cakes at the tempting *Maryellens* café, built into the wall of the Pool Garden.

Llandeilo and around

Beautifully set below the magnificent Black Mountain, the quiet market town of **LLANDEILO** is becoming known as an upmarket rural retreat for urbanites from Swansea, Cardiff and beyond, with a couple of boutique hotels, some fancy shops and galleries on King Street, and a handful of delis, cafés and restaurants. It also hosts an up-and-coming **music festival** in mid-July (ⓦ llandeilomusicfestival.org.uk), and the Festival of the Senses (ⓦ fos.wales) in mid-November, when you can eat, drink, shop and enjoy music.

Church of St Teilo

Bridge St, SA19 6BH • **Church** Tues–Sat 11am–4pm; open for services at other times • **Llandeilo Fawr Gospels** Easter–Oct Tues–Sat 11am–4pm • Free

Don't overlook the parish **church of St Teilo** (established in the seventh century and rebuilt from 1848 by George Gilbert Scott), home to a pair of eighth-century Celtic crosses and an interactive display on the **Llandeilo Fawr Gospels**, an eighth-century parchment manuscript that contains the earliest known example of written Welsh. The book itself is in Lichfield Cathedral in England, but you can browse its digitized text and learn something of both these gospels and the closely related (and more famous) Lindisfarne Gospels.

2

Dinefwr Castle

Dinefwr Park, 1 mile west of Llandeilo, SA19 6RT • Open access • Free

The strategic importance of the Tywi Valley is underlined by the tumbledown ruins of **Dinefwr Castle**, set high on a wooded bluff above the river. Built in 877 by Rhodri Mawr, King of Wales, the castle became the seat of the rulers of Deheubarth. It was rebuilt in stone from 1165 by the Lord Rhys (Rhys ap Gruffudd), who united the warring Welsh princes against the Normans, and then strengthened by Edward I after 1282; from the seventeenth century it was allowed to fall into "Romantic" ruin.

The ruins give stunning views across the valley and, in the other direction, to Newton House. With a car, you'll have to pay to park at Newton House and follow the well-marked half-mile walk from there; otherwise, there's free access by public footpaths through the lovely **Dinefwr Park**. Mostly landscaped in the 1770s following suggestions by Capability Brown, the park now contains rare white park cattle and fallow deer; the National Trust has created two excellent loop trails, of one and 1.5 miles long.

Newton House

One mile west of Llandeilo, SA19 6RT • Mid-March to Oct daily 10am–6pm; Nov to mid-March Fri–Sun 10am–4pm • £7.27; NT • ☎ 01558 825412, ⓦ nationaltrust.org.uk/dinefwr

By Tudor times Dinefwr Castle had become ill suited to the needs of the Lord Rhys' descendants, who built a new residence nearby. Now named **Newton House**, it was much transformed over the centuries, being rebuilt in the 1660s and given corner towers in the 1750s and a new "Venetian-Gothic" facade in the 1860s; it then fell into disrepair before being saved in the 1990s. It isn't the most distinguished of stately homes, but the basement and ground floor have been imaginatively set up as though it were a Sunday in 1912. Below stairs you can try your hand at brushing a top hat or correctly folding a shirt before progressing upstairs, where a formal lunch is laid out and a gramophone plays in the drawing room. Up the splendid staircase there are interesting displays on the Rhys family genealogy, the estate's heritage and the impact of World War II.

Carreg Cennen Castle

Four miles southeast of Llandeilo, SA19 6UA • Daily: April–Oct 9.30am–6pm; Nov–March 9.30am–5pm • £5.50; CADW • ☎ 01558 822291, ⓦ carregcennencastle.com

Isolated in Llandeilo's rural hinterland is the most magnificently located castle in Wales. **Carreg Cennen Castle** was constructed on its fearsome outcrop in 1248 (though Sir Urien, one of King Arthur's knights, is said to have built a fortress here earlier), but fell to Edward I in 1277. It remained in use until 1462, when it was partly destroyed by the Earl of Pembroke for being a rebel base.

The castle's most striking aspect is its vertiginous location, 300ft above a sheer drop to the Cennen River. From the car park and **farm**, with rare breeds of cows and sheep, a path climbs sharply upwards, with astounding **views** towards the severe purple lines of the Black Mountain, contrasting with the velvety green Tywi and Cennen valleys. The castle seems impenetrable, its crumbling walls merging with the limestone on which it defiantly sits. After the views, the highlight of a visit is the long, damp descent into a pitch-black **cave** that served as a shelter in prehistoric times. Torches (which can be rented for £1.50 from the excellent tearoom near the car park) are essential; continue as far as possible and then turn them off to experience absolute darkness.

ARRIVAL AND DEPARTURE	LLANDEILO AND AROUND

By train The train station, on the eastern edge of town on Heol yr Orsaf, is on the scenic Heart of Wales Line, from Swansea and Llanelli to Llandovery and Shrewsbury.

Destinations Llandovery (5 daily; 20min); Llandrindod Wells (4 daily; 1hr 20min); Llanelli (5 daily; 40min); Shrewsbury (4 daily; 2hr 50min); Swansea (5 daily; 1hr 10min).

By bus Buses stop on New Rd. Note that buses between Carmarthen and Llandeilo give access to Aberglasney.

Destinations Carmarthen (8 daily; 40min); Llandovery (8 daily; 40min); Swansea (6 daily; 90min).

ACCOMMODATION

Abermarlais Caravan Park A40, 6 miles east, SA19 9NG ☏01550 777868, ⓦ abermarlaiscaravanpark .co.uk. Spacious rural campsite near Llangadog – it's perfect for families. Closed Nov–Feb. **£15**

The Cawdor 70 Rhosmaen St, SA19 6EN ☏01558 823500, ⓦ thecawdor.com. Llandeilo's focal point, this former coaching inn has been given a modern makeover

with delightful, simply decorated rooms (all different) and stunning attic suites (£200). **£85**

Plough Inn Rhosmean, SA19 6NP ☏01558 823431, ⓦ ploughrhosmaen.com. Just a mile north of town, this well-established pub/restaurant (see below) has a modern extension with large, comfortable rooms, gym and sauna. **£100**

EATING AND DRINKING

★Angel Hotel 62 Rhosmaen St, SA19 6EN ☏01558 822765, ⓦ angelbistro.co.uk. Convivial pub serving real ales and superb bar meals (mains £12–20), with a slightly more formal restaurant at the rear where you'll pay £10 for one course, £14 for two or £16 for three. Mon–Sat 11.30am–3pm & 6–11pm; kitchen Mon–Sat 11.30am–3pm & 6–9pm.

The Cawdor 70 Rhosmaen St, SA19 6EN ☏01558 823500, ⓦ thecawdor.com. Excellent semi-formal restaurant serving sumptuous two- or three-course lunches (£20/£25) and dinners (£25/£30), which might include grilled duck breast with sautéed celeriac and a red wine sauce. Good wine, guest ales and deep leather sofas also attract a broad clientele – the bar snacks and cream teas aren't bad, either. Restaurant Wed–Sat noon–2pm & 7–9pm, Sun noon–2pm & 7–8pm; bar snacks daily 11am–8pm.

Ginhaus 1 Market St, SA19 6AH ☏01558 823030, ⓦ ginhaus.co.uk. In addition to the best coffee, breads, cheese, charcuterie, antipasti and wines in town, this deli

also offers baguettes, wraps and flatbreads, quiches and pies, and specials such as chilli con carne to take away or eat at the tables in front. Oh, and they stock 250 gins, too. Mon–Thurs 8am–6pm, Fri & Sat 8am–10pm.

Heavenly 60 Rhosmaen St, SA19 6EN ☏01558 822800, ⓦ heavenlychoc.co.uk. Great organic ice cream and handmade chocolates that are, well, heavenly. Mon 1–5pm, Tues–Thurs 9.30am–5pm, Fri, Sat & school hols 9.30am–5.30pm, Sun 11.30am–4pm.

Plough Inn Rhosmaen, SA19 6NP ☏01558 823431, ⓦ ploughrhosmaen.com. Just a mile north of town, the best local ingredients are used in starters such as cheese terrine or chicken liver parfait (both around £7), mains such as lasagne, curry, root vegetable falafels or Welsh lamb (£13–20), steaks (£23–27) and desserts (£5–7). There's also a vegan menu (£11.50 for one course, £16.50 for two or £21.50 for three) and a two-/three-course roast Sun lunch (£18.20/£20.95). Pub & kitchen Mon–Fri 7am–9.30pm, Sat 8am–9.30pm, Sun 8am–9pm.

Llandovery and around

Twelve miles northeast of Llandeilo, the former cattle drovers' town of **LLANDOVERY** (Llanymddyfri) makes a natural base for exploring the Tywi Valley and the breathtaking countryside around Llyn Brianne and Dolaucothi to the north and west. The town has changed little for centuries, the main Broad Street lined with solid early nineteenth-century townhouses and older inns, much as it was when itinerant writer George Borrow visited in 1854, remembering it as the "pleasantest little town in which I have halted in the course of my wanderings". The market hall, built in 1840, now houses the **Dinefwr Crafts Centre** (daily 10am–5pm), with a café and stalls selling crafts such as wicker furniture, love spoons and raku pottery.

The castle ruins

South side of Broad St, SA20 0AR • Open access • Free

The scant ruins of a twelfth-century **castle**, atop a grassy mound, give fine views over Llandovery's huddled grey buildings and the Bran River. The real draw, though, is a ridiculously shiny stainless-steel **sculpture** of local lord Llywelyn ap Gruffydd Fychan, the "Welsh Braveheart", raised on the six-hundredth anniversary of his execution in the Market Square – in front of the English king Henry IV – for helping the rebel Owain Glyndŵr escape in 1401.

Local History Exhibition

Castle Hotel, Kings Rd, SA20 0AP • Easter–Sept daily 9.30am–5pm; Oct–Easter Mon–Sat 10.30am–12.30pm, Sun 2–4pm • Donation appreciated

The community-run **Local History Exhibition** contains interesting displays on the legend of the Lady of the Lake from Llyn y Fan Fach and her descendents, the Physicians of Myddfai (see p.146); sixteenth-century outlaw Twm Sion Cati, the "Welsh Robin Hood"; seventeenth-century vicar Rhys Prichard, author of *Canwyll y Cymry* ("The Welshmen's Candle"); and the cattle drovers and their Black Ox bank, now part of Lloyds TSB. The area's droving and sheep-farming tradition is celebrated in the entertaining Llandovery Sheep Festival (ⓦllandoverysheepfestival.co.uk) on the last weekend of September.

Talley

Nine miles west of Llandovery on the B4302, the crumbling twelfth-century tower of Wales' only Premonstratensian **abbey** (daily 10am–4pm; free; CADW; ⓦcadw.gov.wales/daysout/talleyabbey) dominates the village of **TALLEY**, also home to the serene lakeside **church of St Michael**, rebuilt in 1773 (largely from the stones of the abbey) and still including its original box pews. Talley's more recent claim to fame is as the home of Wales' famous **Tipi Valley**, a hippy encampment set up in the 1970s just south near Cwmdu (which has a brilliant community-run pub). Controversy has dogged the place ever since, but there now seems to be a stoic truce between the locals and the tepee dwellers.

Dolaucothi Gold Mines

Pumsaint, 10 miles northwest of Llandovery, SA19 8US • Daily: mid-March to June, Sept & Oct 11am–5pm; July & Aug 10am–6pm; underground tours (1hr) mid-March to Oct daily 11am–5pm • £7.70, tours free; NT • ☎ 01558 650171, ⓦnationaltrust.org.uk/dolaucothi-gold-mines

West of Llandovery the countryside is blissfully quiet, with a web of lanes that see little traffic. The principal route is the A482, which heads eight miles from Llanwrda, on the A40 between Llandeilo and Llandovery, to the **Dolaucothi Gold Mines**.

This is the only place in Britain where we can be sure the **Romans** mined gold, using remarkably advanced systems to extract the precious metal from the rock; an opencast mine and a few water channels can still be seen. The mine lay abandoned from around 350 AD until 1872, when new shafts were sunk and sporadically exploited until 1938. The site appears much as it was in the 1930s, and there are good displays, but you'll get a much better appreciation by taking a hard-hat **underground tour**.

Near the entrance is a stone used by the Romans for crushing gold ore; it's marked with indentations supposedly left by five saints who slept here one night. This event gives its name to the adjacent village of **Pumsaint** (Five Saints), where the National Trust owns the community-run *Dolaucothi Arms* **pub** and B&B.

Gwenffrwd-Dinas Nature Reserve

Eleven miles north of Llandovery, SA20 0PG • Open access • Free

Four miles beyond the village of Rhandirmwyn, at the Ystradffin chapel, there's a car park for the RSPB's **Gwenffrwd-Dinas Nature Reserve**, from where a spectacular trail loops through the gorge and ancient woodland, home to woodpeckers, nuthatches, sandpipers, dippers, redstarts and pipits. A short **side-trail** leads up to the reputed hideout cave of Twm Sion Cati (see above)

Llyn Brianne

Twelve miles north of Llandovery, SA20 0PG

The **Llyn Brianne** reservoir, built in the 1970s to supply Swansea, fits well into the region's hilly contours and offers peaceful shoreline walks and a cycling loop. The land to the north is remote and spectacular, with walks following the Tywi Valley into the Elenydd hills and to the *Elenydd Wilderness Hostels* in Dolgoch (see p.225).

ARRIVAL AND INFORMATION

By train Llandovery's train station is on the A40 just west of town.

Destinations Llandeilo (5 daily; 20min); Llandrindod Wells (4 daily; 1hr); Llanelli (5 daily; 1hr 10min); Shrewsbury (4 daily; 2hr 30min); Swansea (5 daily; 1hr 30min).

By bus Buses leave from the car park by the castle, also calling at the train station.

Destinations Brecon (3 daily; 40min); Carmarthen (8 daily; 1hr 20min); Dolaucothi (6 weekly; 25min); Lampeter (8

LLANDOVERY AND AROUND

weekly; 45min); Llandeilo (8 daily; 40min).

Tourist information The joint tourist office and Brecon Beacons National Park visitor centre, at the central car park off Kings Rd, is well stocked with leaflets on local walks and natural history, and has an interpretive centre on the Black Mountain (Easter–Oct daily 10am–1pm & 1.45–4pm, high season to 5pm; ☎ 01550 720693, ✉ llandovery.ic @breconbeacons.org).

ACCOMMODATION

HOTELS AND GUESTHOUSES

Cwmgwyn Farm Llangadog Rd (A4069), 2 miles southwest, SA20 0EQ ☎ 01550 720410, ✉ cwmgwyn -holidays.co.uk. Charming farmhouse B&B with spacious rooms, tasty breakfasts and a wood-beamed lounge complete with inglenook fireplace. **£70**

Cynyll Farm Off the A4069, 5 miles southwest, SA19 9BB ☎ 01550 777316, ✉ cynyllfarm.co.uk. Great-value, long-standing B&B in a seventeenth-century farmhouse and nearby barn and bungalow, just northeast of Llangadog, where there are some great pubs. **£62**

The Drovers 9 Market Square, SA20 0AB ☎ 01550 721115, ✉ droversllandovery.co.uk. Six elegantly individual rooms and a huge lounge with books and board games, in an eighteenth-century townhouse; very welcoming owners serve superb locally sourced breakfasts. **£78**

Henllys Estate 2 miles northwest, SA20 0EW ☎ 01550 721332, ✉ henllysestate.co.uk. The best value of the area's rural B&Bs, with lovely oak-floored en-suite bedrooms, in converted barns, with digital TVs and good breakfasts. There's also access to their woodland reserve. **£75**

New White Lion 43 Stone St, SA20 0BZ ☎ 01550 720685, ✉ newwhitelion.co.uk. An understated exterior hides

Llandovery's finest accommodation, combining modern style and selected antiques, plus an honesty bar featuring speciality gins. Excellent breakfasts and dinners available. **£120**

Royal Oak Inn Rhandirmwyn, 7 miles north, SA20 0NY ☎ 01550 760201, ✉ theroyaloakinn.co.uk. Tucked away on quiet lanes, this popular pub's five rooms make a perfect base for walking, mountain-biking or just enjoying rural peace. **£78**

HOSTEL AND CAMPSITES

Erwlon 1 mile east, off the A40, SA20 0JU ☎ 01550 720332, ✉ erwlon.co.uk. The nearest campsite to town (300yd from a supermarket), with caravan sites and camping. Freezer space available plus wi-fi across the site. **£14**

Gellifechan 7 miles north, 2 miles beyond Rhandirmwyn, SA20 0PF ☎ 01550 760397. A basic tap-in-a-field and portaloo campsite, but in an idyllic dark-skies site by the Iron Bridge (1913) and associated *Towy Bridge Inn*. **£10**

The Level Crossing A40, opposite the station, SA20 0BE ☎ 01550 721155, ✉ thelevelcrossingllandovery-uk.co .uk. An independent hostel with dorm beds, en-suite doubles and family rooms, a bar-bistro with pizza and tapas on Fri nights, and occasional live music. Dorms **£19**, doubles **£75**

EATING AND DRINKING

Castle Hotel Kings Rd, SA20 0AP ☎ 01550 720343, ✉ castle-hotel-llandovery.co.uk. The town's leading hotel has been given a cool makeover and is now also its classiest place to eat. There are plenty of leather sofas where you can enjoy coffee, cakes and sandwiches, plus bar areas with open fires and a more formal restaurant. The menu covers familiar favourites, but the daily specials (starters £5.50–6.50, mains £14–17) might include vegetable tagine, pasta and wild mushroom bake or various fish dishes such as seared fillets of John Dory. Restaurant Mon–Thurs noon–3pm & 6–9.30pm, Fri & Sat noon–3pm & 6–10pm, Sun noon–3pm & 6–8.30pm; café daily 11am–6pm.

Indian Lounge 34 High St, SA20 0PU ☎ 01550 720022. Great curry restaurant with a standard selection of north Indian curries plus set meals (from £17 for two). Daily noon–2.30pm & 5.30–11pm.

King's Head Inn 1 Market Square, SA20 0AB ☎ 01550

720393, ✉ kingsheadllandovery.co.uk. Come to this former drovers' inn for traditional bar meals (£6–10), ox-cheek Wellington (£13.50), Greek lamb and orzo (£15) or various vegetarian options. Daily 10am–11pm; kitchen Mon–Sat noon–2.30pm & 6–9.30pm, Sun noon–2.30pm & 6–8.30pm.

The Old Printing Office 1 Broad St, SA20 0AR ☎ 01550 720690. In a covered courtyard at the rear of a gift shop (also dealing in women's clothes, picture framing and dry cleaning), this friendly little café serves light lunches (soup, sandwiches, sweetcorn fritters), excellent tea and coffee and home-made cakes and crumpets. Mon–Sat 9am–5.30pm.

Royal Oak Inn Rhandirmwyn, 7 miles north, SA20 0NY ☎ 01550 760201, ✉ theroyaloakinn.co.uk. This country pub is well worth the trip for the beer – it's a regular winner of CAMRA's Carmarthenshire pub of the year award

– and for the imaginative menu, ranging from laverbread and potato cake (£4) or cawl (£7.50) via veggie pasta or Welsh beef burger (both around £9) to harissa- and lime-baked salmon (£12.50). Tues–Sat noon–2pm & 6–11pm, Sun noon–2pm & 7–10pm; kitchen Tues–Sat noon–2pm & 6.30–9pm, Sun noon–2pm & 7–9pm.

Southern Carmarthenshire

Frequently overlooked in the stampede towards the Pembrokeshire resorts, **southern Carmarthenshire** is a quiet part of the world, its coastline broken by the triple estuary of the Tywi, Taf and Gwendraeth rivers. **Llansteffan** huddles below its ruined castle alongside the Tywi, while the Taf estuary is home to lovely **Laugharne** – far more than simply a place of pilgrimage for Dylan Thomas lovers.

Llansteffan

Pretty **LLANSTEFFAN**, on the Tywi estuary ten miles southeast of Carmarthen, is overshadowed by a dramatic ruined **castle** (unrestricted access; free). This prime example of Norman fortifications was built between the eleventh and thirteenth centuries, on the site of an Iron Age fort. The entrance used today is not the original gatehouse, which was converted into living quarters in the fourteenth century. In both gatehouses, however, the portcullis and murder holes can still be seen. Atop the towers, it's easy to appreciate the site's defensive position, with far-reaching **views** in all directions. Returning from the castle to where the path doubles back to the right near a house, continue ahead (west) for half a mile then left down the lane towards the **beach**. The door in the wall on the right conceals **St Anthony's Well** (Bwthyn Sant Antwn), which can supposedly heal lovesickness. At anything but high tide you can return via the beach.

ARRIVAL AND DEPARTURE   LLANSTEFFAN

There are regular **buses** between Llansteffan and Carmarthen (Mon–Sat 6 daily; 20min).

ACCOMMODATION AND EATING

Inn At The Sticks High St, SA33 5JG ☎ 01267 2410566, ⓦ innatthesticks-llansteffan.com. At the village's central junction, this authentic and friendly free house (with beer garden) serves excellent food at weekends, presenting the best of local produce in a bright, modern way. There are also five rooms, decorated in a warm, contemporary style. Tues 4–11pm, Wed & Thurs noon–11pm, Fri & Sat noon–midnight, Sun noon–11pm; kitchen Thurs–Sat noon–2.30pm & 6.30–9pm, Sun noon–2.30pm. **£90**

Mansion House Hotel Pantyrathro, 2 miles north, SA33 5AJ ☎ 01267 241515, ⓦ mansionhousellansteffan .co.uk. Set in five acres of garden overlooking the estuary, with spacious, comfortable rooms and a fine restaurant serving à la carte meals or one-/two-/three-course menus (£13/£15/£17) that might list thick-cut beef with curly kale, a couple of fish dishes or black garlic risotto. The Sun lunch menu has similar options, as well as one- to three-course roasts (£14.50/£17.50/£20.50) and platters (£30 for two/£60 for four). Mid-Feb to Oct Mon–Sat noon–2.15pm & 6–8.45pm, Sun noon–2.30pm & (guests only) 6–8.45pm; Nov to mid-Feb Tues–Sat noon–2.15pm & 6–8.45pm, Sun noon–2.30pm. **£114**

Pant-yr-Athro International Hostel 2 miles towards Carmarthen, SA33 5AJ ☎ 01267 241014, ⓦ llansteffan .com/pantyrathro-international-hostel. Slightly poky hostel-style accommodation plus one double room, with a bar serving Mexican food. The adjoining hotel also serves food. Dorms **£17**, double **£34**

The Village Store High St, SA33 5JY ☎ 01267 241367. Behind the post office shop and deli is this offbeat little restaurant serving breakfasts, light lunches (and a full Sun lunch), sandwiches, coffee and home-baked cakes; they also do themed evenings, such as tapas or Chinese food. April–Oct Mon, Tues, Thurs & Fri 8.30am–4.30pm, Wed 8.30am–1pm, Sat 8.30am–2pm, Sun 9am–noon; Nov–March Mon, Tues, Thurs & Fri 8.30am–2.30pm, Wed & Sat 8.30am–1pm, Sun 9am–noon.

★**Yr Hen Dafarn** High St, SA33 5JY ☎ 01267 241656. This superb restaurant is a real labour of love, with a seasonal (handwritten) menu specializing in fish and game (and malt whisky). Portions are large, with mains usually costing about £15. It's open just two evenings a week and booking is essential. Fri & Sat eve; call for hours.

Laugharne

When quiet, the village of **LAUGHARNE** (Talacharn) is a delightful spot, with a ragged **castle** looming over the reeds and tidal flats and narrow lanes snuggling in behind. However, it has increasingly been taken over by the legend of **Dylan Thomas**, the nearest Wales has to a national poet, making it hard to value the place for its own sake.

From The Strand, beneath the castle, you can follow **Dylan's Birthday Walk** south around the shoulder of St John's Hill, retracing the route he took on his 30th birthday (a mile each way); he described it in *Poem in October* and quotations from the poem are inscribed on benches along the way.

2

Dylan Thomas Boathouse

Dylan's Walk, SA33 4SD • Daily: April–Sept 10am–5pm; Oct–March 10.30am–3pm • £4.20 • ☎ 01994 427420, ⓦ dylanthomasboathouse.com

Down an exceedingly narrow lane (no cars) beside the estuary stands the **Dylan Thomas Boathouse**, the simple home of Thomas, his wife Caitlin and their three children from 1949 until his death in 1953. It's an enchanting museum, offering a feeling of inspirational peace above the ever-changing water. In the bedrooms upstairs you can see a video on Thomas' life and a selection of local artists' views of the estuary and the village. Downstairs, the parlour has been preserved intact, with the rich tones of the man himself reading his work via a period wireless set. A small tearoom and outdoor terrace overlook the water.

Back along the lane, it's possible to peer into the **writing shed**, a green garage where Thomas wrote: a wood-burning stove, curling photographs of literary heroes, a pen collection and numerous scrunched-up balls of paper under the cheap desk suggest that he's just popped out for a pint.

St Martin's church

Church St, SA33 4 QP • Usually open

Thomas is buried with Caitlin, who died in 1994, in the graveyard of **St Martin's church** at the northern end of the village, marked by simple white crosses. Inside the church door is a painting by Benjamin West (the Anglo-American second president of the Royal Academy), plus a tenth-century Celtic cross in the south transept.

Tin Shed Experience

Clifton St, SA33 4QG • May–Oct Wed–Fri 10am–5.30pm; Nov–April by appointment • £3 • ☎ 01994 106157, ⓦ tinshedexperience.co.uk

Just north of the village centre (note the doorways of the fine Georgian townhouses), the **Tin Shed Experience** is literally a tin garage housing mementos of the 1940s and World War II; it's a key venue for **The Laugharne Weekend** (ⓦ thelaugharneweekend.com), a popular and relaxed arts festival in early April that atracts big names from John Cooper Clarke to Irvine Welsh.

Laugharne Castle

Wogan St, SA33 4SA • April–Oct daily 10am–5pm • £4; CADW • ☎ 01994 427906, ⓦ cadw.gov.wales/daysout/laugharnecastle

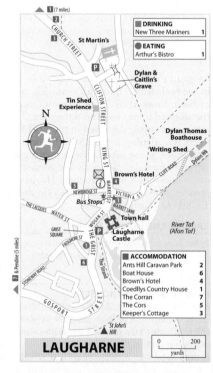

LAUGHARNE

■ DRINKING
New Three Mariners 1

● EATING
Arthur's Bistro 1

■ ACCOMMODATION
Ants Hill Caravan Park 2
Boat House 6
Brown's Hotel 4
Coedllys Country House 1
The Corran 7
The Cors 5
Keeper's Cottage 3

0 — 200 yards

2

DYLAN THOMAS

Dylan Thomas (1914–53), born into a snugly middle-class family in Swansea, was the quintessential Celt – fiery, verbose, richly talented and habitually drunk. His first glimmers of literary talent came when he worked as a cub reporter on the *South Wales Evening Post* in Swansea; some of the most popular tales in his *Portrait of the Artist as a Young Dog* were inspired by his newspaper days.

Rejecting Swansea's provincialism, Thomas arrived in London as a broke 20-year-old in 1934, weeks before the appearance of his first volume of **poetry**. Another soon followed, cementing the engaging young Welshman's reputation. Married in 1937, he and his wife Caitlin returned to Wales, settling in the backwater of Laugharne before moving to New Quay in Cardiganshire for some of World War II. **Short stories** – crackling with rich and melancholy humour – tumbled out as swiftly as poems, widening his base of admirers, although they remained relatively few until well after his death. Despite his evident hedonism, spending many days boozing in *Brown's Hotel*, Thomas was a disciplined writer, honing some of the twentieth century's most instantly recognizable poetry. Perhaps better than anyone, he wrote in an identifiably Celtic, rhythmic wallow. Although Thomas knew little Welsh – he grew up when the native language was stridently discouraged – his writing is definitively Welsh in its cadence and bold use of language.

Thomas, especially in public, liked to adopt the persona of an archetypal stage Welshman: sonorously loquacious, romantic and fond of a stiff tipple. This role was particularly popular in the **United States**, where he made lucrative lecture tours, and where he died in 1953. His death was attributed to "a massive insult to the brain" (spurred by numerous whiskies), but it's possible he was a victim of pneumonia or diabetes and incompetent doctors. Just one month earlier, he had put the finishing touches to what many regard as his masterpiece: the "play for voices" **Under Milk Wood**. Describing the dreams, thoughts and lives of a Welsh seaside community over 24 hours, the play has never dipped out of fashion and has lured Wales' greatest stars, including Richard Burton, Anthony Hopkins and Michael Sheen, to the narrator's role. The small town of Llareggub (spelt Llaregyb by the BBC, which wouldn't allow the use of the expression "bugger all" backwards) is loosely based on Laugharne and New Quay, with a vast dose of Thomas' own imagination.

Laugharne's main street courses down to the imposing ruins of **Laugharne Castle**. Built in the twelfth and thirteenth centuries, most of the original buildings were obliterated in Tudor times when Sir John Perrot (possibly the illegitimate son of Henry VIII) transformed it into a splendid mansion. The "castle brown as owls" (as Dylan Thomas put it) was largely destroyed in the Civil War. The mix of medieval might and Tudor finery is intriguing, especially in the **Inner Ward**, dominated by two towers, the domed roof of one giving sublime views over the huddled town. This is now surrounded by an attractive formal garden with fine mature trees; a gazebo contains an explanatory panel on another Welsh writer, Richard Hughes, best known for his novel *A High Wind in Jamaica*, who rented the adjoining Castle House from 1934 to 1942 and first brought Thomas to Laugharne.

ARRIVAL AND INFORMATION   LAUGHARNE

By bus Buses stop on Market St in Laugharne (Mon–Sat 5 daily; 30min) on their run from Carmarthen to Pendine.

Tourist office At Corran Books, opposite *Brown's Hotel* on King St (April–Oct Mon–Sat 10am–5pm; ☏ 01994 427444).

ACCOMMODATION

HOTELS AND GUESTHOUSES

Boat House 1 Gosport St, SA33 4SY ☏ 01994 426938, ⓦ theboathousebnb.co.uk. Stylish, comfortable four-room B&B, full of local art, and right in the centre. Great breakfasts might include vanilla waffles or smoked salmon. **£85**

Brown's Hotel King St, SA33 4RY ☏ 01994 427688,

ⓦ browns.wales. Dylan's old boozing hole, built in 1752, is now a "bar-with-rooms" – and the "genuine" Dylan Thomas dartboard has been reinstated. Rooms are in a retro 1950s style, but with modern gadgets. There's a good breakfast and a basic menu for lunch and dinner, with a soup of the day (£6.50), toasties, pizzas and curries (£8–9). Daily

11am–11pm; kitchen noon–3pm & 6–8.30pm. £95

★**Coedllys Country House** Llangynin, 7 miles north, SA33 4JY ☎01994 231455, ⓦcoedllyscountryhouse .co.uk. Wonderful, thoughtfully run Georgian farmhouse with three rooms, each with antique furniture, classy bedding and a comfy sofa. Visit their animal sanctuary and then take afternoon tea, with home-made Welsh cakes. £90

The Corran East Marsh, SA33 4RS ☎01994 427417, ⓦthecorran.com. This isolated luxury resort, with a lovely skylit restaurant and a spa, based around a sixteenth-century core, has recently been extended, with twenty more rooms. £175

The Cors Newbridge Rd, SA33 4SH ☎01994 427219, ⓦthecors.co.uk. This small, gracious country house was long known as one of the classiest restaurants around;

now, however, they offer simpler brasserie-style food and tapas for B&B guests (by arrangement), private parties and special events. The three comfortable rooms are newly refurbished, and there's an eclectic art collection as well as lovely gardens. £90

Keeper's Cottage Just north of town, A4066, SA33 4QN ☎01994 427404, ⓦkeepers-cottage.com. Friendly B&B with three good-sized rooms and a full breakfast featuring scrambled eggs with smoked salmon. £85

CAMPSITE

Ants Hill Caravan Park A4066 1 mile north, SA33 4QN ☎01944 427355, ⓦantshill.co.uk. The closest camping and caravan park to town, with laundry and games rooms and a swimming pool. Closed Nov–Feb. £20

EATING

Arthur's Bistro 6 Grist Square, SA33 4SS ☎01994 427422. Named after the owner's father, painter Arthur Lewis, whose land- and seascapes are on sale, this friendly café serves breakfasts (until 11.30am) then soups,

sandwiches, rarebit, pizza, fish and chips. Four evenings a week there's a choice of antipasti followed by fairly standard mains (£8–14). Mon & Wed 10am–3pm, Thurs–Sun 10am–3pm & 6.30–9pm.

DRINKING

New Three Mariners High St, SA33 4SE ☎01994 427426, ⓦnewthreemarinersinn.co.uk. Cheery pub

that offers the best drinking in town, as well as bar meals and pizzas. Mon–Fri 3–11pm, Sat & Sun noon–11pm.

Narberth and the Landsker Borderlands

As you head west into Pembrokeshire, the first town of any significance is **Narberth**, a cheerful little place with a burgeoning reputation for its upmarket shopping. It's also the "capital" of the **Landsker Borderlands**, a quiet, charming region dotted with beautiful but little-visited villages. *Landsker* is a Norse word meaning "frontier", referring to the division between Cymric north Pembrokeshire and the anglicized south. The division goes back to the Norman colonization of the south of the county, though the name has only been used since the 1930s.

Narberth

According to *The Mabinogion*, a collection of ancient Celtic folk tales and legends, **NARBERTH** (Arberth) was the court of Pwyll, and its **castle** was probably home to the Welsh princes. Today, though, it has a growing reputation as Pembrokeshire's prime boutique **shopping** destination, with a dozen or so delis, galleries and clothing and homeware shops along High Street, and a lively farmer's market on Thursday afternoons in the Queen's Hall (see p.157). You'll certainly notice the curious, spiky **town hall**, midway down High Street, built in the 1830s with a clock tower added in 1881, and now housing a gift shop. Outside, a plaque marks the cell where the leaders of the Rebecca Riots (see p.230) were imprisoned.

Narberth Museum

Church St, SA67 7BH • May–Oct Tues–Sat 10am–5pm, plus spring and summer public hols; Nov–April Wed–Sat 10am–5pm • £3.50 • ☎ 01834 860500, ⓦ narberthmuseum.co.uk

Water Street, with views to the castle ruins, leads down from the town hall to Church Street, where you'll find the fine **Narberth Museum**. It's housed in the former Bonded

2

LITTLE ENGLAND BEYOND WALES

Ever since the Normans stormed their way through Wales, securing their rule with castles, Pembrokeshire has been effectively divided. But its colonization began even earlier, when seaborne Viking raiders seized the best land – the sandy southern coast and the fertile pasture of the Daugleddau estuary – and the Normans only continued an established practice by intermingling with the Vikings (to produce a very English racial mix) and restricting the Celtic Britons (the Welsh) to the northern part of the country.

This racial divide is still evident, delineated by what has become known as the **Landsker Line**, a vestigial boundary through the heart of Pembrokeshire. Along the line are some sixteen castles or castle mounds (from Amroth to Roch, via Narberth and Haverfordwest), and village names on either side are either demonstrably Welsh or anglicized. The area south of the line, dubbed "**Little England Beyond Wales**", has long appealed to English migrants and tourists, while the north tends to attract Celts and other Europeans. Whereas the Tenby and Pembroke area has inclined towards the most Unionist of UK parties, the Conservatives (who hold very little sway in the rest of southern Wales), the north dallies between the old Liberal tradition and modern Welsh nationalism in the shape of Plaid Cymru.

Stores, where whisky, brandy, port and sherry were diluted and bottled. Upstairs, displays include house interiors, items from old shops and businesses – especially brewing and bottling – as well as nineteenth- and twentieth-century fans, costumes and military uniforms, and a geared penny-farthing bicycle, one of just six in the world.

ARRIVAL AND GETTING AROUND   NARBERTH

By train The train station is on the edge of the town, a mile east from High St; bus #381 (every hour or so; 4min) will take you to the centre.
Destinations Carmarthen (every 2hr; 30min); Pembroke (every 2hr; 45min); Swansea (every 2hr; 1hr 25min); Tenby (every 2hr; 30min).
By bus Buses stop at the top of High St.
Destinations Cardigan (3 daily; 1hr); Carmarthen (3 daily;

40min); Haverfordwest (hourly; 20min); Tenby (hourly; 45min).
Bike rental Pembrokeshire Bikes, 1 Rushacre Enterprise Park, Redstone Rd, 0.5 mile north on the B4313 (Mon–Fri 9am–5.30pm; ☎01834 682755, ⓦpembrokeshirebikes .co.uk). Hybrid bikes can be rented from £15/day, here or in Croesgoch (on the A487 south of Porthgain), or they can deliver, by arrangement.

ACCOMMODATION

Canaston Oaks A4075, just off the A40, SA67 8DE ☎01437 541254, ⓦcanastonoaks.co.uk. A luxury B&B in converted farm buildings, featuring beautifully furnished rooms (all different) with iPod docks, and a fabulous breakfast. **£95**
The Grove Molleston, 2 miles southwest, SA67 8BX ☎01834 860915, ⓦthegrove-narberth.co.uk. Derelict in 2007, this Georgian mansion has been restored as one of Wales' finest country-house restaurants-with-rooms.

Rooms (and bathrooms) are spacious and plushly furnished, and the Modern British food (see below) is great. **£175**
Plas Hyfryd Country Hotel Moorfield Rd, SA67 7AB ☎01834 869006, ⓦplashyfrydhotel.com. Comfortable hotel at the top of town, in a former rectory with fourteen rooms (including family and executive suites), bar and restaurant, with terrace dining. **£90**

EATING AND DRINKING

The Angel 43 High St, SA67 7AS ☎01834 860579, ⓦtheangelnarberth.co.uk. The best spot in town for pub food such as all-day breakfasts (£5.25) or cod and chips (£9); there's also a beer garden. Daily 11am–11pm; kitchen 11am–9pm.
The Grove Molleston, 2 miles southwest, SA67 8BX ☎01834 860915, ⓦthegrove-narberth.co.uk. The restaurant at this country-house hotel (see above) offers superb Modern British choices for vegetarians and carnivores. Dinner £64 for three courses, £94 for eight, with

a wine flight at £48. Daily noon–2.30pm & 6–9.30pm.
Jabajak Banc y Llain, Llanboidy Rd, 3 miles north of Whitland, SA34 0ED ☎01994 448786, ⓦjabajak.co.uk. Bare-board and rock-walled restaurant-with-rooms where the food is local, seasonal and often foraged (edible flowers are a feature) – pan-fried scallops (£9) might be followed by Welsh lamb with an orange, port and red berry sauce (£24). The wine list, featuring their own white wine, is very good. Advance reservations only. Mon–Sat from 6.30pm.
Kirkland Arms St James St, SA67 7BU ☎01834

860423. Cheery memorabilia-filled pub at the top of town. It's great for a beer or a game of pool; there's also basic food. Mon–Sat 11am–midnight, Sun noon–10.30pm.

Plum Vanilla 2 St James St, SA67 7DB ☏ 01834 862762, ⊚ plumvanilla.com. Very popular new boho-styled café and deli, serving home-made organic food with lots of veggie choices; breakfast is served until 11.30am, after which you'll find soup of the day, ciabattas, jacket potatoes, salads (falafel, perhaps, or halloumi and beetroot) and hot dishes such as meat or veg tagines. Mon–Sat 9am–5pm.

Sospan Fach 44 High St, SA6 7AS ☏ 01834 862767. Modern café-restaurant in the Queen's Hall, serving tasty breakfasts, snacks, soups, rarebit, salads, mussels (£9.50) and a Mediterranean platter (£9). Mon & Wed 9.30am–5pm, Tues & Thurs 11.30am–5pm, Fri & Sat 9.30am–8pm.

★ **Ultracomida** 7 High St, SA76 7AR ☏ 01834 861491, ⊚ ultracomida.co.uk. Perfect for lunch, this little slice of Spain tucked in behind a fabulous deli has hams hanging from the ceiling, large shared tables and a menu featuring delicious authentic tapas or larger *raciones* (£4–7), as well as salads and sandwiches, all to be washed down with Iberian wines or sherries. Mon–Sat: deli, drinks & takeaways 10am–6pm; restaurant 10am–5pm.

ENTERTAINMENT

The Queen's Hall 44 High St, SA67 7AS ☏ 01834 861212, ⊚ thequeenshall.org.uk. One of Pembrokeshire's best venues, hosting concerts, comedy and theatre plus art exhibitions in the Oriel Q gallery. Wed–Sat 10am–5pm.

The Eastern Cleddau

West of Narberth, quiet lanes wind down towards the muddy banks of the Cleddau estuary. The **Eastern Cleddau** is a charming landscape, dotted with little settlements and great, if occasionally overgrown, walking following the waymarked **Knight's Way** and **Landsker Borderlands Trail**.

Lawrenny

Pretty **LAWRENNY** village, eight miles southwest of Narberth, is dominated by the magnificent twelfth-century **St Caradoc's church**. Half a mile away, the Cresswell and Carew rivers meet at **Lawrenny Quay** from where a lovely **loop walk** (3 miles; 1–2hr; 200ft ascent) weaves through the ancient sessile oaks of Lawrenny Wood, giving fine views of privately owned **Benton Castle** across the estuary. The waymarked Landsker Borderlands Trail and South of the Landsker Trail also pass through Lawrenny Quay.

ACCOMMODATION AND EATING LAWRENNY

Knowles Farm 1 mile north, SA68 0PX ☏ 01834 891221, ⊚ knowlesfarmhouse.com. A great farmhouse B&B, serving organic breakfasts and handy for some wonderful walks (there's even a slipway that you can use if you bring your own boat). £78

Lawrenny Village Hostel Near the church, SA68 0PW ☏ 01646 651270, ⊚ lawrennyhostel.com. A community-owned hostel in a Victorian schoolhouse, with dorms and family rooms plus a kitchen and lounge with books and games. Dorms £16, family rooms £36

Quayside Lawrenny Quay, SA68 0PR ☏ 01646 651574, ⊚ quaysidelawrenny.co.uk. The staff here really care about their food: super-fresh baguettes compete with mushroom tart, smoked mackerel or crab sandwiches (£8), served either in the airy pine interior or outside, with a view of the passing yachts. Easter–Sept Tues–Sun 11am–5pm.

Carew

The picturesque village of **CAREW** (Caeriw), on the banks of the Cleddau estuary four miles east of Pembroke, is famed for its 13ft **Celtic cross**, by the road just south of the river crossing. Erected as a memorial to Maredydd, ruler of Deheubarth, who died in 1035, the gracefully tapering shaft is covered in fine tracery of ancient Welsh designs.

Carew Castle and Tidal Mill

In the centre of the village, SA70 8SL • Castle & mill April–Oct daily 10am–5pm; Nov–March castle only Mon–Fri 11am–3pm • April–Oct £5.50; Nov–March £4 • ⊚ carewcastle.com

An Elizabethan walled garden houses the ticket office for **Carew Castle and Tidal Mill**. Here you can pick up an explanatory leaflet and audio guide (free) for the roofless castle, a hybrid built from defensive necessity (c.1100) and Elizabethan whimsy. It offers an excellent example of the organic nature by which castles grew, with a Norman tower (probably the original gatehouse) and thirteenth-century battlements, and a Tudor gatehouse and Elizabethan mansion grafted onto them.

2

Carew Tidal Mill

A few hundred yards west of the castle is the **Carew Tidal Mill**, probably established in the sixteenth century, rebuilt around 1800 and last used in 1937. The impressive exterior of the only restored tidal mill in Wales belies the pedestrian exhibitions and moderately interesting audiovisual displays of the milling process inside.

ARRIVAL AND DEPARTURE   CAREW

Carew is served by **buses** from/to Tenby (9 daily; 30min) and Pembroke (4 daily; 10min).

ACCOMMODATION AND EATING

Carew Inn Opposite the castle, SA70 8SL ☎01646 651267, ⓦcarewinn.co.uk. A fine traditional inn for real ale and pub grub; the pleasant garden hosts a barbecue and live music on Thurs and Sun, with more music on alternate Sat. Daily 11am–11pm; kitchen Mon–Sat noon–2pm & 6–9pm, Sun noon–3pm & 6–9pm.

Cresswell House Cresswell Quay, SA68 0TE ☎01646 651435, ⓦcresswellhouse.co.uk. In an idyllic waterfront setting across the bridge from the pub, this large Georgian house has just two stylish rooms, with excellent breakfasts, and a self-catering cottage (sleeping four; weekend and week-long breaks available; from £40/night). **£90**

South Pembrokeshire coast

The southern zigzag of the **South Pembrokeshire coast** on either side of **Tenby** is a strange mix – caravan parks and Ministry of Defence shooting ranges above some spectacularly beautiful bays and gull-covered cliffs. For walkers, the coast is constantly beguiling, as it nips and tucks past some excellent, comparatively quiet beaches, many of which are also accessible by car.

Northeast of Tenby, **Saundersfoot** and **Amroth** have popular beaches, separated by cliffs topped by caravan parks. West of Tenby, worthwhile destinations include **Manorbier**, with its dramatic castle above a small bay, and charming **St Florence**. You can stroll along the beautiful sandy **Barafundle Bay** and past the **Bosherston lily ponds** at the National Trust's **Stackpole Estate**, then cross MOD land to the ancient **St Govan's chapel**, squeezed into a rock cleft above the crashing waves. The limestone sea arch known as the **Green Bridge of Wales** is the pick of the area's dramatic scenery, which gradually softens towards the village of **Angle**, facing the petrochemical installations across the harbour of Milford Haven.

Saundersfoot and around

At the Carmarthenshire county boundary, six miles northeast of Tenby, the Welsh Coast Path joins up with the long-established Pembrokeshire Coast Path (where the scallop markings change to acorns). From the tiny beachside village of Amroth to Tenby the cliffs are lined with caravan parks, although the Coast Path and cycle route pass below them from Wiseman's Bridge to Saundersfoot through former tramway tunnels. The only break is the picturesque harbour of **SAUNDERSFOOT**, built in the 1830s for the export of coal and anthracite. The industry has long since folded and a predictable clutch of cafés, tacky shops and boisterous pubs make the town a popular, good-natured place to hang out beside the wide yawn of sand.

Colby Woodland Garden

One mile inland from Amroth, SA67 8PP • Daily: mid-Feb to mid-Nov 10am–5pm; mid-Nov to mid-Feb 10am–3pm • £6.30; NT • ☎01834 811885, ⓦnationaltrust.org.uk/colby-woodland-garden

THE PEMBROKESHIRE COAST NATIONAL PARK AND COAST PATH

Of Britain's fifteen national parks, the **Pembrokeshire Coast National Park**, established in 1952, is the only one that's largely coastal, made up of a discontinuous set of patches of shoreline and inland scenery. Starting from the southeast, the first segment clings to the shore from Amroth through to the Milford Haven waterway, an area of sweeping limestone cliffs and fabulous beaches. The second (and much the quietest) part covers the pastoral Daugleddau estuary, plunging deep into Pembrokeshire's rural heart southeast of Haverfordwest. The third section includes the scenic cliffs and beaches of St Bride's Bay, a great chunk scooped out of Wales' westernmost land. Finally, beyond Fishguard to the north, the park boundary runs far inland to encompass the Mynydd Preseli, a barren but invigoratingly beautiful range of hills dotted with ancient relics.

Following almost every wriggle of the coast, the **Pembrokeshire Coast Path** winds 186 miles from Amroth in the southeast to its northernmost point at St Dogmael's near Cardigan; it's by far the most spectacular section of the Welsh Coast Path. Mostly it clings to the clifftops, overlooking seal-studded rocks, craggy islands, unexpected gashes of sand and shrieking clouds of sea birds. Only on the Castlemartin peninsula, occupied by army camps and firing ranges, does the path veer substantially inland; it also ducks briefly inland along the Milford Haven estuary, where the huge expanse of water lined by oil refineries provides one of the route's many surprises.

The Coast Path's most ruggedly **inspiring** segments are the stretch from the castle at Manorbier to the tiny cliff chapel at Bosherston along the southern shore; around the Marloes peninsula and St Davids Head, either side of St Bride's Bay; and the undulating contours, massive cliffs and tiny coves along the northern coast, either side of Fishguard. These offer miles of windswept walking among flashes of gorse and heather, with close-up views of thousands of sea birds. Basking seals frequent some of the more inaccessible beaches, particularly in autumn when their pups are born.

Spring is perhaps the finest season for walking: the crowds have yet to arrive and the clifftop flora is at its most vivid. The national park's excellent free newspaper *Coast to Coast*, detailing special walks, boat trips and other events, is published every spring and can be picked up from visitor centres across the area. The best **websites** are the park's general site Ⓦ pembrokeshirecoast .org.uk, and Ⓦ nt.pcnpa.org.uk, which has more practical trip-planning advice.

For people with walking difficulties, the *Easy Access Routes* booklet (£3) details flatter sections, many remodelled with gates rather than stiles.

2

The attractive **Colby Woodland Garden** is wedged into a wooded valley in an area that was extensively mined for anthracite and iron ore from the fourteenth century until 1949. Highlights include the sloping walled garden and gazebo and, in May and June, the explosion of colour in the numerous rhododendron bushes. Between April and October there are art and craft galleries and a useful tearoom. There are also marked woodland walks (and an MTB loop) leading to the coast and inland almost to the A40.

ARRIVAL AND INFORMATION

SAUNDERSFOOT

By train Saundersfoot is served by trains between Swansea and Pembroke Dock; the station is more than a mile northwest up The Ridgeway.

Destinations Carmarthen (every 2hr; 40min); Narberth (every 2hr; 12min); Pembroke (every 2hr; 35min); Swansea (every 2hr; 90min); Tenby (every 2hr; 8min).

By bus Buses from/to Tenby (roughly hourly; 15min) stop in the centre of the village.

Tourist office At the community centre, one block inland up Milford St (Easter–Oct Mon–Sat 10am–1pm & 2–4pm, Thurs & Fri 10am–1pm & 2–6pm; Ⓣ 01834 813672, Ⓦ visit-saundersfoot.com).

ACCOMMODATION AND EATING

Cliff House Wogan Terrace, SA69 8HA Ⓣ 01834 813931, Ⓦ cliffhousebbsaundersfoot.co.uk. A lovely former ship-owner's home, this B&B has great sea views from some rooms and the sitting-room balcony, plus excellent breakfasts. **£79**

coast Coppet Hall Beach, just north, SA69 9AJ Ⓣ 01834 810800, Ⓦ coastsaundersfoot.co.uk. This fresh and informal beachfront restaurant is one of the finest in Wales, especially for seafood. Starters (£11–16) might include crab, king scallops, slow-poached salmon or new potato veloute, while for a main (£18–23) you could choose lamb, red mullet fillet or white beetroot and dill risotto. There's a vegetarian menu, too, and a tasting menu (£65, plus £40 for a matching flight of wines). Easter, May bank hols/ half-term & July–Sept daily noon–2.30pm & 6.30–9pm; rest of year closed Mon & Tues.

Mulberry Brewery Terrace, SA69 9HG ☎01834 811313, ⓦmulberry-restaurant.co.uk. Near the harbour, this lively bistro serves fish, steak and good three-course menus (£17 lunch/£20 dinner), with specials such as shoulder of Preseli lamb, salmon fillet or Thai-style monkfish. There's a splendid Sun lunch, with tapas (£4–5) on weekday lunchtimes. Mon–Sat noon–2.30pm & 6–9pm, Sun noon–2.30pm (also Sun 6–9pm school hols & bank hols).

Old Chemist Inn The Strand, SA69 9ET ☎01834 813982, ⓦfacebook.com/TheOldChemistInn. A lively pub with a beer garden backing onto the beach, this serves a range of grills, burgers and vegetarian options; there is live music in the cellar bar at weekends. Daily 11am–

midnight; kitchen noon–9pm.

Royal Oak Inn Corner of High St and Wogan Terrace, SA69 9HA ☎01834 812546, ⓦtheroyaloaksaunders foot.co.uk. A homely, central free house for good beer and snacky food (sandwiches, toasties and jacket potatoes £5–6), plus burgers or pasta. Daily noon–11pm; kitchen Mon–Thurs 11am–3pm & 6–9pm, Fri & Sat noon–5pm & 5.30–9pm, Sun noon–5pm & 6–9pm.

St Brides Spa Hotel St Brides Hill, SA69 9NH ☎01834 812304, ⓦstbridesspahotel.com. High on the hill overlooking the beach, this is one of Pembrokeshire's finer hotels, with contemporary style, an elegant restaurant and a spa with an infinity hydrotherapy pool. Restaurant noon–9pm. **£160**

Wiseman's Bridge Inn 1.5 miles north, SA69 9AU ☎01834 813236, ⓦwisemansbridgeinn.co.uk. A thoroughly enjoyable beachside pub, good for a drink or a fairly standard pub meal, with friendly service. Daily 11am–11pm; kitchen noon–2.30pm & 6–9pm.

Tenby

Beguilingly old-fashioned **TENBY** (Dinbych-y-Pysgod), wedged on a promontory between two sweeping beaches fronting an island-studded seascape, is everything a seaside resort should be. Narrow streets wind downhill from the medieval centre to the harbour, past miniature gardens fashioned to catch the afternoon sun. Steps down the steeper slopes give magical views of the dockside arches, while rows of brightly painted houses and hotels are strung along the clifftops. Simply walking around the streets and along the beaches is a delight, but Tenby is best visited at quiet times such as May or late September – in busy months, you'll be fighting for space with hordes of fellow holiday-makers.

Tenby is also one of the major stopping-off points along the **Pembrokeshire Coast Path** (see box, p.159), providing walkers with a welcome urban interlude amid mile upon mile of undulating cliff scenery. A few miles offshore from Tenby, the monastic **Caldey Island** makes for an appealing day-trip.

Brief history

Tenby's pedigree is long. First mentioned in a ninth-century bardic poem, the settlement grew after the Normans erected a **castle** on the headland. The town was sacked by the Welsh three times in the twelfth and thirteenth centuries; the last time, in 1260, by Prince Llewelyn himself. In response, the castle was refortified and the stout town walls were built. Tenby prospered as a **port** between the fourteenth and sixteenth centuries, and although decline followed, the arrival of the railway in 1863 brought renewed prosperity as it became a fashionable **resort**. Now firmly middle-market, Tenby caters to both retirees and rumbustious fun-seekers – although it is trying to quell its popularity with hen and stag parties.

The old town walls

Tenby's old centre is triangular, with two sides meeting at the castle and the third following the remaining **town walls**, built in the late thirteenth century and massively strengthened in 1457 by Jasper Tudor, Earl of Pembroke and uncle of Henry VII. Tenby was further fortified in the 1580s, when it was seen as a likely target for the Spanish Armada. The only town gate still standing is the **Five Arches** (roughly halfway along the wall), a semicircular barbican with hidden lookouts and acute angles to surprise invaders, now busy with oblivious pedestrians. The wall continues south to the Esplanade, a line of snooty hotels facing out over South Beach.

St Mary's church

Between Tudor Square and St George's St, SA70 8AP • Usually open • Free

The town centre's focal point is the 152ft spire of the largely fifteenth-century **St Mary's church**. Its light triple-naved interior shows off the chancel's elaborate ceiling bosses, while fifteenth-century tombs attest to Tenby's mercantile tradition. On the church's western side runs Upper Frog Street, replete with craft shops and an arcaded indoor market.

Tudor Merchant's House

Quay Hill, SA70 7BX • 11am–5pm: Feb half-term & Aug daily; March, Nov & Dec Sat & Sun; April–Oct Wed–Mon • £5; NT • ☎ 01834 842279, ⓦ nationaltrust.org.uk/tudor-merchants-house

Quay Hill runs down towards the harbour past some of Tenby's oldest dwellings, including a **Tudor Merchant's House**, built in the late fifteenth century when Tenby was second only to Bristol as a west-coast port. The compact house with its Flemish-style chimneypieces is on three floors; you're welcome to sit on the reproduction Tudor chairs and benches. The herb garden at the back gives a good view of the huge Flemish chimney.

The harbour and Castle Hill

When it's not too crowded, the **harbour**, fringed by pastel-hued Georgian and Victorian houses, can look idyllic. Sheltered by the curving headland, it's ideal for an evening stroll; by day, it's the departure point for numerous excursion boats, especially the short trip to Caldey Island. Above it is the headland of **Castle Hill**, its grassy slopes rife with Victoriana in the form of huge beds of flowers (including an indigenous small daffodil in springtime), benches, a bandstand and a pompous memorial to Prince Albert – upstaging the ruins of the Norman **castle**, notable for the all-round view from

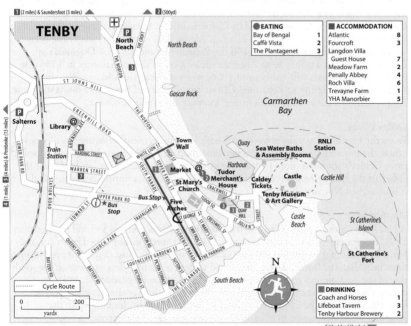

its windswept tower. On the north side of the headland, the modern RNLI **lifeboat station** (daily 8.30am–5.30pm; donations) has photos of wrecked ships, videos, a viewing gallery and a schedule of launch exercises, plus a souvenir shop.

Tenby Museum & Art Gallery

Castle Hill, SA70 7BP • April–Oct daily 10am–5pm; Nov–March Tues–Sat 10am–5pm • £5 • ☎ 01834 842809, ⓦ tenbymuseum.org.uk

The **Tenby Museum & Art Gallery** presents a broad history of the town and harbour since Precambrian times. The geology section includes ancient axes and a skull dating from c.1300 BC, there are books written in the 1550s by locally born mathematician Robert Recorde, the first to use the "equals" symbol, and a scale model shows Tenby in 1586, before it burst the town walls. The real attraction, though, is the **art collection**, featuring work by Tenby-born Augustus John and Nina Hamnet, as well as John Piper and Augustus' sister Gwen.

Sea Water Baths and Assembly Rooms

Returning to the harbour from Castle Hill, you'll pass the **Sea Water Baths and Assembly Rooms** on Harbour Square, built in 1806 and 1811 by Sir William Paxton. Having made money in India, and built Middleton Hall, now the National Botanic Garden of Wales (see p.145), Paxton then invested heavily in reviving Tenby as a bathing resort, leaving it set for Victorian prosperity even after the end of the Napoleonic Wars reopened access to the continental spas and resorts.

South Beach

Castle Hill offers great views over the quieter **South Beach**, where the sea recedes so far at low tide that tiny **St Catherine's Island** (no access) becomes fully beached. It's topped by the remains of the 1869 St Catherine's Fort, one of Palmerston's Follies (see box, p.164).

Caldey Island

Two miles offshore • Boats leave Tenby Harbour (or Castle Beach when the tide is out) every 20min (10am–5pm: Easter–Oct Mon–Fri plus Sat May–Sept; 20min each way; £12 return; ☎ 01834 844453, ⓦ caldey-island.co.uk); tickets sold at the kiosk at the harbour

Caldey Island (Ynys Pyr) was settled by Celtic monks in the sixth century, perhaps as an offshoot of St Illtud's monastery at Llantwit Major. This community may have been wiped out in Viking raids, but in 1136 the Benedictine monks of St Dogmael's at Cardigan founded a priory here. After the dissolution of the monasteries in 1536, the island changed hands willy-nilly until 1906, when it was again sold to a Benedictine order, and subsequently to Reformed Cistercians. The island has been a **monastic home** almost constantly ever since, with fifteen monks currently in residence.

Caldey Village

From the island's jetty a short woodland walk leads to its main settlement: a tiny post office, the popular tea gardens and a **perfume shop** selling the herbal fragrances distilled from Caldey's abundant flora by the monks. The narrow road to the left leads past the abbey to the heavily restored **chapel of St David**, whose most impressive feature is the round-arched Norman door.

The old priory

A lane leads south from the village to the **old priory**, abandoned in 1536 and restored after 1897. Its centrepiece is the twelfth-century **St Illtud's church**, distinguished by its curiously blunt (and leaning) steeple, and by the presence of one of the most significant pre-Norman finds in Wales. The **Ogham Stone**, discovered under the stained-glass window on the south side of the nave, bears a runic inscription from the sixth century (added to, in Latin, during the ninth). The church's rough sixth-century flooring consists largely of pebbles from the island's beaches. From here, the lane continues south, climbing up to the gleaming white lighthouse, built in 1828 – views from here are memorable.

2

TENBY FESTIVALS

The week-long **Tenby Arts Festival** (ⓦtenbyartsfest.co.uk) in late September is fairly highbrow, but has a rowdy and lively Fringe; the three-day **Tenby Blues Festival** (ⓦtenbyblues.co.uk), meanwhile, in mid-November is gaining in profile.

ARRIVAL AND GETTING AROUND   TENBY

By train The train station is just west of the town centre, at the bottom of Warren St.

Destinations Carmarthen (9 daily; 50min); Lamphey (9 daily; 20min); London (1 daily; 5hr); Narberth (9 daily; 20min); Pembroke (9 daily; 20min); Pembroke Dock (9 daily; 30min); Saundersfoot (9 daily; 10min); Swansea (8 daily; 1hr 45min); Whitland (9 daily; 30min).

By bus Local buses stop on South Parade at the top of Trafalgar Rd and on Upper Park Rd; National Express coaches call on Upper Park Rd.

Destinations Amroth (8 daily; 40min); Carew/Cresswell (4 daily; 40min); Carmarthen (1 daily; 1hr); Haverfordwest (hourly; 1hr); Manorbier (hourly; 20min); Narberth (hourly; 45min); Pembroke (hourly; 45min); Saundersfoot (every 30min; 15min).

By car Cars are banned in central Tenby between 11am and 5pm from mid-July to early Sept. Use the Salterns and North Beach car parks (both pay-and-display), to the west and north of the town centre respectively.

By taxi Tenby Taxis (☎01834 842371).

INFORMATION

Tourist office By the bus shelter on Upper Park Rd (June–Aug Mon–Fri 9am–5pm, Sat 10am–5pm, Sun 10am–4pm; Sept–May Mon–Fri 9am–1pm & 1.45–5pm, Sat 10am–1pm & 1.45–5pm; ☎01437 775603, ⓔtenby.tic@

pembrokeshire.gov.uk).

Internet Free access at the library on Greenhill Ave (Mon, Thurs & Fri 10am–5pm, Tues 10am–6pm, Sat 10am–12.30pm) and at *Caffè Vista* (see below).

ACCOMMODATION

HOTELS AND GUESTHOUSES

Atlantic The Esplanade, SA70 7DU ☎01834 842881, ⓦatlantic-hotel.uk.com. South Beach's best hotel, with fine rooms (some with sea views), the good *Salt Cellar* restaurant and a pool and spa. **£115**

Fourcroft North Beach, SA70 8AP ☎01834 842886, ⓦfourcroft-hotel.co.uk. Decent three-star hotel with forty rooms, sun terraces, an outdoor pool (April–Oct), spa pool and sauna all year, plus an adequate restaurant. **£110**

Langdon Villa Guest House 3 Warren St, SA70 7JU ☎01834 849467, ⓦlangdonguesthousetenby.co.uk. Handy for the station, this four-star B&B has a range of double and twin rooms and offers a hearty breakfast. **£70**

Penally Abbey 1 mile west, close to Penally station, SA70 7PY ☎01834 843033, ⓦpenally-abbey.com. Luxurious country-house hotel on the site of a sixth-century abbey, with great sea views. Standards are very high, but the atmosphere is relaxed and the food unpretentious. **£140**

Roch Villa 1 Harding Villas, SA70 7LL ☎01834 843096, ⓦrochvillabandb.com. Budget accommodation with three rooms with shared bathrooms and video or DVD

player. Limited parking, but it's near the train station. **£50**

YHA Manorbier Skrinkle Haven, 5 miles west, SA70 7TT ☎0345 371 9031, ⓦyha.org.uk/hostel/manorbier. Modern hostel in an old MOD building on the cliffs near the Manorbier bus route. Meals, private rooms and camping facilities available. Closed Nov–Feb. Dorms **£13**, doubles **£59**

CAMPSITES

Meadow Farm Northcliffe, less than a mile north, SA70 8AU ☎01834 844829, ⓦmeadowfarmtenby.co.uk. North of town on the Coast Path, this dog-free campsite in a grassy field has limited facilities but long views over the town towards Caldey Island – a great alternative to the family-fun-park-style places. Closed Nov–March. Per person **£9**

Trevayne Farm Monkstone, 2 miles from the A478 New Hedges roundabout, SA69 9DL ☎01834 813402, ⓦtrevaynefarm.co.uk. Family-oriented caravan and campsite with superb views over Saundersfoot and the sandy arc sweeping round to Amroth and Pendine. Closed Nov–March. **£16**

EATING

Bay of Bengal 1 Crackwell St, SA70 7HA ☎01834 843331, ⓦbayofbengaltenby.com. You get reliable food at this curry restaurant; there's no licence, so bring your own alcohol. Ask for a seat downstairs, for great bay views. Service can be variable. Cash only. Daily 5.30–11pm.

Caffè Vista 3 Crackwell St, SA70 7HA ☎01834 849636. Great little Greek-/Australian-run, licensed café with excellent panini, pies, espresso and cakes, plus a small list of hot dishes such as beef or butterbean stew. Good harbour views from the small terrace, and free wi-fi.

2

PALMERSTON'S FOLLIES

The coast of southern Britain, and particularly of south Pembrokeshire, is littered with the nineteenth-century coastal defences known as **Palmerston's Follies**. As prime minister in 1860, Lord Palmerston felt that Britain was ill prepared to withstand an attack by Napoleon III, newly equipped with iron-clad battleships. Britain's navy had barely been upgraded since Nelson's victory at Trafalgar half a century earlier, so a Royal Commission recommended building a series of forts to protect naval dockyards while the navy modernized.

Palmerston wholeheartedly backed the recommendation and had forts built right along the south coast of England and around Milford Haven and Pembroke. By the time they were completed in the 1880s, Anglo-French relations had improved, and the forts were never attacked. Arguably, the forts had been an effective deterrent, but the public saw them as expensive follies.

The best examples around Pembrokeshire are at Tenby, West Angle Bay, West Blockhouse Point and Milford Haven; others are mostly inaccessible to the public.

Summer school hols Mon–Wed & Sun 9am–5pm, Thurs–Sat 9am–10.30pm; rest of year daily 9am–5pm. ★**The Plantagenet** Quay Hill, SA70 7BX ☎01834 842350, ⊚plantagenettenby.co.uk. This cosy and enjoyable restaurant makes optimum use of local produce.

It's in one of Tenby's oldest houses – ask for a table inside the massive tenth-century Flemish chimney. Dinner mains go for £21–27 (vegetarian £16), but lunch is cheaper (£8–13). You could also just have a drink in the intimate bar. Daily noon–2.30pm & 5–10pm.

DRINKING

Coach and Horses Upper Frog St, SA70 7JD ☎01834 842704. Animated, wooden-beamed pub (said to be the oldest in Tenby) with good beer, well-prepared bar meals and a commendable menu of tasty Thai dishes. Daily noon–11pm; kitchen noon–3pm & 6–9pm.
Lifeboat Tavern St Julian's St, SA70 7AD ☎01834 844948. Popular and enjoyable pub, with a youthful clientele and family-friendly food such as steaks, fish and chips, and burgers; live music Tues and Sun. Daily

noon–midnight; kitchen Mon–Fri noon–9pm, Sat & Sun noon–7pm.
Tenby Harbour Brewery Sergeants Lane, SA70 7BU ☎01834 845797, ⊚harbwr.wales. In an eighteenth-century warehouse on an alley behind the Tudor Merchant's House, the brewery's taproom serves a wide range of Harbwr beers, from pale ale to stout, as well as food (sandwiches, salads and specials). Fri 4.30–10pm, Sat & Sun noon–10pm.

Manorbier and around

Proceeding west, the Coast Path passes Lydstep Beach, privately owned and lined with caravans; it's worth paying to park and explore the caves in craggy Lydstep Point, immediately south (some are only accessible at low tide, but the **Smugglers' Cave** is safe at all times). Then the path veers inland to avoid the artillery range on Old Castle Head, before reaching the quaint village of **MANORBIER** (Maenorbŷr; pronounced "manner-beer"). Giraldus Cambrensis, or "Gerald of Wales" (see box, p.376), was born in the castle here in 1146, which he later described as "excellently well defended by turrets and bulwarks, and ... situated on the summit of a hill extending on the western side towards the sea".

Manorbier Castle

Above the village, SA70 7SY • Feb & Oct half-terms & April–Sept daily 10am–4pm • £5.50 • ☎01834 870081, ⊚manorbiercastle.co.uk

Founded in the early twelfth century as a baronial residence and little changed since, the **Manorbier Castle** sits above the village and its beach on a hill of wild gorse. The Norman walls are very well preserved, ringing walled gardens and a grass courtyard in which the extensive remains of the castle's chapel and staterooms jostle for position with the nineteenth-century domestic residence. Views from the ramparts are wonderful, taking in the corrugated coastline, bushy dunes, deep-green fields and the village's smoking chimneys. There's a warren of dark passageways to explore, occasionally opening out into little cells populated by lacklustre wax figures, including Gerald himself.

Church of St James the Great
Church Lane, SA70 7SZ • Easter–Sept daily 9.30am–6pm

The lane below the castle leads to the Norman **church of St James the Great**, whose curious, elongated tower has been rendered with a "buttermilk limewash" to mimic how the whole church would apparently once have looked – a striking sight, but not universally popular.

The beaches
From the car park between church and castle, a path leads to Manorbier's shell-shaped **cove**. For more secluded bathing, follow the path on the left of the beach (as you face the sea) over the headland called the Priest's Nose, past a Neolithic cromlech (burial chamber) known as the **King's Quoit**, and round for just over half a mile to the steep steps down to often-deserted **Presipe Beach**. High tides can cover the whole beach, so check times. Alternatively, follow the Coast Path 2.5 miles right (west) to **Swanlake Bay**, known for its stunning rock pools and formations.

St Florence
The village is served by buses from/to Tenby (4 daily; 15min)

Three miles north of Manorbier is the delightful little village of **ST FLORENCE**, whose whitewashed stone cottages, many with medieval "Flemish" chimneystacks, huddle around tiny lanes. St Florence was a port until the river was dammed in 1820, leaving a lovely walk down to Penally (on the edge of Tenby, three miles southeast) beside the usually dry bed of the Ritec stream.

ARRIVAL AND DEPARTURE · MANORBIER

By train The railway station is a mile north of town. Destinations Carmarthen (every 2hr; 1hr); Narberth (every 2hr; 30min); Pembroke (every 2hr; 10min); Swansea (every 2hr; 1hr 50min); Tenby (every 2hr; 12min).
By bus Buses stop on the B4585 in the village centre, 400yd east of the castle. Destinations Haverfordwest (hourly; 1hr 15min), Lamphey (hourly; 15min), Pembroke (hourly; 20min) and Tenby (hourly; 20min).

Mid-Pembrokeshire

Mid-Pembrokeshire is generally ignored by visitors intent on reaching the more obvious coastal pleasures to the south and west. The towns here are not especially interesting, but they're the county's largest settlements. Historically, the most significant is **Pembroke**, the old county town with its formidable **castle**, plus the nearby ruins of the Bishop's Palace at **Lamphey**. Just north is **Pembroke Dock**, on the southern shore of the magnificent Daugleddau estuary, from where ferries leave for Ireland. Across the massive Milford Haven waterway, described by Nelson as the world's greatest natural harbour, American Quakers founded the town of **Milford Haven**, which has a dramatic setting and a good museum but probably won't detain you long.

Seven miles north, the region's chief town, **Haverfordwest**, is an important market and transport centre. Despite some handsome architecture, it remains rather soulless, though it benefits from its proximity to **Scolton Manor** and **Picton Castle**.

Pembroke and around

The old county town of **PEMBROKE** (Penfro) grew up solely to serve its **castle**, the mightiest in the chain of Norman strongholds across southern Wales and the base for the invasion of Ireland in 1171. Stretched along a ridge, the walled town flourished as a port shipping local goods to all parts of Britain, as well as Ireland, France and Spain.

Though it chose the winning side during the Wars of the Roses, Pembroke was less fortunate in the Civil War, being besieged and captured by Cromwell.

A centre for leather-making, weaving, dyeing and tailoring, Pembroke was a prosperous port in the eighteenth century, when many of its simple Georgian houses were built; however it was in grave decline by the twentieth century, its port long since overtaken by nearby rivals. Happily, this means that central Pembroke was spared postwar redevelopment, although the town's fringes are largely modern and bland.

The town's sole thoroughfare, **Main Street** stretches from the train station (as Station Rd) in the east to the mighty castle walls. From the thirteenth-century **St Mary's church** (open daily; free), just before the castle, Northgate Street drops to the bridge and the lovely **Mill Pond**, now a nature reserve (unrestricted access; free) and home to swans and otters. A pondside promenade leads past the most impressive remnants of the thirteenth-century town **walls** to the ruined **Barnard's Tower** and a path back up to the east end of Main Street.

Pembroke Castle

Westgate Hill, SA71 4LA • Daily: April–Aug 9.30am–5.30pm; March, Sept & Oct 10am–5pm; Nov–Feb 10am–4pm • £6 • ☎ 01646 681510, ⓦ pembrokecastle.co.uk

After the Norman Conquest, Rhys ap Tewdwr, ruler of Deheubarth (west Wales), held off the Normans for a while, but after his death in battle in 1093, Lord Roger de Montgomery invaded and raised a castle, rebuilt in stone after 1189. Surrounded by water on three sides, **Pembroke Castle** proved impregnable for four centuries. In 1452 Henry VI granted it to Jasper Tudor, whose nephew Harri was born here, later becoming the Lancastrian claimant to the throne and, in 1485, King Henry VII. During the Civil War, Pembroke was a Parliamentarian stronghold until switching to the Royalist side in 1648. Cromwell's 48-day siege of the town only succeeded after he cut off its water supply. There's a café, gift shop and a brass-rubbing centre here – very handy on a rainy day.

The gatehouse

Despite Cromwell's battering and centuries of subsequent neglect, the castle's sheer, bloody-minded bulk still inspires awe, even if it's largely due to extensive restoration over the last century. You enter through the soaring **gatehouse**, home to some excellent displays on the history of the castle, the Tudor empire and the Civil War. The walls and towers contain many walkways and dark passages that give ample chance to chase around spiral stairways into great oak-beamed halls. Eventually you'll descend into the large, grassy courtyard, enclosed by battlements and punctuated by hulking towers where the town walls once joined the fortress.

The keep

In the inner ward, the 75ft-high Norman **keep** has walls 18ft thick and a high domed interior; it's the largest and most impressive thirteenth-century keep in Britain. Alongside, you can peer down into the gloomy cell below the Dungeon Tower, housing a model of its last prisoner.

Wogan Cavern

Steps beside the Dungeon Tower lead far down into **Wogan Cavern**, a huge natural cavern, dank and slimy, lit by a barred hole in the wall above the waterside path. Inhabited at least twelve thousand years ago, the cavern was fortified by the Normans, who built the spiral staircase by which you enter.

ARRIVAL AND INFORMATION   PEMBROKE

By train The train station is off Upper Lamphey Rd, east of the town centre.

Destinations Lamphey (9 daily; 3min); Manorbier (9 daily;

12min); Pembroke Dock (9 daily; 10min); Swansea (8 daily; 2hr 10min); Tenby (9 daily; 20min).

By bus Buses stop near the castle on Main St.

2

Destinations Angle (May–Sept 4 daily; Oct–April Mon, Thurs & Sat 2 daily; 30min–1hr 25min); Bosherston (May–Sept 6 daily; Oct–April Mon, Thurs & Sat 4 daily; 35min–1hr); Carew/Cresswell (4 daily; 20min); Castlemartin (May–Sept 6 daily; Oct–April Mon, Thurs & Sat 4 daily; 40min–1hr 10min); Haverfordwest (hourly; 55min); Manorbier (hourly; 20min); Milford Haven (hourly; 50min); Pembroke Dock (every 20min; 10min); Stackpole (May–Sept 6 daily; Oct–April Mon, Thurs & Sat 4 daily; 30min–

1hr 15min); Tenby (hourly; 40min).

Tourist office The library (Easter–Oct Mon–Wed, Fri & Sat 10am–1pm & 2–5pm, Thurs 10am–1pm & 2–7pm; Nov–Easter Tues–Sat 10am–1pm; ☎ 01646 776499, ✉ pembroke.tic@pembrokeshire.gov.uk) on Commons Rd, offers a useful free town guide and information on the Pembrokeshire National Park and Coast Path; there is also free internet access.

ACCOMMODATION AND EATING

Cornstore Café North Quay, SA71 4NG ☎ 01646 684290, ⊕ thecornstore.com/cafe. Attached to the eclectic Cornstore furnishings shop, with riverside seating, this serves good espresso, light meals and fantastic home-made cakes. Mon–Sat 10am–5pm.

Food at Williams 18 Main St, SA71 4NP ☎ 01646 689990, ⊕ foodatwilliams.co.uk. A stylish licensed café, serving fine coffee and cakes, breakfasts till noon and light lunches such as Glamorgan sausages or mackerel pâté (£6.50), sandwiches and daily specials. Mon–Fri 9am–4.30pm, Sat 9am–4pm, Sun 10am–3pm.

Old King's Arms 13 Main St, SA71 4JS ☎ 01646 683611, ⊕ oldkingsarmshotel.co.uk. Good pub grub, tapas and

more substantial restaurant dishes; they also have four decent en-suite rooms. Daily 11am–11pm; kitchen noon–2.15pm & 6.30–9.15pm. **£80**

Penfro 111 Main St, SA71 4DB ☎ 01646 682753, ⊕ facebook.com/Penfro-BB-239277051946. Three large rooms in a fine Georgian townhouse, some without bathroom or TV; there's a lovely and spacious garden at the rear. **£75**

Tregenna 7 Upper Lamphey Rd, SA71 5JL ☎ 01646 621525, ⊕ tregennapembroke.co.uk. Some 900yd beyond the train station, this B&B offers four en-suite rooms plus covered bike storage and a drying room. **£70**

Pembroke Dock

Workaday **PEMBROKE DOCK** (Doc Penfro), three miles north of Pembroke, is principally of interest for its **naval dockyard**, active from 1814 to 1926 and now slowly awakening from suspended animation – **ferries** sail from here to **Rosslare** in Ireland.

Pembroke Dock Heritage Centre

Meyrick Owen Way (A4139), SA72 6WS • Mid-Feb to mid-Dec Mon–Sat 10am–4pm • £5 • ☎ 01646 684220, ⊕ sunderlandtrust.org.uk

Shipbuilding was swiftly followed by "PD" becoming the world's largest flying boat base during World War II, and both are recalled by the **Pembroke Dock Heritage Centre** in the newly restored **Garrison Chapel**, the only Neoclassical Georgian church in Wales. In addition to the informative panels, models and relics from sunken planes, you can talk to enthusiasts restoring Pegasus engines and discuss their hopes of ultimately restoring a Sunderland, and view flying boat models, photos, medals and uniforms. You can also ask whether the **Gun Tower**, one of Palmerston's Follies (see box, p.164), on Front St at the eastern end of the docks, has reopened after repairs.

ARRIVAL AND DEPARTURE
PEMBROKE DOCK

By train Pembroke Dock's train station is in the centre of town, 0.5 mile east of the ferry terminal.
Destinations Carmarthen (every 2hr; 1hr 20min); Pembroke (every 2hr; 8min); Swansea (every 2hr; 2hr 15min); Tenby (every 2hr; 30min).

By bus Buses stop on Laws St, just west of the train station.

Destinations Carew (4 daily; 15min); Haverfordwest (hourly; 40min); Milford Haven (hourly; 30min); Pembroke (every 20min; 10min); Tenby (hourly; 1hr).

By ferry Irish Ferries (☎ 08717 300500, ⊕ irishferries .com) currently sail to Rosslare at 2.45am and 2.45pm; the crossing takes 4hr.

ACCOMMODATION

Cleddau Bridge Hotel Essex Rd, SA72 6EG ☎ 01646 685961, ⊕ cleddauhotel.co.uk. Fairly utilitarian and not

that close to the ferry port, but it's the best there is. There's an adequate restaurant, and bar food. **£70**

2

CLEDDAU BRIDGE

One of the most impressive sights in mid-Pembrokeshire is the view from the 1970s **Cleddau Bridge** (car toll 75p) between Pembroke Dock and Neyland on the north bank; it's open to pedestrians and cyclists, with National Cycle Network route 4 continuing to Haverfordwest on the traffic-free Brunel Trail. The views are magical, especially at sunset, with the masts of boats far below and the full skies reflected in the clear water. Even the refineries look attractive from up here.

Lamphey

The village of **LAMPHEY** (Llandyfai), two miles east of Pembroke, is best known for the ruined **Bishop's Palace**, off a quiet lane to the north of the village.

Bishop's Palace

Off the A4139, SA71 5NT • Daily 10am–4pm • April–Oct £3.50; Nov–March free; CADW • ☏ 01646 672224, ⓦ cadw.gov.wales/daysout/lampheybishopspalace

Dating from at least the thirteenth century and abandoned at the Reformation, Lamphey's **Bishop's Palace** was the country retreat of the bishops of St Davids. Stout walls surround the scattered ruins, and many of the buildings are long lost under the grassy banks. Most impressive are the freestanding bell tower and the remains of the fourteenth-century Bishop Gower's **Great Hall** at the site's eastern end, topped by his hallmark arcaded parapets, similar to those of the Bishop's Palace of St Davids. Lit only by narrow slits, the gloomy undercroft below the Great Hall has the feeling of a crypt.

ARRIVAL AND DEPARTURE

LAMPHEY

By train The station is on the A4139 in the centre of the village.
Destinations Carmarthen (every 2hr; 1hr 10min); Pembroke (every 2hr; 5min); Pembroke Dock (every 2hr; 15min); Swansea (every 2hr; 2hr); Tenby (every 2hr; 20min).

By bus Buses stop at the church, between the train station and the lane to the Bishop's Palace.
Destinations Haverfordwest (hourly; 1hr); Pembroke (hourly; 8min); Tenby (hourly; 40min).

ACCOMMODATION

Lamphey Court Hotel & Spa 0.5 mile north, SA71 5NT ☏ 01646 672273, ⓦ lampheycourt.co.uk. This small mansion (built in 1822), in a lovely park opposite the palace ruins, offers grand if slightly over-the-top accommodation, with a spa and decent restaurant. **£98**
Lamphey Park About a mile northeast of the train station, SA71 5PD ☏ 01646 672906, ⓦ lampheypark .co.uk. A characterful and very welcoming Georgian farmhouse, with three bedrooms (with good modern bathrooms) and outbuildings converted into self-catering cottages (sleeping two to five; from £70/night). **£65**
Portclew House 2 miles south, SA71 5LA ☏ 01646 672800, ⓦ portclewhouse.co.uk. Half a mile from the superb beach of Freshwater East, this Grade II-listed Georgian house offers seven spacious rooms and good, hearty breakfasts. **£98**

Stackpole Estate

One of the best starting points for breathtaking clifftop walks is the National Trust's **Stackpole Estate**, five miles south of Pembroke, encompasssing spectacular coast and beautiful inland waterways and woods. The old mansion is long gone, but there's an **exhibition** on the estate's history in the former dairy, brewery and game larder, and you can visit the adjacent **walled gardens** (March–Oct daily 10am–5pm; Nov–Feb Mon–Thurs 10am–4pm, Fri 10am–3.30pm; free; ⓦ stackpole-walledgardens.co.uk), where adults with learning disabilities grow and sell produce and run a pleasant café. Just across the river from here, pretty **Stackpole Village** consists of little more than a fine pub and a few houses.

Stackpole Quay and Barafundle Bay

Road access to the coast is at two main points on either side of Stackpole Village, the more easterly being the gorgeous harbour of **Stackpole Quay**. It's one of the tiniest harbours you'll find anywhere, with barely room for four boats between its slabs of stratified limestone. A half-mile walk south brings you to **Barafundle Bay**, inaccessible by car and one of Britain's finest beaches, with clear water and a soft sand fringed by wooded cliffs pierced by three arches.

Stackpole Head and Broadhaven South

2

South of Barafundle Bay, a spectacular stretch of the Coast Path leads to **Stackpole Head**, a tufted plateau on craggy arches jutting into the sea. This is a good place to see choughs, with around twenty resident pairs. The path continues through the dunes of **Stackpole Warren** to **Broadhaven South** – the next spot on the coast accessible by car – where a nice small beach overlooks several rocky islets owned by the National Trust.

Bosherston Lily Ponds

Just inland from Broadhaven South, by the village of Bosherston, SA71 5DN

The **Bosherston Lily Ponds**, three reed-fringed fingers of water created in the late eighteenth century for coarse fishing, are now beautifully landscaped, though lilies no longer carpet the surfaces as they once did. The westernmost lake remains the prettiest, especially in June and July, when the flowers are in full bloom. Despite a growing otter population, you can still fish here (Jan, Feb & July–Dec), though you'll need a permit (£7/day) from the National Trust estate office (see below) or *Ye Olde Worlde Café* in Bosherston.

St Govan's chapel

One mile south of Bosherston, SA71 5DR • Open access • Free

From Bosherston it's a mile to the coast across the **army training grounds**, by a road that's generally closed on weekdays but open at weekends and evenings (firing orders are posted at the Bosherston car park and outside *Ye Olde Worlde Café*; or see ⓦ gov.uk/government/collections/firing-notice or call ☎ 01646 662367 after 4.30pm for the next day's programme). Continue from the MOD checkpoint to a parking spot overlooking the cliffs where **St Govan's chapel** is wedged. This tiny grey structure is at least eight (and possibly as much as fourteen) centuries old. Legend has it that when St Govan was attacked here by pirates in the sixth century, the cliffs opened up and folded gently around him, saving him from certain death; he later chose to be buried here. Steps descend into the sandy-floored chapel, with its simple stone altar, and thence to a small cell hewn from the rock, containing the fissure that reputedly sheltered Govan. The steps continue all the way down to the spume-flecked sea for a magnificent close-up of the precarious crags, caves and arches.

ARRIVAL AND INFORMATION

STACKPOLE ESTATE

By bus The #387 and #388 Coastal Cruiser make a loop from Pembroke (around 30min), calling three times daily at Bosherston and Stackpole Village and twice at St Govan's and Stackpole Quay; in winter the service runs on Thurs and Sat only.

By car The Stackpole Estate is off the B4319 south of Pembroke. There are NT car parks at Bosherston Lily Ponds, Stackpole Village, Broadhaven South and Lodge Park (for the estate office and exhibition); all charge £5/day (free to NT members and after 5.30pm) and tickets are transferable between car parks.

Tourist information The National Trust estate office by Lodge Park car park can give out maps, walking leaflets and other information (Mon–Fri 10am–5pm; ☎ 01646 661359, ⓦ nationaltrust.org.uk/stackpole).

ACCOMMODATION AND EATING

Boathouse Tearoom Stackpole Quay, SA71 5LS ☎ 01646 661359. Tasty lunches (of local crab and produce from the Stackpole estate) and teas served in a sheltered, sunny courtyard by the quay. Mid-Feb to March & Nov Fri–Sun noon–3pm; April–Oct daily 10am–5pm.

Stackpole Inn Jason's Corner, Stackpole village, SA71

2

5DF ☎01646 672324, ⓦstackpoleinn.co.uk. Real ales and superb pub meals with straightforward lunches (mains £5–8) and more elaborate dinners (mains £13–20) such as pan-fried sea bass or Moroccan lamb cutlets. They also have spacious and pleasant nautically themed rooms. Mon–Fri noon–3pm & 6.30–11pm, Sat noon–11pm, Sun noon–4pm & 6–11pm; kitchen Mon–Sat noon–2.15pm, Sun noon–4pm (snacks only 2.30–4pm) & 6.30–9pm. **£90**

The Castlemartin Ranges

The area west of Broadhaven South is made up of the army's **Castlemartin Ranges**, entirely out of bounds except for a four-mile clifftop strip on which the Coast Path and bridleway lead past the striking cleft of **Huntsman's Leap** and two isolated beaches at **Bullslaughter** and **Flimston Bay**, to **Stack Rocks**. This area, known as Range East, is open to the public when firing is not taking place – generally at weekends, bank holidays, in August, at Christmas and New Year, and most evenings after about 4.30pm (see ⓦgov.uk/government/collections/firing-notice or call ☎01646 662367 for recorded information or ☎01646 662496 for the Range Office). National Park rangers lead occasional walks here and in the otherwise closed Range West (☎01834 845040; £5/evening, £10/day); despite the military activity, the ranges are rich in wild flowers, butterflies and choughs. An inland alternative is the trail from Bosherston to the army camp of **MERRION**, on the B4319. The only vehicle access to the coast is a lane (open only as above) from Merrion to Stack Rocks past the mournful little chapel at **FLIMSTON**, a hamlet forcibly abandoned to the army.

Stack Rocks jut out of the sea here like a series of tall, guano-spattered stepping stones. On a quiet day, your only company will be the hundreds of guillemots, razorbills and kittiwakes swooping to their nesting spots on the limestone ledges. A hundred yards further west (as far as you're allowed to go), a graceful limestone arch known as the **Green Bridge of Wales** rises from a wave-flattened rock platform.

Freshwater West and around

Castlemartin, SA71 5HW • ☎01646 661640, ⓦnationaltrust.org.uk/freshwater-west-and-gupton-farm

The Coast Path (and the Coastal Cruiser bus) follows the B4319 a couple of miles to **Freshwater West**, a beach that's great for **surfing**, though the currents can be too strong for swimming. Indeed, there's a memorial to 73 men drowned here in 1943 while training for amphibious assaults. Behind the beach, desolate wind-battered dunes, recently used as locations for *Robin Hood* and *Harry Potter* films, make for interesting walking; there's also good birdwatching. At **Gupton Farm**, just west of Castlemartin, there's a National Trust interpretation centre (May–Sept daily 24hr; ☎01646 623110, ⓔguptonfarm@nationaltrust.org.uk) and simple accommodation (see below).

ACCOMMODATION AND EATING — **FRESHWATER WEST**

Café Môr Freshwater West Beach Car Park, SA71 5AH ☎07422 535345, ⓦcafemor.co.uk. This food cart comes as a welcome surprise in this off-grid location, with fine concoctions of locally grown and foraged ingredients, notably the beef burger with laverbread. Easter–Sept daily 10am–4pm (9am–7pm in school summer hols).

Gupton Farm Just west of Castlemartin, SA71 5HW ☎01646 623110, ⓔguptonfarm@nationaltrust.org.uk. Rustic NT campsite (non-members pay £10 extra) and rooms in the farmhouse. Camping **£12**, campervan **£18**, doubles **£56**

Angle

The B4320 from Pembroke meets the B4319 near the **Devil's Quoit**, a Neolithic burial chamber topped by an impressive capstone, and continues down the final finger of the peninsula to the remote village of **ANGLE**. This consists of one long street, bounded by old, colourful cottages, at the western end of a wide curve of mud and eelgrass known as **Angle Bay**, frequented by migrating waders such as redshank, curlew, whimbrel, dunlin and turnstone. **West Angle Bay**, a secluded spot a mile west of the village, is better for swimming, and overlooks one of Lord Palmerston's forts (see box, p.164) on **Thorn Island**. In fact, the area is rich in military history, starting with the fourteenth-century tower house just north of the church; from here a track leads past the famed *Old Point House* pub (see below) to the lifeboat station, with a path continuing to **Chapel Bay Fort** (Easter–Oct Fri–Sun 10am–4pm; £5; ⑩chapelbayfort.com), built in 1890 and now being restored by volunteers. It's full of weapons and bomb-disposal kit, all explained in a forty-minute tour. From here a new road leads back to the western end of the village, allowing a one-hour loop walk.

ARRIVAL AND DEPARTURE   ANGLE

By bus Angle can by reached on the Coastal Cruiser bus from Pembroke (May–Sept 2 daily; Oct–April Thurs &

Sat 2 daily; 30min).

EATING AND DRINKING

Old Point House 10min east along the shore, SA71 5AS ☎01646 641205. A delightful rustic inn (reached by walking behind the church and 10min east along the shore), whose fire is said to have burned continuously for more than three hundred years until the mid-1990s, since when it has only been lit in winter. Quality meals come in

large portions: the specials board usually includes several examples of the day's catch. Easter & summer hols daily noon–3pm & 6–10.30pm; rest of year Wed noon–3pm, Fri & Sat noon–3pm & 6–10.30pm, Sun noon–4pm; kitchen same days noon–3pm & 6–8pm.

Milford Haven

Taking its name from the waterway, or natural harbour, the town of **MILFORD HAVEN** (Aberdaugleddau), four miles west of Neyland, was founded in 1790 by Quakers from Nantucket, brought here to work as whalers. The grid pattern they established – principally three streets rising sharply parallel to the waterway – survives today. The town stagnated until developing as a major fishing port from the 1880s; these days, despite a magnificent location and interesting heritage, the centre hasn't got much going for it. The **waterside** is undeniably impressive, however, with ferries and tankers ploughing the glittering waters of the haven that stretch out below the pleasant public gardens.

Milford Haven Museum
The Marina, SA73 3AF • Easter–Oct Mon–Sat 10.30am–4pm • £3 • ☎01646 694496, ⑩facebook.com/MilfordHavenMuseum

Public funding has transformed the old docks into a lively café-lined **marina** (⑩milfordmarina.com), where the old Customs House (1797) houses the interesting **Milford Haven Museum**. Exhibits include photographs and mementos from the fishing trade, details of the town's Quaker origins and some fascinating material on Milford Haven during the world wars, when massive convoys formed here.

ARRIVAL AND INFORMATION   MILFORD HAVEN

By train Milford Haven station is below the Hakin road bridge, next to the docks.
Destinations Carmarthen (11 daily; 1hr); Haverfordwest (11 daily; 15min); Swansea (8 daily; 2hr 20min).
By bus Buses stop at Tesco near the train station and on Charles St (westbound) or Hamilton Terrace (north/eastbound).
Destinations Dale (3 daily; 30min); Haverfordwest (every

30min; 25min); Marloes (3 daily; 40min); Pembroke (hourly; 50min).
Tourist information Limited information is available at the library at 19 Cedar Court, in the retail park just west of the train station (Mon, Wed & Fri 10am–5pm – plus Tues in summer holidays – Thurs 10am–6pm, Sat 10am–1pm; ☎01437 771888, ⑥milford.tic @pembrokeshire.gov.uk).

ACCOMMODATION AND EATING

Belhaven House 29 Hamilton Terrace, SA73 3JJ ☎01646 695983, ⑩milford-havenhotel.com. One of

the nicer places in town, overlooking the gardens and haven, with very welcoming owners. The rooms feel dated

2

but are spacious and en suite. **£70**

Foam Food & Drink Barrallier House, SA73 3AA ☎01646 698985. At the far end of the marina, in a spacious 1907 building with a waterfront deck, this café serves breakfast until 11.30am and all day on Sun (£8.95), a set lunch (£10.95) such as teriyaki chicken breast, and tapas on Fri and Sat evenings; service is variable. Mon–Wed & Sun 9am–4pm, Thurs 9am–10pm, Fri & Sat 9am–11pm.

Martha's Vineyard Cleddau House, Milford Marina, SA73 3AA ☎01646 697083, ⓦmarthasvineyard restaurant.co.uk. A good eating option with a balcony

overlooking the marina, offering soups and sandwiches (around £4), salads and lots of pasta choices (£11) as well as fish and sirloin (£17–25). Daily noon–11pm.

Sandy Haven Herbrandston, 4 miles west, SA73 3ST ☎01646 698844, ⓦsandyhavencampingpark.co.uk. A quiet little waterfront site with free boat parking available. Closed mid-Sept to Easter. **£12**

Upper Neeston Lodges Upper Neeston Farm, Dale Rd, 2 miles west, SA73 3RY ☎01646 690750, ⓦpembrokeshirebunkhouse.co.uk. These comfy energy-efficient barn conversions comprise two family-sized units and two for couples. **£18**

Haverfordwest and around

Ancient but dull **HAVERFORDWEST** (Hwlffordd), seven miles north of Milford Haven, grew up around the castle that dominates the skyline to this day. Built in earth and timber by the Flemish Tancard for the Earl of Pembroke around 1110, it was rebuilt in stone and then refurbished by Queen Eleanor in 1289–90, and demolished after the Civil War. This was one of Wales' largest towns in Tudor times, prospering as a port and trading centre, but the Civil War and an outbreak of plague in 1651–52 put a halt to that. Haverfordwest is once again the county town of Pembrokeshire, but despite a slew of fine architecture from its glory days, it's hardly a place in which to linger. From the diminutive **Castle Square**, at the town's heart, a small alleyway ascends to the **castle**, which fails to live up to the expectations created by the views from below; there's little left but the bare shell of the thirteenth-century inner ward.

Haverfordwest Town Museum

Castle St, SA61 2EF • Easter–Oct Mon–Sat 10am–4pm • £2 • ☎01437 763087, ⓦhaverfordwest-town-museum.org.uk

In the imposing governor's house (1779) next to the castle is the **Haverfordwest Town Museum**, a motley collection of fairly interesting local history exhibits, such as the first ballot paper used here, Nelson's freedom of the borough charter, and lots of good historical photos.

The lower town

Below the castle, in the **lower town**, the Riverside Shopping Centre follows the River Cleddau from Castle Square to the Old Bridge, by the bus station and tourist office. The more appealing parts of Haverfordwest lie up the handsome High Street, rising from the grand Old Shire Hall (1835) and Castle Square towards the thirteenth-century **St Mary's church** (10am–5pm daily; free), the north arcade of which is one of the finest early Gothic works in Wales, with beautifully carved capitals.

Scolton Manor

B4329, 4 miles northeast of Haverfordwest, SA62 5QL • **House** April–Oct daily 11am–5pm • £3.50 • **Park** Daily: April–Oct 9am–6pm; Nov–March 9am–4.30pm • ☎01437 731328, ⓦscoltonmanor.co.uk

A modest mansion completed in 1842, **Scolton Manor** is nominally home to the Pembrokeshire County Museum, but due to cuts you can currently only view its fine collection of agricultural and railway machinery through the viewing windows of the museum store, beyond the main car park at the bottom of the site. In the house itself the gilt, brocade and fine furnishings upstairs contrast with the servants' quarters below; beside it is an agreeable café specializing in cawl. Finally, check out the surrounding **country park**, where the visitor centre stresses environmental awareness.

Picton Castle

Rhos, 5 miles east of Haverfordwest, SA62 4AS • April–Oct daily 9am–5pm (1hr castle tours noon, 1pm & 2pm); also Feb & Oct half-terms & pre-Christmas events; grounds all year daylight hours • £10 including tours; grounds only £7 • ⓣ 01437 751326, ⓦ pictoncastle.co.uk

Three miles east of Haverfordwest on the main A40, signs lead two miles south to **Picton Castle**, a chunky mansion built between 1295 and 1308 and remodelled between 1790 and 1800. Set in glorious **grounds** with a walled garden, maze and play area, the castle still has its original contents, notably wonderful marble fireplaces, a circular library and long thin chapel, family portraits (some by Graham Sutherland) plus a Renoir and the earliest-known fake Van Gogh (from the 1920s). There's an excellent **deli/café** in the courtyard, too (see below).

2

ARRIVAL AND DEPARTURE — HAVERFORDWEST AND AROUND

By train The train station is a 10min walk to the east.

Destinations Cardiff (7 daily; 2hr 25min); Carmarthen (11 daily; 40min); Milford Haven (11 daily; 25min); Swansea (7 daily; 1hr 30min).

By bus The bus station is across the Old Bridge from the town centre, near the tourist office.

Destinations Broad Haven (6 daily; 20min); Cardigan (hourly; 1hr 20min); Carmarthen (3 daily; 1hr); Dale (3 daily; 55min); Fishguard (hourly; 40min); Manorbier (hourly; 1hr 10min); Milford Haven (every 30min; 25min); Narberth (hourly; 20min); Newgale (hourly; 25min); Newport, Pembrokeshire (hourly; 1hr); Pembroke (hourly; 55min); Rosebush (1 on Tues only; 45min); St Davids (hourly; 45min); Solva (hourly; 40min); Tenby (hourly; 1hr).

INFORMATION AND GETTING AROUND

Tourist office On Dew St, behind the library, where there is also wi-fi (Mon, Wed & Fri 10am–5pm – also Thurs during summer holidays – Tues 10am–7pm, Sat 10am–1pm; ⓣ 01437 775244, ⓔ haverfordwestlendinglibrary@pembrokeshire.gov.uk).

Bike rental Mike's Bikes, 17 Prendergast (Mon–Sat 9am–5.30pm; ⓣ 01437 760068, ⓦ mikes-bikes.co.uk), 400yd northeast of the bus station, rents out mountain bikes and hybrid tourers (both £12/day) with panniers, lock and helmet, and tag-a-longs for kids.

ACCOMMODATION

Boulston Manor 3 miles southeast, SA62 4AQ ⓣ 01437 764600, ⓦ boulstonmanor.co.uk. On a stunning site overlooking the Western Cleddau, this top-end B&B has just three rooms, all furnished in Georgian style but with modern comforts. **£75**

College Guest House 93 Hill St, SA62 1QL ⓣ 01437 763710, ⓦ collegeguesthouse.com. This Georgian town house, with eight rooms on three storeys, is one of several decent B&Bs at the top of Hill St (with plenty of free parking). **£80**

Lower Haythog Farm Spittal, SA62 5QL ⓣ 01437 731279, ⓦ lowerhaythogfarm.co.uk. Comfortable farmhouse B&B and self-catering cottages near Scolton Manor, with welcoming hosts and lovely gardens. **£70**

Rising Sun Inn Pelcomb Bridge, St Davids Rd (A487), 2 miles northwest, SA62 6EA ⓣ 01437 765171, ⓦ therisingsunwest.co.uk. A spacious campsite with all facilities. It sits behind the pub, which serves filling and family-friendly meals and also has two rooms (£70 B&B). **£20**

EATING AND DRINKING

The Creative Common 11 Goat St, SA61 1PX ⓣ 01437 779397, ⓦ thecreativecommon.co.uk. Linked to a co-working space, this attractive coffee shop has great coffee and tea (served with a timer), delicious cakes and enthusiastic staff. Mon–Fri 8am–2.30pm, Sat 10am–3pm.

The George's 24 Market St, SA61 1NH ⓣ 01437 766683, ⓦ thegeorges.uk.com. A good option for lunch, taking a wholefood approach to delicious peasant dishes. You can eat in a lovely walled garden if the weather allows, or the cellar bistro if not. Tues–Sat 10am–5.30pm.

Hotel Mariners Mariners Square, SA61 2DU ⓣ 01437 76335, ⓦ hotelmariners.co.uk. Despite external appearances and the shoddy hotel itself, this is actually one of the most popular and reliable places to eat in town. The menu contains few surprises, with specials such as lamb shank or duck breast costing around £15. Daily noon–2pm & 7–9pm.

★ **Maria's@Picton** Picton Castle, SA62 4AS ⓣ 01437 751346, ⓦ pictoncastle.co.uk/for-visitors/marias-courtyard-restaurant. A long-standing fixture in Haverfordwest, Maria recently moved her classy deli/bistro to Picton Castle, selling Spanish, French and Welsh cheeses, meats and olives, and with a café serving soups, pies, panini, tapas and daily specials. There's also a takeaway shop for sandwiches, salads, ices and drinks. Her Fri-night tapas evenings are an institution (reservations required). April–Oct Mon–Thurs 9am–5pm, Fri from 7.30pm; Nov–March Mon–Thurs noon–3pm, Fri from 7.30pm.

2

St Bride's Bay

At the westernmost end of Wales, **St Bride's Bay** is one of the country's most enchanting areas, with rocky outcrops, islands and broad, sweeping beaches curving around between two headlands that sit like giant crab pincers facing out into the warm Gulf Stream. The southernmost of these, St Ann's Head, offers calm, east-facing sands at **Dale**, sunny expanses of south-facing beach at **Marloes** and wilder west-facing sands at **Musselwick**. From **Martin's Haven**, boats depart for the islands of **Skomer**, **Skokholm** and **Grassholm**.

The golden sands of the main scoop of St Bride's Bay are backed by popular holiday villages such as **Little Haven**, **Broad Haven** and **Newgale**. From here, the lacerated coast veers west as **St Davids peninsula**, the stunning cliffs interrupted only by occasional gashes of sand. Just north of **St Non's Bay**, the tiny cathedral city of **St Davids**, founded in the sixth century by Wales' patron saint, is a justified highlight. Rooks and crows circle above the impressive ruins of the huge **Bishop's Palace**, beside the more delicate bulk of the **cathedral**, the most impressive in Wales. The peninsula, more windswept and elemental than any other part of Pembrokeshire, tapers out just west of the city at the popular **Whitesands Bay** and the hamlet of **St Justinian's**, facing the crags of **Ramsey Island**.

Dale and around

The tiny but ancient village of **DALE**, fourteen miles west of Haverfordwest, huddles at the head of a huge bite out of the coast. Dale is blighted by views of oil refineries, but it's surprisingly sunny and its sheltered, east-facing beach makes it a popular yachting and **watersports** centre. The bay's calm waters are deceptive, though, and as you head south towards **St Ann's Head** the weather gets wilder – this was where the tanker *Sea Empress* was wrecked in 1966.

Around the Dale peninsula

The **Dale peninsula** offers invigorating **walking**. The Coast Path sticks tight to the undulating coastline, passing tiny bays en route to St Ann's lighthouse. Tucked in the eastern lee of St Ann's Head is **Mill Bay**, where Henry VII landed in 1485, marching the breadth of his native Wales and gathering an army to defeat Richard III at Bosworth Field.

The coast turns north from St Ann's Head to reach sandstone-backed **West Dale Bay**, less than a mile from Dale on the opposite side of the peninsula; the seven-mile walk around the peninsula is highly worthwhile, but swimming here is hazardous, due to currents and hidden rocks.

ARRIVAL AND DEPARTURE   DALE

Dale is served by three daily **buses** from/to Haverfordwest (55min) and Milford Haven (30min).

ACCOMMODATION

Allenbrook Castle Way, SA62 3RN ☎01646 636254, ⓦallenbrook-dale.co.uk. A luxurious, charming, but somewhat timewarped country house; all rooms have sea views across the lawns. **£80**

Griffin Inn Waterfront, SA62 3RB ☎01646 636227, ⓦgriffininndale.co.uk. This traditional waterfront pub, with a modern extension and open deck above, has built a strong reputation above all for its fish specials (mostly perfectly fresh and lightly steamed), but it also works as a real village pub where you can relax and chat freely. May–Sept daily noon–11pm; Oct–April Tues–Sun noon–11pm; kitchen same days noon–2.30pm & 6–8.30pm.

WATER ACTIVITIES AROUND DALE

Water activities around Dale are focused on the beachside shack of West Wales Wind, Surf and Sailing (☎01646 636642, ⓦsurfdale.co.uk), which offers lessons (April–Oct; £35–70/half-day) in **windsurfing**, **sailing** and **kayaking**. With adequate proficiency you can rent equipment: a basic windsurfer costs £40 a half-day; a superior ensemble £60; and a kayak £20.

Point Farm Campsite A 5min walk south of the village, SA62 3RD ☎01646 636842, ⓦpointfarmdale .co.uk. This peaceful little waterfront campsite, on the Coast Path, has spaces for tents and campervans, and excellent toilet facilities. **£20**

Marloes and around

A mile north of Dale, the village of **MARLOES** backs the great sandy curve of **Marloes Sands** (ⓦnationaltrust.org.uk/marloes-sands-and-mere), known for its stunning cliffs of grey, gold and purple folds of rock, alternate layers of grey shale and old red sandstone. At **Three Chimneys**, two-thirds of the way along the beach, three vertical lines of hard Silurian sandstone and mudstone were formed horizontally and forced up by ancient earth movements.

Gateholm Island

Accessible at mid-tide and lower; a 5min walk from the National Trust's Marloes Sands car park (£5), SA62 3BH

The beach at Marloes is crowned at its western end by **Gateholm Island**, where more than 130 Iron Age hut circles, pottery and pieces of jewellery have been found on what seems to have been an ancient monastic community. Today, Gateholm is powerfully atmospheric, though getting topside involves a tricky scramble: head around the left side as you look at the island.

Martin's Haven

The road west from Marloes ends after two miles at **Martin's Haven**, a basic jetty that is the main departure point for **boat trips** to the islands of Skomer, Skokholm and Grassholm (see p.176). Just above are a battered **Celtic ring cross**; a small cottage (April–Oct 10am–6pm; free) where **Natural Resources Wales** has displays on marine life, including videos; and the Wildlife Trust of South and West Wales' **Lockley Lodge** (Easter/April to mid-Sept Tues–Sun 8.30am until the last boat returns; ☎01646 636800), where you can get boat tickets, snacks and information. Covering the coast of the headland as well as the island, the **Skomer Marine Conservation Zone** harbours soft coral, forty species of sea anemone and more than seventy species of sponge, as well as octopus, crabs and lobster. A gateway in the wall just beyond the car park gives access to the **Deer Park**, the sublime headland at the western tip of this peninsula (bypassed, alas, by the Coast Path). It was never actually stocked with deer; the National Trust now grazes it with Welsh mountain ponies, creating habitat for choughs and peregrine. Paths radiate across the headland, all with stunning views over St Bride's Bay and the islands, and the prospect of a glorious sunset.

Musselwick Sands and St Bride's Haven

Musselwick Sands, just north of Marloes, is a beautiful and unspoilt beach, though it vanishes at high tide. Further north along the peninsula is **St Bride's Haven**, a tiny, sheltered beach at the end of the lane that peters out by the tiny chapel of St Bridget (c.1291) and the Pump House (built in 1904 to supply fresh water to the Victorian St Bride's Castle), where the gleaming pumps are still in full working order. There are some good rock pools around the beach.

ARRIVAL AND DEPARTURE	**MARLOES AND AROUND**

By bus The Puffin Shuttle runs between St Davids and Marloes (May–Sept 3 daily; Oct–April Thurs & Sat 3 daily; 1hr 30min); it also stops at Martin's Haven, 5min later.

ACCOMMODATION AND EATING	

Beach Hut Café Marloes, SA62 3AZ ☎01646 636968, ⓦfacebook.com/marloesvillagestoreandbeachhutcafe. At the village shop and post office (and definitely not a beach hut!), this lovely little café sells teas and coffees, cakes and toasties, as well as arts and crafts. Winter Mon & Sun 10am–noon, Tues–Sat 9am–4pm; rest of year Mon–Sat

8am–5pm, Sun 9am–1pm.
West Hook Farm 0.5 mile east of Martin's Haven, SA62
3BJ ☎01646 636424, ⊛westhookfarm-camping

.co.uk. Spacious but simple site (coin-op showers, no
electric hook-ups) usefully placed right beside the Coast
Path. Closed Nov–Easter. **£14**

Skomer, Skokholm and Grassholm

A boat trip around the **offshore islands** is a real highlight on this stretch of coast. While
wildlife- and bird-spotting trips head out to all three, the only island that day-trippers
can land on is **Skomer**; it also greets overnighters, as does **Skokholm**, but no landings at
all are allowed on **Grassholm**.

Skomer

Skomer, a 722-acre flat-topped island that dominates the near horizon, boasts the
largest **sea bird** colonies in southern Britain, the remains of hundreds of ancient
hut circles, a stone circle, collapsed defensive ramparts and settlement systems
and a Bronze Age standing stone, known as Harold's Stone, near the narrow neck
where boats land. The stars are the two hundred thousand-plus **Manx shearwaters**
(a third of the world population), which only emerge at night, though day-visitors
can see live footage from one of their burrows. There are also **puffins** (best
May–July), gulls, guillemots, razorbills, storm petrels, cormorants, shags and
kittiwakes. Land birds include buzzards, skylarks, jackdaws, chough, owls and
peregrines. There's a good chance of seeing **grey seals** on Skomer's north side,
especially from late August to October. Risso's dolphins and harbour porpoise can
be seen offshore, with whales further out, and in spring and early summer, wild
flowers carpet the island.

Skokholm

Two miles south of Skomer is the 240-acre island of **Skokholm**, whose warm red
sandstone cliffs are a sharp contrast to Skomer's grey severity. Britain's first bird
observatory was founded here in the 1930s, and the island is still rich in **birdlife**, above
all puffins, Manx shearwaters and storm petrels.

SKOMER, GRASSHOLM AND SKOKHOLM BOAT TRIPS

All boats operate from April to October. The only company authorized to land on **Skomer** is
Dale Sailing (☎01646 603109, ⊛pembrokeshire-islands.co.uk), operating from Martin's
Haven (Tues–Sun & bank holidays 10am, 11am & noon, returning from 3pm; £21), which
gives you several hours to explore the island. The company also has round-the-island cruises
(daily 1pm; 1hr; £12), an evening trip that's great for spotting sea birds (mid-April to July
Tues, Wed & Fri 7pm; 2hr; £16) and jaunts in fast, rigid inflatables such as the Skomer &
Skokholm Safari (April–July daily 2pm & 4pm; 90min; £30); the Skomer & Skokholm Evening
Safari (April–July daily 6pm; 2hr; £45) and the Pembrokeshire Islands Safari (Aug–Sept daily
10.30am, 1pm & 3.30pm; 2hr; £45). From Neyland, beyond Milford Haven, Dive
Pembrokeshire (☎01646 600200, ⊛dive-pembrokeshire.com) offers a trip down the haven
to Skomer and Skokholm (4hr; £42), while Thousand Islands Expeditions (☎01437 721721,
⊛thousandislands.co.uk), based at St Justinian's, near St Davids, runs a Skomer puffin-
viewing excursion (hourly; 2hr; £48).

For **Grassholm**, Dale Sailing offers a Grassholm Cruise (mid-April to late Sept Mon 1pm; 3hr;
£35) and a Grassholm Gannetry Experience (April–July daily 11.30pm; 2hr; £45). Thousand
Islands Expeditions, meanwhile, runs a day-tour to Grassholm and Ramsey Island with an RSPB
warden (April–Oct Tues 9.30am; £57), and a whale- and dolphin-watching trip to Grassholm and
beyond (daily 9am, 3.15pm & 4.15pm; 3hr; £60). Check out also Ramsey Island Cruises, Venture
Jet and Voyages of Discovery, all of which include Grassholm in their itineraries (see box, p.184).

At present no day-trips land on **Skokholm** but that may change – contact the Wildlife Trust
of South and West Wales (☎01239 621600, ⊛welshwildlife.org).

Grassholm

Six miles west of Skomer, the tiny islet of **Grassholm** resembles a small iced cake. From April to September the "icing" is, in fact, a swarming mass of forty thousand **gannets**, one of the northern hemisphere's largest colonies, covering well over half the island; at other times it's their guano.

ACCOMMODATION — SKOMER AND SKOKHOLM

Wildlife Trust of South and West Wales bunkhouses
Skomer and Skokholm ☎0156 724100, ⓦwelshwildlife
.org. Self-catering accommodation in old farm buildings on Skomer and Skokholm; perfect for birders and anyone in

search of solitude. The boat to Skokholm costs £25 return (Mon & Fri only), while the boat to Skomer costs £11 return (9am daily); they leave from Martin's Haven (see p.175). Closed Nov—March. Per person: Skokholm £33, Skomer £35

Little Haven to Solva

The long, straight west-facing back of St Bride's Bay, with its sublime Atlantic surf, is flanked by dramatic stretches of cliffs from **Little Haven** to Druidston, and on either side of the miniature fiord of **Solva**.

ARRIVAL AND DEPARTURE — LITTLE HAVEN TO SOLVA

By bus Buses from Haverfordwest to St Davids (Mon—Sat 11 daily) pass through Newgale and Solva. The Puffin Shuttle runs between St Davids and Marloes via Solva,

Newgale, Druidston, Broad Haven, Little Haven and St Brides (May—Sept 3 daily; Oct—April Thurs & Sat 3 daily).

ACTIVITIES

Big Blue Experience Newgale, SA62 6AS ☎07816 169359, ⓦbigblueexperience.co.uk. Kitesurfing courses (£99/day) and land-based kiteboarding (£45/2hr) from April to Oct.
Haven Sports Marine Rd, Broad Haven, SA62 3JR ☎01437 781354, ⓦhavensports.co.uk. Rental of sit-on-top kayaks and bodyboards. Daily 9am—6pm.

Newsurf Newgale, SA62 6AS ☎01437 721398, ⓦnewsurf.co.uk. Rental of kayaks and surfing gear, plus surfing lessons (£35/2hr 30min); open year round.
Nolton Stables Just inland from Nolton Haven, SA62 3NW ☎01437 710360, ⓦnoltonstables.com. Fantastic beach riding, particularly to Druidston (1hr 30min; £49).

Little Haven

Five miles north of Marloes, steep streets descend to the sheltered stony beach of **LITTLE HAVEN**, a picturesque old fishing village and former coal port that's extremely popular with divers and swimmers in summer. At low tide, walks along the shore towards Broad Haven are superb – there's some striking geology on show, with alternating bands of hard and soft rocks producing caves and blowholes.

EATING AND DRINKING — LITTLE HAVEN

The Swan Point Rd, SA62 3UL ☎01437 781880, ⓦtheswanlittlehaven.co.uk. This beachside gastropub offers quality bar meals at lunch (faggots or fish and chips for £11) and more refined dining in the evening, featuring

unusual fish such as sand sole or superb spider crab (£15–19) or perhaps belly pork (£15). Daily 10am—11pm; kitchen noon—9pm.

Broad Haven

The Coast Path cuts inland from Little Haven for a mile to reach brash **BROAD HAVEN**, a dramatic contrast to its unassuming neighbour, especially in summer, when cars cruise its waterfront and holiday-makers spill out of its pubs. Still, it has a wide beach fringed by fissured and shattered cliffs.

ACCOMMODATION — BROAD HAVEN

Belmont Barn Long Lane, a mile inland, SA62 3LD ☎01437 781372, ⓦbelmontbarn.co.uk. This B&B has two

rooms (sharing a shower), each with a kitchenette and lounge with balcony, all upstairs and with big sea views. £80

Bower Farm 0.5 mile southeast, SA62 3TY ☎ 01437 781554, ⓦ bowerfarm.co.uk. A welcoming farmhouse B&B, reached by a narrow twisty road from Broad Haven. **£80**

YHA Broad Haven Northern end of the village, SA62 3JH ☎ 0345 371 9008, ⓦ yha.org.uk/hostel/broad-haven. Almost on the seafront, this modern, spacious hostel comes with a good-value café-bar; some doubles are en suite. Closed Nov–Feb. Dorms **£13**, doubles **£50**

Druidston Haven

A couple of miles north of Broad Haven, the quiet sandy beach at **DRUIDSTON HAVEN**, hemmed in by cliffs, is reached along small paths from the bottom of the sharply sloping lane from Broad Haven or – ideally – from the unique *Druidstone Hotel* (see below).

ACCOMMODATION AND EATING   DRUIDSTON HAVEN

★ **Druidstone Hotel** SA62 3NE ☎ 01437 781221, ⓦ druidstone.co.uk. A rambling and easy-going place on the cliff, with a quirky array of B&B rooms, some with superb sea views, self-catering cottages (sleeping two to four; minimum one week; from £85/night), including an old circular croquet pavilion, and a cellar bar that spills out onto the clifftops. Under the stairs is the smallest bookshop in Wales. It's frequently booked up months in advance, especially at weekends. The restaurant has a nightly changing dinner menu that might include anything from lamb kofte (£8) to sea bass with tapenade (£20). Tues is feast night, with a buffet of, say, Cajun or Jamaican food for £16.50 (vegetarian £14.50). Daily 12.30–2.30pm & 7–9.30pm (Fri to 10pm). **£60**

Shortlands 200yd inland in Druidston hamlet, SA62 3NE ☎ 01437 781234, ⓦ shortlandsfarm.co.uk. This small, friendly campsite is on a rare-breeds organic farm with great sea views. It also has a static caravan (sleeps six) and a low-allergen self-catering cottage (sleeps eight), both let by the week or for short breaks outside high season. Camping **£15**, caravan **£67**, cottage **£140**

Newgale

The next bay north of **Nolton Haven** (little more than a pub and a few houses and caravans around a sheltered shingle cove) is the vast, west-facing **Newgale Sands**, virtually untouched at its southern end, but popular with families and surfers around the uninspiring **NEWGALE**. Nearby, Brandy Brook marks the boundary of "Little England Beyond Wales" (see box, p.156) and the limit of Norman colonization of Pembrokeshire.

ACCOMMODATION AND EATING   NEWGALE

Newgale Camping Site Wood Farm, SA62 6AR ☎ 01437 710253, ⓦ newgalecampingsite.co.uk. Just across the road from the beach, and very popular with surfers; there are coin-op showers and a few electric hook-ups, but no fires and no dogs. Closed Oct–Easter. **£16**

Sands Café Main road, SA62 6UU ☎ 01437 729222. A great place for baguettes, panini, espresso, ice creams and smoothies, plus light meals such as green pea and pesto soup (£5) or smoked mackerel pâté (£6.50). Daily 9.30am–4.30pm.

Solva

Beyond Newgale the coast turns west, rising abruptly to craggy cliffs that make a wilder, more Celtic landscape than that of southern Pembrokeshire. The Coast Path from Newgale to **SOLVA**, four miles west, is marvellous, with easy clifftop walking, magnificent coastal views and a secluded sandy beach at **Porthmynawyd**. Solva itself is a touristy, picture-postcard village at the top of an inlet running down to **Gwadn beach**. Above this, the **Gribin Headland** between the valleys of the Solva and Gribin rivers gives memorable views and has an imposing Iron Age earthwork on its summit.

ACCOMMODATION AND EATING   SOLVA

Cambrian Inn 6 Main St, SA62 6UU ☎ 01437 72120, ⓦ thecambrianinn.co.uk. With five decent B&B rooms, this once traditional pub now offers fine dining. Starters might include mango and brie filo parcels or local pastrami (£7), followed by the likes of Catalan fish stew or hake fillet on wild mushroom, cockle and laverbread pearl barley risotto, as well as gourmet burgers and classic bar meals from lasagne to scampi. Mains from £12.50. Daily noon–11pm; kitchen April–Sept noon–3pm & 5.30–9.30pm; Oct–March noon–3pm & 6–9pm. **£100**

Lavender Café The Old Chapel, Main St, SA62 6UU ☎ 01437 721907, ⓦ lavendercafesolva.wordpress.com. Run by a husband-and-wife team – a Cuban artist/ musician and a photographer – this is a great place for soup, tapas, sandwiches and cakes; there's often live music. April–Sept daily 10.30am–5pm.

St Davids

Perched at the very western point of Wales on a windswept, treeless peninsula, **ST DAVIDS** (Tyddewi) is really just a large village, with 1800 inhabitants, but was officially granted city status in 1995. It clusters around its **cathedral**, Wales' spiritual and ecclesiastical centre and formally independent of Canterbury. Founded by Wales' patron saint himself in 550, the shrine of **St David** has drawn **pilgrims** – including William the Conqueror and Edward I – for almost a millennium and a half; in 1124 Pope Calixtus II decreed that two journeys to St Davids were spiritually equivalent to one to Rome. The cathedral was built from 1181, the settlement growing around it; St Davids today still relies on the imported wealth of newcomers to the area, attracted by its savage beauty.

St Davids High Street courses down to the triangular Cross Square, with its centrepiece **medieval cross**, and continues under the medieval **Tower Gate**, entrance to the serene **Cathedral Close**. The cathedral lies down to the right, hidden for safety in a hollow by the babbling River Alun, beyond which lie the ruins of the Bishop's Palace.

There are numerous small commercial **art galleries** and craft outlets: some are tacky, but most reflect the quality of the many artists attracted here by the unique quality of the light. The best is **Oriel y Parc**, a landscape gallery (daily 10am–4pm; free) at the National Park visitor centre (see p.181), which features works by Graham Sutherland and rotating loans from the National Museum of Wales.

St Davids cathedral

The Close, SA62 6RD • Mon–Sat 8.30am–5.30pm, Sun 12.45–5.30pm; guided tours (Aug Mon 11.30am & Fri 2.30pm, other times by appointment; 1hr) are arranged at the bookshop in the nave • £3 donation requested; guided tours £4 • ☎ 01437 720202, ⓦ stdavidscathedral.org.uk

The gold-and-purple stone tower of **St Davids cathedral** is approached down the Thirty-Nine Steps (traditionally named after the Thirty-Nine Articles, the key tenets of Anglicanism), descending from the fourteenth-century **Tower Gate** (Porth y Twr), with a history exhibition (daily 10am–5pm; £1) above a tiny display of carved stones (free). Alongside, a thirteenth-century tower now houses the cathedral's bells, removed from the main tower in 1730 when it was near collapse. The tower has clocks on only three sides (the people living to the north couldn't raise enough money for one facing them), and is topped by pert pinnacles that seem to glow a different colour from the rest of the building.

The cathedral hosts a superb classical **music festival** in late May/early June (ⓦ stdavidscathedralfestival.co.uk).

The nave, crossing and choir

The most striking feature of the low twelfth-century **nave** is its intricate latticed oak roof, built to hide sixteenth-century emergency repairs. The support buttresses inserted in the northern aisle still look incongruously temporary and

ST DAVIDS

Whitesands Bay (2 miles) & Fishguard (16 miles)

Solva (4 miles) & Haverfordwest (16 miles)

St Justinian's (2 miles)

Porth Clais (1.5 mile)

River Alun

Bishop's Palace

St Davids Cathedral

Bell Tower

THE PEBBLES

TOWER HILL

GOAT STREET

National Trust visitor centre

FFYNNON WEN

BRYN TEG

QUICKWELL HILL

NUN STREET

ST PETERS LANE

GOSPEL LA

CROSS SQUARE

Bus Stop

BRYN ROAD

TOWN HALL LA

NEW STREET

Oriel y Parc/ National Park visitor centre

HIGH STREET

FEIDR PANT

Y-BRYN

CAERFAI ROAD

N

0   200
        yards

St Non's (1 mile)   Caerfai Bay (1 mile)

■ ACCOMMODATION		● EATING	
The Coach House	2	The Bench	2
Twr y Felin	4	Blas	5
The Waterings	3	Cwtch*	4
Y Glennydd	1	The Refectory	1
■ DRINKING		St Davids Food & Wine	3
Farmers Arms	1		

the floor has a clear slope. At the crossing, an elaborate **rood screen** was constructed by fourteenth-century Bishop Henry Gower to incorporate his own tomb. Behind the screen and the organ, the choir sits directly under the tower's magnificently bold and bright lantern, also added by Gower. The Norman round arch over the organ contrasts with the other three supporting the tower, which are pointed and date from the 1220s. At the back of the right-hand choir stalls is a unique **monarch's stall**, complete with royal crest, for, unlike any other British cathedral, the queen is an automatic member of the cathedral Chapter. The misericords under the choir seats display earthy medieval humour; there's one of a chaotic wild boar hunt and another of someone being seasick.

The treasury

Off the north transept, the **treasury** recounts the cathedral's history through a small, well-presented display of its treasures. Also in the north transept, the tomb of St Caradog has two pierced quatrefoils in which people probably inserted diseased limbs in the hope of a cure.

The presbytery

Separating the choir and the presbytery is an unusual **parclose screen** of finely traced woodwork; beyond this is the tomb of Edmund Tudor, father of King Henry VII. On the right/south side is a carved sedilla, a seat for the priest and deacon celebrating Mass, and the tombs of two thirteenth-century bishops. On the other side of the sanctuary is the disappointingly plain thirteenth-century tomb of St David, largely destroyed in the Reformation. The back wall of the **presbytery** was once the cathedral's eastern end, as shown by its windows. The upper row is intact, while the lower three were filled with delicate gold mosaics in the nineteenth century. The colourful fifteenth-century roof, with its deceptively simple medieval pattern, was restored by Sir George Gilbert Scott in the 1860s.

Bishop Vaughan's chapel

Behind the filled-in lancets at the back of the presbytery altar is the Perpendicular **Bishop Vaughan's chapel**, with an exquisite fan tracery roof completed in 1522. Bishop Vaughan's statue occupies the niche to the left of the altar. To the right is an effigy of Giraldus Cambrensis, Gerald of Wales, a mitre placed not on his head, but at his feet – a reminder that he never attained the status of bishop to which he evidently aspired. Opposite, a peephole looks west into the presbytery. The four crosses around the opening may well predate the Norman church: the bottom one is largely obscured by a casket, reputedly containing some of the intermingled bones of St David and his friend, St Justinian. Behind Bishop Vaughan's Chapel is the ambulatory and the simple **Lady Chapel** with its sentimental Edwardian stained glass.

Bishop's Palace

The Close, SA62 6PE • March–June, Sept & Oct daily 9.30am–5pm; July & Aug daily 9.30am–6pm; Nov–Feb Mon–Sat 10am–4pm, Sun 11am–4pm • £4; CADW • ☎ 01437 720517, ⓦ cadw.gov.wales/daysout/stdavidsbishopspalace

From the cathedral, a path leads over the river to the splendid **Bishop's Palace**, built by bishops Beck (1280–93) and Gower (1328–47). A huge quadrangle is enclosed by an array of ruined buildings in extraordinarily rich colours: the green, red, purple and grey tints of volcanic rock, sandstone and many other types of stone. The **arched parapets** along the top of the walls were a favourite motif of Gower, who was largely responsible for transforming the palace into an architectural and political powerhouse. Beck's **Bishop's Hall** is ruinous yet still impressive, while Gower's enormous **Great Hall**, with its glorious rose window, overlays dank vaults housing an interesting exhibition on the palace and the indulgent lifestyles of its occupants. The palace's destruction was largely due to Bishop Barlow (1536–48), who supposedly stripped off the lead roofs to provide dowries for his five daughters' marriages to bishops.

ACTIVITIES AROUND ST DAVIDS

As well as offering **boat trips** to the outlying islands (see p.176), St Davids is a centre for outdoor activities of all description. In addition to the operators listed below – chief among them **TYF** – other companies offering **coasteering** and **sea kayaking** include Cardigan Bay Adventures (Cardigan; ☎01239 612133, ⓦcardiganbayactive.co.uk); Sealyham Activity Centre (Wolfscastle; ☎01348 840763, ⓦsealyham.com) and The Real Adventure Company (Trehenlliw Farm; ☎07421 831462, ⓦtherealadventurecompany.com).

Ma Simes Surf Hut 28 High St, St Davids, SA62 2SD ☎01437 720433, ⓦmasimes.co.uk. The place to rent surfboards (£12/day) or book a lesson (£35/half-day).

Pembrokeshire Sea Kayak Guides The Old School House, Carnhedryn, SA62 6XT ☎01437 720859, ⓦseakayakguides.co.uk. The go-to people for guided sea and surf kayaking, with guides who are knowledgeable about the local birds and seals. £95/person/day for two or more, £150 for one.

Preseli Venture 10 miles east of St Davids, near Mathry, SA62 5HN ☎01348 837709, ⓦpreseliventure.co.uk. Coasteering, sea kayaking, surfing, walking and biking (all half-day £52; £98/day). They also serve lunch and offer superb hostel-style accommodation in their *Eco Lodge* (£39 B&B, £62 full board).

TYF 1 High St, SA62 6SA ☎01437 721611, ⓦtyf.com. This outdoor operator pioneered coasteering, an exhilarating multisport combo that involves scrambling over rocks, jumping off cliffs and swimming across the narrow bays of St Davids peninsula. It's possible for just about anyone (there are even itineraries for non-swimmers) and is offered by TYF throughout the year, as is surfing, kayaking and rock climbing (all £58/half-day, £99/day). They can also organize multiday sessions and longer courses.

ARRIVAL AND INFORMATION   ST DAVIDS

By bus From mid-April to Sept, the Celtic Coaster bus (#403) connects the Grove car park (by the tourist office) and the centre of St Davids with Whitesands Bay, St Justinian's and Porth Clais. Buses from/to Fishguard and Whitesands Bay stop on New St (arriving) and Nun St (departing).

Destinations Broad Haven (3 daily; 45min); Fishguard (7 daily; 50min); Haverfordwest (hourly; 45min); Marloes (3 daily; 1hr 20min); Porthgain (3 daily; 30min); Solva (hourly; 10min); Whitesands Bay (mid-April to Sept hourly; late May to Aug every 30min; 30min).

Oriel y Parc/National Park visitor centre As it comes in from Haverfordwest, the main A487 (here called the High St) passes the National Park's visitor centre (daily: March–Oct 9.30am–5pm; Nov–Feb 10am–4.30pm; ☎01437 720392, ⓦstdavids.co.uk), where you'll also find an art gallery, café and toilets.

National Trust visitor centre Captain's House, Cross Square (Mon–Sat 9am–5pm, Sun 9am–4pm; ☎01437 720385, ⓦnationaltrust.org.uk/st-davids-visitor-centre-and-shop).

ACCOMMODATION

There are numerous places to **stay** on and around St Davids peninsula, including campsites, with fairly high prices in season at the larger hotels, but falling dramatically for the rest of the year. We've listed accommodation outside St Davids itself in our **St Davids peninsula** section (see p.185).

The Coach House 15 High St, SA62 6SB ☎01437 720632, ⓦthecoachhouse.biz. An unpretentious, central B&B with a good range of rooms plus a small cottage for families, and excellent breakfasts. **£85**

Twr y Felin Caerfai Rd, SA62 6QT ☎01437 725555, ⓦtwryfelinhotel.com. Built around a nineteenth-century windmill, this luxurious art-hotel, the finest in town, is the flagship for a group of three local hotels: *Penrhiw Hotel*, a Victorian rectory in the woods just beyond the cathedral, is quieter, while *Roch Castle*, 9 miles east, is a Norman fortress on a volcanic outcrop where the six sleek minimalist rooms are popular for romantic breaks. The hotel's public rooms have almost too much modern art packed in; rooms are decorated in subtle shades of grey with surroundsound TVs,

USB sockets and iPod docks. There's a fine restaurant, too (see p.182). **£170**

The Waterings Anchor Drive, SA62 6BW ☎01437 720876, ⓦwaterings.co.uk. Very comfortable en-suite rooms and suites in a former marine research establishment, which retains a maritime theme. The grounds are lovely, and you can play croquet on the lawn. **£90**

Y Glennydd 51 Nun St, SA62 6NU ☎01438 870487 or ☎01437 720576, ⓦglennyddhotel.co.uk. Welcoming two-star hotel (built for coastguard officers in the 1880s) with eleven rooms (some with shared bathrooms) and a restaurant (£17 for two courses, £20 for three). **£65**

2

2

WALKS AROUND ST DAVIDS

There's some fabulous **walking** around St Davids, largely on the Coast Path, and the Celtic Coaster bus service means that you won't need to retrace your steps. The National Park visitor centre in St Davids (see p.181) stocks a number of leaflets (50p), each detailing a short coastal walk. One good and relatively leisurely **day walk** is from Caerfai Bay, past Porth Clais and round Treginnis Head to St Justinian's. At half tide the waters between here and Ramsey Island churn up into an impressive maelstrom. Another good day walk loops from Whitesands Beach around St Davids Head, one of the most mysterious and magical places in Wales. Evidence of ancient civilization is everywhere, and many mystics have pinpointed the area as a focus of the earth's natural energies. Highlights include the rocky summit of **Carn Llidi** (595ft), approached on the south side past two cromlechs, and **Coetan Arthur** (Arthur's Quoit), a 6000-year-old burial chamber almost hidden on its western slope.

EATING

The Bench Corner High St and New St, SA62 6SB ☏07855 327196, ⓦfacebook.com/pg/benchcafe. Aka *Gianni's*, this sells the best gelato in Pembrokeshire, made with local organic milk in an amazing range of flavours such as Kinder Bueno or gin and elderflower. Daily 9.30am–6pm.

Blas Caerfai Rd, SA62 6QT ☏01437 725555, ⓦtwryfelinhotel.com. The *Twr y Felin* hotel's formal and highly efficient restaurant serves beautifully crafted starters such as goat's curd with olive caramel, tapenade tuile and baby gem (£8) and mains such as sautéed wild mushroom with fresh egg linguine, spinach and black truffle (£18). Daily 8–10am, 11.30am–4.30pm & 6–9.30pm.

★**Cwtch*** 22 High St, SA62 6SD ☏01437 720491, ⓦcwtchrestaurant.co.uk. Some of the finest dining in Pembrokeshire can be found at *Cwtch** (pronounced "cutsh"), an intimate and easy-going restaurant that's all slate, wood and blackboard menus. Top-quality local ingredients are sourced for unfussy dishes such as roasted

red pepper and tomato soup or hake with lime and anchovy butter. Dinner £27/£33 for two/three courses; £23/£27 if you arrive within 45min of opening. Booking recommended. Mid-Feb to Easter, Nov & Dec Wed–Sat 6–9.30pm (last orders), Sun noon–2.30pm; Feb half-term, Easter & Oct Mon–Sat 6–9.30pm, Sun noon–2.30pm; post-Easter to Sept daily 5/6pm–9.30pm.

The Refectory St Davids Cathedral, SA62 6PE ☏01437 721760, ⓦstdavidsrefectory.co.uk. The beautiful St Mary's Hall is a great spot for tea and cakes, classy sandwiches (£6) and mains such as burgers, faggots or fish skewers (all £10). Free wi-fi. Daily: Nov–Easter 11am–4pm; Easter–Nov 10.30am–4.30pm.

St Davids Food & Wine High St, SA62 6SB ☏01437 721948, ⓦstdavidsfoodandwine.co.uk. A splendid deli, selling organic local cheeses and more than thirty Welsh beers; it's the best place to pick up filled rolls or picnic ingredients. Mon–Sat 9am–5pm; summer hols Mon–Sat 8.30am–5.30pm, Sun 10am–5pm.

DRINKING

St Davids is a magnet for surfers, outdoor types and musicians, and has a lively **drinking** scene – in the summer, and over Christmas/New Year, parties can break out just about anywhere.

Farmers Arms 14 Goat St, SA62 6RF ☏01437 721666, ⓦfarmersstdavids.co.uk. Lively and very friendly pub, with a terrace overlooking the cathedral – ideal for a summer's evening. Good food available (summer only), such as panini,

salads, jacket potatoes and mains for £7–12. Easter–Sept daily 11am–midnight; Oct–Easter Mon–Thurs 4pm–midnight, Fri 3pm–midnight, Sat & Sun 11am–midnight; kitchen Easter–Sept daily noon–2.30pm & 6–9.30pm.

St Davids peninsula

Surrounded on three sides by inlets, coves and rocky stacks, St Davids is an easy base for excellent walking around the headland of the same name. A mile south, the popular **Caerfai Bay** is a sandy gash (vanishing at high tide) in the purple-sandstone cliffs, from which masonry for the cathedral was quarried. Half a mile to the west is the craggy indentation of **St Non's Bay**, with the ancient harbour of Porth Clais just beyond.

Dr Beynon's Bug Farm

Lower Harglodd Farm, just over a mile northeast of St Davids on the A487, SA62 6BX • School hols daily 10.30am–4.30pm; rest of year Sat & Sun 10.30am–4.30pm • £6.50 • ☎ 07966 956357, ⊕ thebugfarm.co.uk

Dr Beynon's Bug Farm is a scientific research centre and working farm investigating the role of insects in agriculture and sustainable enterprises. It is now the flagship of the movement for **entomophagy**, or eating insects, as part of a drive to reduce the global environmental impact of producing more and more meat. It's also a lot of fun, with a one-room museum full of juicy insect facts and a Victorian collection of iridescent butterflies; a bug zoo featuring monsters such as Chilean rose tarantulas, rainbow stag beetles and Madagascan hissing cockroaches as well as land snails and hermit crabs; an art gallery; and the outdoor Pollinator Trail. A former cowshed houses an insect-focused **restaurant** (see p.185).

2

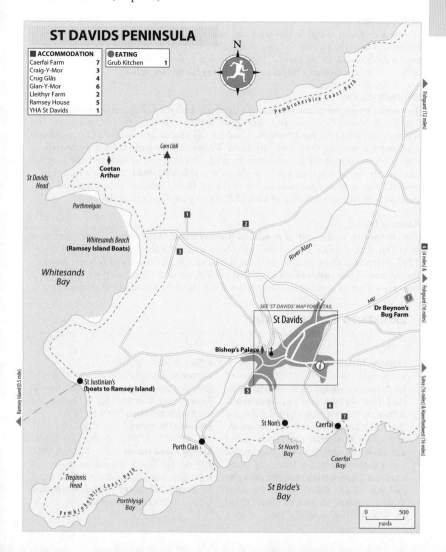

2

St Non's Bay

Legend tells that St Non gave birth to St David in what is now **St Non's Bay**, a mile south of St Davids, during a tumultuous storm around 500 AD. A spring opened up between her feet, and despite the crashing thunder all around, an eerily calm light filtered down onto the scene. Pilgrims have come here for centuries, resulting in the foundation of a tiny Celtic chapel, whose successor's thirteenth-century ruins now lie in a field to the right of the car park, beyond the simple well and shrine at the birthplace of Wales' patron saint. The 1934 **chapel**, in front of the austere 1929 **Retreat House**, was built in plain Pembrokeshire style from the rocks of ruined houses, which, in turn, had been built from the stone of ancient, abandoned churches. Just to the west, **Porth Clais** was the city's main harbour from Roman times, the spruced-up remains of which can still be seen at the bottom of the turquoise river creek.

St Justinian's

Running due west out of St Davids, Goat Street ducks past the ruins of the Bishop's Palace and over the plateau for two miles to the harbour at **St Justinian's**, little more than a roofless chapel (no access), lifeboat station (summer daily 10am–4pm) and ticket hut for the frequent **boats** over to **Ramsey Island** (see below).

Whitesands Bay

Two miles to the north and reached via the B4583 off the Fishguard road, **Whitesands Bay** (Porth Mawr) faces west and offers good **surfing**, especially for intermediates. The spectacularly beautiful **Porthmelgan**, a narrow slip of cove reached by a fifteen-minute walk northwest along the Coast Path from Whitesands car park, is far less crowded, largely on account of the dangerous swimming. The thin spit of rock and cliff that juts out into the ocean less than a mile to the west is **St Davids Head**, site of an Iron Age coastal fortress, its outline most visible in spring. Rising behind Whitesands and Porthmelgan, the gnarled crag of **Carn Llidi** tops a pastoral patchwork of fields.

Ramsey Island

The enchanting dual-humped plateau of **Ramsey Island** (Ynys Dewi), three miles west of St Davids and half a mile offshore, has been under the able care of the RSPB since 1992. Peregrines and choughs circle the skies above it, but the island is better known for the tens of thousands of sea birds that noisily crowd the sheer cliffs on the western side. Grey seals laze on the beaches, below paths worn by a herd of red deer. There's

---

CRUISES TO RAMSEY ISLAND

Several operators run **boat trips** to Ramsey either from St Justinian's or Whitesands Beach; some also offer trips to Grassholm (see p.177).

Thousand Islands Expeditions Cross Square, St Davids, SA62 6SL ☎01437 721721, ⊛thousand islands.co.uk. The only operator allowed to land on the island. Boats (April–Oct daily; £18) depart from St Justinian's at 10am and noon, returning at noon and 4pm; you can come back on either boat, allowing you up to six hours of exploration, or you can take a guided walk with an RSPB warden (£25). Perhaps the best deal is their combined "Landing & Around" trip (10am; returning at 1.30pm, 4pm or 5.30pm; £38), which gives you a good look at the wildlife. There's also the evening "Puffin & Shearwater" trip (6pm; 1hr 30min; £30) and the "Whale & Dolphin experience" (9am, 3.15pm &

4.15pm; 2hr 30min–3hr; £60).

Venture Jet ☎01348 837764 or freephone ☎0800 0854786, ⊛venturejet.co.uk. Jet boats from St Justinian's and Whitesands Bay to Ramsey and Grassholm, from £25 for an hour to £60 for 3hr.

Voyages of Discovery 1 High St, St Davids, SA62 6SA ☎01437 721911, ⊛ramseyisland.co.uk; **Ramsey Island Cruises** New St, St Davids, SA62 6SW ☎01437 721423 or freephone ☎0800 028 6212, ⊛ramseyislandcruises.co.uk). Both charge from roughly £25 for an hour's trip to Ramsey Island to £60 for a 2hr 30min trip to Grassholm.

something to see all year round, but spring is great for nesting birds (especially puffins and shearwaters), and autumn for seals with their pups. Two loop paths can be combined as a three-hour full island circuit.

| ACCOMMODATION | ST DAVIDS PENINSULA |

HOTEL AND GUESTHOUSES

Craig-Y-Mor Whitesands Bay, SA62 6PT ☎01437 720431, ⊛stdavidsbandb.co.uk. Excellent B&B whose three rooms each have a lounge area as well as an artfully designed bathroom; you get views across the golf course to St Davids Head, and classy breakfasts. **£110**

★**Crug Glâs** 4 miles northeast of St Davids off the A487, SA62 6XX ☎01348 831302, ⊛crug-glas.co.uk. Luxurious country house on a working farm, with five large rooms elaborately decorated with gold fittings, tasselled cushions and half-tester or four-poster beds, plus a spacious attic suite (£190). Breakfasts are excellent (great bacon) and dinners are very classy, with starters such as Abercastle crab cake and mains such as cannon of lamb, plus a good long wine list. **£150**

Ramsey House Lower Moor, on the road from St Davids to Porth Clais, SA62 6RP ☎01437 720321, ⊛ramseyhouse.co.uk. Quality B&B, with six boutique-style rooms and excellent breakfasts (featuring eggs from their own hens and ducks). They also have a bar. Closed Dec–Feb. **£100**

HOSTEL AND CAMPSITES

Caerfai Farm Caerfai Bay, 1 mile south of St Davids, SA62 6QT ☎01437 720548, ⊛cawscaerfai.co.uk. The best campsite around, on an organic dairy farm (with shop) with stunning coastal views. You get a £2 discount if you arrive on foot or by bike. Closed late Sept to late May. **£16**

Glan-Y-Mor Caerfai Rd, 0.5 mile south of St Davids, SA62 6QT ☎01437 721788, ⊛glan-y-mor.co.uk. This is the nearest campsite to town, with spacious pitches and a log cabin, and bookings and transfers for surfing lessons. Closed Oct–March. Camping **£14**, cabin **£60**

Lleithyr Farm Just off the B4583 between St Davids and Whitesands Bay, SA62 6PR ☎01437 720245, ⊛lleithyrfarm.co.uk. High-quality campsite and caravan park, with a good shop (Easter–Sept) plus heated shower rooms in the colder months. Closed Nov–Feb. **£18**

YHA St Davids Llaethdy, 2 miles northwest of St Davids, SA62 6PR ☎0345 371 9141, ⊛yha.org.uk/hostel/st-davids. Large, renovated hostel in a former farmhouse. Daytime lockout and 11pm curfew. Closed Nov–March. Dorms **£15**, doubles **£50**

EATING

Grub Kitchen Dr Beynon's Bug Farm, Lower Harglodd Farm, just over a mile northeast of St Davids, SA62 6BX ☎07986 698169, ⊛grubkitchen.co.uk. A former cowshed at the bug farm (see p.183) houses this quirky restaurant serving dishes such as cricket-flour cookies, bug burgers and bug felafels, as well as more standard offerings – vegetarian, vegan or sustainable, local lamb and beef. Bookings required for dinner. School hols Mon–Thurs & Sun 10.30am–4.30pm, Fri & Sat 10.30am–4.30pm & 6–9.30pm; rest of year Sat & Sun 10.30am–4.30pm & 6–9.30pm.

North Pembrokeshire coast

The **North Pembrokeshire coast**, forming the very southern sweep of Cardigan Bay, is noticeably less commercialized than the touristy littoral of south and mid-Pembrokeshire. From the crags and cairns above St Davids Head, the Coast Path perches precariously on the cliffs, where only the thousands of sea birds have access.

Although the area's major source of income is now tourism, the remains of old mines, quarries and ports at **Abereiddi** and **Porthgain** bear witness to the slate and granite industries that once employed hundreds of people. Industry dies down towards **Trefin** and up to the more remote beaches and inlets that punctuate the coast as it climbs up to the splendid knuckle of **Strumble Head**. To the east is **Carregwastad Point**, the site of the last invasion of Britain in 1797 – also remembered in the port town of **Fishguard**, where the invading French surrendered at the *Royal Oak Inn*.

Abereiddi to Abercastle

The fantastic stretch of coast northeast of St Davids, from **Abereiddi to Abercastle**, combines rugged cliffs and birdlife with remnants of long-closed industry and even more ancient cultures.

2

Abereiddi

Five miles north of St Davids, a small lane tumbles down into the bleak hamlet of **ABEREIDDI**, where you can find tiny fossilized animals in the shale of the black-sand beach. At the back of the beach are remains of workers' huts and a tramway that once looped around the hill to Porthgain, all part of the slate quarry that closed in 1910. The quarry was then dynamited for safety reasons, producing a "blue lagoon" due to the minerals suspended in the seawater – it's popular with coasteering groups and cliff-divers.

Porthgain

Continuing parallel to the coast, the lane leads to tiny **Llanrhian**, where a left turn takes you a mile down to the rambling village green of **PORTHGAIN**. This fascinating little port grew up from 1850 below its slate works, the stumpy remains of which huddle around the tiny quay, together with an old brickworks, lime kiln and eerie ruins of workers' cottages. It also has toilets, a couple of small galleries and the *Sloop Inn* (see below). There's a superb circular walk (4 miles; 2hr) back to Abereiddi, which is largely level after the steep climb out of Porthgain; it returns inland (or you can take the Strumble Shuttle bus).

Abercastle

The coastal lane continues east across through Trefin and drops to **ABERCASTLE**, passing the footpath to the 4500-year-old **Carreg Samson** cromlech at Longhouse Farm, precariously topped by a 16ft capstone. If you're walking, continue past the cromlech and down to the Coast Path to Abercastle, an attractive little cove once used for the export of limestone and coal. From there, one of the most scenic parts of the Coast Path zigzags east for about two miles along wild, vertiginous cliffs to the point at **Trwyn Llwynog**.

ARRIVAL AND GETTING AROUND	ABEREIDDI TO ABERCASTLE
By bus The Strumble Shuttle (bus #404) connects St Davids with Fishguard via coastal villages such as Abereiddi, Porthgain and Trefin (May–Sept 3 daily;	Oct–April Thurs & Sat 2 daily). Bus #413 (Mon–Sat 6 daily) runs from St Davids to Fishguard via Trefin.

ACCOMMODATION AND EATING

★**Caerhafod Lodge** 0.5 mile north of Llanrhian, SA62 5BD ☎01348 837859, ⍵caerhafod.co.uk. Within walking distance of Porthgain, this is a brilliant independent hostel with a tranquil atmosphere, good views and helpful hosts. They offer self-catering facilities and mostly four-bedded rooms (sheets supplied). **£20**

Celtic Camping and Bunkhouse Pwllcaerog Farm, 0.5 mile west of Abereiddi, SA62 6DG ☎01348 837405, ⍵celtic-camping.co.uk. This glorious campsite sits on the cliffs with wonderful sunset views over tiny Aberpwll beach; there are good facilities for campervans and caravans as well as secluded tent-hiding spots, and also bunkhouses and dorms for groups. Open all year. **£20**

Old School Hostel Ffordd-yr-afon, Trefin, SA62 5AU ☎01348 831800, ⍵oldschoolhostel.com. A mile or so east of Porthgain, this ecologically minded place is a former YHA hostel that has been revamped and rejuvenated. It

offers bunks and ultra-cheap private rooms, as well as light breakfasts and packed lunches. Dorms **£16**, doubles **£36**

The Shed Porthgain, SA62 5BN ☎01348 831518, ⍵theshedporthgain.co.uk. As well as a tearoom and deli selling fresh fish and cheese, this is a classy fish and chips restaurant, with most of the fish (from £10.50) caught locally. Shop & tearoom Easter to mid-Oct daily 10am–5pm; restaurant March–Sept daily noon–3pm & 5.30–10pm; Oct–April Mon–Thurs noon–3pm, Fri–Sun noon–3pm & 5.30–10pm.

Sloop Inn Porthgain, SA62 5BN ☎01348 831449, ⍵sloop.co.uk. This charming eighteenth-century pub has numerous photographs of the port in its sepia heyday and a perfect terrace to while away the evening, as well as good bar food and a Sun roast. Mon–Fri & Sun 9.30am–11pm, Sat 9.30am–11.30pm; kitchen daily 9.30–11.30am, noon–5.30pm & 6–9.30pm.

Strumble Head

The headland – known as **Pen Caer** – that rises to the north of Abercastle, peaking at Strumble Head, is delightful: tiny hedge-backed lanes bump around between rocky cairns, with fields of wild flowers and sudden glimpses of shimmering sea. This remote and spectacular section of the Coast Path gives access to the sandy stretch of **Aber Mawr**, smaller **Aber Bach** and the west-facing gash of **Pwllcochran**.

Nearly two miles further north, there's the simple but fabulously sited *Pwll Deri* YHA **hostel** (see below). Looming large on the inland side of the hostel are the three crags of **Garn Fawr** (699ft): by following a path from the car park at their eastern edge, on the lane up to Strumble Head, you'll find a spectacular Iron Age fort, with ditches, ramparts and hut circles.

STRUMBLE HEAD itself, just over a mile north of Garn Fawr, is reached either by the rugged Coast Path – with astounding views over the two-mile-long "wall" of cliffs to the south – or along a floral country lane. At the headland, the 1908 **lighthouse** perches atop **Ynys Meicel**, connected to the mainland by a metal footbridge that's closed to the public. It's a peaceful yet invigorating spot that's perhaps the best in Wales for **sea bird spotting**, with gannets, kittiwakes, guillemots and fulmars, and five types of shearwaters, as well as porpoises. On land you may see stonechats, linnets, choughs, peregrines, buzzards and ravens.

ACCOMMODATION	STRUMBLE HEAD
YHA Pwll Deri Castell Mawr, Trefasser, SA64 0LR ☎0345 371 9536, ⊛yha.org.uk/hostel/pwll-deri. Splendidly located self-catering hostel (4 miles west of	Goodwick and the nearest shops), with en-suite dorms and a couple of private twin rooms. Closed Oct–March. Dorms <u>£18</u>, twins <u>£49</u>

Llanwnda and Carregwastad Point

Almost three miles beyond Strumble Head, the hamlet of **LLANWNDA** was the site of the last invasion of Britain (see box below). Its very simple **St Gwyndaf church** (usually open) is also worth a visit for its charming setting, an ancient history which winds back beyond the eighth century, and the collection of pre-Norman carved stones embedded in its walls. The 1.5-mile **walk** to **Carregwastad Point** is fabulous, coasting gently down fields and across the top of a craggy cwm. Start by crossing the stile up the track from the church entrance. At the coast turn left to reach the point and the plaque commemorating the invasion, or right to **Aber Felin**, a bay where you may see grey seals.

Fishguard

FISHGUARD (Abergwaun) occupies a lofty headland between the pretty Lower Town and the port of **Goodwick** (Wdig), just under a mile northwest. The huge port was built

THE LAST INVASION OF BRITAIN

In 1797, while Napoleon was off fighting in Italy, a newly formed Franco-Irish revolutionary command was trying to make its mark in Paris. Believing that the oppressed countryfolk of Britain would sympathize with their revolutionary views and join their cause, a motley band of "liberators" – some just out of prison and still shackled – launched a madcap plan to invade Britain. Winds blew their ships from their planned landing at Bristol and they ended up at **Carregwastad Point**, just west of Fishguard. The disorganized army of 1400 made its base at Trehowel Farm, midway between Strumble Head and Llanwnda, which was stocked with food and drink for an imminent family wedding. Indeed most local farms were full of contraband liquor plundered from a recent Portuguese shipwreck. The would-be conquerors set to with gusto, swiftly becoming too drunk to do anything except loot the silver plate in Llanwnda's church.

After two days the invasion had collapsed and the invaders surrendered on February 24 to a local militia at the **Royal Oak** in Fishguard, claiming they had seen "troops of the line to the number of several thousand". No such army was in the vicinity and some say the bleary-eyed French mistook several hundred local women clad in stovepipe hats and red flannel shawls for British Redcoats. While that may not be true, it's a fact that fourteen soldiers were rounded up with a pitchfork by 47-year-old Jemima Nicholas – dubbed ever since the "Welsh Heroine".

2

by the Great Western Railway in 1906 as the shortest route to the United States as well as southern Ireland; fittingly, Goodwick was also the departure point in 1912 for the first flight from Wales to Ireland. Though often seen only as somewhere from which to catch the Irish **ferry**, it's an enjoyably arty place, with fine views from the easy coastal walks around town.

In the centre of town, the **Royal Oak Inn** was the scene of the surrender of the "last invasion of Britain" in 1797. The episode's heroine, Jemima Nicholas (see box, p.187), is buried beside the Victorian **parish church** behind the pub.

Last Invasion Gallery

Main St • April–Sept Mon–Wed & Fri 9.30am–5pm, Thurs 9.30am–6pm, Sat 9.30am–4pm; Oct–March Mon–Wed & Fri 9.30am–5pm, Thurs 9.30am–6pm, Sat 9.30am–1pm • Free

Inside the town hall, the **Last Invasion Gallery** contains the 100ft-long **Fishguard Tapestry**, inspired by the famous Bayeux model and made to mark the event's bicentenary in 1997. The tapestry offers a wonderful depiction of the invasion, including debauched French soldiers, with one unfortunate thief shown on the lower border with his throat cut. A video tells the story of the local artists and embroiderers who made it all happen, and the bicentenary re-enactment.

Lower Town

Main Street plummets down to **Lower Town** (Y Cwm), a cluster of old-fashioned cottages around a muddy, thriving, herring-fishing and pleasure-boat port. From above there are superb views over the town headland and out to the breakwater. Lower Fishguard's moment of glory came in 1971, when Richard Burton and Elizabeth Taylor filmed Dylan Thomas' *Under Milk Wood* here.

ARRIVAL AND INFORMATION

FISHGUARD

By train Trains call at Fishguard & Goodwick station on Station Hill in Goodwick (occasional buses to Fishguard stop across the road, except on Sun) and terminate at Fishguard Harbour, in Goodwick.
Destinations Cardiff (6 daily; 2hr 45min); Carmarthen (7 daily; 50min); Swansea (7 daily; 1hr 45min).
By bus Buses stop by the town hall in the central Market Square, right outside Fishguard's tourist office, and at Station Hill and The Parrog in Goodwick.
Destinations Cardigan (hourly; 40min); Haverfordwest (hourly; 40min); Newport, Pembrokeshire (hourly; 15min); Rosebush (1 on Tues; 25min); St Davids (6–8 daily; 45min); Trefin (6–8 daily; 30min).

By ferry Fishguard harbour, for ferries to Rosslare, Ireland (2 daily; 3hr 30min), is on Quay Rd in Goodwick. Most buses stop 0.5 mile away at Station Hill. A taxi (☎01348 873075 or 875129 or 870288) into Fishguard costs about £4 from the harbour.
Tourist office In the town hall on the central Market Square (June–Aug Mon–Fri 9am–5pm, Sat 10am–4pm; Sept–May Mon–Fri 9am–1pm & 1.45–5pm; ☎01347 776636, ✉fishguard.tic@pembrokeshire.gov.uk). It has free internet access (15min maximum); for longer sessions visit the library upstairs (Mon–Wed, Fri & Sat 10am–5pm, Thurs 10am–6pm).

ACCOMMODATION

★**Cefn-y-Dre** 1 mile south along Hamilton and Wallis Streets, SA65 9QS ☎01348 875663, ⊕cefnydre.co.uk.

There's a relaxed and understated elegance to this lovely country house, with just three rooms, partly dating from the

> ## FISHGUARD'S FESTIVALS
>
> Theatr Gwaun on West Street (☎01348 873421, ⊕theatrgwaun.com) mainly shows films but also hosts the occasional music or drama event –notably the increasingly popular **Fishguard Folk Festival** (⊕pembrokeshire-folk-music.co.uk), held over the bank holiday weekend at the end of May. There's also the **Fishguard International Music Festival** (⊕fishguardmusic festival.co.uk) in late July, combining classical, choral, jazz and blues; the **Aberjazz Festival** in late August (⊕aberjazz.com); and **Fishguard's Autumn Festival** (⊕fishguardsautumnfestival .co.uk) around the first weekend of November.

early sixteenth century. Attractive grounds, tasty breakfasts and superb home-cooked meals (reserve in advance; not high season) prepared by wonderful hosts. £90

Gwaun Vale Caravan Park 1.5 miles southeast, on the B4313, SA65 9YA ☎ 01348 874698, ⊛ gwaunvale.co.uk. Well-appointed site on the fringes of Cwm Gwaun that is relatively wind-free even when the Coast Path is getting battered. £20

Hamilton Lodge 23 Hamilton St, SA65 9HL ☎ 01348 874797, ⊛ hamiltonbackpackers.co.uk. Cosy, very central

and well-set-up hostel with rooms for two, three and four (light breakfast included), a private double and self-catering for groups in the old chapel next door. Bed linen provided; towels can be rented. Dorms £20, double £49

Manor Town House 11 Main St, SA65 9HG ☎ 01348 873260, ⊛ manortownhouse.com. This lovingly restored Georgian house in the centre of town is an award-winning guesthouse with fantastic beds and superb, locally sourced breakfasts. £85

EATING AND DRINKING

Ffwrn 8 Main St, SA65 9HH ☎ 01348 875412. This quirkily decorated Franco-Welsh café-bakery serves delicious tapas, pastries and crêpes and is also a music venue. Tues–Sun 10.30am–4pm.

The Gourmet Pig 32 West St, SA65 9AD ☎ 01348 874 404, ⊛ gourmetpig.co.uk. A very classy deli, selling breads, meats and cheeses, gluten-free cakes, barista coffees, wine and beer; head for the tin shed-style upper dining area to enjoy deli sandwiches, platters and pies. Mon–Fri 9.30am–3.30pm, Sat 9.30am–4.30pm.

Pepper's aka Café Celf 16 West St, SA65 9AE ☎ 01348 873867, ⊛ peppers-hub.co.uk. Arty café with a range of spaces (bistro, art gallery, cocktail bar, jazz basement) that's great for tapas or a bistro meal. Mains (£15–18)

might include lamb meatballs or chicken with saffron, almonds, raisins and spices. Popular music nights, too. Mon–Sat 10am–10.30pm.

Royal Oak Market Square, SA65 9HA ☎ 01348 873355, ⊛ facebook.com/trofishguard. Historic pub with real ales and good pub lunches. There's also a long-established folk night on Tues – participants very welcome. Mon–Thurs & Sun 11am–12.30am, Fri & Sat 11am–1.30am; kitchen daily noon–4pm.

Ship Inn 3 Newport Rd, Lower Town, SA65 9ND ☎ 01348 874033. Eccentric pub with interesting clutter all over the walls and ceiling, including black-and-white photos of the filming of *Under Milk Wood* and *Moby Dick*. There's often music on Fri nights. Daily noon–midnight.

Mynydd Preseli

Pembrokeshire is famed for its magnificent coastal scenery, but its interior is frequently overlooked. The **Mynydd Preseli** (Preseli mountains) occupy a triangle of land in the north of the county, flecked with prehistoric remains and roughly bounded by the coast in the north, the B4313 to the west and the A478 to the east.

The main A487 coast road is the area's only major **bus** route, cruising from Fishguard to Cardigan through delightful **Newport**, handy for the historic peak of **Carn Ingli**, the bucolic church at **Nevern** with its "bleeding" yew, and the reconstructed Iron Age settlement at **Castell Henllys**. This is also the final (or initial) stretch of the Pembrokeshire Coast Path and the cognoscenti's favourite, with awesome solitude, abundant natural life and stunning cliff formations.

Inland from Fishguard, the **Gwaun River** wriggles southeast through its green cwm, with tiny villages and remote churches seemingly untouched by modernity. Formed around two hundred thousand years ago, this is Europe's oldest glacial meltwater valley and the subject of many a geology field trip. The brooding mountains hereabouts shelter innumerable standing stones, stone circles, hillforts, cairns and earthworks, several linked by a hike along the **Golden Road**.

Newport and around

The A487 winds through **NEWPORT** (Trefdraeth), an ancient, proud and wealthy little town that without doubt makes the best base in north Pembrokeshire. On a gentle slope coursing down to the estuary of the Afon Nyfer, it is a quietly enjoyable place, with superb accommodation, food and drink, welcoming inhabitants and a selection of fine coastal and hill walks on its doorstep. Newport still appoints a mayor annually, a legacy of its days as the seat of the Norman Marcher Lordship of Cemaes. Another manifestation of this heritage is the annual custom, on the third Friday of August, of "Beating of the Bounds", when the mayor marks out the town's boundaries. The town's **festival**, Ffair Gurig, is held the week of June 27, with a carnival on its last Saturday.

South of the main thoroughfare, **Bridge Street**, a number of pretty lanes rise up to the intriguing **castle** (private), a nineteenth-century residence fashioned out of the thirteenth-century gatehouse. The other obvious landmark, just to the west, is **St Mary's church** (usually open), with a Norman font, a massive thirteenth-century tower, and a history display in the north transept.

The Nyfer estuary and beaches

Long Street and Lower St Mary Street head down to the **Nyfer estuary**, over which squawking gulls circle and skim the water's edge. A path hugs its southern shore – turn east (or take Parrog Road if you're driving) for a gentle stroll to the **Parrog**, Newport's nearest beach, mostly shingle but with sandy stretches at low tide. A better beach is the vast dune-backed **Traethmawr**, on the north side of the estuary, reached over the Iron Bridge down Feidr Pen-y-Bont – note the pilgrims' stepping stones upstream from the bridge. The footpath along the river, marked as the Pilgrims' Way, makes a delightful stroll for a couple of miles east to Nevern (see opposite). Just short of the bridge, on the town side, **Carreg Coetan Arthur**, a well-preserved capped burial chamber, can be seen behind holiday bungalows.

Carn Ingli

Follow Church Street past St Mary's for the relatively easy two-hour ascent of **Carn Ingli** (Hill of Angels), once the core of an active volcano and one of Wales' holiest mountains. It gets its name from the angels who supposedly kept St Brynach company as he lived here in quiet contemplation. More certainly, stone embankments of the Iron Age hillfort and the nearby Bronze Age hut circles prove that the hill once had a sizeable community. There's also access from the Sychpant Woods car park to the north in the Gwaun Valley.

ARRIVAL AND INFORMATION   **NEWPORT**

By bus Buses stop on Bridge St in the town centre. The Poppit Rocket (May–Sept 3 daily; Oct–April Thurs & Sat 3 daily) runs to the Parrog and Trefdraeth beaches as well as Poppit Sands.
Destinations Cardigan (hourly; 20min); Fishguard (hourly; 15min); Haverfordwest (hourly; 1hr).
Tourist office The National Park tourist office (April–Oct

Mon–Sat 10am–5.30pm; Nov–March Mon–Sat 10.30am–1pm & 1.30–5.30pm, Sat 10.30am–1.30pm; ☎01239 820912, ✉newportTIC@pembrokeshirecoast .org.uk), on Long St, offers paid internet access.
Bike rental Carn Ingli Bike Hire, at the Carningli Centre, East St (Mon–Sat 10am–5.30pm; ☎01239 820724, ⓦcarningli .co.uk), has bikes for £15/day and tag-alongs for kids for £10.

ACCOMMODATION

HOTELS AND GUESTHOUSES

Cnapan East St, SA42 0SY ☎01239 820575, ⓦcnapan .co.uk. Five comfortable rooms and an old-fashioned friendly welcome are the hallmarks of this B&B, a long-standing favourite. Closed Jan–March. **£95**
The Globe Upper St Mary St, SA42 0PS ☎01239 820296, ⓦtheglobebedandbreakfast.co.uk. A former pub with two rooms with shared bathroom and a pleasant garden; continental breakfast included. **£73**
★ **Llys Meddyg** East St, SA42 0SY ☎01239 820008, ⓦllysmeddyg.com. Comfy-chic restaurant-with-rooms fashioned from a Georgian coaching inn, displaying fine local art. All rooms have great bedding, classy toiletries and individual decor. The food's good, too (see opposite). **£120**

Y Bryn Fishguard Rd, 200yd west, SA42 0TY ☎01239 820288, ⓦbrynbedandbreakfast.co.uk. Great-value B&B with four unfussy rooms, all with private bathroom (three also have sea views); the spacious attic room is particularly appealing. A full breakfast is served and there's off-street parking. **£75**

HOSTEL AND CAMPSITE

Morawelon The Parrog, 300yd northwest of town, SA42 0RW ☎01239 820565, ⓦcampsite-pembrokeshire .co.uk. Seaside campsite, in pleasant gardens and with its own café overlooking the beach, and coin-op showers. Closed Nov–Feb. **£18**
YHA Newport Lower St Mary St, SA42 0TS ☎0345 371

9543, ⓦyha.org.uk/hostel/newport-pembrokeshire.
Classy conversion of an old school with dorms and a couple

of private rooms. Self-catering only. Closed Oct–March.
Dorms __£15__, doubles __£78__

EATING AND DRINKING

Blas at Fronlas Market St, SA42 0PH ☎01239 820065,
ⓦblasatfronlas.com. There's a cosy licensed café-deli at
this B&B, serving breakfast and lunch, including baguettes
and panini, quiche of the day and cawl (£8). Reserve for
dinner. Mon–Thurs & Sun 9am–4.30pm, Fri & Sat
9am–4.30pm & dinner from 7pm.

Golden Lion East St, SA42 0SY ☎01239 820321,
ⓦgoldenlionpembrokeshire.co.uk. Bare stone and
timber-beamed pub with real ales and a superb menu of
carefully prepared pub meals (£12) and fancier restaurant-
style dishes (£13–22), both served either in the bar or
more formally at the back. Daily noon–midnight; kitchen
noon–2pm & 6–9pm.

Llys Meddyg East St, SA42 0SY ☎01239 820008,

ⓦllysmeddyg.com. A Georgian dining room, a cellar bar
or a partly walled kitchen garden (July & Aug) provide
settings for exquisite dinners, which might start with crab
with green apple and fennel (£9) followed by a fish stew or
local lamb with asparagus (£16). Lunches are equally
appealing. They also offer guestrooms (see opposite).
April–Sept Tues–Sat noon–3pm & 6–9pm, Sun noon–
3pm; Oct–March Wed–Sat noon–3pm & 6–9pm.

Morawelon The Parrog, SA42 0RW ☎01239 820565.
Waterfront café specializing in seafood, with crab and
prawn sandwiches (£5–8.75) and cod and chips (£10), as
well as vegetable tagine (£9.50), waffles (£5) and cream
teas (£4). April–Sept daily 9am–5pm; Oct & Dec–March
Wed–Sun 10am–4pm.

The Coast Path from Newport

Either side of Newport, the **Coast Path** runs through some sublime scenery. Two miles
west of town, a very narrow road leads to the popular strand at **Cwm-yr-Eglwys**, where
the scant seafront ruins of the twelfth-century **St Brynach's church** are all that survived a
huge storm on the night of October 25, 1859, when the rest of the church and 114
ships at sea were wrecked. From here or **PWLLGWAELOD**, on the far side of the
headland, where the *Old Sailors*, an ancient smugglers' inn (Tues & Sun 11am–6pm,
Wed–Sat 11am–10pm), sits above a grey-sand beach, you can take a three-mile walk
around **Dinas Head**, offering splendid views over the huge cliffs, where thousands of sea
birds nest between May and mid-July.

The stretch of path running **east** from Newport to the fringes of Cardigan at St
Dogmael's is perhaps the wildest and toughest of the whole Coast Path: it plummets and
climbs past rocky outcrops, blowholes, caves, natural arches, ancient defensive sites and
thousands of sea birds. The only road access is at the spectacularly folded cliffs of **Ceibwr
Bay**, eight miles from Newport near the pretty pastel village of **MOYLEGROVE** (Trewyddel).

Nevern

Just over a mile east of Newport by road, about double that by a riverside walk, the
darkly atmospheric village of **NEVERN** (Nanhyfer) has a couple of intriguing sights.

Church of St Brynach

B4582, in the centre of the village, SA42 0NF • Daily • Free

The brooding bulk of the **church of St Brynach**, founded in the sixth century and with a
massive Norman tower, has many features of interest. The churchyard's ancient yews
give it a dank, dark presence. Note the second on the right, the famous "**bleeding
yew**", so called for the brown-red sap that oozes mysteriously from its bark. Legend has
it that it will continue to bleed until a Welsh lord of the manor is reinstated in the
village castle – unlikely any time soon, given its tumbledown state. Also outside the
church, just by the south transept, are the stunning **Great Cross of St Brynach**, an
inscribed tenth-century Celtic masterpiece standing some 13ft high, and the **Vitalianus
Stone**, with a Latin inscription recording a sixth-century burial. Inside, two ancient
inscribed stones have been built into the south transept's windowsills: the **Maglocunus
Stone**, with Latin and Ogham inscriptions from about the fifth century AD, and the
Cross Stone, marked with a very early Celtic cross.

Nevern Castle
North side of the village • Open access • Free

High above the village, the ruins of the Norman **Nevern Castle**, built in 1108 and abandoned in 1195, are being excavated and restored a bit; visitors are welcomed at the dig in June or July. A circular walk from the church gate crosses the stream and climbs to the large motte, on top of which is the circular base of a stone keep raised in the 1170s by the Lord Rhys (Rhys ap Gruffudd), who ended up imprisoned here by his own sons before they burnt the castle to prevent its falling into Anglo-Norman hands.

Pentre Ifan
Two miles south of Nevern • Open access • Free

The well-signposted cromlech at **Pentre Ifan** is a vast Neolithic communal grave – the largest in Wales – with its 16-tonne arrowhead top-stone precariously balanced on three stone legs. The views of the stark, eerie Mynydd Preseli and the pastoral rolling countryside to the east are superb.

Castell Henllys
Off the A487, 2 miles east of Nevern, SA41 3UR • Easter–Oct daily 10am–5pm; Nov–Easter Mon–Fri 11am–3pm; guided tours (1hr; free) April–Oct 11.30am & 2.30pm • Easter–Oct £5.50; Nov–Easter £4 • ☎ 01239 891319, ⓦ castellhenllys.com

Excavations of the Iron Age village of **Castell Henllys** are turning up more and more of its past. Four roundhouses and a granary, complete with thatch, have been reconstructed on their 2000-year-old foundations, and throughout the summer the National Park lays on opportunities to watch ancient skills and learn about Iron Age life here. Children's activities during school holidays give kids a chance to try wool dyeing and basket making or train as a warrior. A sculpture trail through the woods and river valley brings to life the folk tales of *The Mabinogion*, and further trails lead into the ancient oak woodlands of the adjacent Pengelli Forest; there's also a busy café.

Cwm Gwaun and the inland hills

Cwm Gwaun, the valley of the burbling River Gwaun, is one of the great surprises of Pembrokeshire – a bucolic vale of impossibly narrow lanes, shouldered by bare mountains. It is a timeless place whose residents retain an attachment to the pre-1752 Julian calendar, celebrating New Year on January 13.

Pontfaen

Three miles off the B4313 you reach the scattered settlement of **PONTFAEN**, complete with its time-warped pub, the remote *Dyffryn Arms* (see opposite). Turning sharp right before the pub and following the lane across the river and up a sharp hill for a quarter-mile, you'll reach Pontfaen's exquisitely restored **church** (daily; free), dedicated, like so many round here, to St Brynach. The circular graveyard indicates pre-Christian origins before the church was founded, according to tradition, by the wandering Breton saint in 540 AD. In the graveyard are two impressive but very worn stone crosses, dating from between the sixth and ninth centuries.

Gerddi Penlan-Uchaf
Two miles northeast of Pontfaen, SA65 9UA • March–Nov daily dawn–dusk • £3 • ☎ 01348 881388, ⓦ carnedward.co.uk/the-gardens

Well tucked away, the delightful **Gerddi Penlan-Uchaf** is a set of hillside **gardens** cut through by a stream with wonderful views over the valley. They contain thousands of miniature flowering and alpine plants, and acres of herbs and wild flowers together with some impressive dwarf conifers. You can also buy their fresh Carn Edward lamb and longhorn beef, as well as soup, cake and cream teas.

| ACCOMMODATION AND DRINKING | CWM GWAUN AND THE INLAND HILLS |

★**Dyffryn Arms** Pontfaen, SA65 9SE ☎01348 881305. You can enjoy good company here in an old-fashioned living room; the pub is known as *Bessie's* after its venerable proprietor. There's a small beer garden, or you can take your drinks into the riverside field across the road. Daily.

Erw-Lon Farm B4313 between Pontfaen and Rosebush, SA65 9TS ☎01348 881297, ⊛erwlonfarm .co.uk. Welcoming B&B with three comfortable rooms, a lounge and a garden with huge views. **£70**

Gwaun Valley Brewery Kilkiffieth Farm, Pontfaen, on the B4313 5 miles from Fishguard, SA65 9TP ☎01348 881304, ⊛gwaunvalleybrewery.co.uk. Friendly micro-brewery serving a wide range of bitters plus a porter. They also have a simple, all-year campsite. Daily: March–Oct 10am–6pm; Nov–Feb noon–4pm; evenings on request, acoustic music sessions Sat 7–10pm. **£8**

2

Rosebush

As you head east, the brooding nature of the Mynydd Preseli makes itself most apparent. This is bleak, invigorating countryside, the wild, open hills scattered with the relics of ancient civilizations. The characteristic **Preseli bluestone**, which was used between 2000 and 1500 BC to construct Stonehenge, some 140 miles away, came from these slopes.

Slate is also found hereabouts, and was quarried until 1905 near the weird little village of **ROSEBUSH**, just off the B4313 around ten miles southeast of Fishguard. Its Klondike atmosphere is partially due to its being built quickly as a would-be resort following the arrival of a railway (now closed) in 1876.

| ARRIVAL AND DEPARTURE | ROSEBUSH |

By bus Services are sparse: bus #644 runs from Rosebush to Haverfordwest on Tues (45min); #645 from Crymych to Fishguard on Thurs (45min); and the #642 from Crymych to Haverfordwest on Fri (1hr) passing through Maenclochog, just south of Rosebush. All head in to town in the morning and return in the afternoon.

| ACCOMMODATION AND EATING | |

Rosebush Caravan Park Y Bwthyn, SA66 7QT ☎01437 532206, ⊛rosebushholidaypark.co.uk. Well-maintained, adults-only site by two fishing lakes. Campers, caravans and motorhomes are all welcome. Closed Nov to mid-March. **£15**

Tafarn Sinc Y Bwthyn, SA66 7QU ☎01437 532214, ⊛tafarnsinc.co.uk. A large red corrugated-iron shack houses the wood-panelled "Zinc Tavern", a good spot for a pint and a meal (£8–11) in the garden on a fine day. Tues–Sun noon–11pm; kitchen Tues–Sat noon–2pm & 6–9pm, Sun noon–2pm.

The Golden Road

The main range of the Preselis lies just northeast of Rosebush, crossed by an ancient track, in use for at least four thousand years, known as the **Golden Road**. The Pantmaenog car park, at the northern entry to Rosebush, gives access to 7.5 miles of trails, plus a hike that takes in the best section of the Golden Road (8 miles one way; 4–5hr; 1000ft ascent), past old slate quarries, through the coniferous Pantmaenog Forest and up onto the ridgeline. Turn right to reach many of the Preselis' cairns and ancient sites, such as **Beddarthur**, an eerie stone circle that is supposed to be the great king's burial place; **Carn Menyn**, probably the quarry from which most of the Stonehenge bluestones were cut; and **Foeldrygarn** (the "Hill of Three Cairns"), with its hugely impressive Iron Age ramparts and hut circles. Public transport is of little use, so plan for a full day out and hike both ways: the perspective is quite different on the way back.

Another good hike runs from the southern edge of the village along the eastern edge of Pantmaenog Forest to the 1760ft summit of **Foel Cwmcerwyn** (4 miles return; 2hr; 800ft ascent), the highest point in Pembrokeshire. Topped by a Bronze Age cairn, the rounded hill sits above Craig y Cwm, the most recently glaciated valley (c.8000 BC) in the area. Continuing northwards, it's just half a mile to the Golden Road.

The Brecon Beacons and Powys

199 Brecon Beacons National Park

224 The Wells towns

229 North and east Radnorshire

236 Montgomeryshire

SUGAR LOAF, NEAR ABERGAVENNY

The Brecon Beacons and Powys

The vast inland county of Powys takes up a full quarter of Wales. Often traversed quickly en route to the coast, it's well worth exploring in its own right. The most popular area is the Brecon Beacons National Park, at the county's southern end, an area of moody heights, wild, rambling moors and thundering waterfalls. The main centres within the Beacons are Wales' culinary capital, Abergavenny, in the far southeast, and Brecon. The bleaker part of the Beacons lies to the west, around the raw peaks of the Black Mountain (Mynydd Ddu) and Fforest Fawr geopark, and includes the immense Dan-yr-ogof caves and the mighty waterfalls around Ystradfellte. Architecturally charming towns such as Crickhowell and Talgarth, set in quiet river valleys, also make good bases for walkers. At the northern corner of the national park, the border town of Hay-on-Wye is famous for its secondhand bookshops and attracts thousands to its annual literary festival.

3

Northwest of Hay lie the old spa towns of Radnorshire and Brecknockshire, the most appealing of which are **Llanwrtyd Wells** and **Llandrindod Wells**. Crossed by spectacular mountain roads such as the **Abergwesyn Pass** from Llanwrtyd, the countryside to the north is supremely beautiful, dotted with ancient churches and remote hill-farming hamlets, from the lively border communities of **Presteigne** and **Knighton** to inland centres like **Rhayader**, the nearest centre of population for the grandiose reservoirs of the **Elan Valley**.

The northern portion of Powys, **Montgomeryshire**, is as sparsely populated and remote as its two southern siblings. In common with most of mid-Wales, country towns here, such as **Llanidloes**, have a sizeable stock of New Age health-food shops, healing groups and arts activity. To the west, the inhospitable mountain of **Plynlimon** is flecked with boggy heathland and gloomy reservoirs, beyond which the spirited town of Machynlleth (covered in Chapter Four) lies on the westernmost margins of Powys. The eastern side of Montgomeryshire is home to the anglicized old county town, **Montgomery**, between the robust towns of **Welshpool** and **Newtown**, the former the site of one of the country's mightiest castles. The northern segment of the county is even quieter, with the only crowds being found along the banks of **Lake Vyrnwy**, a flooded-valley reservoir.

The Beacons Way p.199	**Black Mountains summits** p.220
A walk around Llanddeusant p.201	**Richard Booth and the Hay book**
A circular walk around Corn Du and	**business** p.221
Pen y Fan p.204	**Hay Festival** p.223
The Taff Trail p.206	**Llanwrtyd Wells' Wacky events** p.225
Brecon festivals p.208	**Royal Welsh Show** p.227
A circular walk around the eastern	**Llandrindod festivals** p.229
Beacons p.209	**Presteigne Festival** p.234
Crickhowell's festivals p.214	**Glyndŵr's Way** p.235
Abergavenny Market p.216	**Offa's Dyke** p.237
Abergavenny's festivals p.218	**Robert Owen, pioneer socialist** p.240

BRECON BEACONS NATIONAL PARK

Highlights

❶ Brecon Beacons There are terrific hikes to be had through these frequently glorious mountains, while the park itself is now an acclaimed stargazing site. **See p.199**

❷ Ystradfellte waterfalls Explore the trio of great waterfalls in the limestone country around Ystradfellte. **See p.202**

❸ Glasbury Canoe downstream along the tranquil River Wye to Hay. **See p.211**

❹ Abergavenny Enjoy locally surced Welsh cuisine from some of the country's finest chefs or simply graze your way through the town's prestigious food festival. **See p.215**

❺ Hay-on-Wye You can browse millions of secondhand books at more than thirty bookshops in this bibliophile's paradise; or just dive into the world-famous festival itself. **See p.221**

❻ Llanwrtyd Wells This small town is the home of wacky Welsh events including the Man versus Horse Marathon or the Real Ale Wobble. **See p.224**

❼ Offa's Dyke A walk along this massive earthwork, through the ever-changing borderlands, is one of Wales' most rewarding expeditions. **See p.237**

❽ Powis Castle While undoubtedly one of the country's most sumptuous castles, the real glory of Powis is its stunning gardens. **See p.244**

HIGHLIGHTS ARE MARKED ON THE MAP ON P.198

THE BRECON BEACONS & POWYS

HIGHLIGHTS

1. Brecon Beacons
2. Ystradfellte waterfalls
3. Glasbury
4. Abergavenny
5. Hay-on-Wye
6. Llanwrtyd Wells
7. Offa's Dyke
8. Powis Castle

Trawsfynydd

Bala

Llangollen

Dee

Oswestry

Pennant
Melangell

Pistyll
Rheadr

Llangynog

Llanrhaeadr-ym-
Mochnant

Lake
Vyrnwy

Llanwddyn

Llanfyllin

Llanmynech

River Severn

Mallwyd

Llanfair-
Caereinion

Welshpool

Powis
Castle

Welshpool
& Llanfair
Light Railway

Berriew

Machynlleth

Dylife

Staylittle

Caersws

Gregynog Hall

Dolforwyn
Castle

Montgomery

ENGLAND

Plynlimon
(2469ft)

Llyn
Clywedog

Newtown

HAFREN FOREST

Llanidloes

Llangurig

Abbeycwmhir

Llananno

Knighton

Elan Valley

Rhayader

RADNOR
FOREST

Presteigne

Claerwen
Reservoir

Elan

Cross Gates

Llanfihangel
Rhydithon

Old Radnor

Abergwesyn Pass

Disserth

Llandrindod
Wells

New
Radnor

Abergwesyn

Beulah

Cilmeri

Builth Wells

Garth

River Wye

Llanwrtyd Wells

Llangammarch
Wells

Glasbury

Hay-on-
Wye

Llyswen

Mynydd
Eppynt

Talgarth

Capel-y-ffin

Sennybridge

Brecon

Llangorse
Lake

Llanthony

Black
Mountains

Partrishow

Black
Mountain

BRECON
BEACONS
NATIONAL PARK

Pen y Fan
(2907ft)

Tretower castle
and court

Bwlch

River Usk

Crickhowell

Dan-yr-ogof

Craig-y-nos Castle
and Country Park

FFOREST FAWR

Ystradfellte

BRECON BEACONS

Abergavenny

Coelbern

0   2
miles

N

By train Services are restricted to the Heart of Wales line from Shropshire to Swansea via Knighton, Llandrindod Wells, Llanwrtyd Wells and smaller stops in between, and the Shrewsbury–Machynlleth route through Welshpool and Newtown.

By bus Many larger centres such as Brecon, Llanidloes, Rhayader and Hay-on-Wye rely on sporadic bus services, although most places can be reached via a handful of daily services. One of the most useful long-distance buses is the T4 (Mon–Sat), which runs from Cardiff up to Newtown, calling in at Pontypridd, Merthyr (both covered in Chapter One), Brecon, Builth Wells and Llandrindod Wells on the way up.

Brecon Beacons National Park

With the lowest profile of Wales' three national parks, the **Brecon Beacons** are refreshingly uncrowded, primarily attracting local urban walkers. Spongy hills of grass and rock tumble and climb around river valleys peppered with glassy lakes and villages that seem to have been hewn from one rock. Known for the vivid quality of their light, the Beacons hills disappear and re-emerge from hazy blankets of cloud, with shafts of sun sharpening the lush green patchwork of fields.

Covering 520 square miles, the national park straddles southern Powys and northern Monmouthshire from west to east. The most remote parts are around the **Black Mountain** peaks to the west, with miles of tufted moorland and bleak, often dangerous, summits plummeting to the porous limestone country in the southwestern section, a rocky terrain of rivers, deep caves and spluttering waterfalls. To the northeast, the lonely **Black Mountains** (not to be confused with the entirely separate Black Mountain to the west) are separated from the Beacons themselves by the Monmouthshire and **Brecon Canal**, which forges a passage along the Usk Valley. Built around the beginning of the nineteenth century to support coal mining, iron ore and limestone quarrying, the canal is an impressive feat of engineering, successfully steering a 25-mile lock-free stretch (Britain's longest) through some of the most mountainous terrain in Wales.

In 2013, the park was granted **International Dark Sky Reserve** status, the first in Wales and one of just eleven in the world. Understandably, it has become a major destination for stargazers, with regular events organized by the authorities (ⓦbreconbeacons.org).

By car If you don't have your own car – which is by far the best way to get the most out of this part of Wales – then you might consider an innovative new scheme run by Eco Travel Network (ⓦecotravelnetwork.co.uk), which offers two-seater electric cars that you can rent for between a day and a week from seven locations in the Brecon Beacons; don't expect to fit much (in fact, any) luggage in, though.

By train Abergavenny is the only town with a train station, though Merthyr Tydfil, on the southern flank of the park, is well connected by rail to Cardiff.

By bus With relatively frequent services (often 4–6 daily) along the major routes, buses are a much better bet than trains; a smattering of services only run on certain days. The main routes are from Brecon to Crickhowell and Abergavenny (#X43); Brecon to Talgarth, Hay-on-Wye and Hereford (#39); and Brecon to Swansea via Sennybridge, the Dan-yr-ogof caves, Craig-y-nos and Ystradgynlais (#T6).

By bike The relatively compact nature of the region, the profusion of narrow lanes and the many opportunities to get off-road make this a great place to travel by bike: rental

---

THE BEACONS WAY

The OS 1:25,000 Explorer map OL12 (Brecon Beacons – Western area) and 1:25,000 Explorer map OL13 (Brecon Beacons – Eastern area) are recommended.

Established in 2005 (but revised in 2016), the 95-mile-long **Beacons Way** (ⓦbreconbeacons parksociety.org) offers the perfect way to get to grips with this stunning landscape, but it's by no means an easy trek. Starting in Abergavenny, the walk zigzags across the park in an east–west direction, comprising stiff climbs, undulating ridges, peat bogs and open moorland (not all of it is waymarked), before winding up at Llangadog. To do it all in one go takes about eight days, though it's best undertaken over a more leisurely ten to twelve days.

3

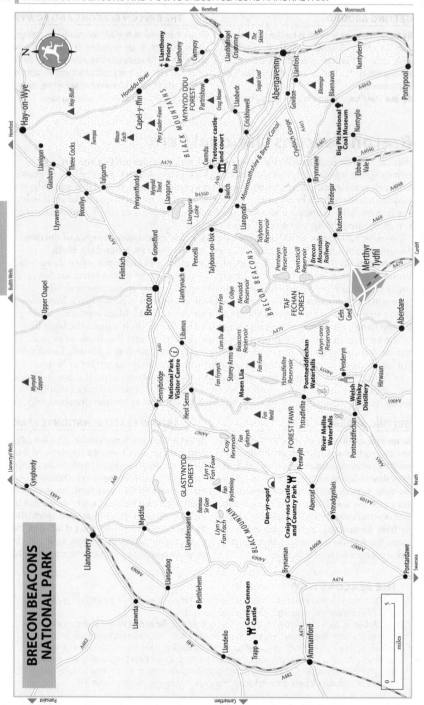

BRECON BEACONS
NATIONAL PARK

locations include Brecon, Abergavenny, Talybont-on-Usk and Hay-on-Wye.

By horse Horseriding is extremely popular and well organized; see the listings throughout this chapter or visit ⓦ horseridingbreconbeacons.com.

INFORMATION

Brecon Beacons National Park Visitor Centre Six miles southwest of Brecon, off the A470 (turn off at Libanus), the visitor centre (Mon–Thurs 9.30am–4.30pm, Fri–Sun 9.30am–5pm; ☏01874 623366, ⓦbrecon beacons.org) is chiefly useful for its well-stocked shop of maps, books and guides, though most of the complex is taken up with local crafts displays. Staff can give experienced hikers details of walks tackling the more challenging peaks of Corn Du and Pen y Fan (see p.204). Otherwise, you can walk straight out from the door onto

Mynydd Illtud Common, laced with gentle paths looking across to some major peaks. An excellent café serves hot meals (daily 9am–5pm). The #T4 bus from Brecon stops in Libanus, but it's an arduous 25min uphill walk from here to the centre (follow the signs).

Brecon Beacons Park Society The Park Society (ⓦbreconbeaconsparksociety.org) organizes walks and events each summer; particularly useful if you don't fancy going it solo.

ACCOMMODATION

The National Park offers plenty of **accommodation**, including low-budget choices; ⓦbreconbeacons.org/stay covers all kinds of options, including B&Bs, hostels, bunkhouses and campsites. The best **self-catering** companies locally are Brecon Beacons Holiday Cottages (ⓦbreconcottages.com) and the Abergavenny Farm Holidays Group (ⓦabergavennyfarmholidays.co.uk).

The western Beacons

The **western Beacons** comprise the bleak uplands of Black Mountain and Fforest Fawr, and the sparsely populated valleys in between. This is clearly limestone country: caves, sinkholes and waterfalls dot the map. From the valleys, invigorating walks or bike rides thread up to the lonely moors for sweeping views across the mountains.

Black Mountain

The most westerly expanse of upland in the national park is known as the **Black Mountain** (Mynydd Ddu). Despite being named in the singular (as distinct from the Black Mountains further east), the "mountain" actually covers an unpopulated range of barren, smooth-humped peaks that break suddenly at rocky escarpments towering over quiet streams and glacial lakes.

The area provides the most challenging and exhilarating **walking** in south Wales. Paths cross the wet, wild landscape from the Dan-yr-ogof caves in the east (see p.203) and from the soaring ruins of Carreg Cennen Castle, just short of Llandeilo in the west (see p.148). Other good starting points for forays into the open Black Mountain uplands are Tyhwnt, near Ystradgynlais, in the south and, in the north, the hamlet of **LLANDDEUSANT**, seven miles south of Llandovery. In Llanddeusant you'll find the **Red Kite Feeding Centre** (daily

---

A WALK AROUND LLANDDEUSANT

The OS 1:25,000 Explorer map OL12 (Brecon Beacons – Western area) is recommended.
Passing both Llyn y Fan Fach and Llyn y Fan Fawr, this bleak and lonely ascent (12 miles; 4–5hr; 1400ft ascent) weaves through classic post-glacial scenery: valleys slashed with tumbling streams cut between purple hills, while occasional mounds and moraines of rock debris indicate the force of the ice that pushed through the valleys. Such heaps sometimes grew large enough to form a natural dam, building up lakes, such as Llyn y Fan Fach, in their wake.

The walk starts in Llanddeusant and climbs steeply to Llyn y Fan Fach, from where a precarious path leads around the top of the escarpment, following the ridge to **Fan Brycheiniog** (2630ft), above the glassy black waters of Llyn y Fan Fawr. Return the same way.

feeding 3pm, 2pm in winter; £4; ⓦredkiteswales.co.uk); the hides are about 250yd from the old *Cross Inn* pub (which is where you park) out on the road towards Myddfai.

Fforest Fawr

Covering a vast expanse of hilly landscape between the Black Mountain and the central Beacons southwest of Brecon, **Fforest Fawr** (Great Forest) seems something of a misnomer for an area of largely unforested sandstone hills dropping down to a porous limestone belt in the south; the "forest" tag refers more to the old definition of a forest as land used as a hunting ground. Fforest Fawr is administered by UNESCO as a **geopark**, one of a Europe-wide network of areas of outstanding geological heritage that also promote sustainable practices. A great way to get to know more about the park and its features is through the annual Geofest (end May; ⓦfforestfawrgeopark.org.uk/geofest), a two-week-long series of walks and talks.

The hills rise up to the south of the A40 west of Brecon, with the dramatic A4067 Sennybridge–Ystradgynlais road scoring the western side of the range and the A470 Brecon–Merthyr road defining the Fforest's eastern limit.

Maen Llia and Ystradfellte

From the hamlet of **Heol Senni**, five miles southwest of the National Park Visitor Centre (see p.201), a wonderful, twisting mountain road threads its way up to the **Devil's Elbow**, a dramatic switchback offering stunning views back down the valley. From here the road plateaus onto open moorland, where the distinctive **Maen Llia** slowly hoves into view; the finest of the Beacon's many standing stones, this huge, almost diamond-shaped red sandstone block, reckoned to be at least 4000 years old and probably an old boundary marker, stands 13ft – legend has it that, on Midsummer's Eve, Maen Llia heads down to the nearby River Mellte to drink. From Maen Llia, the road drops down into the valley of the Afon Llia and the limestone crags around the hamlet of **YSTRADFELLTE**. Little more than a handful of houses, a church and a pub, this is, nonetheless, a phenomenally popular centre for walking, as a result of the dazzling countryside on its doorstep. Lush, deep ravines – a total contrast to the barren mountains immediately north – carve through the limestone ridge south of the village, with great pavements of bone-white rock littering fields next to cradling potholes, disappearing rivers and thundering **waterfalls**.

River Mellte waterfalls

A mile south of Ystradfellte, the River Mellte tumbles into the dark and icy mouth of the **Porth-yr-ogof** cave, emerging into daylight a few hundred yards further south by the Cwm Porth car park. From here a signposted path heads south into the green gorge of the River Mellte, where you can follow the **Four Falls Trail**, which officially starts at the Gwaun Hepste car park, a short way east. Continue for little more than a mile to the first of its three great waterfalls, **Sgwd Clun-Gwyn** (White Meadow Fall), where the river crashes 50ft over two huge, angular steps of rock before hurtling down course for a few hundred yards to the other two falls, the graceful **Sgwd Isaf Clun-Gwyn** (Lower White Meadow Fall) and, a little further on, the mighty **Sgwd y Pannwr** (Fall of the Fuller).

The path continues through the foliage to the confluence of the rivers Mellte and Hepste, half a mile further on. A quarter of a mile along the Hepste is arguably the most impressive of the area's falls, the **Sgwd yr Eira** (Fall of Snow), where the rock below the main tumble has eroded back 6ft, allowing people to walk directly behind a dramatic 20ft curtain of water – particularly dazzling in afternoon or evening light. From Sgwd yr Eira you can return to either the Cwm Porth or Gwaun Hepste car parks or continue south, following a trail down to Pontneddfechan.

Pontneddfechan waterfalls

Just off the A465 along the forested valley of the River Nedd (or Neath), near the village of **PONTNEDDFECHAN**, are some spectacular waterfalls. The most accessible walk is the Elidir Trail, from Pontneddfechan to Pont Melin-Fach, a round trip of around five miles, for which you should allow three hours; starting at the information board opposite the *Angel* pub, it's an easyish mile's walk along the river to the pretty **Sgwd Gwladus** (Lady Falls), which, like Sgwd yr Eira, overhangs enough to allow you to walk behind; this should be just enough for those with young families, but from here, you can continue up to **Sgwd y Bedol** (Horseshoe Falls), **Sgwd Ddwli Isaf** (Lower Gushing Falls) and **Sgwd Ddwli Uchaf** (Upper Gushing Falls), before reaching the car park at Pont Melin-Fach.

Penderyn Welsh Whisky Distillery

Penderyn, CF44 0SX • Tours (hourly; 1hr) daily 9.30am–5pm • £8.50, booking advised • ☎ 01685 810650, ⊛ penderyn.wales

Four miles east of Pontneddfechan in the village of **PENDERYN** is the **Penderyn Welsh Whisky Distillery**. When it opened in 2000, Penderyn became Wales' first working distillery for more than one hundred years, and today it produces three single malt whiskies, matured in bourbon barrels and finished in Madeira wine casks. **Guided tours** take in an exhibition on the working of the distillery, an explanation of the distillation and bottling processes and, of course, a little taster at the end. Uniquely, the process here involves the use of a single copper pot still – as opposed to the conventional two or three – before the whisky is matured for between four and seven years. The distillery also produces a Brecon gin, vodka and cream liqueur.

Dan-yr-ogof Showcaves

Glyntawe, just west of the A4067, SA9 1GJ • April–Oct daily 10am–3.30pm • £15 • ☎ 01639 730284, ⊛ showcaves.co.uk

The upper reaches of the Afon Tawe, Swansea's river, mark the limestone belt, as seen in the hamlet of **GLYNTAWE** at the **Dan-yr-ogof Showcaves**. Discovered by two local farmers in 1912, and opened to the public in 1939, the caves, it's claimed, form the largest system of subterranean caverns in northern Europe.

Following a self-guided tour, with commentary resonating from loudspeakers, you are first led into the **Dan-yr-ogof** cave. Known to be around ten miles long (though you'll be steered around a circular route of about a mile), it's the longest showcave in Britain, a warren of caverns framed by stalactites and frothy limestone deposits. One of the more intriguing formations is the "curtain", a transparent, wafer-thin sheet precariously angled on a sloping wall formed when water runs down the roof of the cave. Back outside, you pass a re-created Iron Age "village" and walk past some of the many life-size fibreglass dinosaurs lurking within the forested hillside to reach **Cathedral Cave** (discovered in 1953), where a long, snaking passage leads to the "cathedral" itself, an impressive 150ft-long, 70ft-high cave inside of which are two 65ft-high waterfalls; these are particularly impressive after heavy rainfall.

Reachable via a steep and awkward path behind the dinosaur park is **Bone Cave**, the third and final cavern, known to have been inhabited by Bronze Age tribes, with some 42 human (and many animal) skeletons found here. There's plenty more to see and do in the complex, especially for kids, including a museum, shire horse centre, playground and farm.

Craig-y-nos Castle and Country Park

Glyntawe, 400yd south of Dan-yr-ogof Showcaves, SA9 1GL • Free access • Historian led-tours of the castle daily 10.30am (1hr) • Tours £10 (booking essential) • ☎ 01639 731167, ⊛ craigynoscastle.com

Craig-y-nos Castle, a grand folly built in 1842, was fancifully extended from 1878 when it was bought by the celebrated Italian-American opera singer Adelina Patti (1843–1919). In her forty years of residence, she turned the place into a diva-esque castle, even adding a scaled-down version of London's Drury Lane opera house for performances. After Patti's reign, Craig-y-nos became a hospital before suffering years of chronic neglect; it was bought in the mid-1990s and turned into a hotel and wedding venue. Even if you're not staying here, you're free to wander around the **ground floor**, which includes the *Patti Bar*, complete with fireplace tiles depicting the novels of Walter Scott, the Grade I-listed opera house and a gloriously sunny conservatory overlooking the River Tawe – if you want to see more you'll need to book a **guided tour**.

Some 44 acres of the castle grounds form part of the Brecon Beacons National Park and operate as **Craig-y-nos Country Park** (free access). From the car park, where there's a tearoom, signposted walks lead around a landscaped site along the banks of the young River Tawe.

The central Brecon Beacons

The **central Brecon Beacons** – after which the whole national park is named – are well set up for walking and pony trekking. The area, to the immediate south of Brecon town, centres on the two highest peaks in south Wales, **Pen y Fan** (2907ft) and **Corn Du** (2863ft), half a mile to the west. Although neither reaches 3000ft, the terrain is unmistakably and dramatically mountainous: classic old red sandstone country with sweeping peaks rising out of glacially carved land.

The **combined ascent** of Pen y Fan and Corn Du is the most popular walk in the park. The most direct route up is the well-trampled red-mud path that starts from Pont ar Daf, half a mile south of Storey Arms on the A470, midway between Brecon and Merthyr Tydfil. The ascent is a comparatively easy five-mile round trip, gradually climbing up the southern flank of the two peaks. A longer and generally quieter route leads up to the two peaks from the **"Gap" route** (see box below) – the pre-nineteenth-century (and possibly Roman) main road winding north from the Neuadd reservoirs through the only natural break in the central Beacons' sandstone ridge to the bottom of the lane. The route eventually joins the main street in the Brecon suburb of Llanfaes as Bailihelig Road. Although the old road is no longer accessible to cars, car parks at either end open out onto the track for an eight-mile round-trip ascent up Pen y Fan and Corn Du from the east.

Brecon and around

The handsome Georgian buildings of **BRECON** (Aberhonddu) stand at the northern edge of the Beacons, bearing testimony to the town's past importance. A Roman fort was built near here, but the settlement only started to grow with the building of a Norman castle and Benedictine monastery, founded in 1093 on the banks of the Honddu River (which gives Brecon its Welsh name); it also became a regional market centre and cloth-weaving town. In the seventeenth-century Civil War, the townsfolk

---

A CIRCULAR WALK AROUND CORN DU AND PEN Y FAN

The OS 1:25,000 Explorer map OL12 (Brecon Beacons – Western area) is recommended.

Few walkers visiting the Brecon Beacons for the first time can resist making an ascent of the two highest peaks: **Corn Du** and **Pen y Fan**. Most take one of the shorter routes from the A470 south of Brecon, but connoisseurs prefer this longer and infinitely more rewarding circular **"Gap" route** (8 miles; 4–5hr; 1400ft ascent) that makes an anticlockwise circuit around a ridge-top horseshoe of the Beacons.

The hike starts at the car park by the late Victorian Neuadd reservoirs and crosses the dam of the lower, smaller reservoir, then climbs westwards up the hill in front. Head right (north) along a well-defined path along the ridge-top including Graig Fan Ddu. Follow the obvious path that strikes up the sandstone ridge to the first summit, then down to a shallow saddle and up again to the peak of Pen y Fan, the highest point in south Wales. Either carry on to the next summit, Cribyn, and then descend to the Gap, or turn right by the stream in the valley between Pen y Fan and Cribyn, around the base of Cribyn and then back to the Neuadd reservoirs.

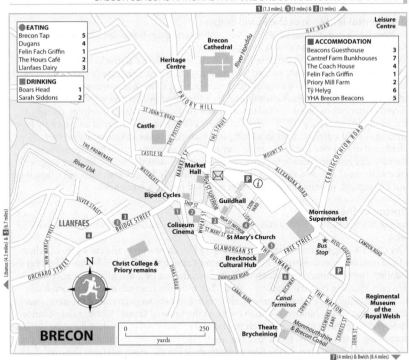

BRECON

demonstrated their neutrality between the forces of Parliament and the Crown by demolishing most of the castle and large sections of the town walls, dissipating the appeal for either side of seizing their town. Today, it's a lively base for walkers and less active visitors alike, with good accommodation, and a reasonable array of places to eat and drink.

Brecon's imposing central square, at the western end of **The Bulwark**, is flanked by the solid, red sixteenth-century tower of **St Mary's church**, an assortment of old-fashioned shop frontages and the elegant Georgian portico of the **Wellington Hotel**. The grid of streets north and west of The Bulwark is packed with delightful Georgian and Victorian buildings. Northwest, at the crossroads of High Street Inferior, Ship Street descends down to the **River Usk**, the bridge crossing the Usk next to the point where the smaller Honddu River flows in from the north.

Brecknock Cultural Hub

Captain's Walk, LD3 7DS

At the junction of The Bulwark and Glamorgan Street is the neo-Grecian frontage of the Brecknock Shire Hall, which, at the time of writing, was closed pending a major renovation. The complex, which will feature a new, modern wing, is due to open in 2018 or 2019 as the **Brecknock Cultural Hub**, incorporating the **Brecknock Museum** and the **tourist office**. So far as the museum goes, expect to see comprehensive galleries on town and rural life, an archeology section featuring inscribed stones dating back to the fifth century and a selection of painstakingly carved Welsh love spoons – some more than four hundred years old – that were betrothal gifts for courting Welsh lovers. The prize exhibit, however, is a remarkably well-preserved, 15ft-long *crannog* (log boat or dugout canoe), dredged up from Llangorse Lake in 1925 and reckoned to date from around 760 AD.

Regimental Museum of the Royal Welsh

The Watton, LD3 7EB • April–July & Sept Mon–Fri 10am–5pm, Sat 10am–4pm; Aug Mon–Fri 10am–5pm, Sat & Sun 10am–4pm; Oct– March Mon–Fri 10am–5pm • £5 • ☎ 01874 613310, ⓦ royalwelsh.org.uk

Beyond the foreboding frontage of the South Wales Borderers' **barracks** is the **Regimental Museum of the Royal Welsh**, packed with mementos from the regiment's 330 years. As well as an extraordinary stash of armoury and medals, there's thorough coverage of campaigns in Burma, the Napoleonic, Crimean and Boer wars, and both world wars, as well as more recent operations in Northern Ireland, Iraq and Afghanistan. Most absorbing, though, is the room devoted to the 1879 Zulu War when 140 Welsh soldiers faced an attack by four thousand Zulu warriors at Rorke's Drift. Ten Victoria Crosses were awarded in the aftermath of that one battle, the most ever received in a single action by one regiment. Remarkable exhibits include the battered flag that flew over the British forward supply base at Rorke's Drift and the headdress worn by the Zulu king, Cetshwayo; elsewhere there are Zulu spears, powder horns and bibles retrieved from the battlefield.

Brecon Cathedral

Cathedral Close, Priory Hill, LD3 9DP • Daily 8.30am–6.30pm; lunchtime recitals Mon 1pm • Free • ☎ 01874 623857, ⓦ breconcathedral .org.uk

Over the rushing waters of the Honddu, Priory Hill climbs up to the stark grey buildings of the monastery settlement, centred on **Brecon Cathedral**, or Priory Church of St John the Baptist. The cathedral's surprisingly lofty interior, framed by a magnificent timber roof, is graced with a few Norman features – these date from the eleventh-century priory, itself built on the site of a probable earlier Celtic church. At the western end of the nave, near the entrance, sit the hulking Norman font and the unusual **Cresset Stone**, a large boulder indented with thirty scoops in which to place oil or wax candles; it's thought to be the last remaining in the country. From here the south aisle runs down to the most interesting of the many family memorials, the **Games monument** (1555), made up from three oak beds and depicting an unknown woman whose hands remain intact in prayer, but whose arms and nose have been unceremoniously hacked off.

Architecturally, the most impressive aspect of the cathedral is the Early English-style **chancel**, distinguished by three long, high windows extending up to the superb vaulted ceiling; no less striking is the relatively modern, stone carved reredos (1936), depicting the Crucifixion, other biblical scenes and Welsh saints.

Heritage Centre

Cathedral Close, opposite the cathedral, LD3 9DP • April–Oct Mon–Sat 10.30am–4.30pm, Sun 12.15–4.15pm; Nov–March Mon–Sat 10.30am–4.30pm • Free • ☎ 01874 625222

A converted seventeenth-century tithe barn houses the cathedral's **Heritage Centre**, holding a small and intermittently interesting collection of gilded vestments, bibles, crucifixes and the like. The star piece is an oversized chair believed to have been used by King Charles I when he stayed at Priory House in 1645. The attached *Pilgrims* tearoom is extremely popular.

THE TAFF TRAIL

Running from **Brecon** to **Cardiff Bay**, the 55-mile **Taff Trail** passes through a spectacular cross section of southern Welsh scenery: the Usk Valley, the Brecon Beacons uplands, the former coal-mining Taff Valley and urban parkland. Most of the route – which is open to hikers and bikers – is on forest trails, designated pathways and country lanes and is seldom steep. Perhaps the best way to tackle the whole trail is by bike, starting in Brecon (where there's bike rental), cycling to Cardiff – downhill much of the way – then catching a train back to Merthyr Tydfil and riding the fifteen miles back over the hills to Brecon. Keen cyclists could do this in a day, though you might prefer to break the journey in Pontypridd or Cardiff. For more information, check ⓦ sustrans.org.uk.

ARRIVAL AND GETTING AROUND
BRECON

By bus Buses stop above the car park on Heol Gouesnou. Destinations Aberdulais (Mon–Sat hourly, Sun 5; 1hr 15min); Abergavenny (Mon–Sat hourly; 40min–1hr); Builth Wells (Mon–Sat 7 daily; 45min); Cardiff (Mon–Sat 7 daily; 1hr 50min); Craig-y-nos/Dan-yr-ogof (Mon–Sat hourly, Sun 5; 40min); Crickhowell (Mon–Sat hourly; 30–50min); Hay-on-Wye (Mon–Sat 7 daily; 40min); Libanus (Mon–Sat hourly, Sun 2; 15min); Llandrindod Wells (Mon–Sat 7 daily, Sun 1; 1hr); Merthyr Tydfil

(Mon–Sat 10 daily, Sun 2; 40min); Sennybridge (Mon–Sat hourly, Sun 5; 15min); Swansea (Mon–Sat hourly, Sun 5; 1hr 50min); Talgarth (Mon–Sat 7 daily; 25min); Talybont-on-Usk (Mon–Sat 6 daily; 20min).

By bike Bikes for all ages and levels can be rented for around £25 a day at Biped Cycles, 10 Ship St (Mon–Sat 9am–5.30pm; ☎01874 622296, 🌐bipedcycles.co.uk); they can deliver.

INFORMATION AND TOURS

Tourist office The tourist office is due to move to the new Brecknock Cultural Hub (see p.205) in 2018 or 2019, but for the time being it's in the large car park off Lion St (Mon–Sat 9.30am–5pm, Sun 10am–4pm; ☎01874 622485, 🌐breconbeacons.org). Its vast stock of material includes a comprehensive range of walking maps for the Brecons.

Canal cruises A series of colourful terraced streets runs down to the town's theatre and the northern terminus of the Monmouthshire and Brecon Canal, where afternoon cruises aboard the *Dragonfly* (March–May Tues–Sun

noon; June Mon–Sat noon; July & Aug daily noon & 3pm; Sept Tues & Wed noon, Sat & Sun noon & 3pm; Oct Tues, Wed, Sat & Sun noon; £7.80; ☎07712 253432, 🌐dragonfly-cruises.co.uk) ease their way out of town for enjoyably relaxed 2hr 30min trips. Inside the old tollhouse at the same spot, Beacon Park Boats (☎0800 612 2890, 🌐beaconparkboats.com) rents six- and eight-seat electric boats (£40/2hr, £50/half-day) and three-seat Canadian canoes (£20/2hr, £25/half-day).

3

ACCOMMODATION

Accommodation to suit all pockets exists in Brecon, though the most enticing possibilities are in the suburb of **Llanfaes**, across the river from the centre, and just outside town itself. Similarly, for hostels and camping you'll have to head a little further out of town.

HOTELS AND GUESTHOUSES

Beacons Guesthouse 16 Bridge St, Llanfaes, LD3 8AH ☎01874 623339, 🌐thebreconbeacons.co.uk. This former boarding house for boys from the college opposite now conceals run-of-the-mill, fairly priced, rooms (£63), some with their original fireplaces, all leading off a central spiral staircase; two cheaper rooms on the top floor share a bathroom. **£52**

The Coach House 12/13 Orchard St, Llanfaes, LD3 8AN ☎01874 620043, 🌐coachhousebrecon.com. High-class and very hospitable guesthouse with rooms painted in smooth creams and browns and boasting designer furnishings; thoughtful touches include low-key floor lighting in the bathrooms for that occasional nocturnal visit. The breakfast menu is something else, with some especially scrumptious variations on Welsh rarebit. **£80**

★**Felin Fach Griffin** Felinfach, A470, 3 miles northwest, LD3 0UB ☎01874 620111, 🌐eatdrink sleepltd.uk. Seven sublime, countrified rooms with beamed ceilings, oak-floored bathrooms and sumptuous beds and chairs dressed in soft Welsh blankets; instead of TVs, you've got Roberts radios, books to browse and magazines to pore over while enjoying freshly ground coffee or loose leaf tea. This also has to be one of the dog-friendliest places in the country; pooches even get their own supply of biscuits. The restaurant is even better (see p.208). **£135**

Tŷ Helyg 39 The Watton, LD3 7EG ☎01874 623321, 🌐tyhelygguesthouse.co.uk. Handsome Georgian corner guesthouse offering nine sparkling, white-on-white rooms (some four-poster) offset with dark-wood furnishings and splashes of grey; the warming guest lounge has a woodburner, honesty bar and Nespresso machine. Cycle storage and drying room, too. **£75**

HOSTEL, BUNKHOUSE AND CAMPSITE

Cantref Farm Bunkhouses Cantref Pony Trekking Centre, 4 miles southeast off the A40, LD3 8LR ☎01874 665223, 🌐cantref.com. Dorm-style accommodation in two large stone farm buildings. One (with kitchen and lounge) has 24 beds and is for groups only; the other (with kitchen) has ten beds spread across double, triple and quad rooms. They also offer camping space, with a separate shower block. Camping/person **£8**, doubles **£44**

Priory Mill Farm Hay Rd, LD3 7SR ☎01874 611609, 🌐priorymillfarm.co.uk. Lovely, low-key riverside campsite, with wooden cabins for showers and trays for log fires. It's on the northern edge of town, a 10min walk along the riverbank; there's some lovely wildlife hereabouts, and a good chance of seeing herons and kingfishers on the river. There are just twenty pitches, so you'll need to get in early. Closed Nov–Feb. Per person **£8**

BRECON FESTIVALS

Held over the second or third weekend of August, the **Brecon Jazz Festival** (ⓦbreconjazz .club) has more than thirty years under its belt, and while it's not the force it once was, the line-up invariably remains strong. Running concurrently with the jazz festival, but even more popular, is the **Brecon Fringe Festival** (ⓦbreconfringe.co.uk), which encompasses alternative – predominantly local – bands playing cafés, pubs and galleries, with a healthy dose of comedy, dance and performance art. A relatively recent addition is the **Brecon Baroque Festival** (ⓦbreconbaroquefestival.com) at the end of October, five days of top-drawer concerts at the cathedral and Theatr Brycheiniog, alongside other Baroque entertainment, particularly dance.

3

YHA Brecon Beacons 7 miles southwest of Brecon, near Libanus, LD3 8NH ☎01874 624261, ⓦyha.org .uk/hostel/brecon-beacons. Traditional farmhouse hostel surrounded by woodlands and overlooking the River Tarell, just off the A470 and main bus route to Merthyr (the #T4 bus stops on the road above the hostel). They offer variously sized dorms, en-suite doubles and, up behind the hostel, two wooden pods sleeping four (a double futon and two singles), as well as a wild woodland campsite; fires allowed. Home-cooked food and bottled ales, too. Breakfast £6.25. Nov–Feb closed Mon & Tues. Camping/person **£11**, dorms **£13**, doubles **£50**, pods **£89**

EATING

Brecon Tap 6 Bulwark, LD3 7LB ☎01874 623888, ⓦbreconinns.co.uk. There are two great reasons to visit this cheerfully informal restaurant/bar owned by the local Brecon Brewing company: their superb range of beers, including the core keg ales Golden Brecon and Three Beacons, as well as unusual offerings such as the bottled Brecon Bamboo (yep, made from bamboo); and their pies (Moroccan lamb, for example or chicken, leek and Pearl Las cheese), which you get with a choice of two sides, perhaps mustard mash and roasted root veg (£9.75). Mon–Sat 11am–11pm, Sun noon–11pm; kitchen daily noon–3pm & 6–9pm.

Dugans Pegasus Lane, LD3 7BH ☎01874 623113, ⓦdugans.co.uk. Cracking patisserie with a homespun interior of oak flooring, kitchen-style tables and chairs and artwork splashed across the whitewashed walls. The food, be it savoury (leek, cheese and walnut quiche) or sweet (salted caramel and pear tart or rolled apple and cinnamon strudel), tastes every bit as good as it looks. Mon 10am–5pm, Tues–Sat 9am–5pm.

★ **Felin Fach Griffin** Felinfach, A470, 3 miles northwest, LD3 0UB ☎01874 620111, ⓦeatdrink sleepltd.uk. The *Griffin* offers some of the finest Modern Welsh cuisine anywhere in the region, with sustainable sourcing at the heart of its short, seasonal menus – for example, fish delivered from Cornwall and fruit and greenery from the kitchen garden. Scrumptious dishes might include silver mullet with confit potato and Savoy cabbage, or smoked ox tongue with pickled red cabbage, horseradish and beetroot. Three-course set menu £29. Beyond the restaurant is the pubby bit, a tiny bar fronting a couple of farmhouse tables laden with newspapers, crumpled leather sofas and a crackling log fire (whatever the time of year). Daily 11am–11pm; kitchen noon–2.30pm & 6–9pm.

The Hours Café 15 Ship St, LD3 9AD ☎01874 622800, ⓦthe-hours.co.uk. Cheerful daytime café-cum-bookshop, with sloping floors and black timber beams, where you can enjoy warm salads and toasted sandwiches, hearty soups, cakes and a range of free-trade coffees. Upstairs you'll find secondhand books and the occasional art exhibition. Tues–Sat 10am–5pm.

Llanfaes Dairy 19 Bridge St, LD3 8AH ☎01874 625892, ⓦllanfaesdairy.com. Colourful ice-cream parlour in a slightly odd location just across the river, but worth venturing to for its exotic home-made flavours like apple and cinnamon, hazelnut truffle or toffee nut crunch. Feb–Dec daily 11am–5.30pm.

DRINKING

The town's **drinking** options are fairly low-key, its pubs generally frequented by off-duty soldiers.

Boars Head Ship St, LD3 9AN ☎01874 622856. Two very different bars: the front is basic and frequented mainly by locals, while the back bar is younger and louder; there's also a not altogether convincing stone terrace overlooking the water. Mon–Thurs & Sun noon–midnight, Fri & Sat noon–2am.

Sarah Siddons 47 High St Inferior, LD3 7AP ☎01874 610666. Named after the famous actress, born here in 1755 when the pub was then known as the *Shoulder of Mutton*. It's a small, fairly ordinary-looking boozer, but it's extremely popular with locals and soldiers alike. Mon–Thurs & Sun 11am–midnight, Fri & Sat 11am–1.30am.

ENTERTAINMENT

Coliseum Cinema Wheat St, LD3 7DG ☏01874 622501, ⓦcoliseumbrecon.co.uk. Screening since 1925, the agreeably old-fashioned Coliseum, with its vaguely Art Deco frontage, offers a good mix of both mainstream and independent film.

Theatr Brycheiniog Canal Wharf, LD3 7EW ☏01874 611622, ⓦbrycheiniog.co.uk. One of the country's foremost theatres offers a rich programme of music, comedy, theatre and dance.

Usk Valley

Home to the majority of the national park's residents, and the greatest concentration of facilities for visitors, the wide, fertile **Usk Valley** leads southeast from Brecon, running parallel to the Monmouthshire and Brecon Canal and effectively dividing the Brecon Beacons proper from the Black Mountains to the northeast. The A40 connects Brecon and Bwlch with Tretower, Crickhowell and Abergavenny, providing a backbone for dozens of minor lanes that twist south over the Brecon Beacons or north into the bucolic headwaters of some of the Usk's tributaries.

Talybont-on-Usk and around

Six miles southeast of Brecon, **TALYBONT-ON-USK** is idyllically situated for walks, bike rides or canal trips. The lane heading south of the village over the canal heads towards a number of **reservoirs**, starting with the 323-acre **Talybont Reservoir**. It then wiggles up onto the rocky hillsides, past the waterfalls on the Nant Bwrefwr and beyond to the isolated and hauntingly beautiful Neuadd (or Beacons) reservoirs to the north, a good starting point for walks to the summits of Pen y Fan and Corn Du along the old "Gap" route. To the south lie the more popular (and hence busier) **Pentwyn** and **Pontsticill** (aka Taf Fechan) **reservoirs**. Two eastbound paths at either end of the Pontsticill Reservoir allow you to escape from fellow walkers in favour of a fairly steep climb up the rocky slopes for wonderful views over the lakes.

Brecon Mountain Railway

Pant Station, Pontsticill Rd, CF48 2DD • Feb & March Sat & Sun 3 trains daily; April–June, Sept & Oct Mon–Thurs, Sat & Sun 3 trains daily; July & Aug 4 trains daily • £12 return • ☏01685 722988, ⓦbmr.wales

From Pant station, just below Pontsticill, the tiny **Brecon Mountain Railway** shuttles passengers along a five-mile section of track on the eastern bank of the reservoir up to Torpantau (1313ft) before the return trip, stopping (for 25min) at Pontsticill station on the way; here you'll find a sweet little steam museum, snack bar, picnic site and play area. If you want to look around Pontsticill, you can always wait for the next train to

---

A CIRCULAR WALK AROUND THE EASTERN BEACONS

The OS 1:25,000 Explorer map OL13 (Brecon Beacons – Eastern area) is recommended.

A very rewarding walk around the **eastern Brecon Beacons** (but requiring careful map-reading) takes in Craig y Fan Ddu and the path skirting the top of the moorland rim beyond it, around the Caerfanell Valley. By starting at the Blaen-y-glyn car park (grid reference SO 064169), on the lane between Talybont-on-Usk and Pontsticill/Merthyr Tydfil, you begin the ascent through forest. The walk starts across the road, follows the River Caerfanell, crosses a concrete bridge and forks left uphill, first along the edge of the forest, then through the forest itself, then left at the Torpantau car park entrance, and up the steep bank. You later face a hard climb up to the ridge of Craig y Fan Ddu, then carry on north a mile to Bwlch y Ddwyallt, where five paths converge. Bear southeast, past a monument, lying between two heaps of twisted metal, marking the spot of a wartime RAF plane crash. Climb to the top of the ridge and then walk southeast along the rim. After half a mile, at a spur of land, head straight on, down the steep grassy slope, later following a fence, down into the valley. You then walk alongside the river on a path past some little waterfalls towards the starting point.

take you back to Pant. Visitor facilities at Pant include a restaurant. The return trip takes around ninety minutes.

ARRIVAL AND GETTING AROUND   TALYBONT-ON-USK

By bus Regular Brecon–Crickhowell buses stop at Talybont.

By bike Bikes for all ages and levels can be rented for £25

a day at Bikes & Hikes, next to the Talybont Stores (July & Aug daily 9am–5.30pm; Sept–June Wed–Sun 9am–5.30pm; ☎07909 968135, ⍵bikesandhikes.co.uk).

ACCOMMODATION

White Hart Inn ☎01874 676227, ⍵whitehartinn talybont.co.uk. Pressed up hard against the canal, this big pub has an upstairs bunkhouse with four- and six-bed rooms and shared shower facilities, as well as a communal kitchen, drying room and bike storage – hence its popularity with walkers and cyclists. Breakfast £7. Dorms **£20**

YHA Danywenallt Around a mile south of Talybont, at the northern end of the reservoir ☎01874 676677,

⍵yha.org.uk/hostel/brecon-beacons-danywenallt. A converted farmhouse offering small, bright dorms, as well as doubles, plus two well-furnished bell tents (May–Sept; sleeping five) and camping in the apple orchard. There's also a lounge with warming woodstove, self-catering kitchen and meals by request. Breakfast £6.25. Closed Dec and Jan. Camping/person **£13**, dorms **£15**, doubles **£39**, bell tents **£60**

DRINKING

Star Inn ☎01874 676635, ⍵thestarinntalybont.com. Despite its grubby exterior, this is the most convivial of the village pubs, which stands out for its lengthy list of real

ales, regular beer festivals and lively music nights. Daily 11am–11pm.

Llangorse and around

North of Talybont and Bwlch, the B4560 threads its way four miles through rolling countryside to **LLANGORSE** (Llangors), sheltered in the western lee of the Black Mountains. The village is a mile northeast of the reed-shored **Llangorse Lake** (Llyn Syfaddan), which was notorious in medieval times for its supernatural properties (blood-red water, eerie sounds and a mythical lost city). Its *crannog* (artificial lake island), the only one of its kind in Wales, is thought to have been a ninth-century seat of the royal house of Brycheiniog. Today, a reconstructed *crannog* at the water's edge has information panels interpreting the lake's history and legends. The lake is rich in **birdlife**, so twitchers should stake out the hide on the lake's southern shore, near Llangasty, where you're likely to see, among others, gooseander, great crested grebes and little egrets, as well as Canadian geese and grey herons. A lengthy (12-mile) circular walk, starting and ending in Bwlch, takes in the lake and Llangorse.

ACTIVITIES   LLANGORSE AND AROUND

Llangorse Multi Activity Centre Experienced climbers can rent gear cheaply at this centre, in Gilfach, a mile southeast of Llangorse (Mon–Sat 9.30am–10pm, Sun 9.30am–5pm; ☎0333 600 2020, ⍵activityuk .com), and for beginners there are climbing sessions (£20/1hr; £30/2hr). Multi-activity indoor sessions (climbing, abseiling, caving and bouldering) cost £30 for

half a day and £54 for a full day, while outside there's a high ropes challenge course and a zip wire (both £30/ half-day). There's also off-road horseriding for beginners and intermediates (£37/half-day) and hacking for experienced riders (£50/half-day). They have a campsite, too (see below).

ACCOMMODATION

Lakeside Caravan and Camping Llangorse Lake, LD3 7TR ☎01874 658226, ⍵llangorselake.co.uk. Well-equipped site with modern shower blocks, laundry, play area, shop, bar and restaurant. Also has rowing boats, stand-up paddles (both £14/hr), kayaks (£12/hr) and Canadian canoes (£20/hr) to rent. Electric hook-up £4.25 extra. Closed Nov–March. Per person **£7.80**

Llangorse Multi Activity Centre Gilfach Farm, 1 mile southeast of Llangorse, LD3 7UH ☎0333 600 2020, ⍵activityuk.com. The Activity Centre (see above) has a small, neat year-round campsite overlooking the lake, with toilets and showers. A mile away in Llangorse village they've got a lovely bed and breakfast, *Pen-y-Bryn House*, which also has a self-catering unit in the garden, sleeping

four (two-night minimum; from £70/night). Camping/person £5.50, doubles £75
Star Bunkhouse Brecon Rd, Bwlch, ☎ 01874 730080, ⓦ starbunkhouse.com. Super-welcoming bunkhouse offering mostly four-bed dorms with triple-sleeper bunks

(a double below and a single up top), as well as communal kitchen and lounge, the latter with woodburner, games and guidebooks. There's also a drying room and laundry. The owners, who are trained mountain leaders, also offer guided walks. £19

Talgarth

Five miles north of Llangorse, **TALGARTH** is a spirited and friendly village built around its unusual town hall and the hulking **St Gwendoline's church** tower, constructed in the fourteenth century but harking back to Talgarth's position as a defence centre against the Norman invasion.

Talgarth Mill

The Square, LD3 0BW • Tues–Sun: April–Oct 10am–4pm; Nov–March 11am–4pm; optional guided tours (30–45min) take place as and when visitors turn up • £4; tours free • ☎ 01874 711352, ⓦ talgarthmill.com

Local records suggest that there's been a mill in the village since the twelfth century, though the **Talgarth Mill** originally dates from 1780. It ceased functioning in the 1940s as the milling industry fell into decline, and was eventually abandoned. An almost total rebuild was required to bring it back to anything like the condition it was once in – only the water wheel is original – and today it again harnesses the waters of the Ennig to grind the grain to produce flour for the on-site bakery. This in turn supplies the adjoining *Baker's Table* café with a delicious array of breads and cakes (see below).

ARRIVAL AND INFORMATION   TALGARTH

By bus The #39 bus between Brecon and Hereford stops on the main square.
Tourist information The friendly, independently run information centre is inside the Tower Shop on the main

square (April–Oct Mon–Sat 10am–4pm, Sun 10am–1pm; Nov–March Mon–Sat 10.30am–3.30pm, Sun 10.30am–1pm; ☎ 01874 712226, ⓦ visittalgarth.org.uk).

ACCOMMODATION AND EATING

Baker's Table The Square, LD3 0BW ☎ 01874 711352, ⓦ talgarthmill.co.uk. Perched over the river, the mill's adjoining café is a lovely spot to rest up following a tour of the site. Delicious sandwiches and cakes aside, they also offer more substantial food such as Black Mountain smoked mackerel salad (£6.75). Tues–Sun 10am–4pm.
Castle Hotel Bronllys Rd, LD3 0AA ☎ 07789 682335, ⓦ talgarthhotel.co.uk. Beyond town in the direction of

Bronllys, this roadside hotel/pub has five smart rooms with snazzy bathrooms. They also own the cracking little fish and chip shop next door. £65
Strand Café Regent St, LD3 0DB ☎ 01874 711195. Part café, part secondhand bookshop, this quaint establishment offers a gamut of snacky-style meals, from pies and salads to pizzas and puddings. Mon 11am–2pm, Thurs–Sat 11am–9pm, Sun 11am–4pm.

ENTERTAINMENT

★**The Tabernacle** Regent St, LD3 0DD ☎ 07795 473883, ⓦ thetabernacle.co.uk. This mid-nineteenth-century Baptist chapel was bought by former Creation Records boss Alan McGee in 2014, who proceeded to

convert it into a brilliant community and performance space. Events (acoustic gigs, readings, plays, pop-up restaurants) are often scheduled at the last minute – check the website.

Glasbury and around

Just off the A438 on the B4350, four miles northeast of Talgarth, the riverside village of **GLASBURY** lies on a lovely stretch of the Wye; there are some great places to **eat** and **sleep** aorund here. At **Wye Valley Canoes** (April–Oct; ☎ 01497 847213, ⓦ wyevalley canoes.co.uk) you can rent a kayak (single, double or Canadian canoe) to paddle its gentle currents. Rental for a five-mile trip downstream to Hay-on-Wye (around 2hr 30min to 3hr) costs £25 including minibus pickup at the end – longer trips are also possible. Bike rental is also available (£20/half-day).

★**Llangoed Hall** 6 miles west of Glasbury on the A470, LD3 0YP ☎01874 754525, ⓦllangoedhall.co.uk. This luxurious pile is actually an ancient castle remodelled in the early twentieth century by Portmeirion's Clough Williams-Ellis (see p.373). The large, decadent rooms are furnished in fabrics by Elanbach (the on-site textile printing company founded by Bernard Ashley, former husband of Laura and one-time owner of Llangoed) and adorned with lovely touches such as antique mirrors, Roberts radios and decanters of sherry. You can play snooker or croquet, admire the remarkable art collection (which includes several pieces by Whistler) and take a stroll around the extensive kitchen garden. **£175**

River Café Wye Valley Canoes, Glasbury, HR3 5NP ☎01497 847007, ⓦtherivercafeglasbury.co.uk. Four

bright, simple en-suite rooms above the restaurant (see below), with splendid views across to the river. A few paces away, on the water's edge, the *River Room* comprises four single beds and minimal furnishings, and is ideally suited to walkers or canoeists. The neighbouring chapel has been converted into a bunkhouse, but this is generally reserved for large groups. *River Room*/person **£50**, *River Café* doubles **£90**

Wye Knot Stop Llyswen, 4 miles west of Glasbury, LD3 0UR ☎01874 754247, ⓦwyeknotstop.co.uk. This village café (see below) also provides restful B&B accommodation, with three tidy en-suite rooms: a double upstairs and, downstairs, a larger option sleeping up to four (and it's wheelchair friendly; £80) and a tiny single that's ideal for walkers (£50). **£65**

Honey Café 4 miles southeast of Glasbury, LD3 0LH ☎01874 711904, ⓦhoneycafe.co.uk. A fixture since 1933, this striking red- and orange-painted café/restaurant remains hugely popular for its home-made cakes and desserts, though the real pull is its spicy Tex-Mex evening menu. Daily 9am–9pm.

River Café Wye Valley Canoes, Glasbury, HR3 5NP ☎01497 847007, ⓦtherivercafeglasbury.co.uk. Very fine restaurant right by the river, whose creditable menu might include charred asparagus with smoked trout, or

pork belly with polenta and roasted beetroot (£14.50) – alternatively, stop by for a heart-starting coffee and a home-baked treat out on the terrace. Mon–Sat 8.30am–11.30pm, Sun 8.30am–4pm.

Wye Knot Stop Llyswen, 4 miles west of Glasbury, LD3 0UR ☎01874 754247, ⓦwyeknotstop.co.uk. Breezy café serving the best coffee for miles, alongside cream teas, cakes and pastries and a belter of an all-day breakfast (£5.50). Feb–Dec Mon & Thurs–Sun 9.30am–5.30pm.

Tretower castle and court

Three miles northwest of Crickhowell, NP8 1RD • April–Oct daily 10am–5pm; Nov–March Thurs–Sat 10am–4pm • £6.50; CADW • ☎ 01874 730279, ⓦ cadw.gov.wales/daysout/tretowercourtandcastle

Rising from the valley floor twelve miles south of Talgarth, the solid round tower of the **castle and court** at **TRETOWER** (Tre-twr) was built to guard the valley pass, and still dominates the skyline from both the A40 and the A479. Having replaced an earlier Norman fortification, the high, circular thirteenth-century tower is pretty much all that remains of the castle building, alongside a few sections of wall adjoining a farm. More impressive is the late fourteenth-century manor house, whose downstairs rooms feature a grand hall with inlaid wooden panels, a mock-up kitchen, pantry and buttery. Accessed via an upper-level walkway, the upstairs rooms are now totally stripped bare, but still retain a certain faded grandeur.

Crickhowell

One of the gems of the Brecon Beacons, **CRICKHOWELL** (Crucywel; locally referred to as "Crick") lies on the northern shore of the wide and shallow Usk. Many a local myth has been spawned by its magnificent eighteenth-century **bridge**, the longest stone bridge in Wales – curiously, there are thirteen arches on one side and twelve on the other. From the river, Bridge Street rises up to the uninspiring mound of the ruined **castle** and the wide **High Street**, which is lined with coloured, rough-hewn tenements, handsome shops – including the venerable Webb's department store – and several old-fashioned butchers.

Table Mountain

Crickhowell's spectacular northern backdrop is **Table Mountain** (1481ft), whose brown cone presides over the rolling green fields below. The most scenic route up is

CRICKHOWELL'S FESTIVALS

Crickhowell stages a handful of superb annual festivals. The big one is the **Green Man Festival** (Ⓦgreenman.net), a three-day jamboree in mid-August that features some of the biggest names in folk, indie and Americana music, plus drum workshops, literary events, a cinema tent, kids' activities, performance art, comedy and a "healing field". At the end of February/beginning of March, Crickhowell hosts a terrific nine-day **Walking Festival** (Ⓦcrickhowellfestival.com), with guided walks ranging from tough all-day treks to easy strolls; special-interest walks and talks are also on offer. The town's thriving artistic community is celebrated at the end of May with the popular **Crickhowell Open Studios**, when local artists open up their workspaces for public viewing. Last but by no means least, there's the **Crickhowell Literary Festival** (Ⓦcricklitfest.co.uk) at the beginning of October, a welcome, lower-key alternative to Hay but still featuring some stellar names and with a determinedly Welsh bent.

along the path that goes off by the electricity substation past The Wern off Llanbedr Road. At the summit are remains of the 2500-year-old hillfort (*crug*) of Hywel, from which Crickhowell takes its name. A steeper, and far shorter, route to Table Mountain starts from the village of **LLANBEDR**, some two miles north of Crickhowell, and heads up alongside the stream behind the *Perth-y-pia* bunkhouse. The views are among the best in the area. Many walkers follow the route to the north from Table Mountain, climbing two miles up to the plateau-topped limestone hump of **Pen Cerrig-calch** (2302ft).

ARRIVAL AND INFORMATION   CRICKHOWELL

By bus Buses (#43 and X43) set down on the main square at the top of the High St.
Destinations Abergavenny (Mon–Sat hourly; 20min); Brecon (Mon–Sat hourly; 30–50min).
Tourist office The super-helpful Crickhowell Resource and Information Centre on Beaufort St (Mon–Sat

10am–5pm, Sun 10am–1.30pm; Ⓣ01873 811970, Ⓦvisitcrickhowell.co.uk) has loads of info on local walks, including *Cracking Walks around Crickhowell* (£3); there's also a café and, upstairs, a fabulous little gallery selling quality local art.

ACCOMMODATION

Bear Hotel Beaufort St, NP8 1BW Ⓣ01873 810408, Ⓦbearhotel.co.uk. A grand old coaching inn whose architectural quirks have led to some highly idiosyncratic rooms. Those in the main building possess the most character, especially the pricier "Unique Feature" options (£182), while those in the old courtyard stables are a touch more polished. **£107**
Dragon Inn 47 High St, NP8 1BE Ⓣ01873 810362, Ⓦdragoninncrickhowell.com. Salmon-pink building at

the quieter, far end of the High St, with sharply furnished rooms sporting silver and grey trimmings and Welsh art. Relaxing, friendly and great for families. **£85**
Park Farm Camping Llangattock, less than a mile south, NP8 1HT Ⓣ01873 812183, Ⓦparkfarm-campsite.co.uk. This simple, attractively located parkland site has a stream running through it; basic facilities include a shower and toilet block. Per person **£7**

EATING AND DRINKING

Bear Hotel Beaufort St, NP8 1BW Ⓣ01873 810408. The romantic candlelit restaurant is ideally suited to winter dining, while the garden is just the job for a summertime splurge; the menu is strong, in game and fish. The hotel's low-beamed pub, scattered with bentwood armchairs and big squishy sofas, sports bags of charm and serves terrific beer. Daily 11am–11pm; kitchen Mon–Sat noon–2.15pm & 6–10pm, Sun noon–2.15pm.
★Book-ish 18 High St, NP8 1BD Ⓣ01873 811256, Ⓦbook-ish.co.uk. If you like books and coffee, this enthusiastically run indie bookshop-cum-café should be

your first port of call. Once done browsing – there's a fabulous children's/young adults section in the basement – head through to the rear and the light-filled mezzanine, where you can kick back with a book and a brew, or perhaps a glass of wine. Lots of literary and musical events, too. Mon–Sat 9am–5.30pm, Sun 10am–4pm.
Bridge End Inn Bridge St, NP8 1AR Ⓣ01873 810338, Ⓦthebridgeendinn.com. Comprising part of the town's former tollhouse, this is a truly old-fashioned pub with flagstone flooring, a stone fireplace and brass, copper pots hanging from the walls and ceilings, and a sweet riverside

garden. Daily 11am–11.30pm.

The Vine Tree Legar House, Llangattock, NP8 1HG ☎01873 812277, ⓦthevinetreellangattock.com. Classy restaurant just across the bridge in Llangattock, with lots of bare brick and slate throughout its trio of dining areas – bag one of the four tables fronting the open kitchen

if you can. Offerings range from comfort dishes (pulled pork burger with chilli jam; £13) to more sophisticated creations such as poached monkfish with Wye Valley asparagus and a lobster glaze (£20). Daily 11am–11pm; kitchen Tues–Sat noon–2.30pm & 6–9.30pm, Sun noon–4pm.

Abergavenny and around

Six miles southeast of Crickhowell, **ABERGAVENNY** (Y Fenni), Wales' culinary hub, is a vibrant, confident town, though its history is somewhat chequered. Today, the combination of urban amenities and countrified setting makes it an ideal jumping-off point for forays into the central and eastern sections of the Brecon Beacons.

Brief history

The first main settlement was around the **Norman castle**, which was built by the English king Henry I's local appointee, Hameline de Ballon, with the express aim of securing enough power to evict local Welsh tribes from the area, an important through route into Wales. Hostility to the Welsh reached its peak at Christmas 1175, when William de Braose, then lord of the town, invited Gwent chieftains to the castle, only to murder them all. The town was shaken badly by the Black Death (1341–51) and a

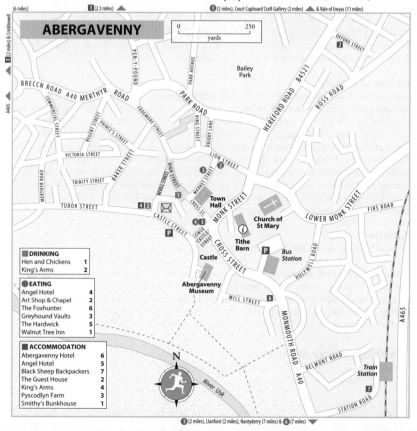

routing by Owain Glyndŵr in 1404, but continued to grow, thanks largely to the weaving and tanning trades that developed from the sixteenth century. The industries prospered alongside Abergavenny's flourishing **market**, still the focal point for a wide area (see box below).

The castle

Castle St, NP7 5EE • Free access

Any street heading south off Cross or High streets leads to Castle Street, where the dark, fragmented remains of Abergavenny's medieval **castle** languish serenely above the River Usk. Entrance to the eleventh-century castle is through the sturdy, though now roofless, gatehouse, to the right of which stands an extensive portion of the curtain wall. The keep, remodelled in the nineteenth century, sits in the middle of the forsaken ruins like an incongruous Lego model. Glorious views aside, the grounds are a lovely spot for a picnic.

Abergavenny Museum

July–Sept daily 10am–4pm; Oct–June Mon, Tues & Thurs–Sun 10am–4pm • Free • ☎ 01873 854282, ⓦ abergavennymuseum.co.uk

While in the castle it's worth visiting the quirky **Abergavenny Museum**, where displays cover the town's history using photographs, billboards and re-created interiors including a saddlery, a sanitized Border farmhouse kitchen of 1885 and Basil Jones's grocery shop, which once stood on Main Street. One of the more unexpected exhibits is a Red Cross parcel sent to Rudolf Hess while he was imprisoned in Maindiff Court Military Hospital between 1942 and 1945. In a quite remarkable episode, Hess flew to the UK in May 1941 – ostensibly to broker a peace deal – but crash landed at Eaglesham, in Scotland, and was subsequently arrested and incarcerated at the Tower of London before being transferred to Abergavenny.

Church of St Mary

Monk St, NP7 5ND • Mon–Sat 9am–4pm • Free • ☎ 01873 858787, ⓦ stmarys-priory.org

Abergavenny's parish **church of St Mary** contains effigies and tombs spanning the entire medieval period. Originally built as the chapel of a small twelfth-century Benedictine priory, the existing building goes back only as far as the fourteenth century, although some of the monuments within predate the building itself. The interior boasts a wealth of outstanding detail, not least the **Jesse Tree**, one of the finest late medieval sculptures in Britain; a recumbent, twice-life-size statue of King David's father, it would once have formed part of an altarpiece tracing the family lineage from Jesse to Jesus. Take a look, too, at the finely crafted fifteenth-century choir stalls, complete with (relatively) contemporary eighteenth-century graffiti.

Tithe Barn

Monk St, NP7 5ND • Mon–Sat 9am–4pm • Free • ☎ 01873 858787, ⓦ stmarys-priory.org

Next to St Mary's church, the splendidly restored fourteenth-century **Tithe Barn** has variously functioned as a coach house, a theatre for travelling actors and even a disco. It's now a heritage centre, with a well-put-together exhibition on the history of Abergavenny; it's all somewhat overshadowed by the **Abergavenny Tapestry**, an expansive, brightly coloured visual record of the town's past. Set against the backdrop of the three local mountains – Blorenge, Skirrid Fawr and Sugar Loaf – are

---

ABERGAVENNY MARKET

Next to the turreted Victorian Gothic town hall on the High Street, Abergavenny's wonderful covered **market** sells produce on Tuesdays, Fridays and Saturdays (8am–4pm). It's also home to a flea market on Wednesdays, a farmers' market on the fourth Thursday of every month and regular weekend antiques fairs.

representations, among others, of the Jesse Tree sculpture, the 1952 Olympic gold-medal-winning horse *Foxhunter* with his rider Harry Llewellyn, and Owain Glyndŵr sacking the town.

Court Cupboard Craft Gallery

New Court Farm, Llantilio Pertholey, off the A465, 2 miles northeast of Abergavenny, NP7 8AU • Daily: Jan–March 10.30am–4pm; April–Dec 10.30am–5pm • Free • ☎ 01873 852011, ⊛ courtcupboardgallery.co.uk

Housed within a 500-year-old farm, and occupying the old stables, piggery and milking parlour, the **Court Cupboard Craft Gallery** is a superbly conceived artist's enclave of workshops, selling anything from leather crafts (including beautiful handmade bags), ceramics and glass to jewellery, pottery and watercolours. You can often chat with the artists as they work, and the gallery also mounts regular exhibitions along with arts and craft courses.

ARRIVAL AND DEPARTURE

ABERGAVENNY AND AROUND

By train Abergavenny's train station is 0.5 mile southeast of the centre on Station Rd.

Destinations Cardiff (every 30min–1hr; 45–55mins); Hereford (every 30–45min; 25mins); Newport (every 30min–1hr; 30mins).

By bus Buses depart from Swan Meadows bus station, at the bottom of town on Cross St.

Destinations Brecon (Mon–Sat hourly; 40min–1hr); Cardiff (Mon–Sat hourly, Sun 2; 1hr 40min–2hr 45min); Crickhowell (Mon–Sat hourly; 20min); Llanfihangel Crucorney (Mon–Sat 7 daily; 15min); Merthyr Tydfil (Mon–Sat hourly, Sun 3; 1hr 40min); Monmouth (Mon–Sat 7 daily, Sun 4; 45min); Raglan (Mon–Sat 7 daily, Sun 4; 35min).

INFORMATION AND GETTING AROUND

Tourist office Tithe Barn, Monk St (Mon–Sat: April–Oct 10am–4pm; Nov–March 10am–2pm; ☎ 01873 853254, ⊛ visitabergavenny.co.uk). It also functions as a branch of the Brecon Beacons National Park office.

By bike Hopyard Cycles in Govilon, a couple of miles west of town (☎ 01873 830219, ⊛ hopyardcycles.co.uk; mountain bikes from £15/day), can deliver bikes (for a small charge) throughout the area.

ACCOMMODATION

HOTELS AND GUESTHOUSES

Abergavenny Hotel 21 Monmouth Rd, NP7 5HH ☎ 01873 859050, ⊛ abergavennyhotel.com. Handsome red-brick and stone Victorian building with twenty rooms of effortless charm, decorated in soothing greys and creams, and featuring dazzling white-on-white bathrooms with capacious showers. Continental breakfast (included) is taken in the snazzy bar. **£80**

★**Angel Hotel** 15 Cross St, NP7 5EN ☎ 01873 857121, ⊛ angelabergavenny.com. Occupying an old coaching inn, the homely *Angel* is a warren of corridors with a range of classy rooms fitted out in soft beige, with plush carpets, big comfy beds with cashmere throws and large bathrooms with posh toiletries; there are also two cottages in the nearby castle grounds. There's invariably a terrific buzz around the place, be it locals supping a pint in the panelled *Foxhunter* bar, or guests tucking into the *Angel's* renowned high tea (see p.218) in the *Wedgwood Room*. Service is impeccable. **£105**

The Guest House 2 Oxford St, NP7 5RP ☎ 01873 854823, ⊛ theguesthouseabergavenny.co.uk. Fun, popular guesthouse with six sunny rooms each named after local peaks. There's a guest lounge with Sky Sports and a Wii console, resident parrots Alfie and Eric in the dining room, and a backyard petting area with chickens; hence the lovely fresh eggs for breakfast. **£80**

King's Arms 29 Neville St, NP7 5AA ☎ 01873 855074, ⊛ kingsarmsabergavenny.co.uk. Limewash beams, bare, sloping wood floors and low, crooked doorways are all quirky features of this pleasing, sixteenth-century coaching inn. The neatly conceived pod-like bathrooms, meanwhile, feature roll-top or jacuzzi baths. **£105**

HOSTEL, BUNKHOUSE AND CAMPSITE

Black Sheep Backpackers 24 Station Rd, NP7 5HS ☎ 01873 859125, ⊛ greatwesternabergavenny.com. A few paces down from the station, this converted railway hotel has accommodation in four- to ten-bed dorms (with shared showers), as well as en-suite doubles. There are self-catering facilities and a launderette across the road. Continental breakfast included. Dorms **£17.50**, doubles **£60**

Pyscodlyn Farm Llanwenarth Citra, 2 miles west, off the A40, NP7 7ER ☎ 01873 853271, ⊛ pyscodlyncaravanpark .com. Easy to reach – all Brecon and Crickhowell buses pass by – this is primarily a caravan site, but there is one sheltered field for campers, with separate shower blocks for males and females. Closed Nov to mid-March. **£14**

3

ABERGAVENNY'S FESTIVALS

Abergavenny's annual **Food Festival** (ⓦ abergavennyfoodfestival.com), in mid-September, is one of the most prestigious in Britain, comprising two bumper days of markets, masterclasses, tastings and talks, and pretty much any other take on food you can think of. There are several spin-off events throughout the year; check the website for details. The town's other key annual event is the week-long **Festival of Cycling** (ⓦ abergavennyfestivalofcycling.co.uk) at the end of June. Wales' most important two-wheeled gathering draws some of the biggest names in the sport for town-centre races; there's plenty going on for non-elite riders and children, too, including tandem and handcycle races through town, and cyclocross.

Smithy's Bunkhouse Lower House Farm, Pantygelli, NP7 7HR ☎ 01873 853432, ⓦ smithysbunkhouse.co.uk. Self-catering dorm accommodation under the slopes of the Sugar Loaf a couple of miles north of town. Comprehensive facilities include a well-equipped kitchen, a drying room and a common room with wood-burning stove. **£15**

3

EATING

Abergavenny's reputation as a culinary hotbed is fully justified; the town boasts one of the finest concentrations of **restaurants** in Wales. The best of these, though, are outside town, so you will need your own transport.

★**Angel Hotel** 15 Cross St, NP7 5EN ☎ 01873 857121, ⓦ angelabergavenny.com. High tea in the hotel's gracious *Wedgewood Room* (or courtyard terrace) is reason enough to come to Abergavenny; the lavish spread (£27.80) includes sandwiches and savouries, freshly baked cakes and pastries, scones with jam and cream, and tea or coffee. Reservations recommended. Meanwhile, the delicious waft of fresh bread will send you straight to the hotel's next-door bakery, which sells all sorts of artisan breads and pastries, including some spectacular sourdoughs. Tea Mon–Fri 2–4pm, Sat & Sun 2–5.30pm; bakery Tues–Sat 8am–4pm.

Art Shop & Chapel Market St, NP7 5EH ☎ 01873 736430, ⓦ artshopandgallery.co.uk. Occupying the basement of a former (nineteenth-century) chapel (the church itself is used as an occasional performance space), this artistic gallery-cum-café makes for a splendid late breakfast or lunch stop. With dishes such as Turkish eggs with chorizo and yoghurt, or Welsh rarebit with leek and rhubarb ketchup on sourdough (£7.80), plus home-made cordials, craft ales and biodynamic wines, you've got many great reasons to visit this marvellous little enterprise. Tues–Sat 10am–5pm.

The Foxhunter Nantyderry, 7 miles southeast, NP7 9DN ☎ 01873 881101, ⓦ thefoxhunterinn.com. Named after a locally bred, 1952 Olympic-gold-medal-winning horse, this lovingly restored former stationmaster's house is now a comely pub and restaurant; it's nothing flash or fancy, but dishes such as sirloin with stilton sauce and roasted field mushrooms (£19) are tremendously satisfying. Mon 5.30–11pm, Tues–Thurs 11.30am–3pm & 5.30–11pm, Fri–Sun 11.30am–11pm; kitchen Mon 6–9pm, Tues–Sat noon–3pm & 6–9pm, Sun noon–4pm.

Greyhound Vaults Market St, NP7 5SD ☎ 01873 858549. Don't be fooled by the dull, pub-like exterior and earthy interior, this place serves a wide range of tasty, moderately priced Welsh and English specialities, such as Welsh Black steak with leeks, and topside of beef with Yorkshire pudding. Tues–Thurs 12–2.30pm, Fri & Sat 12–2.30pm & 6–9.30pm, Sun 12–2.30pm.

The Hardwick Old Raglan Rd, 2 miles east, NP7 9AA ☎ 01873 854220, ⓦ thehardwick.co.uk. Headed up by chef Stephen Terry, this fabulous-looking pub offers brilliantly simple but fantastically presented dishes such as deep-fried pork belly and black pudding with pickled fennel and apple and mustard sauce (£18). The Sunday three-course set lunch is superb value at £28. Daily 11am–11pm; kitchen noon–3pm & 6.30–10pm.

★**Walnut Tree Inn** B4521, Llanddewi Skirrid, 2 miles north, NP7 8AW ☎ 01873 852797, ⓦ thewalnuttreeinn .com. A highly regarded foodies' paradise under the helm of Shaun Hill, this restaurant, with one Michelin star, has been drawing diners from afar for years. A three-course dinner menu might consist of smoked leeks with goat's cheese croquettes, followed by veal kidneys with streaky bacon and cassis sauce (£22), and a pistachio crème brûlée to finish. The lack of pretension – there's no rigid formality or dress code – adds to the easy-going charm. Tues–Sat noon–3pm & 7–11pm.

DRINKING

Hen and Chickens Flannel St, off High St, NP7 5EG ☎ 01873 853613. Timeless, traditional pub popular with locals and visitors alike, serving some of the best beer in town and staging regular live music, including jazz on Sun afternoons and pop/rock on alternate Fris. Mon–Sat 10.30am–11pm, Sun noon–10.30pm.

King's Arms 29 Neville St, NP7 5AA ☎01873 855074, ⓦkingsarmsabergavenny.co.uk. Very handsome pub combining the old (stone fireplace and wonderful curving beams on the low ceiling) and the new (neat modern furnishings) to smart effect. Good local beer from the Wye

Valley and creditable food in the restaurant section; dressed Devonshire crab with potato and apple salad, for example (£15.25). Mon–Thurs & Sun 11am–11pm, Fri & Sat 11am–1am; kitchen daily noon–3pm & 6–9.30pm.

Black Mountains

Appearing only partly tamed by human habitation, the northeastern-most section of the Brecon Beacons National Park, known as the **Black Mountains** (plural, as distinct from the Black Mountain, forty miles west) is made up of a series of high, finger-like ridges enclosing remote, secretive valleys dotted with tiny villages. The wide valley of the River Usk divides the Beacons heartland from the Black Mountains, whose sandstone range rises to more clearly defined individual peaks than those in the western end of the park.

The **Vale of Ewyas** stretches along the extreme eastern boundary of the National Park, making one of the most enchanting and reclusive regions in Wales, most memorably seen by car on the narrow road past Llanthony Priory, over the Gospel Pass and on to Hay-on-Wye.

The most rewarding areas to **walk** are around Llanthony and the hilltops above, Hay Bluff, and along the southern band of peaks – notably Pen Cerrig-calch, Table Mountain and the Sugar Loaf. The mass of rippling hills in the centre and to the north is less easy to reach, although a couple of good paths follow the contours around them.

Llanfihangel Crucorney

Six miles north of Abergavenny, on the main village street of **LLANFIHANGEL CRUCORNEY** (Llanfihangel Crucornau; the "Sacred Enclosure of Michael at the Corner of the Rock"), are a fifteenth-century **church** and the reputedly haunted *Skirrid Mountain Inn* (see below).

EATING AND DRINKING   **LLANFIHANGEL CRUCORNEY**

Skirrid Mountain Inn Llanfihangel Crucorney, NP7 8DH ☎01873 890258, ⓦskirridmountaininn.co.uk. First mentioned in 1110 and thought to be the oldest pub in Wales. During the seventeenth century, some 180 people are believed to have been hanged here – you can still see

the beam inside the inn, which bears the scorch marks of the rope. It's an atmospheric spot for a drink, particularly in winter when the fireplaces roar into life. Mon 5.30–11pm, Tues–Fri 11.30am–2.30pm & 5.30–11pm, Sat 11am–11pm, Sun noon–10pm.

Partrishow church

From Llanfihangel Crucorney, the main road through the valley heads north into the Vale of Ewyas. After a mile, a lane heads west towards the enchanting valley of the **Grwyne Fawr**, lost deep in the middle of quiet hills. The road is well worth following to the hamlet of **PARTRISHOW**, where a bubbling tributary of the Grwyne Fawr trickles past the delightful **church** and **well** of St Issui – you'll need to confirm opening times with the Abergavenny tourist office (see p.217).

Founded in the eleventh century, the tiny church features a lacy fifteenth-century **rood screen**, carved out of solid Irish oak and adorned with crude symbols of good and evil, most notably in the corner, where an evil dragon consumes a vine, a symbol of hope and well-being – the rest of the whitewashed church breathes simplicity by comparison.

Of special note are the **wall texts** painted over the apocalyptic picture of a skeleton and scythe. Before the Reformation, such images were widely used with the intent of teaching an illiterate population about the scriptures; however, King James I ordered it to be whitewashed over and repainted with scripture texts. Here, the ghostly grim reaper is once again seeping through the whitewash. Encased in glass by the pulpit is a rare example of a 1620 bible in Welsh.

3

BLACK MOUNTAINS SUMMITS

Blorenge (1834ft) The simplest way up is from the road that strikes off the B4246 a mile short of Blaenafon: the open road climbs the shale- and sheep-covered slopes to the car parks near the radio masts. An easy walk from here leads across boggy heathland to a long cairn at the summit, from where there are some glorious views. There is a steeper ascent of the Blorenge from Llanfoist, a mile southwest of Abergavenny, which cuts past the church and under the canal before zigzagging up the mountain.

Sugar Loaf (1955ft) Probably the most popular local walk is the broad and smooth cone of Sugar Loaf, which commands the Black Mountains foothills to the northwest of Abergavenny. The easiest ascent is from the south, taking the right fork of Pentre Lane off the A40, half a mile west of Abergavenny, and following the road that climbs beyond the Sugar Loaf Vineyard to the Llanwenarth car park. From the car park, it's initially a gentle stroll through open moorland before the impressive mountain face opens up and the climb becomes increasingly steep and rocky; from the summit, there are fantastic views of the brooding Brecon mountains to the west.

The Skirrid (1595ft) Shooting up from the Gavenny Valley, three miles northeast of Abergavenny, the Skirrid (Ysgyryd Fawr) is the most eye-catching mountain in the area. The Skirrid has long been held to be holy; the almighty chasm that splits the peak is said to have been caused by the force of God's will on the death of Christ, a theory that drew St Michael and legions of other pilgrims to this bleak but breathtaking spot. Another theory claims that Noah's Ark clipped it as it passed by. The best path, although it's still a steep ascent, leads from the lay-by on the B4521 just short of the *Walnut Tree Inn*. At the summit, a few leaning boulders are all that remains of a clandestine chapel built by persecuted Catholics.

Hay Bluff (2220ft) Giving terrific views from its often windy summit, this is easily climbed from the top of the road at the Gospel Pass south of Hay-on-Wye. A prominent track runs up to the summit cairn, from where you can continue southeast around the rim of the hill until turning left down the Offa's Dyke Path, which drops steadily to the road to make a magnificent three-mile circuit.

Cwmyoy

If you're prepared for some adventurous driving, take the little lane that peels off the Vale of Ewyas road down over the river and into the village of **CWMYOY**. The main feature here is the wonky **parish church of St Martin**, which has subsided substantially due to geological twists in the underlying rock. Nothing squares up: the tower leans at a severe angle from the bulging body of the church and the view inside from the back of the nave towards the sloping altar, askew roof and straining windows is unforgettable. No less stunning are the views back down through the valley.

Llanthony Priory

Llanthony, NP7 7NN • Daily 10am–4pm • Free; CADW • ☏ 01443 336000, ⊚ cadw.gov.wales/daysout/llanthonypriory

In the heart of the Vale of Ewyas is the secluded hamlet of **LLANTHONY**, where a handful of houses, an inn and a few farms cluster around the remains of **Llanthony Priory**. The ruins retain a real sense of spirituality and peace, set against an inspiring backdrop of river and mountain. It's believed the priory was founded on the site of a ruined chapel around 1100 by Norman knight William de Lacy, who was allegedly so captivated by the site that he renounced worldly life and founded a hermitage, attracting like-minded recluses and forming Wales' first Augustine priory. The church and outbuildings still standing today were constructed in the latter half of the twelfth century. Roving episcopal envoy Giraldus Cambrensis visited the emerging priory church in 1188, noting that "here the monks, sitting in their cloisters, enjoying the fresh air, when they happen to look up at the horizon behold the tops of mountains, as it were touching the heavens". A track behind the ruins winds up to the Offa's Dyke Path, which runs along a lofty, windy ridge.

Llanthony Priory Hotel Llanthony, NP7 7NN ☎ 01873 890487, ⍟ llanthonyprioryhotel.co.uk. Fashioned out of part of the tumbledown priory, this hotel was built in the eighteenth century as a hunting lodge. Even the most easily accessed of the four antique-laden rooms (with shared bathrooms) involves scaling a narrow spiral staircase, and the tower rooms are several steep flights up. Tucked away down beneath the medieval arches, the hotel's restaurant and cellar bar has bags of charm. Restaurant/bar hours are convoluted – check the website. **£90**

Capel-y-ffin

From Llanthony, the road climbs alongside the narrowing Honddu River before coasting by ruined farmhouses for four miles to the isolated hamlet of **CAPEL-Y-FFIN**. Locked in the middle of sheer hills, it has a devotional feel, comprising little more than two tiny chapels (one with a congregation of just twenty) and a curious ruined monastery. A lane forks off by the phone box, leading up to the ruins of the privately owned (and confusingly named) **Llanthony Monastery**, founded in 1870 by the Reverend Joseph Lyne. The religious order failed to survive his death in 1908, but the place later became a self-sufficient outpost of the art world when, in 1924, it was bought by English sculptor and typeface designer Eric Gill, whose commune, a motley collection of artists and their families, drew much of their creative inspiration from the area.

Gospel Pass

From Capel-y-ffin, the hedge-lined road narrows further still as it weaves a tortuous route up into the **Gospel Pass** and out onto the glorious roof of the Black Mountains. A howling, windy moor by **Hay Bluff**, five miles up from Capel-y-ffin, gives panoramic views and terrific walking over springy hills. The road drops just as suddenly as it climbs, descending five miles into Hay-on-Wye.

The Grange Capel-y-ffin, NP7 7NP ☎ 01873 890215, ⍟ grangetrekking-wales.co.uk. A comfortable, friendly B&B with three en-suite rooms, a glamping pod (sleeping two), a shepherd's hut (sleeping three) and extensive gardens in which you can pitch a tent; campers are free to use the showers. Guests can also get well-priced evening meals, and staff can organize pony trekking (£20/hr). Closed Nov–Easter. Camping/person **£6**, hut/person **£17**, pod **£34**, doubles **£76**

Hay-on-Wye

The quaint border town of **HAY-ON-WYE** (Y Gelli), at the northern tip of the Brecon Beacons, is synonymous with secondhand **books**. Since the first bookshop opened here

---

RICHARD BOOTH AND THE HAY BOOK BUSINESS

Richard Booth, whose family originates in the area, opened the first of his Hay-on-Wye **secondhand bookshops** in 1961. Since then, he has built an astonishing empire and attracted other booksellers to the town, turning it into the greatest market of used books in the world.

Whereas so many mid-Welsh and border towns have seen populations ebb away over the past half-century, Hay is booming on the strength of its bibliophilic connections. Booth views this transformation of a hitherto ordinary little market town as a prototype for reviving rural economies, based on local initiatives and unusual specialisms. This, coupled with Hay's geographical location slap-bang on the Wales–England border and Booth's own self-promotional skills, led him to declare Hay independent of the UK in 1977, with himself, naturally, as king. He appoints his own ministers and offers "official" government scrolls, passports and car stickers to visitors. Although such a proclamation carries no weight officially, most of the people of Hay seem to have rallied behind King Richard and are delighted with the publicity – and visitors – that the town's high profile attracts.

Booth's avant-garde ideas and the events surrounding the 1977 declaration are laid out in his entertaining autobiography, *My Kingdom of Books*.

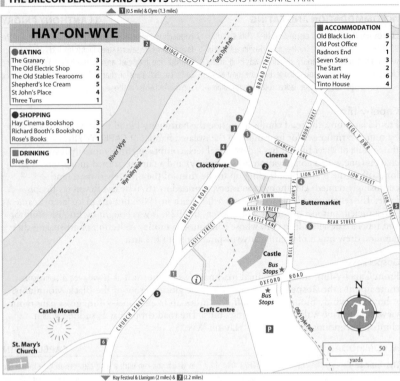

HAY-ON-WYE

● **EATING**
The Granary	3
The Old Electric Shop	2
The Old Stables Tearooms	6
Shepherd's Ice Cream	5
St John's Place	4
Three Tuns	1

● **SHOPPING**
Hay Cinema Bookshop	3
Richard Booth's Bookshop	2
Rose's Books	1

■ **DRINKING**
| Blue Boar | 1 |

■ **ACCOMMODATION**
Old Black Lion	5
Old Post Office	7
Radnors End	1
Seven Stars	3
The Start	2
Swan at Hay	6
Tinto House	4

in the 1960s, just about every spare inch has been given over to the trade, including the old cinema, houses and most shops. There are now well over thirty bookshops in town, most of which cluster on and around Castle Street. Many are highly specialized, including those dedicated solely to travel, poetry, children and even "murder and mayhem". The annually updated leaflet *Hay-on-Wye Booksellers, Printsellers & Bookbinders* (free), detailing all the town's booksellers and literary happenings, is available from the tourist office. In addition to the bookshops you'll find antique shops, galleries and an increasing number of fine-food haunts.

The castle

Castle St, HR3 5DF · Guided tours (1hr) Thurs 11am · £5

The **castle**, a fire-damaged Jacobean mansion built into the walls of a thirteenth-century fortress was owned, until recently, by Hay's ruling "monarch", Richard Booth (see box, p.221). Now run by the Hay Castle Trust, it is undergoing extensive renovation, expected to be finished in 2019. In the meantime, **guided tours** take in the second floor and roofed section of the castle, though you'll actually learn more about the history and the characters that have inhabited the place.

ARRIVAL AND GETTING AROUND   HAY-ON-WYE

By bus Buses from Brecon and Hereford stop by the Oxford Rd car park, near the tourist office.

Destinations Brecon (Mon–Sat 7 daily; 45min); Hereford (Mon–Sat 7 daily, Sun 3; 1hr); Talgarth (Mon–Sat 7 daily; 25min).

Bike rental Drover Cycles, Forest Rd (£20/half-day, £30/day;

☏ 01497 822419, ⓦ drovercycles.co.uk), has a superb range of bikes, offers servicing and repairs, and can deliver for free. They've also got a great little café for a post-cycle pick-me-up.

INFORMATION

Tourist office Chapel Cottage, Oxford Rd (daily: Easter–Oct 10am–4.30pm; Nov–Easter 11am–3pm; ☎01497 820144, ⓦhay-on-wye.co.uk). Staff can advise on and make reservations for local accommodation.

ACCOMMODATION

Hay is well served for accommodation, although prices are a little higher here than nearby, and there are no hostels. It goes without saying that you should book any accommodation several months in advance for the **Hay Festival**.

HOTELS AND GUESTHOUSES

Old Black Lion Lion St, HR3 5AD ☎01497 820841, ⓦoldblacklion.co.uk. Very well-regarded thirteenth-century inn with charming en-suite rooms above the pub and in a neighbouring annexe; the latter are slightly more appealing. **£79**

Old Post Office Llanigon, 2 miles south, HR3 5QA ☎01497 820008, ⓦoldpost-office.co.uk. A wonderful seventeenth-century, vegetarian B&B, with three good-looking rooms leading off a spiral oak staircase. Well placed for local walks, including the Offa's Dyke Path. Two-night minimum at weekends. **£80**

Seven Stars 11 Broad St, HR3 5DB ☎01497 820886, ⓦtheseven-stars.co.uk. Former town pub near the clock tower, with eight modest, cosy rooms (including a triple and a quad), some with original oak beams and window frames. There's also an indoor swimming pool and sauna. **£94**

The Start Hay Bridge, HR3 5RS ☎01497 821391, ⓦthe-start.net. Neatly renovated Georgian house on the riverbank, with three rooms boasting antique furnishings and linen, and handmade quilts. The vegetable garden provides many of the ingredients for breakfast, including scrummy Glamorgan sausages and organic porridge. **£80**

Swan at Hay Church St, HR3 5DQ ☎01497 821188, ⓦswanathay.co.uk. A hostelry of sorts since 1812, this graceful, pale-grey stone Georgian hotel has undergone a recent renovation, resulting in nineteen light-filled rooms with beautifully upholstered furnishings and sparkling bathrooms with toiletries supplied by Myddfai, a local social enterprise for adults with learning disabilities. Some rooms have garden views. A lounge and bistro, alongside a couple of snugs and a pretty garden, completes this classy ensemble. **£125**

Tinto House 13 Broad St, HR3 5DB ☎01497 821556, ⓦtinto-house.co.uk. The splendid Regency frontage of this charming old house conceals two large and sumptuous rooms, each a different style and colour; there is an equally attractive self-contained unit (£100) in the old stable block, with fabulous garden views. **£90**

CAMPSITE

Radnors End 10min walk from town across the Wye bridge on the road to Clyro, HR3 5RS ☎01497 820780, ⓦhay-on-wye.co.uk/radnorsend. Small, neat field in a beautiful setting overlooking Hay, with on-site showers, laundry facilities and a kids' play area. Closed Nov–Feb. Per person **£7**

EATING

The Granary Broad St, HR3 5DB ☎01497 820790. White rough-hewn walls and simple wooden tables and chairs mark out this unpretentious café and bistro as one of the most enjoyable in town. There's a wide range of excellent vegetarian and meat-based meals (£10), many made from local produce. Save space for the desserts and espresso. Daily 9am–5.30pm.

The Old Electric Shop 10 Broad St, HR3 5DB ☎01497 821194, ⓦoldelectric.co.uk. This agreeably incoherent space incorporates a shop – selling vintage clothing and furniture, gifts and books – and a licensed veggie café that also serves terrific coffee and home-baked treats. Occasional pop-up cocktail bars and music sessions, too. Daily 10am–5pm.

The Old Stables Tearooms Bear St, HR3 5AN ☎01497 821557, ⓦoldstablestearooms.co.uk. Barely half a dozen tables are crammed into this delightful place; chalk boards list superb Welsh produce, including a fantastic array of speciality teas and home-made tarts. On a warm day, the flower-filled yard is a lovely spot. Tues–Sat 11am–5pm.

HAY FESTIVAL

Hay bursts at the seams in the last week of May, when the international literati decamp here for the **Hay Festival** (ⓦhayfestival.com), Britain's leading literary gathering bar none. Dubbed the "Woodstock of the mind" by former festival attendee, Bill Clinton, the festival incorporates a raft of high-profile keynote readings alongside top-rank music and comedy, with loads of events for children of all ages. Running concurrently, the innovative **HowTheLightGetsIn** festival (ⓦhowthelightgetsin.org) gathers together some of the world's leading thinkers in music and philosophy.

Shepherd's Ice Cream 9 High Town, HR3 5AE ☎ 01497 821898. Popular café/ice-cream parlour doling out local ice cream made from sheep's milk, often in offbeat flavours like raspberry cheesecake or rhubarb and custard. The less calorie-conscious might want to try the waffle topped with ice cream and whipped cream. Mon–Fri 9am–5.30pm, Sat 9.30am–6pm, Sun 10.30am–5.30pm.

★ **St John's Place** 3 Lion St, HR3 5AA ☎ 07855 783799, ⓦ stjohnsplacehay.tumblr.com. Occupying an old chapel, *St John's* is a little bit special. The menu is essentially whatever takes the fancy of chef Julia Robson, but there are usually three options for each course: to start you might have ox heart with red chilli and coriander, followed by a main of sea trout with shrimp, hispi cabbage and seaweed and, to finish, jasmine pannacotta with strawberries and shortbread. Expect to pay around £30 for three courses. Booking essential. Fri & Sat 6–10pm.

Three Tuns Broad St, HR3 5DB ☎ 01497 821855, ⓦ three-tuns.com. Set in Hay's second-oldest building (after the castle); the ancient stonework, outdoor terrace and crackling open fires make for an atmospheric dining spot. Local creations include Wye Valley asparagus and chive hollandaise (£8), and Black Mountain smoked salmon with crayfish and capers. Daily 11am–11pm; kitchen Mon–Sat noon–2pm & 6.30–9pm, Sun 12.30–3pm.

DRINKING

Blue Boar Castle St, HR3 5DF ☎ 01497 820884. In the absence of anywhere truly exciting to drink in Hay, the *Boar* does the job: a tasteful, wood-panelled real ale pub centred around a gently curving bar and two stone fireplaces, with a separate dining area to one side. Daily 9.30am–11pm.

SHOPPING

Hay Cinema Bookshop Old town cinema, Castle St, HR3 5DF ☎ 01497 820071, ⓦ haycinemabookshop .co.uk. Secondhand, antiquarian and remaindered books across all subjects and at very low prices. Mon–Sat 9am–6pm, Sun 10am–5.30pm.

Richard Booth's Bookshop 44 Lion St, HR3 5AA ☎ 01497 820322, ⓦ boothbooks.co.uk. Although no longer owned by Booth, Hay's largest bookshop still trades under his name; before entering, take a look at the beautiful glazed tiles on the facade, painted with agricultural motifs. Once you're done browsing this superb emporium, which pretty much covers every conceivable subject, pop into the bright café for a drink or bite to eat. At the back of the bookshop, a little cinema screens arthouse movies at weekends. Mon–Sat 9.30am–5.30pm, Sun 10.30am–5.30pm.

Rose's Books 14 Broad St, HR3 5DB ☎ 01497 820013, ⓦ stellabooks.com. A wonderful stock of rare and collectable children's and illustrated books. Daily 10am–5.15pm.

The Wells towns

Straddling the old border of Brecknockshire and Radnorshire, around fifteen miles north of Brecon, mid-Wales' former spa towns – known as the **Wells towns** – are strung out along the Heart of Wales rail line and the main A483. All were obscure villages up until the eighteenth century, when royalty and nobility spearheaded the fashion for "taking a cure". Once the railway arrived, the Welsh spas became much more egalitarian, each developing its own distinct clientele and atmosphere.

The westernmost spa of **Llanwrtyd Wells**, hunkered down beneath the hills, is best known for its offbeat festivals and unusual events, while **Llandrindod Wells** is worth a stop thanks to some exceptional Victorian-era architecture and a brilliant cycle museum.

Llanwrtyd Wells

Historically, the spa town of **LLANWRTYD WELLS**, around twenty miles northwest of Brecon, was the base for Welsh visitors – farmers from Dyfed and the Nonconformist middle classes from Glamorgan – travelling to the great eisteddfodau in the valley of the Irfon. One of the smallest towns in Britain, these days it's better known for being the Welsh capital of wacky events (see box opposite) and, along with Abergavenny, it boasts the finest restaurants in mid-Wales.

Main Street runs through the centre of town, crossing the Irfon River just below the main square, **Y Sgwar**, which is framed by boldly coloured buildings and dominated by a striking sculpture of a red kite. Although the sulphurous aroma had been apparent in the area for centuries, it was "discovered" in 1732 by the local priest, Theophilus Evans, who drank from a vile-smelling spring after seeing a healthy frog pop out of it. The spring, named **Ffynnon Drewllyd** (Stinking Well), bubbles up among the dilapidated spa buildings on Dolecoed Road.

Llanwrtyd District Heritage and Arts Centre

3 Ffos Rd, LD5 4RG • Thurs–Sun 10am–4pm • Free • ☎ 01591 610067, ⓦ llanwrtydhistorygroup.webs.com

Just up from the main square, and occupying the former chapel (which functioned as such until 2009), the wonderful **Llanwrtyd District Heritage and Arts Centre** recalls the town's colourful past through a chronological timeline from the spa years via World War II through to more recent traditions – including, of course, the wacky events (see box below). Particularly eye-catching is the beautifully shot *Now and Then* slide show, a series of images of local landmarks taken by F.D. Shackley in the early twentieth century, alongside their modern equivalents. The upstairs gallery holds rotating exhibitions of artists from all over mid-Wales.

3

ARRIVAL AND INFORMATION   LLANWRTYD WELLS

By train The train station is a 5min walk east of town on Station Rd.
Destinations Builth Wells (Mon–Sat 4 daily, Sun 2; 20min); Knighton (Mon–Sat 4 daily, Sun 2; 1hr 10min); Llandrindod Wells (Mon–Sat 4 daily, Sun 2; 30min); Shrewsbury (Mon–Sat 4 daily, Sun 2; 2hr 10min); Swansea

(Mon–Sat 4 daily, Sun 2; 1hr 50min).
By bus Buses, serving Builth Wells (5 daily; 25min), stop on the main square.
Tourist information There's no official tourist office, but the heritage centre (see above) has plentiful information.

ACCOMMODATION

★ **Ardwyn House** Station Rd, LD5 4RW ☎ 01591 610768, ⓦ ardwynhouse.co.uk. Stunning turn-of-the-twentieth-century period piece with three, richly detailed en-suite rooms, all with a double aspect and variously featuring roll-top baths, cast-iron fireplaces and antique light fittings. Downstairs, there's a marvellous book-lined billiards room and honesty bar, and tea and cake upon arrival, too. £80

Drover's Rest The Square, LD5 4RA ☎ 01591 610264, ⓦ food-food-food.co.uk. The bridgeside *Drover's* offers four sweet, cottage-like rooms (including one single)

tastefully furnished in beautiful fabrics and with splashes of artwork on the walls. It also has a wonderful riverside restaurant (see p.226). £70

Elenydd Wilderness Hostels Dolgoch, SY25 6NR ☎ 01440 730226, Ty'n Cornel, SY25 6PH ☎ 01980 629259, ⓦ elenydd-hostels.co.uk. Two converted farmhouses with clean dorms (four-, six- and ten-bed dorms at Dolgoch; two eight-bed dorms at Ty'n Cornel) with space for camping at both. They close periodically in winter, so check in advance. Camping/person £8, dorms £12

LLANWRTYD WELLS' WACKY EVENTS

Belying its sleepy appearance, Llanwrtyd Wells has its distinctly zany moments. Although a host of events takes place here throughout the year, three in particular take precedent. In mid-June, the **Man Versus Horse Marathon** is a punishing 22-mile endurance test between man (and woman) and beast over various types of terrain; for the record, the last time a human won was 2007. At the end of August, it's the turn of the **World Bog-Snorkelling Championships**, in which competitors must complete two lengths of a water-filled trench cut through a peat bog – the current world record, achieved here in 2014, is one minute and 22 seconds. In November there's the **Real Ale Wobble**, two days of combined mountain biking and beer drinking, an event for the somewhat less serious-minded cyclist. It goes without saying that all these events are accompanied by lots of drinking, eating and general merriment. Visit ⓦ green-events.co.uk for full listings.

A fourth major event takes place bi-annually (every even-numbered year); in the wake of the 2012 Olympic Games in London, organizers decided to set up their own **World Alternative Games** (ⓦ worldalternativegames.co.uk), two weeks of more than sixty madcap events including belly flopping, gravy wrestling and husband dragging.

Lasswade Station Rd, LD5 4RW ☎01591 610515, ⓦlasswadehotel.co.uk. A lovely Edwardian residence overlooking lush fields, with eight tranquil, flowery rooms. After a good night's sleep, enjoy a cracking breakfast in the conservatory with its delightful views. There's a five percent discount if you arrive by train. They have a tip-top restaurant, too (see below). __£85__

Stonecroft Lodge Dolecoed Rd, LD5 4RA ☎01591 610332, ⓦstonecroft.co.uk. This self-catering guest-house, adjoining the pub, looks positively grubby from the outside, but it has a perfectly acceptable selection of triple-, quad- and six-bed dorms, all with shared shower facilities. There's also a lounge and fully equipped kitchen. __£16__

EATING AND DRINKING

Carlton Riverside Irfon Crescent, LD5 4SP ☎01591 610248, ⓦcarltonriverside.com. The food at this well-regarded restaurant is traditional Welsh, prepared with flair and imagination – pan-fried venison with potato fondant, punchnep (root vegetables) and a port *jus*, for example (£21) – with a wine list to match. There are just half a dozen well-spaced, crisply laid tables offering river views. Mon–Sat 6.30–10pm.

★**Drover's Rest Riverside Restaurant** The Square, LD5 4RA ☎01591 610264, ⓦfood-food-food.co.uk. Bric-a-brac fills this warm, cottagey restaurant, which specializes in wholesome traditional Welsh food with a continental flourish; try Brecon venison in red wine and mushroom gravy (£17.50), braised lamb rump in a Madeira and redcurrant sauce, or any of the delicious cheese-based veggie dishes. On a warm day, it's lovely to be able to dine out on the wooden deck perching precariously over the Irfon river. They run cookery and art classes, too. Reservations essential. Wed–Sun 10.30am–3.30pm & 7.30–10pm.

★**Lasswade** Station Rd, LD5 4RW ☎01591 610515, ⓦlasswadehotel.co.uk. Run by an award-winning chef, this consummate organic restaurant sources most of its food from its own kitchen and cottage gardens. The daily changing menu typically comprises three choices per course and may feature treats such as duck *rillettes* with onion marmalade and watercress, or pan-roasted saddle of venison with bubble and squeak and a port wine. Three-course menu £34. Booking essential. Daily 7.30–9pm.

Neuadd Arms The Square, LD5 4RB ☎01591 610236, ⓦneuaddarmshotel.co.uk. This lively pub is home to the Heart of Wales brewery, which produces eight fabulous regular ales (including Welsh Black, a delicious stout), plus lots of seasonal offerings. The bar food is good, too, including great curries. It was here, in 1980, that the Man versus Horse Marathon was conceived, hence the many wonderful photos of the town's various crazy events lining the walls. Daily 11am–midnight; kitchen noon–2.30pm & 6–9pm.

Mynydd Epynt

South of Llanwrtyd Wells, the remote **Crychan Forest** and the rippling mountains of the **Mynydd Epynt** (which translates as "Place of Horses") make up the northern outcrops of the Brecon Beacons, best seen from the roads that snake across the moors from the towns of Garth and Builth. In 1939, the bulk of the Epynt was appropriated by the Ministry of Defence, as evidenced by the many red flags stiffly flying, warning you not to stop or touch anything. However, there's ample compensation in the form of the fifty-mile **Epynt Way** (ⓦepyntway.org), which tracks a course around the perimeter of the military zone. Suitable for both walkers and cyclists, the trail is divided into eight sections, each one beginning with an access point from a public road; if you can get your hands on one, the *Epynt Way Official Route Guide* (£4.99) is an invaluable resource.

Abergwesyn Pass

From Beulah, five miles north of Llanwrtyd Wells, it's six miles to the riverside hamlet of **Abergwesyn**. From here, a magnificent winding road twists up to the **Abergwesyn Pass**, threading its way up through dense conifer forests to wide, gorse- and heather-strewn valleys bereft of any sign of human habitation, framed by craggy peaks and waterfalls. At the little bridge over the tiny Tywi River, a track heads south past the wonderfully isolated, gaslit *Elenydd Wilderness Hostel* at **Dolgoch**.

On the other side of the river, a new road channels past the thick forest on to Llyn Brianne (see p.150), a couple of miles further on. This is as remote walking as can be had in Wales – paths lead from Dolgoch through the forests and hillsides to the

---

ROYAL WELSH SHOW

The former spa town of **Builth Wells**, thirteen miles east of Llanwrtyd Wells, doesn't have an awful lot going for it these days, but for four days in late July, it becomes the focus for Europe's largest agricultural fair. Taking place at the enormous **Royal Welsh Showground** (Ⓦ rwas .co.uk), across the river from town, the animated **Royal Welsh Show** attracts more than one hundred thousand visitors, here to enjoy livestock shows, sheep dog trials, shearing, woolhandling and falconry displays, among many other things; even if you have no interest in matters agricultural, this is quite some event.

---

exquisitely isolated chapel at **Soar-y-Mynydd** and beyond, over the mountains to the next *Elenydd Wilderness Hostel* at Ty'n Cornel (also spelt Tyncornel), five strenuous miles from Dolgoch.

From Dolgoch, the road continues over expansive terrain before dropping down along the rounded valley of the Berwyn River and into Tregaron. Although the entire Llanwrtyd–Tregaron route is less than twenty miles long, it takes a good hour for drivers to negotiate the twisting, narrow road safely.

Llandrindod Wells

Following the 1864 arrival of the railway, **LLANDRINDOD WELLS** (Llandrindod; locally referred to as "Llandod" or simply "Dod") was once Wales' most elegant spa resort. Its Victorian heyday is a distant memory, however, although many of the fine buildings from the era still stand, and it's well worth a stop to admire the faded glamour of its ornate architecture. There are a couple of very worthwhile **museums**, too, and a fantastic Victorian **park**.

Radnorshire Museum

Temple St, LD1 5DL • April–Sept Tues–Sat 10am–4pm; Oct–March Tues–Fri 10am–4pm, Sat 10am–1pm • £1 • ☎ 01597 824513, Ⓦ powys.gov.uk/radnorshiremuseum

The small but hugely entertaining **Radnorshire Museum** evokes the area's history with exhibits ranging from archeological finds to items from Victorian spa days. Star sights include the Sheela-na-gig, a typically crude, remarkably well-preserved, carved relief of a vulva, found in the local parish church, and a log-boat dredged up from the Ifor River in 1929 and thought to date from around 1200 AD. Elsewhere, look out for the original clock from the station signal box, and an elegant needle shower of the kind used at the old pump room.

National Cycle Museum

Temple St, LD1 5DL • Tues, Wed & Fri 10am–4pm • £5 • ☎ 01597 825531, Ⓦ cyclemuseum.org.uk

The marvellous **National Cycle Collection** is a nostalgic collection of some 240 velocipedes, including "ordinaries" (aka penny-farthings), trikes, racers and an 8ft-high "Eiffel Tower" advertising bike from 1899. The museum holds some notable machinery, not least a bike belonging to the little-known George Nightingale, the first man to ride 25 miles in under an hour (in 1938). There are also bikes belonging to another serial record-breaking time trialist, Eileen Sheridan, and 1992 Olympic gold medallist Chris Boardman (with his racing skin). Look out, too, for the pneumatic tyred racer dating from 1890, its front wheel larger than the rear, which, some experts believe may have been used in the first modern Olympics, in 1896.

Rock Park

Ⓦ therockpark.org

Quietly tucked away on the southwest side of town, and accessed via several paths, **Rock Park** is a delightful spot for a leisurely ramble. Part Victorian arboretum (including Douglas fir and Japanese red cedar), part native woodland, and bisected by the frothing Arlais Brook, it's also the site of numerous mineral-rich springs – check out the chalybeate spring, with its ornate pink marble fountain and drinking basin. At the heart of the park, the once-lavish **spa pump room** is now a conference centre, though the iron-and-glass-framed pavilion, connecting the pump room and old treatment centre remains an impressive site. From here, a path leads to "**Lovers' Leap**", a Victorian fake cliff overlooking the river. There's also a **tree trail**, outlined in a leaflet available from the **café** next door to the pump room (Thurs–Sat 10.30am–4pm), an enjoyable spot to kick back with a coffee.

ARRIVAL AND INFORMATION   LLANDRINDOD WELLS

By train The train station is in the heart of town between the High St and Station Crescent.
Destinations Builth Wells (Mon–Sat 4 daily, Sun 2; 10min); Knighton (Mon–Sat 5 daily, Sun 2; 40min); Llanwrtyd Wells (Mon–Sat 4 daily, Sun 2; 30min); Shrewsbury (Mon–Sat 5 daily, Sun 2; 1hr 30min); Swansea (Mon–Sat 4 daily, Sun 2; 2hr 30min).

By bus Buses leave from outside the train station.
Destinations Brecon (Mon–Sat 8 daily, Sun 1; 1hr); Builth Wells (Mon–Sat hourly; 20–30min); Newtown (Mon–Sat 6 daily, Sun 1; 50min); Rhayader (Mon–Sat 7 daily; 30min).
Tourist office Inside the town council building in front of the Radnorshire Museum on Temple St (Mon–Fri 10am–1pm; ☎ 01597 822600, ⊛ llandrindod.co.uk).

ACCOMMODATION

The Cottage Spa Rd, LD1 5EY ☎ 01597 825435, ⊛ thecottagebandb.co.uk. Handsome Edwardian property fronted by a pretty, tree-filled garden, with seven differently configured rooms, all laden with period-style furnishings. No TVs in the rooms, but guests are welcome to

use the lounge. Exceptional value. **£68**
Greylands High St, ☎ 01597 822253, ⊛ greylands guesthouse.co.uk. A tall Victorian red-brick house in the town centre, near the station, with seven comfortable, good-value rooms, including singles,

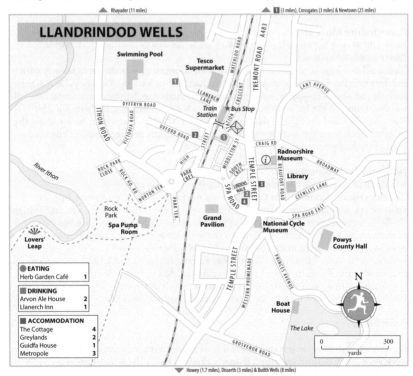

▲ Rhayader (11 miles)   ▲ 🅱 (3 miles), Crossgates (3 miles) & Newtown (25 miles)

LLANDRINDOD WELLS

Swimming Pool
Tesco Supermarket
WATERLOO ROAD
A483
TREMONT ROAD
LLANERCH LANE
LANT AVENUE
DYFFRYN ROAD
Train Station ✭ Bus Stop
IFTHON ROAD
VICTORIA ROAD
OXFORD ROAD
STATION CRESCENT
HIGH STREET
MIDDLETON ST
CRAIG RD
Radnorshire Museum ℹ
BROADWAY
River Ithon
ROCK PARK CLOSE
ROCK NO RD
PARK CRES
SOUTH CRES
TEMPLE STREET
BEAUFORT ROAD
Library
CEFNLLYS LANE
LINDENS WALK
SPA ROAD
NORTON TER.
PARK TER.
Rock Park
Spa Pump Room
Grand Pavilion
National Cycle Museum
SPA ROAD EAST
Lovers' Leap
Powys County Hall
TEMPLE STREET
PRINCES AVENUE
WESTERN PROMENADE

● **EATING**
Herb Garden Café   1

■ **DRINKING**
Arvon Ale House   2
Llanerch Inn   1

■ **ACCOMMODATION**
The Cottage   4
Greylands   2
Guidfa House   1
Metropole   3

Boat House

The Lake

N

0   300
yards

GROSVENOR ROAD

▼ Howey (1.7 miles), Disserth (3 miles) & Builth Wells (8 miles)

LLANDRINDOD FESTIVALS

Llandrindod Wells' town's strong Victorian heritage is celebrated each August in the vibrant, week-long **Victorian Festival** (ⓦ victorian-festival.co.uk), with concerts, plays, guided walks, food and craft tents, a Victorian fair and circus and, of course, Victorian costume parades; the week culminates in a fireworks display over the lake. However, just as popular these days is the three-day **Radnor Fringe Festival** (ⓦ radnorfringefestival.com) at the end of June, comprising an exciting and original programme of music, comedy, art, theatre and dance, most of which takes place in the lovely surrounds of Rock Park.

---

twins, doubles and family options. **£60**

Guidfa House Crossgates, 3 miles north on the A44, LD1 6RF ☎ 01597 851241, ⓦ guidfa-house.co.uk. This relaxing Georgian guesthouse, set in deep countryside, has six pretty rooms, each thoughtfully designed and neatly presented. There's also an elegant sitting room with log fire, and the hosts can provide simple, snacky meals made from local produce. **£99**

Metropole Temple St, LD1 5DY ☎ 01597 823700, ⓦ metropole.co.uk. Fronted by a splendid Art Nouveau canopy, this imposing hotel has been a prominent fixture in town since 1896. Despite its size, and obvious business-/group-oriented approach, the personal touch remains (it is privately owned) and the rooms are spot on. There's also a spa, as well as a very decent bar/brasserie and restaurant. **£126**

EATING

Herb Garden Café 5 Spa Centre, LD1 5BB ☎ 01597 823082, ⓦ herbgardencafe.co.uk. Delightful community-run café/diner with squashy sofas and big windowsills heaving with greenery; the accent here is on fresh,

organically grown (mostly) veggie food, such as salads and platters (mango and avocado salad £7.90), juicy house burgers (cashew or lamb burger £6) and a stack of sweet treats. Mon–Sat 9.30am–5pm.

DRINKING

★**Arvon Ale House** Temple St, LD1 5DL ☎ 07477 627267. Occupying an old shop premises, this small, neat pub is the business, typically offering five real ales as well as two or three real ciders and perrys, plus an impressive selection of gins. The interior is fun, too, with old postcards plastered over the walls and ceilings, while evenings of folk and acoustic music add to the general air of bonhomie. Wed, Thurs & Sun 4–10pm, Fri & Sat 4–11pm.

Llanerch Inn Llanerch Lane, LD1 6BZ ☎ 01597 822234, ⓦ thellanerchinn.co.uk. Directly opposite the train station, this sixteenth-century hostelry predates most of the surrounding town by quite some time. A pint in front of the stone fireplace or a well-cooked, classic pub meal are two good reasons to come. Daily 11am–11pm; kitchen noon–2.30pm & 6–9.30pm.

North and east Radnorshire

Before the reorganization of British counties in 1974, Radnorshire was the most sparsely populated county in either Wales or England, and it's still a remote area, especially to the north and east. In the northwest, **Rhayader** is the only settlement of any size. Most people base themselves here to explore the wild countryside to the west, a hilly patchwork of waterfalls, bogland, bare peaks and the four interlocking reservoirs of the **Elan Valley**, built at the beginning of the twentieth century and displaying a grandiose Edwardian solidity.

The countryside northeast of Rhayader is tamer, with lanes and bridlepaths delving in and around the woods and farms, occasionally brushing through minute settlements like the village of **Abbeycwmhir**, named for the scant ruins of the Cistercian abbey in the dank, eerie valley of the Clywedog Brook. From here, the hills roll eastwards towards the English border and some of the most intact parts of **Offa's Dyke**, the eighth-century King of Mercia's border with the Welsh princes. The handsome border town of **Knighton** is well geared-up for walkers and cyclists. Seven miles south and just inches from England, the dignified town of **Presteigne** contains some intriguing reminders of its former role as the county capital. The River Lugg flows through

Presteigne from the Radnorshire hills, passing the isolated church at **Pilleth**, where Owain Glyndŵr captured Sir Edmund Mortimer, agent of the English king, in 1402.

Rhayader

Ten miles west of Llandrindod Wells lies the bustling small town of **RHAYADER** (Rhaeder Gwy, literally "waterfall on the Wye"). Although the waterfall suggested by the town's name virtually disappeared when the bridge was built in 1780, the Wye still frames the centre, running in a loop around the western and southern sides. Rhayader was a hub of the mid-nineteenth-century "**Rebecca Riots**", when local farmers disguised themselves in women's clothing in order to tear down tollgates that were prohibitively expensive for travellers and local workers. Rhayader's four main streets – named North, South, East and West – meet at a small clock tower in the centre of town.

3

Gigrin Farm Red Kite Feeding Station

Off South Rd (the A470 from Builth) on the outskirts of Rhayader, LD6 5BL • Tues–Sun 12.30–4pm • £6 • ☎ 01597 810243, ⓦ gigrin.co.uk

One of the best places anywhere in Europe to watch **red kites feeding** is at **Gigrin Farm**. Each day at 3pm (2pm in winter), these magnificent birds are lured here (ravens and buzzards join in the frenzy, too), with as many as five hundred descending at any one time – it's a fantastic sight. A handful of hides (all wheelchair accessible) are used for viewing; you can prebook to use a specialized photography/filming hide (£15–25). There's also a scenic 1.5-mile-long nature trail, and a small café/shop.

Gilfach Farm Nature Reserve

Three miles north of Rhayader, just off the A470, LD6 5LF • Interpretation centre daily 24hr • Free • ☎ 01597 823298, ⓦ rwtwales.org

A quiet little outpost, the peaceful **Gilfach Farm Nature Reserve** is the showpiece of the Radnorshire Wildlife Trust. Within its 418 acres are meadows, oak forest, moorland, an old railway tunnel that's home to bats, and river habitats supporting a huge variety of wildlife and flora. The main walk hereabouts is the **Marteg Valley Nature Trail**, a most enjoyable 2.5-mile circular walk beginning at the bridge just as you turn off the A470 into the reserve; following the course of the river, it takes in a Bronze Age burial site and an otter hide and passes near the old farmyard; here the restored byre has been kitted out as an (unmanned) **interpretation centre**, with leaflets, boards showing wildlife sightings and an honesty box for refreshments.

ARRIVAL, INFORMATION AND GETTING AROUND

RHAYADER

By bus Buses stop in the main Dark Lane car park behind the leisure centre; they serve Builth Wells (Mon–Sat hourly; 20min) and Llandrindod Wells (Mon–Sat 7 daily; 30min).

Tourist office Inside the small town museum on East St, 400m from the main crossroads (Mon–Fri 10am–4pm, Sat 10am–1pm; ☎ 01597 810561, ⓦ rhayader.co.uk); the

museum itself is worth a brief look for its local history displays and occasional temporary exhibitions.

Bike rental Clive Powell Bikes on West St, on the road out towards the Elan Valley (daily 9am–5.30pm; £6/hr, £24/day; ☎ 01597 811343, ⓦ clivepowell-mtb.co.uk) also offers servicing and repairs.

ACCOMMODATION

HOTEL AND GUESTHOUSE

Elan Hotel West St, LD6 5AF ☎ 01597 810109. Recently refitted, this (not too noisy) pub has eight well-insulated rooms, one furnished in pastel tones and simple pine, with wall-mounted TVs and decent bathrooms. **£80**

Ty Morgans East St, LD6 5BH ☎ 01597 811666, ⓦ tymorgans.com. Superb mid-seventeenth-century building housing nine effortlessly cool rooms, most of which still feature their original bare brick walls and oak-beamed ceilings. Thick carpets, low-slung beds and numerous mod cons complete the stylish ensemble. **£80**

FROM TOP RED KITE (ABOVE); MAN VERSUS HORSE MARATHON, LLANWRTYD WELLS (P.225) >

BUNKHOUSE AND CAMPSITES

Beili Neuadd 2 miles northeast, off the B4518, LD6 5NS ⓣ01597 810211, ⓦbeilineuadd.co.uk. A laidback farmhouse B&B with a sixteenth-century stone barn bunkhouse containing three rooms (two sleeping six and one sleeping four), each with their own bathroom; there's a kitchen and lounge, too. Walkers and cyclists are particularly welcome. Breakfast costs £8 for bunkhouse guests. Dorms £19, doubles £80

Gigrin Farm Off South Rd (the A470 from Builth), LD6 5BL ⓣ01597 810243, ⓦgigrin.co.uk. Quiet, very basic option (flush toilets, hot water, but no showers) at the red kite feeding station (see p.230). They've also got one cool wooden pod (minimum two-night stay) sleeping two adults and two children, which is heated and has a TV. Camping closed Nov–Feb, pod available all year. Camping £5, pod £40

Wyeside Immediately north, off the A470, LD6 5LB ⓣ01597 810183, ⓦwyesidecamping.co.uk. On the banks of the Wye, this is a smart site with separate camping and caravan areas and clean, modern amenities. Closed Nov–March. £17

EATING AND DRINKING

Crown Inn North St, LD6 5BU ⓣ01597 811099. The most agreeable of the town's several boozers, serving Brains beer and with lots of small, dark wooden tables gathered around a large stone fireplace. Daily noon–11pm.

Old Swan Corner West and South sts, LD6 5AB ⓣ01597 811060. Tuck into chunky pasties and sugary home-made treats (baklava, carrot cake, cream scones) in this agreeably old-fashioned, cluttered tearoom. Mon–Sat 9am–5pm, Sun 11am–5pm.

Ty Morgans East St, LD6 5BH ⓣ01597 811666, ⓦtymorgans.com. The pick of the town's few eating places, this buzzy bar/bistro offers mouthwatering burgers (including a pork, honey and mustard variety) along with sophisticated dishes such as braised rabbit with potatoes and leeks (£13.95). The bistro leads through to the bustling *Strand* coffeehouse and deli. Bar/bistro daily 8am–9pm (kitchen 8am–2.30pm & 5–9pm); coffeehouse daily 8am–7pm.

3

Elan Valley

Until the last decade of the nineteenth century, the untamed countryside west of Rhayader received few visitors, although the poet Shelley did holiday here. Shelley's honeymoon retreat at Nantgwyllt was among the couple of dozen buildings submerged by the waters of the **Elan Valley** reservoirs, a nine-mile-long string of four lakes created between 1892 and 1903 to supply water to the rapidly growing industrial city of Birmingham, 75 miles away; in the 1950s, a supplementary reservoir at Claerwen, to the immediate west, was opened. Although the lakes enhance an already beautiful and idyllic part of the world, the colonialist way in which Welsh valleys, villages and farmsteads were seized and flooded to provide water for England is something tourist promotions prefer to gloss over.

The appeal of the Elan Valley is, nonetheless, extremely strong, not only for the landscape but also for the profusion of rare plants and **birds** in the area. **Red kites** are especially cherished – in the 1930s, when numbers were down to just a couple of breeding pairs, the Elan Valley looked set to enter the history books as their last outpost in Britain. Loss of habitat, along with nest robbing by collectors and poisoning at the hands of farmers, was largely to blame, but conservation work undertaken by a few dedicated individuals saved the day. Since then, these birds of prey have staged an impressive recovery, becoming so common they've started repopulating surrounding areas. Other birds of prey to be found in the Elan Valley include kestrels, peregrines, merlins, buzzards, goshawks and sparrowhawks.

Claerwen Reservoir

From the Elan Valley visitor centre, a road tucks in along the bank of Caban Coch to the **Garreg Ddu** viaduct, from where you can follow the bank for four spectacular miles – initially along a heavily wooded shoreline before opening up into rocky moorland – to the vast 1952 dam on **Claerwen Reservoir**. More remote and less popular than the Elan lakes, Claerwen is a good base for the more determined walker, with paths for eight to ten miles across the harsh terrain to the abbey of Strata Florida or the lonely **Teifi Pools**.

Pen y Garreg

From the Garreg Ddu viaduct, a more popular road continues north along the long, glassy finger of **Garreg Ddu Reservoir**, before doubling back on itself just below the awesome **Pen y Garreg** dam and reservoir; if the dam is overflowing, the vast wall of foaming water is mesmerizing. At the top of Pen-y-garreg lake, it's possible to drive over the dam at **Craig Goch** for a close-up view of its gracious curve, elegant Edwardian arches and green cupola. The lake beyond it is fed by the Elan River, which the road crosses just short of a junction. A bleak, invigorating moorland pass heads west from here before dropping into the eerie moonscape of Cwmystwyth, while the eastbound road funnels into a beautiful valley back to Rhayader. On the way back, fork off the Elan Valley Road in Rhayader onto the smaller Aberystwyth Road. Look out for the **Dam Open Days**, run by rangers from the visitor centre; held on selected days throughout the year (£1 donation), these offer visitors the opportunity to enter the central tower of the Pen y Garreg dam and to enjoy an amazing birds-eye view of the dam wall itself.

INFORMATION   **ELAN VALLEY**   **3**

Elan Valley visitor centre Just below the dam of the first reservoir, Caban Coch (daily 9.30am–4.30/5pm; ☎ 01597 810898, ⓦ elanvalley.org.uk), the centre has stacks of info on the valley (including a series of leaflets on local walks; the website also lists ten downloadable routes), an exhibition about the history and ecology of the area, bike rental (£6/1hr, £24/day), a play area and a tearoom. The centre also runs a series of excellent ranger-led events, most of which are free to attend; they're very popular, however, so it's best to call in advance.

Abbeycwmhir

ABBEYCWMHIR (Abaty Cwm Hir), seven miles northeast of Rhayader, takes its name from the **abbey** whose meagre ruins (open access; free) lie beneath the village. Cistercian monks founded the abbey in 1146, planning one of the largest churches in Britain, whose 242ft nave has only ever been exceeded in length by the cathedrals of Durham, York and Winchester. Destruction by Henry III's troops in 1231 scuppered plans to continue the building, however. The sparse remains of what they did build – a rocky outline of the floorplan – lie in a conifer-carpeted valley alongside a gloomy green lake, lending weight, if only by atmosphere, to the site's melancholic associations. Llywelyn ap Gruffydd's body, after his head had been carted off to London, was rumoured to have been brought here from Cilmeri (near Builth Wells) in 1282, and a new granite slab, carved with a Celtic sword, lies on the altar to commemorate this last native prince of Wales. It should look incongruous, but somehow it only adds to the eerie presence of the ruins and the village.

The Hall at Abbeycwmhir

Abbeycwmhir, LD1 6PH • Tours (1hr) March–Sept, Nov & Dec Mon–Thurs, Sat & Sun 10.30am & 2pm; booking essential • Tours £16, gardens only £5 • ☎ 01597 851727, ⓦ abbeycwmhir.com

Presiding over the ruins at Abbeycwmhir is the resplendent, privately owned manor house **The Hall at Abbeycwmhir**, set in twelve acres of flower-filled gardens and woodlands. Built in 1834 by Thomas Wilson, this Gothic Victorian pile possesses 52 rooms – mostly restored in the late 1990s – all of which can be viewed on a guided tour conducted by one of the family members. Among the highlights is the beautifully tiled entrance hall with its decorative plasterwork, the magnificent snooker room with stained-glass ceiling, and themed bedrooms and bathrooms. Afterwards, wander around the gardens and grounds, with their silky lawns and terraces, woodland, lake and waterfall.

Presteigne

Twenty miles east of Llandrindod Wells, the charming town of **PRESTEIGNE** (Llanandras) has attracted escapees from the rat race since the 1960s, which partly accounts for the

3

> **PRESTEIGNE FESTIVAL**
>
> In the last week of August, the prestigious **Presteigne Festival** (ⓦ presteignefestival.com) features classical music in venues such as the church of St Andrew and the Assembly Rooms, along with other churches in nearby villages.

laidback cafés and craft, antique and book shops occupying the town's gracious, old-fashioned buildings. The town tucks in between the B4362 town bypass and the River Lugg, the border with England, which flows under the seventeenth-century bridge at the bottom of Broad Street. Just before the bridge, the solid parish **church of St Andrew** contains Saxon and Norman fragments, as well as a sixteenth-century Flemish tapestry.

At the end of the High Street stands the town's most impressive building, the Jacobean **Radnorshire Arms**, built as a private home for Sir Christopher Hatton, Lord Chancellor of England and, allegedly, lover of Queen Elizabeth I, who owned neighbouring property; it's been a hostelry of some description since 1792.

Judge's Lodging

Broad St, LD8 2AD • March–Oct Tues–Sun 10am–5pm; Nov Wed–Sun 10am–4pm; Dec 1–22 Sat & Sun 10am–4pm • £7.95 • ☎ 01544 260650, ⓦ judgeslodging.org.uk

Presteigne's standout attraction is the **Judge's Lodging**, a fabulously interpreted trawl through the rooms where circuit judges stayed while presiding over the local assizes. Before entering the lodging proper, take a peek at the old holding cells, which replaced the original underground cells located beneath the dock in 1900. Evocative photos recall the history of the Radnorshire Constabulary, which started its days in 1847 as the smallest force in Britain, merged with Brecknockshire in 1948 to become the Mid-Wales constabulary and in 1968 joined several regional forces to become the Dyfed-Powys police force, now the second largest in Britain.

Armed with a good old-fashioned Walkman, you'll be introduced to various characters along the way; nothing is roped off or hidden, and it feels more like visiting a private home than a museum, with the oil lamps on the upper floors and the gas-flame lighting in the servants' quarters providing a whiff of authenticity. You finally emerge in the courtroom, where an alleged thief that you've "met" in the cells is being tried for allegedly stealing ducks and poultry.

ARRIVAL AND INFORMATION   PRESTEIGNE

By bus Buses from Knighton, Kington and Leominster stop outside the *Radnorshire Arms* or at the coach park on the bypass.

Tourist office Inside the Judge's Lodging on Broad St

(March–Oct Tues–Sun 10am–5pm; Nov Wed–Sun 10am–4pm; Dec 1–22 Sat & Sun 10am–4pm; ☎ 01544 260650, ⓦ presteigne.org.uk).

ACCOMMODATION AND EATING

Hat Shop Restaurant 7 High St, LD8 2BA ☎ 01544 260017, ⓦ thehatshoprestaurant.co.uk. This perky, two-floored place, sporting bright-orange and sunflower-yellow wood-panelled walls is a delightful spot to try comforting, meaty dishes such as game sausages in red-wine gravy (£9.75). Look out for themed food nights. Mon–Sat 10am–3pm & 6–9pm.

The Moroccan Delicatessen Broad St, LD8 2BE ☎ 01544 598531. A somewhat unexpected find in this part of the world, but hugely enjoyable all the same, thanks to its combination of informality, a cheery proprietor and knockout food, which is usually served in traditional clay-fired patterned bowls; try a sizzling

meatball tagine with tomato and chickpea sauce (£9.90) followed by a deliciously sticky slice of *baklava*. Tues–Thurs 9am–2pm, Fri & Sat 6–10pm.

Old Vicarage Norton 2 miles north, on the road to Knighton, LD8 2EN ☎ 01544 260038, ⓦ oldvicarage-nortonrads.co.uk. Sumptuous Victorian country house designed by Sir George Gilbert Scott with three gorgeous, antique-furnished rooms (no TVs but vintage radios) with fine views across the Marches, and a wonderful garden. Tea and cake upon arrival. Minimum two-night stay at weekends. **£112**

Radnorshire Arms High St, LD8 2BE ☎ 01544 267406, ⓦ radnorshirearmshotel.com. Despite its tatty frontage, the "Rad" is a lovely, historic boozer boasting oak-panelled walls, an open fire and a superb choice of real ales. The warm restaurant is a good spot for house burgers or steaks, as is the family-friendly tented beer garden. There are distinguished period guestrooms (thick, plush carpets and oak panelling) in the main building, and a modern set of rooms in the surprisingly cosy garden lodge to the rear. Pub daily 11am–11pm; kitchen Mon–Sat noon–3pm & 6–9pm, Sun noon–7pm. **£115**

Old Radnor

Just off the A44, six miles southwest of Presteigne, **OLD RADNOR** was once the home of King Harold, killed at the Battle of Hastings by William the Conqueror's troops. The site of his vanished castle is down the lane running southeast from the large, very English-looking **church of St Stephen**, gazing across to Radnor Forest. Inside, beyond the elaborately carved fifteenth-century rood screen is Britain's oldest organ case, dating from the sixteenth century (though the organ is newer), and a chunky pre-Norman font on four stone feet.

ACCOMMODATION AND EATING OLD RADNOR

Harp Inn Old Radnor LD8 2RH ☎01544 350655, ⓦ harpinnradnor.co.uk. In a rambling, fifteenth-century former longhouse, the *Harp* serves somewhat refined pub offerings such as smoked duck with red cabbage slaw or sea trout fillet with mash and watercress butter sauce (£15); the real ales are exceptional, best enjoyed in the garden, looking across the valley. It has five rooms, all with marvellous views: one retains the original timber beams and has a four-poster bed (but is not en suite), while the rest are surprisingly modern. Pub & kitchen Wed & Thurs 6–11pm, Fri–Sun noon–3pm & 6–11pm. **£105**

Radnor Forest

North of New Radnor, the deep ravines and wooded hillsides of **Radnor Forest** offer memorable high-level walking and birdwatching. A good starting point is the village of **New Radnor**, from where a lane called Mutton Dingle gives access to a couple of routes around the isolated summit of **The Whimble** and above spectacularly deep Harley Dingle towards the prominent mast on Black Mixen. Further west, just off the A44, a track signposted from the car park leads into a thick forest and to the rushing cascade of the **Water-Break-Its-Neck Waterfall**, at its icicle-adorned best in winter.

Knighton

Lively, attractive **KNIGHTON** (Tref-y-clawdd, "the town on the dyke"), six miles north of Presteigne, straddles King Offa's eighth-century border and the modern Wales–England divide, and has come into its own as a base for anyone walking the **Offa's Dyke Path** and the **Glyndŵr's Way** footpath (see box below).

So close is Knighton to the border that the town's **train station** is actually in England. From here, Station Road crosses the River Teme into Wales and climbs a couple of hundred yards into the town, joining the pretty Broad Street at Brookside Square. Further up the hill is the town's Victorian clock tower, where Broad Street becomes

> ### GLYNDŴR'S WAY
>
> The fabulous **Glyndŵr's Way** (ⓦ nationaltrail.co.uk/glyndwrsway) weaves 135 miles through the solitary rural landscapes of Montgomeryshire and northern Radnorshire, from Knighton to Welshpool. Well signposted all the way, though depending rather a lot on lane and road walking, Glyndŵr's Way is far quieter than the Offa's Dyke Path, both in the number of settlements en route and the number of hikers on the trail. Varied scenery includes barren bog, exhilarating uplands, reservoirs, undulating farmland and sections of river-valley walking. You can pick up an official route guide (£13.95) from tourist offices in the region or order it online at ⓦ shop.nationaltrail.co.uk

West Street and the steep High Street soars off up to the left, past rickety Tudor buildings and up to the mound of the old **castle**.

ARRIVAL AND DEPARTURE
KNIGHTON

By train The train station is at the bottom of Station Rd, a few minutes' walk from the centre.
Destinations Llandrindod Wells (Mon–Sat 5 daily, Sun 2; 40min); Llanwrtyd Wells (Mon–Sat 4 daily, Sun 2; 1hr 10min); Shrewsbury (Mon–Sat 5 daily, Sun 2; 55min);

Swansea (Mon–Sat 4 daily, Sun 2; 3hr 10min).
By bus Buses stop at the station on Bowling Green Lane, between the train station and the centre.
Destinations Ludlow (Mon–Sat 5 daily; 1hr); Presteigne (Mon–Sat 8 daily; 20min).

INFORMATION AND GETTING AROUND

Tourist information The Offa's Dyke Centre on West St (daily except Tues: Easter–Oct 10am–5pm; Nov–Easter 10am–4pm; ☏01547 528753, ⓦoffasdyke.org.uk or ⓦvisitknighton.co.uk) has all the information you need, both on the town and the Dyke itself; there is an interesting exhibition on the latter, as well as a café.

By bike The nearest bike rental firm, Wheely Wonderful (£20 day/£15 half-day; ☏01568 770755, ⓦwheelywonderfulcycling.co.uk), is over the border in Shropshire at Petchfield Farm, Elton, near Ludlow, but will deliver to Knighton for a small fee.

ACCOMMODATION AND EATING

Horse and Jockey Wylcwm Place, LD7 1AE ☏01547 520062, ⓦthehorseandjockeyinn.co.uk. The town's main hostelry is this fourteenth-century coaching inn, whose warming snug is a lovely spot to hunker down with a pint. The restaurant features the usual pub standards like cod in crispy beer batter (£9.75). Daily noon–11pm; kitchen noon–2pm & 6–9pm.

Knighton Hotel Broad St, LD7 1BL ☏01547 520530, ⓦtheknighton.com. This smart hotel offers sixteen beautifully appointed rooms around a gorgeous double staircase and an equally stunning double-height balcony. £130

Offa Dyke House 4 High St, LD7 1AT ☏01547 528886, ⓦoffadykehouse.com. Homely, accommodating guesthouse whose proprietor is an author – hence the bookish atmosphere. The three rooms (two have bathrooms in the corridor) are appealingly furnished with writing desks, handsome beds and thoughtful touches like fresh fruit and flowers. It's tricky to find; the entrance is by the little gate opposite the clock tower. £80

Panpwnton Farm Panpwnton Half a mile up the lane

that forks left at the station, LD7 1TN ☏01547 528112. Cheap camping in a field across the river; basic facilities include one shower, one sink and one toilet. Per person £5

★**Red Lion** West St, LD7 1EN ☏01547 428080, ⓦredlionknighton.co.uk. The somewhat chilly grey-brick exterior of this former pub conceals four gorgeous rooms – each named after a former prince of Powys – brimming with colour and thoughtful touches including ground coffee and fresh milk. The good-looking restaurant is by far the best place to eat in town, with a menu based on fantastic local produce – wild mushroom fricassée with truffle oil, perhaps, or duo of belly pork with home-made black pudding, mustard mash and cider sauce (£17). Wed–Sat 5.30–9pm, Sun noon–4pm. £75

Tower House Gallery 29 High St, LD7 1AT ☏01547 529530, ⓦgalleryknighton.co.uk. Well-regarded local social enterprise comprising a cheerfully cluttered gallery-cum-shop (Welsh books, bags, cards and textiles) and a comfy café serving Fairtrade coffee, a choice selection of leaf teas and infusions and irresistible home-made cakes. Wed–Sat 10am–5pm.

Montgomeryshire

The northern part of Powys is made up of the old county of **Montgomeryshire**, an area of enormously varying landscapes and few inhabitants. The best base for the spartan and mountainous southwest of the county is the spirited little town of **Llanidloes**, ten miles north of Rhayader on the River Severn (Afon Hafren), which arrives in the town after rising nearby in the dense **Hafren Forest** on the bleak slopes of **Plynlimon**. From Llanidloes, one of Wales' most dramatic roads rises past the chilly shores of the **Llyn Clywedog Reservoir**, squeezed into sharp hillsides, and up through the remote hamlet of **Dylife**. East of here, **Newtown** serves as a good transport interchange and will interest followers of **Robert Owen**; close by lie the dank hilltop remains of **Dolforwyn Castle**.

OFFA'S DYKE

George Borrow, in his classic book *Wild Wales*, noted that it was once "customary for the English to cut off the ears of every Welshman who was found to the east of the dyke, and for the Welsh to hang every Englishman whom they found to the west of it". Certainly, **Offa's Dyke** has provided a potent symbol of Welsh–English antipathy ever since it was created in the eighth century as a demarcation line by King Offa of Mercia, ruler of the whole of central England; it appears that the dyke was an attempt to thwart Welsh expansionism.

Up to 20ft high and 60ft wide, the earthwork made use of natural boundaries such as rivers in its run north to south, and is best seen in the sections near Knighton in Radnorshire and Montgomery. Today's England–Wales border crosses the dyke many times, although the basic boundary has changed little since Offa's day. The glorious **long-distance footpath** (ⓦnationaltrail.co.uk/offas-dyke-path) runs from Prestatyn on the north Clwyd coast for 177 miles to Sedbury Cliffs, just outside Chepstow, and is one of the most rewarding walks in Britain – neither too popular to be unpleasantly crowded, nor too monotonous in its landscapes.

3

This stark, uplifting scenery contrasts with the gentler, greener contours that characterize the east of the county, where the muted old county town of **Montgomery**, with its fine Georgian architecture, perches above the border and Offa's Dyke. In the north of the county, **Welshpool** is the only major settlement, packed in above the wide flood plain of the Severn and linked by an impossibly cute toy rail line to **Llanfair Caereinion**. On the southern side of Welshpool is Montgomeryshire's one unmissable sight, the sumptuous **Powis Castle** and its exquisite terraced gardens. The very north of the county is pastoral, deserted and beautiful, particularly around **Lake Vyrnwy**.

Llanidloes and around

Transforming itself from rural village to weaving town and, more recently, into a centre for artists and craftspeople, **LLANIDLOES** (pronounced Thlann-idd-loiss) has managed to avoid the decline of so many other small market towns. It's a charming, if sedate, little place that receives few visitors, but is well worth a detour.

The town centres on four main streets, which all meet at the market hall – the main thoroughfare is **Great Oak Street**, a wide, handsome road framed by well-proportioned, two- and three-storey buildings accommodating shops, restaurants and tenements. Running in the opposite direction, west of the market hall, is **Short Bridge Street**, a line of fine buildings running down to the River Severn, past two imposing nineteenth-century chapels staring across the road at each other. North and south of the **old market hall** are China Street and Long Bridge Street – the latter is good for interesting little shops.

Old market hall

Great Oak St, SY18 6HU • Late May–Sept Tues–Sun 11am–4pm • Free • ☎ 01686 412388

At the junction of the town's four main streets is the superb black-and-white **old market hall**, built on timber stilts around 1600, allowing the market – now long since moved – to take place on the cobbles beneath. The only surviving timber-framed market hall in Wales, it's also known as the Booth Hall, and remained a popular trading place until the early twentieth century, as well as functioning variously as a law court, a Quaker meeting place, a flannel store and the local Working Men's Institute.

Today it houses an **exhibition** with a fascinating display on timbered buildings in Llanidloes and further afield. A free leaflet outlines the town's many timbered structures, including the building on the corner of Great Oak Street and China Street; built in 1926 to complement the market hall, and sporting a similarly striking black-and-white frontage, this was formerly a bank building, but now stands redundant, forlornly awaiting its fate.

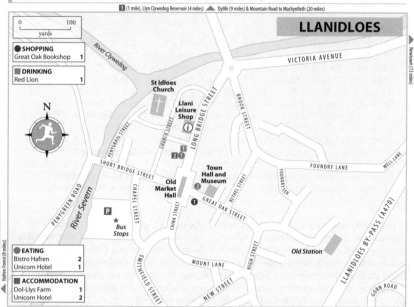

(1 mile), Llyn Clywedog Reservoir (4 miles) — Dylife (9 miles) & Mountain Road to Machynlleth (20 miles)

LLANIDLOES

VICTORIA AVENUE

Newtown (13 miles)

SHOPPING
Great Oak Bookshop   1

DRINKING
Red Lion   1

St Idloes Church

Llani Leisure Shop

Town Hall and Museum

Old Market Hall

Bus Stops

FOUNDRY LANE   WELL LANE

LLANIDLOES BY-PASS (A470)

Old Station

GORN ROAD

EATING
Bistro Hafren   2
Unicorn Hotel   1

ACCOMMODATION
Dol-Llys Farm   1
Unicorn Hotel   2

Hafren Forest (8 miles)

River Clywedog · River Severn · Pengreen Road · Penygraig Street · Church Street · Short Bridge Street · Chapel Street · China Street · Long Bridge Street · Brook Street · Bethel Street · Foundry Ter · Great Oak Street · High Street · Mount Lane · Smithfield Street · New Street

St Idloes church

Church St, off Bridge St, SY18 6EE • Daily 10.30am–3.30pm

The glory of **St Idloes church** is its impressive fifteenth-century hammerbeam roof (also known as the "Angel Roof"). Recent tree-ring dating refutes the previously held theory that it was poached from Abbeycwmhir; the pillars and arches, though, were most certainly taken from the abbey following its dissolution in 1536. The adjoining mid-fourteenth-century tower, meanwhile, is typical of those found in the county, a massive square block crowned by a wooden belfry and pyramidal roof.

Town hall and museum

Great Oak St, SY18 6BN • Museum Tues, Thurs & Fri 11am–1pm & 2–4pm, Sat 11am–2pm • £1 • ☎ 01686 413777

The **town hall** was originally built as a temperance hotel to challenge the boozy *Trewython Arms*, now the smart *Trewython Hotel*, opposite. Nowadays the complex houses an eclectic **museum** that offers a diverting collection, from old local prints and mementos, including pictures of boomtown Dylife, to a stuffed two-headed lamb born nearby in 1914.

A plaque by the entrance to the *Trewython Hotel* commemorates Llanidloes as an unlikely-seeming place of industrial and political unrest, when, in April 1839, Chartists stormed the building, dragging out and beating up special constables who had been dispatched here in a futile attempt to suppress the political fervour of the local flannel weavers.

Llyn Clywedog Reservoir

Four miles northwest of Llanidloes, the beautiful **Llyn Clywedog Reservoir**, built in the 1960s, has settled well into the folds of the Clywedog Valley. At its southern end, the modern concrete dam is Britain's tallest (237ft), towering menacingly over the remnants of the **Bryntail lead mine**, through which a signposted path runs. The roads along the southern shores of Clywedog wind around into the dense plantation of **Hafren Forest**, the only real sign of life and vegetation on the bleak, sodden slopes of **Plynlimon** (Pumlumon Fawr; 2469ft). There's a car park at **RHYD-Y-BENWCH**, in the heart of the forest; the most popular of the **walking paths** that fan out from here is a six-mile round trip following the River Severn up through the trees, past a waterfall and out to its source, a saturated peat bog in some of the harshest terrain in Wales.

Dylife

Nine miles northwest of Llanidloes, old mine workings herald the approach to **DYLIFE** (pronounced Duh-levah). In the mid-nineteenth century, this was a lead-mining community of almost two thousand people, with a reputation as a lawless gambling pit. The mine closed in 1896, and the population has since dwindled to around just twenty (it features on the excellent historical website, Abandoned Communities, at ⓦabandonedcommunities.co.uk).

Good walks from Dylife include that up to Pen-y-crocbren, the mine-pocked slope that rises to the south of the village, and west to **Glaslyn**, or "blue lake", and the reedy shores of **Bugeilyn**. The scenically varied **Glyndŵr's Way** footpath (see box, p.235) crosses this patch on its way to Machynlleth. A popular viewpoint on the road two miles west of Dylife has been furnished with a cheery memorial to broadcaster and author **Wynford Vaughan-Thomas** (1908–87), whose outstretched slate hand points to the dozens of rippling peaks and verdant valleys.

3

ARRIVAL, INFORMATION AND TOURS	LLANIDLOES

By bus China St curves down to the car park from where all bus services operate.
Destinations Aberystwyth (Mon–Sat 3 daily; 1hr); Newtown (Mon–Sat 8 daily; 30min); Welshpool (Mon–Sat 6 daily; 1hr 20min).
Tourist information There's no tourist office, but the

Llani Leisure shop, 16 Long Bridge St (Tues–Sat 10am–5pm; ☎01686 414893, ⓦllanidloes.com), stocks literature on the town and surrounds.
Guided walks Free guided town walks set off from the town hall (June–Sept Wed–Sat 10.30am).

ACCOMMODATION

Dol-Llys Farm Trefeglwys Rd, SY18 6JA ☎01686 412694, ⓦdolllyscaravancampsite.co.uk. Large site around a 15min walk north of town, with pitches on the level field near the facilities and in a more secluded spot down by the river, where campfires are permitted. There are excellent play areas, and free fishing is available on site.

Closed Nov to Easter. Per person **£7.50**
Unicorn Hotel 4 Long Bridge St, SY18 6EE ☎01686 411171, ⓦunicornllanidloes.co.uk. A small hotel of considerable charm, hosting six crisp, generous and impeccably clean rooms. Substantial breakfasts, too. **£90**

EATING

Bistro Hafren 2 Great Oak St, SY18 6BN ☎01686 414936, ⓦbistrohafren.com. Unfussy restaurant with little decor to speak of, but whose food is very much worth a punt – medallions of pork with cider and cream sauce (£10.95), for example, as well as a tempting trio of steak dishes (£13–15) and good-value set menus, not least a three-course dinner for £15. Mon & Wed–Sat 9am–3pm & 6–11pm, Sun noon–2pm.

Unicorn Hotel 4 Long Bridge St, SY18 6EE ☎01686 411171, ⓦunicornllanidloes.co.uk. This hotel's perky evening bistro offers a tempting steak menu and deliciously sauced dishes including roasted duck leg with Cointreau and orange gravy (£13.75) and spicy Moroccan nut roast with tomato and red pepper sauce (£10.50). Tues–Sat 6–9.30pm.

DRINKING

Red Lion 8 Long Bridge St, SY18 6EE ☎01686 412270. The most agreeable of the town's pubs, with a lounge bar sporting comfy leather seating huddled around an

imposing stone fireplace festooned with brass, and another, noisier room used principally for bar games. Daily 11am–midnight.

SHOPPING

Great Oak Bookshop 35 Great Oak St, SY18 6BW ☎01686 412959, ⓦgreatoakbooks.co.uk. This bookshop sells loads of Celtic and Welsh-interest titles,

with a barn full of high-quality new and secondhand fiction. Mon–Fri 9.30am–5.30pm, Sat 9.30am–4.30pm.

Newtown and around

Despite its name, **NEWTOWN** (Y Drenewydd), thirteen miles northeast of Llanidloes, was founded in the thirteenth century, growing steadily until experiencing a massive population explosion in the 1800s as a centre for weaving and textiles. Today, its activity is much reduced and it's hardly awash with great amenities, but the compact town centre, straddling the River Severn, has a certain faded appeal. The main thoroughfare is Broad Street, which intersects with High Street by the nineteenth-century red terracotta **clock tower**. A few paces down High Street, it's worth popping into the **W.H. Smith** shop, which opened in 1927. It was decided, amid the company's modernization programme in the 1970s, to restore this particular branch to its original state, hence the oak shelving and other 1920s fixtures and fittings. Take a look, too, at the original tiling on the frontage.

Robert Owen Memorial Museum

The Cross, Broad St, SY16 2BB • July & Aug Mon–Sat 11am–3pm; Sept–June Mon–Fri 11am–3pm • Free • ☎ 01686 625544, ⓦ robert-owen-museum.org.uk

A plaque on the wall of the Barclays Bank near the clock tower denotes the birthplace (the original house has long since gone) of early socialist **Robert Owen** (see box below). His remarkable life is celebrated in the **Memorial Museum** directly opposite, its visitors' book indicating just how much of a shrine the place has become, with a roll call of socialist politicians and trade unionists scrawling their thanks for Owen's work in its pages. Among the personal effects are furniture, many letters, his funeral procession card and a lock of hair. A two-minute walk down the road, on the outside wall of St Mary's church, is Owen's tomb, enclosed by a high black railing.

Textile Museum

5–7 Commercial St, SY16 2BL • May–Sept Tues, Thurs & Fri noon–4pm, Sat 10.30am–4pm • £1 • ☎ 01938 622024, ⓦ newtowntextilemuseum.co.uk

Over the river from the town centre, the **Textile Museum** sits above six cramped old weavers' cottages. Exhibits show the dramatic ebb and flow of the town's staple trade, focusing on the flannel and handloom factories of the 1790s, the social unrest and

---

ROBERT OWEN, PIONEER SOCIALIST

Born in Montgomeryshire in the late eighteenth century, **Robert Owen** (1771–1858) left Wales to enter the Manchester cotton trade at the age of 18 and swiftly rose to the position of mill manager. His business acumen was matched by a strong streak of philanthropy; fundamentally, he believed in social equality between the classes and was firmly against the concept of competition between individuals. Poverty, he believed, could be eradicated by cooperative methods. Owen recognized the potential of building a model workers' community around the New Lanark mills in Scotland and joined the operation in 1798, swiftly setting up the world's first infant school, an Institution for the Formation of Character and a model welfare state for its people.

Owen's ideas on cooperative living prompted him to build up the model community of New Harmony in Indiana, USA, which he established between 1824 and 1828 before handing the still-struggling project over to his sons. Before long, and without the wisdom of its founder, the idealistic tenets of New Harmony collapsed under the weight of greed, ambition and vested interests. Undeterred, Owen, by now back in Britain, was encouraging the formation of the early trade unions and cooperative societies, as well as leading action against the 1834 deportation of the **Tolpuddle Martyrs**, a group of Dorset farm labourers who withdrew their labour in their call for a wage increase. Owen's later years were dogged by controversy, as he lost the support of the few sympathetic sections of the British establishment in his persistent criticism of organized religion. He gained many followers, however, whose generic name gradually changed from Owenites to "socialists" – the first usage of the term. Owen returned to Newtown in his later years, and died there in 1858.

industrial decline of the 1830s and 1840s (Wales' first Chartist demonstration took place here in 1838), the revival of trade thanks to local entrepreneur Pryce Jones' world-first mail-order service, and finally its dwindling to nothing by 1935. Try and time your visit with one of the spinning or weaving demonstrations, held on selected dates between June and early September.

Oriel Davies Gallery

The Park, SY16 2NZ • Mon–Sat 10am–5pm • Free • ☎ 01686 625041, ⓦ orieldavies.org

Next to the car park and bus station, the **Oriel Davies Gallery** is a contemporary arts and crafts gallery that hosts imaginative temporary exhibitions, ranging from multimedia to ceramics and experimental artworks. There's a decent café, too (see p.242).

Gregynog Hall

Five miles north of Newtown, SY16 3PW • Gardens daily 8am–8pm, café March–Oct daily 10am–4pm • £3 • ☎ 01686 650224, ⓦ gregynog.org

Mock-Tudor **Gregynog Hall** was home from 1920 to Gwendoline and Margaret Davies, aesthete sisters who inherited a fortune from their port-building father and spent much of it on a world-class art collection, most of which now resides in Cardiff's National Museum of Wales. Gregynog became the headquarters for their artistic revival, including the establishment of a world-famous small press, Gwasg Gregynog, which is up and running once more. The hall is now best known for hosting the prestigious **Gregynog Music Festival** (ⓦ gregynogfestival.org) in the second half of June, a high-class feast of classical music. The building itself is not open to the public, but the beautiful **gardens** are bursting with rhododendrons and azaleas, with some delightful woodland walks; there's also a sunny courtyard café that makes a lovely pit stop.

Mid Wales Arts Centre

Caersws, 6 miles west of Newtown, SY17 5SB • Thurs–Sun 10am–4pm • Free • ☎ 01686 688369, ⓦ midwalesarts.org.uk.

The lively, privately run **Mid Wales Arts Centre** stages a good array of events, exhibitions and workshops. You can also see a wide selection of paintings and sculptures by the owner's late husband, the internationally renowned Polish-born artist Stefan Knapp. They offer B&B accommodation, too (see below).

ARRIVAL AND DEPARTURE

By train Newtown's train station is on the southern edge of the town centre.
Destinations Aberystwyth (9–10 daily; 1hr 15min); Machynlleth (9–10 daily; 40min); Welshpool (9–10 daily; 15min).
By bus A path heads past the Victorian parish church of St

NEWTOWN AND AROUND

David and up Back Lane to the bus station.
Destinations Llandrindod Wells (Mon–Sat 6 daily; 50min); Llanidloes (Mon–Sat 8 daily; 30min); Machynlleth (Mon–Sat 6 daily; 50min); Montgomery (Mon–Sat 8 daily; 25–40min); Welshpool (Mon–Sat hourly; 40min).

ACCOMMODATION

Maesmawr Caersws, 6 miles west, SY17 5SB ☎ 01686 688369, ⓦ midwalesarts.org.uk. The Mid Wales Arts Centre (see above) offers delightful farmhouse accommodation in four rooms, each with wonderful views and containing original pieces of artwork, some of which is for sale. **£90**

Yesterdays Severn St, SY16 2AG ☎ 01686 622644, ⓦ yesterdayshotel.com. In the square behind the clock tower, this sweetly old-fashioned B&B offers a mix of single, double and triple rooms and locally sourced Welsh breakfasts. **£70**

EATING AND DRINKING

Mirrens 17 Parker's Lane, SY16 2LT ☎ 01686 621120, ⓦ mirrensrestaurant.co.uk. This colourful, Spanish-style *cantina* oozes charm, its wood-lined interior adorned with abstract art. The small plates, such as merguez sausage (£6) and crab *crostini* (£5), are on the money. On Fri and Sat

the upstairs lounge hosts sophisticated cocktail evenings and Sun afternoons are given over to open-mic sessions in the sunny courtyard. Wed 6–10.30pm, Thurs & Fri noon–3pm & 6–11pm, Sat noon–3pm & 6pm–midnight, Sun noon–5.30pm.

3

Oriel Café Oriel Gallery, SY16 2NZ ☏ 01686 625041. The location, next to the bus station, is far from glorious, but the funky-coloured, atrium-like interior of this gallery café is a fun place to try an imaginative (typically vegetarian) daily special, like roast nut burger in a garlic and herb bun (£6.95), perhaps, or something from the tapas menu.

Mon–Sat 10am–4pm.

The Sportsman 17 Severn St, SY16 2AQ ☏ 01686 623978. The town's standout pub has a rough-hewn red-brick frontage and a clean, good-looking interior serving many fine ales from the local Monty's brewery; there's a smart little pool room, too. Tues–Sun noon–11pm.

Montgomery and around

Eight miles northeast of Newtown, the tiny, anglicized town of **MONTGOMERY** (Trefaldwyn) lies at the base of a dilapidated **castle** on the Welsh side of Offa's Dyke and the present-day border. Construction of the castle began in 1233 under the English king, Henry III, and today's remains are not on their own worth the steep climb up the lane at the back of the town hall, although the view over the gargantuan green bowl of hills around the town is stunning.

Montgomery is near one of the best-preserved sections of **Offa's Dyke**, which the long-distance footpath shadows either side of the B4386 a mile east of the town. Ditches almost 20ft high give one of the best indications of the dyke's original look, twelve hundred years after it was built. The heart of Montgomery is Broad Street, the symmetrical main thoroughfare that's actually more square than street. Framed by handsome red-brick Georgian buildings, it swoops up to the dignified **town hall**, crowned by a trim clock tower.

Old Bell Museum

Arthur St, SY15 6RA • April–July & Sept Wed–Fri & Sun 1.30–5pm, Sat 10.30am–5pm; Aug Mon–Fri & Sun 1.30–5pm, Sat 10.30am–5pm • £1 • ☏ 01686 668313, ⓦ oldbellmuseum.org.uk

A few paces from the town hall is the **Old Bell Museum**, formerly a temperance house and butcher's, but now an unusually enjoyable local history collection. Crammed into every nook and cranny of this marvellous little building are artefacts from excavations, scale models of local castles, mementos from Montgomery civic life and displays on the region's various trades, with prominence given to the likes of clogmakers, clockmakers, carpenters and tanners.

Cloverlands Model Car Museum

Arthur St, SY15 6RA • Thurs 10am–1pm, Fri 2–5pm, Sat 9.30am–1pm, Sun 2–4.30pm • £2.50 • ☏ 01686 668004, ⓦ cloverlandsmuseum.org.uk

Opposite the Old Bell Museum, the **Cloverlands Model Car Museum** holds the remarkable collection of Gillian Rogers, a local motoring fanatic who started acquiring miniature cars as a young girl in the 1950s – the result is in excess of 1500 models, including classics, old timers, sports cars, fire engines, trams and much more; look out, too, for the rare Scalex clockwork cars, the forerunner to the modern Scalextrics. Not only was Rogers an inveterate collector, but she also worked in the automotive industry (which was extremely rare for a woman in those days) and built model cars – on display here is a 1:4 scale model of the 1935 Singer Le Mans she owned for forty years and which she regularly drove down to Le Mans.

Church of St Nicholas

The Rectory, Lion Bank, SY15 6PT • Daily 8am–6pm • Free

The rebuilt tower of Montgomery's parish **church of St Nicholas** dominates the diminutive buildings around it. Largely thirteenth-century, the highlights of its spacious interior include the 1600-canopied tomb of local landowner Sir Richard Herbert, his wife, Magdalen, and their eight children (including Elizabethan poet George Herbert). The two medieval effigies on the floor at the end of the tomb are of uncertain origin, although the farther one is thought to be of Sir Edmund Mortimer ("revolted Mortimer", as Shakespeare had him), son-in-law of Owain Glyndŵr, brother-in-law of Hotspur and once Constable of Montgomery Castle. Equally impressive are the elaborately carved fifteenth-century double screen and accompanying loft, believed to have been built from sections removed from a priory over the border in Chirbury.

Dolforwyn Castle

Four miles southwest of Montgomery, just off the A483, SY15 6JJ · Daily 10am–4pm · Free; CADW · ☎ 01443 336000, ⓦ cadw.gov.wales/daysout/dolforwyncastle

Described by Jan Morris as "the saddest of all the Welsh castles", **Dolforwyn Castle** was the last fortress to be built by a native Welsh prince on his own soil – Llywelyn ap Gruffydd, in 1273 – as a direct snub to the English king, Edward I, who had forbidden the project. Llywelyn built his fortress and started to construct a small adjoining town as a Welsh fiefdom to rival heavily anglicized Welshpool, just up the valley. Dolforwyn only survived four years in Welsh hands before being overwhelmed after a nine-day siege by the English, and the castle was left slowly to rot. In the past twenty years, the remains have been excavated and significant portions of the fragile old castle have emerged on the wind-blown hilltop, with astounding views over the Severn Valley, 400ft below. Drivers should note that the castle is a stiff fifteen-minute uphill climb from the car park.

ARRIVAL AND INFORMATION

MONTGOMERY AND AROUND

By bus Buses pick up and drop off in front of the Town Hall at the bottom of Broad St.
Destinations Newtown (Mon–Sat 8 daily; 30min); Shrewsbury (Mon–Sat 4 daily; 55min); Welshpool (Mon–Sat 5 daily; 25min).

Tourist information There's no tourist office in Montgomery, but the grey telephone box, on a grassy triangle as you enter the town on the Welshpool road, has leaflets and information on local events.

ACCOMMODATION

Brynwylfa 4 Bishops Castle St, SY15 6PW ☎ 01686 668555, ⓦ brynwylfa.co.uk. Just off the main square, this beautiful Georgian town house has just two rooms: a twin with exposed brick walls and a double with a gorgeous roll-top bath. Upon arrival, guests receive tea and cake, while breakfast is taken in the garden-facing conservatory. Closed June–Aug. **£80**

★ **The Checkers** Broad St, SY15 6PN ☎ 01686 669822, ⓦ checkerswales.co.uk. The five understatedly elegant rooms of this erstwhile coaching inn are characterized by higgledy-piggledy beams and low ceilings and doorways.

Free-standing baths and wet rooms (with L'Occitane toiletries), Egyptian cotton sheets and duck-down duvets are all standard, with further thoughtful touches like freshly ground coffee and home-made shortbread. **£125**

Dragon Hotel Market Square, SY15 6PA ☎ 01686 668359, ⓦ dragonhotel.com. Next to the town hall, the rambling, seventeenth-century black-and-white *Dragon* has a good complement of rooms at a range of prices (generally according to size), but throughout you'll find timber beams and frames, soft grey carpets and lilac walls, and the occasional four-poster bed. Indoor pool, too. **£79**

EATING

Bistro 7 Dragon Hotel, Market Square, SY15 6PA ☎ 01686 668359, ⓦ dragonhotel.com. Nicely filling the gap between high-end *Checkers* and the snacky *Castle Kitchen*, this agreeable bistro offers an enterprising menu listing the likes of pork and pesto lasagne (£11.50) and spiced Iranian vegetable stew (£10.95). It's a great-looking space, with big square tables set well apart from each other. Daily 7.30–9.30am, 11.30am–3pm & 6–9pm.

Castle Kitchen 8 Broad St, SY15 6PH ☎ 01686 668795, ⓦ castlekitchen.org. Sociable café/deli with an open kitchen doling out savoury (soups, quiches and tarts) and sweet (cakes and pastries) delights. The busy downstairs area extends to a vine-covered terrace, and upstairs is all

wonky flooring and stripey walls. A welcome spot to refuel after trekking Offa's Dyke. Mon–Sat 9.30am–4.30pm, Sun 11am–4.30pm.

★ **The Checkers** Broad St, SY15 6PN ☎ 01686 669822, ⓦ checkerswales.co.uk. Outstanding, pleasingly informal Michelin-starred restaurant, whose nicely spaced, stripped-down wooden tables make an inviting setting. From the premeal canapés to the classically French seasonal menus – asparagus *velouté* with chive cream and truffle oil; roasted breast of Gressingham duck with *pain d'epices* (spiced bread), pak choi and pineapple – you're in for a special evening. Six-course menu £65. Booking essential. Tues–Sat 7.15–10pm.

SHOPPING

Bunners Arthur St, SY15 6RA ☎01686 668308, ⓦbunners.co.uk. You'd be remiss not to visit this extraordinary ironmonger's shop, just a few paces from the town hall, which has been trading since 1892. There's almost nothing that you *can't* buy in this labyrinthine emporium; you'll end up spending more time here than you intended. Mon–Sat 9am–5.30pm.

Welshpool

Three miles from the English border and five miles north of Berriew, eastern Montgomeryshire's chief town, **WELSHPOOL** (Y Trallwng), was formerly known merely as Pool, acquiring its prefix in 1835 to distinguish it from the English seaside town of Poole in Dorset. The town's well-proportioned roads are lined with some Tudor and many good Georgian and Victorian buildings, but it's sumptuous **Powis Castle**, one of the greatest Welsh fortresses, that puts Welshpool on most people's agenda. The main thoroughfare is Broad Street, with the ponderous Victorian town hall and its dominating clock tower overlooking Tudor and Jacobean town houses.

Powysland Museum

Canal Wharf, SY21 7AQ • June–Aug Mon–Fri 10.30am–1pm & 2–5pm, Sat 10.30am–3pm; Sept–May Mon, Tues, Thurs & Fri 11am–1pm & 2–5pm, Sat 11am–2pm • £1 • ☎01938 554656

In the nineteenth century, some thirty warehouses lined this stretch of the canal. One of them, now restored, houses the **Powysland Museum**, an impressively wide local history collection. The entrance, heralded by Andrew Logan's spangly outsized handbag, leads to a range of displays including Roman remains and archeological finds from a local Neolithic timber circle, exhibits showing the changing patterns of domestic and civic life, and some surprises – an intricate model of a guillotine carved from mutton bones, left behind by prisoners of the Napoleonic Wars, for example, and a slice of wallpaper that was allegedly taken from Napoleon's residence on St Helena. There's also a nostalgic look at the Welshpool & Llanfair Railway, with a ceremonial spade and bugle.

Welshpool & Llanfair Railway

Raven Square, SY21 0SF • Generally 3–5 trains on operating days: April & Oct hols & weekends only; May, June & Sept Tues–Thurs, Sat & Sun; July & Aug daily • £13.50 rover ticket • ☎01938 810441, ⓦwllr.org.uk

Broad Street changes name five times as it rises up the hill towards the tiny Raven Square terminus station of the **Welshpool & Llanfair Railway**, half a mile beyond the town hall. The eight-mile narrow-gauge line originally operated for less than thirty years, closing in 1931 – these days, scaled-down engines once more chuff along the equally small-scale valleys of the Sylfaen Brook and Banwy River to the quiet village of **Llanfair Caereinion**; the round journey takes two hours.

Powis Castle

A mile southwest of Welshpool up Park Lane, SY21 8RF • Daily: March castle 12.30–4pm, gardens 11am–4pm; April–Sept castle 11am–5pm, gardens 10am–6pm; Oct–Dec castle 11am–4pm, gardens 10am–4pm • Castle and gardens £12.50, gardens only £9.25; NT • ☎01938 551944, ⓦnationaltrust.org.uk/powis-castle-and-garden

Located on the site of an earlier Norman fort, the outstanding **Powis Castle** was started in the reign of Edward I by the Gwenwynwyn family; to qualify for the site and the barony of De la Pole, they had to renounce all claims to Welsh princedom. In 1587, Sir Edward Herbert bought the castle and began to transform it into the Elizabethan palace you see today.

After buying your ticket from the **Old Coach House**, take a look at the stagecoach that belonged to the third Earl of Powis, complete with a magnificent silver-plate harness and buttercup-yellow silk lining. In the castle itself, the sumptuous period rooms are undoubtedly impressive, from the vast and kitsch frescoes by Lanscroon above the

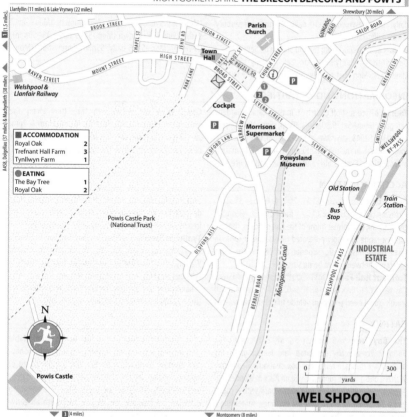

Map of Welshpool with the following labels:

Llanfyllin (11 miles) & Lake Vrynwy (22 miles)
Shrewsbury (20 miles)
BROOK STREET
CHAPEL ST
UNION STREET
Parish Church
GUNGROG ROAD
SALOP ROAD
HIGH STREET
JEHU RD
HALL ST
BERRIEW ST
CHURCH STREET
Town Hall
PUZZLE SQ
MILL LANE
GREENFIELDS
RAVEN STREET
MOUNT STREET
PARK LANE
BROAD STREET
SEVERN STREET
P
Welshpool & Llanfair Railway
Cockpit
Morrisons Supermarket
SMITHFIELD RD
WELSHPOOL BY-PASS
Shrewsbury (20 miles)
A458, Dolgellau (37 miles) & Machynlleth (38 miles)

■ ACCOMMODATION
Royal Oak 2
Trefnant Hall Farm 3
Tynllwyn Farm 1

● EATING
The Bay Tree 1
Royal Oak 2

OLDFORD LANE
P
Powysland Museum
SEVERN ROAD

Powis Castle Park (National Trust)

Old Station
★ Bus Stop
Train Station

3

OLDFORD RISE
Montgomery Canal
WELSHPOOL BY-PASS
INDUSTRIAL ESTATE

BERRIEW ROAD

N

Powis Castle

0 ____ 300
yards

WELSHPOOL

3 (4 miles)
Montgomery (8 miles)

balustraded staircase to the mahogany bed, brass-and-enamel toilets and decorative wall hangings of the state bedroom; the bed itself is set within its own alcove behind an ostentatious balustrade, said to be modelled on the one in Versailles and the only one of its kind in the country. Many rooms were remodelled in the Jacobean style in the early 1900s on the orders of the fourth earl, George Herbert, hence the proliferation of oak panelling and elaborate plasterwork ceilings. There are some notable paintings, too, including one of Henrietta Herbert (wife of Edward Clive) by Joshua Reynolds, and a Gainsborough *Little Boy* in the Oak Drawing Room.

The former ballroom houses the **Clive Museum** – named after the diplomat Robert Clive (aka Clive of India) and his son Edward, who married into the family in 1784; it's a remarkable collection, providing a lively account of the British in India through diaries, notes, letters, paintings, tapestries, weapons and jewels. No less impressive is part of the campaign tent belonging to Tipu Sultan, ruler of the Kingdom of Mysore.

Designed by Welsh architect William Winde, the **gardens** are spectacular in their own right, dropping down from the castle in four huge stepped terraces. The design has barely changed since the seventeenth century, with a charmingly precise orangery and topiary. Summertime concerts, frequently with firework finales, take place in the gardens.

ARRIVAL AND DEPARTURE
WELSHPOOL

By train The train station is at the bottom of Severn Rd, with the neo-Gothic turrets of the old Victorian station just in front.

Destinations Aberystwyth (9–10 daily; 1hr 30min); Birmingham (6–8 daily; 1hr 30min); Machynlleth (9–10 daily; 1hr); Newtown (9–10 daily; 15min); Shrewsbury (9–10 daily; 25min).

By bus Buses depart from the Old Station on Severn Rd.
Destinations Llanfyllin (Mon–Sat 4 daily; 35min); Llanidloes (Mon–Sat 6 daily; 1hr 20min); Llanymynech

(Mon–Sat 5 daily; 35min); Montgomery (Mon–Sat 7 daily; 25min); Newtown (Mon–Sat 9 daily; 35–50min); Oswestry (Mon–Sat 5 daily; 55min); Shrewsbury (Mon–Sat 6 daily; 50min).

INFORMATION AND ACTIVITIES

Tourist office Just off Church St, in the Vicarage Gardens car park (Mon–Sat 9.30am–4.30pm, Sun 10am–4pm; ☎01938 552043, ⓦ visitwelshpool.org.uk). One of the few tourist offices in the region, offering stacks of information and a National Express bus- and train-booking service.

Canal trips It's possible to take trips along the Montgomery Canal (April–Sept Sat & Sun 11am & 2pm; 2hr; £8 including teas, coffees and soft drinks); tickets must be bought in advance from the tourist office.

ACCOMMODATION

Royal Oak The Cross, SY21 7DG ☎01938 552217, ⓦroyaloakwelshpool.co.uk. Traditional Georgian coaching inn and former home of the Earl of Powis, the *Oak* offers a range of crisply presented rooms, which come in three categories; classic, superior and deluxe, the main difference between them being size. **£99**

Trefnant Hall Farm 4 miles southwest, beyond Powis Castle, SY21 8AS ☎01686 640262, ⓦtrefnanthall .co.uk. You'll need your own vehicle to get to this isolated

Georgian farmhouse, whose three flowery rooms have delightful views towards green sloping fields. Guests are free to use the lounge with its gorgeous fireplace. **£65**

Tynllwyn Farm Groes-Pluen, 1 mile west on the A490, SY21 9BW ☎01938 553175, ⓦtynllwynfarm.co.uk. Warmly run B&B offering five sizeable, homely rooms, a fabulous breakfast and generous hospitality. There are also a handful of self-catering cottages sleeping four to six (from £270 for a minimum of three nights). **£60**

EATING

The Bay Tree 5–6 Church St, SY21 7DL ☎01938 555456. Eccentrically decorated café featuring, among many other things, a telephone box, seating culled from a Waltzer, and a whole room themed on Alice in Wonderland – once you've digested all that, settle back with a cuppa and a sandwich or, on Fri and Sat evenings, something a little stronger in the upstairs lounge, sinking into a Chesterfield sofa as you do so. Mon–Thurs 9am–5pm, Fri & Sat 9am–midnight.

Royal Oak The Cross, SY21 7DG ☎01938 552217,

ⓦroyaloakwelshpool.co.uk. The hotel's comfortable restaurant offers a cracking grazing menu (try the honey-and-mustard mini-sausages; £6) and a fuller menu of seasonal dishes (rump of lamb with creamed potatoes and rosemary gravy, for example; £16). The adjoining café/bar is a relaxing spot to kick back with an early-morning coffee or early-evening glass of wine. Breakfasts, too. Daily: restaurant noon–3pm & 6–10pm; café/bar 9am–11pm.

Llanfyllin

The hills and plains of northern Montgomeryshire conceal a maze of deserted lanes and farms as the land rises towards the foothills of Denbighshire's Berwyn mountains. The only settlement of any size is **LLANFYLLIN**, a handsome and friendly hillside town ten miles northwest of Welshpool in the valley of the River Cain. The **High Street** is busy with bright pubs, cafés, shops and a weekly Thursday market, while the square-cut, red-brick parish **church** is a rare example of eighteenth-century church building in Wales.

Llanfyllin Workhouse

One mile southeast of Llanfyllin on the A490, SY22 5LD • Daily 10am–5pm • Free • ☎01691 649062, ⓦ the-workhouse.org.uk

Following a decade-long restoration project, the **Llanfyllin Union Workhouse** reopened in 2016. Workhouses were conceived following the Poor Law Amendment Act 1834, which intended to ease the pressure on the welfare system – conditions were intentionally grim so that only the poorest, most vulnerable felt compelled to come here; by the end of the nineteenth century, there were more than five hundred workhouses in England and Wales. Llanfyllin opened in 1839, with a simple, effective design: a quad each for men, women, boys and girls with, in a spot of architectural cunning, the master's house in the centre, comprising three floors and diagonally facing windows for uninterrupted views of all four wings. Although workhouses were officially abolished in 1930, many, such as Llanfyllin, were simply transferred to local authority control. Conditions thereafter were certainly more benign and Llanfyllin itself continued to function in various capacities (in later years as a home for the elderly) until 1982, when it fell into disrepair. The complex today remains a work in progress, though it has become a well-used communal facility accommodating artists and musicians and hosting drama productions, concerts and fairs.

Before looking around the buildings (there's little of substance to see), pop into the reception area, where a film, *Ghosts of the Workhouse*, provides illuminating insights into the workhouse's operations and the many – often thoroughly nasty – characters who ran the place.

ARRIVAL AND DEPARTURE	LLANFYLLIN

By bus Buses stop on the High St.
Destinations Llanrhaeadr-ym-Mochnant (Mon–Sat 3 daily; 20min); Oswestry (Mon–Sat 4 daily; 35min); Welshpool (Mon–Sat 5 daily; 35min).

ACCOMMODATION AND EATING

Cyfie Farm Llanfihangel, 7 miles southwest, SY22 5JE ☎01691 648451, ⏍ cyfiefarm.co.uk. The tranquil, ivy-draped seventeenth-century *Cyfie Farm* has four self-catering cottages sleeping between two and four (three-night minimum), each with glorious countryside views. Its terraced gardens are something of an attraction themselves. **£100**

Seeds 5 Penybryn Cottages, High St, SY22 5AP ☎01691 648604. Sixteenth-century seed merchant's house that now boasts a superb restaurant. Take your place at one of the six small tables in front of the log burner and enjoy warm black pudding salad with blackcurrant, or sea bass on a sweet potato and chilli mash; there's a serious wine list to boot. Three-course menu £28.95. Thurs–Sat noon–2pm & 7–11pm.

Llanrhaeadr-ym-Mochnant and Pistyll Rhaeadr

The small, low-roofed village of **LLANRHAEADR-YM-MOCHNANT**, six miles north of Llanfyllin, is best remembered as the parish of Bishop William Morgan, who translated the Bible into Welsh in 1588, a pivotal act that ensured the survival of the old tongue.

Llanrhaeadr lies at the foot of the wild walking country of the southern Berwyn mountains. From the middle of the village, Waterfall Street becomes a lane that courses northwest for four miles to a dead end at the enchanting **Pistyll Rhaeadr**, Wales' highest waterfall at 240ft. The river tumbles down the crags in two stages, flowing under a natural stone arch known as the Fairy Bridge. It's well worth walking the twenty or so minutes to the top of the falls for the dizzying views down the valley, as well as the chance to follow further paths leading up into the remote and moody Berwyns; little explored, these mountains were once a major centre for lead-mining, and have always has strong links to spiritualism. Pistyll Rhaeadr is rich in legend, which you can absorb at the riverside café *Tan-y-Pistyll* (see below).

ACCOMMODATION AND EATING	LLANRHAEADR AND PISTYLL RHAEADR

Bron Heulog Waterfall St ☎01691 780521, ⏍ bronheulog.co.uk. Grand Victorian house hidden behind a lush garden, with three beautifully decorated B&B rooms set off a gorgeous spiralling oak staircase. Each is themed around a different type of flower: bluebell, sunflower and orchid. **£75**

Plough Inn ☎01691 780654, ⏍ ploughcountryinn .com. Delightful country pub that's a great spot for a pint and a bite – home-made Caerphilly and leek pancakes, perhaps, or pan-fried salmon in lemon butter sauce (£12). Pub & kitchen Mon–Fri 4–11pm, Sat & Sun noon–11pm.

Tan-y-Pistyll Café Pistyll Rhaeadr ☎01691 780392, ⏍ pistyllrhaeadr.co.uk. Easy-going café with a range of accommodation (all requiring either a minimum two- or three-night stay). Choose between two en-suite rooms, a cottage sleeping five, a superbly restored showman's caravan and a lovely, low-key campsite in the back field, which has a shower block and where fires are allowed (note, thought, that you must pay a one-off £25 "membership" fee in order to camp here). Daily: summer 10am–5pm; rest of year 10am–4pm. Camping/person **£7.50**, cottage **£90**, caravan **£113**, doubles **£120**

Sycarth and around

East of Llanrhaeadr, the B4396 runs along the Tanat Valley and through the village of **Llangedwyn**. A mile or so beyond the village, few visitors make it up one of the left turns leading to **SYCARTH**. Just a mile from the English border, here lies one of the most Welsh of all shrines: a grass mound marks the site of **Owain Glyndŵr's ancestral court**, reputedly a palace of nine grand halls. Bard Iolo Goch immortalized this Welsh Shangri-la as a place of "no want, no hunger, no shame/No one is ever thirsty at Sycarth".

Just east of Sycarth, the English–Welsh border tightly encircles the 740ft limestone crag of **Llanymynech Rocks** (now a nature reserve), before cutting down to run right through the village of **Llanymynech**.

Llangynog and Pennant Melangell

Heading northwest from Llanrhaeadr, the B4391 hugs the river as far as the sleepy former mining village of **LLANGYNOG**, where it heads north into the Berwyn mountains and Denbighshire. A lane by the bridge leads to a stunning four-mile hike over the top of Y Clogydd and down to Pistyll Rhaeadr.

You can walk (or, less strenuously, drive) two miles further up the Tanat Valley from Llangynog to the hamlet of **PENNANT MELANGELL**, sitting low in a quiet, sheer-sided valley of sparkling brooks, and the site of one of Wales' most enduring sites of pilgrimage. Legend has it that the eighth-century saint Melangell was praying in the valley when a hare being chased by a hunt pack led by Prince Brochwel took refuge in her skirts. The hounds drew to a sudden stop before her and fled howling. The prince drew his horn to his lips to call them, only to find himself unable to remove it. The prince was so moved by Melangell's gentle humanity that he granted her the valley, in which she built a religious community.

The little **church** here dates from the eighth century; inside, a twelfth-century shrine and supposed effigy of St Melangell lie beneath an exquisite barrel roof. Melangell's grave is in the semicircular *cell y bedd* at the back of the church. Intact Norman features include a window in the main church, the south door porch and the font.

Lake Vyrnwy

A few miles south of Pennant Melangell, the magnificent **Lake Vyrnwy** (Llyn Efyrnwy) combines its functional role as a water supply for Liverpool with Victorian self-aggrandizement in the shape of the huge nineteenth-century dam and turreted straining tower. Constructed during the 1880s, Vyrnwy was the first of the massive reservoirs of mid-Wales. The village of **Llanwddyn** was flattened and rebuilt at the eastern end, its people receiving meagre compensation for the loss of their homes.

The lake also makes a terrific base for **birdwatching**, with three hides for enthusiastic twitchers; up at the northern end of the lake, some five miles from the RSPB Visitor Centre (see opposite), the Centenary and Lakeside hides are dedicated to spotting peregrines, typically between April and July, as well as buzzards, kestrels, redstarts and pied and spotted flycatchers. In the small Coed-y-Capel hide across the road from the visitor centre, you can sit and watch forest birds attacking the feeders outside the windows. The lake is well stocked with fish, particularly brown trout; fishing in boats is permitted and these can be rented from *Lake Vyrnwy Hotel* (see opposite).

Half a dozen colour-coded walking **trails** fan out around the lake, ranging from a gentle one-mile circular stroll through woodland, to a couple of five-mile treks along the lakeside and up into the forest – pick up a leaflet from the visitor centre.

INFORMATION
LAKE VYRNWY

Tourist information On the western side of the dam, the RSPB Visitor Centre (daily 10.30am–4pm; ☎01691 870278, ⓦrspb.org.uk/lakevyrnwy) is really just a shop, but the knowledgeable staff can advise on the best places to birdwatch and offer free guided walks of the lake and environs (phone for details).

ACTIVITIES

Bike rental From the *Artisans Coffee Shop* just below the RSPB Visitor Centre (£5/hr, minimum 2hr; ☎01691 870317, ⓦartisans-lakevyrnwy.co.uk); last rental is at 2pm.

Fishing Between mid-March and mid-Oct, fishing permits can be obtained from *Lake Vyrnwy Hotel* (£42/person/day including boat, £57 for two).

Canoeing and kayaking From a boathouse about 100m along from the visitor centre, Bethania Adventure (Easter–Sept Sat & Sun, summer school hols daily; ☎01691 870615 or ☎07816 036358) offers canoe (£15/hr) and kayak (£10/hr) rental and guided trips out on the lake.

ACCOMMODATION AND EATING

Artisans Coffee Shop The Old Sawmill, just below the visitor centre, SY10 0NA ☎01691 870317, ⓦartisans-lakevyrnwy.co.uk. Large, well-stocked café-cum-gift shop serving teas, coffees, cakes, snacks and ice cream. Daily 10am–4.30pm.

Fronheulog At the top of the hairpin bends, 2 miles from the lake on the road to Llanfyllin, SY10 0NN ☎01691 870662, ⓦfronheulog-caravan-park.co.uk. Although this adults-only site is almost totally geared up for caravans, there is a separate field here for campers. Note, though, that there are no facilities beyond toilets and tap water. Closed Nov–March. Per person £5

Lake Vyrnwy Hotel Above the southeastern shore, SY10 0LY ☎01691 870692, ⓦlakevyrnwy.com. The lake's most prominent accommodation is this lavish spa retreat overlooking the waters above the southeastern shore. Rooms have either a garden or lake view; if you're going to spend this much money anyway it's worth the extra splurge for the glorious vistas from the lakeside rooms. The *Tower* restaurant is no less accomplished, its three-course evening dinner good value at £35. Daily noon–3pm & 6.30–9pm. £175

The Cambrian coast

255 From Cardigan to Aberaeron

264 Teifi Valley

271 Aberystwyth and around

276 Vales of Rheidol and Ystwyth

279 North from Aberystwyth

281 Southern Cadair Idris and the Dyfi and Talyllyn valleys

292 Northern Cadair Idris and the Mawddach estuary

298 Ardudwy

THE COAST NEAR ABERYSTWYTH

The Cambrian coast

Cardigan Bay (Bae Ceredigion) takes a huge bite out of Wales' west coast, bordered by the Pembrokeshire peninsula in the south and the Llŷn in the north. Between these two rugged projections lies the Cambrian coast, which starts where the rugged seashore of Pembrokeshire ends, continuing in much the same vein of great cliffs, isolated beaches and swirling sea birds, punctuated with sarnau, stony offshore reefs largely exposed at low tide. This coast is split by tumbling rivers, while the bulwark of the Cambrian mountains lies to the east. Before the nineteenth-century construction of the railway and improved roads, these served to isolate this stretch of coast from the rest of Wales, with only narrow passes and cattle-droving routes pushing through the rugged terrain to the markets in England. Today, development is still low-key, with large sand-fringed sections sprinkled with enchanting coastal resorts.

North of the charismatic town of **Cardigan**, the coast breaks at some popular seaside resorts – the best being **Llangrannog** and **New Quay** – before the tiny Georgian harbour town of **Aberaeron**, with its concentration of good places to stay and eat. A bucolic **inland** alternative to the coastal resorts follows the **River Teifi**, which meets the sea at Cardigan and meanders eastwards through lush meadows past a clutch of small towns: the stalwart market centre of **Newcastle Emlyn**, the pint-sized university town of **Lampeter** and the charmingly old-fashioned **Tregaron**.

The coastal and inland routes connect at the cosmopolitan "capital" of mid-Wales, **Aberystwyth**, built on the estuary of the **Rheidol**, a fast-flowing river with dramatic ravines that make for great walking country. A narrow-gauge railway, an attraction in itself, climbs out of Aberystwyth to **Devil's Bridge**, where three bridges, one on top of the other, span a plunging chasm of cascading waterfalls.

Machynlleth, at the head of the Dyfi estuary, was once the seat of Owain Glyndŵr's putative fifteenth-century Welsh parliament and is still a thriving market centre. Just outside the town is the **Centre for Alternative Technology**, Britain's renowned showpiece for sustainable living and renewable energy.

The train line and narrow coastal road then skirt west around **Cadair Idris**, the monumental mountain that dominates the southern third of **Snowdonia National Park**. Each of the mountain's crag-fringed faces invites exploration, but it is best approached from the south, where the narrow-gauge **Talyllyn** rail line reaches the tiny settlement of **Abergynolwyn**, a great base for the unhurried delights of the **Dysynni Valley**. Cadair Idris'

Ceredigion Coast Path p.257
Dylan Thomas in New Quay p.261
Dolphin-spotting near New Quay p.261
Walking the Coast Path: New Quay to
   Llangrannog p.262
Festivals in Aberaeron p.263
Cycling the Vale of Rheidol and the
   Ystwyth Trail p.277
Owain Glyndŵr, Welsh hero p.283

Mountain biking in Mac p.286
Cadair Idris: the Minffordd Path p.291
Walking and cycling around Dolgellau
   p.294
The Big Session p.295
Walks from Barmouth p.296
Three Peaks Yacht Race p.297
Walks on the Rhinogs p.299

CADAIR IDRIS

Highlights

❶ New Quay Follow Dylan Thomas' footsteps through the salty seaside town that inspired *Under Milk Wood*. **See p.260**

❷ Aberaeron Colourful Georgian harbour town, lined with great places to eat and sleep; superb seafood festival, too. **See p.263**

❸ Aberystwyth Hang out in this lively seaside university town rooted firmly in Welsh culture and language. **See p.271**

❹ Bwlch Nant yr Arian Visit mid-afternoon for the impressive sight of dozens of red kites squabbling over a heap of beef and lamb, and then follow that with some of the best single-track mountain biking in Wales. **See p.277**

❺ Devil's Bridge Ride the scenic narrow-gauge, steam-powered Vale of Rheidol Railway from Aberystwyth to this towering triplet of bridges and series of cascades. **See p.278**

❻ Machynlleth Learn about ways to reduce your impact on the planet at the cutting-edge Centre for Alternative Technology. **See p.282**

❼ Cadair Idris Hike up southern Snowdonia's highest peak for swooping views. **See p.281**

❽ Harlech Take a stroll around the grounds of this buzzy little town's formidable castle while savouring glorious views of the Cambrian coast and the Llŷn Peninsula. **See p.300**

HIGHLIGHTS ARE MARKED ON THE MAP ON P.254

northern flank slopes down to the market town of **Dolgellau**, the best base for visiting the superb running and mountain-biking trails at **Coed-y-Brenin**. Dolgellau is at the head of the scenic Mawddach estuary and linked by waterside path to the likeable resort of **Barmouth**. The coastal strip then broadens out with complex dune systems protecting the approaches to **Harlech** and its virtually intact castle, the southernmost link in Edward I's chain of thirteenth-century fortresses, perched high on its rocky promontory.

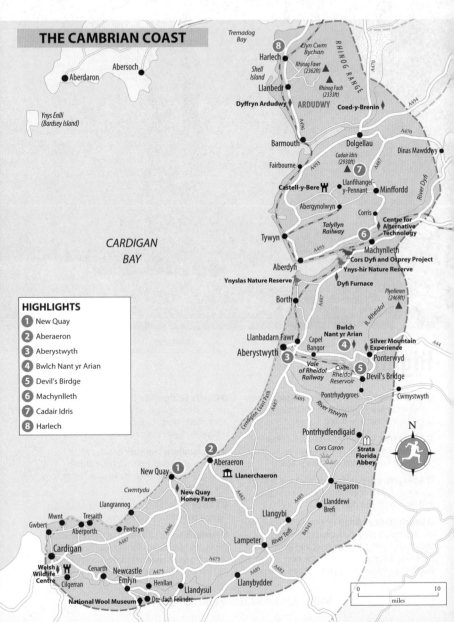

THE CAMBRIAN COAST

Tremadog Bay

8 Harlech

Llyn Cwm Bychan

Aberdaron

Abersoch

Aberdaron

Rhinog Fawr (2362ft)

RHINOG RANGE

A470

Shell Island

Llanbedr

Rhinog Fach (2333ft)

Ynys Enlli (Bardsey Island)

Dyffryn Ardudwy

ARDUDWY

Coed-y-Brenin

A494

Barmouth

Dolgellau

Dinas Mawddwy

Fairbourne

A493

Cadair Idris (2930ft)

7

A487

River Dyfi

A470

Castell-y-Bere

Llanfihangel-y-Pennant

Minffordd

Abergynolwyn

Corris

Centre for Alternative Technology

Talyllyn Railway

6

CARDIGAN BAY

Tywyn

A493

Machynlleth

Cors Dyfi and Osprey Project

Aberdyfi

Ynys-hir Nature Reserve

Ynyslas Nature Reserve

A487

Dyfi Furnace

Plynlimon (2469ft)

Borth

R. Rheidol

HIGHLIGHTS

1 New Quay
2 Aberaeron
3 Aberystwyth
4 Bwlch Nant yr Arian
5 Devil's Birdge
6 Machynlleth
7 Cadair Idris
8 Harlech

Llanbadarn Fawr

Bwlch Nant yr Arian

Capel Bangor

4

Silver Mountain Experience

A44

Aberystwyth

3

Vale of Rheidol Railway

Cwm Rheidol Reservoir

5

Ponterwyd

Devil's Bridge

Ceredigion Coast Path

A487

A485

River Ystwyth

Pontrhydygroes

Cwmystwyth

Pontrhydfendigaid

N

Cors Caron

Strata Florida Abbey

2 Aberaeron

New Quay **1**

🏛 **Llanerchaeron**

Tregaron

Cwmtydu

New Quay Honey Farm

Llangrannog

A486

A485

Llanddewi Brefi

Mwnt

Tresaith

Penbryn

Llangybi

Gwbert

Aberporth

A487

River Teifi

Lampeter

A485

A482

B4343

Cardigan

A475

A475

Llanybydder

Welsh Wildlife Centre

Cenarth

Newcastle Emlyn

A475

Henllan

Llandysul

Cilgerran

National Wool Museum

Dre-fach Felindre

0   10

miles

GETTING AROUND   **THE CAMBRIAN COAST**

By train The most relaxing way to get fairly swiftly to, and along, the Cambrian coast is on the Cambrian Line (ⓦ thecambrianline.co.uk) from Shrewsbury in England through Welshpool and Newtown to Machynlleth. At Machynlleth, the line splits: one branch runs south to Aberystwyth, from where you can pick up the Vale of Rheidol line to Devil's Bridge; the other swings north, calling at 25 stations in less than sixty miles before terminating at Pwllheli on the Llŷn. The Day Ranger ticket (see box, p.28) offers flexible travel at moderate prices.

By bus All towns and many villages in the region can be reached by bus, though there are few services on Sun. The most useful routes are the #T1 (Carmarthen–Lampeter–Aberaeron–Aberystwyth); the #T2 (Aberystwyth–Machynlleth–Dolgellau–Porthmadog–Caernarfon); and the #T5 (Aberystwyth–Aberaeron–Cardigan–Fishguard–Haverfordwest). There's also the handy Cardi Bach bus (service #552), which connects all the villages and coves between Cardigan and New Quay (see p.260).

From Cardigan to Aberaeron

The southern section of the Ceredigion coastline has Wales' highest sea-cliffs, safe, sheltered beaches, great coastal walking, and a resident pod of bottlenose dolphins. Many of the coast's settlements retain a timeless, salty charm: the one-time smuggler's port of **New Quay** uncoils down the hair-raisingly steep hillside to the craggy coastline, while smaller places like **Llangrannog**, **Penbryn**, **Mwnt** and **Tresaith** juxtapose rolling pastoral countryside and wide, sweeping beaches, and brightly painted cottages huddle around the boat-filled harbour at **Aberaeron**. Just inland, at the mouth of the Teifi, is the pretty and cheerful old county town of **Cardigan**.

4

Cardigan and around

Until the River Teifi silted up in the nineteenth century, **CARDIGAN** (Aberteifi) was one of the greatest sea ports in Britain, although these days there's little evidence of its former status. It is, however, a sprightly little town, with some great diversions and a relaxed ambience. The picturesque High Street leads up to the spiky turrets of the **Guildhall** and the bustling **covered market** (daily except Wed & Sun), an eclectic mix of locally produced food and browsable oddities. Leading off the High Street, narrow thoroughfares come crammed with Georgian and Victorian buildings.

Cardigan Castle

Green St, SA43 1JA • Daily: April–Sept 10am–4pm; Oct–March 11am–3pm • £4.50 • ☎ 01239 614131, ⓦ cardigancastle.com

The main focus of town, and just a stone's throw from Cardigan's **medieval bridge**, is **Cardigan Castle**, whose spectacular decade-long renovation was completed in 2017. Although there was a castle of sorts in Cardigan in 1093, this was the first Welsh castle to be made of stone, in 1171 by Lord Rhys, and despite the presence of four of the seven original towers, it doesn't much resemble a castle at all these days – though that's not to detract from its charm.

At the heart of the complex is **Castle Green House**, a handsome Georgian pile dating from 1808 that has undergone a dramatic transformation as part of the recent renovation. It now accommodates several superb exhibitions, one of which focuses on the castle's last resident, **Barbara Wood**, who lived here from 1940 until 1999, by which time the place was virtually uninhabitable – on display is her rather bashed up doll's house, rusting typewriter and items of correspondence. Cardigan was the site of the first Welsh **eisteddfod** in 1176 (see box, p.452) – though the term, eisteddfod, wasn't used until 1523 – and another exhibition makes great play of this, with artefacts pertaining to this most cherished of Welsh traditions; the last time the eisteddfod was held in Cardigan, however, was 1976. Another room recalls the town's history, and in particular its prestigious **shipbuilding** heritage. Between

1792 and 1840, more than 140 vessels were built here; with the port came emigration and it was from Cardigan, during this same period, that some six thousand of the rural poor left for the Americas.

Fronting the house are the perfectly manicured lawns of the **Regency Gardens**, around which are dotted various objects of interest, including a whalebone arch, an oversized replica of the eisteddfod chair from 1176 and, peeking over the battlements, a World War II pillbox, positioned here in the event of a German offensive emanating from Ireland. Once you've absorbed all that, kick back a while in the agreeable *1176 restaurant* (see p.258).

Teifi Marshes Nature Reserve

The extensive **Teifi Marshes Nature Reserve** hugs the banks of the Teifi right on the fringes of Cardigan. It encompasses several important habitats – reed beds, meadows, marshes and untouched oak woodland – for otters, badgers, butterflies and birds, including Wales' largest resident group of Cetti's warblers. A herd of **buffalo**, brought in to control invasive bulrushes, wanders incongruously among the native inhabitants and can be seen from the various trails which access viewing hides.

You can drive from Cardigan (a very roundabout route of about four miles), but the best approach is to simply walk (or cycle) from the town's river bridge along the bed of an old railway. It is an inviting route past reed beds and a couple of bird hides, and in fifteen minutes you'll be at the **Welsh Wildlife Centre**.

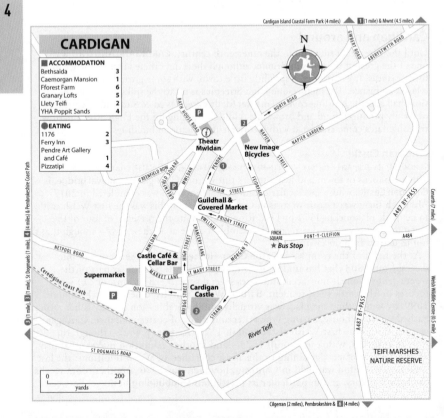

CEREDIGION COAST PATH

Cardigan is the start and end of both the Pembrokeshire Coast Path and the **Ceredigion Coast Path** (ⓦceredigioncoastpath.org.uk), which follows the coast for some sixty wind-blown miles from Cardigan to Ynyslas on the edge of the Dyfi estuary; both sections form part of the Wales Coast Path. You can walk the whole thing over several days making use of the Cab-a-bag service, whereby local taxis deliver your luggage to your next stop for around £1.50 a mile. Alternatively, just walk short sections using the Cardi Bach buses (see p.255) to loop back to your starting point. Tourist offices sell leaflets detailing short sections of the route, or you can download descriptions from the website. There is no shortage of wonderful walking, but some of the most **dramatic sections** are from Llangrannog north to New Quay.

Welsh Wildlife Centre

Teifi Marshes, SA43 2TB • Daily: Easter–Oct 10am–5pm; Nov–Easter 10am–4pm • Free • ☎01239 621600, ⓦwelshwildlife.org

The elegant, modern timber-and-glass structure in the centre of the Teifi Marshes is the **Welsh Wildlife Centre**, home to informative displays, an airy café with expansive views over the reserve and an adventure playground to keep kids entertained. You can easily spend half a day here exploring the four themed trails – the shortest is an easy ten-minute walk around the meadow, the longest a forty-five minute trail through the wetlands. There are also seven observation hides (including an otter hide), with binocular rental available (£3.50). This area is best explored, however, on **canoe trips** run by Heritage Canoes (☎01239 613961, ⓦheritagecanoes.squarespace.com), who are based in Slate Cottage, just below the wildlife centre; they offer tours of the river and Cilgerran Gorge (2hr 30min; £35/person), with an emphasis on spotting local wildlife (see opposite).

Cardigan Island Coastal Farm Park

Gwbert, 4 miles north of Cardigan, SA43 1PR • April–Oct daily 10am–6pm • £3.90 • ☎01239 623637, ⓦcardiganisland.com

The B4548 follows the Teifi estuary north to the straggling seaside village of **GWBERT**, a peaceful spot with fabulous sea views best enjoyed from the **Cardigan Island Coastal Farm Park**, which keeps a curious mixture of animals, including llamas, pigs and emus, as well as more traditional British stock – ponies, chickens, ducks, goats and donkeys. From the park, there's a coastal walk from which it's possible to spot dolphins and grey seals, plus peregrines, gannets and choughs; there are lovely views across to Cardigan Island, a nature reserve that's off limits to the public.

ARRIVAL AND DEPARTURE   CARDIGAN

By bus Buses stop on Finch Square. The Poppit Rocket bus (#405) runs to Fishguard via St Dogmaels and Poppit Sands car park (May–Sept 3 daily; Oct–April Thurs–Sat 3 daily).
Destinations Aberaeron (Mon–Sat hourly, Sun 3; 1hr); Aberystwyth (Mon–Sat hourly, Sun 3; 1hr 45min); Carmarthen (Mon–Sat hourly, Sun 3; 1hr 30min); Cenarth (Mon–Sat hourly; 15min); Cilgerran (Mon–Sat 5 daily; 10min); Llangrannog (2 daily; 1hr 10min); Newcastle Emlyn (Mon–Sat hourly; 20min); New Quay (Mon–Sat hourly, Sun 5; 45min).

INFORMATION AND GETTING AROUND

Tourist office Theatr Mwldan, Bath House Rd (term time Tues–Sat 10am–1pm & 2–4pm; hols Mon–Sat same times; ☎01239 613230, ⓦvisitcardigan.com).
Bike rental New Image Bicycles, 29 Pendre (Mon–Sat 10am–5pm; £15/half-day, £20/day; ☎01239 621275, ⓦbikebikebike.co.uk), offers standard or hybrid bikes; it also does repairs and maintenance.

ACCOMMODATION

HOTELS, GUESTHOUSES AND SELF-CATERING

★**Bethsaida** High St, St Dogmaels, just over a mile west, SA43 3EQ ☎01239 615749, ⓦbethsaida.wales. This erstwhile Baptist chapel – much of which remains *in situ* (the pulpit functions as the reception desk) – has been brilliantly converted into a top-drawer guesthouse, hosting five stunningly original rooms; stained-glass windows, pre-loved furnishings and pew headboards are just several features. Breakfast, meanwhile, is taken in the dining area

4

(the old organ space) behind the pulpit or, when it's warmer, in the pretty garden terrace. **£99**

★**Caemorgan Mansion** Caemorgan Rd, 1 mile northeast, just off the A487, SA43 1QU ☎01239 613297, ⓦcaemorgan.com. An outstanding level of comfort and hospitality awaits at this marvellous guesthouse, whose five rooms are appointed to the highest order, with luxury Egyptian cotton bedding, underfloor heating and smart drinks stations with fresh milk. You'll not find better cooked Welsh breakfasts anywhere. **£120**

Granary Lofts Teifi Wharf, SA43 3AA ☎01239 623633, ⓦcoldatnight.co.uk. Occupying the old maritime warehouses, these five self-catering loft apartments – four have two floors and one is open plan – have been superbly converted, with exposed brick walls, slate flooring and reclaimed pitch pine furnishings; the views, as you'd expect, are marvellous. Minimum two-night stay. **£120**

Llety Teifi Pendre, SA43 1JU ☎01239 615566, ⓦlletyteifi-guesthouse.co.uk. A raspberry-pink boutique guesthouse with ten good-sized, contemporary rooms in a Victorian town house. Breakfast is taken in the wonderful conservatory. **£75**

HOSTEL AND GLAMPSITE

Fforest Farm Cwnplysgog, Cilgerran, just off the A478 at Pen y Bryn, 2 miles south, SA43 2TB ☎01239 623633, ⓦcoldatnight.co.uk. Outdoor luxury at this wonderful farmland site beside the Teifi Marshes. All manner of tents are available (sleeping at least four) – dome, Kata cabin, bell, all with their own fully equipped cooking area – along with Crog Lofts (former crofter's cottages). There's loads of privacy but also an on-site "pub", sauna and occasional meals. Breakfast (included) is served in the Fforest Lodge. Minimum two-night stay. **£120**

YHA Poppit Sands Poppit, 4 miles northwest, SA43 3LP ☎01239 612936, ⓦyha.org.uk/hostel/poppit -sands. Remote hostel at the northern end of the Pembrokeshire Coast Path, with glorious views across the water to Cardigan Island. There are male and female dorms, all with six beds and shared shower facilities, plus doubles, and a self-catering kitchen. Both the Poppit Rocket bus service (see p.257) and the #407 bus will get you as far as Poppit Sands car park, from where it's a stiff 15min walk uphill. Closed Nov–Easter. Dorms **£15**, doubles **£50**

EATING

1176 Cardigan Castle, Green St, SA43 1JA ☎01239 562002, ⓦcardigancastle.com. Elegant, glassed-in café/ restaurant overlooking the castle's gardens on one side and the Teifi on the other – though the setting's not the only reason to visit. Sample Welsh rarebit with onion marmalade (£6.75) as a mid-morning snack, or perhaps garlic mushrooms on brioche toast for lunch; alfresco afternoon tea (£13.95) is also tempting. Daily 10am–4pm.

Ferry Inn St Dogmael's, just over a mile west, SA43 3LF ☎01239 615172, ⓦferry-inn.co.uk. Enviably sited right beside the Teifi, this rambling delight of a pub offers loads of seating areas (including upper and lower alfresco decks) where you can enjoy a range of tasty meals such as the house bouillabaisse or fish pie (£14.95). Great beer, too. Daily noon–11.30pm; kitchen noon–3pm & 6–9pm.

Pendre Art Gallery and Café 35 Pendre, SA43 1JL ☎01239 615151. Formerly a minor shopping complex – hence the compartmentalized, booth-like spaces – this place is heaps of fun, from the 70s retro tables and sofas at the front through to the back room arranged with furnishings culled from pallets and coffee sacks. Fri nights are given over to tapas, while Sat is cocktail night. Mon–Thurs 10am–5pm, Fri & Sat 10am–5pm & 6.30pm–late.

Pizzatipi 1 Cambrian Quay, SA43 1EZ ☎01239 612259, ⓦpizzatipi.co.uk. The main reason to visit this easy-going waterside café is to dine on wood-fired pizza (£8) and craft beer under the ingeniously conceived pizza tepee. Occasional live music and events. June–Sept daily noon–9.30pm.

ENTERTAINMENT

Castle Café & Cellar Bar 25–26 Quay St, SA43 1HU ☎01239 621882, ⓦthecellarcardigan.com. Good daytime café with great music – lunchtime acoustic happenings, open mic on Thurs, and all sorts on most Fris and Sats. Café daily 9am–6pm; gig nights 7.30–11pm.

Theatr Mwldan Bath House Rd, SA43 1JY ☎01239 621200, ⓦmwldan.co.uk. Cardigan's main cultural centre offers much more than a town of this size should reasonably expect, including a full programme of theatre, dance, comedy, music and film. Days and hours vary.

Mwnt to Llangrannog

Between Cardigan and New Quay, the coast is a mass of impossibly narrow, hedgerow-hemmed lanes leading down to gorgeous little bays – especially **Mwnt**, **Tresaith**, **Penbryn** and **Llangrannog** – that aren't much more than clefts in the rugged cliffs; they all offer great, family-safe swimming, with lifeguards on the beaches at Tresaith and Llangrannog between June and August.

Mwnt

Five miles north of Cardigan • Free, but parking £3/day; NT • ⓦ nationaltrust.org.uk/mwnt

Five miles north of Cardigan, tiny lanes bump down to the isolated little hamlet of **MWNT**, where the exquisite sandy beach and cliffs are under the custodianship of the National Trust. Set in windswept solitude above the cliffs, the tiny, whitewashed **church** (open 24hr) is the oldest in Ceredigion, founded in the sixth century, although most of today's thickset building dates from the thirteenth century. Inside, seek out the wall-bound pieces of timber from the fifteenth-century rood screen, featuring carvings of human heads (possibly depicting disciples) with traces of red and green colouring. Mwnt's finest hour came in 1155, when invading Flemings landed here only to be routed by the Welsh. The occasion, which became known as **Sul Coch y Mwnt**, the Bloody Sunday of Mwnt, has been periodically remembered through the intact skeletons and other human bones that have been unearthed en masse in the vicinity.

Tresaith

At the scenic hamlet of **TRESAITH**, six miles east of Mwnt, there's a great little beach, a kiosk renting wetsuits and aquatic playthings, and the *Ship Inn*. Fifty yards around the rocks to the east, a sandy cove has its own natural after-sea shower – a **waterfall** crashing down from the River Saith above. There's often good **surf** (heed the signs if you're swimming), as well as **dinghy races** on calmer summer Sundays.

Penbryn

One mile northeast of Tresaith • Free, but parking £3/day; NT • ⓦ nationaltrust.org.uk/penbryn

The wide, sandy, National Trust beach at **PENBRYN** is accessed by impossibly narrow lanes (and by the clifftop Ceredigion Coast Path). Almost a mile in length, its unspoilt shallow waters make it ideal for children. Parking is 400yd back from the beach beside the café (see p.260).

4

Llangrannog

Three miles northeast of Penbryn, **LLANGRANNOG** is the busiest and most attractive village on the Ceredigion coast, wedged between hills covered with bracken and gorse. The very narrow streets wind their way to the tiny seafront, catering for visitors with a couple of cafés and pubs and assorted sporting activities. The beach can become congested in midsummer, though the madness is easily escaped on a clifftop walk.

ARRIVAL AND DEPARTURE

MWNT TO LLANGRANNOG

By bus The Cardi Bach bus (see p.255) travels from Cardigan (daily except Thurs 8.45am & 2.10pm) to Mwnt car park, Tresaith, Penbryn car park and Llangrannog.

ACCOMMODATION AND EATING

Blaenwaun Farm Mwnt, SA43 1QF ☎ 01239 613456, ⓦ blaenwaunfarm.com. Well-equipped family-run caravan site a walk up through the wooded ravine from the Mwnt church. There's a modern amenities block with showers, washing and laundry facilities, a kids' play area and a well-stocked shop. Campfires allowed. Closed Nov–Feb. **£15**

Ffynnon Fendigaid Rhydlewis, 3 miles south of Llangrannog, SA44 5SR ☎ 01239 851361, ⓦ ffynnonf .co.uk. Eighteenth-century farmhouse in extensive semi-wild grounds offering an eclectic assortment of accommodation, including the guesthouse itself; a beautifully furnished circus wagon sleeping two (complete with a parlour and adjoining shepherd's hut which functions as the bathroom; £80); and a Swedish lodge with a 1960s, retro-inspired interior (sleeping four; from £85/ night). Walkers and cyclists are particularly welcome, with pick-ups and drop-offs on offer. **£80**

Llety Caravan Park Tresaith, SA43 2ED ☎ 01239 810354, ⓦ lletycaravanpark.co.uk. Amid the static caravans there's a wonderful (if significantly sloping) clifftop field for tents and tourers with a pretty footpath that descends straight to the beach. Friendly and with masses of information to hand, and excellent shower blocks. Closed Dec–Feb. **£17**

Pentre Arms Llangrannog, SA44 6SP ☎ 01239 654345, ⓦ pentrearms.co.uk. A pebble's throw from the beach, this warming pub offers seven rooms – three with sea views and two dog-friendly rooms – in addition to a creditable menu of grilled fish (the day's catch), a decent range of wines and a changing roster of real ales. Daily 11am–11pm; kitchen noon–2pm & 6–9pm. **£95**

★ **The Plwmp Tart** Penbryn Beach, SA44 6QL ☎ 01239 758100. Fun name aside (pronounced "plump"), this comely café, occupying an old National Trust cottage by the car park, is an essential stop if you're in the area, thanks to its delicious savoury snacks – the crab sandwiches are a big hit – and lush cakes like mixed berry and polenta or carrot

and walnut. April–Sept daily 10am–5pm; Oct–March Sat & Sun 10am–5pm.

Tŷ Gwyn Min-y-Mor, Mwnt, SA43 1QH ☎ 01239 614518, ⓦ campingatmwnt.co.uk. Around 400yd beyond the Mwnt church, and with wonderful sea views, this otherwise basic campsite has few facilities beyond showers. Come supplied, as there are no shops nearby. Closed Nov–Feb. **£17**

New Quay

NEW QUAY (Cei Newydd) lays claim to being the original Llareggub in **Dylan Thomas'** *Under Milk Wood*. Certainly, it has the little tumbling streets, pastel-painted Victorian terraces, cobbled harbour and dreamy isolation that Thomas evoked so successfully in his "play for voices", as well, perhaps, as the darkly eccentric characters he describes.

New Quay's main road cuts through the upper, residential part of town, past **Uplands Square**, from where acutely inclined streets plunge down to a pretty harbour, formed by its sturdy stone quay, and with a small, curving main beach. Back from the sand, the higgledy-piggledy lines of multicoloured shops and houses comprise the lower town, the more traditionally seaside part of New Quay, full of standard-issue cafés, pubs and beach shops.

Cardigan Bay Marine Wildlife Centre (CBMWC)

Glanmor Terrace, SA45 9PS • April–Oct daily 9am–5pm • Free • ☎ 01545 560224, ⓦ cbmwc.org

Tucked away down the slipway above the main harbour beach, the **Cardigan Bay Marine Wildlife Centre (CBMWC)** contains some interesting exhibits on the dolphins,

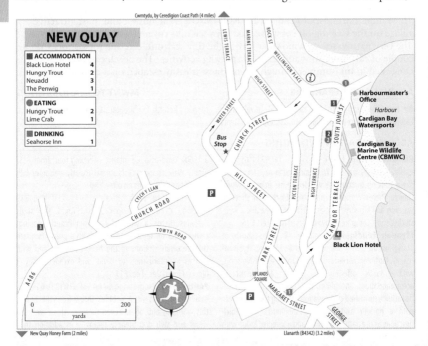

DYLAN THOMAS IN NEW QUAY

Dylan Thomas and his young family lived in New Quay during the last half of World War II, and his experiences here showed him the odder side of human nature. Thomas' metropolitan ways and poetic demeanour did not go down too well in such a close-knit little town, particularly so with an ex-commando officer, fresh home from the war, with whom he had a row in the *Black Lion* pub. The soldier, convinced that his wife was in a *ménage à trois* with Thomas and his wife Caitlin, followed the writer home and shot at his rented bungalow, the Majoda, with a machine gun, while the family was inside. The officer was charged with attempted murder in June 1945, and acquitted. Dylan Thomas and family left the area soon afterwards. The story forms the centrepiece of the 2008 film *The Edge of Love*, much of which was filmed in the area.

Two free leaflets from the tourist office highlight places where the poet spent time: *Dylan Thomas' Ceredigion*, which guides you through local villages, and *Dylan Thomas' New Quay* **walking trail**, concentrating on places he lived and his favourite pubs. One of these was the *Black Lion Hotel*, on Glanmor Terrace, where you'll find lots of photos of Thomas lining the walls (see p.262).

sea birds and seals that inhabit the bay – better still, you can have a go at an underwater virtual reality experience. Staff will point you to the best spots on land from which to see dolphins, though you'll have more luck on their boat trips (see box below).

New Quay Honey Farm

Off the A486 at Cross Inn, 2 miles inland from New Quay, SA44 6NN • Easter–Oct Tues–Sat 10am–5pm • £3.75 • ☎ 01545 560822, ⓦ thehoneyfarm.co.uk

The **New Quay Honey Farm** does a great job of illustrating the life and works of bees, with several glassed-in colonies of the creatures busily creating hives in tree branches and logs, one of which opens up upon the press of a button to show what a colony looks like inside. More compelling is the very active leaf-cutter ant colony, where you can watch a steady procession of these insects marching back and forth along a piece of rope with oversized pieces of vegetation to bury in their underground fungus farm. The on-site meadery farms a variety of delicious honey wines, many of which are sold in the well-stocked shop, or you can simply content yourself with a pot of tea and a slice of honey cake in the **tearoom**.

ARRIVAL AND DEPARTURE   NEW QUAY

By bus Buses stop at the top of Church St. **Destinations** Aberaeron (Mon–Sat hourly, Sun 3; 20min); Aberystwyth (Mon–Sat hourly, Sun 3; 1hr); Cardigan (Mon–Sat hourly, Sun 5; 50min).

DOLPHIN-SPOTTING NEAR NEW QUAY

One of just two pods in Britain, the Cambrian coast's **bottlenose dolphins** are among New Quay's major attractions, and can often be seen frolicking by the harbour wall, particularly when the tide is high and the weather calm; you may also see harbour porpoises and Atlantic grey seals here. A mile-wide strip of the coastal waters forms the **Ceredigion Marine Heritage Coast**, which in summer is plied by boat trips geared around sightings.

Dolphin Spotting Boat Trips Harbourmaster's office, harbour wall ☎01545 560800, ⓦnewquay boattrips.co.uk. Trips with this outfit cost £10 for 1hr, £16 for 2hr. April–Oct daily.
Dolphin Survey Boat Trips Glanmor Terrace, SA45 9PS ☎01545 560032, ⓦdolphinsurveyboattrips .co.uk. Part of the CBMWC (see opposite), this is the best operator, going further offshore, and higher up the heritage coast, than most companies. Fees (£17.50 for 90min, £20 for 2hr, £38 for 4hr, £60 for 8hr) go towards marine mammal research, partly undertaken by the on-board ranger. April–Oct daily.

WALKING THE COAST PATH: NEW QUAY TO LLANGRANNOG

The OS 1:25,000 Explorer map OL198 (Cardigan & New Quay) is recommended.
It's easy to escape New Quay's bustle (such as it is) using one of the most spectacular sections of the **Ceredigion Coast Path**, easily broken into two very manageable sections. The terrain is fairly undulating the whole way; explanatory leaflets are available at local tourist offices, while the Cardi Bach bus service (see p.255) provides access to Cwmtydu and Llangrannog.
New Quay to Cwmtydu (4 miles; 2–3hr). Start around the rocky promontory of New Quay Head, where an invigorating path steers along the top of the sheer drops to Bird Rock, aptly named for the profusion of razorbills and guillemots nesting here. There's a good chance of seeing dolphins, too. Continue past Cwm Soden, an area of interesting folded geology, and on to Cwmtydu. Once a smuggler's cove, Cwmtydu is the site of a glorious cave-walled beach, and is often visited by dolphins and seals; the mainly shingle beach makes a relatively safe spot for watersports.
Cwmtydu to Llangrannog (6 miles; 3–4hr). A wonderful section of path, often cut into the coastal slopes high above the water with long views both ways. It also runs through the National Trust lands of Ynys Lochtyn and can be turned into a loop walk using an alternative route through a wooded valley.

INFORMATION AND ACTIVITIES

Tourist office At the corner of Church St and Wellington Place (Easter & summer holidays only Mon–Sat 10am–1pm & 2–4pm; ☎01545 560865, ⓦ discoverceredigion.co.uk).
Watersports Cardigan Bay Watersports, Main Beach (April–Oct but check website for exact opening days and times; ☎01545 561257, ⓦ cardiganbaywatersports.org .uk) offers various watersports courses and rents paddleboards (£18), windsurfs (£20), sailing dinghies (from £15) and single and double kayaks (£15–25) – the last perfect for exploring the rocky coast to the south.

ACCOMMODATION

HOTELS

Black Lion Hotel Glanmor Terrace, SA45 9PT ☎01545 561144, ⓦ blacklionnewquay.co.uk. Thomas's favourite New Quay watering hole – there are photos and pictures throughout – has been smartened up considerably, with nine rooms (five with superlative sea views, though these cost £30 extra) characterized by high ceilings, sash windows and stripy, boldly coloured curtains. £75
Hungry Trout 2 South John St, SA45 9NG ☎01545 560680, ⓦ thehungrytrout.co.uk. Set above New Quay's best (seafood) restaurant, there are just two rooms here, only one of which is en suite (£110), though both offer sea views; as you might expect, breakfast is delicious. £95

The Penwig South John St, SA45 9NN ☎01545 560910, ⓦ penwig.co.uk. For a Brains pub, the seven rooms (including two family options) are surprisingly accomplished, and three have fabulous sea views; moreover, it's not nearly as noisy as you might expect, given that it's right above one of the town's busiest bars. £80

CAMPSITE

Neuadd Behind the Penrhiwllan Inn at the top of the hill, on the A486 to Synod Inn, SA45 9TY ☎01545 560709, ⓦ neuaddcaravanpark.com. The nearest campsite to town, with tent pitches on a grassy site overlooking the rooftops and the sea. Closed Nov–Feb. £15

EATING

Hungry Trout 2 South John St, SA45 9NG ☎01545 560680, ⓦ thehungrytrout.co.uk. Don't expect to find a seat easily at New Quay's finest seafood restaurant, especially on the cramped balcony terrace. Dishes are rustled up according to the day's catch, but expect the likes of surf clams pan fried in garlic and white wine, and smoked Teifi sewin (sea trout) with asparagus (sorrel) and capers. Daily 9am–3pm & 6–9pm.

Lime Crab South John St, SA45 9NP ☎01545 561400, ⓦ limecrab.com. Justifiably popular fish and chip shop that offers a slightly more refined take on your average chippie, with the likes of scallops, salt-and-pepper squid and mackerel goujons, all for around £7–8 each; at £9.99 the two-person seafood platter is great value. They've even got gluten-free fish and chips. Daily noon–8pm.

DRINKING

Seahorse Inn Margaret St, SA45 9QJ ☎01545 560736. This fine, traditional local, a world away from the holiday bustle down the street, is little more than one room with exposed stonework, fake beams, pool and a limited range of good ales. It was known to Dylan Thomas as the *Commercial* and was the model for the *Sailor's Arms* in *Under Milk Wood*. Daily 11am–11.30pm.

Aberaeron and around

In contrast to the precipitous, zigzagging streets of New Quay, **ABERAERON**, seven miles up the coast, faces away from the ocean, its brightly coloured Georgian houses and level streets clustered instead around the town's internal harbour. It is a beguiling sight, which, combined with a stack of superb places to stay and eat, has helped make Aberaeron *the* weekend getaway of the Cambrian coast. Well-heeled visitors from Cardiff, Swansea and even London descend for a few days of good eating and breezy walks along the coast path.

Aberaeron's harmonious appearance results from its being built en masse after the 1807 Harbour Act paved the way for port development. Reverend Alban Gywnne spent his wife's inheritance dredging the Aeron estuary as a new port for mid-Wales and constructing a formally planned town around it – reputedly from a design by John Nash. To see the best of the town's Georgian buildings, head to the central **Alban Square**, with its graceful, small-scale terraces of quoin-edged buildings and the odd pedimented porch.

From the square, a grid of narrow streets stretches away to the sea at **Quay Parade**, a neat line of brightly coloured houses on the seafront. The southern end of Aberaeron's stony **beach** is marginally better than its northern extent, but the most agreeable activity is simply ambling around the waterfront and grazing in the cafés and pubs.

ARRIVAL, INFORMATION AND GETTING AROUND
ABERAERON

By bus The main bus stop is on the north side of Alban Square, from where it's a short walk across the road down towards the harbour area.

Destinations Aberystwyth (Mon–Sat every 30min, Sun 3; 40min); Cardigan (Mon–Sat hourly, Sun 3; 1hr); Carmarthen (Mon–Sat hourly, Sun 3; 1hr 30min); Lampeter (Mon–Sat hourly; 30min); New Quay (Mon–Sat hourly, Sun 3; 20min).

Tourist office Down by the harbour at 3 Pen Cei

(Mon–Wed, Fri & Sat 10am–4pm; school summer holidays daily 10am–4pm; ☎01545 570602, ⓦdiscoverceredigion .co.uk); staff can book local accommodation.

Bike rental Cyclemart, Cilcennin, 6 miles east (Tues–Sat 10am–6pm; ☎01570 470079, ⓦcyclemart.co.uk), offers a wide range of bikes from £10 a day. You can also rent bikes (£13/half-day, £19/day; ☎07896 895366) from the car park at Llanerchaeron.

ACCOMMODATION

★**3 Pen Cei** 3 Pen Cei, SA45 0BT ☎01545 571147, ⓦpen-cei-guest-house.co.uk. The deep navy-blue exterior of these former shipping offices conceals five dashing rooms, each named after a local river, and variously painted in shades of pink and mauve, with leather sofas, oak-panelled wardrobes and marble- and glass-topped dressing tables. Breakfast can be taken in the garden. £105

Drefnewydd Farm A487, 400yd north of town, SA46 0JR ☎07773 769318, ⓦcampingonthefarm.co.uk. Laidback, family-run campsite in a plum spot right on the shoreline; facilities are limited, but there are clean toilets and hot showers. Closed Oct–March. £18

★**Harbourmaster Hotel** 1 Pen Cei, SA46 0BT ☎01545 570755, ⓦharbour-master.com. Wonderful hotel with thirteen ultramodern rooms spread across three buildings; seven of them are in the Grade II-listed harbourmaster house itself. Exposed stone walls, leather armchairs and vintage Welsh blankets all feature prominently, and there are splendid views. £145

Llys Aeron Lampeter Rd, 1 mile south, SA46 0ED ☎01545 570276, ⓦllysaeron.co.uk. You'll get fresh flowers in your spacious room, a warm welcome and a top-quality breakfast at this upscale B&B on the outskirts of town. Coast Path walkers might fancy the hot tub in the

FESTIVALS IN ABERAERON

The town is positively hopping during its fun-filled **festivals**, notably the annual **Seafood Festival** (ⓦaberaeronfishfest.com) on the second or third Sunday in July, with big-name Welsh chefs rustling up free food alongside great live entertainment. Other festivities include the **Cob Fair** (mid-Aug; ⓦaberaeronfestival.co.uk), with horse displays in Alban Square and local art and crafts taking over the streets; and the **Aberaeron Carnival**, on the August Bank Holiday Monday, when the town swings to live jazz. Another event not to be missed if you're around at the beginning of August is a mass **Tug of War** across the harbour, with the losers getting a serious dunking.

4

4

back garden (£4/person) and there's also self-catering for four available (£130/night; minimum two nights). **£85**
The Monachty Market St, SA46 0AS ☎ 01545 570389, ⓦ monachtyaberaeron.co.uk. A respectable semi-budget option in a town full of otherwise pricey establishments. Seven light-filled rooms come with big dollops of colour, and despite being above a pub, are well insulated. Dog-friendly, too. **£80**

EATING AND DRINKING

Cadwgan 10 Market St SA46 0AU ☎ 01545 570149. This unmissable, raspberry-pink building is a fabulous, unpretentious local that provides a wonderful antidote to Aberaeron's gentrification. It's like walking into someone's living room – someone who serves a rotating roster of real ales and a few bar snacks, that is. Daily noon–11.30pm.
Harbourmaster Hotel 1 Pen Cei, SA46 0BT ☎ 01545 570755, ⓦ harbour-master.com. Two places in one. The convivial bistro/bar, set around a cool, brushed-steel bar, is perfect for sinking into a sofa with one of their excellent Welsh ales or something from the extensive list of wines by the glass. There's no attempt to be flash, but the cooking is executed with aplomb. The restaurant (£35 for three courses) serves the likes of Cardigan Bay crab cake with pink grapefruit and ginger mayo, or you might plump for crispy cockles with chilli vinegar salt in the bistro, which also serves breakfast until 11.45am. Bistro daily 8am–late; restaurant daily noon–2.30pm & 6–9pm.
★**The Hive** Cadwgan Place, SA46 0BU ☎ 01545 570599, ⓦ thehiveaberaeron.com. Buzzy waterside café and bar/grill with several seating areas; the best is the sunny gravel terrace with brightly painted tables and benches. With an adjoining fishmonger's, the seafood menu is strong – the fish pie or the crab and chilli risotto are good places to start – but there's plenty more. Treat yourself, too, to some wonderful honey ice cream sold from the kiosk. Live music Fri evenings. Mon–Sat 10am–late, Sun 10am–4pm; kitchen daily noon–3pm & 6–9pm; kiosk daily 10.30am–6pm.
Naturally Scrumptious 18 Market St, SA46 0AX ☎ 01545 574733. Excellent deli groaning with Welsh cheese, pies, posh sausages and panini; otherwise, content yourself with the best cakes in town (hazelnut and amaretti, raspberry and almond) and a freshly brewed coffee in the breezy café to the rear. Mon–Sat 9.30am–4.30pm.
New Celtic 8 Market, St SA46 0AS ☎ 01545 570369, ⓦ newceltic.co.uk. The best fish and chips around (including gluten-free), to take away or eat in on their terrace; breakfasts, coffee and cakes, and an ice-cream parlour too. Daily 8am–9pm.

Llanerchaeron

Ciliau Aeron, A482, 3 miles east of Aberaeron, SA48 8DG • **House** April–Oct daily 11.30am–4pm • **Parkland** Daily 10.30am–5pm • March–Oct £7.45; Nov–March £3.75 (parkland only); NT • ☎ 01545 570200, ⓦ nationaltrust.org.uk/llanerchaeron • Bus #T1 stops on the main road, 1 mile from the site; alternatively, you can cycle or walk here along the Aeron Valley Trail, which begins just off South Rd in Aberaeron – bikes can also be hired from here (see p.263)

A remarkable example of a type of holding once common in these parts, **Llanerchaeron** is the substantially restored remains of a late eighteenth-century Welsh country estate. Over the last decade or so, a century of decline has been arrested and partially reversed, leaving the Nash-designed main house in pristine shape. The original, mostly Edwardian set-piece rooms only hint at the fact that just three decades ago this was someone's home; this is much more apparent in the servants' quarters and the serviced courtyard.

On the opposite side of the estate, you'll find the **Geler Jones** collection (Wed & Fri only), an impressive, if rather random, assemblage of nineteenth-century agricultural, industrial and domestic machinery belonging to a former Cardigan-based saddler; the undoubted highlight is a superb Fowler steam engine dating from 1923. The estate is also a working organic farm, with a considerable vegetable- and fruit-growing enterprise in the **walled garden**, a time capsule of horticultural history, featuring early greenhouses and hotbeds with underground heating styled on Roman hypocausts.

Teifi Valley

The meandering Teifi is one of Wales' most eulogized rivers for its spawning fish, otter population and the coracles that were a regular feature from pre-Roman times. The river flows through the **Teifi Valley**'s undulating, vivid-green countryside to the estuary at Cardigan, dotted with a string of pleasant little market towns with a strong Welsh ambience. This is the centre of Welsh **cheesemaking**, so you'll often find the good stuff on restaurant cheese platters; look out for Caws Cenarth.

The river is tidal almost as far up as the massive ramparts of **Cilgerran Castle**, though it narrows appreciably by the time it reaches the rapids at **Cenarth**. Further upstream, it swirls around three sides of another fortress at **Newcastle Emlyn**, and takes in the tiny university town of **Lampeter**. Beyond here, it passes through harsher landscapes to **Tregaron**, a good base for nearby **Llanddewi Brefi**, with some fine walks up into the Abergwesyn Pass and the reedy bogland of **Cors Caron**. The river's infancy can be seen in the solid village of **Pontrhydfendigaid**, famed for its annual eisteddfod, and the nearby ruins of **Strata Florida Abbey**, beyond which the river emerges from the dark and remote **Teifi Pools**.

Cilgerran Castle

Cilgerran, SA43 2SF • Daily: April–Oct 10am–5pm; Nov–March 10am–4pm • April–Oct £4; Nov–March free; CADW • ☎ 01239 621339, ⓦ cadw.gov.wales/daysout/cilgerran-castle

Just a couple of miles up the Teifi from Cardigan (four miles by road) is the commandingly situated village of **CILGERRAN**. Park considerately on the wide main street to visit the massive ramparts of **Cilgerran Castle** that rise on a high wooded bluff above the river, which was still navigable for seagoing ships during the castle's construction in 1100. In 1109, Nest (the "Welsh Helen of Troy") was abducted here by a lovestruck Prince Owain of Powys; her husband, Gerald of Pembroke, escaped by slithering down a toilet waste chute through the castle walls.

The massive dual-entry **towers** still dominate the castle, and the outer walls are some 4ft thicker than those facing the inner courtyard. Walkways high on the battlements – not for vertigo-sufferers – connect the other towers. The outer ward is a good example of the evolution of the keepless castle throughout the thirteenth century. Any potential attackers would be waylaid instead by the still-evident ditch and the outer walls and gatehouse, of which only fragmentary remains can be seen. Another ditch and drawbridge pit protect the inner ward underneath the two entry towers.

4

Cenarth

A lure for tourists since the nineteenth century, tiny **CENARTH**, six miles upstream from Cilgerran, is still chock-full of tearooms and gift shops thanks to its pretty (albeit rather tame) **rapids**, caused by the Teifi tumbling and churning its way over the craggy limestone. It's worth following the delightful, mile-long **nature trail**, which starts at the bridge and heads up along the river's edge and into the gorge before looping back down again – there's a good chance of seeing otters and kingfishers among other local wildlife; pick up a leaflet from the **National Coracle Centre**. Otherwise, there are a couple of stony **beaches** down by the bridge where you can dip your toes and enjoy a picnic (there are tables and benches) on a warm summer's day.

On the last Sunday of July, Cenarth becomes a hive of activity courtesy of the good-natured **River Festival**, which sees a variety of happenings in and around the water, such as coracle and duck races, make voice choirs and the like.

National Coracle Centre

Cenarth Mill, SA38 9JL • Easter–Sept Mon–Fri & Sun 10.30am–5.30pm; other times by appointment • £3.50 • ☎ 01239 710980, ⓦ coraclemuseum.co.uk

The riverside **National Coracle Centre** is a delightful small museum with intriguing displays of original coracles from all over the world, many of them from Wales. There are some fascinating stories here, not least in the bamboo coracle from Vietnam that was used to transport a handful of refugees hundreds of miles across the South China Sea to Hong Kong. The heyday of the coracle fishing industry in Wales was the early twentieth century, when some two hundred vessels would ply the waters hereabouts. Commercial practices started to wane at the end of the 1980s, though between April and August you may still see people fishing for salmon from these traditional boats, which the fishermen strap to their backs to haul upstream. Your best bet, though, if you want to see coracles in action, is to attend Cilgerran's fun annual **coracle races**, which take place in mid-August.

Newcastle Emlyn and around

An ancient farming and droving centre, **NEWCASTLE EMLYN** (Castell Newydd Emlyn) still retains an agricultural feel, particularly during the busy and bellowing Thursday market. The swooping meander of the Teifi River made the site a natural defensive position, first built on by the Normans. The "new" **castle** – of which only a few stone stacks and an archway survive – replaced this original fortress in the mid-thirteenth century. Although the ruins aren't impressive, the river setting, surrounded by grazing sheep and rugby fields, is quintessentially Welsh. The castle is tucked away at the bottom of dead-end Castle Terrace, which peels off the main street by a squat little stone **market hall**. That's about it for sights, but there are some decent cafés and pubs, along with a strong sense of community, an eclectic range of shops and an unhurried charm.

National Wool Museum

Dre-fach Felindre, 3 miles southeast of Newcastle Emlyn, SA44 5UP • April–Sept daily 10am–5pm; Oct–March Tues–Sat 10am–5pm • Free • ☎ 029 2057 3070, ⓦ museumwales.ac.uk

At the beginning of the twentieth century, the village of Dre-fach Felindre was at the heart of the Welsh wool trade, with 43 working mills in and around the village; today there are just thirteen fully operational mills remaining in Wales. One of these, the Cambrian Mills, has been turned into the marvellous **National Wool Museum**, which recalls the lower Teifi's prolific past as a weaving centre. Excellent exhibits span the entire process – from the different wools produced by Wales' eleven million sheep through to the machinery itself. Dobcross looms, willowing machines (for untangling wool), carding engines (which combs the wool after willowing) and spinning machines are on show; you may also get to see the "Mighty Mule" in action, which, with its four hundred spindles spinning the wool into yarn, is quite a sight at full throttle.

The **textile gallery**, meanwhile, displays stunning examples of the finished flannels, shawls and blankets, alongside Celtic couture and fashion accessories – look out for a selection of woollen dresses from Mary Quant. Here, too, is **Melin Teifi**, the museum's on-site commercial mill, whose clattering you can hear emanating from the weaving shed – you can view the men at work from the gallery, though such is the noise that you'll not want to hang around.

Teifi Valley Railway

Station Yard, Henllan, SA44 5TD, 4 miles east of Newcastle Emlyn • 11am–4.30pm: June to mid-July & Sept Tues–Thurs & Sun; mid-July to Aug daily • £2.50 • ☎ 01559 371077, ⓦ teifivalleyrailway.wales

A section of the old Newcastle Emlyn branch of the Great Western Railway has been converted into the delightful **Teifi Valley Railway**, where two vintage engines chunter along a short stretch of the old trackbed to Forest Halt, some two miles distant; plans are afoot to extend this, though at present it's roughly a twenty-minute round trip. There's also a sit-on Pixie train which shuttles back and forth along a short length of track, as well as a children's play area, crazy golf and café.

ARRIVAL AND DEPARTURE   NEWCASTLE EMLYN

By bus The #460, which stops by the Cattle Market on New Rd, serves Cardigan (Mon–Sat hourly; 30min) and Carmarthen (Mon–Sat hourly; 1hr 10min).

ACCOMMODATION AND EATING

The Daffodil A475, Penrhiwllan, 4.5 miles east, SA44 5NG • 01559 370343, • thedaffodilinn.co.uk. This large and summery village inn comprises a handsome, olive-green restaurant with skylight, cosy bar and, best of all, a raised wooden deck with fabulous valley views. Eye-catching dishes might include pea and asparagus ravioli with black truffle foam or local smoked trout fillet with orange and fennel salad (£16.95), and the two-course Sunday roast is tremendously popular (£18.95). Daily 11.45am–11pm; kitchen noon–2pm & 6–9pm.

Emlyn Hotel Bridge St, SA38 9DU • 01239 710317, • emlynhotel.co.uk. Nicely refurbished old coaching inn with stylish, modern rooms, plus gym, sauna and jacuzzi. The hotel's smart *Y Bistro* restaurant (mains from £12.95) is easily the best place to eat in town; there are also two informal bars where you can grab a light meal and a pint or glass of wine. Daily: restaurant noon–2.30pm & 6–9pm; bar 11am–11pm. **£120**

La Calabria Ffostrasol, 6 miles northeast, SA44 5JT • 01239 851101, • la-calabria.co.uk. Run by a Welsh-Italian in the converted cowshed of a farm, this place offers rustic southern Italian food – *pollo marsala*, *saltimbocca* (sirloin stuffed with Parma ham with ratatouille, £16.95), pasta and pizza – and caters well for kids. Be sure to try the ice cream made with milk from the owner's herd. Tues–Sat noon–2pm & 6–10pm.

Riverside Café Adpar, SA39 9ED • 01239 710404. Nestled up against the bridge at the northern end of town, this mint-coloured building, with a cooling tree-shaded terrace overlooking the Teifi, rustles up a comprehensive, all-veggie menu of light lunches – spinach and feta pie, for example, or leek and potato bake, all for around £6 – as well as cakes and other goodies. Mon–Sat 9.30am–4.30pm.

Lampeter

The old-fashioned town of **LAMPETER** (Llanbedr Pont Steffan), twenty miles east of Newcastle Emlyn, is best known as a remote outpost of the British university system, known as Trinity St David. It was founded in 1822 by the Bishop of St Davids to aid Welsh theological students unable to travel to England for their education. Though the town has fewer than three thousand residents, it's a lively place, with frequent gigs and theatre performances and an eclectic population of students, graduates who forgot to leave, hippies and farmers. At the end of July, the university grounds are taken over by the hugely enjoyable **Lampeter Food Festival**.

The town's three main streets – High, Bridge and College – meet at **Harford Square**, named after the local landowning family responsible for the construction of the early nineteenth-century **Falcondale Hall**, now an opulent hotel on the northern approach to Lampeter.

Lampeter Museum

College St, SA48 7ED • April–Oct Tues, Thurs & Sat 10am–4pm • Free • 01570 422769, • haneslambed.org.uk

Off College Street are the main university buildings, which include C.B. Cockerell's **St David's Building**, the original stuccoed quadrangle dating from 1827 and modelled along the lines of an Oxbridge college. Tucked right underneath the main buildings, the motte of Lampeter's long-vanished **castle** forms an incongruous mound amid such order. Occupying the old porter's lodge is the **Lampeter Museum** – possibly the country's smallest museum – which has rotating exhibitions on the town and area's history; these could cover anything from textiles and costume to furnishings and photography, and are usually a minor delight.

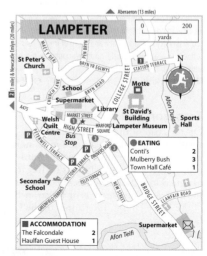

Welsh Quilt Centre

High St, SA48 7BB • **Galleries** Mid-March to Nov Tues–Sat 11am–4.30pm • **Shop** Tues–Sat 11am–4.30pm • £6 • ☎ 01570 422088, ⓦ welshquilts.com

The **Welsh Quilt Centre** shop-cum-gallery, brainchild of American antique dealer Jen Jones, is housed within Lampeter's old town hall. In the main gallery – which occupies the old courtroom – a new exhibition of antique or historic Welsh quilts is unveiled each year. Gallery two, which also stages a fresh exhibition each year, usually offers a contemporary slant, while, in the third gallery, which is basically an extension of the shop, you can buy the items on display. All the specimens amply illustrate what a colourful and artistic contribution the Welsh quilting industry has made to national culture.

ARRIVAL AND INFORMATION

LAMPETER

By bus Buses stop outside the NatWest Bank on High St. Destinations Aberaeron (Mon–Sat hourly; 30min); Aberystwyth (Mon–Sat every 45min–1hr; 1hr 15min); Carmarthen (Mon–Sat hourly, Sun 4; 1hr); Tregaron (Mon–Sat 9 daily; 30–40min).

Tourist information There's no tourist office in town, but staff at the Lampeter Museum can furnish you with local information, though they have very limited opening hours (see p.267).

ACCOMMODATION

The Falcondale Falcondale Drive, a mile or so west, SA49 7RX ☎ 01570 422910, ⓦ thefalcondale.co.uk. Italianate Victorian mansion in spacious parkland. Rooms (which vary enormously) are beautifully opulent; the most inspiring offer valley views. The meals are wonderful, too; mackerel with tomato jam, or woodland pork with fondant potato and fennel (£28) are sample offerings. Non-guests can enjoy afternoon tea (2.30–5pm; £15) or the excellent Sun lunch (£20 for two courses); booking required for all meals. Daily noon–2pm & 6.30–9pm. **£125**

Haulfan Guest House 6 Station Terrace, SA48 7HH ☎ 01570 422718, ⓦ haulfanguesthouse.co.uk. The only worthwhile option in the town centre, this quiet, family-run B&B has four rooms (two of which share a bathroom), the pick of which is the one just below street level. **£70**

EATING

Conti's 5 Harford Square, SA48 7HD ☎ 01570 422223. Venerable, Italian-run café whose rich, home-made, organic ice creams (salted caramel, Welsh honey) and sorbets (lemon, mango) have been pulling in the punters for the best part of seventy years – indeed, you'll find their ice cream widely distributed throughout the region. On a cooler day, try hot fudge cake and a cup of freshly roasted coffee and watch the world go by through the big bay windows. Mon–Sat 9am–5pm.

Mulberry Bush 2 Bridge St, SA48 7HG ☎ 01570 423317. Airy café above a long-standing wholefood shop, serving tasty vegetarian dishes such as Perl Las cheese and pepper quiche, or cashew nut risotto (£7.50). Occasional music nights. Mon–Sat 9am–5.30pm.

Town Hall Café High St, SA48 7BB ☎ 01570 421599. Smart, light-filled café and deli next to the Welsh Quilt Centre, offering filled sandwiches, baguettes and paninis, alongside charcuterie, pork pie and cheese boards (all £7), as well as good coffee and cakes. Mon–Sat 9am–4pm.

Tregaron and around

On the cusp of the verdant Teifi Valley and the desolate moors rising above it, the small town of **TREGARON**, ten miles northeast of Lampeter, was for long seemingly untouched by the modern world, but is now gradually being drawn into the twenty-first century. All roads to Tregaron lead into the spruced-up **market square**, hemmed in by solid eighteenth- and nineteenth-century buildings. The **statue** in the centre of the square is of Tregaron-born Henry Richard (1812–88), the founder of the Peace Union, forerunner of the League of Nations and, subsequently, the United Nations.

Rhiannon Welsh Gold Centre

Cnr Dewi Rd & Market Square, SY25 6JL • Mon–Sat 9.30am–5pm • ☎ 01974 298415, ⓦ rhiannon.co.uk

Tregaron-born Rhiannon Evans has been designing Celtic-inspired jewellery for the best part of forty years, and there's every chance that you'll get to see her at work in the classy **Rhiannon Welsh Gold Centre**. The items you see here are fashioned from both silver and gold, with some Welsh gold mined in north Wales. Displays are backed up with an art gallery exhibiting predominantly Welsh artists, and a museum of Celtic art: among the many beautiful pieces on show are clasps, brooches and fasteners, invariably featuring an animal symbol and/or the *triskele*, a triple spiral motif. There's also a good café.

Cors Caron

B4343, 2 miles north of Tregaron, SY25 6JF • Open access • Free • ⓦ ccw.gov.uk

The Afon Teifi meanders through a wide, flat valley into the eerie wetland of **Cors Caron** (Tregaron Bog), a national nature reserve of peatland that was once cut for fuel. It is one of the most prodigious wildlife areas in Wales, home to rare marsh grasses, black adders, buzzards, red kites and hen harriers. A couple of walks lead off from a parking area beside the **Ystwyth Trail** (see box, p.277), which follows part of the old Great Western Railway line along the bog's flanks. Easiest is a wheelchair-accessible **boardwalk** (two-mile loop; 1hr; flat) that weaves out through cotton grass, bog mosses and birch to a hide with huge windows. Part-way round you can spur off on the **Riverside Walk** (four miles; 2–3hr; uneven), which extends into a large loop along the infant Teifi and back along the disused railway.

Strata Florida Abbey

Six miles north of Tregaron, SY25 6ES • Daily: April–Oct 10am–5pm; Nov–March 10am–4pm • April–Oct £4; Nov–March free; CADW • ☎ 01974 831261, ⓦ cadw.gov.wales/daysout/strata-florida-abbey

In glorious rural solitude against wide-open skies and sheep-flecked hills stand the atmospheric ruins of **Strata Florida Abbey**, originally located in Ystrad Fflur, "the valley of the flowers", two miles away, but relocated in its early years to this equally fertile spot. Founded in 1164, the Cistercian abbey swiftly grew into a centre for milling, farming and weaving, and became an important political centre for Wales. In 1238, a dying Llywelyn the Great, fearful that his work of unifying Wales under one ruler would disintegrate, summoned the lesser Welsh princes here to command them to pay homage to his son, Dafydd.

Although very little survived Henry VIII's dissolution of the monasteries, the huge, Norman west doorway gives some idea of the church's vast dimensions. Fragments of side-chapels include beautifully tiled medieval floors, and there's also a serene cemetery. A yew tree in the neighbouring graveyard shades the spot where Dafydd ap Gwilym, fourteenth-century bard and contemporary of Chaucer, is said to be buried.

ARRIVAL AND DEPARTURE   TREGARON

By bus Services from and to Aberystwyth (Mon–Sat 10 daily; 1hr 10min) and Lampeter (Mon–Sat 8 daily; 30–40min) arrive at and leave from the market square.

ACCOMMODATION AND EATING

Llew Du Mill St, Pontrhydfendygaid, 1 mile west of Strata Florida, SY25 6BE ☎ 01974 831624, ⓦ black lionhotel.co.uk. The "Black Lion" is a great local pub, particularly welcoming to cyclists and walkers, with a roaring fire when the temperature drops. Bar meals are unsophisticated but well made, and there are comfortable B&B rooms. Daily 11am–11pm. **£70**

Talbot Hotel Market Square, SY25 6JL ☎ 01974 298208, ⓦ ytalbot.com. Dominating the main square, this classically symmetrical old drovers' inn has been given a smooth contemporary gloss, its thirteen rooms stylishly spare and well appointed. The classy Modern British restaurant uses local produce to wonderful effect in dishes like the tart made of Pantysgawn goat's cheese, caramelized onion and beetroot; the same menu is served in the lovely old bar, which retains its low timber beams, slate flooring and inglenook fireplace. The Welsh ales and ciders are terrific. Daily: bar 11am–11pm; restaurant noon–2.30pm & 6–9pm. **£120**

Aberystwyth and around

Midway along the Cambrian coast, spirited **ABERYSTWYTH** (or "Aber", as it's known locally) is a blast of fresh sea air. Two long bays skirted by pebbly beaches curve between twin rocky heads: **Constitution Hill** to the north, and **Pen Dinas** to the south above the town harbour's marina, where both the Rheidol and Ystwyth rivers empty into the sea. East of the town centre, the hillside suburb of **Penglais** is home to the graceful Portland stone buildings of Wales' **National Library** – the presence of which makes the city home, it's claimed, to more books per capita than anywhere else in the world – and the modernist blocks of Aberystwyth University, one of the UK's most prestigious educational institutions (the Prince of Wales, Prince Charles, studied here). There are plenty of other cultural and other diversions in town, as well as an array of Victorian and Edwardian seaside trappings, including a **cliff railway**.

Pubs – and there are loads – stay open late, the political scene is green-tinged, and the town is emphatically Welsh (the *Cymdeithas yr Iaith*, or Welsh Language Society, was founded in Aberystwyth in 1963 and is still here). It's an easy-going and enjoyable place to gain an insight into the national psyche.

The precursor of Aberystwyth is the inland village of **Llanbadarn Fawr**, the seat of Wales' oldest bishopric between the sixth and eighth centuries, whose massive parish church still reeks of past power. Aberystwyth and Llanbadarn grew together around the church and the thirteenth-century seafront castle, minting its own coins and headquartering Owain Glyndŵr's revolutionaries in the Middle Ages.

4

Constitution Hill and the cliff railway

Cliff Terrace, SY23 2DN • Railway April–June, Sept & Oct daily 10am–5pm; July & Aug daily 10am–6pm; winter hours are unpredictable so call or check online in advance • £5 return • ☎ 01970 617642, ⊕ aberystwythcliffrailway.co.uk

The 430ft-high **Constitution Hill** (Y Graig Glais) rises sharply from the rocky beach at the long Promenade's northern end. It's accessible on foot, though if you don't fancy the invigorating but stiff walk, you can take the clanking 1896 **cliff railway**, which creeps up the crooked tracks at scarcely more than walking pace from the grand terminus building at the top of Queen's Road, behind the Promenade. Originally employing a water balance system, it was electrified in 1921, and remains Britain's longest electric funicular railway. On a clear day, the views of Cardigan Bay are fantastic.

Camera obscura

Cliff Terrace, SY23 2DN • April–Oct daily 11am–4pm • £1 • ☎ 01970 617642, ⊕ aberystwythcliffrailway.co.uk

At the top of Constitution Hill you'll find a café, picnic area, telescopes and an octagonal **camera obscura**, a device that uses a mirror and hefty lens to project close-up and long-shot views over the town, the surrounding mountains and bays. It also offers a vista of the hordes of caravans to the north, resembling legions of tanks poised for battle. The existing structure was built in 1985 on the ground plan of the Victorian original, but with its scale expanded to make it the largest of its type in the world.

Ceredigion Museum

Terrace Rd, SY23 2AQ • Mon–Sat: Easter–Oct 10am–5pm; Nov–Easter noon–4.30pm • Free • ☎ 01970 633088, ⊕ ceredigion.gov.uk

The **Ceredigion Museum** is atmospherically housed over three floors in the ornate Edwardian Coliseum music hall, which functioned as a variety theatre until the 1930s and then as a **cinema** until 1977; much to the delight of the locals, screenings resumed here in 2016, and there are usually fortnightly showings (typically, and fittingly, old classics).

ABERYSTWYTH

6 (3 miles), Borth (5 miles) & Machynlleth (20 miles)

ACCOMMODATION	
Aberystwyth University	7
Bodalwyn	1
Conrah Hotel	8
Glan y Môr Leisure Park	6
Gwesty Cymru	4
Maes-y-Môr	3
Richmond Hotel	2
Yr Hafod	5

EATING	
Agnelli's	4
Gwesty Cymru	1
Pysgoty	5
Treehouse	3
Ultracomida	2

DRINKING	
Rummers	3
Ship and Castle	1
Yr Hen Lew Du	2

CEFN LLAN

Aberystwyth Arts Centre

Students Union

Aberystwyth University

A487

PENGLAIS ROAD

Drwm

National Library of Wales

A44

▶ Church of St Padarn, Llanbadarn Fawr (0.5 mile)

▶ Aberystwyth Rugby Club (0.5 mile)

Bronglais Hospital

LLANBADARN ROAD

University Sports Ground

BOULEVARD ST. BRIEUC

Constitution Hill (0.5 mile) ▲

Cliff Railway

QUEENS AVE

MARINE TERRACE

North Beach

NORTH ROAD

Town Hall

QUEEN'S ROAD

BATH STREET

PORTLAND ST

NORTH PARADE

PORTLAND ST

NORTHGATE ST

POPLAR ROW

STANLEY ROAD

School of Art Gallery and Museum

TERRACE ROAD

Ceredigion Museum

CAMBRIAN STREET

ELM TREE AVENUE

Bus Station

ALEXANDRA ROAD

Train Station

Vale of Rheidol Railway

PARK AVENUE

Pier

MARKET STREET

EASTGATE

DARKGATE STREET

GRAYS INN RD

QUEENS ST

MILL STREET

Pavilion

Old College

NEW ST

PIER ST

BRIDGE ST

HIGH ST

Market

VULCAN ST

St Michael's

KING STREET

SOUTH ROAD

PENPARCAU ROAD

NEW PROMENADE

Castle

SEA VIEW PL.

War Memorial

NEW PROMENADE

SOUTH MARINE TER.

Marina

River Rheidol

TREFECHAN RD

PEN-YR-ANGOR

A487

South Beach

CARDIGAN BAY

▶ 8 (3 miles) & Cardigan (40 miles)

▶ Pen Dinas (1.5 miles) & Tanybwlch

N

0   200   yards

Mementos of the building as a theatre and cinema give a sense of place to an otherwise wonderfully disparate collection. A fascinating section charts the seafaring exploits in the bay, where more than a thousand ships were built during the eighteenth and nineteenth centuries – look out for the barometer designed by Robert Fitzroy, captain of HMS *Beagle* during Darwin's voyage to Tierra del Fuego. There's much more besides, including an interesting look at the history of time-keeping.

Old College

King St, SY23 2AY • ☎ 01970 623111, Ⓦ aber.ac.uk/en/oldcollege

West of Marine Terrace and the spindly **pier**, the seafront is dominated by the dazzling, John Nash-designed, turreted villa known as the **Old College**. Dating from 1790, the villa was massively extended in the 1860s as a hotel, designed to soak up the anticipated masses arriving on the new rail line – the hotel failed, however, and in 1872 it was sold to the fledgling university, whose property it remains. Indeed, it was the focus of most university activity until the 1960s, when work began to develop the Penglais campus (see p.274). Plans are afoot to redevelop the college into a cultural hub, but in the meantime it's always worth checking to see what exhibitions they've got on.

The castle

Open access • Free

At the southern end of the Promenade, a rocky headland is occupied by the **castle** ruins, which stare blankly out to sea. Built by Edward I as part of his conquest of Wales, the thirteenth-century fortress is more notable for its breezy position than for the buildings themselves, of which the two outer gates are the most impressive remains.

4

The harbour and Pen Dinas

South of the castle is the quiet, sandy beach along South Marine Terrace, which peters out by the wide **harbour**, the mouth of the Rheidol and Ystwyth rivers. The quietest beach is further south still, across the other side of the rivers' mouth, at **Tanybwlch**. High above the shingle strand is the Iron Age hillfort of **Pen Dinas** (413ft), crowned with what looks like a chimney – actually an 1853 memorial to the Duke of Wellington. Paths lead to the top from the car park at Tanybwlch.

School of Art Gallery and Museum

Buarth Mawr, SY23 1NG • Mon–Fri 10am–5pm • Free • ☎ 01970 622460, Ⓦ aber.ac.uk/en/art/gallery-museum

Aberystwyth's splendid **School of Art** is housed inside the Edward Davies building. Originally bequeathed to the university by the Davies sisters of Gregynog Hall (see p.241), this impressive Edwardian building, topped with a distinctive cupola, has been the home of the university's art department since 1995. The **public galleries** on the ground floor mount touring exhibitions and rotating exhibitions from the university's extensive permanent collection, with an emphasis on Welsh art.

National Library of Wales

Penglais Rd, SY23 3BU • Mon–Fri 9.30am–6pm, Sat 9.30–5pm; guided tours (1hr) Mon 11am & Wed 2.15pm • Free; guided tours £5 • ☎ 01970 632800, Ⓦ llgc.org.uk • Bus #03 (Mon–Fri every 20min; Sat & Sun hourly) from the bus station

Housed in a massive white stone Edwardian building overlooking the town, the **National Library of Wales**, established in 1907, possesses fine manuscripts including the oldest extant Welsh text, the twelfth-century *Black Book of Carmarthen*, and the earliest manuscript of *The Mabinogion* – these are occasionally on show in the excellent temporary exhibitions. Displays from the library's permanent collection of books, manuscripts and papers include the **World of the Book**, which looks at the history of the written word and publishing in Wales. Also here is the **Nanteos Cup**, an ancient mazer bowl, or chalice, discovered at Strata Florida Abbey around 1880. Actually little more than a fragment of wood, albeit one with alleged healing properties, the cup (named after the nearby mansion in which it was kept, by a group of monks, for many years) is believed by some to be the holy grail, though it more likely dates from the fourteenth or fifteenth century; regardless, its mythological status ensures a steady stream of devotees.

As one of the UK's copyright repositories, the library holds copies of every new book published in Britain. If you're tracing family history you'll want access to the **Reading Rooms**, for which you'll need two forms of ID, including one that shows your current address. Otherwise, all manner of (often free) events are held at the library, including films, exhibitions, live performances and lectures – and there's a good café to boot. You could easily spend a few hours here.

Aberystwyth Arts Centre

Penglais Rd, SY23 3DE · ☎ 01970 623232, ⊚ aberystwythartscentre.co.uk

The excellent **Aberystwyth Arts Centre**, a quarter of a mile uphill from the National Library, sits in the middle of the university's main campus. A curious mix of 1960s brutalism and postmodern elegance, the centre is a great place to while away an hour or two, taking in the temporary art and photographic exhibitions, browsing the designer crafts and bookshops, catching a film or enjoying a drink in the café, which affords sublime views over the town and bay.

Church of St Padarn

Llanbadarn Fawr, just off the A44, 1 mile southeast of Aberystwyth, SY23 3QY · Generally daily 10am–4pm · ☎ 01970 612944, ⊚ st-padarns.llanbadarn.org.uk

The suburb of **Llanbadarn Fawr**, the original settlement from which Aberystwyth grew, warrants little attention but for the stunning sight of the massive, thirteenth-century **church of St Padarn**. The site's religious association goes back to the Breton St Padarn who established a monastic settlement here in the second half of the sixth century, decades before even St Augustine's mission to the English of 597 AD.

Inside the church, opposite the main door, hangs an enlargement of a page from *Rhygyfarch's Psalter* of 1079, one example of the beautifully decorated texts for which the monks of Llanbadarn became renowned. In the south transept, there's a fascinating exhibition on St Padarn's monastic foundation and the area's history that includes two fine tenth-century crosses, moved inside from the churchyard in 1916. The taller one, about 8ft high, is woven with exquisite Celtic tracery. Perhaps the most entertaining part of the exhibition deals with poet **Dafydd ap Gwilym** (c.1320–70) and his upbringing in Llanbadarn parish. His poem *Merched Llanbadarn* ("Women of Llanbadarn") tells of his frustration at sitting in the church watching the beautiful parish girls:

Plygu rhag llid yr ydwyf,
Pla ar holl ferched y plwyf!
Am na chefais, drais drawsgoed,
Onaddun'yr un erioed,
Na morwyn fwyn ofynaig,
Na merch fach, na gwrach, na gwraig.

Passion doubles me over,
Plague take all the parish girls!
Because, frustrated trysting,
I've had not a single one.
No lovely, longed-for virgin,
Not a wench nor witch nor wife.

ARRIVAL AND INFORMATION	**ABERYSTWYTH**
By train The train station is in the centre of town on Alexandra Rd, a 10min walk from the seafront.	Destinations Borth (10–12 daily; 12min); Machynlleth (10–12 daily; 30min).

By bus The main bus station is next to the train station on Alexandra Rd.

Destinations Aberaeron (Mon–Sat every 30min, Sun 3; 40min); Borth (Mon–Sat hourly; 30min); Cardigan (Mon–Sat hourly, Sun 3; 1hr 45min); Carmarthen (Mon–Sat hourly; 2hr 20min); Lampeter (Mon–Sat hourly; 1hr 15min); Machynlleth (hourly; 40min); New Quay (Mon–Sat hourly, Sun 3; 1hr); Pontrhydfendigaid (Mon–Sat 5 daily; 45min); Tregaron (Mon–Sat 10 daily; 1hr); Ynyslas (Mon–Sat hourly; 35min).

Tourist office Sharing the entrance with the Ceredigion Museum, Terrace Rd (Mon–Sat 10am–5pm; ☎01970 612125, ⊛discoverceredigion.gov.uk), the tourist office can help with accommodation and sells tickets for local events.

ACCOMMODATION

Aberystwyth has a healthy, if largely uninspiring, stock of accommodation, with **guesthouses** and B&Bs predominating. It's generally reasonably priced; that said, anywhere on the **seafront** is likely to charge a premium. Note that everywhere fills up during **graduation week** (usually the second or third week of July), when prices invariably jump.

HOTELS AND GUESTHOUSES

Bodalwyn Queens Ave, SY23 2EG ☎01970 612578, ⊛bodalwyn.co.uk. Quiet and roomy guesthouse blending contemporary furnishings with original features such as decorative fireplaces. All seven rooms have well-appointed en-suite bathrooms, and breakfast is served in a sunny conservatory. **£85**

Conrah Hotel A487, 4 miles south, SY23 4DF ☎01970 617941, ⊛conrah.wales. This stately Georgian hotel has a bit of a businessy feel, but the rooms – either in the main house or within the spacious grounds – are very comfortable and the restaurant and lounges have great views; you'll also see red kites nesting in the grounds. **£90**

★**Gwesty Cymru** 19 Marine Terrace, SY23 2AZ ☎01970 6122252, ⊛gwestycymru.com. The town's most appealing place to stay by far, this classy guesthouse offers eight colour-themed, artfully designed rooms (four with sea view), each with handcrafted oak furnishings inlaid with slate, crisp white cotton sheets, and applestone-tiled bathrooms; the feel is most definitely modern Welsh. Breakfast is served in the half-basement restaurant. **£90**

Richmond Hotel 45 Marine Terrace, SY23 2BX ☎01970 612201, ⊛richmondhotel.uk.com. Traditional seafront hotel with tidy rooms, most of which are sea-facing, though there's no premium for these; there's a convivial bar and restaurant, too. **£85**

Yr Hafod 1 South Marine Terrace, SY23 1JX ☎01970 617579, ⊛yrhafod.co.uk. Good-value seafront accommodation, with six spacious, well-maintained, plainly furnished rooms (some en suites and several with sea views), appealingly situated south of the castle. There's also a snug little lounge with a large-screen TV and loads of travel books. **£70**

HOSTEL, CAMPING AND SELF-CATERING

Aberystwyth University Penglais, SY23 3FL ☎01970 621960, ⊛aber.ac.uk/en/visitors. During the university's summer recess (mid-June to Aug) the university offers single-bed en-suite accommodation in self-contained flats with bed linen, cooking facilities and access to the university facilities, including two sports halls and a heated pool. Prebooking required. Per person **£36**

Glan y Môr Leisure Park Clarach Bay, 3 miles north, SY23 3DT ☎01970 828900, ⊛sunbourne.co.uk. Situated on the other side of Constitution Hill, with a variety of options including on-site caravans and tent pitches affording fabulous sea views, plus a superb range of leisure facilities including (for an extra fee) a heated indoor pool and gym, plus bar. **£25**

Maes-y-Môr 25 Bath St, SY23 2NN ☎01970 639270, ⊛maesymor.co.uk. Brightly painted and very central hostel-cum-guesthouse offering nine rooms (seven twins, a double and a family option) with shared bathrooms. There's a guest kitchen and laundry facilities. No breakfast. **£50**

EATING

Aberystwyth has a limited but excellent selection of restaurants, many of which have a strong **Mediterranean** influence, while daytime café culture is thriving.

★**Agnelli's** 3 Bridge St, SY23 1PY ☎07969 959466. You'll find the best espresso for miles around at this warm and welcoming Italian-run deli/café, which goes down a treat with a slice of Sicilian cannoli with vanilla; there's more substantial food, too, such as grilled Tuscan sausages with pancetta, or baked aubergines in a Parmesan crust (£6.95). Mon–Sat 10am–8pm.

Gwesty Cymru 19 Marine Terrace, SY23 2AZ ☎01970 6122252, ⊛gwestycymru.com. Accomplished slate-floored half-basement restaurant with an exciting modern Welsh menu featuring the likes of Welsh lamb rump with sautéed kale, leeks and Parmentier potatoes (£19.50), and Welsh honey and lavender crème brûlée. The seaview terrace out front is an ideal spot for a pre-dinner drink on a warm evening. Mon–Sat noon–2.30pm & 6–9pm, Sun noon–2.30pm.

★**Pysgoty** The Harbour, South Promenade, SY23 1JY ☎01970 624611, ⊛pysgoty.co.uk. Located in a former public convenience (yes, really), the "Fish House" fully deserves its many plaudits. It's a tiny space, with just four tables inside (which must be booked) and a further half a dozen out on the breezy deck, with invigorating sea views. The food is more or less whatever comes in off the boat that day, so you might end up with wild turbot with chorizo mash or fillet of John Dory with pea and mint risotto (£18), but you'll usually find a couple of house staples such as Cardigan Bay lobster with herb butter (£18.50). Tues & Wed 10am–5pm, Thurs–Sat 10am–10pm.

Treehouse 14 Baker St, SY23 2BJ ☎01970 615791, ✆ treehousewales.co.uk. Upbeat café above a bustling little organic shop. While the lunchtime menu is largely vegetarian, there is usually one daily meat-based special,

and there are gluten-free options (mains £7.50). It's no less enjoyable for coffee and home-made cakes. Mon–Fri 10am–5pm, Sat 9am–5pm.

★**Ultracomida** 31 Pier St, SY23 2LN ☎01970 630686, ✆ ultracomida.co.uk. Spain comes to Aber in this fabulous deli, its wall lined with Iberian wines, meats and olives, alongside French and Welsh cheeses and all manner of other treats. You can sample tapas (£4–5), like *croquetas* with Welsh cheddar and chilli jam, or deep-fried Basque peppers in tempura batter, in the casual restaurant/bar at the rear, which is also a cool spot to kick back with a coffee. Deli Mon–Sat 10am–6pm, Sun noon–5pm; restaurant Mon 10am–5pm, Tues–Sat 10am–10pm, Sun noon–4pm.

DRINKING

Aberystwyth's nightlife is a cosmopolitan, year-round affair, thriving on students in term time and visitors in the summer. With lots of good **pubs**, the town is also a good place to hear Welsh **music** and a lively centre for theatre and cinema.

Rummers Bridge St, SY23 1QD ☎01970 625177. Studenty, late-closing pub with slate floors, outdoor seating by the river and live music most weekends – it calls itself a wine bar but you're better off sticking to beer and spirits, and they also have an excellent gin menu. Daily 7pm–late.

Ship and Castle Corner of Vulcan and High sts, SY23 1JG ☎01970 612334. Much smarter inside than out, this nicely refurbished, and very welcoming, pub takes considerable pride in having the best selection of real ales

in town; there's a great little pool table, too. Mon 4pm–midnight, Tues–Sun 2pm–midnight.

Yr Hen Lew Du 14 Bridge St, SY23 1PZ ☎01970 615378. "The Old Black Lion" is a boisterous, very Welsh and hugely enjoyable pub that's easily the best place in Aberystwyth to catch an international match on the big screen – there are six of them, and comfy leather sofas from which to watch. Mon–Thurs & Sun noon–midnight, Fri & Sat noon–1.30am.

ENTERTAINMENT

Aberystwyth Arts Centre The University, Penglais SY23 3DE ☎01970 623232, ✆ aberystwythartscentre .co.uk. The main venue for arthouse cinema, touring theatre, classes, events and wide-ranging temporary exhibitions (see p.274). Look out, too, for the Aberystwyth Musicfest in late July, which features mostly classical and jazz. Days and hours vary.

Côr Meibion Aberystwyth Aberystwyth Rugby Cub, Plascrug Ave, SY23 1HL ☎01970 202980, ✆ aberchoir .co.uk. Visitors are welcome to attend rehearsals of the Male Voice Choir. Thurs 7–8.30pm.

Drwm National Library of Wales, Penglais, SY23 3BU ☎01970 632800, ✆ llgc.org.uk. Small but very hip centre for film, lectures and concerts. Days and hours vary.

Vales of Rheidol and Ystwyth

The Rheidol winds its way down to Aberystwyth through the secluded, wooded **Vale of Rheidol**, where occasional old industrial workings have moulded themselves into the contours, past waterfalls and minute villages. Devil's Bridge is easily accessed by the Vale of Rheidol Railway (see below) and the Rheidol Cycle Trail (see box opposite) and by car. For a **day out**, drivers can head straight for Devil's Bridge (along the A4120), then get to the lead mines in time for the kite feeding at **Bwlch Nant yr Arian**. Note, though, that if you stay for the feeding you'll probably be too late for side-trips to the **Cwm Rheidol Reservoir** and the **butterfly house** on the same day.

Vale of Rheidol Railway

Park Ave, Aberystwyth, SY23 1PG • April–Oct 2–4 trains most days • £21 return • ☎01970 625819, ✆ rheidolrailway.co.uk

The glorious Vale of Rheidol is best seen from the 23.5in-gauge **Vale of Rheidol Railway**, a narrow-gauge steam train which huffs and puffs from Aberystwyth to the Devil's

---

CYCLING THE VALE OF RHEIDOL AND THE YSTWYTH TRAIL

You can explore the Vale of Rheidol by bike along the **Rheidol Cycle Trail**, a combination of designated cycle paths and quiet country lanes that runs eighteen miles from Aberystwyth to Devil's Bridge: Aberystwyth's tourist office has a free leaflet outlining the route. Bikes can be taken on the Vale of Rheidol Railway (£5), but may be refused during busier times.

The twenty-mile **Ystwyth Trail** from Aberystwyth to Tregaron is another winner, partly following the trackbed of the Manchester & Milford Railway – which became the Great Western Railway Company – across Cors Caron (see p.270).

Bridge along twelve miles of steep hillsides, climbing more than 650ft in the process. It was built in 1902, ostensibly for the valley's lead mines but with a canny eye on its tourist potential. For many years it operated as part of British Rail's network, running steam trains until 1989 (more than twenty years after steam locos had ceased operating elsewhere). The railway is now owned by a private group that operates it using authentic Rheidol rolling stock. The trip takes one hour each way (though you can break your journey at any of the seven intermediate stations), and is most enjoyable from the comfortable first-class observation carriage (£3 extra each way) or the open-sided "summer car".

Cwm Rheidol Reservoir and Rheidol Power Station

Four miles east of Capel Bangor, SY23 3NF • Visitor centre Easter & May–Sept daily 10.30am–4.15pm; free power station tours (Mon–Fri; 45min) must be prebooked online • Free • ☎ 01970 880667, ⓦ statkraft.com • Vale of Rheidol trains stop (upon request) at the nearby Rheidol halt (see opposite)

Midway along the valley, the Rheidol is dammed at the **Cwm Rheidol Reservoir**, the final element in a small, showpiece hydroelectric scheme that starts high in the headwaters at the Nant-y-moch Reservoir. The history of the Norwegian-owned **Rheidol power station** is explained at the visitor centre, where you can view a handful of items (pulpit, oil lamp and bible) retrieved from the old Blaenrheidol chapel, which was drowned in 1964 as part of the scheme; there's a café here, too. Guided tours take you into the **power station**, where impressive sluices and channels funnel the water according to need.

Magic of Life Butterfly House

Behind the Cwm Rheidol Reservoir visitor centre, 4 miles east of Capel Bangor, SY23 3NB • April–Oct daily 10am–5pm • £7.50 • ☎ 01970 880928, ⓦ magicoflife.org

The **Magic of Life Butterfly House** houses dozens of beautiful butterflies and moths – including the lovely blue morpho – in a wild garden and tropically heated polytunnel. Visitors are encouraged to interact with the butterflies, which are at their most active in the mornings, making this the best time of day to visit. It's pricey for what it is.

Bwlch Nant yr Arian

A44, 9 miles east of Aberystwyth, SY23 3AB • Visitor centre daily 10am–5pm • Free • ☎ 01970 890453, ⓦ naturalresources.wales /bwlchnantyrarian • Bus #525 (Mon–Sat; 20min) from Aberystwyth stops outside

Superbly located deep within the Cambrian mountains, **Bwlch Nant yr Arian** is a prominent activity centre, as well as being one of the country's most important red kite feeding centres. From the **visitor centre**, which has a decent café with a pleasant deck, three well-marked **walking trails** head out into the evergreen forest and among the abandoned detritus of lead mining. The easiest trail (30min; wheelchair accessible) loops around a lake past the kite hide, while the Miners' (1.5 miles; 1hr) and Ridgetop trails (3 miles; 2hr) both require a moderate level of fitness as they feature some climbing. There are also two fabulous **running trails** (3 miles and 6.5 miles), which combine forest roads, singletrack paths and some tarmac.

Above all, the woods here offer top-class **mountain biking**, albeit for experienced riders, with three dedicated trails – two red (5.6 miles and 11 miles) and one black (22 miles; 4–5hr) – and a Skills Park, featuring a series of jumps, berms and rollers catering to all ages and abilities. Unfortunately, there's no bike rental – the nearest is in Cardigan (see p.257) or near Aberaeron (see p.263).

You can view the daily **red kite feeding** (3pm during daylight saving, 2pm at other times) from either the designated hide on the east side of the lake or a kite-viewing area on the opposite side. The latter is better, as this is where the kites – often up to two hundred of them – swoop down above your head before the squabble begins over the 20lb or so of beef and lamb placed on a grassy patch by the lake.

Silver Mountain Experience

A44, 1 mile east of Bwlch Nant yr Arian, SY23 3AB • Daily: April to mid-July, Sept & Oct 10am–4pm; mid-July to Aug 10am–5pm • £12.95 for all surface attractions plus one tour (45min), extra tours (all 45min) £3 • ☎ 01970 890620, ⓦ silvermountainexperience.co.uk • Bus #525 (Mon–Sat; 20min) from Aberystwyth stops outside

Bwlch Nant yr Arian forest's lush foliage makes it difficult to imagine how stark the valley once looked. A truer picture unfolds in the impressively barren scenery around the old Llywernog Silver Mine, which opened in the 1740s before closing in the early twentieth century. The site reopened as a museum in the early 1970s, since when it has expanded in an appropriately rustic manner and is now known as the **Silver Mountain Experience**.

There's a choice of three character-led **tours**: the straightforward, heritage-based "Miner's Life"; the somewhat spookier, fantasy-based "Black Chasm"; and "A Dragon's Tale", suited to younger visitors. Topside, you can enjoy the interactive "Time Lab" show, pan for fool's gold, build a dam or dowse for veins of galena, a silver-rich mineral once mined locally. The remains of waste tips scarring hillsides and shafts pockmarking former sites are now mostly hidden among the evergreens of the Rheidol Forest; in the latter half of the 1800s, the whole of northern Ceredigion lured galena speculators and opportunists by the trainful.

Devil's Bridge

A4120, 12 miles east of Aberystwyth, SY23 3JW • ☎ 01970 890233, ⓦ devilsbridgefalls.co.uk

Folk legend, incredible scenery and travellers' lore combine at **DEVIL'S BRIDGE** (Pontarfynach), a tiny settlement that can be reached by road or, far more scenically, via the Vale of Rheidol Railway, whose upper terminus is here (see p.276). Built largely for the long-established visitor trade, the village can be murderously busy in high season, so to avoid the congestion, you'd do well to visit at the beginning or end of the day, or out of season.

The main attraction is the **Devil's Bridge** itself, where three roads (the A4120, the B4343 and the B4574) converge and cross the churning River Mynach yards above its confluence with the Rheidol to form three bridges, one on top of the other. The most recently built of the three dates from 1901, while, immediately below it and wedged between the rock faces are the stone bridge from 1753, and, at the bottom, the original bridge, dating from the eleventh century and reputedly built by the monks of Strata Florida Abbey (see p.270).

The Punch Bowl and the three bridges

Open access • £1 coin in the turnstile

The classic view of the **three bridges** is from the **Punch Bowl** path. Standing by the modern road bridge with your back to the hotel, take the right-hand turnstile for a ten-minute loop. Slippery steps lead down to the deep cleft in the rock, where the water pounds and hurtles through the gap crowned by the bridges. The Punch Bowl is the name given to a series of rock bowls scooped by the sheer power of the thundering river, which rushes through past bright-green mossy rocks and saturated lichen.

Mynach Falls

Easter–Oct daily 9.30/9.45am–5/6pm; Nov–Easter open access • Easter–Oct £3.75; pay at the ticket office by the entrance to the walks; outside opening hours, and Nov–Easter, pay £2 in the turnstile

There are more extensive trails and many more steep steps across the road from the Punch Bowl. A path leads down into the valley and ultimately to the crashing **Mynach Falls**. The scenery here is magnificent: sharp, wooded slopes rising away from the frothing river, with distant mountain peaks surfacing on the horizon. A platform overlooks the series of falls, from where a steep flight of steps takes you further down to a footbridge dramatically spanning the river at the bottom.

ACCOMMODATION AND EATING	DEVIL'S BRIDGE

Hafod Hotel A4120, SY23 3JL ☏01970 890232, ⓦthehafod.co.uk. A few paces down from the bridge, the *Hafod* is a grand, alpine-style building possessing sixteen differing rooms (some overlooking the gorge), all of which are being upgraded. The agreeable, colonial-style brasserie and bar is the social hub of this scattered community, and does roaring trade from the many visitors; top-drawer food features the likes of pan-fried chicken and chorizo ciabatta from the lunchtime

sandwich menu and Welsh lamb pie (£12.95) from the main menu. Daily 10.30am–9pm. **£90**

Woodlands Caravan Park A4120, SY23 3JW ☏01970 890233, ⓦwoodlandsdevilsbridge.co.uk. Spacious, picturesque and well-run campsite that also has a gypsy pod sleeping three, plus great amenities including modern shower blocks, a laundry, a kids' playground, shop and tearooms. Camping **£18**, gypsy pod **£50**

Vale of Ystwyth

The **Vale of Ystwyth** runs pretty much parallel to the Rheidol, a couple of miles to the south. Four miles south of Devil's Bridge is the quiet village of **PONTRHYDYGROES**, the former centre of local lead-mining activity. The B4574 climbs out of the village and past the country estate of **Hafod**, once the seat of a great house belonging to the wealthy Johnes family. Their last mansion was demolished in 1958 as an unsafe ruin, and all that remains is the beautiful estate Thomas Johnes landscaped and forested two hundred years ago. The church, off the B4574, is the best place to embark on the waymarked **trails** that lead through the estate, past its trickling streams, monumental relics and planted glades, down to the river. A bridge spans the river, where paths fan out along its banks and up through the tiny valley of the Nant Gau.

North from Aberystwyth

The A487 runs **north from Aberystwyth** towards Machynlleth, slicing between the mountains to the east and the flat lands bordering the vast Dyfi estuary. The seaward plain is essentially a raised bog, **Cors Fochno**, visible from the main road but better viewed from the railway line or the coastal B4353. This road sneaks through **Borth**, stretching for nearly two miles along the seafront, to the **nature reserve** at **Ynyslas**, the best place to explore the sand dunes, flanking a supremely scenic **beach** looking across the Dyfi estuary.

Inland, the eighteenth-century iron foundry at **Furnace** heralds **Ynys-hir**, an RSPB nature reserve with an impressive range of bird habitats, and **Cors Dyfi**, where ospreys can be viewed for most of the summer.

Borth

Hemmed in by the sea on one side and a vast peat bog on the other, **BORTH**, five miles north of Aberystwyth, is an old fishing village that gradually adapted to caravan-park tourism. The settlement is strung out along ruler-straight High Street, which regularly gets battered by weather fronts from the Atlantic. Its three-mile-long shallow **beach** is excellent: swimming is fine as long as you don't go too far up towards the mouth of the Dyfi.

Stretching intermittently for a couple of miles between the northern reaches of Borth and Ynyslas is a remarkable **fossilized forest** where, at low tides, the sands near the water's edge are studded with the petrified stumps of a dozen or so 5000-year-old trees, a reminder that the coast was some twelve miles away when these trees were in their prime. A more romantic explanation is the Welsh legend that tells of a drowned land known as Cantre'r Gwaelod which was protected by sea walls and floodgates. Their keeper, Seithenyn, happened to get drunk the night of an almighty storm and the sea burst through, drowning a thousand people and fourteen settlements.

ARRIVAL AND DEPARTURE
BORTH

By train The train station is on Cambrian Terrace, midway along High St.
Destinations Aberystwyth (10 daily; 12min); Machynlleth

(10 daily; 18min).
By bus Bus #512 to Aberystwyth (Mon–Sat hourly; 25min) departs from the train station.

ACCOMMODATION AND EATING

Tir a Mor High St, SY24 5HZ ☎01970 872047. Cheery two-floored café-cum-gallery with squidgy sofas in the painted loft, where you can grab a pair of binoculars and gaze out across the Cors Fochno. It's a terrific ice-cream parlour too. Daily 9am–5pm.

YHA Borth High St, SY24 5JS ☎01970 871498, ⓦyha .org.uk/hostel/borth. Edwardian YHA hostel at the northern end of town, with four- to eight-bed dorms and some family rooms, as well as a kitchen, lounge and licensed bar. Bus #512 passes right outside. Breakfast £6.25. Dorms **£18**

Ynyslas Nature Reserve

Just off the B4353, 3 miles north of Borth, SY20 5JZ • **Visitor centre** Easter–Sept daily 9am–5pm • Free • ☎01970 872901, ⓦ naturalresources.wales

Northwards from Borth, the flat landscape meets the formidable sand dunes that line the southern side of the Dyfi estuary – the road follows the coast a couple of miles to the dramatic estuary-side **Ynyslas Nature Reserve**. In winter, wading and sea birds feed among the dunes and mud flats, while in summer, butterflies flit among vibrant sand plants growing in the grass. The views stretch inland to the mountains, along the estuary and coast, and over the river to the colourful huddle of Aberdyfi. Nestled among the dunes, the reserve's **visitor centre** is the starting point for a couple of lovely circular walks: the wheelchair-accessible "Dune" (1hr), and the more extensive "Ynyslas" (2hr), which takes in both the dunes and the saltmarshes. There are also free guided walks and tours most Sundays between May and September, which generally focus on the local flora and fauna, for example saltmarsh flowers, butterflies and sand lizards.

Dyfi Furnace

A487, 11 miles north of Aberystwyth, SY20 8PD • Open access • Free; CADW • ☎01443 336000, ⓦ cadw.gov.wales/daysout/dyfifurnace

During the latter half of the eighteenth-century, the barn-like **Dyfi Furnace** was the centre of the silver- and iron-smelting activities in Wales; charcoal, limestone and iron ore were brought here from Cumbria, before being cast into pig iron and shipped across to the forges in the Midlands. The power of the Einion River was harnessed using an immense water wheel driving the bellows, and with the recent installation of a generator this magnificent (albeit not original) wooden water wheel is once again producing power. Take two minutes to stroll around the back to a picturesque waterfall that feeds the water wheel.

Ynys-hir Nature Reserve

A487, 0.5 mile north of Dyfi Furnace, SY20 8TA • **Reserve** Daily 9am–9pm or dusk if earlier • £5 • **Visitor centre** Daily: April–Oct 9am–5pm; Nov–March 10am–4pm • ☏ 01654 700222, ⓦ rspb.org.uk/wales • Bus #X28 from Aberystwyth (30min) stops in the village of Eglwys-fach, from where it's a 15min walk to the visitor centre

The 2000-plus-acres of **Ynys-hir Nature Reserve** comprise five distinct habitats. Redstarts, pied flycatchers and lapwings flit about the ancient hanging oak woodland so typical of mid-Wales, while cormorants flock to the estuarine salt marshes, and red-breasted mergansers and elusive otters inhabit the freshwater streams and pools – in winter, there's the impressive sight of up to one hundred white-fronted geese descending upon the marshes. The remnant peat bogs are a riot of wild flowers in spring; winter brings water rails to the reed beds to join the herons. The attractions are obvious to the birders who return time and again to the network of hides and viewing points, but there's enough along the three one- or two-hour designated trails to interest anyone; you can rent binoculars (£5).

ACCOMMODATION AND EATING   YNYS-HIR

★**Ynyshir Hall** A487, beside the Ynys-hir Nature Reserve, SY20 8TA ☏ 01654 781209, ⓦ ynyshir.co.uk. Sublime country-house hotel in expansive manicured grounds – it's gracious without being the slightest bit stuffy. As gorgeous as the ten rooms are, the emphasis is very much on the food; the Michelin-starred restaurant, headed by chef Gareth Ward, presents sublime Modern British dishes using seafood from the Dyfi estuary, river fish and local game, as well as ingredients plucked from the kitchen garden and surrounding woods. Dishes such as pollock with black bean, crab with elderflower and wild strawberry, or sheep's yoghurt with olive oil and wood sorrel are listed on a nine-course lunch menu (£55), eighteen-course dinner menu (£110) or, for the ultimate gastronomic experience, the Chef's Table (£130). Booking essential. Tues 6.30–9pm, Wed–Sat noon–2pm & 6.30–9pm. **£210**

Cors Dyfi and the Osprey Project

A487, 5 miles north of Dyfi Furnace, SY20 8SR • **Cors Dyfi** Daily 10am–6pm • Free • **Osprey Project** April–Sept daily 10am–6pm • £3 • ☏ 01654 781414, ⓦ dyfiospreyproject.com

At the **Cors Dyfi** reserve, a short wheelchair-accessible boardwalk leads out among the reeds, ponds and bog plants. During the summer parts of the reserve are inhabited by water buffalo, which have been brought in to manage the invasive birch and willow that would otherwise turn the place into a forest. The best reason to visit, however, is for the **Osprey Project**; two ospreys, Monty and Glesni, nesting on the top of a pole, some 220yd away from the 360° observatory, which affords wonderful views of the Dyfi Valley and the Snowdonian mountains. There are currently four pairs of breeding ospreys in Wales, including the pair here, though, surprisingly, it wasn't until 2004 that these magnificent birds were first officially recorded in the country. In the visitor centre, CCTV cameras give you fabulous close-ups of the nest (livestreamed on the website): in May you might see the chicks hatch, while they typically fledge in August.

Southern Cadair Idris and the Dyfi and Talyllyn valleys

The southern coastal reaches of Snowdonia National Park are almost entirely dominated by **Cadair Idris** (2930ft), a five-peaked massif standing defiant in its isolation. Tennyson claimed never to have seen "anything more awful than the great veil of rain drawn straight over Cader Idris", but catch it on a good day, and the views from the top – occasionally stretching as far as Ireland – are phenomenal. During the last Ice Age, the heads of glaciers scalloped out two huge cwms from Cadair Idris' distinctive dome, leaving 1000ft cliffs dropping away on all sides to cool, clear lakes. The largest of these amphitheatres is Cwm Gadair, the **Chair of Idris**, which takes its name from a giant warrior poet of Welsh legend, although some prefer the notion that Idris' Chair refers to a seat-like rock formation on the summit ridge, where anyone spending the night (specifically New Year's Eve, some say) will become a poet, go mad or die.

Cadair Idris' southern limits are lapped by the broad expanse of the Dyfi estuary, which in turn bleeds into the grand, green scenery of the **Dyfi Valley**. The valley's focal point is the engaging town of **Machynlleth**, which lies just south of the renowned **Centre for Alternative Technology**.

There's pleasure in staying at small-scale coastal resorts such as **Aberdyfi**, a good base for exploring the inland cormorant colony at **Craig yr Aderyn**, the brooding thirteenth-century **Castell-y-Bere** and the quaint narrow-gauge **Talyllyn Railway**, which runs seven miles up the **Talyllyn Valley** to **Abergynolwyn** at the foot of Cadair Idris.

Machynlleth and around

MACHYNLLETH (pronounced Mah-hun-cthleth, and referred to locally as Mac) is Wales' "alternative" capital in more ways than one. Shortlisted as a possible capital of Wales in the 1950s and site of **Owain Glyndŵr**'s totemic fifteenth-century Welsh parliament, it retains some handsome architecture, while the town's excellent facilities, lively atmosphere and proximity to the coast make it an ideal jumping-off point for exploring

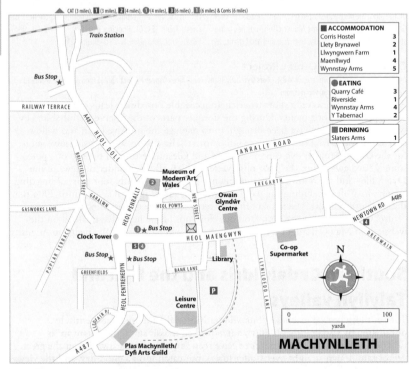

OWAIN GLYNDŴR, WELSH HERO

No name is so frequently invoked in Wales as that of **Owain Glyndŵr** (c.1349–1416), a potent figurehead of Welsh nationalism ever since he rose up against the occupying English in the first few years of the fifteenth century.

Little is known about the man described in Shakespeare's *Henry IV, Part I* as "not in the roll of common men". There seems little doubt that the charismatic Owain fulfilled many of the mystical medieval prophecies about the rising up of the red dragon. He was of **aristocratic** stock – descended from the princes of Powys and Cyfeiliog – and had a conventional upbringing, part of it in England, of all places. He studied in London and became a distinguished soldier of the English king before returning to Wales and marrying a local woman.

Wales in the late fourteenth century was a turbulent place. The brutal savaging a century earlier of Llywelyn the Last and Edward I's stringent policies of subordinating Wales had left a discontented, cowed nation where any signs of **rebellion** were sure to attract support. Glyndŵr became the focus of the rebellion when his neighbour, the English Lord of Ruthin, seized some of his land. When the courts failed to back him, Glyndŵr took matters into his own hands. With four thousand supporters and a new declaration that he was "Prince of Wales", he attacked Ruthin, and then Denbigh, Rhuddlan, Flint, Hawarden and Oswestry, before encountering an English resistance at Welshpool. As Glyndŵr consolidated his position in north Wales, English king Henry IV imposed punitive laws on Welsh land ownership, even outlawing Welsh-language bards and singers. Glyndŵr's support swelled enough for him to take the castles at Conwy, Harlech and Aberystwyth. By the end of 1403, he controlled most of Wales.

In 1404, Glyndŵr assembled a **parliament** of four men from every *commot* (community) in Wales at Machynlleth, drawing up mutual recognition treaties with France and Spain. He also had himself crowned ruler of a free Wales. A second parliament in Harlech took place a year later, with Glyndŵr making plans to carve up England and Wales into three as part of an alliance against the English king: Glyndŵr would rule Wales and the Marches of England. He then demanded independence for the Welsh Church from Canterbury and set about securing alliances with English noblemen who had grievances with Henry IV. This last, ambitious move heralded his downfall.

The English army concentrated with increased vigour on destroying the Welsh uprising, and the Tripartite Indenture was never realized. From then on, Glyndŵr lost battles, ground and castles and was forced into hiding – dying, it is thought, in Herefordshire.

Anti-Welsh laws stayed in place until the accession to the English throne of Henry VII, a Welshman, in 1485. Wales became subsumed into English custom and law, and Glyndŵr's uprising became an increasingly powerful symbol of frustrated Welsh independence. In modern times, the shadowy organization that surfaced in the early 1980s to burn the holiday homes of English people and English estate agents dealing in Welsh property took the name Meibion ("the sons of") Glyndŵr.

The figure of Glyndŵr, his trademark double-pointed beard to the fore, can often be seen gracing Welsh pub signs of inns called the Prince of Wales – as distinct from those who, by dint of being the first-born son of the reigning British monarch, have occupied the title ever since.

4

the area. It also boasts a long tradition of progressive and environmentally conscious thinking and innovation, long before such concerns became fashionable.

The wide main street is **Heol Maengwyn**, busiest on Wednesdays, when a lively **market** swings into action. Heol Maengwyn comes to an end at a fanciful **clock tower**, built in 1873 by local landowner, the Marquess of Londonderry, to commemorate his son and heir's coming of age.

Owain Glyndŵr Centre

Heol Maengwyn, SY20 8EE • Easter–Sept Mon–Sat 11am–3pm • Free • ☎ 01654 702932, ⓦ canolfanglyndwr.org

Glyndŵr's partly fifteenth-century **Parliament House**, a modest-looking black-and-white-fronted building concealing a large interior, is now home to the **Owain Glyndŵr Centre**. Displays chart the course of his life, military campaigns and downfall, and of the town's 1404 parliament, when he controlled almost all of what is now known as

Wales and even negotiated international recognition of the sovereign state (see box, p.283). The sorriest tales are from 1405 onwards, when tactical errors and the sheer brute strength of the English forced an ignominious end to the great Welsh uprising. The most important exhibit is a reproduction of the "Pennal Letter", sent by Glyndŵr to King Charles of France in 1406, in which he lays out his plans for an autonomous Welsh nation while simultaneously pledging his support for the idea of a French pope – the original letter resides in Paris.

Plas Machynlleth

Y Plas, SY20 8ER • Dyfi Arts Guild gallery Mon–Sat 11am–4pm • Free • ☎ 01654 702571, ⓦ dyfiartsguild.co.uk

Opposite the Owain Glyndŵr Centre, a path leads into the landscaped grounds of **Plas Machynlleth**, the elegant seventeenth-century mansion of the Marquess of Londonderry. Its solitude is entirely intentional: in the 1840s the marquess bought up all the surrounding buildings and had them demolished, and rerouted the main road away from his grounds. Today, the house accommodates the bright **Dyfi Arts Guild** gallery and shop, where you can view and buy a wide range of works of art; there's a super café here, too.

Museum of Modern Art, Wales

Heol Penrallt, SY20 8AJ • Mon–Sat 10am–4pm • Free • ☎ 01654 703355, ⓦ moma-machynlleth.org.uk

The **Museum of Modern Art, Wales** (MOMA Cymru) is housed in Y Tabernacl, a serene old chapel that hosts temporary exhibitions, including some from its own growing collection. It is also the place to go for theatre, comedy, concerts, good coffee and the highbrow **Gŵyl Machynlleth festival** (last week in Aug; ⓦ machynllethfestival.co.uk), which combines classical and folk music with theatre and debate.

Centre for Alternative Technology

A487, 3 miles north of Machynlleth, SY20 9AZ • Daily: April–Oct 10am–5pm; Nov–March 10am–4pm; guided tours (1hr; free) daily 2pm in the school hols • April–Oct £8.50; Nov–March free • ☎ 01654 705950, ⓦ cat.org.uk • Bus #34 (Mon–Sat every 1–2hr) from Machynlleth

After the inception of the **Centre for Alternative Technology** (CAT or *Canolfan y Dechnoleg Amgen*) during the oil crisis of 1974, seven acres of a once-derelict slate quarry were turned into an almost entirely sustainable community. At one stage, eighty percent of the power was generated from wind, sun and water, but this is no back-to-the-land hippie commune. The idea has always been to embrace technology – much of the on-site equipment was developed and built here, reflecting the centre's achievements in this field. With the general rise of eco-consciousness the emphasis has shifted more towards promoting its application in urban situations and, with this in mind, they've used low-carbon-footprint techniques – timber construction with lime-and-hemp cladding, for example – in building the Wales Institute for Sustainable Education (WISE) on this site. Its 22ft rammed-earth wall is the highest in Britain.

CAT's water-balanced **cliff railway** (Easter–Oct only) whisks visitors 200ft up from the car park to the main site, sensitively landscaped using local slate and wood; you can easily spend half a day sauntering around. There's plenty for kids, including a **children's theatre** (mainly mid-July to Aug), while the vegetarian **café** turns out delicious food and the excellent **shop** stocks a wide range of alternative literature, along with crafts and intriguing toys. The **Quarry Trail** – broken up into three routes, from thirty to sixty minutes – invites visitors to explore features of the former quarry site, though there are steep gradients in places.

Corris

CORRIS, a small former slate-quarrying settlement six miles north of Machynlleth in the middle of the Dyfi Forest, is home to the sweet little **Corris Railway**. Half a mile further up the valley, the **Corris Craft Centre** occupies a former slate mine, and houses half a

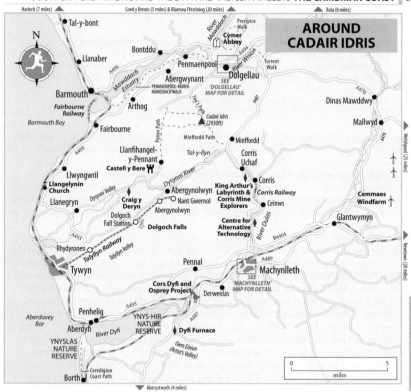

dozen or so craft shops, a gin distillery, café, children's playground and two of the area's main attractions.

Corris Railway and Museum

Station Yard, SY20 9SH • **Trains** Hourly 11am–4pm: May–July & Sept Sat, Sun & bank hols; Aug Mon, Tues, Sat & Sun • £6 return • **Museum** May–July & Sept Sat, Sun & bank hols; Aug Mon, Tues, Sat & Sun 10.30am–5pm • Free • ☎ 01654 761303, ⓦ corris.co.uk • The #34 bus from Machynlleth runs to Corris (Mon–Sat every 1-2hr; 15min)

Built in 1859 as a horse-hauled tramroad, and subsequently used to transport passengers until 1930, the **Corris Railway** today shuttles passengers along a half-mile stretch of the 27in-gauge line that linked the slate quarries of the Dulas Valley with the main line at Machynlleth. Starting at Station Yard, the train takes ten minutes to reach **Maespoeth**, where you have around thirty minutes to look around the old engine shed and workshop before the return. Housed inside the Station Yard terminus is a small **museum** with a nostalgic collection of rusting quarry wagons, station signs, vintage luggage and beautifully engraved brass plates; there's also a shop and café here.

King Arthur's Labyrinth

Corris Craft Centre, SY20 9RF • April–Oct daily 10am–5pm; call for winter hours • Labyrinth £11.50, Lost Legends £4.95, combined ticket £11.80 • ☎ 01654 761584, ⓦ kingarthurslabyrinth.co.uk • The #X27 from Machynlleth to Dolgellau runs to Corris Craft Centre (Mon–Sat every 45min–1hr, Sun 2; 15min)

Deep within the flooded tunnels of a former slate mine, **King Arthur's Labyrinth** is a fun subterranean jaunt through the legends around the mythical king. Following a short DVD presentation, you are led (with hard hat) into the mine proper by a guide dressed

MOUNTAIN BIKING IN MAC

Machynlleth has become one of the country's most important **mountain biking** centres, with a number of excellent purpose-built tracks nearby. The most impressive is a few miles southwest in **Derwenlas**, where there's the Mach 1 trail (10 miles; moderate), while, in **Ceinws**, just north of the CAT centre, there's the superb Cli-machx trail (9 miles; difficult to severe), which has one of the longest single-track descents in the UK; see ⓦ dyfimountainbiking.org.uk for more info. Unfortunately, nowhere in town offers **bike rental**; the closest is in Dolgellau (see p.294).

as a monk; a boat then carries you into the heart of the atmospherically lit mountain, where you proceed through several caverns complete with *son et lumière* tableaux illustrating various Welsh legends.

Up above ground, the cleverly conceived **Lost Legends of the Stone Circle** outdoor floral maze reveals "mystical stories echoing across the ages" by way of various iconic sculptural figures from Welsh folklore, alongside druid ruins and the stone circle itself; it's is a great way to help ensure these Welsh stories are retained by younger generations.

Corris Mine Explorers

Corris Craft Centre, SY20 9RE • Tours all year on demand, book ahead • Taster (50min) £12.50, Explorer (2hr) £27, Expedition (4hr) £52 • ☎ 01654 761244, ⓦ corrismineexplorers.co.uk • The #X27 from Machynlleth to Dolgellau runs to Corris Craft Centre (Mon–Sat every 45min–1hr, Sun 2; 15min)

With **Corris Mine Explorers** you head into different levels of the same old slate mine that houses King Arthur's Labyrinth, though the experience could hardly be more different. Sporting a climbing harness and miner's helmet, you'll ideally spend at least a couple of hours in the cool, dark tunnels that have been barely touched since the miners downed tools for the last time back in 1970. Ancient tallow candles are stuck to the walls, hand drills lie scattered along the passageways and winch flywheels still spin at the slightest touch. There's no production-line feel about these trips: all are tailored to the fitness of the group. You'll also hear fascinating stories about the lives of the miners, while adventurous parties could find themselves clipped into safety wires as they sidle along the steeply shelving walls of a vast slate cavern. Wear something warm and prepare to have fun.

ARRIVAL AND INFORMATION

By train Trains stop at the station, a 5min walk up Heol Penrallt from the clock tower.

Destinations Aberdyfi (8 daily; 20min); Aberystwyth (10–12 daily; 30min); Barmouth (8 daily; 1hr); Birmingham (8 daily; 2hr 15min); Borth (10–12 daily; 20min); Harlech (8 daily; 1hr 25min); Porthmadog (8 daily; 2hr); Shrewsbury (10 daily; 1hr 10min).

By bus Buses stop close to the clock tower, and many also

MACHYNLLETH AND AROUND

call at the train station.

Destinations Aberdyfi (Mon–Sat 7 daily, Sun 2; 25min); Aberystwyth (Mon–Sat hourly, Sun 3; 45min); Corris (Mon–Sat every 45min–1hr, Sun 2; 15min); Dolgellau (Mon–Sat hourly, Sun 2; 30min); Tywyn (Mon–Sat 7 daily, Sun 2; 35min).

Tourist information There is no tourist office, but staff at the Owain Glyndŵr centre may be able to help.

ACCOMMODATION

HOTEL AND GUESTHOUSES

Llety Brynawel Tower Rd, Pennal, 4 miles west, SY20 9DP ☎ 01654 791206, ⓦ lletybrynawel.co.uk. En route to Aberdyfi, this Georgian guesthouse offers four effortlessly cool rooms with period furnishings, cast-iron fireplaces and lush fabrics including soft Welsh blankets and cushions; caffeine fiends will enjoy the Nespresso machines. Breakfast is taken in their superb sister restaurant, the *Riverside*, a 2min walk away (see opposite). **£75**

Maenllwyd Newtown Rd, SY20 8EY ☎ 01654 702928, ⓦ maenllwyd.co.uk. Comfortable, low-key B&B in a

former manse with eight super-clean and well-maintained rooms, including a family room with DVD player. There's a large garden plus off-street parking. **£70**

Wynnstay Arms Heol Maengwyn, SY20 8AA ☎ 01654 702941, ⓦ wynnstay.wales. You'll want to shop around as there's considerable variation in the twenty-odd rooms at this early nineteenth-century coaching inn; some have heavy beams, creaky floors and a four-poster, others are relatively modern. The hotel is effectively the heart of the town's social life and there are cosy guest lounges where you can curl up with a book. **£95**

HOSTEL AND CAMPSITE

Corris Hostel Old Rd, Corris, SY20 9TQ ☎ 01654 761686, ⓦ corrishostel.co.uk. There's a strong ethical philosophy and a spiritual tenor to this low-key hostel, which occupies a wonderful old school building on a steep road just up in from the centre of the village. Accommodation is in two large single-sex dorms, doubles and several family rooms, and there are excellent self-catering facilities, though home-cooked (mostly vegetarian) meals are available. The garden, with a firepit, backs out onto thick woods. Groups only Oct–March. Breakfast £4.25. Dorms £16, doubles £38

Llwyngwern Farm Pantperthog, 3 miles north, near the Centre for Alternative Technology, SY20 9RB ☎ 01654 702492. Machynlleth's closest campsite, in a grassy field beside oaks and the burbling Afon Dulas. Facilities are limited to little more than toilets and hot showers. Closed Oct–March. Per person £8.50

EATING

Quarry Café 13 Heol Maengwyn, SY20 8EB ☎ 01654 702624, ⓦ thequarrycafemachynlleth.co.uk. This popular wholefood café offers a cracking veggie menu featuring the likes of chilli with Welsh yoghurt and the "Big Mach" burger (lentil patty, soya mayonnaise and a wholesome salad; £5.75). Mon–Fri 9am–4pm, Sat & Sun 10am–3pm.

Riverside Pennal, 4 miles west, SY20 9DW ☎ 01654 791285, ⓦ riversidehotel-pennal.co.uk. By some distance the best place to eat round these parts, this spruce pub has several eating areas (and a riverside garden) where you can enjoy scrumptious, simple dishes such as goat's cheese and red pepper salad (£6.50) or a rather wonderful spiced Mediterranean fish stew (£14). Daily 11am–11pm; kitchen noon–2.30pm & 6–9.30pm.

Wynnstay Arms Heol Maengwyn, SY20 8AA ☎ 01654 702941, ⓦ wynnstay.wales. While the classic slate-floored restaurant itself is justifiably popular (try grilled plaice with capers and mint butter; £14.50), most people are here for the superb pizzeria (£8–10) in an adjoining building. The bar is a fine place to cosy up in with a beer. Bar daily 11am–11pm; restaurant daily noon–2pm & 6.30–9pm; pizzeria Wed–Sun 4.30–9.30pm.

Y Tabernacl Museum of Modern Art, Heol Penrallt, SY20 8AJ ☎ 01654 703355. This refined little museum café doles out delicate cakes and excellent coffee in peaceful, arty surrounds. Mon–Fri 10am–3pm.

DRINKING

Slaters Arms Corris, SY20 9SP ☎ 01654 761324. Welcoming old village pub that comprises Corris' social centre – straightforward bar meals, a pool table, dominoes and fine, locally brewed ales. Daily 5pm–midnight.

Aberdyfi

The proud maritime heritage of **ABERDYFI** (sometimes anglicized to Aberdovey) has largely been replaced by its status as a well-heeled resort. Backed by lush mountains and with a south-facing aspect across the Dyfi estuary, Aberdyfi has one of the highest proportions of holiday homes anywhere on this coast. There's no watercraft rental, nor much else in the way of activities, but the deep, golden beach is fabulous. Swimming is possible; tidal currents make it potentially hazardous in town, so head about a mile and a half north to the safer waters of **Cemetery Beach**. It also makes a great base for exploring the delights of the Talyllyn and Dysynni valleys to the north.

In the mid-nineteenth century, the town, with its seamlessly joined eastern neighbour, **Penhelig**, built shallow-draught coastal traders for the inshore fleet, a past remembered in the small historic and **maritime display** in the tourist office (see below). Otherwise, take a look under the jetty, where you may chance upon Aberdovey's **Time and Tide Bell**, said to be linked to the legend of a submerged lost kingdom somewhere beneath Cardigan Bay, and which you can hear ringing at high tide.

ARRIVAL AND INFORMATION   ABERDYFI

By train Aberdyfi is served by two train stations: the request-only Penhelig, 0.5 mile east (the most convenient for the centre of town), and Aberdyfi, 0.5 mile west of the tourist office.
Destinations Barmouth (8 daily; 45min); Machynlleth (9 daily; 20min); Porthmadog (8 daily; 1hr 30min); Tywyn (8 daily; 15min).

By bus The #28 & #X29 stop close to the tourist office.
Destinations Machynlleth (8 daily; 20min); Tywyn (8 daily; 10min).

Tourist office Wharf Gardens (Easter–Oct daily 9.30am–1pm & 1.30–5pm; ☎ 01654 767321, ⓔ tic .aberdyfi@eryri.llyw.cymru).

ACCOMMODATION AND EATING

Britannia Inn 13 Seaview Terrace, LL35 0EF ☎ 01654 767426, ⊚ britannia-aberdovey.co.uk. Lively town-centre pub, especially fun when the sun comes out and everyone piles onto the deck with a pint of real ale for the sunset. Meals, a cut above the usual pub grub, might include Aberdyfi crab (£12.95). Mon–Wed 11am–midnight, Thurs–Sat 11am–1am, Sun noon–midnight.

Cartref Guest House Penrhos, LL35 0NR ☎ 01654 767273, ⊚ cartref-aberdovey.co.uk. Quality B&B in a large Edwardian house just a few steps from the train station. The five rooms (including one single) are done in muted tones with crisp white linen; breakfasts are excellent. Closed Nov–Feb. **£95**

Llety Bodfor 1 Bodfor Terrace, LL35 0EA ☎ 01654 767475, ⊚ lletybodfor.co.uk. The fairly typical frontage of this townhouse does little to suggest that within lies Aberdyfi's swankiest accommodation: singles, doubles and suites, all with sea views. The guest lounge, meanwhile, is equipped with a piano, games, DVDs and a stack of old vinyl. Breakfast £12. **£80**

Y Bwtri Blasus 7 Seaview Terrace, LL35 0EE ☎ 01654 767470. Great little deli and café that makes a fine place to hang out over a coffee and a slice of cake, or to stock up on picnic essentials. The bread and quiches (£5.95) are freshly made locally and they'll whip up a sandwich with whichever filling you desire. Daily 8.30am–5.30pm.

Talyllyn Valley

Around four miles north of Aberdyfi, two connected valleys – the Talyllyn and Dysynni – spur northeast from the coast towards Cadair Idris. The scenery hereabouts is monumentally beautiful, and there's superb lowland and mountain walking, particularly on Cadair Idris itself.

The **Talyllyn Valley**, which starts at the faded resort town of Tywyn, is initially traced by the delightful Talyllyn Railway, the first of Wales' restored narrow-gauge lines. There are several diversions along the course of the line, not least the lovely **Dolgoch Falls**, beyond which there are trails at both **Abergynolwyn** and **Nant Gwernol**; the valley ends at the placid waters of Tal-y-Llyn.

Talyllyn Railway

Station Rd, Tywyn, LL36 9EY • April–Oct 2–7 trains daily; also some winter weekends (check website for details) • £17.50 unlimited one-day travel • ☎ 01654 710472, ⊚ talyllyn.co.uk

An excellent way to experience the lower Talyllyn Valley is aboard the cute 27in-gauge **Talyllyn Railway**, the inspiration for Thomas the Tank Engine. The railway tootles seven miles inland from Tywyn through the delightful wooded valley to the old slate quarries at Nant Gwernol. From 1865 to 1946, the line hauled slate to Tywyn Wharf station. Five years after the quarry's closure, rail enthusiasts took over, making it the world's first volunteer-run railway. Of the original rolling stock, two steam engines and all five of the oak and mahogany passenger carriages still run up to Nant Gwernol.

The round trip (at a maximum 15mph) takes around two and half hours (with a pause), but you can get on and off as frequently as the schedule allows, taking in some fine broadleaf **forest walks**, best at Dolgoch Falls. At the end of the line, more woodland walks take you around the site of the old slate quarries. In mid-August each year, the schedule is disrupted by the "Race the Train" event, when runners attempt to beat the train to Abergynolwyn and back (a total of fourteen miles). Some do.

Narrow-Gauge Railway Museum

Tywyn Wharf station, LL36 9EY • April–Oct daily 10am–4.30pm • Free • ☎ 01654 710472, ⊚ narrowgaugerailwaymuseum.org.uk

Leave half an hour to peruse the superb **Narrow-Gauge Railway Museum** at Tywyn Wharf station. Along with the history of the railway and a re-created study of Thomas the Tank Engine inventor, Reverend W. Awdry, the museum holds some fine rolling stock from the Talyllyn and other narrow-gauge lines around the British Isles, including a Guinness shunter.

FROM TOP ABERAERON HARBOUR (P.263); HARLECH CASTLE (P.300) >

Dolgoch Falls, Abergynolwyn and Nant Gwernol

Five miles northeast of Tywyn, reachable via the B4405 and Talyllyn Railway, are the lovely **Dolgoch Falls**, where three trails (maximum 1hr) lead off through oak woods to the lower, mid and upper cascades. Pied flycatchers and redstarts can often be seen flitting about.

The Dysynni Valley joins the Talyllyn two miles northeast of Dolgoch Falls at the twin valleys' only real settlement, **Abergynolwyn**. Here, a few dozen quarry workers' houses crowd around a small visitor centre, a café, a pub and the Talyllyn Railway station. It is a short stroll up from here to the Talyllyn Railway's **Nant Gwernol** station, from where you can start the Quarryman's Trail (4 miles; 2–3hr; 800ft ascent), an excellent loop through quarry remains and a couple of waterfalls. Beyond Nant Gwernol and the tranquil Tal-y-Llyn, the B4405 meets the A487 right by the start of the Minffordd Path (see box opposite).

ARRIVAL AND DEPARTURE   TALYLLYN VALLEY

Having your own vehicle gives you the best flexibility, but it is possible to explore the Talyllyn Valley using the **Talyllyn Railway** and **bus** #30 (Mon–Sat 3–4 daily) which runs from Tywyn to Abergynolwyn and continues to Minffordd (where you can catch #32 or #X32 to Dolgellau or Machynlleth).

ACCOMMODATION AND EATING

Dôl Einion B4405 at Minffordd, just before the A487 junction, LL36 9AJ ☏01654 761312. Conveniently located around 400yd along from the entrance to the Minffordd Path, this very basic campsite is just the ticket if you intend overnighting before taking on Cadair Idris. Toilets, showers and electric hook-ups available. **£14.50**

Dolffanog Fawr B4405 at the north end of Tal-y-Llyn, LL36 9AJ ☏01654 761247, ⊛dolffanogfawr. co.uk. This charmingly run B&B makes for a great getaway, with four rooms offering mountain views, plus a big lounge, outdoor hot tub and inviting grounds. Three-course evening meals (Wed–Sat; £28) are available, along with a very good wine selection. Closed Nov–Feb. **£110**

Railway Inn Lichfield Terrace, Abergynolwyn, LL36 9YN ☏01654 782279. Great little pub with a cosy interior and outdoor seating with idyllic valley views. They serve the best range of real ales for miles, and good food; book for dinner (mains from £10) and Sun lunch. Daily 11am–11pm.

Dysynni Valley and around

Running almost parallel to the Talyllyn Valley, the idyllic **Dysynni Valley** meets the A493 near the church at Llanegryn. From there you can head upstream past the birds at **Craig y Deryn** then either turn southeast to join the Talyllyn Valley at Abergynolwyn or continue up the Dysynni to the ruins of Castell-y-Bere and the church of St Michael at Llanfihangel-y-Pennant. A few miles north up the coast, Llangelynin is worth a brief stop for its time-warped church.

Llanegryn and around

Half a mile northwest of the village of **LLANEGRYN**, just off the A493, the little hilltop **Llanegryn church** (generally open in the daytime) has an unexpectedly beautiful rood screen, probably carved in the fifteenth century, which is said to have been carried overnight from Dolgellau's Cymer Abbey after its dissolution.

Three miles northeast of Llanegryn at **Craig y Deryn** (Birds' Rock), around thirty breeding pairs of cormorants colonize a stunning 760ft-high cliff some four miles from the coast. As the sea has gradually withdrawn from the valley, the birds have remained loyal to their home, making this Europe's only inland cormorant nesting site. It's reachable via a signposted path (2 miles; 1hr; 750ft ascent).

Castell-y-Bere

Five miles northeast of Llanegryn, short of Llanfihangel-y-Pennant, LL36 9TS · Daily 10am–4pm · Free; CADW · ☏01443 336000, ⊛cadw.gov.wales/daysout/castell-y-bere

CADAIR IDRIS: THE MINFFORDD PATH

The OS 1:25,000 Explorer map OL23 (Cadair Idris & Llyn Tegid) is recommended.

The most dramatic ascent of Cadair Idris follows the **Minffordd Path** (6 miles; 5hr; 2900ft ascent), a justifiably popular route that makes a full circuit around the rim of **Cwm Cau**, probably the country's most impressive mountain cirque.

The path starts just west of the *Minffordd Hotel* at the junction of the A487 and the B4405. From the car park, follow the signs along an avenue of horse chestnuts until you come to the **Visitor Centre and Ty Te Cadair Tea Room** (Easter–Oct 10am–5pm; holidays daily, term time Wed–Sun; ☎01654 761505, ⍟cadairidriswales.com), with an exhibition on the various stages of the climb up the mountain, as well as a live feed of the lesser horseshoe bat roost ensconced in the attic.

From the visitor centre, continue up through the woods, heading north. At a fork, take the left path, which wheels around the end of Craig Lwyd into Cwm Cau. Before you reach the lake, fork left and climb onto the rim of Cwm Cau, following it round to **Penygadair** (2930ft), the highest point on the massif. Here, there's a circular shelter and a tin-roofed hut originally built for dispensing refreshments to thirsty Victorians, and now affording none-too-comfortable protection from wind and rain.

The shortest descent follows the summit plateau northeast, then down to a grassy ridge before ascending gradually to **Mynydd Moel** (2831ft), from which you get a magnificent view down into a valley and Llyn Arran, the smallest of Cadair's lakes. The descent starts beside the fence which you cross just before the summit – follow the fence south all the way to the fork below Cwm Cau.

With large slabs of the main towers still standing, there's plenty of opportunity to poke around at **Castell-y-Bere**, a native Welsh fortress built by Llywelyn ap Iorwerth (Llywelyn the Great) in 1221 to protect the mountain passes. After being besieged twice in the thirteenth century, this – one of the most massive of the Welsh castles – was consigned to seven centuries of obscurity and decay. Castell-y-Bere seems to rise almost imperceptibly out of the rock on which it was built – it is a great place just to sit or picnic, with good views to Cadair Idris and Craig y Deryn.

Church of St Michael

Llanfihangel-y-Pennant, a few hundred yards beyond Castell-y-Bere, LL36 9TP • ⍟ llanfihangel-y-pennant.org.uk

The stocky little **church of St Michael** has a couple of interesting exhibits in its vestry, including a fabulous 3D map of the valley, 14ft long and built to a scale of one foot to one mile from patchwork and cloth. There are also exhibits centred on **Mary Jones** – famed for her 1800 bible-buying walk to Bala (see box, p.322) – whose ruined cottage, **Tŷn-y-ddôl**, is just up the lane and marked with a monument.

Llangelynin church

A493, 7 miles north of Tywyn, 0.5 mile short of Llangelynin, LL32 8LJ • Generally daily 9am–5pm

Half a mile from the hamlet of Llangelynin, a track descends seawards off the main road to the ancient **Llangelynin church**: a mainly eleventh-century building on the foundations of an eighth-century structure, and bare but for a few basic pews and a bier which was carried by horses. Look out for the ancient board inscribed with the Ten Commandments in Welsh, and the wall painting of a skeletal **figure of death** with his scythe, probably painted in the seventeenth century. Just outside the porch is the grave of Abram Wood, patriarch of Y Teulu Wood, a clan of Romanies who settled in Wales at the beginning of the eighteenth century.

ARRIVAL AND DEPARTURE
DYSYNNI VALLEY

There is **no public transport** in the Dysynni Valley, so your best bet is to make your way by train or bus to Tywyn and head on from there.

ACCOMMODATION

Cae Du A493, Llangelynin, just over 2 miles west of Llanegryn, LL36 9ND ☎01654 711234, ⬡caedufarmholidays.co.uk. Wonderfully dramatic clifftop site that's pretty simple but has hot showers and access down to a beach and allows campfires. The slope means you'll need to pick your site carefully, and it is pretty exposed when the wind gets up. Closed Nov–Easter. £̲1̲5̲

Llanllwyda Near the start of the path to Craig y Deryn, LL36 9TN ☎01654 782627. Well-equipped caravan and campsite (toilets, showers) in grassy fields on a working farm; campfires are allowed. Closed Nov–Feb. £̲1̲0̲

Northern Cadair Idris and the Mawddach estuary

Gouging their way deep into the heart of the mid-Wales mountains, the **Mawddach estuary**'s broad tidal flats create dramatic backdrops from every angle. With the sun low in the sky and the tide ebbing, the constantly changing course of the river trickles silver through the golden sands. That colour isn't just an illusion: the sands actually do contain gold, albeit in tiny amounts, as the abandoned mines littering the hills around testify.

Spasmodic gold fever still occasionally hits the region's main town, **Dolgellau**, but most people come here for excellent **walking** up Cadair Idris and along the estuary, the **mountain biking** at **Coed-y-Brenin** to the north, or to hit the beaches, particularly at **Barmouth**, the area's main resort.

Fairbourne

The blink-and-you'll-miss-it settlement of **FAIRBOURNE**, on the southern side of the Mawddach estuary, was developed in the late nineteenth century as the country estate of the chairman of the McDougall's flour company. There's a decent beach and sublime views along the coast and across the estuary, but otherwise the only attraction is the **steam-hauled railway**.

Fairbourne Railway

Beach Rd, LL38 2EX • April–Oct 4–8 trains most days; museum hours dependent on train schedule • £9.50 day rover • ☎01341 250362, ⬡fairbournerailway.com

Travelling between Fairbourne and Barmouth is easy on the mainline train that crosses the Mawddach Rail Bridge. More fun, however, is the tiny, 12in-gauge **Fairbourne Railway**, which runs along the seafront for just a mile between Fairbourne and the Barmouth Ferry station; here, connecting passenger ferries (£4 return) cross the estuary mouth to Barmouth itself (see p.296).

Midway along, a halt on the line boasts the name Gorsafawddacha'idraigodanhed dogleddollônpenrhynareurdraethceredigion ("The station on the Mawddach with dragon's teeth on the north Penrhyn Drive on the golden Cardigan sands"). The "dragon's teeth" are, alas, a set of grim concrete defences left over from World War II. Before you depart, spend a few moments looking around the **museum** inside the terminal at Fairbourne, which has some lovely model railways.

ARRIVAL AND DEPARTURE · FAIRBOURNE

By train Fairbourne is well served by trains; the station is in the centre of town, off Beach Rd.

Destinations Aberdyfi (8 daily; 30min); Barmouth (8 daily; 10min); Machynlleth (9 daily; 50min); Tywyn (9 daily; 20min).

EATING

Indiana Cuisine 3 Beach Rd, LL38 2PZ ☎01341 250891, ⬡indianacuisinewales.uk. Fairbourne is one of the last places you'd expect to find one of the UK's finest Indian restaurants, but here it is, run by Noorie, the wife of

Bollywood superstar Mayur Verma (Raj). The north Indian cuisine is all cooked fresh, and the execution is way above the norm – try, for example, charcoal-smoked fillet of salmon with mint chutney, or coconut lamb with mustard seed and curry leaves (£8.95). Mon & Wed–Fri 6.30–10pm, Sat & Sun noon–3pm & 6.30–10pm.

Dolgellau and around

The old county town of Meirionethshire, **DOLGELLAU** still maintains an air of unhurried gravitas, never more so than when the area's farmers roll up for market every Thursday morning. Its dark buildings gleam forebodingly in the frequent downpours, but in fine weather, the lofty crags of Cadair Idris perfectly frame the stone squares and streets.

There's little to see or do in town itself, but it's the most convenient access point to the southern reaches of Snowdonia National Park. The local **walks** are superb, the **Mawddach Trail** offers some of the finest easy cycling around, and nearby **Coed-y-Brenin** has become a major centre for **mountain bikers** and trail runners.

Brief history

Dolgellau is much older than appearances suggest, lying at the junction of three Roman roads that converged on a now vanished military outpost. It was here that **Owain Glyndŵr** assembled the last Welsh parliament in 1404, and later signed an alliance with Charles VI of France for providing troops to fight against Henry IV of England (see box, p.283). Seventeenth-century Quakers sought freedom from persecution here, and in the 1860s Dolgellau became the focus of numerous **gold rushes**, drawing waves of prospectors to pan the estuary or blast levels into Clogau shale or mudstone sediment under the Coed-y-Brenin forest. The quartz veins yielded some gold, but in quantities too small to make much money.

Cymer Abbey

Two miles north of Dolgellau, signposted off the A470, LL40 2HE · Daily 10am–5pm · Free; CADW · ☎ 01443 336000, ⓦ cadw.gov.wales/daysout/cymer-abbey

Gold frenzy first hit Dolgellau when the Romans found flecks glinting in the Mawddach silt. Later, the thirteenth-century Cistercian monks based at **Cymer Abbey** were given "the right in digging or carrying away metals and treasures free from all secular exaction". The fine location at the head of the Mawddach estuary is typical of this austere order, but unfortunately the surrounding caravan site mars the effect of the remaining Gothic slabs. A path beside the abbey makes an alternative approach to the Precipice Walk (see box, p.294).

Coed-y-Brenin

A470, 8 miles north of Dolgellau, LL40 2HZ · **Forest** Open access · Free · **Visitor centre** April–Oct daily 9.30am–5pm; Nov–March Mon–Fri 9.30am–4.30pm, Sat & Sun 9am–5pm · ☎ 01341 440747, ⓦ naturalresources.wales/coedybrenin

One of the most popular activity spots in southern Snowdonia, the vast **Coed-y-Brenin** forest park is home to some of Wales' finest mountain biking, as well as the UK's first bespoke trail-running centre; there are also superb walking trails, orienteering and geocaching courses, and innovative kids' play areas.

Mountain biking takes place in the evergreens of "The King's Forest", with

4

miles of old trackways, roads and eight purpose-built trails crisscrossing the hillsides, offering lung-busting uphill rides and adrenalin-pumping descents. They're all graded like ski runs: black for experts, red and blue for intermediates and green for family riders. Highlights include the Dragon's Back (20 miles; difficult) and the aptly named Beast (25 miles; severe), but there's plenty for beginners, families and the disabled.

Just as exciting are the **running trails**, five waymarked routes ranging from a mile-long shoe-test route to a half-marathon distance on a mixture of forest roads and single tracks. You can buy maps and obtain information on any aspect of the trails, as well as the many walking routes – which range from one to seven miles – from the **visitor centre**; here too you can pick up a map to get a taste of **geocaching**, essentially using a GPS (they rent them for £5/day) to find one of four little boxes of treasure hidden in the woods.

At the Beics Brenin shop you can **rent bikes** (hardtails £25/3hr, £30/day – book in advance; ☎01341 440728, ⍟beicsbrenin.co.uk) and have your cycle repaired; there's also a trail-running store (☎01341 440798, ⍟runcoedybrenin.com) where you can rent running shoes to test out on the one-mile shoe-test route, showers (£1) and an excellent **café**.

ARRIVAL AND GETTING AROUND

DOLGELLAU AND AROUND

By bus Dolgellau is well served by buses, which pull into Eldon Square. Most services head north past Coed-y-Brenin. To stick to the coast, pick up the train at Barmouth (see p.296).

Destinations Bala (Mon–Sat 10 daily, Sun 5; 40min); Barmouth (Mon–Sat hourly, Sun 5; 25min); Llangollen (Mon–Sat 10 daily, Sun 5; 1hr 30min); Machynlleth (Mon–Sat hourly, Sun 3; 30min); Porthmadog (Mon–Sat 7 daily, Sun 4; 50min).

Bike rental Dolgellau Cycles, Smithfield St (March–Oct daily 9.30am–5pm; Nov–Feb closed Mon & Sun; ☎01341 423332, ⍟dolgellaucycles.co.uk), rents bikes suitable for the Mawddach Trail (£13/half-day, £20/day) and offers repairs and servicing.

ACCOMMODATION

While there is commendable accommodation in Dolgellau itself (some of it catering to the legions of mountain-bikers here for Coed-y-Brenin), there are more appealing options scattered nearby, some so close to **Cadair Idris** that you can start your hike at the back door.

DOLGELLAU

Ffynnon Love Lane, LL40 1RR ☎01341 421774, ⍟ffynnontownhouse.com. Six impeccable rooms in this

former Victorian rectory, variously furnished with mahogany beds, slipper baths and French chandeliers, but all with separate sitting areas and great views. Rates

---

WALKING AND CYCLING AROUND DOLGELLAU

Cadair Idris: Pony Path The OS 1:25,000 Explorer map OL23 (Cadair Idris & Llyn Tegid) is advised. If the weather is fine, don't miss this classic and enjoyable ascent of Cadair Idris (9 miles; 4–5hr; 2800ft ascent). The walk starts from the car park at Tŷ Nant, three miles southwest of Dolgellau along Cadair Road (no buses). Early views to the craggy flanks of the massif are tremendous, but they disappear as you climb steeply to the col, where you turn left on a rocky path to the summit shelter on Penygadair (2930ft).

Mawddach Trail (10 miles from Dolgellau to Barmouth; flat). Follow this beautiful combined walking and cycle route beside the Mawddach estuary's broad sands along a disused rail line. Walkers seeking the most interesting section should start from Penmaenpool (catch bus #28), two miles west. Highlights include the wooden toll bridge and George III Hotel (see p.opposite) at Penmaenpool, an RSPB wetland walk at Arthog and the Barmouth bridge.

Precipice Walk (3–4 miles; 2hr; negligible ascent). Starting three miles north of Dolgellau off the road to Llanfachreth, the path on this easy-going loop is narrow in places, and there are some steep banks, but it is a little precipitous. There are great views to the 1000ft ramparts of Cadair Idris and along the Mawddach estuary – best in late afternoon or early morning sun.

Torrent Walk (2 miles; 1hr; 100ft ascent). Attractive lowland stroll following the cascading, bedrock-carved Clywedog River through gnarled old woodland that drips with antiquity. It starts on the B4416, just off the A470, three miles east of Dolgellau (bus #32/X32).

THE BIG SESSION

Dolgellau's **Sesiwn Fawr** (W sesiwnfawr.cymru) or "Big Session" festival in mid-July was once huge, but has now returned to its smaller Celtic folk roots. Held in the meadows west of the river bridge, it features much of the best of Welsh and wider Celtic folk, as well as comedy and literature. For more music, it's always worth checking out what's going on at **Ty Siamas** (☎ 01341 421800, W tysiamas.com) – the National Centre for Welsh Folk Music – on Eldon Square.

---

include afternoon tea on arrival and daily newspapers. Two-night minimum stay at weekends. **£150**

★**Tan y Gader** Meyrick St, LL40 1LS ☎ 01341 421102, W tanygader.co.uk. This sociable guesthouse offers three startlingly original rooms – each named after a children's book (Secret Garden, Alice and Narnia) – crammed with playful elements alongside a host of thoughtful touches like fresh coffee and shortbread, bedside hand cream and eye masks. Guests are encouraged to use the cosy drawing room, chock-full of books and games, which is also where tea and home-made cake are served upon arrival. **£85**

★**Y Meirionnydd** Smithfield Square, LL40 1ES ☎ 01341 422554, W themeirionnydd.com. This solid stone Georgian townhouse has been re-fashioned as a chic five-room hotel with light tones and blond woods offset by feature cushions and curtains; the retro Roberts radios are a great addition. The smart little bar leads through to a distinguished restaurant where the cracking breakfast is served. **£85**

AROUND DOLGELLAU

Coed Cae A496 at Taicynhaeaf, 4 miles west, LL40 2TU ☎ 01341 430628, W coedcae.co.uk. Sustainability and appreciation of the outdoors are the watchwords at this three-room B&B, handily located for the Mawddach Trail, just across the toll bridge. Guests are free to enjoy the lounge with its superb log burner, while locally sourced meals and packed lunches are available on request. Bike rental £20/day. **£85**

George III Hotel A493, Penmaenpool, 2 miles west, LL40 1YD ☎ 01341 422525, W georgethethird.co.uk. Handsome seventeenth-century hotel superbly situated at the head of the Mawddach estuary (bus #28), with six rooms in the main hotel building and five smartly updated ground-level rooms in the Lodge, the former train station buildings. **£110**

★**Graig Wen** A493, 5 miles west, near Arthog, LL39 1YP ☎ 01341 250482, W graigwen.co.uk. Access is steep but the Mawddach estuary views make it all worthwhile at this wonderfully tranquil campsite with B&B. You can camp in either the upper (closed Feb) or lower (car-free; closed Oct–April) field, the latter offering a wilder camping experience with compost toilets and campfires. There's plenty of comfort available, too, courtesy of a handful of yurts, a bell tent (minimum three nights), and a two-person "caban" timber pavilion (minimum two nights); the *Slate Shed B&B* is yet another step up in the comfort stakes. Bike rental available, too. Closed Jan & Feb. Camping/person **£9**, yurt **£70**, bell tent **£75**, caban **£80**, B&B **£110**

Tyddyn Mawr Farmhouse Islawrdref, 3 miles southwest, LL40 1TL ☎ 01341 422331, W wales -guesthouse.co.uk. Eighteenth-century farmhouse on the slopes of Cadair Idris, at the foot of the Pony Path, with one ground-floor room with its own patio and a first-floor room with balcony and mountain views. Complimentary tea and cakes on arrival and a superb breakfast. Closed Dec & Jan. **£86**

YHA Kings Penmaenpool, 4.5 miles west, LL40 1TB ☎ 0345 371 9327, W yha.org.uk/hostel/kings. Large country house a mile up a delightful wooded valley off the #28 Tywyn bus route (last bus around 6pm), with six-bed dorms and a self-catering kitchen. An ideal base for the Pony Path up Cadair Idris. Reception 8–10am & 5–10.30pm. **£14**

EATING

DOLGELLAU

★**Gwin Dylanwad** Smithfield St, LL40 1ET ☎ 01341 422870, W dylanwad.com. Part café, part bar, this charmingly run establishment is highly respected for the quality of its wines, which go down a treat with the small plates (around £6–8) – herring with mustard mayonnaise, for example, or goat's cheese with apple and Welsh honey. The place itself oozes atmosphere, above all in the adjoining glass conservatory. Tues & Wed 10am–6pm, Thurs–Sat 10am–11pm.

Royal Ship Queen's Square, LL40 1AR ☎ 01341 422209, W robinsonsbrewery.com. Large, cheerful old coaching inn, with good beer, alfresco seating and a range of moderately upscale dishes such as mussels in whisky cream with chips (£12.50). Daily 7.30am–11pm; kitchen 8–10am & noon–9pm.

★**Siop Coffi T.H.** Bridge St, LL40 1BD ☎ 01341 423573. This big, perennially busy café was once the town's ironmongers, as the wonderful old fixtures and fittings testify: a long, raised wooden table where nowadays folk tap away on laptops, and the former glassed-in office, which is now a snug. They serve fresh baguettes and paninis, sumptuous cakes and freshly roasted coffee. Mon–Sat 9am–5.30pm, Sun 10am–4pm.

AROUND DOLGELLAU

George III A493, Penmaenpool, 2 miles west, LL40 1YD ☎01341 422525, ⓦgeorgethethird.co.uk. Superb spot for a pub meal overlooking the Mawddach estuary or a sunset drink in the dark-wood bar. Meals might include lamb shank, fish and chips or bacon-wrapped chicken. Daily 11am–10.30pm; kitchen noon–2.30pm & 6–9pm.

Mawddach A496, 2 miles northwest, LL40 2TA ☎01341 421752, ⓦmawddach.com. Dark and slate-floored downstairs, airy with bare boards and exposed beams upstairs, this contemporary restaurant occupies a converted barn with fabulous head-on views of Cadair Idris. The menu comprises simply prepared and beautifully cooked dishes such as wild sea trout fillet with brown butter breadcrumbs and salsa verde (£17). Thurs–Sat noon–2.30pm & 6.30–9.30pm, Sun noon–2.30pm.

Barmouth and around

Cluttered with shops selling takeaway food, buckets and spades and pleasure-beach sideshow attractions, lively **BARMOUTH** (Abermaw) tucks in beneath steep cliffs, lapped by both estuary and sea. It was popularized by nineteenth-century English Midlands sea-bathers who mostly arrived over the 2253ft-long **Barmouth Bridge**, which traverses 113 spindly wooden spans across the Mawddach estuary south of town. Barmouth was once a shipbuilding centre, and a maritime air lingers around the quay at the south end of town, departure point for a **passenger ferry** to Fairbourne and the miniature railway (see p.292).

Backed by high dunes, the long, wide and sandy **beach** is perfect for families. If you prefer something more energetic, try your hand at **paddleboarding**, which is extremely popular here: at the Merioneth Yacht Club in the harbour, SUP Barmouth (☎07787 585561, ⓦsupbarmouth.co.uk) offers lessons starting at £25 for one hour.

There is also a lot of good **walking** in these parts; the ten-day **Barmouth Walking Festival** (ⓦbarmouthwalkingfestival.co.uk), in mid-September, offers a series of great guided walks (£8.50 each), ranging from five to 21 miles.

The Last Haul
Corner The Quay and Church St

The most famous of many **shipwrecks** along this coast was that of the 700-ton Genoese galleon known locally as the *Bronze Bell*, which sank in 1709 complete with its cargo of finest Carrara marble. Forty or so two-ton blocks of marble still lie on the sea bed but one piece was raised in the 1980s, and fashioned by local sculptor Frank Cocksey into **The Last Haul**. Three centuries beneath the sea have left the surface fabulously

---

WALKS FROM BARMOUTH

Barmouth–Fairbourne loop (5 miles; 2–3hr; 300ft ascent). A rewarding low-level coastal circuit, this easily managed walk around Barmouth and Fairbourne gives superb mountain, estuarine and coastal views all the way. You cross the rail bridge (90p return toll; £1.50 with a bike) to Morfa Mawddach station, then follow the lane to the main road, cross it onto a footpath that rises around the back of a small wooded hill to Pant Einion Hall, then follow another lane back to the main road near Fairbourne. Turn north then left down the main street of Fairbourne to the sea; from here you can return to Barmouth either by taking the Fairbourne Railway, or by walking north along the beach and catching the ferry.

Panorama Walk and Dinas Oleu (3 miles; 2hr; 400ft ascent). A bracing walk taking in a fine viewpoint over town and estuary plus Dinas Oleu (Fortress of Light), the cliffs immediately above Barmouth. Essentially the route follows Gloddfa Road off High Street onto the exposed clifftops, where there is a map of the reserve. Go through the metal gate and follow the path past Frenchman's Grave to a road where you turn left to the Panorama Viewpoint. Return by the same route.

THREE PEAKS YACHT RACE

Every June, the highly competitive **Three Peaks Yacht Race** (w threepeaksyachtrace.co.uk) – a two- to three-day amateur monohull yachting event entailing navigation to Caernarfon, the English Lake District and Fort William in Scotland, and a run up the highest peak in each country – starts in **Barmouth**. The current record, set in 2002, is two days, fourteen hours and four minutes.

pockmarked, though the quality of marble comes through in the carved section, which depicts three fishing generations working together to haul in a catch.

Tŷ Gwyn Museum

The Quay, LL42 1EU • June–Sept daily 1–4.30pm • Free

A medieval tower house where Henry VII's uncle, Jasper Tudor, is said to have plotted Richard III's downfall now houses **Tŷ Gwyn Museum**. It contains explanatory panels on local shipwrecks plus a few artefacts, including the 1677 bronze bell that gave the nameless galleon its local moniker (see opposite).

Tŷ Crwn Roundhouse

The Quay, LL42 1EU • Daily 10.30am–5pm • Free

A few paces away from the Tŷ Gwyn Museum, the **Tŷ Crwn Roundhouse** acted as a lockup for drunken sailors in the nineteenth century. The circular design, with two cells on opposite sides (one for men, one for women), was reputedly conceived to prevent the Devil lurking in any corners and further tempting the incarcerated mariners.

4

ARRIVAL AND GETTING AROUND   BARMOUTH

By train The train station is on Station Rd, right in the centre.
Destinations Aberdyfi (9 daily; 35min); Harlech (8 daily; 25min); Llanbedr (8 daily; 15min); Machynlleth (9 daily; 55min); Porthmadog (8 daily; 50min).
By bus Buses to Dolgellau (Mon–Sat hourly, Sun 5; 25min) and Harlech (Mon–Sat hourly, Sun 2; 30min) stop on

Jubilee Rd, near the train station.
By ferry Passenger ferries run from the harbour to Fairbourne (Easter–Oct; as frequently as custom demands; £3 return).
Bike rental Birmingham Garage, Church St, rents out basic machines that are ideal for the Mawddach Trail (£10/half-day, £14/day; ☎ 01341 280644).

ACCOMMODATION AND EATING

Bae Abermaw Hotel Panorama Hill, LL42 1DQ ☎ 01341 280550, w baeabermaw.co.uk. Very un-Barmouth, this former Victorian hotel is now contemporary, with minimalist white-on-white rooms, almost all with unfurling views over Cardigan Bay, and an elegant bare-boards lounge. The restaurant, with comfy chairs, wooden floors, white walls and a wintertime fire serves good Modern British cuisine. Mon–Sat 6–9pm, Sun noon–2.30pm. £100

Hendre Mynach Llanaber Rd, 1 mile north, LL42 1YR ☎ 01341 280262, w hendremynach.co.uk. Barmouth's closest campsite, a large level site just off the beach with comprehensive facilities including modern shower blocks, launderette, shop and a cool kids' play area. Closed Jan & Feb. £23

Last Inn Church St, LL42 1BN ☎ 01341 280530, w lastinn-barmouth.co.uk. Locals and tourists alike mingle happily in this flower-bedecked former cobbler's, where you can also get good pub meals such as

beer-battered cod and chips. The outdoor tables catch the afternoon sun. Live music on Tues. Daily noon–11pm.

Llwyndû Farmhouse Hotel Llanaber, 2 miles north, LL42 1RR ☎ 01341 280144, w llwyndu-farmhouse .co.uk. A gem of a B&B with en-suite rooms in the seventeenth-century farmhouse building (complete with mullioned windows and inglenook fireplace), the converted barn or the granary. Delicious evening meals (available to non-guests) are served in the romantic dining room, with candles flickering on the tables. Local ingredients are the order of the day on the two-/three-course menus (£25/£30). Mon–Sat 7–10pm. £100

Sandpiper 7 Marine Parade, LL42 1NA ☎ 01341 280318, w thesandpiperguesthouse.co.uk. Just a few steps from the train station, this is one of many B&Bs along the seafront, a well-presented guesthouse with a mix of singles, doubles and family rooms, many with sea views. Closed Nov–Feb. £60

Ardudwy

North of Barmouth, the coast opens out to a narrow coastal plain running a dozen miles towards Snowdonia and flanked by the heather-covered slopes of the Rhinog mountains, five miles inland. This is **Ardudwy**, a fertile land used as a fattening ground for black Welsh cattle on their way to the English markets, and now tamed by caravan sites and golf courses.

No modern road crosses the Rhinogs to the east, but until the construction of coach roads in the early nineteenth century, the existence of two mountain passes made this a strategic and populous area, as the numerous minor Neolithic burial chambers testify. Further up the coast, the town of **Harlech** was built as one link in Edward I's chain of magnificent fortresses. It's the only real town in the region, followed in importance by **Llanbedr**, from where a road runs west to the dune-backed camping resort on **Shell Island**, and another rises east, splitting into two delightfully remote valleys.

Llanbedr and around

LLANBEDR, seven miles north of Barmouth, isn't much in itself, but is central to a diverse bunch of scattered sites from **Neolithic burial chambers** and wild **dunes** to a disused **slate quarry** and a pair of gorgeous valleys from where hikes lead up into the wild **Rhinog** range.

Morfa Dyffryn National Nature Reserve

Off the A496, 2 miles southwest of Llanbedr • Open access • Free

The constantly changing coastal dunes of **Morfa Dyffryn National Nature Reserve** stretch from Llandwyne four miles north to the edge of Shell Island. Notable for its flora, particularly the marsh helleborine, this is a fragile zone and large areas are fenced off, but there's beach access across a boardwalk. Follow the path from Dyffryn Ardudwy station through the caravan parks and the dunes to the splendid, vast **beach**. A section of shore a few hundred yards to the north serves as Wales' only official **naturist beach** (when it's warm enough).

Dyffryn Ardudwy Burial Chamber

Signposted behind the school in Dyffryn Ardudwy off the A496, 3 miles south of Llanbedr, LL46 6LF • Daily 10am–4pm • Free; CADW • ☎ 01443 336000, ⓦ cadw.gov.wales/daysout/dyffrynardudwyburialchamber

Dyffryn Ardudwy Burial Chamber comprises two supported capstones lying among a bed of small boulders, the base stones of a mound thought to have been 100ft long; the site dates from around 3500 BC. Finds from a dig here in the 1960s – including pottery, finely polished stone plaques and bones – are on display at the National Museum in Cardiff.

Shell Island

Two miles west of Llanbedr • No access at high tide, check website for times • ☎ 01341 241453, ⓦ shellisland.co.uk

A lane from Llanbedr snakes its way alongside the babbling Afon Artro, past the train station and redundant airfield, to **Shell Island**, or Mochras. A peninsula at anything other than high tide, the island is reached by a tidal causeway and offers the chance to swim, sail, look for wild flowers or scour the beach for some of the two hundred varieties of shell found here. At low tide you can see a line of rocks in the sea leading out towards Ireland, known as Sarn Badrig (St Patrick's Causeway) and traditionally thought to be the road to a flooded land known as the Cantre'r Gwaelod ("The Low Hundreds").

Llyn Cwm Bychan

A narrow road dives six miles northeast of Llanbedr through gorgeous woods as it follows the Afon Artro to the waters of **Llyn Cwm Bychan**, deep in the heather and

WALKS ON THE RHINOGS

The OS 1:25,000 Explorer map OL18 (Harlech, Porthmadog & Bala) is recommended.
The northern **Rhinogs** offer some surprisingly tough walking. At less than 2500ft, they're hardly giants, but the typically large, rough, gritstone rocks hidden in thick heather make anything but the most well-worn paths hard-going. The rewards for your efforts are long views across Cardigan Bay, a good chance of stumbling across a herd of feral goats and a strong sense of achievement. The two walks described here start at the head of different valleys (see p.288 & p.290), but share a common summit, that of **Rhinog Fawr**.

RHINOG FAWR AND THE ROMAN STEPS FROM CWM BYCHAN

For this walk (5 miles return; 3–4hr; 1900ft ascent), start at the car park in **Cwm Bychan** (see opposite) and follow signs up through a small wood onto the open moor. The **Roman Steps** (see below) guide you up to a pass, Bwlch Tyddiad, giving views east to Bala and beyond. The terrain then becomes steeper and the path less well defined. You may have to use your hands to finally reach **Rhinog Fawr** (2362ft). Return by the same route.

RHINOG FAWR AND RHINOG FACH FROM CWM NANTCOL

This demanding walk (6–7 miles return; 5–6hr; 2900ft ascent) begins by the Maes-y-Garnedd farmhouse at the head of Cwm Nantcol for a fairly rugged circuit over Rhinog Fawr and Rhinog Fach. Follow the track north from the car park to the house, into the fields and over the stile, then turn northeast and walk gradually towards the base of the rocky southwest ridge, following the white marker posts. Eventually, the path turns north to a cairn on the skyline, then east following more cairns up the ridge to the summit trig point of **Rhinog Fawr**.

After an arduous descent into Bwlch Drws Ardudwy (The Pass of the Door of Ardudwy), cross the stone wall and start on a fairly clear line up **Rhinog Fach** (2236ft). Explore the summit ridge to get the best views of the coast then descend to Cwm Nantcol by first walking to a rocky ledge overlooking Llyn Hywel to the south. From here you should be able to see a scrappy path running very steeply down to the lake on the right-hand edge of the ledge. You'll have to use your hands at times, and there are sections of scree, but you're soon on a clear path that skirts north around the base of Rhinog Fach towards Bwlch Drws Ardudwy and back to Cwm Nantcol.

4

angular rocks of the Rhinog range. Pay the farmer to park on the property here to take the path up to the **Roman Steps** – most likely a medieval packhorse route, made of flat slabs cutting through the range – onto **Rhinog Fawr** (see box abvoe). Branching off the Cwm Bychan road a mile out of Llanbedr, another delightful road leads to **Cwm Nantcol**, the next valley south. Two hundred yards up the lane, **Capel Salem** is a Baptist chapel immortalized by Sidney Curnow Vosper's 1908 painting of the same name – a copy hangs inside.

ARRIVAL AND DEPARTURE

LLANBEDR AND AROUND

By train Llanbedr is on the Cambrian coast line; the station is in the centre of the village.
Destinations Barmouth (8 daily; 15min); Harlech (8 daily; 10min); Porthmadog (8 daily; 35min).

By bus Llanbedr is served by the #38 bus from Barmouth (every 2hr; 20min), which continues along the coast to Harlech then heads inland to Blaenau Ffestiniog.

ACCOMMODATION AND EATING

★ **Nantcol Waterfalls** 2 miles east, LL45 2PL ☎ 01341 241209, ⓦ nantcolwaterfalls.co.uk. Blissfully secluded tent and caravan site at the base of the Rhinogs and beside a burbling river. Facilities include a shower block, laundry and basic shop; campfires are allowed (you'll need to bring your own firewood or buy it here), and in the summer holidays there's a stone oven pizza stand. Best of all are the lovely woodland and riverside walks leading off from the site. Closed Nov–Feb. Per person **£10**

Shell Island Campsite Along the beach from the harbour down to Morfa Dyffryn, LL45 2PJ ☎ 01341 241453, ⓦ shellisland.co.uk. Massive 300-acre tent and motorhome campsite (no caravans) that spreads along the beach to the vast dunes of Morfa Dyffryn. It is Europe's biggest, and although it can get crowded during the holiday season, campers must pitch tents a minimum of 20yd from each other (unless agreed with your neighbours), guaranteeing relative solitude amid spectacular scenery, with some of the best sunsets in north Wales. No walk-ins; you must have a vehicle. Closed Nov–Feb. Per person **£9.25**

Shell Island Restaurant and Tavern Bar Shell Island, LL45 2PJ ☏ 01341 241453, ⓦ shellisland.co.uk. People come from miles around for the three-course Sun lunches (£15) in the restaurant, while there are also good meals available at the adjacent tavern, which serves excellent Purple Moose ales from Porthmadog just up the coast.

March–Oct: restaurant Sun noon–2.30pm; tavern bar daily noon–11pm.

Victoria Inn Llanbedr, LL45 2LD ☏ 01341 241213, ⓦ vic-inn.co.uk. Stone-built village pub that's a winner for the beer garden and meals made from produce from its own market garden. The five rooms are well above average for your typical pub. Mon–Thurs 8.30am–11pm, Fri & Sat 8.30am–midnight, Sun 8.30am–10.30pm; kitchen daily 8.30am–9pm. **£80**

Harlech

HARLECH, three miles north of Llanbedr, is one of the highlights of the Cambrian coast and makes a dramatic first impression. Its commanding castle clings to a rocky outcrop, while the charming township cloaking the hill behind takes in one of Wales' finest views: over the Morfa Harlech dunes across Cardigan Bay to the Llŷn, and north to the jagged peaks of Snowdonia.

Harlech's **sand dunes** and **beach** are among the finest on this coast, reached via Beach Road, which shoots off the main road through town, directly below the castle. On the way to the sands, you'll swing by the exclusive **Royal St David's golf course**, venue of many championships (ⓦ royalstdavids. co.uk). There's a handful of inviting places to eat (though relatively few places to stay) in the town's steep and narrow streets, plus wonderful walking country and more superb beaches on the doorstep.

Harlech Castle

Castle Square, LL46 2YH • March–June, Sept & Oct daily 9.30am–5pm; July & Aug daily 9.30am–6pm; Nov–Feb Mon–Sat 10am–4pm, Sun 11am–4pm • £6.50; CADW • ☏ 01766 780552, ⓦ cadw.gov.wales/daysout/harlechcastle

Harlech's showpiece is its substantially intact **castle**, rising mightily on its 200ft bluff – the entrance is through a new **visitor centre**, itself linked to the castle by an equally impressive curving pedestrianized bridge suspended over the moat. Intended as one of Edward I's Iron Ring of monumental fortresses (see box, p.405), Harlech castle was begun in 1283, just six months after the death of Llywelyn the Last. It was built of a hard Cambrian rock, known as Harlech grit, hewn from the moat. One side of the fortress was originally protected by the sea – the waters have now receded, though, leaving the castle dominating a stretch of duned coastline.

The castle has seen a lot of action in its time: it withheld a siege in 1295, was taken by Owain Glyndŵr in 1404, and the youthful, future Henry VII – the first

■ ACCOMMODATION		● EATING			
Castle Cottage	1	As.Is	2	Hufenfa'r	
Pen Y Garth	2	Castle Cottage	1	Castell	3
		Cemlyn Tea Shop	4		

Welsh king of England and Wales – withstood a seven-year siege here at the hands of the Yorkists from 1461 to 1468, until the castle was again taken. It subsequently fell into ruin, but was put back into service for the king during the Civil War, and in March 1647 it became the last Royalist castle to fall.

The first defensive line comprised the three successive pairs of gates and portcullises built between the two massive half-round towers of the **gatehouse**, where an **exhibition** outlines the castle's history. Much of the outermost ring has been destroyed, leaving only the 12ft-thick curtain walls rising up 40ft to the exposed battlements, and only the towering gatehouse prevents you walking the full circuit. The views stretching away over the golf course towards Snowdonia and the Llŷn Peninsula are magnificent.

ARRIVAL AND DEPARTURE   HARLECH

By train Trains stop by the A496 below the castle.
Destinations Barmouth (8 daily; 25min); Machynlleth (8 daily; 1hr 25min); Porthmadog (8 daily; 25min).

By bus Buses to Barmouth (Mon–Sat hourly, Sun 3; 30min) and Porthmadog (Mon–Sat 7 daily; 25min) generally call at the train station.

INFORMATION

Tourist information There's no tourist office in town, but the castle's visitor centre (see opposite) can provide all the information you need on the town and area.

ACCOMMODATION

★**Castle Cottage** Y Llech, LL46 2YL ☎01766 780479, ⓦcastlecottageharlech.co.uk. Established restaurant-with-rooms with a contemporary yet cosily informal feel. The seven rooms are decorated in natural tones and very well appointed (big TVs, high-flow showers, leather sofas) but otherwise totally different, many with massive weathered beams and slate floors. Residents get a discount on dinner (see below)

and on green fees at the local golf course. **£130**
Pen Y Garth Old Llanfair Rd, LL46 2SW ☎01766 781352, ⓦpen-y-garth.co.uk. High-quality, and super-friendly, B&B in a former YHA with three, mostly all-white, rooms, each with a view of either the castle or coast. It's popular with cyclists, golfers and walkers – they can provide packed lunches. **£75**

EATING

As.Is Castle Square, LL46 2YH ☎01766 781208, ⓦasis -harlech.com. Marvellous little bistro with tables culled from pallets and filament bulbs strung across the ceiling. Food combinations are refreshingly original, and might include radish, mustard and red pepper strudel with kale and walnut puree (£11.50), or lamb Henri with parmesan polenta and salsa verde. Mon, Tues & Thurs–Sat 5.30–9pm.
★**Castle Cottage** Y Llech, LL46 2YL ☎01766 780479, ⓦcastlecottageharlech.co.uk. There's wonderful food on offer at this unpretentious Modern British restaurant, its walls lined with Welsh art. Two- or three-course menus (£35/£40) include canapés followed by the likes of pan-seared scallops with avocado and poppy-seed dressing, or roasted porchetta with black pudding and calvados jus.

They offer guest rooms, too (see above). Daily 7–9pm.
Cemlyn Tea Shop Stryd Fawr, LL46 2YA ☎01766 780425, ⓦcemlynteashop.co.uk. Upmarket café serving a terrific range of loose-leaf teas and espresso drinks, plus home-made gluten- and dairy-free cakes, and afternoon tea (£6.20). If you can, grab a table on the sunny terrace and soak up the coastal views. Mid-March to Dec Wed–Sun 9.30am–5pm.
Hufenfa'r Castell Castle Square, LL46 2YH ☎07810 164547, ⓦhufenfa.co.uk. The "Castle Creamery" serves up the best ice cream for miles around, made on the premises and with flavours like Welsh fudge, butter pecan and chocolate cherry truffle; delicious sorbets include a wonderful mandarin variety. April–Oct daily 9.30am–5pm.

4

The Dee Valley and around

306 Wrexham and around

310 Chirk and around

312 The Dee Valley

323 Mold and the Vale of Clwyd

VALLE CRUCIS

5

The Dee Valley and around

The Dee Valley and its immediate environs is a region with something of a split identity, encompassing both industrialized flatlands that spill over the border from England and attractive folds of green hill countryside that are as Welsh as anywhere. There's plenty to see here, but few of the sights top most people's list, and visitors often travel through with their minds set firmly on the more obvious destinations further west. The two main routes through the region – the Dee Valley and the Vale of Clwyd – both start in the border country known as the Marches, long contested by the Welsh and English.

At the region's heart is its largest town, **Wrexham**, its industrial hinterland leavened by the mining and smelting heritage along the **Clywedog Valley**. The only surviving Marcher fortress of note is **Chirk Castle**, a potent reminder of the centuries following the Norman conquest of England, when powerful barons fought the Welsh princes for control of these fertile lands.

This makes a fine introduction to the **Dee Valley**, running between the Welsh borders and the rugged mountains of Snowdonia. Its undoubted highlight is **Llangollen**, with the **International Eisteddfod** folk music festival each July and a broad selection of ruins, rides and rambles to tempt visitors throughout the rest of the year. The Dee Valley remains more firmly Welsh than the Marches, and three hundred years after the Normans' arrival this was the site of the first big revolt against them. From his base near **Corwen**, Wales' greatest hero, Owain Glyndŵr, attacked the property of a nearby English landowner, sparking a fourteen-year campaign which, at its height, saw Glyndŵr ruling most of Wales. Little remains to commemorate the era, and most people drive through oblivious of its heritage, making straight for **Bala** with its lake, watersports and cascading rapids.

The bucolic lands to the north reward a leisurely approach. The historic but dull market town of **Mold** is the gateway to the bald tops of the **Clwydian Range**, easy walking country overlooking the pastoral **Vale of Clwyd**. Its sights include the appealing town of **Ruthin** with its fine medieval buildings and lively jail tour, and **Denbigh**, surmounted by its craggy castle.

GETTING AROUND

THE DEE VALLEY AND AROUND

By train Wrexham and Chirk are served by the Chester–Shrewsbury rail line.

By bus Wrexham and surrounding towns are linked by excellent bus services. Bala and the upper Dee Valley are served by the #T3 from Wrexham to Barmouth (via Llangollen). There is no easy connection between Llangollen and Snowdonia: follow the north coast to Llandudno Junction or Bangor and change there.

A short walk from Chirk p.311
The Llangollen International Eisteddfod p.312
The Ladies of Llangollen p.314
Walks from Llangollen p.315
Thomas Telford p.316
Bala in legend p.321

Thomas Charles, Mary Jones and Michael D. Jones p.322
Rafting and watersports around Bala p.323
Walks to Foel Fenlli and Moel Famau p.325
Mountain biking at Coed Llandegla p.327

PONTCYSYLLTE AQUEDUCT

Highlights

❶ Erddig Hall Amble around the most interesting stately home in Wales, complete with finely preserved servants' quarters, outbuildings and gardens. **See p.309**

❷ Llanarmon Dyffryn Ceiriog Enjoy great accommodation and food in a tiny village on the edge of bleak moors. **See p.310**

❸ Plas Newydd, Llangollen An elegant monument to romantic friendship, Plas Newydd always inspires. **See p.314**

❹ Castell Dinas Brân, Llangollen Hike up to this ragged ruin of a Welsh castle for a breath of air and fantastic views. **See p.315**

❺ Pontcysyllte Aqueduct, Llangollen Cruise over Thomas Telford's wonderful aqueduct, part of the Llangollen Canal, one of the great late-Georgian feats of engineering. **See p.317**

❻ Rug Chapel and Llangar Church, Corwen Buy one ticket to visit two small churches – a finer pair you couldn't hope to find. **See p.320**

❼ Ruthin This compact hilltop town offers a cluster of diverting sights and easy access to gentle walks on the Clwydian hills. **See p.326**

HIGHLIGHTS ARE MARKED ON THE MAP ON P.306

5

Wrexham and around

While not classically pretty, **WREXHAM** (Wrecsam), the largest town in north Wales, has a boisterous charm and some fine older buildings amid the identikit chain stores. It has long looked more to the industrial northwest of England than its own Welsh hinterland, so Wrexham's Welshness is obvious only when the national football team plays at the town's Racecourse Ground.

A marketplace in medieval times for the fertile lands all around, Wrexham was propelled into the industrial age upon the discovery of iron ore, coal and lead nearby. The legacy of these times is best seen to the south and west of town in the Clywedog Valley and at the splendidly evocative **Erddig Hall** stately home.

St Giles' Church

Church St, LL13 8LY • Daily 10am–4pm; the tower can be climbed on the last Sat of the month – book through the tourist office (see opposite) • Free; £4 suggested donation for tower • ⓦ wrexhamparish.org.uk

Built at the end of the fifteenth century, **St Giles' Church** is topped with a tower with five tiers and four pinnacles. These were replicated in 1921 at America's Yale University, in homage to Wrexham being the ancestral home of the

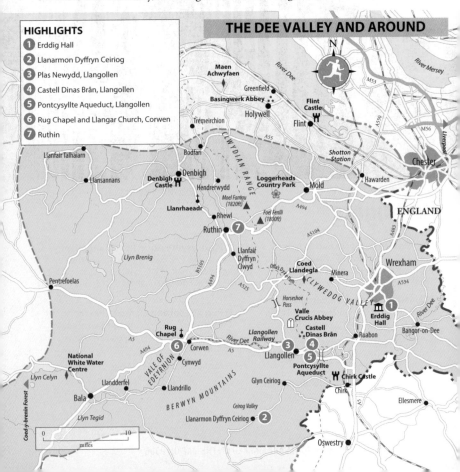

HIGHLIGHTS

1. Erddig Hall
2. Llanarmon Dyffryn Ceiriog
3. Plas Newydd, Llangollen
4. Castell Dinas Brân, Llangollen
5. Pontcysyllte Aqueduct, Llangollen
6. Rug Chapel and Llangar Church, Corwen
7. Ruthin

THE DEE VALLEY AND AROUND

college's benefactor, Elihu Yale. The interior boasts the remains of a mural of the Last Judgement (c.1500) above the entrance to the chancel, and an abundance of Victorian and contemporary stained glass. The church is approached through wrought-iron gates installed in 1718–24 by famed ironworkers Robert and John Davies of Bersham, also responsible for the gates at Chirk Castle and Ruthin church.

Wrexham County Borough Museum

Regent St, LL11 1RB • Mon–Fri 10am–5pm, Sat 11am–4pm • Free • ☎ 01978 297460, ⓦ wrexham.gov.uk/heritage

The small but engaging **Wrexham County Borough Museum** exhibits a miscellany from the town's nineteenth-century boom years, alongside Roman nuggets and the remarkable remains of the Bronze Age **Brymbo Man**, unearthed from a local sandstone burial cist complete with pottery beaker and flint knife. Along with the reconstruction of the grave, look out for the exhibits commemorating the 266 miners who lost their lives in the 1934 Gresford Mine Disaster just north of town.

ARRIVAL AND DEPARTURE   WREXHAM

By train Trains from Bidston (connecting from Liverpool) via Shotton (for the north Wales coast) arrive at Wrexham Central, calling first at Wrexham General (a 10min walk northwest on Mold Rd) to connect with trains from Chester to Shrewsbury (for mid/south Wales).
Destinations Bidston (hourly; 1hr); Chester (hourly; 20min); Chirk (hourly; 15min); London (1 daily; 2hr 40min); Shrewsbury (hourly; 40min).
By bus The bus station on King St is served by frequent

local buses plus some National Express coach services (book online or at the tourist office).
Destinations Bala (8 daily; 90min); Birmingham (1 daily; 2hr 40min); Chester (every 15min; 40min); Chirk (roughly hourly; 40min); Denbigh (hourly; 1hr 15min); Llangollen (5 hourly; 35min); London (1 daily; 6hr); Manchester (1 daily; 1hr 40min); Mold (every 20min; 40min–1hr); Ruthin (hourly; 1hr).

INFORMATION

Tourist office Lambpit St (April to mid-Oct Mon–Sat 10am–5pm; mid-Oct to March Mon–Fri 10am–4pm; ☎ 01978 292015, ⓔ tic@wrexham.gov.uk).

Internet Free at the library and arts centre on Rhosddu Rd (Mon–Fri 9.30am–6pm, Sat 9.30am–4pm).

ACCOMMODATION

★**The Lemon Tree** 29 Rhosddu Rd, LL11 2LP ☎ 01978 261211, ⓦ lemon-tree-hotel-wrexham.com. A Victorian villa converted into a restaurant-with-rooms, with small and simple, tasteful rooms (some, for the same price, with canopy beds and DVD players), and a good restaurant (see below). **£70**

Woodhey 9 Sontley Rd, LL13 7EN ☎ 01978 262555, ⓦ woodhey-guesthouse.com. The best of the central, low-cost B&Bs, with seven rooms in a Victorian house, plus a pleasant lounge and garden and filling breakfasts. Very good value. **£55**

EATING

Anise 1 Smithfield Rd, LL13 8EN ☎ 01978 261273, ⓦ anisewrexham.co.uk. Easily the best curry house in these parts, serving all the usual suspects (£8–16) with aplomb. Mon–Thurs & Sun 5.30–11pm, Fri & Sat 5.30–11.30pm.
Caffi'r Cowt Wrexham County Borough Museum, Regent St, LL11 1RB ☎ 01978 290302. The "Courtyard Café" offers the town's best light lunches – soup, salads, sandwiches, jacket potatoes and rarebits, all celebrating local producers and seasonal ingredients. Mon–Fri 10am–5pm, Sat 11am–3pm.
The Lemon Tree 29 Rhosddu Rd, LL11 2LP ☎ 01978 261211, ⓦ lemon-tree-hotel-wrexham.com. Bustling,

brightly decorated restaurant with an extensive menu of Modern British food such as tandoori salmon with artichoke, cauliflower and hazelnuts, or duck breast with beetroot mashed potato and a blackberry jus (starters and desserts £5–8, mains £13–21). Daily 7am–10pm or later.
Sleepy Panda Farndon St, LL13 8DA ☎ 01978 310700, ⓦ sleepypandawrexham.co.uk. Upmarket Cantonese restaurant (also featuring Szechuan and Beijing dishes) on the edge of the centre opposite the Tesco supermarket (mains £8–12, menus £15–21). Daily 5.30–11.30pm.

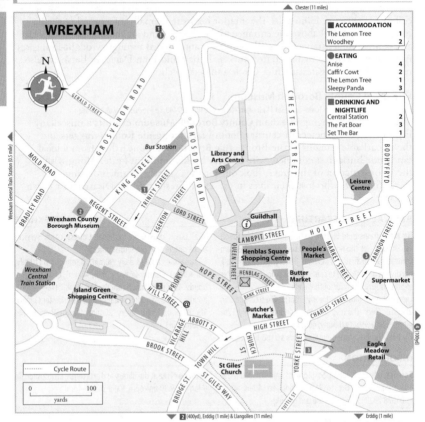

Chester (11 miles)

WREXHAM

N

ACCOMMODATION
| The Lemon Tree | 1 |
| Woodhey | 2 |

EATING
Anise	4
Caffi'r Cowt	2
The Lemon Tree	1
Sleepy Panda	3

DRINKING AND NIGHTLIFE
Central Station	2
The Fat Boar	3
Set The Bar	1

Wrexham General Train Station (0.5 mile)

GERALD STREET

GROSVENOR ROAD

MOLD ROAD

BRADLEY ROAD

CHESTER STREET

BODHYFRYD

Bus Station

Library and Arts Centre @

RHOSDDU ROAD

KING STREET

TRINITY STREET

EGERTON STREET

LORD STREET

REGENT STREET

Wrexham County Borough Museum

Leisure Centre

Guildhall (i)

LAMBPIT STREET

HOLT STREET

MARKET STREET

FARNDON STREET

Henblas Square Shopping Centre

People's Market

QUEEN STREET

HENBLAS STREET

Butter Market

HOPE STREET

Wrexham Central Train Station

Island Green Shopping Centre

HILL STREET

PRIORY ST

BANK STREET

Supermarket

CHARLES STREET

Butcher's Market

VICARAGE HILL

ABBOTT ST

HIGH STREET

YORKE STREET

Eagles Meadow Retail

BROOK STREET

TOWN HILL

CHURCH ST

St Giles' Church

BRIDGE ST

ST GILES WAY

TUTTLE ST

Cycle Route

0   100
yards

Erddig (1 mile)

2 (400yd), Erddig (1 mile) & Llangollen (11 miles)

DRINKING AND NIGHTLIFE

For an evening of quintessentially Welsh entertainment, check at the tourist office for details of the **male voice choirs** that practise in local halls (all year except Aug; Mon, Wed, Thurs & Sun).

Central Station 15 Hill St, LL11 1SN ☎01978 358780, ⓦcentralstationvenue.com. The town's main venue for live bands (£12–20) and club nights; Sat nights feature chart/indie/alternative music. Wed–Sun 7pm–2am.

The Fat Boar 11 Yorke St, LL13 8LW ☎01978 354201, ⓦthefatboarwrecsam.co.uk. This new independent pub, specializing in craft beers and cocktails, is a lively spot for a night out, with live music from 10.30pm on Fri and Sat. Mon–Thurs noon–11pm, Fri & Sat noon–midnight, Sun noon–10.30pm; kitchen Mon–Sat noon–9pm, Sun noon–8pm.

Set The Bar 7 Lord St, LL11 1LF ☎01978 312548 ⓦsetthebarwrexham.co.uk. Above the bus station, this new café-bar is a surprisingly attractive venue for acoustic sessions, bands and open mic nights; there's a rooftop terrace for chilling and a good veggie-/vegan-friendly menu. Tues–Thurs 2–10pm, Fri & Sat noon–late; kitchen Thurs 5–9pm, Fri & Sat noon–9pm.

Clywedog Valley

Tracing an arc around the western and southern suburbs of Wrexham, the **Clywedog Valley** was the crucible of the region's eighteenth-century industrial development. Iron production boomed thanks to abundant ore deposits and cheap water power. As the Industrial Revolution forged ahead and coal became a more important energy source than water, factories moved to be nearer their raw materials, leaving the valley in peace.

5

Clywedog Valley Trail

The long-abandoned industrial ruins in the valley – principally a mine, a mill and an ironworks – have been partly restored and are now waypoints on the nine-mile-long **Clywedog Valley Trail**, easily walked in one long, varied day.

Minera Lead Mines

Minera, 4 miles west of Wrexham, LL11 3DU · Free · ☎ 01978 318970

The surface workings of the **Minera Lead Mines** have largely vanished, and the area is now a country park, but the **engine house**, a pithead derrick and some ore-processing machinery have been rebuilt. For a better impression of the layout, walk up onto the heather-clad hill behind – the edge of a moor called **World's End** – and look back on the valley. In the eighteenth century this was full of mines extracting galena, a silver-and-zinc-rich lead ore, from shafts more than 1200ft deep.

Nant Mill visitor centre

Near Coedpoeth, 3 miles west of Wrexham, LL11 3BT · Easter–Oct daily 10.30am–4.30pm · Free · ☎ 01978 752772

The Clywedog Valley Trail leads a mile and a half east along the river from Minera Lead Mines to the child-oriented **Nant Mill visitor centre**, where you can pick up leaflets for nature trails leading to a very visible section of **Offa's Dyke** in the nearby Pas Power Woods.

Bersham Ironworks

Bersham Rd, LL14 4LP · April to mid-July Sat & Sun noon–5pm; mid-July to Aug Mon & Thurs–Sun noon–5pm · Free · ☎ 01978 318970

The Clywedog Valley Trail runs through woodland to the seventeenth-century **Bersham Ironworks**, expanded by Cumbrian ironmaster John "Iron-Mad" Wilkinson who, in 1775, patented a method for horizontally boring out cylinders. This produced the first truly circular – and thus highly accurate – smooth-bore cannons, hundreds of which were made here for the Napoleonic and American Civil Wars. The works also produced fine-tolerance steam cylinders, for which engineer James Watt was a big customer, creating steam engines that eventually put water-powered sites such as Bersham out of business. The old **foundry** survives largely intact, and around it the ironworks' remains are being unearthed after nearly two centuries of neglect, revealing a broad area of knee-high foundations.

A ten-minute walk east, the **Bersham Heritage Centre** has closed, but outdoor equipment from the agricultural revolution and Bersham Coal Mine are still visible outside.

Erddig Hall

One mile southwest of Wrexham, LL13 0YT · Daily: house late March to July, Sept & Oct 12.30–3.30pm; Aug 10am–5pm; Nov to late March 11am–2.30pm; garden, shop and restaurant late March to Oct 10am–5pm; Nov to late March 11am–4pm · Late March to Oct £11.80, garden only £7.60; Nov to late March £5.60 (kitchens, outbuildings only), garden only £3.70; NT · ☎ 01978 355314, Ⓦ nationaltrust.org.uk/erddig

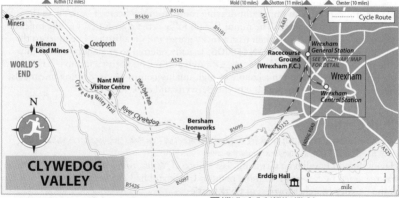

5

Erddig Hall, built in the 1680s, is one of the most fascinating stately homes in Wales. Ever since the Yorke family – all seemingly called Simon or Philip – took over in 1733, they took a hands-off attitude, especially the fourth Simon Yorke, who inherited in 1922. He failed to install electricity, running water, gas or a phone, and ignored the chronic damp that had the Chinese block-print paper peeling off the walls. The National Trust took charge in 1973, restoring the house to its 1922 appearance and returning the jungle of a garden to its formal eighteenth-century plan.

The Servants' Hall

The house itself isn't especially distinguished, but, as nothing was ever thrown away, it holds a collection of fine furniture and portraits, most notably a Gainsborough of the first Philip Yorke. The real interest, though, lies below stairs, particularly in the **Servants' Hall**, where portraits of eighteenth- and early nineteenth-century staff members are accompanied by evocations in verse by a Yorke. You can also see the smithy, stables, laundry and kitchen, and the still-used bake house.

The walled garden

Don't miss the **walled garden**, saved from the worst of the eighteenth-century landscaping craze despite the best efforts of William Emes, a contemporary of Capability Brown, who worked on the surrounding parkland. Manicured yew hedges delineate beds planted with pleached lime trees, the walls support some 150 species of ivy, and apple trees produce fruit celebrated during an apple festival in early October.

GETTING AROUND   **CLYWEDOG VALLEY**

On foot Aside from Minera and Nant Mill, all the sites lie within a couple of miles of Wrexham.
By bus To take in the whole valley in a day (a total of nine miles walking), catch a #9 or #10 bus from Wrexham to Minera, follow the Clywedog Trail to Erddig, then wander the mile and a half back into Wrexham via the *Squire Yorke Inn*.

Chirk and around

The Normans founded **CHIRK** (Y Waun) almost a thousand years ago, their motte remaining as a small tree-covered mound at the southern end of this pleasant enough village, its main street lined with attractive buildings dating from its heyday as a coaching stop where Telford's road to Holyhead entered Wales. The attractive twin-aisled church, full of ornate memorials, is worth a look, as is the war memorial by Eric Gill (1920).

Chirk Castle guards the entrance to the **Glyn Ceiriog** (the Ceiriog Valley), which runs parallel to, and three miles south of, the Dee Valley. This blissfully quiet and beautiful area was for centuries an important droving route from the heart of Wales over the Berwyns and into England. The minor B4500 follows the river for six bucolic miles to the village of Glyn Ceiriog, then past a rocky gorge and on a further five miles to the appealing **LLANARMON DYFFRYN CEIRIOG**. Usually referred to as **Llanarmon DC**, this little spot – nothing but a few houses, a church and the odd artist's studio – has some excellent **accommodation** in a couple of high-quality country inns. Serving fine **meals**, they make good bases for walking in the Berwyns and on Offa's Dyke.

Chirk Castle

Two miles west of Chirk, LL14 5AF • Daily: Jan, March, Oct & Dec 10am–4pm; April–Sept 10am–5pm • Jan & Dec £6.10; March–Oct £12.20; NT • ☎ 01691 777701, ⓦ nationaltrust.org.uk/chirk-castle

Having lured Llywelyn ap Gruffydd, last Prince of Wales, to his death, Roger Mortimer was rewarded by Edward I with the grant of Chirk and in 1295 began the construction of the massive Marcher fortress of **Chirk Castle**.

5

A SHORT WALK FROM CHIRK

On the way back from Chirk Castle you could deviate for a fun **short walk** (1.5 miles return; 30–45min; flat) along the **Shropshire Union Canal**, taking in a canal tunnel, an aqueduct and the English border. About 50yd west of the railway station a short track leads down to the entrance to the 460yd **Chirk Tunnel**. Walk south through the tunnel (a torch is handy but not essential), to emerge at the start of **Chirk Aqueduct** over the River Ceiriog, and a parallel rail viaduct. You can walk to the far end where the canal enters England. Return the same way, or avoid the tunnel by using Station Road, which runs above it.

The gatescreen

Access to the castle is guarded by a magnificent Baroque **gatescreen**, the finest work of the Davies brothers of Bersham, who wrought it between 1712 and 1719. Ebullient floral designs are capped by the Myddleton coat of arms and a red hand, the family's crest and source of the region's many "Hand" hotels. The gates are flanked by a pair of wolves, perhaps a memorial to one of the last wolves in Wales, said to have kept watch over the moat in the 1680s.

The castle

From the gates, an oak-lined avenue (pedestrians and cycles only) leads up to the **castle**, an austere drum-towered place softened only by its mullioned windows. The original plan was probably to mimic Beaumaris Castle, started just a couple of months earlier, but Chirk lacks Beaumaris's purity and symmetry. It seems the southern walls were never completed, perhaps because of the unstable slope, and attackers were able to enter here in 1322 and 1330; the present north gate and south wall were built around 1400 against Owain Glyndŵr's forces.

The castle was bought in 1595 by Sir Thomas Myddelton, whose son found himself besieging his own home in the Civil War after it was seized by Royalist forces; in 1659 he joined a Royalist revolt and was besieged by the Parliamentarians. The Myddeltons added a **Long Gallery** and grand **state apartments**, leaving a legacy of sumptuous rooms reflecting sixteenth- to nineteenth-century tastes, many now returned to their original states after some Victorian meddling by Pugin. The **east wing** includes one of the last great Welsh family libraries, with volumes dating back to 1513.

Note that in January and December only the **Adam Tower** (c.1300) is open, furnished with wooden benches and a truckle bed; you can climb up two flights and further down to the dungeon.

The gardens

Leave time to explore the clipped yew hedges in the beautiful ornamental **gardens** or trace the section of Offa's Dyke that runs across the front of the house (it was flattened in 1758 for use as a cart track).

ARRIVAL AND DEPARTURE

CHIRK

By train The station is on Station Ave, a quarter mile to the west.
Destinations Chester (hourly; 30min); Shrewsbury (hourly; 25min); Wrexham (hourly; 15min).

By bus Buses stop in the town centre on Holyhead Rd.
Destinations Llanarmon DC (3 daily, via Chirk train station; 30min); Llangollen (hourly; 30min); Wrexham (roughly hourly; 40min).

ACCOMMODATION AND EATING

Bridge End Inn Bridge St, Ruabon, LL14 6DA ☎ 01978 810881, ⓦ mcgivernales.co.uk. This traditionally authentic and very friendly little place was CAMRA's real-ale pub of the year in 2011; they are happy to show visitors their brewery at the back. They stock other fine beers and ciders; food is limited to pies and Scotch eggs. Mon–Thurs 5–11pm, Fri 4–11pm, Sat & Sun noon–11pm.

Fron Frys Glyn Ceiriog, LL20 7AA ☎ 01691 718880, ⓦ fronfrys.co.uk. Lovely farmhouse B&B about a mile down the B4579 towards Oswestry; it's dog- and

5

outdoor-activity-friendly, and there's a secluded family wing. **£60**

Hand Hotel Llanarmon DC, LL20 7LD ☎ 01691 600666, ⓦ thehandhotel.co.uk. Converted sixteenth-century farmhouse with a convivial wood-beamed bar, a relaxed dining room and a modern spa. Starters (£5–6) might include cream of tandoori leek soup or a cheese brûlée with Earl Grey-infused dates, while mains (£14.50–26) feature local meats and cod, and a vegetarian dish. The older rooms (£135) – less well-appointed but more atmospheric –have the edge over those in the modern wing. Bar Mon–Sat

11am–11pm, Sun noon–11pm; kitchen daily noon–2.15pm & 6.30–8.45pm. **£95**

West Arms Llanarmon DC, LL20 7LD ☎ 01691 600665, ⓦ thewestarms.co.uk. Ancient farmhouse-turned-inn with stone-flagged floor and a gorgeous inglenook fireplace, plus a public bar and garden. There are a couple of cheaper, more modest rooms, but you'll really want one of the characterful older rooms (£145). Enjoy filling dinners (starters £6–8, mains £15–20) or affordable bar meals (sandwiches £6–7, mains £10–16). Daily noon–late; kitchen noon–9pm. **£75**

The Dee Valley

The **Dee Valley** has long been the main corridor from the English Marches to Snowdonia, and it remains the most interesting route west. The course of the River Dee (Afon Dyfrdwy) is traced by Thomas Telford's A5 road between London and Holyhead, passing **Chirk** with its fine Marcher castle, **Llangollen** with its hilltop castle ruins, broken-down abbey and medieval bridge and **Corwen**, Owain Glyndŵr's stronghold, with a couple of beautiful small churches nearby.

Llangollen

Wedged in the narrow Dee Valley between the Berwyn and Eglwyseg mountains, **LLANGOLLEN** is the embodiment of a Welsh town in both setting and character. Licking the angled buttresses of Llangollen's weighty Gothic bridge, the River Dee cuts a wide arc around the base of **Dinas Brân**, a conical tor surmounted by castle ruins. On its south bank, half a dozen straggling streets form the core of the scattered settlement.

THE LLANGOLLEN INTERNATIONAL EISTEDDFOD

Llangollen is heaving in summer, but never more so than during the first or second week of July, when for six days the town explodes into a frenzy of music, dance and poetry. Unlike the very Welsh National Eisteddfod, the **Llangollen International Eisteddfod** (ⓦ international -eisteddfod.co.uk) draws around four thousand amateur performers from fifty countries, all competing for prizes in their chosen disciplines. Dances and choral performances take place at Plas Newydd, Valle Crucis and just about anywhere that people can gather, though competitive performances are concentrated in the main venue, the **Royal International Pavilion**. When the day's competition is over, headlining stars often pack out the pavilion, and the final Sunday is the all-day party known as Llanfest.

The first public eisteddfod was held in Corwen in 1789, and the international festival has been held in its present form since 1947, when it was started by one Harold Tudor to soothe the social wounds of World War II. Forty choirs from fourteen countries performed at the first (entirely choral) event, and it expanded fast, drawing praise from Dylan Thomas, who declared that "the town sang and danced, as though it were right". Today this town of three thousand people is swamped by up to 120,000 visitors, but there is an irresistible *joie de vivre* as brightly costumed dancers walk the streets and fill the restaurants and cafés.

Tickets for all but the headliners can often be obtained on the day itself. All-day access to the main site, with no guarantee of a seat, costs just £15 a day. Accommodation, however, needs to be booked months in advance, so unless you are going specifically for the festivities, avoid trying to stay in Llangollen during the eisteddfod.

The eisteddfod is followed by the less frenetic **Llangollen Fringe** (ⓦ llangollenfringe.co.uk), with a number of more "alternative" acts – music, dance, comedy and so on – performing in the town hall on Castle Street over the third week in July.

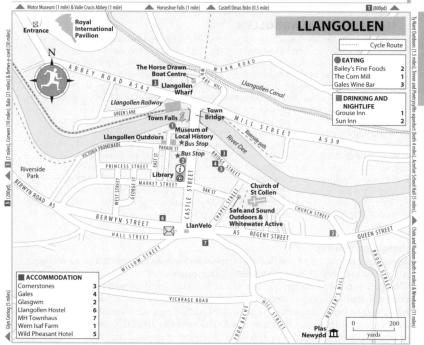

With its wealth of historical sights, canal trips over a fine aqueduct, steam-train rides and enjoyable walks, Llangollen is very popular throughout the summer, particularly in early July when the town barely copes with the thousands of visitors to Wales' celebration of worldwide folk music, the **Llangollen International Eisteddfod** (see box, opposite). This mostly takes place in the **Royal International Pavilion**, its white plastic roof raised in 1992 to evoke the shape of the marquee formerly erected here each year, but looking more like some giant armoured reptile.

Brief history

As the only river crossing point for miles, Llangollen was an important town long before the early Romantics arrived at the end of the eighteenth century, when the Napoleonic Wars cut off their European Grand Tours. Turner came to paint the swollen river and the Cistercian ruin of **Valle Crucis**, a couple of miles up the valley; John Ruskin found the town "entirely lovely in its gentle wildness"; and George Borrow made Llangollen his base for the early part of his 1854 tour detailed in *Wild Wales* (see p.459). The rich and famous came not only for the scenery, but to visit the celebrated **Ladies of Llangollen**, an eccentric couple who became the toast of society from their house, **Plas Newydd** (see box, p.314). But the town's rural charm had already been gnawed at by one of the century's finest engineers, Thomas Telford (see box, p.316), who squeezed both his **London–Holyhead trunk road** and the **Llangollen Canal** alongside the river, spanning the valley with the majestic **Pontcysyllte Aqueduct**.

Town bridge and Town Falls

Few visitors can resist admiring the view from the **town bridge** which, though widened and strengthened over the years, has spanned the river since 1345. Upstream, the Dee pours through the fingers of shale that make up the unimaginatively dubbed **Town Falls**. Castle Street continues south from the bridge, passing the tourist office.

5

THE LADIES OF LLANGOLLEN

Lady Eleanor Butler and Sarah Ponsonby – better known as the **Ladies of Llangollen** – were Anglo-Irish aristocrats who twice failed to elope together, dressed in men's clothes. In 1778 they were grudgingly allowed to leave home with an annual allowance of £280, enough to settle in Llangollen, where they became the country's most celebrated lesbians – though apparently they were affronted by the suggestion that their relationship was anything other than chaste. Regency society was captivated by their "model friendship" in what Simone de Beauvoir called "a peaceful Eden on the edge of the world".

Despite their desire for a "life of sweet and delicious retirement", they didn't seem to mind the constant stream of gentry who called on them. They found the Duke of Wellington a "charming young man, hansom, fashioned tall and elegant", and also approved of Walter Scott, though he deemed them to be "a couple of hazy or crazy old sailors" in manner, and like "two respectable superannuated clergymen" in their mode of dress. Thomas de Quincey humoured the ladies, if only to earn forgiveness for his friend Wordsworth, who had displeased them by referring to their house as "a low roofed cot" in an inelegant poem composed in the grounds. Gothic oriel windows and porches were added by the ladies to a simple farm cottage, but the mock-Tudor half-timbering was added after their time.

Llangollen Railway

Llangollen station, Abbey Rd, LL20 8SN • April–Sept Mon–Fri 3 services daily (usually steam), plus most Sat & Sun year-round up to 7 steam and diesel services daily • £15 return • ☎ 01978 860979, Ⓦ llangollen-railway.co.uk

Wherever you are in Llangollen, the hills echo to the shrill cry of steam engines easing along the standard-gauge **Llangollen Railway**. Shoehorned into the north side of the valley, it runs from Llangollen's time-warped station past the Horseshoe Falls to Corwen, ten miles west. Using a restored section of the disused Ruabon–Barmouth line (pushed through Llangollen in 1865), belching steam engines (and diesels and railcars) haul ancient carriages sporting the liveries of their erstwhile owners.

Most visitors simply ride to the end of the line and back (1hr 40min), but consider getting off partway along and walking back to town along the Dee Valley Way (see box, opposite), perhaps stopping for a pint in the riverside *Grouse Inn* at Carrog. Equally, from Berwyn station you can cross the rebuilt Chain Bridge to the Horseshoe Falls (see p.316) and stroll back along the canal towpath to Llangollen.

Museum of Local History

Parade St, LL20 8PW • Daily 10am–5pm • Free • ☎ 01978 862862, Ⓦ llangollenmuseum.org.uk

Llangollen's Tardis-like **Museum of Local History** occupies a ring of alcoves, centred on a replica of Eliseg's pillar, each covering a topic such as Valle Crucis, the eisteddfodau, the Ladies of Llangollen (see box abvoe) and the railway. There are lots of historic photos and documents, as well as an animatronic scribe.

Church of St Collen

Church St, LL20 8HY • Late May to Sept Tues–Sat 2–6pm

Llangollen takes its name from the **Church of St Collen**, dedicated to its sixth-century founder. Rebuilt in the thirteenth century, it has a fine sixteenth-century oak hammerbeam roof, said (wrongly) to have come from Valle Crucis. In the graveyard, don't miss the triangular monument to Mary Carryll erected by her mistresses, the so-called Ladies of Llangollen (see box above), who are also buried here and commemorated on the other two sides of her pillar.

Plas Newydd

Half a mile up Hill St, LL20 8AW • **House** April, May & Sept Mon & Wed–Sun 10.30am–5.30pm; June–Aug daily 10.30am–5.30pm; Oct Mon & Wed–Sun 10.30am–4pm • £6 • **Grounds** Daily 9am–dusk (until 9pm in summer) • Free • ☎ 01978 862834, Ⓦ plasnewyddllangollen.co.uk

For almost fifty years, charming black-and-white **Plas Newydd** was home to the famed **Ladies of Llangollen** (see box above). An excellent, free self-guided audio tour leads you around the house's half-dozen rooms, modest apart from the riot of dark-wood panelling: a wonderful if slightly oppressive effect set off by assorted furniture similar to that owned by the ladies. As a counterpoint you can also visit the spartan attic room of their loyal housekeeper Mary Carryll. Outside, take time to wander through the twelve acres of formal **grounds**, including the **knot garden**, perfectly complementing the front of the house.

Castell Dinas Brân

Above town, LL20 8DY – follow signs from Llangollen Wharf • Open access • Free

It's the views up and down the valley that justify the 45-minute slog up to **Castell Dinas Brân** (Crow's Fortress Castle), perched on a hill 750ft above the town. The lure certainly isn't the few sad but evocative vaulted stumps, a poor testament to what was once the district's largest and most important Welsh fortress. Prince Madog ap Gruffydd Maelor, ruler of northern Powys, raised the castle around 1260 on the site of an Iron Age hillfort. It was abandoned as soon as 1277, during Edward I's first campaign against Llywelyn ap Gruffydd, and left to decay, the antiquarian John Leland finding it "all in ruin" in 1540. Even so, it's a great place to be as the sun sets, imagining George Borrow sitting up here translating seventeenth-century bard Roger Cyffyn:

Gone, gone are thy gates, Dinas Brân on the height!
Thy warders are blood-crows and ravens, I trow;
Now no-one will wend from the field of the fight
To the fortress on high, save the raven and the crow.

Llangollen Motor Museum

Pentre Felin, 1 mile west of Llangollen, LL20 8EE • March–Oct Mon & Fri–Sun 9.30am–5pm • £5 • ☎ 01970 860324, ⓦ llangollenmotormuseum.co.uk

An easy mile's walk west along the canal towpath leads to the **Llangollen Motor Museum**, a former slate-dressing shed that now smells evocatively of engine oil and old leather. Passing through a workshop area, you'll find three dozen bikes from the glory years of British manufacturing and two dozen cars, most of them still road-worthy. Check out the 1957 three-wheeler "bubble car" and what is claimed to be Britain's oldest caravan, a tiny wooden affair.

WALKS FROM LLANGOLLEN

The OS 1:25,000 Explorer map 255 (Llangollen & Berwyn) is recommended.
In addition to the OS map, the following walks are detailed on an excellent free leaflet from the tourist office (see p.317), picking out pubs and points of interest along the way. See also ⓦ deevalleywalks.com.

Llangollen is a great place to explore **on foot**, perhaps using a narrowboat or steam train to shorten a loop; you can in any case walk the towpath east or west.

Dee Valley Way This well-marked route along the north side of the valley between Llangollen and Corwen is thirteen miles long, but can be broken into smaller sections, or shortened by taking the Llangollen Railway to Glyndyfrdwy or Carrog then walking back. You can lunch well at the *Grouse Inn* at Carrog (see p.318).

Llangollen History Trail An easy-to-follow loop (6 miles; 3–6hr; 500ft ascent), initially tracing the canal towpath to Horseshoe Falls, then visiting Valle Crucis Abbey and Eliseg's Pillar before returning via Dinas Brân.

North Berwyn Way A wilder option flanking the south side of the Dee Valley between Llangollen and Corwen, along the wild moorland tops of the Berwyn hills and past an old slate quarry. The full walk is fifteen miles, but shorter versions are outlined in the leaflet from the tourist office, and you can create a loop using parts of the Dee Valley Way.

5

Valle Crucis Abbey

A542, 1.5 miles north of Llangollen, LL20 8DD • Daily: April–Oct 10am–5pm; Nov–March 10am–4pm • April–Oct £4; Nov–March free;
CADW • ☎ 01978 860326, �🌐 cadw.gov.wales/daysout/vallecrucisabbey

The gaunt remains of **Valle Crucis Abbey** stand in Glyn y Groes, the "Valley of the Cross". In 1201, Madog ap Gruffydd Maelor chose this majestic setting for one of the last Cistercian foundations in Wales, as well as Britain's first Gothic abbey. Despite a devastating fire in its first century, and a complement of far from pious monks, it survived until the Dissolution in 1536. The church fell into disrepair and the monastic buildings were employed as farm buildings. Later, Turner painted the abbey, imaginatively shifting it to sit immediately below Dinas Brân.

Valle Crucis greets you with its best side, the church's largely intact west wall pierced by the frame of a rose window. Head through the mostly ruined cloister and past the vaulted chapterhouse to reach the monks' dormitory, where a set of gravestones supposedly includes that of Owain Glyndŵr's resident bard, Iolo Goch. There are also displays on monastic life, and the small white cottage at the back contains an excellent exhibit conjuring up abbey life as it would have been around 1400.

Eliseg's Pillar

A542, 400yd north of Valle Crucis Abbey, LL20 8DF • Open access • Free; CADW • ☎ 01443 336000, �🌐 cadw.gov.wales/daysout/ellisegspillar

The cross that gave Valle Crucis its name is the 8ft-tall **Eliseg's Pillar**, set on a Bronze Age cairn. Erected to a prince of Powys in the early ninth century by his great-grandson, it stood more than 20ft high but was smashed during the Civil War of the 1640s. The stump remains, but you can now see only half of the full 31 lines glorifying the lineage of the princes of Powys, translated from the remaining pieces in 1696.

Llangollen Canal

When it opened in 1806, the **Llangollen Canal** was one of Britain's finest feats of canal engineering, designed both to transport slate from the Horseshoe Pass quarries and as a water supply for the Shropshire Union Canal. It starts at **Horseshoe Falls**, a crescent-shaped weir two miles west of Llangollen, which diverts water from the River Dee into the canal. In recognition of its significance, and its almost entirely intact state, the

---

THOMAS TELFORD

The poet Robert Southey dubbed **Thomas Telford** (1767–1834) the "Colossus of Roads" in recognition of his pre-eminence as the greatest road builder of his day, but he was also one of the greatest canal engineers. Throughout the early nineteenth century, he managed some of the most ambitious projects yet attempted, and there was seldom a public work on which his opinion wasn't sought.

Born in Scotland, Telford was apprenticed to a stonemason in London where he taught himself engineering architecture, eventually earning himself a job with the Ellesmere Canal Company, which aimed to link the Severn, Dee and Mersey rivers. His reputation was forged on the **Pontcysyllte Aqueduct**, part of the **Llangollen Canal**, hailed as innovative even before he had completed it.

Though lured away to build the Caledonian Canal in Scotland and St Katherine's Docks in London, he returned to Wales after the 1800 Act of Union between Britain and Ireland, when a good road was needed to hasten mail and to transport the new Irish MPs to and from parliament in London. What is now the A5 was wedged into the same valley as Telford's Llangollen Canal, then driven right through Snowdonia with its gradient never exceeding 1 in 20. From 1815 the combination of its near-level route and the high quality of its well-drained surface cut hours off journey times, but the Dublin ferries left from Holyhead on the island of Anglesey, separated from the mainland by the Menai Strait. Telford's solution and his greatest achievement was the 580ft-long **Menai Suspension Bridge** (1826), strung 100ft above the strait to allow tall ships to pass under. Though the idea wasn't completely novel, the scale and the balance of grace and function won the plaudits of engineers and admiring visitors from around the world.

eleven miles from Horseshoe Falls across the Pontcysyllte Aqueduct and the Chirk Aqueduct (see box, p.311) to the English border are now a UNESCO World Heritage Site (ⓦpontcysyllte-worldheritage.co.uk).

Pontcysyllte Aqueduct

Four miles east of Llangollen, LL20 7TP · **Boat tours** Easter–Oct daily noon, 1pm, 2pm & 3pm; 45min · £7.50 · ☎01978 824166, ⓦcanaltrip.co.uk

The Llangollen Canal avoids locks for its first fourteen miles, partly thanks to the 1000ft-long **Pontcysyllte Aqueduct**, rising almost 127ft above the Dee and still the world's highest navigable aqueduct. It was designed by the great engineer Thomas Telford (see box opposite), who placed long cast-iron troughs on nineteen great stone piers – a bold move for its time. You can take a vertiginous walk along the **towpath** across the aqueduct or a leisurely **narrowboat ride** across and back.

ARRIVAL AND DEPARTURE   LLANGOLLEN

By car With your own vehicle, the most spectacular way to approach Llangollen is over the 1350ft Horseshoe Pass (A542) from Ruthin.

By train Trains stop 5 miles east at Ruabon, which is served by Llangollen–Wrexham buses.

By bus Buses stop on Parade St, including a daily National Express coach from/to Birmingham and London; tickets are

sold at the tourist office. Note that it's difficult to access central Snowdonia from Llangollen: go via Denbigh and the north coast.

Destinations Bala (9 daily; 1hr); Birmingham (1 daily; 4hr 30min); Chirk (hourly; 20min); Corwen (9 daily; 20min); Dolgellau (9 daily; 1hr 45min); Llanarmon DC (3 daily; 1hr); London (1 daily; 7hr 30min); Wrexham (5 hourly; 35min).

INFORMATION AND GETTING AROUND

Tourist office Y Capel, Castle St (Mon–Sat 9.30am–5pm, Sun 9.30am–4pm; ☎01978 860828, ✉llangollen@nwtic .com, ⓦllangollen.org.uk). Free internet access is available.

On foot Buses are fairly infrequent, but you can easily walk most places: even Valle Crucis, the most distant sight, is

only a mile and a half along the towpath.

Bike rental LlanVelo, 3 Berwyn St (☎01978 806226, ⓦllanvelo.co.uk); Safe & Sound, Chapel St (☎01978 860471, ⓦsasoutdoors.co.uk); Hire Cycles 2 Go, Station Rd, Trevor (☎01691 773532, ✉hirecycles2go@hotmail.co.uk).

ACTIVITIES AND OPERATORS

NARROWBOAT TRIPS

Anglo Welsh Trevor Basin, LL20 7TT ☎0117 304 1122, ⓦanglowelsh.co.uk. Groups of up to ten can rent a self-steer narrowboat from £120/day. You can travel west as far as Llangollen and east across the aqueduct to Chirk; there are a couple of good pubs for lunch.

The Horse Drawn Boat Centre Llangollen Wharf, LL20 8TA ☎01978 860702, ⓦhorsedrawnboats.co.uk. Taster rides in a horse-drawn narrowboat (45min; £7), horse-drawn trips to Horseshoe Falls (2hr; £12.50) and four-mile motorized trips to cross the Pontcysyllte Aqueduct (2hr; £14). Mid-March to Oct daily; Nov & Dec Sat & Sun.

Jones the Boats Trevor Basin, LL20 7TT ☎01978 824166, ⓦcanaltrip.co.uk. Daily 45-minute narrowboat trips across the aqueduct and back (see opposite).

RAFTING AND GORGE WALKING

Llangollen Outdoors The Fringe Shed, Parade St, LL20 8PW ☎01978 897220, ⓦllangollenoutdoors.co.uk. All

sorts of adventure activities including whitewater rafting, canoeing and kayaking, gorge walking and rock climbing (£50–55/half-day); book in advance.

Safe and Sound Outdoors Chapel St, LL20 8NW ☎01978 860471, ⓦsasoutdoors.co.uk. Rafting (£55/3hr session), and gorge walking, climbing/abseiling, mountain biking, kayaking and canoeing (all £50/half-day), plus bushcraft (£95/day).

Ty Nant Outdoors Plas Ifa, Sun Bank, 1.5 miles east, LL20 8AG ☎01978 869326, ⓦtynantoutdoors.com. From £49 for quadbiking (2hr) or canoeing (3hr), £55–59 for a half-day kayaking or gorge-walking/canyoning, or £89 for a day of climbing/abseiling.

Whitewater Active Chapel St, LL20 8NW ☎01978 860763, ⓦwhitewateractive.co.uk. Rafting (£55/2hr session) with several runs down a bouncy but unmenacing 0.5-mile section of the Dee, plus mountain-biking and gorge-walking (£50/half-day) and ropes courses (£40/2hr session).

ACCOMMODATION

Llangollen has plenty of decent places to **stay**. Rooms can be scarce in high summer, especially during the eisteddfod (see box, p.312), though this is alleviated by people letting out rooms at peak times – these can be booked through the tourist office.

5

HOTELS AND GUESTHOUSES

Cornerstones 15–19 Bridge St, LL20 8PF ☏01978 861569, ⓦ cornerstones-guesthouse.co.uk. The over-the-top exuberance of this luxury B&B, spread across three sixteenth-century houses, can easily be forgiven when you see the river views. **£120**

Gales 18 Bridge St, LL20 8PF ☏01978 860089, ⓦ galesofllangollen.co.uk. Large rooms in a very comfortable and central guesthouse – above the restaurant of the same name – some with brass beds and oak beams. **£85**

★**Glasgwm** Abbey Rd, LL20 8SN ☏01978 861975, ⓦ glasgwm-llangollen.co.uk. Extremely relaxed B&B where the relatively modest facilities are compensated for by the engaging hosts, whose good taste is reflected in the decor of the doubles, twin and single (which has its own deep bath). There's a piano and plenty of books, and they offer Offa's Dyke Path pick-ups and drop-offs as well as packed lunches and dinners. **£70**

MH Townhaus Hill St, LL20 8EU ☏01978 860775, ⓦ manorhausllangollen.com. An offshoot of Ruthin's fine *Manorhaus* (see p.327), this is a simpler place, but nevertheless a classy addition to Llangollen's range of B&Bs. **£70**

Wild Pheasant Hotel Berwyn Rd (A5), 0.5 mile west, LL20 8AD ☏01978 860629, ⓦ wildpheasanthotel .co.uk. This comfortable hotel has an older wing with standard rooms and a luxurious, tastefully decorated new wing with rooms from £90; there's also a good restaurant. Guests can use the modern spa pool, steam room and sauna (£10 day pass). Check online for deals. **£80**

HOSTEL AND CAMPSITE

★**Llangollen Hostel** Berwyn St, LL20 8NB ☏01978 861773, ⓦ llangollenhostel.co.uk. Neat bunks in modernized rooms (mostly en suite, with four to six bunks) in a Victorian townhouse. There's a comfy lounge with games and books and a well-equipped kitchen (with free breakfast). Dorms **£18**, doubles **£45**

Wern Isaf Farm Wern Rd, LL20 8DU ☏01978 860632, ⓦ wernisaf.co.uk. Simple but idyllic campsite on the flanks of Dinas Brân (turn right over the canal on Wharf Hill and climb steeply for almost a mile). Some hookups. Closed Nov–March. **£15**

EATING

Bailey's Fine Foods Castle St, LL20 8NU ☏01978 860617, ⓦ baileysfinefoods.com. Stop off at this deli next to the tourist office for fine picnic ingredients from pies, pasties and cold meats to cakes, beer and more. Mon–Sat 9am–5pm, Sun 10.30am–4.30pm.

★**The Corn Mill** Dee Lane, L20 8PN ☏01978 869555, ⓦ brunningandprice.co.uk/cornmill. Superbly converted town-centre mill, with a deck by the falls that catches the afternoon sun. Good all day for coffee, fine ales, sandwiches (£6) and well-prepared café-bar food. Mains (£11–19) might include crispy harissa lamb with couscous salad and felafels; seabass fillets with mussels, samphire and seasonal veg; or spinach and ricotta tortellini with roasted butternut squash. Mon–Sat 11am–11pm, Sun 11am–10.30pm; kitchen Mon–Sat noon–9.30pm, Sun noon–9pm.

★**Gales Wine Bar** 18 Bridge St, LL20 8PF ☏01978 860089, ⓦ galesofllangollen.co.uk. Old church pews, wooden floors, delicious bistro-style food and a good range of wines from around the world make this chilled-out place a long-standing favourite. A la carte dishes all come in starter or main-course portions (£6–8/£11–19), and there's a two-course set lunch (£10). Mon–Sat noon–2pm & 6–9.30pm, Sun noon–2pm.

DRINKING AND NIGHTLIFE

Grouse Inn Carrog, 8 miles west along the A5, LL21 9AT ☏01490 430272, ⓦ thegrouseinncarrog.co.uk. Smart, modernized country pub with outdoor seating overlooking the River Dee, a 5min walk from the Llangollen Railway's Carrog station. Freshly cooked meals are on offer. Daily noon to around midnight; kitchen noon–10pm.

Sun Inn 49 Regent St, LL20 8HN. Convivial slate-floored late-closing locals' pub with a wide range of well-kept beers and live bands (of just about any stripe) most nights. Tues–Fri 7pm–2am, Sat & Sun 5pm–2am.

ENTERTAINMENT

Outside the eisteddfod and its fringe, there's not much **nightlife**, but local bands (and occasionally bigger acts) do play from time to time; check out the scene at the *Sun Inn* (see above).

Côr Meibion Froncysyllte Acrefair School Hall, just off the A539, 5 miles east, LL14 3SH ⓦ fronchoir.com. Côr Meibion Froncysyllte, one of Wales' most exalted male voice choirs, rehearses at this local school hall. Directions are given on their website. Mon & Thurs 7–9pm.

Royal International Pavilion Abbey Rd, LL20 8SW ☏01978 860111, ⓦ llangollenpavilion.co.uk. With a covered stage and smaller hall, the eisteddfod site serves as a year-round venue for anything from choral and classical concerts to comedy and rock gigs.

5

Corwen and around

In the early fifteenth century local landowner Owain Glyndŵr set out from **CORWEN**, ten miles west of Llangollen, to wrest back Wales from Henry IV's English barons. In his time, cattle-droving routes from Anglesey and from Harlech met at Corwen for the final push to the English markets. Later a rail junction, the town declined steadily once the line closed; but the extension of the Llangollen Railway to Corwen is reversing this, making it a handy base for visiting parking-challenged Llangollen. More enticingly, Corwen has on its doorstep two fine **churches** and the bucolic charms of the **Vale of Edeyrnion**.

In the centre of town, a modern equestrian **statue** of Owain Glyndŵr looks set to terrorize his persecutors once again, and he is further recalled at the thirteenth-century church, where a cross incised into the grey stone lintel of the south porch (largely hidden by a grille) is known as **Glyndŵr's Sword**. He is said to have cast it in anger at the townspeople from Pen y Pigyn, the hill behind, though it actually predates him by half a millennium. Just east of the centre, the imposing cruciform **workhouse** (built in 1840) now houses craft shops and a café. Paths from here and the church up to the Coed Pen y Pigyn viewpoint were remade to mark the railway's reopening in 2015.

Corwen Museum

London Rd (A5), LL21 0DR • Mon, Wed & Fri–Sun 10.30am–3.30pm • Free • ⑩ corwenmuseum.org.uk

Opened in 2015 opposite the workhouse, the community-run **Corwen Museum** has interesting displays on Owain Glyndŵr, agriculture and droving, and in particular on the way in which the town was transformed by Telford's A5 (from 1804 until 1848, when the Irish mails were transferred to the coastal railway) and the railway (from 1864 to 1964).

Rug Chapel

A494, 1 mile west of Corwen, LL21 9BT • April–Oct Mon–Fri 10am–5pm • £4 including Llangar Old Parish Church; CADW • ☎ 01490 412025, ⑩ cadw.gov.wales/daysout/rugchapel

Taking its name from the Welsh word for heather, **Rug Chapel** is one of Wales' best examples of an unaltered seventeenth-century church. It gives a charming insight into worship almost four hundred years ago, when Mass was a private clerical devotion, with the congregation kept behind the rood screen.

Little has changed since it was built in 1637 by William Salusbury, former privateer and collaborator on William Morgan's Welsh Bible (see box, p.394). The plain exterior gives no hint of the richly decorated interior: wooden angels support a roof patterned with stars and amoebic swirls, and a painted skeleton represents the transience of life and the inevitability of death. Informative displays in the ticket office give more details.

Llangar Old Parish Church

One mile south of Rug Chapel, LL21 9BT • April–Oct Mon–Fri 12.30–2.30pm; obtain ticket at Rug Chapel • £4 including Rug Chapel; CADW • ☎ 01443 336000, ⑩ cadw.gov.wales/daysout/llangaroldparishchurch

In 1853, parish boundary changes made the fourteenth-century **Llangar Old Parish Church** redundant, saving its extensive fifteenth-century wall paintings and seventeenth-century figure of death from obliteration. The interior woodwork is wonderful, from the beamed roof and minstrel's gallery down to the eighteenth-century box pews.

Vale of Edeyrnion

South of Corwen, the B4401 heads towards Bala through the **Vale of Edeyrnion** past a couple of the area's best country hotels. None of the vale's peaceful villages (Cynwyd, Llandrillo and Llandderfel) is particularly interesting, but all give access to the largely undiscovered Berwyn Range to the east, where you can hike all day without seeing a soul. The rather easier Tegid Way links the three villages with Bala.

ARRIVAL AND DEPARTURE **CORWEN AND AROUND**

The Interchange behind *The Eagles Inn* on the main square acts as a de facto **bus** station.

Destinations Bala (9 daily; 35min); Llandrillo (9 daily; 12min); Llangollen (hourly; 20min); Ruthin (9 daily; 25min, connecting to Rhyl); Wrexham (9 daily; 50min).

ACCOMMODATION AND EATING

Bison Grill A5, 2 miles west of Corwen, LL21 0EH ☏ 01490 411100, ⓦ rhug.co.uk. Next to the Rhug Estate organic farm shop, this excellent bistro serves popular bison burgers, soup (£5), sandwiches (£6–11.50), à la carte meals (£11–34) and Sun roasts; also takeaways. Mon–Thurs & Sun 8am–5.30pm, Fri & Sat 8am–6pm.

Bron-y-Graig A5, east edge of Corwen, LL21 0DR ☏ 01490 413007, ⓦ north-wales-hotel.co.uk. Comfortable, authentically renovated Victorian rooms in a house built for the Sheriff of Denbigh. Most rooms have a sofa and either river or forest views, and there's a reasonable restaurant. Assorted dinner, B&B and multi-night deals. **£69**

Palé Hall Llandderfel, LL23 7PS ☏ 01678 530285, ⓦ palehall.co.uk. This grand mansion, built in 1871 for a railway magnate, is now the finest hotel in north Wales, with large and luxurious rooms and a range of elegant lounges where a piano or harp plays before dinner. The restaurant, supervised by Michael Caines, uses seasonal and largely organic ingredients to produce food that is locally rooted but globally flavoured. Two-/three-course

lunch menus £30/£37; dinner around £60 à la carte. Daily noon–2pm & 7–9pm. **£235**

★ **Tyddyn Llan Country House** Llandrillo, 6 miles southwest of Corwen on the B4401, LL21 0ST ☏ 01490 440264, ⓦ tyddynllan.co.uk. Luxuriate in this elegant restaurant-with-rooms, where a sense of calm descends as you pass through the gate. The thirteen rooms are as comfortable as you need, but the real focus is Bryan Webb's Michelin-starred Modern British food. Two-/three-course lunches £29/£36; three-course dinner menu £65; six-/nine-course tasting menus £75/£90. Mon–Thurs 7–9pm, Fri–Sun 1–2pm & 7–9pm. **£190**

Tyn-y-Fron Llandderfel, LL23 7RA ☏ 01490 440346, ⓔ dee.crogan@btinternet.com. Beautiful glamping spot overlooking the bucolic Vale of Edeyrnion. They have a bell tent with a double futon and two single airbeds (bring sheets), a warming chiminea, gas hob and exterior fire pits; a cabin sleeping four; a shepherd's hut sleeping two (all April–Aug); and a self-catering barn for two (all year; one-week minimum stay in summer). Bell tent **£35**, cabin **£40**, shepherd's hut **£55**, barn **£75**

Bala and around

The little town of **BALA** (Y Bala) sits at the northern end of Wales' largest natural lake, **Llyn Tegid** (Bala Lake). The four-mile-long body of water is perfect for **windsurfing**, with steady winds from the coast whipping up the Talyllyn Valley between the Aran and Arenig mountains that flank the lake.

Bala's second lake, **Llyn Celyn**, five miles northwest, is very much an artificial affair created amid huge controversy in the 1960s, to supply water to Liverpool, in England. A lakeside chapel commemorates the valley-bottom village of Capel Celyn, flooded by the reservoir.

Tomen-y-Bala

On Heol y Domen, off the northern end of High St • Generally daily 9am–dusk • Free

Bala's role in Welsh history far outweighs its current modest status. The Romans built a fort at the southern end of the lake (not open to the public), then Roger Mortimer erected a motte in about 1310. Climbed by a spiral path, the **Tomen-y-Bala** (Bala Mound) gives a panoramic view over the rooftops.

BALA IN LEGEND

Bala sits slightly back from the edge of Llyn Tegid, perhaps to avoid the legendary catastrophe that **drowned** the old town, which stood where the lake is now. The story tells of the **prince Tegid Foel**, who was warned by a voice that because of his cruelty to his people "Vengeance will come". On the birth of his grandson, he held a banquet and hired the best harpist in the land, who heard a voice saying "Vengeance has come". The harpist followed a bird to a hill where he slept, waking to find the town submerged beneath the lake that took the drowned prince's name.

The lake also has a **legendary beast** lurking in its waters, but thankfully the tourist hype about "Tegi" hasn't done to Bala what the Nessie industry has done to Scotland. On the other hand, the lake really is home to a species of fish found nowhere else: the **gwyniad**, or whitefish.

5

Bala Lake Railway

The Station, Llanuwchllyn, LL23 7DD • Easter–Oct 4 trains most days • £7 single, £11 return • ☎ 01678 540666, ⓦ bala-lake-railway.co.uk

The 24-inch-gauge **Bala Lake Railway** follows the level, lakeside course of the former Ruabon–Barmouth standard-gauge line, closed in 1963. Renovated north Wales slate quarry trains are put to use for a pretty, if hardly thrilling, five-mile run. Either walk around the head of the lake to the northeastern end of the line (10min), or drive six miles southwest to the main terminus at Llanuwchllyn where you can combine your train trip with a visit to *The Eagles Inn* (see opposite).

ARRIVAL AND GETTING AROUND

By car With your own vehicle, the best approach is the A4212 from Blaenau Ffestiniog over the wild open moorlands between the twin peaks of Arenig Fawr and Arenig Fach. Unfortunately, this route isn't covered by public transport.

By bus Bala's only bus, the #T3, stops on the High St. It runs from Wrexham through the Vale of Edeyrnion to

BALA AND AROUND

Barmouth.

Destinations Corwen (9 daily; 35min); Dolgellau (9 daily; 35min); Llandrillo (9 daily; 25min); Llangollen (9 daily; 1hr); Wrexham (9 daily; 85min).

Bike rental R.H. Roberts, 7 High St (£15/day; ☎ 01678 520252, ⓦ rhrcycles.magix.net/public).

ACCOMMODATION

HOTELS AND GUESTHOUSES

★**Abercelyn** A494, a mile south of Bala, LL23 7YF ☎ 01678 521109, ⓦ abercelyn.co.uk. The pick of the local mid-range places, this fine country house occupies an eighteenth-century former rectory. Rooms (two with bathtub) are stylishly understated, and there are also three self-catering cottages sleeping up to six (minimum three nights; from £80/night). Discounts for multi-night stays. **£90**

Bryniau Golau Llangower, less than 2 miles south of Bala, off the B4403, LL23 7BT ☎ 01678 521782, ⓦ bryniau-golau.co.uk. Set in extensive grounds across the lake from Bala, this multi-award-winning B&B has

three very spacious rooms richly decorated in antique country style and an elegant lounge; walkers and cyclists are very welcome. **£110**

Monfa 6 Pensarn Rd, Bala (A494), LL23 7SR ☎ 01678 521388, ⓦ monfa.co.uk. At the south end of town, Bala's cheapest B&B maintains high standards with one double and one twin room each with private (not en-suite) bathroom and bathrobes as standard . Good single rates (£50). **£65**

HOSTEL, BUNKHOUSE AND CAMPSITES

Bala Backpackers 32 Tegid St, Bala, LL23 7EL ☎ 01678 521700, ⓦ bala-backpackers.co.uk. This friendly, central

THOMAS CHARLES, MARY JONES AND MICHAEL D. JONES

During the seventeenth and eighteenth centuries, the religious needs of the Welsh were poorly met by the established Church. None of the bishops was Welsh, few were resident, and most regarded their positions as stepping stones to higher appointments. This allowed the rise of the new Nonconformist sects – Quakers, Baptists and Methodists. Itinerant religious teachers improved literacy and the strident sermons of native Welsh-speakers fired their enthusiasm. **Thomas Charles**, the chief protagonist of Methodism in Wales, gave the movement a huge boost in 1804 by founding the British and Foreign Bible Society, a group committed to distributing local-language bibles worldwide.

Charles had already reprinted Bishop Morgan's 1588 original Welsh translation, but was down to his last copy when 16-year-old **Mary Jones**, the daughter of a poor weaver from the far side of Cadair Idris, arrived on his doorstep. She had saved money for six years to buy a bible from him and, in 1800, walked the 25 miles to Bala, barefoot some of the way, prompting Charles to found the society. His statue stands outside Bala's Presbyterian church on Tegid St, while the new **Mary Jones World**, a mile south of town in the former church of Llanycil (April–Oct daily 10am–5pm; £4; ☎ 0808 178 4909, ⓦ bydmaryjonesworld.org.uk) aims to tell the story of Mary and Thomas and to explore the impact of the Bible on Wales and the world; it's family-focussed, with a café, picnic area and playground.

Many of the more pious converts sought greater religious freedom, and in 1865 reformist preacher **Michael D. Jones** recruited around Bala for the 153 Welsh settlers who established Y Wladfa, "The Colony", in the Chubut Valley of Argentine Patagonia. Jones stayed in Wales, setting up the Bala-Bangor Theological College and leading campaigns for Welsh causes; many now regard him as "the father of modern Welsh nationalism".

RAFTING AND WATERSPORTS AROUND BALA

The only real **whitewater rafting** in Wales takes place on the Afon Tryweryn at the **National White Water Centre**, 4 miles northwest of Bala on the A4212 (Jan to mid-Oct & Dec daily 9am–dusk; ☎01678 521083, ⊛ukrafting.co.uk). Water is released on around two hundred days a year, crashing down a mile and a half of Grade III rapids where competitions often take place on summer weekends. It's interesting enough to drop by and watch what's going on; alternatively book ahead to have a go yourself. There are all sorts of options, including a taster (40min–1hr; £35; wetsuit rental extra) involving two runs down the course. The 2hr session (£66) typically gives you four runs, or you can step up a notch to the Orca Adventure (half-day; £88), involving two runs in a normal raft followed by a chance to tackle the rapids in a more challenging two-person inflatable. Proficient **kayakers** with their own gear can take to the water for a fee of £14, and **canyoning** trips (£55 for half a day) are also on offer.

By the shores of Llyn Tegid, the **Bala Adventure and Watersports Centre** (☎01678 521059, ⊛balawatersports.com) runs numerous aquatic courses and rents out kayaks (£12/hr), windsurfers (£18/hr), sailing dinghies (£28/hr) and more.

hostel offers beds (linen rental £3) in small dorms or larger, partitioned rooms. There are also private twins/doubles (some en suite), most of them across the road. Cook for yourself or order breakfast in advance (£4.50). Closed Oct–April except by prior reservation. Dorms **£21**, doubles **£49**

Bala Bunk House Tomen-y-Castell, A494, 1.5 miles north of Bala, LL23 7HD ☎01678 520738, ⊛balabunkhouse.co.uk. Self-catering bunkhouse with small dorms, one self-contained unit sleeping six, and communal lounge and cooking areas, plus an inviting barbecue area in the woods at the back. Use your own sleeping bag or rent a duvet (£2). **£17**

Pen-y-Bont B4319, 1 mile southeast of Bala, LL23 7PH ☎01678 520549, ⊛penybont-bala.co.uk. This well-tended campsite, by the outlet of the lake, is the nearest to town. Along with tent and caravan sites they have a gypsy caravan (bring your own bedding). Closed Nov to mid-March. Camping **£20**, gypsy caravan **£60**

Tyn Cornel A4212, 4 miles northwest of Bala, LL23 7NU ☎01678 520759, ⊛tyncornel.co.uk. Camping and caravan park by the National White Water Centre (see above); it's usually packed with paddlers at weekends. Closed Nov–Feb. **£18**

EATING AND DRINKING

The Eagles Inn Llanuwchllyn, 5 miles southwest of Bala, LL23 7UB ☎01678 540278, ⊛yr-eagles.co.uk. Cosy local 0.5 mile from the Lake Railway station, serving excellent bar meals in hearty portions (mostly £9–12) with several vegetarian options and a kids' menu. You'll need to book at weekends. Also handy for the male voice choir rehearsals in the village hall at 7.30pm on Thurs. Mon–Fri 6–11pm, Sat 11am–midnight, Sun noon–3pm & 6–11pm; kitchen Mon–Fri noon–2pm & 6–9pm, Sat & Sun noon–2pm.

Eco-Caffe 21 Tegid St, LL23 7EH. Opposite *Bala Backpackers*, this is a traditional tearoom that also serves

salad platters, chilli and curry (£7.50) as well as cakes and drinks. April–Oct most days noon–3pm.

Plas-yn-Dre 23 High St, LL23 7LU ☎01678 521256. Spacious bistro popular with locals for dishes such as fettuccine with a seasonal ragoût (£11), lamb cawl or pie of the day (£13). New guest rooms were added in 2017. Daily noon–10pm.

Y Cyfnod 48 High St, LL23 7AF ☎01678 521260. A local legend, this simple café was founded in 1885 and is still going strong for breakfasts, sandwiches, panini, jacket potatoes and cheap, filling lunches. Daily 9am–5pm.

Mold and the Vale of Clwyd

One of the least-travelled paths through northwest Wales leaves the Marches at **Mold**, crosses the soft contours of the **Clwydian Range** – along whose tops, studded with hillforts, runs a section of the long-distance **Offa's Dyke Path** – and approaches the north coast through the wide and fertile **Vale of Clwyd**. Lying between England and Snowdonia, and between Powys and Gwynedd, this was known as Perfeddwlad or the Middle Country and was the heart of Tudor Wales, when many churches were rebuilt in a characteristic double-naved style. Gerard Manley Hopkins eulogized the valley where he studied for the priesthood in the 1870s, celebrating its beauty in some of his

5

best-loved poems, *The Windhover*, *In the Valley of the Elwy* and *Pied Beauty*. Linked by quiet roads through a patchwork of small farms, two attractive market towns of warm-hued stone sit on hills above the valley. **Ruthin** is the pick of the two, with its thirteenth-century castle, compact core of medieval buildings, intriguing jail and host of good places to stay. Seven miles northwest is **Denbigh**, best known for its "hollow crown", the high-walled castle ruin that sits above the town.

Mold

The slow pace of **MOLD** (Yr Wyddgrug) is only disrupted by its Wednesday and Saturday **markets**, when stalls supplant cars along the High Street. Despite much interesting history tied to the town, there's not much reason to linger, unless you're here for a performance at the region's theatrical powerhouse, **Clwyd Theatr Cymru** (⍵ theatrclwyd.com).

Mold was founded during the reign of William Rufus, though only a copse of beeches atop the mound of **Bailey Hill** marks the site of the motte-and-bailey fortifications at the top of High Street. Its commanding view over the River Alyn (Afon Alun) shows the strategic value of the site, which alternated between Welsh and Anglo-Norman control until Edward I's clampdown on the region. In 1465, during the War of the Roses, local lord Rheinallt ap Gruffydd captured the Mayor of Chester, took him back to the Tower in Nercwys and presented him with a pie containing the rope that would hang him.

St Mary's church

High St, CH7 1AZ • Usually summer Wed & Sat mornings; at other times, get the key from J.H. Jones shop, 53 High St • Free • ⍵ moldchurch.org

In gratitude for Henry VII's victory in 1485, his mother, Margaret Beaufort, commissioned the airy Perpendicular **St Mary's church**, set serenely on a grassy hillock. The north aisle retains its original oak roof carved with Tudor roses, and there's a quatrefoil and animal frieze outside beneath the small clerestory windows.

Among the Tudor stained glass, a Victorian window is Mold's meagre memorial to its most famous son (at least to English-speakers) and Wales' greatest painter, the eighteenth-century landscapist **Richard Wilson**, whose grave is outside the church's north entrance. Although Wilson co-founded the Royal Academy in 1768 and was acclaimed by Ruskin, his work was undervalued and he died a pauper.

Mold Museum

Inside the library, Earl Rd, CH7 1AP • Mon & Thurs 9.30am–7pm, Tues, Wed & Fri 9.30am–5pm, Sat 9.30am–1.30pm • Free • ☎ 01352 754791

Local tailor and novelist **Daniel Owen** (1836–95) is commemorated by a statue outside the library, with an inscription stating "Not for the wise and learned have I written but for the common people". While his bluntly honest accounts of ordinary life made him unpopular with the Methodist leaders of the community, Owen, writing only in Welsh, became his country's most prominent writer. Within the library itself, the little **Mold Museum** contains a small but effective display on the man, as well as a replica of the **Mold Cape**, an almost 4000-year-old beaten gold ceremonial garment discovered nearby in 1833. The original is in the British Museum.

Loggerheads Country Park

A494, 3 miles west of Mold, CH7 5LH • Daily 8am–9pm; visitor centre April–Oct daily 10am–4.30pm; Nov–March Sat & Sun 10am–4pm • ☎ 01352 810586, ⍵ clwydianrangeanddeevalleyaonb.org.uk/loggerheads-country-park

For peaceful walks beside the trickling River Alyn it's hard to beat family-oriented **Loggerheads Country Park**. Except for an old water channel and water wheel, you'd barely know that in the nineteenth century this was a busy lead-mining area. A short, fully accessible trail follows a wooded gorge, and a longer 1.5-mile loop climbs to the top of the limestone cliffs.

ARRIVAL AND INFORMATION

By bus Buses stop behind the cattle market on Hallfields, east of High St.
Destinations Chester (every 12min; 50min); Flint (hourly; 20min); Loggerheads (9 daily; 10min); Ruthin (hourly; 25–45min); Wrexham (every 20min; 40–50min).

MOLD

Tourist information Mold tourist office has closed, but you can pick up leaflets and information at Flintshire Connect, in the same building as the library and Mold Museum on Earl Rd (Mon & Thurs 9.30am–7pm, Tues, Wed & Fri 9.30am–5pm, Sat 9.30am–1.30pm; ⓦ discoverflintshire.gov.uk).

ACCOMMODATION

Beaufort Park Hotel Alltami Rd, CH7 6RQ ☏ 01352 758646, ⓦ beaufortparkhotel.co.uk. A modern conference/business hotel with ranks of spacious rooms in a rural setting with a decent restaurant and café. Heavy discounts online (sometimes down to £51 a room). **£130**
Broncoed Uchaf Nercwys, 1 mile south of Mold, CH7 4ED ☏ 01352 700817, ⓦ broncoeduchaf.com. A warm

welcome awaits at this solid farmhouse, with spacious rooms, two lounges, a sheltered garden and excellent breakfasts. **£50**
Tower Nercwys, 1 mile south of Mold, CH7 4EW ☏ 0135 700220, ⓦ towerwales.co.uk. This fortified manor, owned by the same family for five centuries, has just three plush rooms full of antique furniture and family portraits. **£80**

EATING AND DRINKING

Alexander's 52 High St, CH7 6BH ☏ 07912 159802. Facing the church, this buzzy place is ideal for cooked breakfasts, tasty panini, salads and good espresso. Mon–Sat 9am–5pm.
Caffi Florence Loggerheads Country Park, 3 miles west of Mold, CH7 5LH ☏ 01352 759225, ⓦ caffiflorence .co.uk. The lawns outside Loggerheads' excellent café make a great spot for salads, sandwiches, hot lunches and afternoon teas, all made on site. Coffee is Fairtrade, and they are dedicated to sourcing locally. Daily 10am–5pm.
Glasfryn Raikes Lane, 1 mile north of Mold off the

A5119, CH7 6LR ☏ 01352 750500, ⓦ brunningandprice .co.uk/glasfryn. Head here for high-class pub food (mains £11–17) and an ever-changing range of real ales, best enjoyed on the terrace with views over Mold to the hills beyond. Mon–Sat 10.30am–11pm, Sun noon–10.30pm; kitchen daily noon–9.30pm.
Y Delyn 3 King St, CH7 1LB ☏ 01352 759642. Behind a plain red-brick Georgian facade, this cosy bar is renowned for its Belgian beers but also has a good choice of real ales, a fine wine list and tapas on offer (three for £12). Tues–Sat 6pm–1am; kitchen Tues–Sat 6.30–9pm.

The Clwydian Range

Mold is separated from the Vale of Clwyd by the wide-open spaces of the **Clwydian Range**, six miles west of town, easily accessed west of Loggerheads, where the B5429 branches right off the A494. Following an old turnpike route between Mold and Ruthin, it climbs up to **Bwlch Pen Barras**, a shallow pass where it meets the **Offa's Dyke Path** (though not the Dyke itself), which follows the line of a Bronze Age trading route along these bald tops, passing the remains of six Iron Age hillforts. The highest point is the 1820ft **Moel Famau**, topped by a truncated **Jubilee Tower**. The subject of much disparaging comment when it was built in 1810 to celebrate George III's fifty-year reign, the 85ft-high obelisk collapsed in a storm in 1862 and was only partially repaired in 1970; in 2013, new stairs were built to a viewpoint atop the base. On a clear day views as far as Snowdon and Cadair Idris make a walk out here worthwhile (see box below). The relatively gentle terrain makes this a popular spot at weekends: stick to weekdays if possible.

WALKS TO FOEL FENLLI AND MOEL FAMAU

From the car park at **Bwlch Pen Barras** a boad path climbs steeply southwards to loop around the most impressive of the Clwydian hillfort sites on 1800ft **Foel Fenlli** (1.5 miles return; 40min; 500ft ascent). Excavations have uncovered 35 hut circles within earthworks three-quarters of a mile across. The height from ditch bottom to bank top reaches 35ft in places, with triple defences on the more vulnerable eastern flank.

From the same car park and Coed Moel Famau, just below to the east, good paths lead north to **Moel Famau** (3 miles return; 1–2hr; 650ft ascent) and the Jubilee Tower.

For more **information**, pick up the *Clwydian Range* leaflet from Loggerheads (see opposite).

By bus The Clwydian Range is crossed by buses #1 or #X1 between Mold and Ruthin.

Tourist information ⓦ clwydianrangeanddeevalleyaonb .org.uk.

Ruthin

With its attractive knot of half-timbered buildings, a handful of sights and some of the finest food and lodging in the area, **RUTHIN** (Rhuthun), ten miles west of Mold, should not be missed. The town, set on a commanding rise in the Vale of Clwyd, centres on **St Peter's Square**, the heart of the medieval town.

St Peter's Square

The hilltop **St Peter's Square** is surrounded by timber-framed buildings. One of them, on the south side, was built in 1421 as a courthouse and prison and still retains under the eaves the barely visible stump of a gibbet, last used in 1679 to hang a Franciscan priest. It's adjacent to the similar **Exmewe Hall** (now Barclays Bank), outside which sits an unimpressive chunk of limestone known as **Maen Huail**. A less-than-convincing story has King Arthur and Huail, brother of a Welsh chieftain called Gildas, fighting over the attentions of a woman. Huail pierced Arthur's thigh, giving him a permanent limp, but promised never to mention Arthur's loss of face. Inevitably, though, Huail couldn't resist taunting him about it and an incensed Arthur had him beheaded on this stone. Ruthin's most photographed building, now housing **Myddleton Grill on the Square**, was built in 1657 in Dutch style and topped by serried dormer windows known as "The Seven Eyes of Ruthin".

St Peter's church

St Peter's Square, LL15 1BL · Daily 9am–4pm · Free

St Peter's church, rebuilt in 1310, is approached via a photogenic pair of iron gates wrought in 1727 by the Davies brothers (who also made the gates of St Giles' church in Wrexham and Chirk Castle). The ceiling of its north aisle consists of 408 carved black oak panels with Tudor Rose bosses, brought from Basingwerk Abbey (see p.392) after its dissolution by Henry VIII. Ask someone to turn the lights on, if possible. By the altar is a bust of Gabriel Goodman who, in 1574, while Dean of Westminster, re-founded **grammar school** that had been closed by Henry VIII forty years earlier; the building still stands behind the church, next to the Christ's Hospital Almshouses, also established by Goodman in 1590.

Nantclwyd y Dre

Castle St, LL15 1DP · April, May & Sept Mon & Sun 11am–3pm, Sat 11am–5pm; June–Aug Mon & Wed 11am–4pm, Tues & Sun 11am–3pm, Sat 11am–5pm · £5 · ☎ 01824 709822, ⓦ nantclwydydre.co.uk

Timber-framed **Nantclwyd y Dre** partly dates from 1435, making this medieval hall-house the oldest in Wales. Restored from near dereliction using ancient techniques, it's a wonderfully higgledy-piggledy place, with wonky oak floors and interesting nooks and crannies; you feel as if you're nosing around someone's home. The house has been extended and updated over five centuries, its major phases re-created in seven main rooms including Jacobean and Georgian bed chambers, a Stuart study, a Victorian schoolroom and an entrance hall of 1942, looking much as it did when the last family moved out in 1984.

Ruthin Gaol

Clwyd St, LL15 1HP · April–Sept Mon & Wed–Sun 10am–5pm · £5 · ☎ 01824 708281, ⓦ ruthingaol.co.uk

Ruthin Gaol has been a prison site since 1654, but the so-called "Gruelling Experience" on offer focuses on the Victorian era and the four-storey cell block (1868) inspired by London's Pentonville. It was designed to improve living conditions and penal correction, with one prisoner per cell and the requirement to work while incarcerated.

MOUNTAIN BIKING AT COED LLANDEGLA

Some of the best **mountain biking** in northeast Wales is in **Coed Llandegla Forest**, roughly nine miles from Ruthin, Llangollen and Wrexham (late March to late Oct Mon–Thurs 9am–9pm, Fri–Sun 9am–6pm; late Oct to late March Mon, Tues & Thurs–Sun 9am–dusk, Wed 9am–9pm; free; ☎01978 751656, ⓦcoedllandegla.com). Trails range from a gentle, family-friendly loop to technically challenging black runs and extreme freeriding options. Walking and trail-running options are also available, including a section of the Offa's Dyke Path, and a bird hide from where you might see black grouse. There's a **visitor centre** (Tues & Thurs–Sun 9am–5.30pm, Wed 9am–8.30pm) with a café and bike rental (Tues–Sun 9am–4pm; from £25/half-day, £35/day).

Most upper-floor cells now house the county archive, but you can poke around elsewhere, following the free audio guide that traces the prison life of a fictional "Will the Poacher". Panels explain daily prison life along with the real meaning of "screws" and "bobbies" and the source of the expression "money for old rope". One tale tells of John Jones, the "Welsh Houdini", who seemingly spent half his life escaping from prisons. He absconded from Ruthin in 1913 before being shot five days later.

Ruthin Craft Centre

Park Rd (A525), LL15 1BB • Daily 10am–5.30pm • Free • ☎01824 704774, ⓦruthincraftcentre.org.uk

The excellent **Ruthin Craft Centre**, Wales' centre for the applied arts, lies 300yd northeast of St Peter's Square. The modern zinc-and-stone building houses three galleries, six artists' studios, workshops, a shop and an excellent café. Exhibits include superb contemporary glass, textiles and ceramics as well as more traditional woodworking.

Ruthin Castle

Castle St, LL15 2NU • ☎01824 702664, ⓦruthincastle.co.uk

Hidden away in the trees on the southern edge of town lie the red sandstone ruins of **Ruthin Castle**, built for Edward I in 1277. By 1400 it was owned by Lord de Grey of Ruthin, who used his influence with Henry IV to have Owain Glyndŵr declared a traitor and acquire his land. In response, Glyndŵr crowned himself Prince of Wales and stormed Ruthin on market day, plundering the goods being sold by the English and then razing the town. The castle went on to resist the Parliamentarians for eleven weeks during the Civil War, after which it was destroyed. A neo-Gothic mansion was built between 1826 and 1852, with Italian and rose gardens landscaped around the ancient moat and crumbling ruins, and became a **hotel** in 1963. Strictly speaking, the grounds are open to residents and peacocks only, but you can have a wander if you're eating or drinking here (see p.328).

ARRIVAL AND INFORMATION

RUTHIN

By bus Buses stop at the corner of Market St and Wynnstay Rd.
Destinations Corwen (hourly; 30min); Denbigh (every 30min–hourly; 25min); Mold (hourly; 40min); Rhyl (hourly; 75min); Wrexham (hourly; 45min).

Internet Free access at the library on Record St.

ACCOMMODATION

★**Firgrove** B5105, Llanfwrog, a mile southeast, LL15 2LL ☎01824 702677, ⓦfirgrovecountryhouse.co.uk. A large Georgian house with manicured gardens, offering B&B and superb three-course dinners (£38); there's an understated elegance to everything here. **£100**

★**Manorhaus** 10 Well St, LL15 1AH ☎01824 704830, ⓦmanorhausruthin.com. This Georgian house, home to a fine restaurant (see p.328), also has eight boutique rooms each boldly themed by a different artist. Plus a small gym, sauna, bar and a library of DVDs, CDs, books and games.

Excellent last-minute deals online. **£95**
Sarum House 2 Record St, LL15 1DS ☎01824 703886, ⓦsarumhouseruthin.com. In this Grade II-listed seventeenth-century townhouse you'll find six light and spacious rooms, welcoming hosts and a superb breakfast. **£80**
Rhydonnen Llanychan, 3 miles north, LL15 1UG ☎01824 790258, ⓦrhydonnen.co.uk. A well-appointed B&B in a fifteenth-century black-and-white farmhouse with oak beams and inglenooks; there's a pool table and fantastic home baking. **£58**

5

EATING AND DRINKING

★**Leonardo's Deli** 4 Well St, LL15 1AH ☎01824 707161, ⊕leonardosdeli.co.uk. Great Welsh/German deli/bakery where quality is paramount. Take away a delicious stuffed baguette, a steak and red wine pie or a delectable tarte tatin. April–Oct Mon–Fri 8.30am–5pm, Sat 8.30am–4.30pm; Nov–March Mon–Thurs 9am–3.30pm, Fri 9am–4.30pm, Sat 9am–3pm.

★**Manorhaus** 10 Well St, LL15 1AH ☎01824 704830, ⊕manorhausruthin.com. Stylish decor, subdued lighting and understated service make this a superb place for dinner (£25/£30 for two or three courses). After canapés in the lounge you might have a blue-cheese mousse with pear purée, followed by twice-cooked belly pork or seabass fillet with lemon risotto cake, mange tout and samphire. Desserts are delicious, and there's a good wine list. Tues–Sat 6.30–9pm.

On the Hill Restaurant 1 Upper Clwyd St, LL15 1HY ☎01824 707736, ⊕onthehillrestaurant.co.uk. This cosy wood-floored restaurant with oak beams is hard to beat for its personal service and bistro-style meals (mains £14–26). Lunch comes in the form of one, two or three courses (£13.50/16.50/19.50); they also do a great pudding sampler and have a well-thought-out wine list (from £3.50/glass). Mon–Sat noon–2pm & 6.30–9pm, Sun 5–9pm.

Ruthin Castle Castle St, LL15 2NU ☎01824 702664, ⊕ruthincastle.co.uk. Nip into this grand and extensively refurbished baronial castle (see p.327) for afternoon tea, a drink or a bar meal in the panelled library bar, or enjoy a formal dinner at *Bertie's* (named after King Edward VII, a regular visitor). They also put on ersatz Welsh medieval banquets (£55). Mon–Sat 7–9.30pm, Sun 1–4pm & 7–9.30pm.

Ye Olde Cross Keys Mwrog St, Llanfwrog, LL15 2AD ☎01824 308081, ⊕yeoldecrosskeys.co.uk. Welcoming pub serving greatly improved bar meals but at modest prices; also Sun lunch (£11). Pub & kitchen Mon–Wed noon–3pm & 5.30–11pm, Thurs–Sat noon–11pm, Sun noon–10pm.

Denbigh and around

The castle ruins dominating the Vale of Clwyd eight miles north of Ruthin herald **DENBIGH** (Dinbych), in medieval times a fortified hill town, which still tumbles down towards its old centre where the Wednesday **market** takes place.

High Street is lined by a pleasing array of colonnaded medieval buildings which, thankfully, haven't been over-restored, helping retain the feel of a working town. In front of the **County Hall** (built in 1572, and now the library) stands a new statue of Henry Morton "Dr Livingstone, I presume?" Stanley, born here in 1841. From High Street, Broomhill Lane (with various artistic installations) climbs through the crumbling **Burgess Gate**, the town's former northern entry, to the vast grassy ward of ruined **Denbigh Castle**.

Denbigh Castle

Castle Lane, LL16 3NB • Daily: April–Oct 10am–5pm; Nov–March 10am–4pm • April–Oct £4; Nov–March Sun–Wed free, Thurs–Sat £4; CADW • ☎01745 813385, ⊕cadw.gov.wales/daysout/denbighcastle

For a long time, the River Clwyd formed the border between England and Wales, guarded here by a now-vanished Welsh castle, which probably gave the town its name, meaning "small fort". When the area eventually fell to Edward I, he entrusted Denbigh to Henry de Lacy, Earl of Lincoln, who from 1282 employed Edward's experienced military architect, James of St George, to build a fortress.

Today the most imposing remnant of **Denbigh Castle** is the **gatehouse**, with three octagonal towers enclosing an originally vaulted hall, making it one of the finest defensive structures of the era. You enter beneath a weathered statue of Edward I in a niche, flanked on the right by the Prison Tower (stained by five garderobes discharging into a common cesspit) and the Porter's Lodge Tower on the left. From here, you can walk atop the wall as far as the Great Kitchen Tower. On the far side, the Postern Tower was strengthened after the Welsh revolt of 1294, as were the **town walls** that branched from the castle walls to form the outer ward. Continue along the short section of wall walk (get the key from the castle office, the library or the *Glass Onion* café) down to the **Goblin Tower**, from where in 1646 Sir William Salusbury threw the castle keys down to the victorious Roundheads, ending a six-month-long siege after receiving the king's written order to surrender.

In 1563, Elizabeth I sold the castle to her favourite, Robert Dudley, Earl of Leicester, who chose a site just below it for the Puritan church he hoped would supplant St Asaph cathedral, four miles north. Abandoned upon his death in 1588, its shell is now known as **Leicester's Folly**.

St Dyfnog's church

Llanrhaeadr, 3 miles south of Denbigh, LL16 4NN • Daily 10am–4pm or later • Free

St Dyfnog's church seems much too large for this tiny hamlet. In the sixth century St Dyfnog established a hermitage here by a healing well, and donations from pilgrims funded the building of the present church in 1533. Typically for the area it has twin naves and, though heavily restored in 1880, drips with original features, including a glorious carved barrel roof with vine-leaf patterns and outstanding stained glass.

The **Jesse Window**, at the east end of the north aisle, depicts the descent of Jesus through the House of Israel from Jesse, the father of King David. One of the finest in Britain, it draws you in to the Virgin and Child, surrounded by 21 of their bearded, ermine-robed ancestors. The window is believed to be contemporaneous with the church, though it was removed and stored in an oak chest during the Civil War. Its companion in the south aisle was probably destroyed then, but in the nineteenth century fragments which may have belonged to it were found nearby and pieced together to form the west window.

ARRIVAL AND INFORMATION

By bus Buses stop centrally, on High St.
Destinations Rhyl (every 20min; 40min); Ruthin (every 30min; 30min); St Asaph (every 20min; 15min).
Tourist information The library (Mon 9.30am–7pm,

DENBIGH AND AROUND

Tues, Wed & Fri 9.30am–5pm, Thurs 9.30am–1pm, Sat 9.30am–12.30pm) has free internet access and tourist leaflets. The website ⓦ visitdenbigh.co.uk is also useful.

ACCOMMODATION

HOTEL AND GUESTHOUSES

Castle House Bull Lane, LL16 3SN ☎ 01745 816860, ⓦ castlehousebandb.co.uk. Three wonderfully luxurious rooms in one of Denbigh's finest houses – in the grounds of Leicester's Folly just below the castle – all with ornate furnishings and long views. Great guests' lounge and lovely grounds. **£150**

Guildhall Tavern Hall Square, LL16 3NU ☎ 01745 816533, ⓦ guildhalltavernhotel.co.uk. This town-centre coaching inn has not quite lived up to its classy refurb, but its eleven spacious rooms retain plenty of character. There's pub food in the bar downstairs. Mon–Thurs & Sun 4–10.30pm, Fri & Sat 4pm–midnight; kitchen Tues–Sat 5–9pm. **£79**

Pentre Mawr Country House Llandyrnog, 3 miles east, LL16 4LA ☎ 01824 790732, ⓦ pentremawrcountryhouse

.co.uk. Set in 200 acres of parkland, this neat mansion is now a delightful boutique guesthouse with spacious rooms (some with antique furniture and jacuzzi baths; £180), a few minimalist suites (with terraces and hot tubs) and safari-style glamping (also with hot tubs; £180). Dinner available on Fri and Sat. **£120**

CAMPSITE

Station House Caravan Park A541, Bodfari, 4 miles northeast of Denbigh, LL16 4DA ☎ 01745 710372, ⓦ stationhousecaravanpark.co.uk. Denbigh's handiest campsite, in a blissful rural setting close to the Offa's Dyke Path, has good facilities and a couple of pubs within easy walking distance. You can get here on bus #14. Closed mid-Oct to mid-March. **£17**

EATING AND DRINKING

Glass Onion 1 Back Row, LL16 3TE ☎ 01745 813125, ⓦ glassonioncafe.co.uk. Relaxed café, good for inexpensive home-cooked daytime meals (including gluten-free and vegetarian options) plus free wi-fi, community information and local arts and crafts for sale. Mon–Fri 9am–4pm, Sat & Sun 10am–3pm.

★**White Horse Inn** Hendrerwydd, 5 miles southeast of Denbigh LL16 4LL ☎ 01824 790218, ⓦ whitehorse restaurant.co.uk. Superb country gastropub in a sixteenth-century inn. They really care about their food and

drink here, from the British tapas, including Menai mussels (£5), to pub classics such as fish, chips and peas (£12), or pork belly with caramelized apples and black pudding (£16). Mon 6–11pm, Wed–Sun 11am–11pm; kitchen Mon 6–9.30pm, Wed–Sat noon–2pm & 6–9.30pm, Sun noon–7.30pm.

Y Goron Fach 6 Crown Lane, LL16 3SY ☎ 07850 687701. Tiny, cheery micropub (and nanobrewery) serving local real ales plus bottled beers, cider and gin. Thurs–Sat 4–10pm.

Snowdonia and the Llŷn

332 Snowdonia

375 The Llŷn

CWM IDWAL

Snowdonia and the Llŷn

Other regions will argue, of course. But it is in Snowdonia (Yr Eryri) that you see Wales is at its grandest – even at its most Welsh. Chiefly composed of the county of Gwynedd, this compact area is a small, separate world where Welsh is regularly the first language, slate mining remains in the collective consciousness and small villages retain the quiet self-sufficiency born of tough weather and centuries of isolation. It's also a place of picturebook castles, particularly at Caernarfon and Criccieth and, on the beautiful Llŷn peninsula, of fabulous white-sand beaches.

More than anything, this is a region known for its **mountains**. The **Snowdonia National Park**, its 823-square-mile heartland, is a landscape of sharp ridges and glacial valleys, with enough cliffs, peaks and waterfalls to keep walkers and climbers happy for weeks. Those sheer faces belie the fact that the tallest peaks only just top 3000ft – Wales' highest mountain, Snowdon (Eryri), is 3560ft and retains its snow into April. In addition to the vast range of outdoor activities on offer, you can nowadays enjoy a number of nerve-shredding rides in disused quarries and mines, especially around **Blaenau Ffestiniog**, an old slate capital which is fast developing into the adventure sports capital of Britain. The **Llŷn peninsula**, on the other hand, offers something entirely different. A land apart, jutting into the Celtic Sea, it seems imbued with a Celtic spirituality – something to do with its raw pastoral beauty, perhaps, or simply that the peninsula has been a pilgrimage destination since the seventh century. Taking time out here – at **Aberdaron**, on **Tre'r Ceiri** or almost anywhere on the **Llŷn Coastal Path** – you'll enjoy slow travel at its best.

Snowdonia

With everything from woodland strolls to mountain scrambles, **SNOWDONIA** is fabulous walking country, and its small valley settlements make great bases or places to rest. Foremost among them is the Victorian resort town of **Betws-y-Coed**, very much a stop on the coach-tour circuit. The smaller walkers' hamlet of **Capel Curig** feels more rugged, while the main focus of the region is **Snowdon**, reached on foot or by railway from the small town of **Llanberis**. Only slightly less celebrated are **Llyn Idwal** and **Tryfan** and **Glyderau** but in truth your options for walking here are only limited by your imagination; hike for a month and you'd still only scratch the surface.

Snowdonia National Park p.335
Walks around Betws-y-Coed p.342
Hiking Moel Siabod from Capel Curig p.345
Walks from the Ogwen Valley p.346
Activities around Llanberis p.352
Walks up Snowdon p.354
King Arthur and Snowdon p.356
What Prince of Wales? p.359
Welsh Highland Railway trips from Caernarfon p.360
Walks from Beddgelert p.362

Welsh Highland Railway trips from Beddgelert p.363
The Welsh slate industry p.365
A walk down the Vale of Ffestiniog p.368
Easy walks around Porthmadog p.369
The Prisoner convention and Festival No. 6 p.373
Giraldus Cambrensis and his journey through Wales p.376
Watersports on the Llŷn p.379
R.S. Thomas p.381
The isle of twenty thousand saints p.383

Highlights

❶ Tryfan Some of the finest hikes in Snowdonia converge with a scramble up this craggy summit – good luck attempting the leap between the two monoliths at the top. **See p.346**

❷ Cwm Idwal This popular, thirty-minute ascent takes you into a realm of legends, with a lake and peaks straight out of Arthurian myth. **See p.347**

❸ Snowdon Wales' highest mountain, with superb hiking paths and a cog railway, appeals to all: holidaymakers on the steam train, strollers on an easy path and hardcore hikers on the Horsehoe Circuit. **See p.355**

❹ Caernarfon Castle Scramble through the wall passages of the mightiest link in Edward I's chain of Norman castles. **See p.357**

❺ Blaenau Ffestiniog Wales' former slate capital is now an adrenaline centre, with thrilling activities above ground and below. **See p.364**

❻ Ffestiniog Railway The best of the many steam rail journeys in Wales; a thirteen-mile adventure from the coast into the heart of the mountains. **See p.370**

❼ Portmeirion Dream-like and brilliantly eccentric seaside "village" created from bits of rescued architecture. **See p.373**

❽ Aberdaron Experience the spiritual side of the Llŷn – the village was home to pastor-poet R.S. Thomas and has drawn Christian pilgrims for centuries – or simply enjoy the pretty beach setting and local walks. **See p.380**

HIGHLIGHTS ARE MARKED ON THE MAP ON P.334

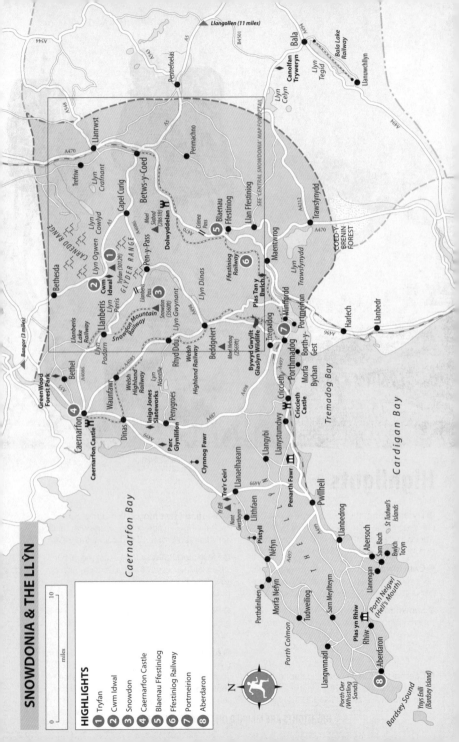

Then there are the more recent arrivals, which have done more than anything to reinvigorate an area that was all hiking boots and cagouls or chintz and doilies, with little in between. Two **zip-line** rides, including the northern hemisphere's longest; a brilliant downhill **mountain-bike descent** and bonkers **underground assault course** at Blaenau Ffestiniog; and the world's first public surfing lake, which lies just outside the boundary of this chapter, are all seeing Snowdonia gunning for a reputation as the adrenaline capital of Britain. You're surprisingly close to the coast, too, specifically the stronghold of **Caernarfon**, where a splendid castle guards the entrance to the Menai Strait.

6

Most settlements here coincide with some enormous mine or quarry, and there remains a self-contained, rugged quality about them despite their embrace of tourism. **Beddgelert**, for example, a former-copper-mining centre living out its dotage as a pretty village, or **Blaenau Ffestiniog**, the former slate capital of north Wales. The most famous of all, however, is the distinctly surreal Italianate hamlet of **Portmeirion**, created by architect Clough Williams-Ellis. It lies where the mountain landscape bleeds into softer coastal contours near the former harbour of **Porthmadog** – the terminus of the magnificent, narrow-gauge **Ffestiniog Railway** and a must-visit for any train buff.

Brief history

For centuries Snowdonia was a redoubt. It was to these mountains that Llywelyn ap Gruffydd, the last true Prince of Wales, retreated in 1277 after his first war with Edward I. It was also here that Owain Glyndŵr held on most tenaciously to his dream of regaining the title for the Welsh. What changed was the arrival of slate barons. Largely English, they built huge fortunes from mining and reshaped the patterns of Snowdonian life forever, as villagers fled the hills for steady work in the towns.

From the late eighteenth century, Snowdonia became the focus for the first truly scientific approach to **geological research**. Its peaks ringed by cwms – huge hemispherical bites out of the mountainsides – and ranges separated by steep-sided U-shaped valleys were interpreted for the first time as evidence of the last Ice Age ten thousand years ago. These pioneer geologists created the rock-type classifications familiar to any students of the subject: Cambrian rock takes its name from the Roman name for Wales, and Ordovician and Silurian rocks from the Celtic tribes of the same names.

Botanists discovered rare alpine flora in Snowdonia, Richard Wilson, Paul Sandby and J.M.W. Turner came to **paint**, and writers produced libraries full of purple prose at a time when the **Romantic ideal** of wild, dramatic landscapes was seizing the public imagination. The leisured classes took heed, flocking to marvel at the waterfalls and to walk the paths of Wales' first and largest national park (see box below).

SNOWDONIA NATIONAL PARK

In recognition of the region's scientific importance, as well as its scenic and recreational appeal, **Snowdonia National Park** (Parc Cenedlaethol Eryri; ⓦ eryri-npa.gov.uk) was established in 1951 as Wales' first, and still largest, national park. Covering 823 square miles of northwest Wales (more than the central part of Snowdonia that we cover in this chapter) it runs all the way from Conwy to Aberdyfi, encompassing the Rhinogs, Cadair Idris and 23 miles of the Cambrian coast. Jagged mountains predominate, but the harsh lines are tempered by broadleaf lowland woods around calm glacial lakes, waterfalls tumbling from hanging valleys and complex coastal dune systems. You won't find wilderness, however: sheep and cattle farming supports many of the 26,000 people who live in the park (some 60 percent of them Welsh-speakers) and another fourteen million people come here each year to tramp almost two thousand miles of designated paths. In apparent contradiction to its name, the national park is 75 percent privately owned by the Forestry Commission and National Trust. However, trespass isn't usually a problem as long as you keep to the ancient rights of way and access areas; most open areas are "access land" where you have freedom to roam anywhere.

GETTING AROUND AND INFORMATION

BY TRAIN

Getting to Snowdonia from elsewhere in Wales is relatively easy: mainline trains run along the coast to nearby Bangor, while the Conwy Valley line branches off at Llandudno Junction to access Betws-y-Coed and then Blaenau Ffestiniog. Here, you could transfer to the Ffestiniog Railway, a scenic tourist heritage service, to Porthmadog. The latter is also a stop on the Cambrian Coast line, which shuttles to Pwllheli on the Llŷn.

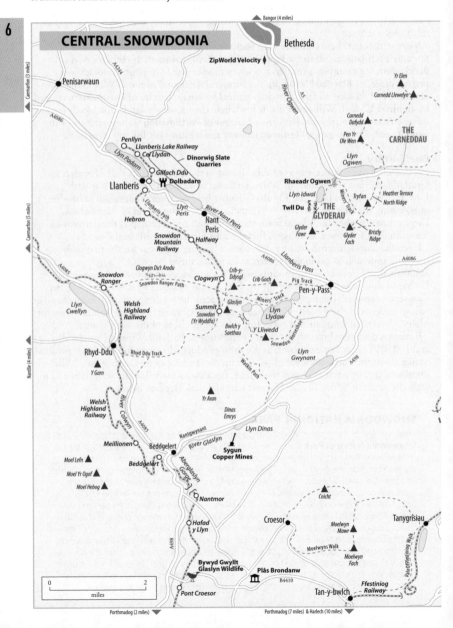

BY BUS

Frequent bus services from Llandudno Junction run up the Conwy Valley to Llanrwst (the region's bus hub) and Betws-y-Coed. From there, Snowdon Sherpa services (see below) provide access to Llanberis, Beddgelert, Porthmadog, Bangor and Caernarfon. Pwllheli is the hub for transport on the Llŷn. Routes and times are online via ⓦ gwynedd.llyw.cymru/transport or in booklets and leaflets from tourist offices and bus stations. Check Basics (see p.28) for details of discount fares and passes (some of which cover the region's narrow-gauge railways).

Snowdon Sherpa bus In central Snowdonia, visitors are

6

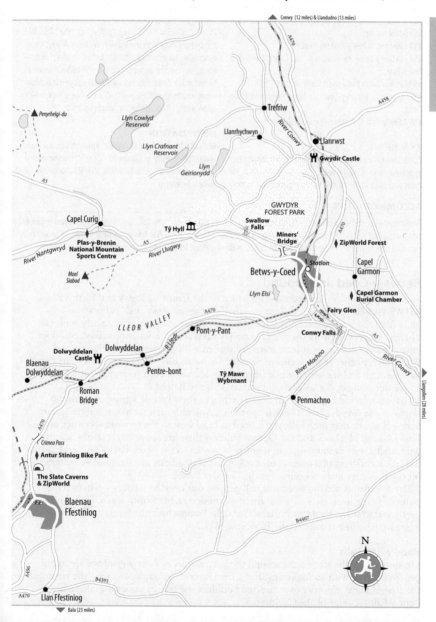

encouraged to park in surrounding towns and access the mountains on the Snowdon Sherpa bus system, comprised of several interconnecting services between Betws-y-Coed, Llanberis, Caernarfon and Porthmadog (timetables via ⓦ gwynedd.llyw.cymru/transport). This avoids having to grapple with full car parks at trailheads (and parking fees) and opens up one-way routes routes using buses to link the paths. Most routes meet at Pen-y-Pass. The Snowdon Sherpa routes are:

#S1 Llanberis to Pen-y-Pass via Nant Peris.

#S2 Betws-y-Coed to Llanberis via Capel Curig and Pen-y-Pass.

#S4 Caernarfon to Beddgelert via Waunfawr.

#S6 Bangor to Betws-y-Coed via Llyn Ogwen and Capel Curig.

#S97 Pen-y-Pass to Porthmadog via Beddgelert.

BY BIKE

Roads are well surfaced but busy, making cycle touring less appealing than it might seem. That said, the views are great and back roads on the Llŷn are perfect for relaxed pedalling. For mountain biking head to Betws-y-Coed, Beddgelert and Blaenau Ffestiniog.

ON FOOT

If you're serious about walking – and some of the walks described in this chapter *are* serious, especially in bad weather (Snowdon gets 200 inches of rain a year) – you need a good map, such as the OS 1:25,000 Explorer map OL17 (Snowdon – Conwy Valley) or the 1:50,000 Landranger map 115 (Snowdon/Yr Wyddfa). Always check mountain weather conditions before setting out – conditions on the summits are often totally different to those further down. Forecasts are usually posted in outdoor shops and touris offices, or visit ⓦ metoffice.gov.uk, which offers weekly forecasts for Snowdon's summit.

INFORMATION

Website Most of the area covered within this chapter falls within the county of Gwynedd – see ⓦ visitsnowdonia .com or the National Park website ⓦ eryri-npa.gov.uk for more information.

ACCOMMODATION

Accommodation is limited inside the Snowdonia National Park; **Llanberis** is the hub. The exception is **Betws-y-Coed**, which is packed with guesthouses that are all busy in summer. There are five YHA **hostels** within 5 miles of Snowdon's summit and a further half-dozen other budget places, making walking from one to another possible.

Betws-y-Coed and around

Spread across a plain around the confluence of the Conwy, Llugwy and Lledr valleys, **BETWS-Y-COED** (pronounced "betus-e-coyd") – the self-described "gateway to Snowdonia" – is almost totally devoted to the needs of visitors, particularly walkers. There is no good grocery shop, and certainly no pharmacy; what Betws-y-Coed does have is outdoor shops – at least seven, all stuffed with gadgets and clothing – and B&Bs (every other house seems to be one). Factor in the number of coach tours that pass through and it's been a while since Wales' leading inland resort felt authentic. If you're not using it as a base, an hour or so is all you'll need.

That's not to say Betws isn't an attractive place. The riverside setting beneath the slopes of the **Gwydyr Forest Park** is appealing. And although no mountain trails start here – if you're after high hills you'll need to head west to the mountain centres of Capel Curig, Llanberis and the Ogwen Valley – there are some lovely strolls nearby, with idyllic wild **swimming**, too, if you're brave. In recent years, Betws-y-Coed has also become something of a magnet for **cycling**, attracting both touring- and mountain-bikers; the latter make a beeline for the Gwydyr Forest.

Any number of activity operators will get you out into the scenery – which is the point of being here, after all – but there are modest sights within reach, including pretty **waterfalls**, a **Neolithic** burial site and, in **Penmachno**, the house of William Morgan, who first translated the Bible into Welsh.

Pont-y-Pair Falls

On sunny days the stone slabs around the low cataract of **Pont-y-Pair Falls** are full of people relaxing with an ice cream after a hard hour in an outdoors shop. The waters of the River Llugwy thunder over assorted boulders and funnel under the adjacent **Pont-y-Pair** ("Bridge of the Cauldron").

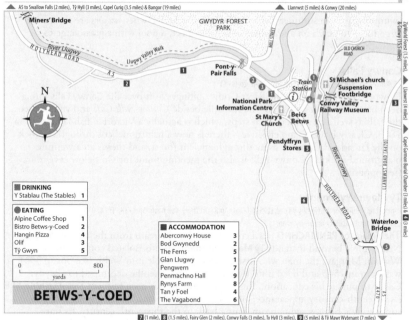

▲ A5 to Swallow Falls (2 miles), Tŷ Hyll (3 miles), Capel Curig (3.5 miles) & Bangor (19 miles)   ▲ Llanrwst (5 miles) & Conwy (20 miles)

DRINKING
Y Stablau (The Stables)   1

EATING
Alpine Coffee Shop   1
Bistro Betws-y-Coed   2
Hangin Pizza   4
Olif   3
Tŷ Gwyn   5

ACCOMMODATION
Aberconwy House   3
Bod Gwynedd   2
The Ferns   5
Glan Llugwy   1
Pengwern   7
Penmachno Hall   9
Rynys Farm   8
Tan y Foel   4
The Vagabond   6

BETWS-Y-COED

▼ 7 (1 mile), 8 (1.5 miles), Fairy Glen (2 miles), Conwy Falls (3 miles), Tŷ Hyll (3 miles), 9 (5 miles) & Tŷ Mawr Wybrnant (7 miles)

Conwy Valley Railway Museum

Old Church Rd, LL24 0AL • Daily 10am–5pm • £1.50; train & tram £2 • ☎ 01690 710568, ⦿ conwyrailwaymuseum.co.uk

Opposite the train station, the old-fashioned **Conwy Valley Railway Museum** sells itself as "layouts, nostalgia, dioramas" – a decent description of a collection of glass-cased memorabilia and miniature steam engines, only slightly enlivened by the opportunity for kids to take a short ride on a miniature train or tram.

St Michael's church

Old Church Rd, LL24 0AE • In theory Easter–Oct daily 10am–5pm; if it's closed during these hours, pick up the key from Conwy Valley Railway Museum • Free • ⦿ stmichaelsbyc.org.uk

A lych gate and ancient yews frame the fourteenth-century **St Michael's church**. It's interesting for its whitewashed interior, specifically the thirteenth-century font and a carved effigy of an armoured knight, whose inscription identifies him as Gruffydd ap Dafydd Goch, the grandson of Llywelyn ap Gruffydd's brother, Prince Dafydd.

Capel Garmon Burial Chamber

0.5 mile south of Capel Garmon, 2 miles southeast of Betws-y-Coed, LL26 0RR • Open access • Free; CADW • ☎ 01443 336000, ⦿ cadw .gov.wales/daysout/capel-garmon-burial-chamber

The **Capel Garmon Burial Chamber**, a heavily reconstructed, multi-chambered Neolithic burial site, was built between 2500 and 1900 BC. It's an atmospheric spot, comprising rough stones lining a series of linked pits, with a central chamber part-covered by an enormous capstone. The site is a five-minute signposted walk across farmland from the road.

Fairy Glen

Signposted off the A470, 2 miles south of Betws-y-Coed, LL24 0SH • Open access • Car park £1, turnstile 50p

South of the village, after negotiating a series of rapids, the waters of the Conwy river flow over a staircase of drops and enter **Fairy Glen**, a lovely cleft in a small wood. It is named after the Welsh fairies, the Tylwyth Teg, once said to live hereabouts. Bring your swimming gear in summer – the narrow gorge is idyllic when waters are slow, with large rocks to perch on and, where two rivers meet, a pool with a grass verge to sunbathe on.

Conwy Falls

A5, 3 miles south of Betws-y-Coed, LL24 0PN • Open access • £1

Downriver of Fairy Glen, the River Conwy plunges 50ft over the **Conwy Falls** into a deep pool. Slip your coins into the turnstile beside *Conwy Falls Café* and you can see the falls as well as a series of rock steps, which is actually a Victorian fish ladder cut in 1863. Clearly it wasn't too effective – there is now a fish tunnel cut through the rock on the far side. Paths track away through ancient forest, and there's an adventure playground for kids. Conwy Falls is also the meeting point for Go Below cave tours (see opposite)

Tŷ Mawr Wybrnant

Penmachno, 7 miles south of Betws-y-Coed, LL25 0HJ • Late April–Oct Thurs–Sun noon–5pm • £4; NT • ☎ 01690 760213, Ⓦ nationaltrust.org.uk/ty-mawr-wybrnant

The village of **PENMACHNO** lies a couple of miles upstream from the Conwy Falls. Nearly three beyond it stands **Tŷ Mawr Wybrnant**. In this isolated cottage, Bishop William Morgan, the man who first translated the Bible into Welsh (see box, p.394), was born in 1545 and lived until his teenage years, when he decamped to Gwydyr Castle to pursue his education. The original cottage has been restored to something like its sixteenth-century appearance: all bare stone and beams, with a gaping fireplace supporting a huge, sagging beam dating back to the thirteenth century. Its star attraction is the collection of bibles and prayer books, including two of the Morgan originals printed in 1588.

Swallow Falls

A5, 2 miles west of Betws-y-Coed, LL24 0DW • Open access • £1.50

Easy access makes **Swallow Falls** (a mistranslation of *Rhaeadr Ewynnol*, or "foaming cataract") one of the region's most-visited sights, but it's really no more than a pretty waterfall in a gorge, enlivened by heavy rainfall the night before or by the appearance of a kamikaze kayaker. A path leads to two viewing platforms.

Tŷ Hyll

A5, 3 miles west of Betws-y-Coed, LL24 0DS • Early to late March Mon & Fri–Sun 10.30am–4pm; late March–Nov daily 10.30am–5.30pm • ☎ 01492 643222, Ⓦ snowdonia-society.org.uk

As the A5 crosses the Llugwy river you can't miss **Tŷ Hyll**, known as the "Ugly House" for its construction from great stone hunks. Decked out with period furniture and surrounded by a wildlife garden and woodland, it is now a historic cafe, *Pot Mêl*, owned by the environmental campaigning group Snowdonia Society, which sells the honeys produced by bees in its pretty cottage garden.

ARRIVAL AND INFORMATION   BETWS-Y-COED AND AROUND

By train Trains from Llandudno Junction arrive via a gorgeously scenic section of track through the Conwy Valley.

Destinations Blaenau Ffestiniog (5 daily; 30min); Llandudno (4 daily; 40–50min); Llandudno Junction (6 daily; 30min); Llanrwst (6 daily; 5min).

By bus Buses (including Snowdon Sherpa services) fan out from near the train station.

Destinations Bangor (3 daily; 50min); Blaenau Ffestiniog (5 daily; 25min); Capel Curig (10 daily; 12min); Llyn Ogwen (3 daily; 20min); Llanberis/Pen-y-Pass (10 daily; 35min); Llandudno (6 daily; 50min); Llanrwst (every 2hr; 10min); Penmachno (4 daily; 30min).

Tourist information The region's largest National Park information centre is in Royal Oak Stables off Station Rd (daily: Easter to mid-Oct 9.30am–5pm; mid-Oct to Easter 9.30am–4pm; ☎ 01690 710426, Ⓔ tic .byc@eryri-npa.gov.uk). It has a film giving a quick overview of Snowdonia and stocks some town flyers alongside its displays.

ACTIVITIES

Fishing There are salmon and sea trout on stretches of the Conwy and Llugwy rivers within the village (mid-March to mid-Oct), and brown and American brook trout on Llyn Elsi, just south (late March to late Oct). Buy rod licences and permits (from £15/£20/day for lake/river) plus a limited range of tackle from Pendyffryn Stores on Holyhead Rd.

Horseriding Gwydyr Riding and Trekking Stables, 4 miles south of Betws-y-Coed in Penmachno (☎01690 760248, ⓦ horse-riding-wales.co.uk), runs scenic hacks with views to Snowdon. Options range from an hour to a full day and include an entertaining pub ride (£22–70).

Mine exploring Go Below, at Conwy Falls (☎01690 710108, ⓦ www.go-below.co.uk) runs two of the best adventure trips in Snowdonia. On the "Challenge" you explore an old mine, learning about its past on a subterranean adventure that takes in zip lines, abseils and a paddle across a small lake – all can be bypasssed if required (book in advance; minimum age 10; £49). The most nerve-jangling trip is the day-long "Extreme", which enters a mine at Blaenau Ffestiniog; at 1600ft it's the deepest part of the UK accessible to the public. This is a raw experience that sees you climb through the caverns as the miners knew them on via ferrata and too-narrow,

dizzyingly high ledges (you're harnessed on) before a steep zip line into the void. There's one trip for over-14s and another for over-18s (£79/£89 respectively).

Mountain biking There's good trail riding in the Gwydyr Forest Park, north and west of the village. The classic route is the Marin Trail (15-mile circuit; 2–4hr) near Llanrwst – single-track heaven with big climbs and swooping descents, ridgelines and deep forest, plus great scenery. Other trails include Dolen Eryri and Dolen Machno near Penmachno. You can rent bikes at Beics Betws (☎01690 710766, ⓦ bikewales.co.uk) behind the post office; hardtails (from £32/day).

ZipWorld Forest ZipWorld Forest (daily: Easter–Oct 10am–4pm; Nov–Easter 10am–1pm; ☎01248 601444, ⓦ zipworld.co.uk), the newest outpost of the ZipWorld group, packs a family's worth of forest adventures into a location a mile east of Betws-y-Coed on the A470. As well as ZipSafari, a high-wire course and zip line through the forest canopy (£40), and Plummet, a 100ft simulated parachute drop (£10), there's the UK's first rail-run toboggan ride, Fforest Coaster; you control the speed of your sled on a 2300ft descent through the trees. Prebook all adventures online or by phone.

ACCOMMODATION

Betws-y-Coed is packed with **B&Bs**, but you'll still need to reserve your bed rather than winging it in summer (and, to be safe, at bank holidays). Since this is the regional hub, we've included several accommodation options in the surrounding area. Check out also **Llanrwst**, five miles north (p.343), for smart rural hotels.

HOTELS AND GUESTHOUSES

Aberconwy House Lôn Muriau, Llanrwst Rd, LL24 0HD ☎01690 710202, ⓦ aberconwy-house.co.uk. The best of several B&Bs grouped on the A470 just outside the centre, this friendly place has been refurbished into a stylish, relaxed option with immaculate five-star en suites and superb views from the front rooms. Room 5 has the best views, room 6 has a four-poster (£105). Two nights minimum in high season. **£85**

Bod Gwynedd A5, 0.5 mile towards Capel Curig, LL24 0BN ☎01690 710717, ⓦ bodgwynedd.com. The downside first: this is hardly the most central option. Its location, on the edge of the village, is made up for by the rooms: en suites with romantic, country-modern style – antique brass frames, king-size mattresses, smart TVs – and by the excellent breakfasts. **£85**

The Ferns Holyhead Rd, LL24 0AN ☎01690 710587, ⓦ ferns-guesthouse.co.uk. A B&B that ticks all the boxes: comfortable en suites individually decorated in contemporary country or romantic French country style (love the cute single in the eaves); accommodating owners; a central location with guest parking; and competitive rates. The only caveat – and it's minor – is that double beds are standards rather than king-size. **£70**

Glan Llugwy A5 towards Capel Curig, 300yd beyond Pont-y-Pair, LL24 0BN ☎01690 710592, ⓦ glanllugwy .co.uk. Though it's unlikely to win any style awards, this traditional, well-maintained B&B is one of the cheapest around; all rooms but one share facilities (en suites cost £10 more). Helpful owners and good breakfasts. Note that it was up for sale when this book went to press. **£60**

★**Pengwern** Allt Dinas, 1.5 miles east on the A5, LL24 0HF ☎01690 710480, ⓦ snowdoniaaccommodation .co.uk. There's relaxed charm by the wheelbarrow load – slate floors, art on the walls – in this spacious, elegant, three-room B&B, formerly the residence of a Victorian artists' colony. Great views down the valley too; book the Richard Gay Somerset room for a bath with a view. In summer they also have a sweet self-contained cottage for two with a wood-burner (three nights minimum; from £80/night). **£84**

Penmachno Hall B4406, Penmachno, 5 miles south, LL24 0PU ☎01690 760410, ⓦ penmachnohall.co.uk. Stay deep in the countryside in this hospitable former rectory, with three spacious bedrooms plus a sunny lounge (with log fire in winter). More home from home than modern luxury. To save a trip into town (or the village pub) they provide light suppers on request (£17.50). **£95**

★ Tan y Foel Capel Garmon, 3 miles east, LL26 0RE ☎ 01690 710507, ⌨ tyfhotel.co.uk. Smart, modern public spaces and stylish accommodation in a sixteenth-century farmhouse make this one of the best boutique B&Bs in the region; a genuine retreat with gorgeous views across 8 acres of grounds to the Conwy Valley. Book online and you get a free bottle of fizz. **£100**

HOSTEL AND CAMPSITE

★ Rynys Farm A5, 3 miles southeast near the Conwy Falls, LL24 0PN ☎ 01690 710218, ⌨ rynys-camping .co.uk. Pure rural bliss on a National Trust-listed farm campsite with plenty of flat sites tucked behind trees or against dry-stone walls, great valley views, good facilities and eco principles. Charming owners, too, who'll sell you farm eggs. There's also a bell tent, yurt and shepherd's hut, all sleeping two, plus a static caravan that sleeps four. Camping/person **£8**, bell tent **£40**, caravan **£40**, hut **£45**, yurt **£50**

The Vagabond Craiglan Rd, LL24 0AW ☎ 01690 710850, ⌨ thevagabond.co.uk. A small independent hostel with four- to eight-bunk dorms and family rooms, plus facilities including secure bike lock-up and off-street parking. Though there's a self-catering kitchen they serve breakfasts (£5) and maintain an inexpensive bar. Bookings recommended at weekends when B&B is obligatory. Dorms **£20**

EATING

Alpine Coffee Shop Betws-y-Coed train station, LL24 0AE ☎ 01690 710747, ⌨ alpinecoffeeshop.co.uk. Going strong since the early 70s, this café has art on the walls and an appealing range of breakfasts and lunches including vegetarian and gluten-free dishes – expect home-made soups and quiche (£7), locally roasted coffee and speciality teas. Daily 8.30am–5.30pm.

Bistro Betws-y-Coed Holyhead Rd, LL24 0AY ☎ 01690 710328, ⌨ bistrobetws-y-coed.co.uk. Owner-chef Gerwyn Williams offers both modern and traditional food in his casual bistro. Either way, the seasonal dishes have a Welsh bias and showcase regional produce. Lunches are light; dinners, such as local lamb marinated in Snowdonian honey (£16.25), up the ante. March–May Wed–Sun 11.30am–2.30pm & 6–9pm; June–Sept daily 11.30am–2.30pm & 6–9pm; Oct–Feb Wed–Fri 6.30–9pm, Sat & Sun 11.30am–2.30pm & 6–9pm.

Hangin Pizza Betws-y-Coed train station, LL24 0AE ☎ 01690 710393, ⌨ hanginpizzeria.co.uk. Locals say that this industrial-styled café/takeaway in the Victorian promenade serves the best pizza in town; traditionally made, Italian style, using a limited range of classic ingredients such as tomato, mozzarella, garlic, oregano,

---

WALKS AROUND BETWS-Y-COED

These two **lowland walks** explore the valleys and waterfalls on the outskirts of the village. Neither is circular, so unless you plan to hitch back, consult local bus timetables first to avoid a long wait for the infrequent services.

Conwy Gorge walk (3 miles; 1hr 15min; descent only). An easy walk that links two of the district's best-known natural attractions, Fairy Glen (see p.339) and the Conwy Falls (see p.340), by way of a cool green lane (once the main road into Betws-y-Coed) giving glimpses of the river through the beech woods. Catch the #19 bus (8 daily) to *Conwy Falls Café*, then after having a look at the falls, walk 150yd back along the road towards Betws-y-Coed and follow a traffic-free lane (the original road into the village) parallel to the river through the trees. After about half an hour, you'll see the gate to Fairy Glen on your left. Returning to the main path, continue to the *Fairy Glen Hotel*, where you can cross the river by Beaver Bridge, turn right and follow a minor road a mile back to Betws-y-Coed.

Llugwy Valley walk (6 miles; 2hr 30min; 600ft ascent). The car park on the north side of the Pont-y-Pair Bridge marks the beginning of a forested path following the twisting river upstream to Capel Curig. With the A5 running parallel to the river all the way, there are several opportunities to cut the walk short and wait for the bus back to Betws-y-Coed. Less than a mile from Pont-y-Pair, you first reach a ford where the Roman road Sarn Helen crossed the river, then pass the steeply sloping Miners' Bridge, which linked miners' homes at Pentre Du on the south side of the river to the lead mines in the Gwydyr Forest. With its plunge pools and rocky diving platforms this is the place to take a dip. The path follows the river on your left for another mile to a slightly obscured view of Swallow Falls. Detailed maps, available from the national park office in Betws-y-Coed, show numerous routes back through the Gwydyr Forest, or you can continue half a mile to the road bridge by Tŷ Hyll and follow the right bank to Capel Curig, passing the scant remains of the Caer Llugwy, a Roman fort, and a couple more treacherous rapids: The Mincer and Cobden's Falls.

grilled peppers, capers and olives (£9). And the name? A percentage of profits goes to great ape conservation. Daily noon–9pm.

Olif Holyhead Rd, LL24 0AY ☎01690 733942, ⓦolifbetws.wales. Never mind the breakfasts, light bites and burgers (tasty though they are). You come to this hip bistro for Welsh (and Spanish) tapas such as Angelsey eggs with mash and leeks, mushroom *bruschetta* or Menai mussels cooked in Taffy cider; plates cost £5–9. Daily: March–Sept 11.30am–2.30pm & 6–9pm; Oct–Feb

Wed–Fri 6–9pm, Sat & Sun 11.30am–2.30pm & 6–9pm.

Tŷ Gwyn A5, 0.5 mile southeast, LL24 0SG ☎01690 710383, ⓦtygwynhotel.co.uk. First choice for historic atmosphere is this former coaching inn, which positively creaks with old oak furniture. Traditional dishes including cottage pie, halibut with creamed leeks and lamb slow-braised over 24hr (mains £13–19) are served in the bar or a snug restaurant. Reservations recommended. Daily noon–2pm & 6–9pm (Jan closed Mon–Wed).

DRINKING

Y Stablau (The Stables) Holyhead Rd, LL24 0AY ☎01690 710219, ⓦstables-bistro.co.uk. The village's liveliest pub, mobbed at weekends with walkers, climbers, bikers and plain old holidaymakers. You're here for simple,

unpretentious stuff: good beer, outdoor seating, sports on the TV and passable pub grub such as home-made lasagne, local beef burgers, pies and fish and chips (mains average £9). Daily 11am–11pm.

Llanrwst and around

It's hard to believe today, but **LLANRWST**, five miles north of Betws-y-Coed via the broad pastoral Conwy Valley, was once the largest wool market in north Wales. It had a spell as a centre for harp manufacture in the eighteenth century, too, and remains the most economically important town in the valley, and a hub of local bus travel. The majority of the population speak Welsh as a first language, which adds to the feel of a proper, solid little market town – refreshing after the village resort of Betws-y-Coed.

St Gwrst Church

Church St, LL26 0BP • Opening hours vary • Free • ☎01492 642550

St Gwrst Church contains an intricately carved rood screen thought to have come from Maenan Abbey, a few miles downstream, after it was dissolved by Henry VIII in 1536; look for the carved pigs. In the south transept (entered through a separate door) lies the thirteenth-century carved stone coffin (minus its lid) of Llywelyn the Great.

Llanrwst almshouses

Church St, LL26 0BP • Officially Mon–Fri 10.30am–3.30pm • £2.50

On the lane just before St Gwrst Church, the **Llanrwst almshouses** date back to 1610 and were still in use until 1976. Two rooms decorated in period style (1610 and 1850) are open to the public as a municipal museum – that's the theory, anyway, though you may often find the place closed.

Tu Hwnt i'r Bont and Pont Fawr

It can seem like half of Llanrwst's visitors are photographing **Tu Hwnt i'r Bont**, a tearoom (see p.345) in a fifteenth-century former courthouse smothered in Virginia creeper. It is approached over **Pont Fawr** (Big Bridge), a beautifully proportioned, humpback bridge designed by the seventeenth-century architect Inigo Jones; he is said to have spent his early years in Llanrwst. It's clear he never planned on summer traffic attempting to cross its single-lane span.

Gwydir Castle

B5106, 0.5 mile west of Llanrwst, LL26 0PN • April–Oct Wed–Sun 10am–4pm • £6 • ☎01492 641687, ⓦgwydir-castle.co.uk

Most of the land around Betws-y-Coed and along the Conwy Valley was once part of the Gwydir estate, owned by the Wynn family. Descended from the kings of Gwynedd, they were the most powerful dynasty in the region until the male line died

6

out in 1678; **Gwydir Castle**, actually a manor house begun around 1490, is a reminder of their might. Despite additions in the sixteenth and nineteenth centuries, and renovations in the twentieth after a serious fire – with parts plundered from the post-dissolution Maenan Abbey – the building is a fabulous model of early Tudor architecture.

Its core is a three-storey tower, whose windows relieve the gloom of the great halls, each with enormous fireplaces and stone-flagged or heavy timber floors. Most of the original fittings and Tudor furniture were sold in 1921, and much of the rest of the house was ruined in a fire a few months later. The subsequent restoration was kept simple – tapestries cover the solid stone walls, a few tables and chairs are scattered about and there's some fine painted glass. Some of the original furnishings have been tracked down, including the heavily carved oak panels, Baroque door-case and fireplace, and the gilded leather chairs of the **dining room**. This room was initially installed by Richard Wynn around 1642, and is attributed to Inigo Jones; its panelling and carving was bought by American newspaper magnate William Randolph Hearst during the 1921 sell-off and shipped across the Atlantic. New York's Metropolitan Museum acquired it in 1956 and kept it boxed up for forty years until it was sold back to the castle in 1996 and re-installed.

Outside, the main attraction is the **Dutch Garden**, one of the only Grade I-listed gardens in Wales, with a fountain, peacocks and cedars of Lebanon which date back to 1625. Gwydir Castle also offers excellent **accommodation** (see below).

Trefriw Woollen Mills

Main Rd, Trefriw, 2 miles northwest of Llanrwst, LL27 0NQ • **Mill** Mid-Feb to mid-Dec Mon–Fri 10am–1pm & 2–5pm • **Museum** Mid-April to Oct Mon–Fri 10am–1pm & 2–5pm • **Shop** April–Oct Mon–Sat 9.30am–5.30pm, Sun 10am–5.30pm; Nov–March Mon–Sat 10am–5pm • Free • ☎ 01492 640462, ⊕ t-w-m.co.uk

The small village of **TREFRIW** is home to the **Trefriw Woollen Mills**, where rugs, throws and bedspreads are made to traditional Welsh geometric designs using late nineteenth-century weaving methods, all driven by the power of Afon Crafnant, which flows right by. The fleece-to-fabric process is explained in the **museum** and you can watch regular weaving demonstrations and have a go yourself during summertime hand-spinning sessions – check the website for schedules. Naturally, there's a large **shop**, open when the museum is closed: double bedspreads start at around £250, but there are cheaper goods on sale, too.

ARRIVAL AND INFORMATION — LLANRWST

By train or bus Trains on the Conwy Valley line and many of the region's buses stop near Ancaster Square.
Internet You can get online for free at the library (Mon & Wed–Fri 9.30am–5pm, Tues 3.30–7.30pm, Sat 10am–1pm) on Station Rd just north of town.

ACCOMMODATION

Gwydir Castle 0.5 mile west, LL26 0PN ☎ 01492 641687, ⊕ gwydir-castle.co.uk. A chance to stay in a Tudor manor – former guests include King George V and Queen Mary (albeit as Duke and Duchess of York) – that still maintains the air of a family home. Two bedrooms have been fitted in baronial style, with four-posters, deep baths and nicely eclectic decor. TVs are anathema. No children under 12. Minimum two nights at weekends. Reservations required. **£95**

Lion Inn Gwytherin, 5 miles east, LL22 8UU ☎ 01745 860123, ⊕ thelion-inn.co.uk. This renovated seventeenth-century inn deep in the hills is the place to come for peace and quiet. No TV, no internet, no mobile coverage in the village (though there is mobile reception in the inn) – sheer bliss. Expect modern rustic furniture and traditional Welsh blankets, lazy meals for guests (reservation required) and snug nights in with a film from the DVD library. No children under 10. Minimum two nights. **£98**

EATING

Caffi Contessa Ancaster Square, LL26 0LG ☎ 01492 640754. A bright little café that's always busy, whether with workmen or locals chatting over coffee. It has a reputation for honest, fresh food: delicious breakfasts and lunches that might feature home-made carrot and coriander soup or mushrooms with creamy pesto. A great choice before or after tackling the Marin mountain-bike trail. Mon–Sat 9am–4pm.

Ffin y Parc Betws Rd, 2 miles south, LL26 0PT ☎ 01492 642070, ⚙ ffinyparc.com. Well-crafted bistro dishes – spinach and caramelized leek quiche (£9), for example – and an elegant atmosphere provide just two good reasons to make for this country-house gallery café. A classy stop

for lunch or afternoon tea. Wed–Sun 10am–5pm.

Tu Hwnt i'r Bont Beside Pont Fawr Bridge, LL26 0PL ☎ 01492 642322, ⚙ tuhwntirbont.co.uk. Old-fashioned, low-beamed tearoom "beyond the bridge" (as it translates from Welsh). A tourist attraction in its own right, it's overpriced – afternoon tea costs £14.50 – but you're here for atmosphere, not culinary brilliance. March & Oct Tues–Sun 10.30am–5pm; April–Sept daily 10.30am–5pm; Nov & Dec Fri–Sun 10.30am–5pm.

Capel Curig

There's scarcely a building in the tiny hamlet of **Capel Curig** that isn't of use to hikers, making it a small but perfect base for keen walkers – the classic trail heads up **Moel Siabod** (see box below). Other routes thread uphill from the two valleys that plunge westwards into the mountains: the A4086 follows Nant Gwryd southwest to the Snowdon massif; the A5 prises apart the Carneddau and Glyder ranges to the northwest, forging through the Ogwen Valley. **Llynnau Mymbyr** is a pleasant option for a dip, with (usually) still waters reflecting views of the Snowdon massif; enter at the little beach near Plas y Brenin.

ARRIVAL AND DEPARTURE   CAPEL CURIG

By bus Capel Curig is served by Snowdon Sherpa buses (see p.337).

Destinations Betws-y-Coed (11 daily; 10min); Llanberis (11 daily; 35min); Pen-y-Pass (11 daily; 15min).

ACTIVITIES

Plas y Brenin: The National Mountain Sports Centre A4086, 400yd south of Capel Curig centre, Plas y Brenin, LL24 0ET ☎ 01690 720214, ⚙ pyb.co.uk. Built around a former coaching inn, the centre runs well-regarded skills training courses in hiking, mountaineering, kayaking,

skiing and rock climbing. Of more interest if you're just passing through, however, are its 3hr family taster sessions in rock climbing, lake canoeing and geocaching, held during the spring and summer school holidays (£30). There's a climbing wall, too (daily 10am–9pm; £6).

ACCOMMODATION

Bron Eryri A5, 1 mile outside the village towards Betws-y-Coed, LL24 0EE ☎ 01690 720240. Four comfortable en suites, all pale greys and parquet floors, plus tea and cake on arrival provided by the friendly owner, a keen walker who fills flasks and prepares packed lunches on request. Communal breakfasts add to the relaxed vibe. There's a pub close to hand; all in all a fine choice. Two-

night minimum at summer weekends. **£70**

Bryn Tyrch Inn A5, 0.3 mile towards Betws-y-Coed, LL24 0EL ☎ 01690 720223, ⚙ bryntyrchinn.co.uk. Sensitively modernized small inn with a relaxed, informal style and tasteful rooms, some with old stone walls. It also has four-bunk en-suite dorms (minimum three in one room). Two-night minimum at weekends. Dorms **£25**, doubles **£90**

HIKING MOEL SIABOD FROM CAPEL CURIG

The OS 1:50,000 Landranger map 115 (Snowdon/Yr Wyddfa) or 1:25,000 Explorer map OL17 (Snowdon – Conwy Valley) are recommended.

Despite Capel Curig's popularity among hikers, the only major **walk** (5 miles; 4hr; 2200ft ascent) from here is up the grassy-backed **Moel Siabod** (2861ft), a challenging ridge walk with views of the Snowdon Horseshoe. Start opposite the *Plas Curig* hostel, cross the concrete bridge and follow the right bank downstream past the falls by *Cobden's Hotel* to the Pont Cyfyng road bridge (30min), an alternative starting point for the walk. Take the road south and turn right on the second path signposted to Moel Siabod. You pass a disued slate quarry before the long scramble up the east ridge, which weaves around outcrops where a moment's inattention could be disastrous. Once you've admired the summit view of the Snowdon Horseshoe, turn northeast and follow the craggy summit ridge, which drops across grass to the moors below, soon rejoining your ascent route for the hike back to Pont Cyfyng.

6

★**Plas Curig** A5, 500yd towards Betws-y-Coed, LL24 0EL ☎01690 720225, ⓦsnowdoniahostel.co.uk. Wales' only independent five-star hostel is as stylish as a boutique B&B: the public areas are beautiful, with slate floors and reclaimed wood, and the dorms are splendid – custom-built bunks have privacy curtains, bed lights and lockable storage. Choose between four- and eight-bed dorms, doubles, twins and family rooms (no en suites), plus a luxury self-catering cottage for up to six (five nights minimum; from £138). Two-night minimum at weekends. Dorms £25, doubles £55

St Curig's Church A5, near the junction in the heart of the village, LL24 0EL ☎01690 720469, ⓦstcurigschurch.com. There's bags of character in this B&B, fashioned from a former church; it retains a gilded mosaic of Christ in the lounge. Though lacking the same wow factor, its six rooms are comfortable and include four-poster doubles. A recess off the lounge has a four-bed bunkroom in the chapel. Dorms £25, doubles £85

EATING AND DRINKING

Bryn Tyrch Inn A5, 0.3 mile towards Betws-y-Coed, LL24 0EL ☎01690 720223, ⓦbryntyrchinn.co.uk. Real ales, high-quality food, garden seating and a view of Snowdon – this lively inn is a winner. The seasonal menu (mains £15–19) might include hake with *patatas bravas* or spicy beef goulash; that said, portion sizes may not hit the sides after a hard day in the hills. Mid-Jan to Easter & Oct to mid-Dec pub & kitchen Fri–Sun noon–3pm & 5.30–9pm; Easter–Sept pub daily noon–11pm, kitchen noon–3pm & 5.30–9.30pm.

★**Moel Siabod** A5, 0.3 mile towards Betws-y-Coed, LL24 0EL ☎01690 720429, ⓦmoelsiabodcafe.co.uk. Preparing to go out? Hard day in the hills? This hangar-like café is the place to come. Busy staff rustle up big breakfasts (£6.95), fresh home-made mains like chilli con carne or beef-and-ale pie (average £12) and home-made cake. Factor in their stock of OS maps and back-issues of climbing magazines and you just might have the best outdoors enthusiasts' caff in Wales. Mon–Fri & Sun 7.30am–6pm (summer hols Mon–Fri till 8pm), Sat 7.30am–8pm.

WALKS FROM THE OGWEN VALLEY

The OS 1:25,000 Explorer map OL17 (Snowdon – Conwy Valley) or the 1:50,000 Landranger map 115 (Snowdon/Yr Wyddfa) are recommended.

Tourists hike up Snowdon, but mountain connoisseurs prefer the sharply angled peaks of the **Glyderau** with their challenging terrain, or **Tryfan** (3012ft) with its scary jump at the summit and fantastic views to Snowdon. We've outlined three walks on Tryfan and one on the Glyderau, but with a map you can plan all manner of variations.

The **Carneddau**, on the other side of the Ogwen Valley, could hardly be in greater contrast. The longest stretch of ground over 3000ft in Wales, they form a rounded plateau extending to the cliffs of Penmaenmawr on the north coast. The sound of a raven and perhaps a wild pony can often be your only company on inclement days, but in fine weather the easy walking and roof-of-the-world views make for a satisfying hike.

TRYFAN

Miners' Track (5 miles; 4–6hr; 2000ft ascent). The standard route up Tryfan, from the car park at Idwal Cottage. Take the path to Cwm Idwal, then, as it bears sharply to the right, keep straight ahead and make for Bwlch Tryfan, the gap on the horizon between Tryfan and Glyder Fach. From there, the South Ridge of Tryfan climbs past the Far South Peak to the summit: this last section is an easy scramble, and you'll need to use your hands. Anyone who has seen pictures of people jumping the 5ft gap between Adam and Eve, two chunks of rhyolitic lava at the summit, will wonder what the fuss is about until they get there and see the mountain plummet on all sides. In theory, the leap is trivial, but the consequences of overshooting would be disastrous. Return the way you came.

Tryfan via Heather Terrace (4 miles; 4–6hr; 2000ft ascent). You'll need a reasonable sense of adventure to enjoy the ascent via Heather Terrace, which follows a fault in the rock running diagonally across the east face. The route starts in the lay-by at the head of Idwal Lake and goes left across rising ground before finding its way onto the exposed "terrace". This ends at the col between South and the Far South peaks, where a right turn then starts your scramble for the summit. Descend the way you came or by the Miners' Track.

North Ridge of Tryfan (3–4 miles; 4–6hr; 2000ft ascent). If you've got the head for it, this is one of the most rewarding scrambles in the country. It's not as precarious as Snowdon's Crib Goch, but you get a genuine mountaineering feel as the valley floor drops rapidly away and

Ogwen Valley

Northwest of Capel Curig the gentle **Ogwen Valley** follows the Ogwen River towards Bethesda, home to one of the last slate quarries in Wales and the longest zip-wire ride in Europe. Most people are here for the mist-shrouded Carnedd range to the north and the spiky Glyder range opposite, featuring the triple-peaked **Tryfan** (see box, below), arguably Snowdonia's most demanding mountain. This forms a fractured spur out from the main range and blocks your view down the valley, the twin monoliths of Adam and Eve that crown Tryfan's summit picked out on the skyline. The courageous (or foolhardy) jump between them as a point of honour on every ascent.

In the middle of the valley is **Llyn Ogwen**, a post-glacial lake formed behind a moraine left by the retreating ice. The only settlement, **IDWAL COTTAGE**, at the western end of the valley, is so small – just a visitor centre with displays on geology and ecology, a café and the cottage itself, now a YHA hostel – that it isn't even named on most maps. The main reason to come here is to tackle some of Wales' most challenging and rewarding hikes, or start the far easier walk to a magnificent glacial cirque, **Cwm Idwal**. As spectacular in its way is **Nant Ffrancon**, further west on the A5. A text-book U-shaped glacial valley carved during the last Ice Age, it's as beautiful as it is popular with geography school groups.

Cwm Idwal

Accessed from Idwal Cottage, LL57 3LZ • Free, but parking 50p/hr; NT • ⓦ nationaltrust.org.uk/carneddau-and-glyderau/trails/cwm-idwal-walk

The Idwal Cottage car park is the starting point of an easy, well-maintained path to **Cwm Idwal** (1.5 miles return; 1hr; 200ft ascent), one of the region's most

---

the views stretch further and further along it. The route starts in the lay-by at the head of Idwal Lake and goes left across rising ground, until you strike a path heading straight up following the crest of the ridge to the 3010ft summit. Return via Heather Terrace or the Miners' Track.

THE GLYDERAU

Glyder Traverse (6 miles; 5–8hr; 2500ft ascent). This day is a fairly rugged undertaking (with some moderate scrambling) but very rewarding. From Idwal Cottage, follow Tryfan's Miners' Track to Bwlch Tryfan where (by adding an extra hour) you can also tick off the summit of Tryfan. From Bwlch Tryfan, scramble up Bristly Ridge, which runs steeply south past some daunting-looking towers of rock. In good conditions it isn't difficult, but it should be avoided in winter unless you're suitably equipped. The ridge ends at the summit of Glyder Fach (3260ft), a chaotic jumble of grey slabs with a massive cantilevered rock.

From Glyder Fach, it is an easy stroll to Glyder Fawr (3280ft), reached by skirting round the rock formations of Castell y Gwynt (the Castle of the Winds), then following a path to the summit of frost-shattered slabs. The descent initially follows loose scree down to Llyn Cwn where you turn north, zigzagging down Twll Du (the Devil's Kitchen) to Llyn Idwal and back to Idwal Cottage.

THE CARNEDDAU

Carnedd Loop (9 miles; 5hr; 3500ft ascent). This fine day out, taking in the range's four mighty southern peaks, has less objective danger than the walks on Tryfan and the Glyderau but is just as exhausting. Start from the lay-by at the head of the lake near Tal y Llyn Ogwen farm and head right of the farm towards a small lake, Ffynnon Lloer, before turning left up the east ridge of Pen yr Ole Wen (3212ft), with its magnificent view down into Nant Ffrancon and back to Tryfan. In clear weather, you can see your route running north past Carnedd Fach, and what looks to be a huge artificial mound, to Carnedd Dafydd (3425ft). After a short easterly descent, the path skirts the steep Ysgolion Duon cliffs, then climbs over stones to the broad, arched top of Carnedd Llywelyn (3491ft), the highest of the Carneddau.

Descend towards Craig yr Ysfa, a sheer cliff that drops away into the vast amphitheatre of Cwm Eigiau to the north. Continuing with care, skirt around the north of Ffynnon Llugwy reservoir and climb to the grassy top of Penyrhelgi-du (2733ft), from where there's a steady broad-ridged descent to the road near Helyg. The mile-long trek back west to the starting point is best done on the old packhorse route running parallel to the A5.

fantastically scenic spots, which, in 1954, became Wales' first **National Nature Reserve**. The evidence of glacial scouring is so clear here that you wonder why it took geologists so long to work out what process created its mountain bowl. Darwin made his excuses when, in 1842, he recalled his visit with the geologist Adam Sedgewick eleven years earlier; they were so awed, he noted, "neither of us saw a trace of the wonderful glacial phenomena all around us". The cwm's floor traps **Llyn Idwal**, which reflects the grey cliffs behind and is accessed by a boardwalk around the lake. There's a pebble beach for a dip on one shore; wade out to a drop off and then swim dwarfed by high crags and slabs. Even better, the lake is open to sunshine. Who knows, you might even see some some.

Twll Du

The back of Cwm Idwal is marked by a dark chasm known as **Twll Du**, literally "black cleft", but dubbed the Devil's Kitchen by Victorian visitors. Down this channel, a fine watery haze runs off the flanks of **Glyder Fawr**, soaking the crevices where early botanists found rare arctic-alpine plants (see p.447). This is one of the few places where you can see the downfolded strata of what is known as the Snowdon syncline, evidence that the existing mountains sat between two much larger ranges some three hundred million years ago. The smooth inclines of the **Idwal Slabs** on their left have been nursery slopes for countless budding rock climbers.

Rhaeadr Ogwen

A five-minute walk down the valley from Idwal Cottage car park, the road crosses a bridge over the top of **Rhaeadr Ogwen** (Ogwen Falls), which cascades down this step in the valley floor. Look under the road bridge and you'll see the simple mortar-free arch of a bridge that was on the original packhorse route through the valley before the road.

ZipWorld Velocity

Signposted off the A5 south of Bethesda, LL57 4YG • Booking centre daily 9am–6pm • £70 • ☎ 01248 601444, ⓦ zipworld.co.uk

Who would have imagined that a disused quarry could be so much fun? Taking its cue from the mountain-bike trails in a former workings at Blaenau Ffestiniog (see p.366), **ZipWorld Velocity**, Europe's longest zip wire, is strung across a former slate quarry to provide a one-mile ride at speeds of up to 70mph – the fastest in the world, it claims. It's an astonishing ride: the land beneath blurs, then plummets away so that you're racing through empty space. Reservations are essential and there are restrictions on weight, height and age. Note, too, that the weather can affect your ride and that ZipWorld offers rescheduling rather than refunds.

ARRIVAL AND INFORMATION	OGWEN VALLEY

By bus From mid-April to Oct the #S6 Snowdon Sherpa runs between Bethesda and Capel Curig (Sat & Sun 3 daily; 30min), continuing either to Betws-y-Coed (20min) or Bangor (30min).
On foot A footpath tracks the valley for 5 miles from Capel

Curig to Idwal Cottage, although it runs parallel to the busy road.
Tourist information There is a staffed information centre covering the local area at Cwm Idwal car park (daily 9am–5pm).

ACCOMMODATION

★**Gwern Gôf Uchaf** A5, 4 miles west of Capel Curig, LL24 0EU ☎ 01690 720294, ⓦ tryfanwales.co.uk. Superbly located campsite right at the base of Tryfan, with a decent shower block, and a good fourteen-berth bunkhouse with a fully equipped kitchen and drying room. Bring a sleeping bag and food. Camping/person **£5**, dorms **£12**
YHA Idwal Cottage A5, 5 miles west of Capel Curig,

LL57 3LZ ☎ 0345 371 9744, ⓦ yha.org.uk/hostel/idwal. Perfectly sited for walkers, this hostel, in an old quarry manager's house, was opened in 1931 as one of Wales' first hostels. It has been well refurbished since then, and offers mostly four-bunk dorms, a double, a single, family rooms and an alcohol licence, but no meals. Opens 5pm for check-in. Limited opening Nov–March (mostly weekends); check the website. Camping **£13**, dorms **£25**, doubles **£59**

Llanberis and around

LLANBERIS is the nearest you'll get in Wales to an alpine climbing village. Its single main street is thronged with walkers and climbers – people march out with rucksacks around 9am, leaving the place quiet during the day, then return from the hills from mid-afternoon. The reason is **Snowdon**, to which Llanberis is inextricably linked, not least because of the five-mile **Snowdon Mountain Railway** to the summit.

At heart, however, this is very much a Welsh rural community, albeit rather depleted now that slate is no longer being mined from Elidir Fawr. For the best part of two centuries, the **quarries** employed up to three thousand men. They closed in 1969, leaving a staircase of 60ft-high platforms and tiers of blue-grey rubble covering the mountainside. Still, there's a glowering beauty about the scene, especially when low cloud roofs the workings and **Dolbadarn Castle** looms from the murk on its hilltop.

When the sun breaks out, hiking competes with a choice of two **narrow-gauge railways** and myriad activities – from messing around in boats on the lake to scrambling and mountain biking.

Snowdon Mountain Railway

Victoria Terrace (on the A4086), LL55 4TT • Mid-March to Oct daily 9am–2.30pm (roughly three ascents): Clogwyn Station mid-March to May; summit May–Oct • Clogwyn Station return £16 (no singles); summit return £29, one-way £22; booking fee £3.50; £6 discount if reserving in advance for 9am train • ☎ 01286 870223, ⓦ snowdonrailway.co.uk

The **Snowdon Mountain Railway** is Britain's only rack-and-pinion railway, completed in 1896. Trains pushed either by century-old steam locos or a dinky diesel engine climb

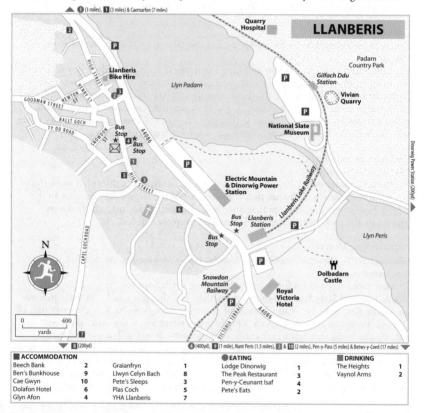

■ ACCOMMODATION				● EATING		■ DRINKING	
Beech Bank	2	Graianfryn	1	Lodge Dinorwig	1	The Heights	1
Ben's Bunkhouse	9	Llwyn Celyn Bach	8	The Peak Restaurant	3	Vaynol Arms	2
Cae Gwyn	10	Pete's Sleeps	3	Pen-y-Ceunant Isaf	4		
Dolafon Hotel	6	Plas Coch	5	Pete's Eats	2		
Glyn Afon	4	YHA Llanberis	7				

to the summit in just under an hour along the most heavily maintained track in the country. The rails follow the shallowest approach to the top of Snowdon, grinding up a mostly one-in-eight gradient for five miles and 1000ft.

Whether steam or diesel, the full round trip takes two and a half hours, with half an hour on top for a cuppa (or a beer) in the summit café *Hafod Eyri*. From mid-March to May (and during high winds) services terminate three-quarters of the way up at **Clogwyn Station**, thirty minutes' walk from the summit.

Demand is high in summer (especially July, Aug and weekends in June and Sept), so book at least a day in advance, especially if you want to ride in the steam train, which has only 35 seats. Walkers who've hiked up to the summit may be able to buy a standby ticket back down but don't count on it – return passengers come first and most trips are full.

Llanberis Lake Railway

Gilfach Ddu, LL55 4TY · Mid-March to June, Sept & Oct 3–5 services daily; July & Aug 4–10 services daily · £8.50 return · ☎ 01286 870549, ⓦ lake-railway.co.uk

From 1843 to 1961, the original Padarn Railway transported slate and workers between the Dinorwig quarries and Port Dinorwig on the Menai Strait. When it closed it was sold for scrap, but enthusiasts subsequently relaid a two-mile stretch along the scenic shores of Lake Padarn as the family-oriented **Llanberis Lake Railway**. Tank engines that once pulled slate around the quarries now take an hour for the sedate round trip, which includes a stop halfway back at **Cei Llydan** station with a picnic spot by the lake. The easiest embarkation point is Llanberis station.

Dolbadarn Castle

Off the A4086, 0.5 mile east of Llanberis centre, LL55 4UB · Open access · Free; CADW · ☎ 01443 336000, ⓦ cadw.gov.wales/daysout /dolbadarncastle

On a rock between Llyn Padarn and Llyn Peris, where it once guarded the mouth of the Llanberis Pass, a single tower and some scattered masonry are all that remain of **Dolbadarn Castle**. Built in the thirteenth century, its construction is usually attributed to Llywelyn ap Iorwerth ("the Great"), and close up there's not a lot to look at. But viewed across Llyn Padarn, framed by the grey crags of the Pass behind, it is easy to see why Richard Wilson and Turner chose it as a subject for their paintings.

Padarn Country Park

Gilfach Ddu, LL55 4TY · Open access · Free

At **Padarn Country Park** lakeside oak woods are recolonizing the discarded workings of the defunct **Dinorwig Slate Quarries**, formerly one of the largest slate quarries in the world. Equipment and engines that once hauled materials up inclined tramways punctuate the paths which link levels chiselled from the hillside.

National Slate Museum

Gilfach Ddu, LL55 4TY · Easter–Oct daily 10am–5pm; Nov–Easter Mon–Fri & Sun 10am–4pm · Free · ☎ 01286 870630, ⓦ museumwales.ac.uk

In what looks more like a fort than maintenance workshops for the former quarry, Wales' **National Slate Museum** relates more than you thought you'd ever want to know about the slate industry. Though most of the equipment dates back to the early part of the twentieth century – not least a 50ft-diameter water wheel that once powered cutting machines through a cat's cradle of lineshafts – it was still in use until the quarries closed. The slate was delivered to dressing sheds via a maze of tramways, cranes and rope lifts. On a self-guided tour you'll learn about the scales used to calculate the price each rock cutter would be paid for his work, before the deductions for the rope and gunpowder he used to extract the slate, from mottled burgundy and bottle green

FROM TOP CAERNARFON CASTLE AND THE SEIONT RIVER (P.357); FFESTINIOG RAILWAY (P.370) >

6

ACTIVITIES AROUND LLANBERIS

Guided climbing and scrambling Several guides in the area offer bespoke trips featuring everything from straightforward hillwalking to scrambling, rock climbing (for all abilities), navigation and winter climbing for people not well equipped or confident enough to get out on the rock alone. Try Paul Poole Mountaineering (☎07786 360347, ⓦpaulpoolemountaineering. co.uk) or Raw Adventures (☎01286 685472, ⓦraw-adventures.co.uk). Expect to pay around £160 a day for a couple.

Mountain biking The Llanberis Path up Snowdon (see box, p.354) is designated a bridleway, making it, the Snowdon Ranger Path and the Pitt's Head Track to Rhyd Ddu accessible to cyclists – unsurprisingly, it's graded a black trail. Note, too, that bikes are banned from summit tracks between 10am and 5pm from May to September. Llanberis Bike Hire, 34 High St (☎07776 051559, ⓦllanberisbikehire.co.uk), rents bikes for £25 a day or £17 a half-day and will deliver to your accommodation.

Watersports Snowdonia Watersports (☎01286 879001, ⓦsnowdoniawatersports.com) will get you on to and into Llyn Padarn in a variety of ways: on a stand-up paddleboard, in a kayak or canoe or just on a supported swim. It offers trips (£40 for half-day) and rents out equipment (£20/2hr) – including wetsuits (£5) should you fancy a dip. It's located in an industrial estate by the lakeshore half a mile northwest of the centre (sat nav LL55 4EL).

---

to every shade of grey. Former quarry workers often demonstrate how they turned an inch-thick slab of slate into perfectly smooth slivers. You'll also discover the slate workers' cottages furnished in various styles over a century of use. To keep everything in working order, the craftsmen here operate a foundry, producing pieces for branches of the National Museum of Wales.

Quarry Hospital

500yd north of the National Slate Museum, LL55 4TY • June–Aug Sat & Sun 11am–4pm • Free

You can pick up leaflets of **waymarked walking trails** from a kiosk near the slate museum, but it's easy just to meander around the old slate workings and through the woodlands of Coed Dinorwig. A goal for a walk in summer is the **Quarry Hospital**, where a resident surgeon patched up miners' injuries. In reality, tuberculosis was far more fatal to miners than gunpowder blasts or falling rock.

Dinorwig Power Station and Electric Mountain

A4086, LL55 4UR • **Underground tours** 4 daily, or 7 daily in the school hols: Easter–May, Sept & Oct 10am–4pm; June–Aug 9.30am–5.30pm; 1hr • £8.50 • ☎01286 870636, ⓦelectricmountain.co.uk • **Electric Mountain** Daily: June–Aug 9.30am–5.30pm; Sept–May 10am–4.30pm • Free

Views north from Llanberis are dominated by the entrance to the **Dinorwig Power Station**, hollowed out of the ground in the mid-1970s, five years after the quarries closed. The power station actually consumes more electricity than it produces, but benefits the national grid by being able to supply electricity instantly, to cope with the early evening surge in demand. Within sixteen seconds it can attain 1300 megawatts by letting the contents of the Marchlyn Mawr reservoir rapidly empty through its turbines into Llyn Peris.

Underground bus tours delve into the innards of the mountain, heading through tunnels hewn from the rock to the powerhouse below, where a film details the scheme's construction. It's a popular option for a rainy day, so book ahead if the weather turns foul.

Tours start from **Electric Mountain**, actually a building beside Llyn Padarn that contains a café and information boards explaining Snowdon's microclimate.

ARRIVAL AND INFORMATION   **LLANBERIS AND AROUND**

By bus Buses stop along High St.
Destinations Bangor (9 daily; 45min); Betws-y-Coed

(10 daily; 50min); Caernarfon (Mon–Sat every 30min, Sun 8; 25min); Capel Curig (10 daily; 35min); Nant Peris

(roughly every 30min; 10min); Pen-y-Pass (roughly every 30min; 10min).

Tourist information There's no dedicated tourist office, but the Electric Mountain (see opposite) doubles as an information point, with leaflets.

ACCOMMODATION

HOTELS AND GUESTHOUSES

Beech Bank 2 High St, LL55 4EN ☎ 01286 871085, ⓦ beech-bank.co.uk. Spacious, comfortable and well-equipped B&B (each room has a drying room and DVD player), with rather sleek modern decor that leans towards boutique. Add welcoming hosts and this ticks most boxes for a relaxing B&B stay. Loaning flasks to guests is a nice touch. **£75**

Dolafon Hotel High St, LL55 4SU ☎ 01286 870993, ⓦ dolafon.com. Budget B&B in a spacious, solid-granite Grade II-listed house. Decor is traditional rather than exciting – no surprise at this price – but rooms are spacious and comfortable, especially the larger front rooms (£85) and the welcome is warm. Excellent value. Closed Nov–Easter. **£65**

Glyn Afon 72 High St, LL55 4HA ☎ 01286 872528, ⓦ llanberisbedandbreakfast.co.uk. A smart and spotless newcomer to Llanberis's B&B market, with extras like nice toiletries and cake on arrival that shift it into the boutique B&B sector, despite the price. Two singles and two twins are useful for walkers. **£75**

Graianfryn Penisarwaun, 3 miles northwest, LL55 3NH ☎ 01286 871007, ⓦ fastasleep.me.uk. This vegetarian and vegan farmhouse B&B offers a spotless, homely rural stay with lovely owners; only one of the three double rooms is en suite. Christine prepares good evening meals of home-grown produce on request. Look online or call for directions. Single guests pay half that of doubles. **£76**

★**Plas Coch** High St, LL55 4HB ☎ 01286 872122, ⓦ plascochsnowdonia.co.uk. Bravo to the owners: having done a top-to-bottom refurbishment to create a beautiful B&B, they've maintained high standards in their seven immaculate, hugely comfortable en-suite rooms. There are vast double beds, an extra shared bathroom with a slipper-tub for post-hike soaks, a drying room and delicious home-made cake on the sideboard for snacks. **£80**

HOSTELS AND CAMPSITES

Ben's Bunkhouse 1 mile southeast, LL55 4UD ☎ 07500 513765, ⓦ bensbunkhouse.co.uk. A good little bunkhouse that sleeps just eighteen in three dorms (bring a sleeping bag), though it can be booked by groups. It also has a great kitchen with an urn of near-boiling water – perfect for a cuppa after the hills – a drying room and wi-fi, which is unusual in a mountain bunkhouse. **£15**

Cae Gwyn Nant Peris, 2 miles southeast, LL55 4UF ☎ 01286 870718. Climbers and bikers make up the bulk of the clientele in this field campsite and very primitive bunkhouse (bring everything). It's almost opposite the *Vaynol Arms* pub and handy for the Pen-y-Pass park-and-ride. Camping/person **£6**, bunkhouse **£12**

Llwyn Celyn Bach 900yd uphill via Capel Coch Rd, LL55 4SR ☎ 01286 870923, ✉ daviesllanberis@aol.com. The good news is that this site spreads over several fields, with views over town to the slate quarries, and sells logs for a campfire. The bad is that flat ground is in short supply and lower fields are boggy after rain – pick your site carefully. The rates go up to £7/person during weekends in July and Aug. Per person **£6**

Pete's Sleeps 40 High St, LL55 4EU ☎ 01286 872135, ⓦ petes-eats.co.uk. Super-central but fairly basic eight-bed dorm above the *Pete's Eats* café, plus a couple of twin rooms (no breakfast), all with access to self-catering facilities. There's a good map library, with UK-wide stock. It can get booked up by groups. Dorms **£16**, twins **£37**

YHA Llanberis 700yd uphill from town along Capel Goch Rd, LL55 4SR ☎ 0345 371 9645, ⓦ yha.org.uk /hostel/snowdon-llanberis. Spacious, well-appointed YHA hostel in a former quarrymaster's house that has benefitted from a recent refurb. They have dorms, twin-bunk rooms and a couple of en-suite doubles; there's a self-catering kitchen, and meals are available (mains £9.95). Closed Dec & Jan. Dorms **£19**, doubles **£59**

EATING

Lodge Dinorwig Dinorwig, 3 miles northwest, LL55 3EY ☎ 01286 871632, ⓦ lodge-dinorwig.co.uk. The awesome terrace views across to Snowdon are appealing, and so is the interior of this old village school, the sort of eclectic café Wales does so well. Food-wise, a small seasonal menu is healthy, fresh and always local: expect home-made fishcakes (£10), *burritos* and cakes. You can walk up here via Padarn Country Park in an hour. Mon–Fri 9am–4pm (till 3pm in winter), Sat & Sun 9am–5pm (till 4pm in winter).

The Peak Restaurant 86 High St, LL55 4SU ☎ 01286 872777, ⓦ peakrestaurant.co.uk. This unflashy open-kitchen restaurant has long served the best food in Llanberis, championing home-made, seasonal and fresh food long before it became fashionable. Sea bass with leek and dill potato cake (£18) typify a Modern British menu which usually finds space for a daily curry and a pie. Booking advised. Wed–Sun 7–10pm.

★**Pen-y-Ceunant Isaf** Snowdon Path, LL55 4UW ☎ 01286 872606, ⓦ snowdoncafe.com. An eighteenth-century cottage café, 400yd up the Llanberis Path, that's been serving Welsh teas, snacks and home-baked cakes in

6

its homely dining room for decades. There are no meals but you're welcome to eat your own sandwiches here if you buy a cuppa. Visit if only to see the gallery, which includes works by Sir Kyffin Williams. Daily: April–Oct 9am–10pm; Nov–March 10am–6pm.

Pete's Eats 40 High St, LL55 4EU ☎01286 870117. A

Llanberis legend for walkers, climbers and bikers for its cheap unpretentious grub – full walker's breakfasts (£5), lamb burgers or fish and chips (£7) – in large portions. There are heaps of magazines and maps to browse and free wi-fi, so it's always busy when the weather turns bad. Daily: summer 8am–9pm; rest of year 6am–8pm.

DRINKING

The Heights 74 High St, LL55 4HB ☎01286 871179, ⓦ heightsllanberis.com. This boozer, in an airy hall-like building, has no pretensions to do anything other than provide a decent place for a pint – including ales from north Wales – and to watch sport on a big screen. Popular

with locals and visitors, it's usually the liveliest place in town. Daily 11am–11pm.

Vaynol Arms Nant Peris, 2 miles southeast, LL55 4UF ☎01286 872672. Slate floors, a fire in the grate, real ales and gutsy pub food the likes of belly pork and Irish stew (£11)

WALKS UP SNOWDON

All the following paths are easy to follow in good weather, but the OS 1:25,000 Explorer map OL17 (Snowdon – Conwy Valley) is still recommended.

LLANBERIS PATH

The easiest, longest and least interesting route up Snowdon, the **Llanberis Path** (5 miles to summit; 3hr; 3200ft ascent) follows the rail line. Victoria Terrace runs off the A4086 opposite the *Royal Victoria Hotel* and becomes a path that soon passes the *Pen-y-Ceunant* tearoom (see p.353). The summit comes into view towards the midway point. From here there are views of Clogwyn Du'r Arddu (The Black Cliff, or "Cloggy" to its friends), a sheet of rock that frames a small lake. The path passes Clogwyn station, then gets steeper, passing the remains of stables where mule trains used to rest. Bwlch Glas (Green Pass) is marked by the "Finger Stone" where the Snowdon Ranger Path (see opposite) and three routes coming up from Pen-y-Pass join the Llanberis Path for the final ascent to Yr Wyddfa.

MINERS' TRACK

The **Miners' Track** (4 miles to summit; 2hr 30min; 2400ft ascent) is the easiest of the three routes up from Pen-y-Pass. Leaving the car park, a broad track leads south then west to the former copper mines in Cwm Dyli. Dilapidated remains of the crushing mill perch on the shores of Llyn Llydaw, a tarn-turned-reservoir with one of the worst eyesores in the national park, an overground pipeline slicing across Snowdon's east face to the power station in Nantgwynant. Skirting around the right of the lake, the path climbs more steeply to the lake-filled Cwm Glaslyn then again to Upper Glaslyn, from where the measured steps of those ahead warn of the impending switchback ascent to the junction with the Llanberis Path.

PIG TRACK

The stonier **Pig Track** (3.5 miles to summit; 2hr 30min; 2400ft ascent) is really just a shorter and steeper variation on the Miners' Track, leaving from the western end of the Pen-y-Pass car park and climbing up to Bwlch y Moch (the Pass of the Pigs), which gives the route its name. Ignore the scramble up to Crib Goch (part of the Snowdon Horseshoe) and traverse below the rocky ridge looking down on Llyn Llydaw and those pacing the Miners' Track, content that you're already 500ft up on them. They'll soon catch up, as the two tracks meet just before the zigzag up to the Llanberis Path. The path is also known as the PYG track, supposedly after the nearby *Pen y Gwryd Hotel*: no one seems able to agree on the matter.

SNOWDON HORSESHOE

One of the UK's finest ridge walks, the **Snowdon Horseshoe** (8 miles round trip; 5–7hr; 3200ft ascent) makes a full anticlockwise circuit around the three glacier-graven cwms of Upper Glaslyn, Glaslyn and Llydaw. It's not to be taken lightly. Every summer's day, dozens of people find themselves straddling the knife-edge traverse of Crib Goch, empty space on either side, frozen to the spot, wishing they weren't there. If it's windy it can be lethal. In

– this traditional pub, with no music to disturb the chat, may be just the ticket for a quiet night. There are old climbing magazines on the shelves for if the conversation flags. Mon–Fri 5–11pm, Sat & Sun noon–11pm; kitchen daily 6–9pm.

Snowdon

The highest British mountain south of the Scottish Grampians, the **Snowdon** massif (3560ft) forms a star of shattered ridges with three major peaks – Crib Goch, Crib-y-ddysgl and Y Lliwedd – and the summit, **Yr Wyddfa**, crowning the lot. Quite apart from the appeal of its sheer height, Snowdon also sports some of the finest walking and scrambling in Wales. Its Welsh name, Eryri, is derived from either *eryr* (land of eagles) or *eira* (land of snow); since the eagles have long gone, the latter feels now more appropriate, with winter snows lingering well into April.

Some hikers dismiss Snowdon. Certainly, it can be **crowded** – a thousand visitors a day press into carriages of the Snowdon Mountain Railway (see p.349) in peak season.

6

winter conditions, an ice axe and crampons are the minimum requirement. The path follows the Pig Track to Bwlch y Moch, then pitches right for the moderate scramble up to **Crib Goch**. If you baulk at any of this, turn back. If not, wait your turn, then painstakingly pick your way along the sensational ridge to Crib-y-ddysgl (3494ft), from where it's an easy descent to Bwlch Glas and on to Yr Wyddfa. Having ticked off Wales' two highest peaks, turn southwest for a couple of hundred yards to a marker stone where the Watkin Path (see below) drops away to the east. Follow it down to the stretched saddle of Bwlch-y-Saethau (Pass of the Arrows), then on to the cairn at Bwlch Ciliau from where the Watkin Path descends to Nantgwynant. Ignore that route, continuing straight up on up the cliff-lined northwest ridge of Y Lliwedd (2930ft), then descend to where you see the scrappy but safe path down to Llyn Llydaw and the Miners' Track.

SNOWDON RANGER PATH

Many of the earliest Snowdon climbers engaged the services of the Snowdon Ranger, who led them up the comparatively long and dull but easy **Snowdon Ranger Path** (4 miles to summit; 3hr; 3100ft ascent), on the now unfashionable south side of the mountain. The path starts from the *YHA Snowdon Ranger Hostel* on the shores of Llyn Cwellyn, five miles northwest of Beddgelert. To the left of the hostel, a path leads up a track then ascends steeply, flattening out to cross sometimes boggy grass and eventually skirting to the right of the impressive Clogwyn Du'r Arddu cliffs. Another steep ascent eventually brings you to the Llanberis Path at Bwlch Glas. Use the Welsh Highland Railway or the #S4 bus for the return journey.

RHYD DDU TRACK

The **Rhyd Ddu Track** (4 miles to summit; 3hr; 2900ft ascent) has two branches, one starting from Pitt's Head Rock, 2.5 miles northwest of Beddgelert, the other from the national park car park in Rhyd Ddu, a mile beyond that. They join up after less than a mile's walk across stony, walled grazing land, and after crossing a kissing gate continue to the northwest up to the stunning final section along the rim of Cwm Clogwyn and the south ridge of Yr Wyddfa. Use the Welsh Highland Railway or the #S4 bus to turn this into a loop.

WATKIN PATH

The most spectacular of the southern routes up Snowdon, the **Watkin Path** (4 miles to summit; 3hr; 3350ft ascent) is also the one with the greatest height gain. From Bethania Bridge, three miles northeast of Beddgelert in Nantgwynant, the path starts on a broad track through oaks opening up to long views of a series of cataracts. Ascend beside what is a disused inclined tramway where the track narrows before reaching the natural amphitheatre of Cwm Llan. The ruins of the South Snowdon Slate Works only briefly distract you from Gladstone Rock, at which, in 1892, the 83-year-old Liberal statesman, then in his fourth term as British prime minister, officially opened the route. A narrower path wheels left around the base of Craig Ddu, then starts the steep ascent past Carnedd Arthur to Bwlch Ciliau, the saddle between Y Lliwedd (see above) and the true summit (Yr Wyddfa), then turning left for the final climb to the top.

Double that number tramps up well-maintained paths, making this Britain's most-climbed mountain; traffic jams of hikers are not unknown on peak weekends. As if the existence of a train up were not insult enough to the hiking purists, there's the fact that they can find themselves at the top among day-trippers in trainers munching oggies and chips bought from the summit café, **Hafod Eryri** ("dwelling place atop Snowdon"). Worse still, it has a gift shop. Still, you try resisting a cuppa – or perhaps a chilled beer – when you get up there. The café also offers a warm place to rest. And however you get up, the **views** can be staggering – over most of north Wales and even to the Wicklow mountains in Ireland on exceptionally clear days.

For walkers, the choice is about how you ascend. The original Llanberis Path remains popular, though most walkers prefer the three shorter and steeper paths from the Pen-y-Pass car park at the top of the Llanberis Pass (see box, p.354). Easily the most dramatic – and most dangerous – route is the wonderful Snowdon Horseshoe, which takes in all four high peaks.

Brief history

The Welsh for the highest point of Snowdon, Yr Wyddfa, means "The Burial Place" – near proof that people have been climbing the mountain for millennia. More recently, **early ascents** were for botanical or geological reasons – 500-million-year-old fossil shells can be found near the summit, dating back from when Snowdon was on the sea dfloor – but the Welsh naturalist **Thomas Pennant** came up here mainly for pleasure, and in 1773 his description of the dawn view from the summit in *Journey to Snowdon* encouraged many to follow. Some were guided by the Snowdon ranger, Evan Roberts, from his house on the south side (now a YHA hostel), but the rapidly improving facilities in Llanberis soon shifted the balance in favour of the easier Llanberis Path, a route later followed by the railway.

The Llanberis Pass and Pen-y-Pass

Most walkers start their ascent from the saddle at the top of the **Llanberis Pass**. It's the deepest, narrowest and craggiest of Snowdonia's passes, running five miles east from Llanberis itself, and worth a visit in its own right for the scenery. It's also the Welsh home of **rock climbing** – you'll almost always see climbers inching their way up the various crags or practising bouldering techniques on roadside rocks.

At the head of the pass, a YHA hostel with a café and a car park, make up **PEN-Y-PASS**, the base for the Miners' Track, the Pig Track and the demanding Snowdon Horseshoe (see box, p.354). All set off from the car park.

KING ARTHUR AND SNOWDON

From the departure of the Romans until the tenth century, Welsh history is pervaded by legends of **King Arthur** (see box, p.93), **Gwrtheyrn** (Vortigern) and **Myrddin**, otherwise known as Merlin (see box, p.144). Arthur's British (as opposed to Anglo-Saxon) blood gives him a firm place in Welsh hearts, and while Caerleon in southeast Wales lays a powerful claim to being the site of Arthur's court, Snowdon is often held to have been his home.

It was atop Dinas Emrys, the seat of Gwrtheyrn's realm near Beddgelert, that the most potent symbol of Welsh independence, the Red Dragon, earned its colours. The Celtic king, Gwrtheyrn, was trying to build a fortress to protect himself from the Saxons, but each night the earth swallowed the masonry. Myrddin divined this to be caused by two dragons sleeping underground: one white, the other red. When woken, they fought unendingly, symbolizing the Red Dragon of Wales' perpetual battle with the White Dragon of the Saxons.

Arthur's domain was higher up the mountain. **Llyn Llydaw** aspires to being the lake into which Bedivere cast Arthur's sword, Excalibur, after Arthur was mortally wounded by an arrow while on the point of vanquishing his nephew Modred at **Bwlch-y-Saethau** (Pass of the Arrows), 1300ft above the lake.

ARRIVAL AND DEPARTURE

By bus The car park at Pen-y-Pass costs £5 for up to 4hr and £10 all day, so consider using the bus. There's also a park-and-ride at the bottom of the pass close to the *Vaynol Arms* (£5 all day) – the frequent #S1 & #S2 Snowdon Sherpa buses (7 daily; 10min) shuttle up to

PEN-Y-PASS

Pen-y-Pass for £1.20.

Destinations Beddgelert (4 daily; 20min); Betws-y-Coed (10 daily; 20min); Capel Curig (10 daily; 10min); Llanberis (hourly or more; 15min); Porthmadog (4 daily; 45min).

ACCOMMODATION AND EATING

★**Pen-y-Gwryd Hotel** 1 mile east, LL55 4NT ☎01286 870211, ⌨pyg.co.uk. This splendid old coaching inn – all aged oak furniture and magnificent Edwardian bathrooms – is legendary as the hotel that the successful Mount Everest team used as a base while training for its 1953 ascent. Edmund Hillary signed the ceiling (as did Chris Bonington and Portmeirion designer Clough Williams-Ellis) and donated mementoes of his trip for the splendid *Smoke Room* bar. The Edwardian double rooms (some en suite) are priced/person – we've quoted the price for two people in a double. In the restaurant – open to non-guests – you can expect solid cooking (£25 for a three-course meal, £30 for five courses) and a congenial, nostalgic atmosphere. Two-night minimum at weekends. Hotel: March to mid-Nov

daily; mid-Nov to Dec Fri–Sun. Restaurant: March to mid-Nov daily noon–2pm & 7.30pm (set dinner time); mid-Nov to Dec Fri & Sat noon–2pm & 7.30pm, Sun noon–2pm. **£90**

YHA Pen-y-Pass Pen-y-Pass, LL55 4NY ☎0345 371 9534, ⌨yha.org.uk/hostel/snowdon-pen-y-pass. The only accommodation at Pen-y-Pass has benefitted from a £1.3m renovation to update what was already a renowned walkers' hostel into a comfy modern option: a couple of six-bed dorms aside, most rooms have two or four beds, and more than half of them are en suite. School groups are shunted into a separate wing. Facilities include a café-bar, a laundry and drying room, but no wi-fi. Curfew 10.30pm. Dorms **£24**, doubles **£60**

6

Caernarfon and around

CAERNARFON, superbly set at the southern entrance to the Menai Strait, has a lot going for it. As the county town of Gwynedd and one of the oldest continuously occupied settlements in Wales – it was once the site of the Romans' most westerly legion post – it retains a genuine sense of gravitas compared to other settlements in the region. That's mostly due to its fantastic **castle**, which remains the undoubted highlight of a visit, just as it has been for centuries. Steam buffs come too for the **Welsh Highland Railway**, which connects the town with the slopes of Snowdon and Porthmadog, while the modern marina development adds **Galeri Caernarfon**, a modest arts centre, to the mix. There's also the pleasure of simply meandering among the seventeenth- and eighteenth-century buildings lining the neat grid of streets, wedged between the **town walls**, that remains nicely scruffy compared to, for example, Conwy. The quayside beneath the castle has been transformed from a car park into a waterside **promenade**, set beneath the town walls (these are as complete as those at Conwy, but there remains no way to access them).

Factor in some great accommodation and a new terminus of the Ffestiniog Railway and Welsh Highland Railway (see box, p.360) for day-trips, and Caernarfon makes a good, central base to explore both sides of Snowdon, the Llŷn and even Anglesey.

Caernarfon Castle

Entrance on Castle Ditch, LL55 2AY • March–June, Sept & Oct daily 9.30am–5pm; July & Aug daily 9.30am–6pm; Nov–Feb Mon–Sat 10am–4pm, Sun 11am–4pm • £8.95; CADW • ☎01286 677617, ⌨cadw.gov.wales/daysout/caernarfon-castle

In 1283, Edward I started work on **Caernarfon Castle**, the strongest link in his Iron Ring (see box, p.405) and the decisive hammerblow to Welsh aspirations of autonomy. Until Beaumaris Castle was built to guard the other end of the Menai Strait, Caernarfon was the ultimate symbol of Anglo-Norman military might and political wrangling. With the Welsh already smarting from the loss of their Prince of Wales, Edward reputedly rubbed salt in the wound by justifying his own infant son's claim to the title, having promised "a prince born in Wales who could speak never a word of

6

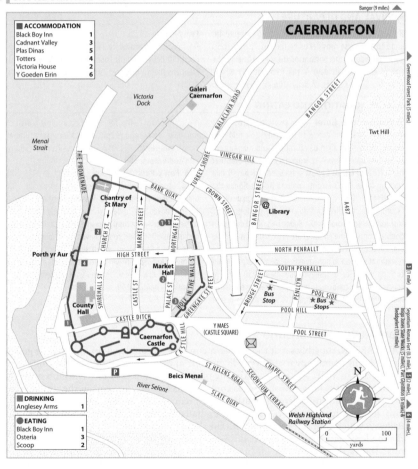

Bangor (9 miles)

CAERNARFON

ACCOMMODATION

Black Boy Inn	1
Cadnant Valley	3
Plas Dinas	5
Totters	4
Victoria House	2
Y Goeden Eirin	6

Greenwood Forest Park (5 miles)

Victoria Dock

Galeri Caernarfon

BALACLAVA ROAD

BANGOR STREET

Twt Hill

Menai Strait

VINEGAR HILL

TURKEY SHORE

BANGOR STREET

A487

THE PROMENADE

BANK QUAY

CROWN STREET

Library

Chantry of St Mary

CHURCH ST.

MARKET STREET

NORTHGATE ST.

NORTH PENRALLT

Porth yr Aur

HIGH STREET

SOUTH PENRALLT

SHIREHALL ST.

CASTLE ST.

PALACE ST.

Market Hall

HOLE IN THE WALL ST.

GREENGATE STREET

BRIDGE STREET

PENLLYN

Bus Stop

POOL SIDE

Bus Stops

County Hall

CASTLE DITCH

Y MAES (CASTLE SQUARE)

POOL HILL

POOL STREET

Caernarfon Castle

CASTLE HILL

P

Beics Menai

ST HELENS ROAD

SEGONTIUM TERRACE

CHAPEL STREET

River Seiont

SLATE QUAY

Welsh Highland Railway Station

N

0   100

yards

Segontium Roman Fort (0.3 mile), Inigo Jones Slate Works (2.5 miles), Parc Glynllifon (6 miles) & Beddgelert (13 miles)

3 (1 mile)

5 (2 miles)

6 (4 miles)

DRINKING

Anglesey Arms	1

EATING

Black Boy Inn	1
Osteria	3
Scoop	2

English". He subsequently presented them with the newborn baby, born in Caernarfon because his pregnant wife had been forced to take up residence there. The story is almost certainly apocryphal, since Edward's son, though born at Caernarfon, wasn't invested until seven years later.

However, Edward attempted to woo the Welsh with gestures to local legends. The Welsh had long associated their town with the eastern capital of the Roman Empire: Caernarfon's old Roman name, Caer Cystennin ("Fort of Constantine"), alludes to the emperor after whom Constantinople was named. Some dreamers once claimed Constantine himself was born here; Edward's architect, James of St George, exploited this connection in the distinctive limestone and sandstone banding and polygonal towers, both reminiscent of the Theodosian walls in Istanbul.

The castle is in an excellent state of repair, thanks largely to a nineteenth-century reconstruction, carried out after Richard Wilson and J.M.W. Turner painted Romantic images of it. The walls and towers are in a much better state than the interior, linked by a splendid honeycomb of wall-walks and tunnels. There are a few historical displays too, but these feel like filler – the interest is in the castle itself.

The King's Gate

As you enter the **King's Gate**, the castle's brute strength is apparent. Between the octagonal towers, embrasures and murder-holes cover no fewer than five gates and six portcullises once you've crossed the moat. They certainly did the job. Seized only once (before it was finished), the castle withstood two sieges by Owain Glyndŵr with a complement of just 28 men-at-arms. Inside, the huge lawn is misleading – a wall originally separated two wards, each filled with wooden buildings.

The Eagle Tower

The **Eagle Tower**, at the western end of the complex, is the highest and most striking of the towers – three slender turrets with heavily eroded eagle sculptures provide superb views of the town. The lower floors feature so-so historical displays on royal lineage plus a dry **Prince of Wales Exhibition**, which includes the slate dais used for the investiture of the current Prince of Wales, Prince Charles (see box below).

The Queen's, Northeast and Black towers

The **Queen's Tower** is entirely taken up by the numbingly thorough **Museum of the Royal Welch Fusiliers**, which details the victories of Wales' oldest regiment through collections of medals, uniforms and a brass howitzer captured from the Russians at the Battle of the Alma in the Crimea in 1854. Crossing the upper ward, you reach the **Northeast Tower**, in which a computer animation narrates a history of Caernarfon. On the same side, an exhibition in the **Black Tower** expands upon Edward's manipulation of Arthurian legend (see box, p.93) for propaganda.

Segontium Roman Fort

Constantine Rd (A4085), LL55 2LF, 0.3 mile east towards Beddgelert • Tues–Sun 12.30–4.30pm • Free; CADW • ☎ 01286 677617, ⓦ cadw.gov.wales/daysout/segontiumromanfort and ⓦ nationaltrust.org.uk/segontium

The western end of the Roman road from Chester terminated at **Segontium Roman Fort**, a five-acre hilltop site that the Romans occupied for three centuries from around 78 AD, though most of the remains are from the final rebuilding after 364 AD. This was the base of Maximus, the Spanish-born pretender to the imperial throne who was declared Emperor by his British troops in 383 AD, and made a failed march on Rome. The remains of Segontium are about as impressive as his attempted coup, seldom more than shin-high – its stone was used to build the castle – with little background information.

WHAT PRINCE OF WALES?

It was in Caernarfon in 1969 that Charles, the current heir to the throne, was theatrically invested as **Prince of Wales**, a ceremony that reaffirmed English sovereignty over Wales in the midst of one of the most nationalist of Welsh-speaking regions. Since 1282, when the English defeated Llywelyn ap Gruffydd, the last Welsh Prince of Wales, the title has been bestowed on heirs to the English throne, usually in a ceremony held either at Windsor Castle or in Westminster Abbey in London. However, in 1911, the machinations of **Lloyd George** – MP for Caernarfon, Welsh cabinet minister and future prime minister – ensured that the investiture of the future King Edward VIII would take place in the centre of his constituency: a paradoxical move for a nationalist, but one that undoubtedly helped to advance his career.

By the time it was Charles's turn, nationalism was on the rise and two extremist members of the **Free Wales Army** blew themselves up trying to attack the Prince's train. In many ways, such acts had a detrimental effect on the nationalist cause, wrongly linking extremism with the more moderate and constitutional methods of the party. Charles's 25-year commemorative return visit in 1994 was a far more low-key affair, remembered, if at all, for the local constabulary ruling that the local joke shop risked committing a public-order offence by selling "wingnut" ears and Prince Charles masks.

GreenWood Forest Park

Y Felinheli (B4366), 3 miles northeast, west of Bethel village, LL35 3AD • Mid-March to Oct daily 10.30am–5pm; Nov to mid-March playbarn only • June–Aug £15.50; reduced prices in mid- and low season • ☎ 01248 670076, ⓦ greenwoodforestpark.co.uk

A sort of eco fun park, **GreenWood Forest Park** will keep children entertained for a day. Activities include a mini roller coaster, zip wires, slides, longbow shooting, treehouses and adventure playgrounds; the **playbarn**, with the usual climbing frames and slides, will entertain younger children. Underlying everything is a conservation message – most activities are human-powered.

Inigo Jones Slateworks

Groeslon, A487, 6 miles south of Caernarfon, LL54 7UE • Daily 9am–5pm • Self-guided audio tours (45min); £5.50 • ☎ 01286 830242, ⓦ inigojones.co.uk

Slate has been fashioned in roadside sheds at the **Inigo Jones Slateworks** since 1861. Many of the inscribed slate plaques on public buildings around north Wales were cut here, which provides an excuse for an exhibition on calligraphy. The exhibition is really a puff piece for the shop, of course, although if ever you wanted to try chiselling odd chips of slate, this is your place.

Parc Glynllifon

A499, 6 miles south of Caernarfon, LL54 5DY • April–Sept daily 10am–5pm; Oct–March Thurs–Sun 10am–5pm • £4 • ☎ 01286 830222

Parc Glynllifon occupies the grounds of nineteenth-century Glynllifon Hall, once home to a local lord and now council owned. The place is enjoyably going to seed; trails weave through the estate's old woodland garden with arboretums, slate buildings, old fountains and bridges to discover. It all feels slightly dream-like.

ARRIVAL AND GETTING AROUND   CAERNARFON

By train There's no national rail link, but the Welsh Highland Railway heritage tourist route (see p.371) ends here on its journey from Porthmadog via Beddgelert and Snowdon.

By bus National Express and local buses stop on Pool Side, northeast of central Y Maes (Castle Square).

Destinations Bangor (every 30min at least; 30min); Beddgelert (Mon–Sat 7 daily; 30min); Llanberis (Mon–Sat every 30min, Sun 8; 25min); Porthmadog (Mon–Sat 14 daily; 50min); Pwllheli (Mon–Sat roughly hourly, Sun 3; 55min).

Bike rental Beics Menai, 1 Slate Quay (Cei Llechi; ☎ 01286 676804, ⓦ beicsmenai.co.uk). All sorts of bikes (including child bikes and tandems) from £10 for a half-day or £15 for 8hr.

ACCOMMODATION

HOTELS AND GUESTHOUSES

Black Boy Inn Northgate St, LL55 1RW ☎ 01286 673604, ⓦ black-boy-inn.com. You have various B&B options here: low-beamed traditional rooms above the inn, said to be the town's oldest building (bar the castle); newer accommodation in an adjacent townhouse, Black Jacks; and en suites with small kitchenettes (though bland Travelodge-esque decor) in Tye Dre, in a neighbouring street. All include free parking. Dynamic pricing system. **£100**

WELSH HIGHLAND RAILWAY TRIPS FROM CAERNARFON

We've covered the **Welsh Highland Railway** in detail in our Porthmadog account (see p.371). Steam- or diesel-hauled trains run from the small station in Caernarfon on St Helen's Road, some of them going the full 25 miles to Porthmadog. The following train routes are good ways to enjoy the railway and to explore the wonderful scenery hereabouts:

Train to Waunfawr Visit the *Snowdonia Parc* microbrewery pub and a pleasant campsite (35min).

Train to Snowdon Ranger One-hour hike up the Snowdon Ranger path (see box, p.354) followed by a stay at the YHA hostel.

Train to Rhyd Ddu Hike the Rhyd Ddu track to Snowdon's summit; peak season timetables give you up to 7hr for the hike.

Train to Dinas Walk the three miles back along Lôn Eifion.

★**Plas Dinas** Bontnewydd, 2 miles south, LL54 7YF ☎01286 830214, ⓦplasdinas.co.uk. Rural peace and understated luxury in an elegant ten-room house, the ancestral home of Lord Snowdon. Very much "an historic home" as billed, it retains a personal feel thanks to its attentive hosts and the oil portraits and antique furnishings clearly pieced together with an eye for romantic glamour. Dinners are on offer Tues–Sat; reservations essential. Great value. **£119**

★**Victoria House** 13 Church St, LL55 1SW ☎01286 678263, ⓦthevictoriahouse.co.uk. This terrific B&B has a large balcony suite with a private deck beside the town walls – ideal for longer stays (£110). Otherwise, it provides immaculate Victorian-style (but modern) en suites (all doubles, no twins), with flatscreen TV/DVD and complimentary drinks in the lounge. There's also a shared town-wall terrace with views over the Menai Strait. **£90**

Y Goeden Eirin Dolydd, 4 miles south, LL54 7EF ☎01286 830942, ⓦygoedeneirin.co.uk. You'll enjoy a very personal stay in this B&B, run by a former university lecturer and packed full with art and books. Expect beautifully curated decor – Welsh art, traditional blankets, Mid-Century Modern pieces – whether in a spacious loft double (£100) or two rooms in an outbuilding. No cards. Find it just uphill from the petrol station. **£90**

HOSTEL AND CAMPSITE

Cadnant Valley Llanberis Rd, 0.5 mile east of Y Maes, LL55 2DF ☎01286 673196, ⓦwww.cwmcadnant valley.co.uk. Pleasant wooded campsite with lots of flat ground that feels more rural than the location – just a 15min walk east of the centre, near the start of the A4086 to Llanberis – suggests. Closed Nov–Feb. **£20**

★**Totters** 2 High St, LL55 1RN ☎01286 672963, ⓦtotters.co.uk. Caernarfon's only backpacker hostel is one of the best in north Wales: centrally located in an airy, modernized house, with friendly owners, clean dorms and inviting communal spaces. There's also a great attic en-suite double with sea views (£55) and a self-contained house available nightly for groups of up to six (from £20/ person). Rates include continental breakfast. Dorms **£18.50**, doubles **£44**

EATING

Black Boy Inn Northgate St, LL55 1RW ☎01286 673604, ⓦblack-boy-inn.com. The closest Caernarfon comes to an old-fashioned British pub, all low beams and swirly carpets, with a choice of two characterful bars serving north Wales craft beers and the best pub grub in town: expect dishes like lamb shank with mash or pan-fried plaice (£12–16). Daily 11am–11pm; kitchen noon–2pm & 7–9pm

Osteria 26 Hole in the Wall St, LL55 1RF ☎01286 674343. With a Tuscan chef-owner, this newish, sweet little restaurant has quickly established itself. The short menu offers genuine, fresh Italian cuisine – *bruschette*, excellent grazing platters (£10), *carpaccio* and authentic pasta dishes that make a virtue of their simplicity (£10). Tues–Thurs 6–9.30pm, Fri & Sat noon–2.30pm & 6–9.30pm.

Scoop 8 Palace St, LL55 1RR ☎01286 673604, ⓦscoopscaernarfon.com. Artisan ice cream (£1.95 a cone) made on site, with interesting flavours alongside plain vanilla or chocolate – try the likes of honey and quinoa, sea buckthorn, or apple and mango frozen yoghurt. The owner's Dutch mother is behind the stove, preparing excellent savoury and sweet crêpes. Tues–Sun 10.30am–4pm; Easter and school hols daily.

DRINKING

Anglesey Arms The Promenade, LL55 1SG ☎01286 672158. While the pub is certainly nothing to quicken the pulse and the beers are largely mass-produced brews, the waterside location makes this an unbeatable spot for a beer on sunny afternoons, with a view over the sea wall to the Menai Strait and Anglesey. Daily 11am–11pm.

ENTERTAINMENT

Galeri Caernarfon Victoria Dock, LL55 1SQ ☎01286 685222, ⓦgalericaernarfon.com. Modern arts and entertainment complex that puts on a wide range of plays, shows mainstream and arty films (mainly on Wed evenings) and includes gallery space and a café/bar (Mon–Sat 8am–9pm, Sun 10am–5pm). Usually daily for cinema, events once or twice/week.

Beddgelert and around

At the confluence of the Glaslyn and Colwyn rivers on the south flank of Snowdon, **BEDDGELERT** is the picture-postcard village of central Snowdonia. Though tiny, it ticks all the boxes for charm: a few dozen grey houses, their window boxes bursting with flowers, a pretty bridge over a burbling river, a number of charming cafés… All this, of course, brings in the crowds; such is the number of tourists on sunny summer days that parking can be tricky – consider making a day of it by visiting from Caernarfon or Porthmadog on the Welsh Highland Railway. Ultimately, however, even the occasional coach tour can't spoil this pleasant spot, ideal for lazy lunches, ice creams and strolls – happy holidays in a nutshell. And with the **Watkin Path** to Snowdon just up the road (see box, p.354), it's a good base for walkers, too.

6

Gelert's Grave

The time-honoured walk in Beddgelert is the 400yd stroll south along the right bank of the Glaslyn to the spot that gives the village its name, **Gelert's Grave** (*bedd* means "burial place"). The story goes this railed-off enclosure marks the final resting place of Prince Llywelyn ap Iorwerth's faithful dog, Gelert. The hound was left in charge of the prince's infant son while he went hunting; on his return, the child was gone and the dog's muzzle was soaked in blood. The impetuous Llywelyn slew Gelert, only to find the child safely asleep beneath its cot and a dead wolf beside him. Llywelyn hurried to his dog, which licked his hand as it died. Nice but baloney: the story is an eighteenth-century invention by a local publican designed to lure in the punters. And it certainly has – the story is more interesting than the site itself. The real source of the name is probably the grave of Celert, a sixth-century British saint who supposedly lived hereabouts.

Sygun Copper Mine

One mile northeast on the A498, LL55 4NE • Self-guided audio tours (45min) daily: summer 9.30am–5pm; rest of year 10am–4pm; closed mid-Nov to Dec except Christmas; last admission 1hr before closing • £8.95 • ☎ 01766 890595, ⓦ syguncoppermine.co.uk

Given its verdant terraces, it's hard to imagine this hillside north of central Beddgelert was mined for ore: first by the Romans, then by nineteenth-century prospectors. The **Sygun Copper Mine** showcases what was once the valley's main source of income on a family-oriented self-guided **tour** through the multiple levels of restored tunnels and galleries (cool at 9°C). To be honest, it's more interesting than exciting; costumed mannequins and a disembodied voice of a miner describing his

---

WALKS FROM BEDDGELERT

The OS 1:25,000 Explorer map OL17 (Snowdon – Conwy Valley) and 1:50,000 Landranger map 115 (Snowdon/Yr Wyddfa) are recommended.

Two good hikes up Snowdon start near **Beddgelert**; there are also a couple of good walks closer to town.

Aberglaslyn Gorge (3 miles return; 2hr; 100ft ascent). This fairly easy walk follows the Glaslyn as it tumbles and cascades through the madly picturesque Aberglaslyn Gorge. Cross a footbridge over the Glaslyn River in the village and follow the left bank downstream until you meet the Welsh Highland Railway. Continue between the railway and the river on the Fisherman's Track as the train line ducks through two tunnels. The path meets the road at Pont Aberglaslyn – the tidal limit before The Cob was built at Porthmadog – from where you can retrace your steps.

Moel Hebog ridge (8-mile loop; 5hr; 2800ft ascent). West of Beddgelert, the lumpish Moel Hebog (Bald Hill of the Hawk; 2569ft) is the highest point on a fine panoramic ridge walk that also takes in the lesser peaks of Moel Lefn and Moel yr Ogof (Hill of the Cave). The final forest section can be a bit disorientating, even in good weather, so be sure you have a compass. Start half a mile northwest of the centre of Beddgelert on the A4085, where Pont Alyn crosses the river to Cwm Cloch Isaf Farm. Follow the signs to a green lane, which soon leads up onto the broad northeast ridge, all the time keeping left of the Y Diffwys cliffs. The summit cairn is joined by two walls, the one to the northwest leading down a steep grassy slope to Bwlch Meillionen, from where you can ascend over rocky ground to Moel yr Ogof. From the top of Moel yr Ogof, it's a clear route north to Moel Lefn, then down to a cairn from where you can plan your descent. The easiest line is to Bwlch Cwm-trwsgl, near the highest point of the Beddgelert Forest, then through the forest to the A4085 and back to Beddgelert.

WELSH HIGHLAND RAILWAY TRIPS FROM BEDDGELERT

Beddgelert is linked to both Caernarfon and Porthmadog by the **Welsh Highland Railway**; we've detailed this in full in our Porthmadog account (see p.371). The route opens up several rewarding day-trips. Note that all but Rhyd Ddu and Waunfawr are request stops.

Lon Gwyfrai cycle and walking track From Beddgelert railway station, walk to Rhyd Ddu (4.5 miles) then catch the train back (30min; £7.50) or rent a bike in Beddgelert (see below) and cycle from the station to Waunfaur (9 miles), returning by train (1hr; £13.20, bikes £3). Views are splendid en route. Trains pass at Rhyd Ddu, so there is almost always a train waiting on the other side of the platform for the return trip.

Train through the tunnels of the Aberglaslyn Gorge to Pont Croesor Pont Croesor, where there is (usually) osprey viewing from late-spring to early summer (30min; £15.40 return).

Train to Nantmor From Nantmor (10min; £4.50) you can walk back to Beddgelert along the Fisherman's Path (1hr).

6

---

working life don't make for too many thrills. Afterwards, you're free to potter around the ore-crushing and separation equipment or to have a go at gold panning or metal detecting (both £2.50).

Nantlle Valley

Eight miles northwest on the A4085 then the B418, LL54 6BP

Having squeezed through a pass west of Rhyd Ddu you descend into the pastoral **Nantlle Valley**, whose former slate hamlets have been overlooked by tourism; after Beddgelert, the peace here comes as something of a surprise. There's good hiking along the nine-mile Nantlle Ridge – a semi-improvised route takes in a fist of peaks south of the B4418, starting at Y Garn, half a mile southwest of Rhyd Ddu.

For a wonderfully scenic wild swim, head to **Llyn Nantlle**. Take the footpath to the lake shore half a mile east of Nantlle village, slip in from the grass bank and swim to the centre. There, framed by the domed back of Myddd Mawr and the Nantlle Ridge crags, is Snowdon – a view memorably captured from the lake's west end by eighteenth-century landscape artist Richard Wilson.

ARRIVAL AND DEPARTURE   BEDDGELERT

By bus Beddgelert is on two bus routes: the #S4 Snowdon Sherpa from Caernarfon and the #S97 between Pen-y-Pass and Porthmadog. Services stop on the main street.

Destinations Caernarfon (Mon–Sat 7 daily; 30min); Pen-y-Pass (2 daily; 20min); Porthmadog (Mon–Sat 8 daily, Sun 3; 30–50min).

INFORMATION AND ACTIVITIES

Tourist information There's a national park visitor centre on the A498 in the village centre (Easter–Oct daily 9.30am–5pm; ☎01766 890615, ⓦ beddgelerttourism .com).

Mountain biking Beddgelert Forest, a mile out on the Caernarfon road and a mile uphill from the *Beddgelert*

Caravan & Campsite (see p.364), has good family-oriented, off-road riding; the trails, which include a 6-mile signposted loop, offer a good half-day of pootling around. Beddgelert Bikes (☎01766 890434, ⓦ beddgelertbikes.co.uk), beside the Welsh Highland Railway train station in the village, rents bikes (£15 for 2hr, £28 for 8hr, less for kids' bikes).

ACCOMMODATION

HOTEL AND GUESTHOUSES

Colwyn Stryd Smith, opposite the bridge, LL55 4UY ☎01766 890276, ⓦ beddgelertguesthouse.co.uk. Central, 300-year-old cottage guesthouse with comfortable (if somewhat cosy) renovated rooms, a beamed lounge and an open fire. Two-night minimum stay at weekends. **£75**

Plas Tan y Graig Stryd Smith, opposite the bridge, LL55 4UY ☎01766 890310, ⓦ plas-tanygraig.co.uk. Central and well-managed B&B that's been refurbished into a homely stylish stay; the twin rooms will appeal to walking friends. Mod-cons in the seven rooms include a small fridge, flatscreen TVs and, in some rooms, CD/DVD players. There's also an honesty bar, a drying room and

6

packed lunches (on request) plus free flask refills. Minimum two nights. **£95**

Sygun Fawr 0.7 mile northeast off the A498, LL55 4NE ☎ 01766 890258, ⊕ sygunfawr.co.uk. The smartest of the local hotels, offering comfy country-styled rooms in a seventeenth-century country house with beams and stone walls. The big draws here are the peace and quiet (no TVs in rooms) and views across to Snowdon from some rooms. Two- and three-night dinner deals in the restaurant are worth investigating. Closed Dec–Feb. **£89**

HOSTEL AND CAMPSITES

Beddgelert Caravan & Campsite A498, 1 mile northwest, LL55 4UU ☎ 01766 890288, ⊕ campinginthe forest.co.uk. Excellent, family-friendly forest campsite with a kids' play area, laundry service, decent on-site shop and a host of other facilities – not least its own (request) stop on the Welsh Highland Line. **£15**

★**Cae Du Camping** A498, 0.5 mile north, LL55 4NE ☎ 01766 890345, ⊕ caeducampsite.co.uk. Spacious and peaceful site that is immaculately maintained without affecting the natural beauty of the area; there are a few lovely stream-side pitches. Good facilities, too: hot showers, some power hook-ups and a small shop. Closed Oct–Feb. **£21**

Llyn Gwynant Campsite A498, 5 miles northeast, LL55 4NW ☎ 01766 890853, ⊕ gwynant.com. A lakeside site, in a gorgeous valley beneath Snowdon, which can host more than three hundred tents at peak times and yet manages to retain its natural appeal. You can access the Watkin Path directly from here, and they rent out kayaks and canoes (June–Sept). Hot showers are free, radios are banned, mobile phones don't work and bookings are not required. Closed Nov to mid-March. Per person **£10**

Red Dragon A498, 2 miles north, LL55 4NH ☎ 01766 890351, ⊕ reddragonholidays.co.uk. These snug camping pods are a good option for a budget stay without a tent. Sleeping two, each comes with feather duvets and pillows (if booked – our quoted price includes this) and access to a shared bathroom block and kitchenette. The caveat: they're beside the road on concrete not grass. **£52.50**

YHA Bryn Gwynant A498, 4 miles northeast, LL55 4NP ☎ 0345 371 9108, ⊕ yha.org.uk/hostel/snowdon-bryn -gwynant. New management had plans to renovate this Victorian mansion in Nantgwynant on our last visit. Even if they don't come to pass it's hugely spacious, cheap and well situated for the Watkin Path. Offers four- to ten-bed dorms and private rooms – those in the old stables are cosiest – plus meals. No wi-fi. Check in from 5pm. Closed Nov–Feb. Dorms **£19.99**, doubles **£59.99**

EATING

Glaslyn Ices/Café Glyndŵr A498, village centre, LL55 4YB ☎ 01766 890339, ⊕ glaslynices.co.uk. One of Wales' finest ice-cream makers produces three dozen flavours plus fruit sorbets on site to take away; the banoffee flavour and mango sorbet have won recent awards. A café behind offers family-friendly food: pizzas and specials such as home-made chilli con carne (£10). Bring your own alcohol. March–Oct: school and bank hols daily 9.30am–8.30pm, otherwise Mon–Fri &

Sun 10am–5pm, Sat 9.30am–8pm.

★**Hebog** Caernarfon Rd, LL55 4UY ☎ 01766 890400, ⊕ hebog-beddgelert.co.uk. This rustic-chic bistro ticks all the boxes. Alongside jacket potatoes and the now requisite gourmet burgers are more ambitious dishes, including lamb with local samphire (£19) or traditional game pie. There are a few tables beside the river – great on warm days. Daily noon–10pm.

Blaenau Ffestiniog and around

The Snowdonia region's most southerly major settlement, **BLAENAU FFESTINIOG** is an anomaly. Despite recent shifts towards tourism, it's gritty, scruffy and genuine, spreading not beneath green slopes but below 1000ft mountains strewn with 150 years' worth of shattered slate. In its heyday thousands of tons of slate were hewn from mines beneath the town and exported worldwide via the Ffestiniog Railway to ships at Porthmadog; today just one surface mine ticks over and the population has dropped to less than half its 1910 peak of twelve thousand. Only that shattered slate and one surface slate quarry remain; the reason why Blaenau was excluded from the Snowdonia National Park boundaries, despite being at at its geographical centre. This fact still rankles with the locals; in 2010 the park authorities voted in principle to reconsider. The trick is to see the slate not as an eyesore but as a monument to the effort of the town's miners. Not convinced? Look again and now consider that every piece of that shattered mountain was dug out by hand.

For years the local economy leaned on a so-so **slate mine tour** and the heritage **Ffestiniog Railway** to attract visitors. No longer. Blaenau Ffestiniog today is quietly transforming itself into the adrenaline capital of Wales. The mine tour has been updated and a world-first **zip wire**, a couple of crazy subterranean adventures and superb **mountain biking** mean that younger visitors are now replacing the coach-tour brigade. Who'd have imagined that slate could be so much fun?

Slate Caverns

A470, 1 mile north of Blaenau Ffestiniog, LL41 3NB • Daily 9.30am–5.30pm, last tour 4.30pm; tours 1hr 15mins, reservations recommended • Each tour £20, combined ticket £30 • ☎ 01766 830306, ⓦ llechwedd-slate-caverns.co.uk

It's hard to understand what slate means to Blaenau Ffestiniog without some sort of a visit to the **Slate Caverns**. There's no charge to watch slate being split, shaped and engraved beyond the gift shop. To visit some of the 25 miles of tunnels and sixteen working levels, however, you'll need to join the **Llechwedd Deep Mine Tour** into the deepest parts of the mine. After donning waterproofs and headgear, you judder down on the steepest cable

6

THE WELSH SLATE INDUSTRY

Slate is as much a symbol of north Wales as coal is of the fabled valleys in the south: it too peaked around the beginning of the twentieth century and shaped society throughout the period of British mass industrialization, drawing thousands from the impoverished hills to the relative wealth of the new towns that sprang up around the quarries.

Slate derives its name from the Old French word *esclater*, meaning "to split" – a perfect description of its most highly valued quality. Six hundred million years ago, what is now north Wales lay under the sea, gradually accumulating a 1000ft-thick layer of fine-grained mud that metamorphosed into the purplish Cambrian slates of the Penrhyn and Dinorwig quarries and the blue-grey Ordovician slates of Ffestiniog.

The Romans used the slate as a cheap and durable **roofing material** for the houses of Segontium in Caernarfon, while Edward I used it extensively in his Iron Ring of castles around Snowdonia. Demand really took off with urbanization during the Industrial Revolution, and throughout the nineteenth and early twentieth centuries millions of tons of slate were shipped around the globe. Hamburg was re-roofed with Welsh slate after its fire of 1842 and it is the same material that gives that rainy-day sheen to interminable rows of English mill-town houses.

By 1898, Welsh quarries – run by the English, like the coal and steel industries of the south – were producing half a million tons of dressed slate a year (and ten times as much slate waste), almost all of it from Snowdonia. At Penrhyn and Dinorwig, mountains were hacked away in terraces, with teams of **workers** negotiating with the foreman for the choicest piece of rock and the selling price for what they produced. They often slept through the week in damp dormitories on the mountain, and tuberculosis was common, exacerbated by slate dust. At Blaenau Ffestiniog, the seams required underground mining, with miners having to buy their own candles. Few workers were allowed to join the Quarrymen's Union, and in 1900, the workers in Lord Penrhyn's quarry at Bethesda went on **strike**. For three years they stayed out – one of Britain's longest-ever industrial disputes – but failed to win any concessions. Those who got their jobs back were forced to work for even less money as a recession took hold, and although the two world wars heralded mini-booms as bombed houses were replaced, the industry never recovered its nineteenth-century prosperity, and most quarries and mines closed in the 1950s.

Welsh slate was firmly established as the finest in the world at the 1862 London Exhibition, where one skilled craftsman produced a sheet 10ft long, 1ft wide and a sixteenth of an inch thick – so thin it could be flexed. Slate is now produced worldwide, and although none beats the quality of north Wales' product, Chinese slate is imported while Welsh slate lies in the ground. The remaining quarries produce relatively small quantities, much of it used for floor tiling, road aggregate or a bizarre array of ashtrays, coasters and wine racks.

More memorable are the roadside fences made from lines of broken, wafer-thin slabs, and the beautifully carved slate fire surrounds and mantelpieces occasionally found in pubs and houses. It's worth noting, too, that Westminster Abbey's memorial to Dylan Thomas is made entirely of **Penrhyn slate**.

railway in Britain and follow a guide to learn about the working and social lives of miners. Audiovisuals and a couple of actors enliven the trip. Just as impressive are the caverns themselves, which culminate in a Tolkein-esque cave with a softly lit pool. The site was the setting for the first Welsh-language film, *Y Chwarelwr* (*The Quarrymen*), in 1935. Perhaps the real stars are the guides, all of whom have a family connection to the mine and usually weave personal memories into their patter. The natural partner to the underground trip is the **Quarry Explorer**, an off-road trip in a 4WD army truck that grinds uphill among the shattered slate tailings to see Llechwedd's man-made mountains – you learn how the quarry was created and pass the last mine operation.

ZipWorld Caverns and ZipWorld Bounce Below

Daily 9.30am–5.30pm; 3–5 tours, up to 3hr (Caverns) and 1hr (Bounce Below); reservations required • ZipWorld Caverns £60, Bounce Below £25 • ☎ 01248 601444, ⓦ zipworld.co.uk

In the mine but operated by a different company, the two ZipWorld adventures re-interpret the vast caverns as huge playgrounds. **ZipWorld Caverns** is the most intrepid of the pair; an Indiana Jones-style adventure that combines the thrill of zip lines (including the steepest in the UK) with rope bridges. A guide is always on hand to coach the nervous. **ZipWorld Bounce Below** is more about fun, letting you explore caverns via a series of slides and huge net trampolines suspended high up in the void. Kids love it.

Antur Stiniog Bike Park

A470, 1 mile north of Blaenau Ffestiniog, LL41 3NB • Thurs–Sun 9am–5.30pm; daily during school hols • Mon–Fri £29; Sat & Sun £32.50; daily £20 half-day • ☎ 01766 238007, ⓦ anturstiniog.com

Launched in 2012, **Antur Stiniog Bike Park**, the newest mountain-bike centre in Wales, is almost as much of a draw as the slate mine next door. An ambitious downhill and free-ride park, it has seven trails – a family-friendly blue-grade trail for novices, plus three red, two black and a double-black run – and its rock sections and big jumps are sufficiently challenging to host international biking championships. All trails offer good views; find time to look up while ripping downhill before catching an uplift (transport that carries you and the bike back up to the trail heads). It's a justifiably popular spot – while walk-up visitors are accommodated, it's worth booking ahead to guarantee a slot. Bike rental is available, and there's a small café.

ZipWorld Titan

A470, 1 mile north of Blaenau Ffestiniog, LL41 3NB • Easter–Sept Mon–Fri 10am–4pm, Sat, Sun & school hols 9am–5pm; Oct to early Nov Mon–Fri 11am–3pm, Sat, Sun & school hols 10am–3pm; reservations required • ☎ 01248 601444, ⓦ zipworld.co.uk

One of the million-pound projects that are transforming Blaenau Ffestinog into north Wales' adrenaline capital, **ZipWorld Titan** is not just the longest zip-line course in the world (thanks to its three runs), but also the only one in Europe that allows you to share the experience. The course, set in an old slate quarry, sees you fly downhill alongside family or friends on three tracks – 890m, 630m and 450m – at speeds of up to around 70mph. Enjoy the panorama of Cadair Idris and Snowdon from the top, because everything afterwards will be a blur. Reservations are essential, and there are restrictions on weight, height and age (children under 18 must be accompanied by an adult); note, too, that the weather can affect your ride and that ZipWorld offers rescheduling, not refunds.

Dolwyddelan Castle

A470, 6 miles north of Blaenau Ffestiniog, LL25 0JD • April–Sept Mon–Sat 10am–5pm, Sun 11.30am–4pm; Oct–March Mon–Sat 10am–4pm, Sun 11.30am–4pm • £4; CADW • ☎ 01690 750366, ⓦ cadw.gov.wales/daysout/dolwyddelan-castle

Dolwyddelan Castle commands the head of the Lledr Valley, over the Crimea Pass from Blaenau Ffestiniog. It appears lonely today, but was a strategic site on the

6

A WALK DOWN THE VALE OF FFESTINIOG

The OS 1:25,000 Explorer map OL18 (Harlech, Porthmadog & Bala) is recommended.
This gentle walk follows a gorgeous section of the **Vale of Ffestiniog** (4–5 miles; 2–3hr; descent only) and completes the loop using the Ffestiniog Railway. Start at Tan-y-Bwlch station and take the train up to Tanygrisiau to start the walk. Turn right out of the station then take the second left – not the road beside the reservoir but the next one following the footpath signs. Cross the train line and pass a car park on your left before turning left down a track and skirting behind the powerhouse. The path then sticks closely to the railway tracks (occasionally crossing them), following the train line to its 360-degree loop, through sessile oak woods and past several cascades all the way to Tan-y-Bwlch, offering great views south to the Rhinogs and west to the Glaslyn estuary en route. Even when there are several paths, you can't go far wrong if you keep the train lines in sight. Recover at the historic *Oakeley Arms* inn near Tan-y-Bwlch station.

---

route from Aberconwy to the north and Ardudwy to the south. Llywelyn ap Iorwerth "the Great" (see p.432) may well have been born here, since his father was reputedly responsible for its construction at the end of the twelfth century. That was a mistake, as it turned out – Edward I seized the castle as a base from which to further subdue the Welsh, and by the end of the fifteenth century it lay abandoned. Its appearance today – a typical Victorian reconstruction featuring fanciful battlements and a new roof – is thanks to the Wynns of Gwydyr. The exhibition on native Welsh castles is eminently missable, but the panoramic view of Snowdonia from its battlements is fantastic.

Vale of Ffestiniog

Slate waste surrounds Blaenau Ffestiniog on three sides, but the fourth drops away into the bucolic **Vale of Ffestiniog**, best explored using the Ffestiniog Railway, or on a walk (see box above). Activity is focused on the railway's Tan-y-Bwlch station, five miles southwest of Blaenau Ffestiniog, where there is a café and woodland play area. Nearby you'll find Snowdonia National Park's study centre, **Plas Tan y Bwlch**, which runs numerous courses throughout the year (see p.50), and the *Oakeley Arms*.

ARRIVAL AND INFORMATION
BLAENAU FFESTINIOG

By train The central train station serves both the Ffestiniog Railway (see p.370) and mainline services.
Destinations Betws-y-Coed (6 daily; 30min); Llandudno (6 daily; 1hr 20min); Llandudno Junction (6 daily; 1hr).
By bus Buses stop outside the train station or along High St.
Destinations Barmouth (3 daily; 1hr 10min); Betws-y-Coed (Mon–Sat 8 daily; 25min); Harlech (Mon–Sat 3 daily;

40min); Llandudno (Mon–Sat 8 daily; 1hr 10min); Porthmadog (Mon–Sat hourly; 30min).
Tourist information The Antur Stiniog mountain bike information centre (Easter & June–Sept Mon–Sat 10am–5pm; Oct–Easter Wed–Sat 10am–4pm; ☏ 01766 832214), on Church St in the heart of the town centre, doubles as a tourist office.

ACCOMMODATION

GUESTHOUSES
★**Bryn Elltyd** Tanygrisiau, 1 mile southwest, LL41 3TW ☏ 01766 831356, ⊚ accommodation-snowdonia .com. The former slate mine manager's house beside the Ffestiniog Railway is now Wales' only carbon-neutral B&B thanks to the efforts of its passionate (and helpful) environmentalist owner – if you want to know about eco living this is the place. Accommodation is in homely rooms or sweet cabins in the garden. **£90**
Isallt Guest House Church St, LL41 3HD ☏ 01766 832488, ⊚ isallt.com. Central B&B in a solid Victorian

house right by the train station – you'll see occasional steam trains chuff past – with six keenly priced rooms (three doubles, one family, a twin and a single), many of which have views of the mountains. **£65**

HOSTEL, BUNKHOUSE AND CAMPSITE
Bryn Tirion Farm A470, 6 miles north, LL25 0JD ☏ 01690 750366, ⊚ price768@btinternet.com. The only camping option nearby is at this hospitable farm run by the custodian of the Dolwyddelan Castle. It also has a tiny, basic self-catering bunkhouse (open all year), with

bedding supplied if required (£4). Closed Nov–Feb. Camping/person £6, bunkhouse £16
CellB Park Square, LL41 3AD ☎01766 832001, ⊚cellb .org. This hub of community life (see below) also maintains

a tiny hostel with a six-bed and three-bed dorm, both with duvets and nice pillows on solid custom-built bunks. The building is the old police station – a drying room and bike store occupy old cells. £22

EATING AND ENTERTAINMENT

CellB Park Square, LL41 3AD ☎01766 832001, ⊚cellb .org. A brilliant community arts centre in a former police station with gigs – the booker has a penchant for reggae – a tiny, hugely popular cinema screening recent Hollywood releases (Wed–Sun) and an informal café/bar that rustles up gutsy home cooking: pasta bakes, lamb burgers, shepherd's pie (£8) and the like. Bar Mon &

Tues 4–10pm, Wed–Sun 8am–11.45pm; café Wed–Sun noon–2.30pm & 6–9.30pm.
Côr Meibion y Brythoniaid Ysgol y Moelwyn school, A470, LL41 3DW ☎01766 830435, ⊚corybrythoniaid .com. The area's best male voice choir practises at this school on the A470 at the south end of town; visitors are welcome to listen. Usually Thurs 7.30pm.

6

Porthmadog and around

In a region crammed with wonderful views, **PORTHMADOG**, at the crook of the Cambrian coast and the Llŷn, has some of the finest – up the Vale of Ffestiniog and across the estuary of the Glaslyn River to the mountains of Snowdonia. Yet the town – formerly north Wales' busiest slate port and large by local standards – makes little of its position. Nor is it any great beauty in and of itself. See it instead as a place you go from, not to; as a gateway to surrounding sights.

Wales' heritage railways obsession reaches its apogee in Porthmadog. As well as the standard Cambrian Coast line, three tourist-oriented narrow-gauge railways operate from here. Best are the peerless **Ffestiniog Railway**, which originally carried slates from Blaenau Ffestiniog, and the **Welsh Highland Railway**, a stunning route that connects to Caernarfon via Beddgelert and the Aberglaslyn Pass. If you're going to do a north Wales steam journey, make it one of these. Better still, do both; they each leave from the same station. There's also the family-oriented **Welsh Highland Heritage Railway** at the opposite end of town.

If steam trains don't toot your whistle, there's plenty more: the Italianate folly of **Portmeirion**, **ospreys** at Glaslyn and walks beside the estuary to pretty **Borth y Gest**.

Brief history

Porthmadog owes its existence to Lincolnshire MP **William Alexander Madocks**. He named the town and Tremadog, a mile north, after himself and the Welsh Prince Madog, who some say sailed from the nearby Ynys Fadog (Madog's Island) to North America in 1170. In 1805, Madocks drained a thousand acres of estuarine mud flats to create grazing land, then built Tremadog town. Buoyed by its success, he sealed off a further 7000 acres off the Glaslyn estuary with a mile-long embankment known as **The Cob**, re routing the Glaslyn River so that it scoured out a deep watercourse close to the north bank – ideal for a slate wharf. The opening of the **Ffestiniog Railway** in 1836 saw the harbour prosper until the middle of the twentieth century; today just a few dozen yachts grace the water.

EASY WALKS AROUND PORTHMADOG

The Cob (2 miles return; 1hr; flat). If the weather is fine, and particularly towards sunset, you can't go far wrong wandering around the harbour then strolling along The Cob, with the occasional steam-hauled Ffestiniog Railway service adding atmosphere to views up the estuary towards Snowdon.

Borth-y-Gest (2 miles return; 1hr; flat). This easy walk beside the Glaslyn Estuary makes a particularly nice summer evening stroll to a meal on the bay – *Moorings Bistro* is our pick (see p.373). Follow Pen Cei south from Porthmadog below the cliffs of Moel-y-Gest.

6

Ffestiniog Railway

Harbour Station, Glaslyn Bridge, LL49 9NF • March–Oct 4–6 services daily; Nov–Feb services depending on maintenance, check website •
Sample fares: all-day Rover £24; return to Tan-y-Bwlch £15.50; single fares two-thirds of a return; one child under 16 travels free with an adult •
☎ 01766 516024, ⓦ festrail.co.uk

The 2ft-gauge **Ffestiniog Railway** twists and loops up 650ft from Porthmadog to the slate mining town of Blaenau Ffestiniog, thirteen miles away. The gutsy little engines chug up steep gradients through stunning scenery, from broad estuarine expanses to the deep greens of the Vale of Ffestiniog before it arrives into the slate-shattered slopes of the upper terminus.

When the line opened in 1836, it used gravity to carry slate from the mines to the port as well as horses to haul the empty carriages back up again. Steam was introduced in the late nineteenth century to cope with the 100,000 tons of slate that Blaenau Ffestiniog churned out annually. After the slate-roofing market collapsed in the 1920s, the line carried passengers until being finally abandoned in

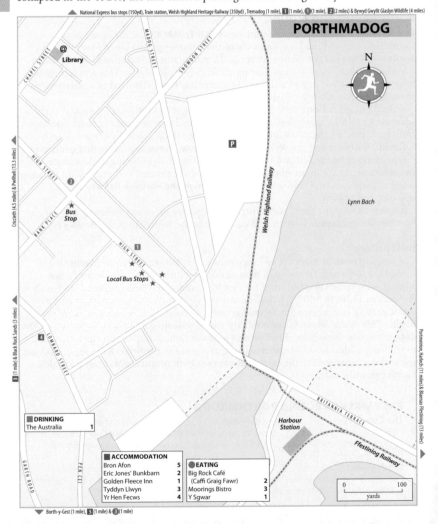

National Express bus stops (150yd), Train station, Welsh Highland Heritage Railway (350yd) , Tremadog (1 mile), **1** (1 mile), **●** (1 mile), **2** (2 miles) & Bywyd Gwyllt Glaslyn Wildlife (4 miles)

PORTHMADOG

N

Criccieth (4.5 miles) & Pwllheli (13.3 miles)

3 (1 mile) & Black Rock Sands (3 miles)

CHAPEL STREET

@ **Library**

MADOG STREET

SNOWDON STREET

HIGH STREET

2

BANK PLACE

★ **Bus Stop**

HIGH STREET

1

★ ★ ★
Local Bus Stops

LOMBARD STREET

P

Welsh Highland Railway

Lynn Bach

4

GARTH ROAD

PEN CEI

BRITANNIA TERRACE

Harbour Station

Portmeirion, Harlech (11 miles) & Blaenau Ffestiniog (13 miles)

Ffestiniog Railway

■ **DRINKING**	
The Australia	**1**

■ **ACCOMMODATION**	
Bron Afon	**5**
Eric Jones' Bunkbarn	**2**
Golden Fleece Inn	**1**
Tyddyn Llwyn	**3**
Yr Hen Fecws	**4**

● **EATING**	
Big Rock Café	
(Caffi Graig Fawr)	**2**
Moorings Bistro	**3**
Y Sgwar	**1**

0   100
yards

▼ Borth-y-Gest (1 mile), **5** (1 mile) & **3** (1 mile)

1946. Most of the tracks and sleepers had disappeared by the time a bunch of dedicated volunteers began to reconstruct the line, starting in 1954 and completing the entire route in 1982.

Leaving Porthmadog, trains cross The Cob then stop at Minffordd, an interchange point for the Cambrian Coast main line and the mile-long walk to Portmeirion. Short **nature trails** spur off from Tan-y-Bwlch (the fourth station), as does the longer Vale of Ffestiniog walk (see box, p.368), which passes Dduallt station by the spiral on its way to Tanygrisiau. The full round trip to Blaenau Ffestiniog takes almost three hours, but a Rover Ticket allows you to get on and off as frequently as the timetable allows. It costs £3 each way for **bikes** (and dogs), but you need to book first. Sit on the right of the carriage going up to get the best view of the scenery; for more legroom or to sit in the observation carriage you'll need to pay £7 each way for a **first-class** upgrade.

6

Welsh Highland Railway

Harbour Station, Glaslyn Bridge, LL49 9NF • March–Oct 2–4 trains daily; Nov–Feb services depending on maintenance, check website • Sample return fares: to Beddgelert £21.90; to Caernarfon £39.80; first-class tickets cost an additional £9–11 each way depending on distance travelled; one child under 16 travels free with an adult; single fares are two-thirds of a return • ☎ 01766 516000, ⓦ festrail.co.uk

The narrow-gauge **Welsh Highland Railway**, the longest heritage railway in the UK, runs the full 25 miles between Porthmadog and Caernarfon, through Beddgelert and along the southern flank of Snowdon, rising from sea level to 650ft. In a land packed with charming railways, this is also one of the most scenic lines. A gorgeous river estuary gives way to oak woods as you approach the **Aberglaslyn Gorge**, where the track hugs the tumbling river. Beyond Beddgelert the line breaks out into open terrain maintaining a 1:40 gradient for six miles – making it the steepest non-funicular track in Britain.

The 2011 opening of this line marked the culmination of fifteen years of volunteer struggle and more than £28 million expenditure, much of it from Millennium lottery and Welsh Assembly sources. It was also a major achievement for having overcome the hurdles put up by farmers with land en route and the ramblers who regularly walked it. The feats of engineering required to reopen the old line were staggering: more than twenty bridges were rebuilt; walking and cycling paths were rerouted; four tunnels down the Aberglaslyn Gorge near Beddgelert needed extensive safety work; and most of the route lies within a national park, with its rigorous planning restrictions.

The irony is that all this effort lasted longer than the original Welsh Highland Railway itself. The line from Porthmadog to Caernarfon ran for just fourteen years (1923–37). It was largely pulled up until two organizations began to run trips on short restored sections of track from Caernarfon and Porthmadog.

Welsh Highland Heritage Railway

Tremadog Rd, LL49 9DY • Late April to Oct 5 services daily • £8.95 ticket valid all day • ☎ 01766 513402, ⓦ www.whr.co.uk

Don't be confused by the name, which is very similar to the more epic journey that starts at the other end of town – the 24in-gauge **Welsh Highland Heritage Railway** is a shorter, cheaper and more child-oriented affair, run by steam enthusiasts. Mostly operating diesel trains – steam makes up roughly a quarter of the service – it operates along almost a mile of track with a stop at a museum in the loco sheds. Fans over 18 can ride the footplate (£15 extra) or have a go at driving a steam train on Saturday evening or full-day sessions (3hr £135; full day £399).

Tremadog

William Madocks' original village of **TREMADOG**, founded in 1805, lies a mile north of Porthmadog. Though really just the intersection of three streets, it is a barely altered example of early town planning, with a central square overlooked by an attractive (former) town hall.

Bywyd Gwyllt Glaslyn Wildlife

Pont Croesor, B4410, 4 miles northeast of Porthmadog, LL49 9SP • Late March to Aug; it is volunteer-run so times vary; call ahead • Free • ☎ 07834 575008, ⊛ glaslynwildlife.co.uk

Established in 2013 to protect the resident **osprey** population, **Bywyd Gwyllt Glaslyn Wildlife** is a small volunteer-run centre with displays on these fish-eating eagles, replica nests, archive footage of the birds and a live webcam on any nesting birds – far more intimate than the telescopes across the lake to see the distant nest. Depending on the time of year, you may see the adults tending the eggs, watch the eggs hatch or see the chicks learning to fly. Almost forgotten is the other wildlife that you can spot here, including otters and woodpeckers.

Borth-y-Gest

The small former boat-building village of **Borth-y-Gest** envelops a picturesque harbour a mile south of Porthmadog, with a semicircle of Victorian houses lining the beach. There's nothing to do as such, but it's a lovely spot to take in the estuary views from one of the waterfront cafés or to enjoy a relaxed B&B stay.

Black Rock Sands

Black Rock Sands, almost three miles southwest of Porthmadog at **Morfa Bychan**, is the best beach for miles: a two-mile swath of golden sand. You come as much for the sublime views down to Harlech and up to the peaks of Snowdonia – "the best view in Europe", painter Sir Kyffin Williams once said, with some justification. At low tide you can explore rock pools and caves.

ARRIVAL AND DEPARTURE   PORTHMADOG AND AROUND

By train The main station is in the northeast of town, near the Welsh Highland Heritage Railway Station; the following destinations exclude Ffestiniog and Welsh Highland services.

Destinations Aberdyfi (8 daily; 1hr 30min–1hr 40min); Barmouth (8 daily; 50min); Criccieth (8 daily; 7min); Harlech (8 daily; 20min); Machynlleth (8 daily; 1hr 55min); Pwllheli (8 daily; 25min).

By bus The Pwllheli-bound National Express buses from London, Manchester and Liverpool stop outside Tesco on

High St. Connecting services to Bangor leave from Caenarfon (see p.357). Note that Dolgellau buses go inland: take the train if you want to stick to the coast. Local buses depart from the High St alongside the park.

Destinations Beddgelert (8 daily; 25min); Blaenau Ffestiniog (Mon–Sat hourly; 30min); Borth-y-Gest (Mon–Sat 9 daily; 3min); Caernarfon (Mon–Sat 6 daily; 40min); Criccieth (Mon–Sat every 30min, Sun 7; 15min); Dolgellau (3–4 daily; 50min); Harlech (Mon–Sat 6 daily; 20min); Pwllheli (Mon–Sat every 30min, Sun 7; 40min).

ACCOMMODATION

HOTEL AND GUESTHOUSES

Bron Afon Borth-y-Gest, 1 mile south, LL49 9TU ☎ 01766 513918, ⊛ bronafon.co.uk. Occupying perhaps the finest location in this pretty village, on a corner of the bay, this traditional B&B has fresh, bright en-suite rooms; pay an extra £5 for one at the front with fabulous views across the estuary to the mountains. Closed Nov–Easter. **£62**

Golden Fleece Inn Market Square, Tremadog, 1 mile north, LL49 9RB ☎ 01766 512421, ⊛ goldenfleeceinn .com. This former coaching inn is slowly spreading through Tremadog, its range of mid-range accommodation now spanning three buildings. Choose from simply furnished rooms above the pub and a neighbouring house or larger, rather theatrical, "Executive King" rooms and King suites (£90) in the Royal Madoc annexe nearby. **£65**

★Yr Hen Fecws 16 Lombard St, LL49 9AP ☎ 01766

514625, ⊛ henfecws.com. Though compact, the en-suite rooms in this B&B are immaculate and comfortable, with fabrics in tasteful shades of dove grey; many of them have ruby-red and exposed stone walls. The owner is a former chef, so breakfasts are good. The best value in the town centre. **£80**

BUNKHOUSE AND CAMPSITES

Eric Jones' Bunkbarn Opposite Eric Jones' Café, near Tremadog, 2 miles north on the A498 to Beddgelert, LL49 9SN ☎ 01766 512199, ⊛ ericjones-tremadog .co.uk. Intended for rock climbers, this place provides very basic accommodation in a bunkbarn – bring sleeping bags – and campsite. The owner's café opposite rustles up breakfast, but it was up for sale at the time of going to press. Camping/person **£6**, dorms **£7.50**

Tyddyn Llwyn Black Rock Rd, Borth-y-Gest, 1 mile

south, LL49 9UR ☏ 01766 512205, ⓦ tyddynllwyn.com. Though intended more for motorhomes and caravans, this site retains a small field for tents. Facilities are clean and there's a "beer and brisket smokehouse" on site. It's a 15min walk along the road to Morfa Bychan, following Bank Place southwest off High St. Campervan serviced pitches cost £32. Closed Nov–Feb. £20

EATING

Big Rock Cafe (Caffi Graig Fawr) 71 High St, LL49 9EU ☏ 01766 512098. Eclectic, cheerful, nicely lived-in café with bare floorboards and sofas in a rear room. Great for coffee and tea, it's also a fine spot for a daily special such as salmon and coriander fishcakes or chorizo and egg – most mains cost around £7–8. Mon–Sat 8.30am–5pm.

Moorings Bistro 4 Ivy Terrace, Borth-y-Gest, 1 mile south, LL49 9TS ☏ 01766 513500, ⓦ moorings bistroborthygest.com. Great little café and bistro, not least for the estuary views from its terrace, which has been a local favourite for years – reservations are recommended. Expect light lunches (£6–11) the likes of falafel wraps or seafood chowder, plus dinners featuring local fish or perhaps a Welsh lamb tagine (mains £14–18). Opening hours occasionally change – call to confirm. April–Sept Mon, Tues & Thurs 11am–3pm & 6–11pm, Fri & Sat 9am–3pm & 6–9pm, Sun 9am–4pm; Oct–March Wed–Sun 11am–3pm plus some evenings (call ahead).

Y Sgwar The Square, Tremadog, 1 mile north, LL49 9RB ☏ 01766 515451, ⓦ ysgwar-restaurant.co.uk. A menu of quick lunches (on average £10) – BLT sandwiches, burgers, bowls of Menai mussels cooked in white wine – ramps up into well-prepared restaurant dishes in the evening, when local beef and lamb star (mains £18–23). Daily noon–2pm & 6–9pm.

DRINKING

The Australia 35 High St, LL49 9LR ☏ 01766 510931. What was once a shabby boozer has been gutted by Porthmadog's Purple Moose brewery and revived as a spacious, hugely welcoming pub. A wide range of its award-winning beers are on tap, from pale ales to interesting seasonal offerings such as elderflower ale. Daily noon–11pm.

Portmeirion and around

Minffordd, 3 miles east of Porthmadog, LL48 6ER • Daily 9.30am–7.30pm; guided tours Easter–Oct daily 10am–3.30pm (20min) • £12; guided tours free; free afternoon entry if you prebook Sun lunch at *Hotel Portmeirion* or lunch at *Castell Deudraeth* • ☏ 01766 770000, ⓦ portmeirion-village.com

If there's one must-see near Porthmadog, it's **PORTMEIRION**. Set on a rocky peninsula in Tremadog Bay, three miles east near Minffordd, the Italianate private village was the brainchild of eccentric architect **Clough Williams-Ellis** – his dream was to build an ideal settlement to enhance rather than blend in with its surroundings, using a "gay, light-opera sort of approach". The result is certainly theatrical: a stage set with a lucky dip of buildings arranged to distort perspectives and reveal tantalizing glimpses of the sea or the expansive sands behind. It all feels rather dream-like, and is why Portmeirion featured as "The Village" in the 1960s British cult TV series *The Prisoner*.

In the 1920s, Williams-Ellis began scouring Britain for a suitable island – he believed only an island could provide the seclusion for his project. Having found nothing he could afford, he was gratified to be offered instead a piece of wilderness four miles from his home, Plâs Brondanw, at Garreg (see p.374). A Victorian house already on the site was turned into a hotel, the income from which provided funds for Williams-Ellis's

---

THE PRISONER CONVENTION AND FESTIVAL NO. 6

For one weekend in April, Portmeirion hosts **The Prisoner convention** (ⓦ portmeiricon.com) when fans book the place out to re-enact scenes from the TV series as best they can – though, as much of the series was shot in the studio, the juxtaposition of Portmeirion's buildings doesn't match that of "The Village".

In a similar vein, September's **Festival No. 6** (ⓦ festivalnumber6.com), named after the number given to the hero of *The Prisoner*, uses the village's venues to good effect during an eclectic festival of left-field music, art and culture, usually pulling in major international names.

"Home for Fallen Buildings". Endangered buildings from all over Britain and abroad were carefully broken down, transported then rebuilt, every conceivable style being plundered: a Neoclassical colonnade from Bristol; Siamese figures on Ionic columns; a Jacobean town hall; a Buddha; and the Italianate touches, a campanile and a pantheon. Williams-Ellis designed his village around a Mediterranean piazza, piecing together a scaled-down nest of loggias, grand porticoes and tiny terracotta-roofed houses, and painting them in pastels: turquoise, ochre and buff yellows. Continually surprising, with hidden entrances and cherubs popping out of crevices, the ensemble is wildly eclectic, yet never quite inappropriate.

More than three thousand visitors a day come to ogle the place in summer, when it can be a delight; fewer appear in winter, when it's just plain bizarre. Much of your time will be spent outside wandering around the buildings or popping into the shops selling *Prisoner* memorabilia, repro vintage homewares and flowery Portmeirion pottery. Guests and visitors can eat at the expensive hotel-restaurant (see below), but most will be content with one of several cafés. Better still, bring a picnic and find a spot on the paths that wind through the exotic forest that backs Portmeirion.

Hotel Portmeirion

Sometimes affectionately named the grandest folly of all, certainly a symbol of Britain's enduring fascination with eccentrics, Portmeirion at least supports Williams-Ellis's guiding principle that natural beauty and profitable development needn't be mutually exclusive. Architectural idealism aside, it was always intended to be self-sustaining and much of the finance comes from lovely waterside **Hotel Portmeirion**, which also utilizes many of the cottages in the village as guest accommodation (see below). Among the reasons to book to stay here is that hotel guests get to see Portmeirion at its best: when the village is closed to the public it becomes wonderfully peaceful, even ghostly.

Plâs Brondanw

Four miles north of Portmeirion, just north of Garreg, LL48 6SW • Easter–Sept daily 10am–5pm • £5.50 • ☎ 01766 772772, ⓦ brondanw.org

Most of the money Clough Williams-Ellis earned went directly to the gardens of his ancestral home **Plâs Brondanw**. "A cheque of ten pounds would come in and I would order yew hedging to that extent, a cheque for twenty and I would pave a further piece of terrace", he said to explain the whimsical topiary around his solid Welsh stone house. The house is closed to the public, leaving just the gardens – immaculate topiary set before a panorama of Snowdonia, juxtaposing civilization with wild countryside, with a lovely café to boot – plus some of the grounds (follow the "To the Tower" sign). A ten-minute woodland walk brings you to the outlook tower, with expansive views of Porthmadog and the Moelwyns.

ARRIVAL AND DEPARTURE   PORTMEIRION

Without your own transport, from Porthmadog you can **walk** to Portmeirion in an hour. Otherwise, catch the #1B bus or the mainline or Ffestiniog trains to **Minffordd**, from where it's a signposted 25min walk.

ACCOMMODATION

Hotel guests receive **free entry** to the Portmeirion village for the duration of their stay. For simple **camping**, try the *Brondanw Arms*, in Garreg (see opposite).

Castell Deudraeth 10min walk north, LL48 6ER ☎ 01766 772400, ⓦ portmeirion-village.com. While the standard modern rooms are smart rather than glamorous, all are spacious, with mod-cons, and provide a comfortable stay. You're here most of all for the joy of staying in a remodelled Victorian "castle" where you're free to roam and use the heated outdoor pool. £174

★ **Hotel Portmeirion** Village centre, LL48 6ER ☎ 01766 770000, ⓦ portmeirion-village.com. The spirit of Clough Williams-Ellis lives on in styling that's equal parts grand and eccentric; the main waterside hotel and cottages throughout Portmeirion village abound in quirky architectural and decorative elements. Though lacking the wow factor of public areas, rooms are excellent, and all

different, many with beautiful views. Former guests include H.G. Wells, George Bernard Shaw and Noël Coward. Breakfast £20. **£204**

EATING AND DRINKING

Brondanw Arms Garreg, 3.5 miles north, LL48 6AQ ☎ 01766 770555, ⓦ robinsonsbrewery.com. If you can drag yourself from the beer garden, which is cupped in the hills, the main reason to come is for the fantastic, historic front bar – slate-floored, with old wood panelling around the woodburner stove. Real ales on tap, plus decent bar meals (£6–14). They'll even let you camp overnight for £5/ person. Daily noon–11pm; kitchen noon–2.30pm & 6–9pm.

Castell Deudraeth 10min walk north, LL48 6ER ☎ 01766 770400, ⓦ portmeirion-village.com. Light, beautiful conservatory brasserie that fuses classical elegance with modern style. Start with cocktails in the panelled bar then choose from a Modern British menu:

evening dishes may include the likes of roast guinea fowl with a Welsh whiskey cream but there's space, too, for lighter lunches and favourites such as fish and chips (mostly £13 at lunch, £13–20 for dinner). Daily noon–2.30pm & 6–9.30pm.

Portmeirion Restaurant Village centre, LL48 6ER ☎ 01766 770480. Delightful, slightly formal restaurant in the *Hotel Portmeirion* with views across the Traeth Bach sands and an inventive modern menu; sea trout with tenderstem broccoli, black garlic, laverbread and browned shrimp butter sauce, are typical (mains average £19). Alternatively just come for afternoon tea on the terrace. Reservations required for dinner – and dress up. Daily noon–3pm & 6.30–9.30pm.

The Llŷn

There's an end-of-the-world magic to the **Llŷn**; few places in Wales feel as remote as its tip. A spur of conical mountains and patchworked green fields jutting from Snowdonia's mountainous heart, it takes its name (roughly pronounced "tleen") from an Irish word for "peninsula", an apt description for this most westerly part of north Wales. This is a staunchly Welsh region – you'll hear only Welsh spoken in most local shops and "Stryd Fawr" is used instead of High Street. While escapism and soul-stirring scenery may draw you here, it is mysticism that will make you linger; the Llŷn is a place of mythological giants, poets and pilgrims. In the Middle Ages the Vatican decreed that three Llŷn pilgrimages – specifically, to Ynys Enlli – equalled one to Rome.

Until the fifth century the Llŷn had a significant Irish population. Their ancestors may have been responsible for the numerous hillforts and cromlechs hereabouts, particularly the hut circles of the **Tre'r Ceiri** hillfort above the Welsh Language Centre at **Nant Gwrtheyrn**. Today it's the beaches that lure most people to the region, specifically to the south-coast resorts of **Criccieth**, **Pwllheli** and **Abersoch**. Yet tiny undeveloped **Aberdaron**, from where pilgrims once sailed for the burial grounds of **Ynys Enlli** (Bardsey Island), probably has most charm. More remote still are the coves that scallop the north coast, notably gorgeous **Porth Oer** and **Porthdinllaen**, with its lonely pub.

With a mazey network of back roads channelled by hedgerows, the Llŷn provides good **cycling** country. However, to truly come in contact with the ancient soul of this peninsula, it's best to discover it on foot. Keen walkers have cottoned on to the **Llŷn Coastal Path**, which, resembling a quieter Pembrokeshire coast path, can be completed in a week; the full 110-mile route tracks along two coasts from Caernarfon to Porthmadog.

ARRIVAL AND DEPARTURE   THE LLŶN

By train and bus Trains and National Express buses serve Criccieth and Pwllheli, leaving an extensive network of infrequent local buses to cover the rest of the peninsula. Easing logistics between April and October is the Llŷn

Coastal Bus, which shuttles along the coastline between Abersoch and Nefyn via Aberdaron and Porth Neigwl (Thurs–Sun 4 daily; ⓦ bwsarfordirllyn.co.uk). It operates on a hail-and-ride basis.

6

Criccieth and around

Though just five miles away, **CRICCIETH** could not be more different from Porthmadog. Instead of a former working town, it is a gentle beach resort, cheerful and uncomplicated, with all the requisite components: a medieval **castle** magnificently sited on a hillock; an arc of golden **sand** and shingle; ice-cream shops; and a smattering of smart guesthouses in tidy streets. The resort began its days with the Victorian fashion for sea-bathing – English families descended on Criccieth's sweeping sand-and-shingle beach and built long terraces of guesthouses (many of which are now retirement homes). These days, the bucket-and-spade brigade go further west, leaving a quietly amiable destination that makes a pleasant stop or convenient touring base. The best view in town is from the hill behind **Marine Terrace**, from where you see the castle set against the backdrop of the Cambrian coast and Rhinog mountains.

Things are particularly lively during the third week of June, when the annual **Criccieth Festival** (ⓦcricciethfestival.co.uk) features jazz and classical music, lectures and art shows in venues all over town.

Criccieth Castle

Castle St, LL52 0DP • April–Oct daily 10am–5pm; Nov–March Mon–Sat 9.30am–4pm, Sun 11am–4pm • April–Oct daily & Nov–March Fri–Sun £5; Nov–March Mon–Thurs free; CADW • ☎ 01766 522227, ⓦ cadw.gov.wales/daysout/criccieth-castle

Criccieth's only real sight is the battle-worn **Criccieth Castle**, dominating the coastline with what remains of its twin, D-shape towered gatehouse – an irresistble subject for painter J.M.W. Turner, who captured it in several works. The castle was started by Llywelyn ap Iorwerth in 1230, but strengthened and finished by Edward I, who too kit in 1283. During his 1404 rebellion, Owain Glyndŵr grabbed the castle back, only to raze it, leaving little besides broken walls and the gatehouse. Nowadays, it's a great spot to sit and look over Cardigan Bay to Harlech or, in the late afternoon, to gaze down over the ripples of the Llŷn coast. There's also a workaday exhibition on Welsh castles and a wonderful animated cartoon in the ticket office based on the twelfth-century Cambrian travels of Giraldus Cambrensis (see box below).

Lloyd George Museum

Llanystumdwy, 1.5 miles west of Criccieth, LL52 0SH • Easter–May Mon–Fri 10.30am–5pm; June Mon–Sat 10.30am–5pm; July–Sept daily 10.30am–5pm; Oct Mon–Fri 11am–4pm; last admission 1hr before closing • £5 • ☎ 01766 522071

Though born in Manchester, the Welsh nationalist, social reformer and British prime minister David Lloyd George (1864–1945) lived in his mother's home village until he was 16. He grew up in Highgate House, the home of his uncle, the village cobbler, which is now part of the **Lloyd George Museum**. Today the rustic two-up, two-down

---

GIRALDUS CAMBRENSIS AND HIS JOURNEY THROUGH WALES

Through his books *The Journey Through Wales* and *The Description of Wales*, Norman–Welsh **Giraldus Cambrensis** (Gerald of Wales, or Gerallt Cymro) has left us with a vivid picture of life in Wales in the twelfth century. Gerald worked his way up the ecclesiastical hierarchy, but failed to achieve his lifelong goal, the bishopric of St Davids, mainly because of his reformist ideals.

Gerald's influence in Wales made him the first choice when Baldwin, the Archbishop of Canterbury, needed someone to accompany him on his 51-day tour around Wales in 1188, preaching the Cross and recruiting for a third Crusade, designed to dislodge the Muslim leader Saladin from Jerusalem. During the tour, Gerald amassed much of the material for his books, where he sensitively portrayed the landscape and its people, judging that "Welsh generosity and hospitality are the greatest of all virtues", but warning "if they come to a house where there is any sign of affluence and they are in a position to take what they want, there is no limit to their demands". But on the whole, he shows sympathy for the Welsh: "if only Wales could find the place it deserves in the heart of its rulers, or at least if those put in charge locally would stop behaving so vindictively and submitting the Welsh to such shameful ill-treatment".

house is laid out much as it would have been in his day, with an informative thirty-minute film on the life of a witty and powerful orator, and displays including his pipes and a personal copy of the Peace Treaty of Versailles, plus an extensive collection of gifts and awards. It's surprisingly moving, not for the exhibits in particular, but more for the idea that so inspiring a politician began life in surroundings so humble. The great man is buried here under a memorial beside the River Dwyfor – a boulder and two simple plaques designed by Portmeirion's creator Clough Williams-Ellis.

Penarth Fawr

Off the A497, 5.5 miles west of Criccieth, LL53 6PR • April–Oct daily 10am–5pm • Free • CADW • ⓦ cadw.gov.wales/daysout/penarthfawrmedievalhouse

Signposted off the A497 down a tiny lane, **Penarth Fawr** is a compact fifteenth-century hall house built to a common standard for the Welsh gentry. Constructed in 1416, the rare aisle truss hall was originally heated by a huge central hearth, replaced in the seventeenth century by the large fireplace you see today. Alterations at that time included the insertion of an upper floor – a dismantled beam from this work is on display, bearing the date 1656.

ARRIVAL AND INFORMATION CRICCIETH

By train Trains serve Porthmadog (8 daily; 10min) and Pwllheli (8 daily; 15min). The station is signposted off the main road, Y Maes, 350yd west of the central crossroads.
By bus Local buses stop on Y Maes.

Destinations Llanystumdwy (Mon–Sat roughly every 30min, Sun 7; 5min); Porthmadog (Mon–Sat roughly every 30min, Sun 7; 15min); Pwllheli (Mon–Sat every 30min, Sun 7; 25min).

ACCOMMODATION

Bron Eifion 0.5 mile west on the A497, LL52 0SA ☎01766 522385, ⓦbroneifion.co.uk. Upmarket, Grade II-listed mansion once owned by a Victorian slate magnate; he exported to the US and imported the Oregon pine for his hall panelling. The decor in the rooms nods to that heritage and adds statement wallpapers. Comfortable rather than glamorous, this is a relaxing stay, set in five acres of grounds. Breakfast not included. **£88**

★**Glyn y Coed** Porthmadog Rd, LL52 0HP ☎01766 522870, ⓦglynycoedhotel.co.uk. Sea views at the front

and ample space make the ten en-suite rooms of this stylishly relaxed B&B the first choice in Criccieth; those views cost £10 extra. Tasty breakfasts use locally sourced bacon. The owner is charming. **£85**

Mynydd Du Porthmadog Rd (A497), 1 mile east, LL52 0PS ☎01766 522294, ⓦmynydddu.co.uk. There are lots of caravans at this campsite (though there's a tents-only field, too), but what a view of Snowdonia and the sea from its sloping fields. Clean modern(ish) shower block and free showers. Closed Nov–Feb. **£18**

EATING AND DRINKING

Cadwalader's Castle St, LL52 0DP ☎01766 523665, ⓦcadwaladers.co.uk. The founding outlet of this regional ice-cream empire has an airy café and great sea views. As well as rich ice creams (from £2.20) in dozens of flavours, they also have coffee, smoothies and tasty pies. Daily: winter 10am–5pm; rest of year 10am–6pm, except late July & Aug 10am–10pm.

★**Dylans** Maes y Mor, LL52 0HU ☎01766 522773, ⓦdylansrestaurant.co.uk. Local mini-chain Dylans has revived Criccieth's Art Deco beach pavilion into the buzziest place in town. Come for coffee or cocktails as much as meals such as seafood linguini (mains £13–24), all served in a bright, crisp dining room with brilliant wraparound views of the castle, coast and Cambrian mountains. Daily 11am–11pm; kitchen noon–10pm.

Poachers 66–68 High St, LL52 0HB ☎01766 522512, ⓦpoachersrestaurant.co.uk. The locals' choice for a

good-value relaxed meal in the centre, this family-friendly place prepares honest bistro meals from local ingredients at good prices (two courses £18.95). Expect fish plates, veg curries, pork shank with sautéed mushrooms or home-made Welsh Black beef lasagne. Mon–Sat 6–9pm.

Tfarn y Plu Llanystumdwy, 1.5 miles west, LL52 0SW ☎01766 523276, ⓦtafarnyplu.com. Classic Welsh heritage pub, a true local, with horse brasses on low beams, a fire in the grate and a warm welcome. The owners prepare home-cooked meals (around £10) using local produce. Wed–Sun 6–11pm; kitchen 6–9pm.

Tir A Môr 1–3 Mona Terrace, LL52 0HG ☎01766 523084, ⓦtiramor-criccieth.co.uk. Delightful small café serving some of Criccieth's best lunches and cakes, freshly prepared with care by an excellent chef: expect the likes of leek and feta quiche, plus classics including gourmet burgers and lasagne (£11). Mon, Tues & Thurs–Sun 8.30am–5pm.

Pwllheli and around

The "capital" of the Llŷn, **PWLLHELI** (pronounced something like "Pooth-heli") is a solid little place that fails to live up either to its seaside location or its illustrious history. Although the town appears largely Victorian, Pwllheli's market charter dates back to 1355: Wednesday and Sunday **markets** still take place on Y Maes. It was also here, in August 1925, that six people met to form Plaid Cymru at the Maesgwyn Temperance Hotel on Penrhydlyniog Street (now a pet shop marked with a plaque). Even in the height of summer, you'll hear far more Welsh spoken than English. However, notwithstanding its Victorian high street, the only real reason to visit is to change buses – this is the **transport hub** of the peninsula.

ARRIVAL AND INFORMATION
PWLLHELI

By train The central train station serves Criccieth (8 daily; 15min), Porthmadog (8 daily; 25min) and other stations down the Cambrian Coast line.

By bus National Express and local buses pull in at Y Maes. Destinations Aberdaron (Mon–Sat 9 daily; 45min); Abersoch (Mon–Sat 10–11 daily, Sun 4; 15–30min); Caernarfon (Mon–Sat roughly hourly, Sun 3; 45min);

Criccieth (Mon–Sat every 30min, Sun 7; 25min); Nefyn (Mon–Sat roughly hourly, Sun 4; 15min); Porthmadog (Mon–Sat every 30min, Sun 7; 40min).

Tourist information There are leaflets in the foyer of the library, Neuadd Dwyfor, on the main drag, Penlan St (May–Sept Mon–Sat 10am–5pm; Oct–April Mon–Sat 10am–3pm; ☎ 01758 613000, ✉ pwllheli.tic@gwynedd.gov.uk).

ACCOMMODATION AND EATING

While there's nothing to detain you in Pwllheli itself, the **surrounding area** includes some of the finest accommodation on the peninsula, with a central location that makes all three coasts accessible.

Away From It All Penfras Isaf, Llwyndyrys, 5.5 miles north, LL53 6NG ☎ 01758 750279, ✇ away-from-it-all .co.uk. Though the central location puts you just 5 miles from either coast, you really do feel away from it all at this farm glamping site. Three geodesic domes sleep four, each with a woodburner and firepit; you share a kitchen and amenities block. Guests receive a hamper of local produce and can collect eggs daily – it's brilliant for kids. Minimum four nights midweek, two nights at the weekend. **£75**

The Old Rectory A497 at Boduan, 4 miles northwest, LL53 6DT ☎ 01758 721519, ✇ theoldrectory.net. Lovely country house in a relaxed setting midway between the north and south coasts, with bright, elegant country-style en-suite rooms and great breakfasts. Well positioned for exploring the tip of the peninsula. **£85**

★**Plas Bodegroes** Efailnewydd, A497, 2 miles north, LL53 5TH ☎ 01758 612363, ✇ bodegroes .co.uk. Probably the finest place to stay on the Llŷn, in a Georgian country house that's full of softly ticking

grandfather clocks and squishy sofas, yet stays feeling fresh with stylish modern accents: dove-grey walls, art on the walls, wild flowers in vases. As well as to decompress, people come here for fine food – expect dishes like wild sea bass with courgette-and-crab risotto, all designed with a touch of theatre (£49 for three courses). Sun lunch costs a modest £20. Tues–Sat 7–9pm, Sun noon–2pm. **£150**

Taro Deg New St (A497), opposite train station, LL53 5HH ☎ 01758 701271. A comfortable daytime café that prepares a soup and quiche each day as well as sandwiches, Welsh rarebit and cake. A good option for a quick bite while changing buses. Mon–Sat 9am–4.30pm.

Whitehall Gaol St, LL53 5RG ☎ 01758 614091, ✇ whitehallpwllheli.co.uk. This restaurant – actually a modestly poshed-up pub – dishes up the best cooking in the town centre. The classic gastropub menu includes the like of fish pie (£11.90), slow-cooked beef and tarragon chicken with creamed mushrooms. Daily 11am–11pm.

Llanbedrog

LLANBEDROG, four miles southwest of Pwllheli, is a modest village worth visiting for its **beach** – featuring Wales' cutest line of beach huts – and to take a look at one of Wales' oldest public **art galleries**.

Oriel Plas Glyn-y-Weddw

Llanbedrog, LL53 7TT • 10am–5pm: May–Sept daily; Oct–April closed Tues except during school hols • Free • ☎ 01758 740763, ✇ oriel.org.uk

Solomon Andrews, a Cardiff entrepreneur who built Pwllheli's Victorian tourist infrastructure, bought the Victorian Gothic **Oriel Plas Glyn-y-Weddw** in 1896 and turned it into a genteel centre for the arts, with pleasure gardens and legendary tea dances. All rooms peel off a spectacular galleried hallway – with its huge stained-glass window and gorgeous hammerbeam oak roof topped with a lantern, it's quite an entrance. The exhibitions combine pieces from the gallery's permanent collection with touring works, often with a Welsh theme. There's also a conservatory **café** in which to sit and gaze out to the distant sea.

Traeth Llanbedrog

Llanbedrog, LL53 7TT · Open access · Free, but parking £4; NT · ☎ 01758 740561, ⓦ nationaltrust.org.uk/llanbedrog-beach

Below the village is **Traeth Llanbedrog**, a sheltered beach lined with primary-coloured beach huts. From the southern end of the beach, a steep, fairly rough **path** climbs through a wooded glen onto a headland known as Mynydd Tir-y-Cwmwd, where the sweeping views are shared by the **Iron Man**, a modern wrought-iron sculpture designed and built locally to replace an 8ft ship's figurehead erected there in 1919.

Abersoch and around

After the solidly Welsh feel of Pwllheli, **ABERSOCH**, seven miles southwest, is a surprise. This former fishing village, pitched in the middle of two golden bays, is a rather glossy resort, catering to yachties and holidaying families from northwest England, with an abundance of cafés and restaurants.

The beaches

One major reason for Abersoch's popularity is its **beaches**. It's just a five-minute walk to the closest, **Main Beach**, a long, clean strand lined by beach huts that are as colourful as they are expensive – one sold for £153,000 in 2015. The powdery sands are busy in peak season but a short walk along the shore leaves most of the crowds behind. For more space, head a few miles south to the wild beaches the locals love. **Porth Ceiriad** is on the south tip downhill from *Nant y Big* campsite; surfers prefer **Porth Neigwl** (Hell's Mouth), two miles southwest. When powerful Atlantic storms push ocean swell north (beware of the undertow if you're swimming) it's the finest **surf** beach in north Wales around mid-tide. Rental and lessons are available (see box below).

ARRIVAL AND DEPARTURE ABERSOCH

By bus Buses from Pwllheli (Mon–Sat 10–11 daily, Sun 4; 20–30min) loop through the middle of Abersoch, stopping on Lôn Pen Cei. To continue to Aberdaron by bus, you must take a Pwllheli-bound service as far as Llanbedrog, then change onto the #17.

WATERSPORTS ON THE LLŶN

Abersoch is a hub for aquatic activities in the region, whether you want **lessons** or simply prefer to **rent** equipment.

SCHOOLS AND OPERATORS

Abersoch Sailing School North end of Main Beach, LL53 7DP ☎ 01758 712963, ⓦ abersochsailingschool .com. The school offers lessons and rents laser dinghies, catamarans, kayaks and pedalos on the town's main beach (dinghies from £45 for 2hr). March–Oct.

Llyn Adventures ☎ 07751 826714, ⓦ llyn adventures.com. Coasteering lessons around the peninsula's superb coastline as well as kayaking and surfing trips (all £40 for 3hr). March–Oct.

Offaxis Town centre, where road turns left behind the harbour, LL53 7HP ☎ 01758 713407, ⓦ offaxis .co.uk. Offaxis runs a paddleboarding, kitesurfing, wakeboarding and surfing academy (£30/lesson) and rents out gear (from £10/day). Summer only.

West Coast Surf Lôn Pen Cei, LL53 7AP ☎ 01758 713067, ⓦ westcoastsurf.co.uk. Rents surfing gear (boards £10, wetsuits £8), offers lessons (£30 for 2hr) and provides paddleboarding rental (£20/2hr, £30/ day). Open year-round.

6

ACCOMMODATION

Accommodation can be tight over **summer** and at **weekends** during spring and autumn. Almost all the **campsites** in villages around Abersoch are family-oriented places, so groups need to look reputable to be admitted.

HOTELS AND GUESTHOUSE

Angorfa Lôn Sarn Bach, LL53 7EB ☎ 01758 712967, ⓦ angorfa.com. Bare boards and white linen characterize this superior budget B&B, the closest to central Abersoch (by 70yd or so). All rooms are en suite; the two attic rooms have the best views. Breakfast is served in the daytime café downstairs. Closed Oct to early March. **£85**

★ **Porth Tocyn** 2.5 miles south, on road through Sarn Bach and Bwlchtocyn, LL53 7BU ☎ 01758 713303, ⓦ porthtocynhotel.co.uk. End-of-the-road escapism in a country-house hotel that brims with laidback style while also catering for families; there's a playroom for kids and an outdoor heated pool. All the rooms are different (we like no. 2) and many have great views of Cardigan Bay (£195). It also has a distant shepherd's hut, Ty Cwtch ("The Cuddle") with views to infinity (£125). Closed Nov to mid-March. **£155**

Venetia Lôn Sarn Bach, LL53 7EB ☎ 01758 713354, ⓦ venetiawales.com. Apart from the view from a couple of the rooms, you'd barely know you were at the seaside at this urban-chic boutique hotel. The five boldly styled rooms, most with king or superking beds, all have plush bathrooms – and those baths could hold a hippo. Note there was talk of the business being put up for sale at the time of research. **£108**

CAMPSITE

★ **Nant y Big** Cilan, 3 miles south, LL53 7DB ☎ 01758 712686, ⓦ nantybig.com. Persevere through the caravans and you come to the panoramic camping field, a lovely low-density site that slopes gently towards Porth Ceiriad – the sea views are outstanding. The narrow valley field is more sheltered and closer to the beach, and there are pitches with hook-ups among the caravans above. Closed Nov–Feb. Per person **£9**

EATING AND DRINKING

Coconut Kitchen Lôn Pont Morgan (main road opposite harbour), LL53 7AN ☎ 01758 712250, ⓦ coconutkitchen.co.uk. It's been going for ages and remains the best Thai place for miles, with dishes served from an open kitchen. As well as classics like beef Massaman or green chicken curry (around £12), it features interesting daily dishes including the likes of Aberdaron crab. Takeaway available. Daily 5.30–10pm.

Porth Tocyn 2.5 miles south, on road through Sarn Bach and Bwlchtocyn, LL53 7BU ☎ 01758 713303, ⓦ porthtocynhotel.co.uk. On sunny days the terrace of this hotel restaurant fits the bill for lunch with a view of sea and mountains. Light lunches of fish pie (£14.50), pasta or deli rolls segue to more formal dinners with international set menus (two courses £40). The "Comfort" supper menu is

simpler and cheaper. Early March to Oct daily 12.15–2.30pm & 6–9.30pm.

Venetia Lôn Sarn Bach, LL53 7EB ☎ 01758 713354, ⓦ venetiawales.com. This smart, award-winning modern restaurant dishes up the best food in central Abersoch, the likes of linguini with local crab, or lobster and chilli – the chef, Marco Fillipi, is half-Italian – along with fish fresh from the boat. Most mains £13–17. Wed–Sun 6.30–10pm.

Zinc Lôn Pen Cei, LL53 7DW ☎ 01758 712880, ⓦ zincabersoch.com. This glossy bar-restaurant exudes metropolitan cool, with a relaxed ambience and a wonderful terrace overlooking the inner harbour. Dishes on the modern menu run the gamut from local haddock with lentils to posh burgers (£9) or Aberdaron lobster. Daily 9am–3pm & 6–11pm, later in summer.

Aberdaron and around

You really feel like you've arrived at the far end of Wales when you come to the lime-washed fishing hamlet of **ABERDARON**, two miles short of the tip of the Llŷn. For the best part of a thousand years, up to the sixteenth century, the inn and church here were the last stops on a pilgrim trail to Ynys Enlli or Bardsey Island, around the headland. Pilgrims gathered in Y Gegin Fawr, the fourteenth-century "Big Kitchen", today a café in the centre, before making the treacherous crossing to Ynys Enlli. With the right mindset it's still possible to sense a numinous quality to the village. Otherwise, Aberdaron is simply a charming, low-key sort of place, with a long spread of pebbly **beach** to enjoy.

Porth y Swnt

In the village centre, at the car park beside the bridge, LL58 8BE • Daily: March & Oct–Dec 10am–4pm; April–June & Sept 9am–5pm; July & Aug 9am–6pm • £2; NT • ☎ 01758 703814, ⓦ nationaltrust.org.uk/porth-y-swnt

The name may translate as "gateway to the sound", but this rather undersells the National Trust's **Porth y Swnt** attraction. Instead, this small display states the case for Aberdaron being the cultural wellspring of the peninsula. Meagre arts and crafts exhibits in the three rooms are brought to life by audio guides, with most exhibits accompanied by an interview with geologists, artists, gardeners, walkers, poets or farmers. The result is an oral history that subtly reveals something of the unique character of the Llŷn. Take your time and it's an impressionistic, even spiritual experience.

6

Church of St Hywyn
Main road, LL53 8BE • Daily: Easter–Oct 9am–6pm; Nov–Easter 10am–4pm • Free

The twelfth-century **church of St Hywyn**, strikingly situated on the cliffs above Aberdaron's beach, has a handsome interior. Its fame, however, is as the ministry of one of Wales' greatest modern poets, R.S. Thomas (see box below). Displays on Thomas have pride of place in a beautifully simple twin-naved interior, beside material on Enlli and its pilgrims, and a pair of Latin-inscribed sixth-century gravestones – among the earliest Christian artefacts in Wales.

Plas yn Rhiw
B4413, 5 miles east of Aberdaron, LL53 8AB • Late March to May & Sept Mon & Thurs–Sun noon–5pm; June & July daily except Tues noon–5pm; Aug daily noon–5pm; Oct Thurs–Sun noon–4pm • £5.20; NT • ☎ 01758 780219, ⊛ nationaltrust.org.uk/plas-yn-rhiw • The Pwllheli–Aberdaron bus #17 (Mon–Sat 9 daily) and the Llŷn Coastal Bus (April–Oct 4 daily; see p.375) stop nearby

In the early years of his retirement, R.S. Thomas lived in a cottage in the grounds of **Plas yn Rhiw**, a Regency manor house on Tudor foundations. The house was derelict in 1938 when it was bought by Thomas's moneyed friends, the Keating sisters. They restored it with the help of Portmeirion architect Clough Williams-Ellis, whose offbeat touch is evident in the flattened arches and a Gothic doorway rescued from a demolished castle. This is a homely and relaxed place, its creaky-floored rooms filled with rustic furniture – note the 1920s oil stove used by Honora Keating until her death in 1981, and her accomplished watercolours. The upstairs sitting room is notable for a 6ft-thick wall containing a fireplace, a spiral staircase and a window nook overlooking gorgeous gardens, all clipped box hedges, fuchsias, hydrangeas, roses and wild flowers.

R.S. THOMAS

The reclusive, Cardiff-born poet **R.S. (Ronald Stuart) Thomas** (1913–2000) was something of a Welsh anti-hero. He worked as a minister in rural parishes throughout Wales, most famously in Aberdaron where he spent his angst-wracked last decades – he is said to have burned his cassock on the beach on retiring. It was Thomas's fourth volume of poetry, published in 1955, that brought him lasting recognition, something consolidated with his best-known collections – *The Bread of Truth* (1963) and *Not that he brought Flowers* (1968).

R.S. Thomas's poetry is frequently dark, spartan and bitter, illuminated by shafts of vision and clarity. Common themes include religion (Christianity in particular), rural and pastoral strands, and the eternal poetic topic of love in human relationships. However, it's in his Welsh-themed work that Thomas most savagely and thrillingly hits the mark.

I never wanted the drab rôle
Life assigned me, an actor playing
To the past's audience upon a stage
Of earth and stone; the absurd label
Of birth, of race hanging askew

About my shoulders. I was in prison
Until you came; your voice was a key
Turning in the enormous lock
Of hopelessness. Did the door open
To let me out or yourselves in?

A Welsh Testament

6

Mynydd Mawr

Two miles southwest of Aberdaron, LL53 0BY • Open access • Free

Having made your way as far as Aberdaron, there's no excuse not to continue via a narrow road to the end of the peninsula and **Mynydd Mawr**, the hill overlooking Bardsey Sound. As the road begins to climb up the hill, make a stop at **Braich-y-Pwll**, a headland from where a short path heads down the cliffs to the ruins of St Mary's church, the crossing point at the end of the Pilgrim's Way. The road continues to Mynydd Mawr, the tip of the Llŷn, with footpaths around the coast and gorgeous seascapes across the sound to Bardsey Island to enjoy. Local folklore identifies Bardsey as King Arthur's Avalon (see box opposite); viewed from this hillside at dusk – a silhouette humped in a silvery sea – that doesn't sound at all far-fetched.

Porth Oer

Two miles north of Aberdaron, LL53 8LG • Open access • Free, but parking £4; NT

The best beach hereabouts is **Porth Oer**, known as "Whistling Sands" for the white sands that squeak as you walk on them. It is a memorable spot, hemmed in by rocky promontories, with easy walks either way along the coast. The only facilities are toilets and a small beach café open in summer. If it's busy, take the coast path north for fifteen minutes to reach Porth Iago, notched in the cliffs.

ARRIVAL AND DEPARTURE
ABERDARON

By bus The #17 bus runs to Aberdaron from Pwllheli (Mon–Sat 9 daily; 40min). Otherwise the Llŷn Coastal Bus (see p.375) shuttles through (April–Oct 4 daily).

ACCOMMODATION AND EATING

Becws Islyn Bakery Pwllheli Rd, LL53 8BE ☎ 01758 760370. Though modern, its walls decorated with murals of local legends, this brilliant family bakery just uphill from the village bridge is all Welsh, preparing the likes of Welsh cakes (get there early, they sell out) alongside home-made cakes and pies, crab sandwiches and jacket spuds. Good breakfasts, too. Summer: daily 7.30am–6pm; other times Mon, Tues & Thurs–Sat 7.30am–5pm.

Mynydd Mawr Llanllawen Fawr, 2 miles southwest, LL53 0BY ☎ 01758 760223, ⓦ aberdaroncaravanand campingsite.co.uk. Just a couple of peaceful grassy fields right by the entrance to Mynydd Mawr, this site is something of a legend among camping afficionados for its sense of escapism and its views across to Ynys Enlli. Hot showers and electricity hook-up available. Closed Nov–Feb. **£18**

Tŷ Newydd Village centre, LL53 8BE ☎ 01758 760207, ⓦ gwesty-tynewydd.co.uk. There's a good reason to choose this modernized hotel – the beach and sea views from the front rooms (£115), the best of which have mini-balconies. Nice touches including iPod docks and superking beds make up for the slightly bland decor. It's a fine choice for eating, too, with a dining terrace over the beach – there's local lobster and herb-crusted cod (£13) as well as pub favourites like Glamorgan bangers and mash (£10.95). Daily noon–2.30pm & 6–8.30pm. **£110**

Ynys Enlli (Bardsey Island)

Ynys Enlli, or **Bardsey Island**, rises out of the ocean two miles off the tip of the Llŷn, separated from it by a strait of unpredictable water. Seen from the mainland it's a siren call for a dose of escapism – certainly it's a place to enjoy seascapes and salt air, to walk paths across coastal grassland and heath, and to spot birdlife and the grey seals that loll in rocky coves.

Most visitors come to Ynys Enlli for the **birdwatching**. Among the dozen or so species of nesting sea birds are Manx shearwaters, choughs, fulmars and guillemots, and an amazing number of vagrants turn up after being blown off course by storms. There are hides dotted around the island.

ARRIVAL AND INFORMATION
YNYS ENLLI

By boat Crossings are dependent on sea conditions and a viable load of passengers: you will need to be flexible. Bardsey Boat Trips (£30 return; ☎ 07971 769895, ⓦ bardseyboattrips.com) sails from Porth Meudwy, a tiny cove a mile south of Aberdaron (sat nav LL53 8DA), in around 15min; the Aberdaron village shop serves as an

THE ISLE OF TWENTY THOUSAND SAINTS

Myth swirls around Ynys Enlli like the currents of the sea: long before the island became a national nature reserve, it was an important **pilgrimage site**. This land was holy for the Celtic druids – one legend holds that it is Avalon, the last resting place of King Arthur. The island's Celtic significance probably inspired the Breton saint St Cadfan to set up a monastery here in the sixth century and, with centuries of religious inhabitation, Ynys Enlli became known as the "the isle of twenty thousand saints". Another tale claimed anyone who who died on the island would not go to hell; small wonder that it became a pilgrimage destination. By the twelfth century, meanwhile, Giraldus Cambrensis was claiming that "no one dies there except in extreme old age, for disease is almost unheard of". Little remains of the early Christian community except the crumbling **bell tower** of the thirteenth-century Augustinian Abbey of St Mary and a few Celtic crosses scattered around it. After the dissolution of the monasteries in 1536, the island became a refuge of pirates for more than a century, before settling down to farming and fishing.

6

unofficial office. The trip gives you around four hours on Enlli.

Services Apart from a dozen seasonal researchers, the island now has just one resident farming family who sell tea, coffee and snacks (11am–1pm); bring your own lunch.

ACCOMMODATION

Bardsey Island Trust ☎ 0845 811 2233, ⊕ bardsey .org. The island's owners rent out eight spartan but substantial electricity-free houses, sleeping two to eight, by the week (Sat to Sat). They're mostly rented out to birders, but also for yoga retreats, photography workshops or simple getaways. Closed early Oct to March. **£68**

The north Llŷn coast

Scalloped by small coves and sweeping beaches between rocky bluffs, the **north Llŷn coast** is quite a contrast to the busier south. There are few settlements of any size here, but plenty of quiet little beaches, the most popular (though seldom thronged) of which is **Porthdinllaen**, with its pub gorgeously sited beside the sand. A rockier coastline is accessible from the Welsh language school at **Nant Gwrtheyrn**, which is overlooked by the heights of **Tre'r Ceiri** with its prehistoric hillfort remains. The road northeast from Tre'r Ceiri towards Caernarfon now bypasses one of north Wales' finest churches, the austere pilgrimage church of St Beuno at **Clynnog Fawr**. Less famous is St Bueno's at **Pistyll** – tiny, but if you want to sense the true atmosphere of medieval pilgramage, this is the place.

Porthdinllaen

Morfa Nefyn car park, LL53 6DAR • Free, but parking £4; NT • ☎ 01758 760469, ⊕ nationaltrust.org.uk/porthdinllaen

There may not be much to recommend **Nefyn**, the largest of the peninsula's northern communities, but the shoreline hamlet of **PORTHDINLLAEN**, reached via **Morfa Nefyn**, is a popular Llŷn destination. Almost chosen in 1839 as the terminus for ferries to Ireland, but losing out to Anglesey's Holyhead, Porthdinllaen today is little more than a calm sweeping bay owned by the National Trust. Backed by a handful of houses and the popular *Tŷ Coch Inn* pub, built in 1828 from old ship's ballast, it's most magical when the coast is sunlit on a sunny late-afternoon or early evening. Access is from the National Trust's Porthdinllaen car park in Morfa Nefyn, half a mile along the beach.

Church of St Bueno (Pistyll)

Pistyll, LL53 6LR • Generally daily 9am–5pm • Free

Blink and you'll miss **PISTYLL** – it's barely a hamlet. Yet it's here, tucked discreetly off the road just north of the village, that you find the pilgrimage **church of St Bueno**. The

6

size of a matchbox, with the atmosphere of a cathedral, this single-nave medieval church served as a resting place and hospice during the fourteenth century, when twenty thousand pilgrims a year trod the path to Ynys Enlli (Bardsey Island). Today, largely unaltered, it's steeped in the Middle Ages. There's a leper squint by the altar on the north side, so afflicted pilgrims could watch the sermon from outside, and the floor is covered in rushes – a hangover from the medieval practice of strewing medicinal herbs. The font, which dates from the eleventh century, is carved with an Anglo-Scandinavian chain design.

Nant Gwrtheyrn

Northeast of Nefyn, the mountains of Yr Eifl rise steeply only to plunge into the sea along **Nant Gwrtheyrn** (Vortigern's Valley), an impressively steep cleft in the hills, its edges chewed away by granite quarries. This is said to be the final resting place of the Celtic chieftain Vortigern, who was responsible for inviting the Saxons to Britain after his magician, Myrddin (Merlin), had seen the struggle of the two dragons – the red of the ancient Britons and the white of the Saxons.

Nant Gwrtheyrn: The Welsh Language and Heritage Centre

1.5 miles north of Llithfaen, 3 miles northeast of Nefyn, LL53 6NL • Daily 9.30am–4.30pm • Free • ☎ 01758 750334, ⓦ nantgwrtheyrn.org

A precipitously steep road corkscrews down towards the coast and **Nant Gwrtheyrn: The Welsh Language and Heritage Centre**, set in rows of converted cottages built in the late nineteenth century, when the valley had three granite quarries. Though the centre is used primarily for residential courses, entirely in Welsh, the valley is also a beautiful spot to spend a couple of hours exploring, either along the Llŷn Coastal Path or around the old mine workings and piles of rock waste; a free leaflet outlines a three-mile **walk**.

To put it all into context, visit the **Heritage Centre** in the original chapel, and the **Quarryman's Cottages**, two rooms set up to look as they might have done in 1910 with dresser, needlework sampler and bible all in pride of place around the hearth. There's also a licensed **café**.

Tre'r Ceiri

Llanaelhaearn, A499 lay-by, LL54 5AG • Open access • Free

Yr Eifl is a trio of mountains that top out at 1850ft. The second highest is crowned by **Tre'r Ceiri** or "Town of the Giants" hillfort, easily the finest **prehistoric remains** on the Llŷn. A massive rampart, 12ft high in places and composed of huge rocks, rings the remains of about 150 dry-stone hut circles. The site dates back to the Bronze Age, but the huts are probably only a couple of thousand years old. Locals refer to them as *Cytiau Gwddelod* or "Irishmen's Huts", possibly recalling the Irish immigrant population on the Llŷn in the first few centuries AD, when five hundred people lived on this inhospitable site. Today, the ruins command a stunning **view** over the whole peninsula.

The summit is reached by a steep **path** (2.5 miles return; 2hr; 800ft ascent) which starts at a lay-by half a mile southwest of Llanaelhaearn.

Church of St Beuno (Clynnog Fawr)

Clynnog Fawr, just off the A499, 4 miles northeast of Llanaelhaearn, LL54 5AQ • Easter–Oct daily, usually 10am–5pm

Light streams in through the clear windows of the large and airy, early sixteenth-century **church of St Beuno**, built on foundations laid by the saint in the sixth century. The monastic settlement, rich in ancient spiritual connections, would have been an important stop for pilgrims bound for Ynys Enlli, ensuring a hefty income that probably financed the impressive church.

The interior combines spartan whitewash and limestone flags with grand flourishes, including the hammerbeam roof with ornamental bosses, choir stalls and imposing chancel. Some 200yd west, at the south end of the village, is **St Bueno's Well**, a walled pool where pilgrims would bathe – it was said to be particularly efficacious at curing rheumatism, warts and epilepsy.

GETTING AROUND   THE NORTH LLŶN COAST

By bus The only option is the request-stop Llŷn Coastal Bus (see p.375), which shuttles from Abersoch via

Aberdaron to Nefyn (April–Oct 4 daily).

ACCOMMODATION AND EATING

6

★**Aberafon** Gyrn Goch, 1 mile south of Clynnog Fawr, LL54 5PN ☎01286 660295, ⓦaberafon.co.uk. There are views to inspire poetry at this beautiful seafront campsite – Tre'r Ceiri on the left, a horizon-busting spread of silvery sea ahead and a tangled wood with a stream burbling behind. The best pitches are on the Beach Field, which puts a private beach almost within touching distance – pure magic at sunset. Closed Oct–Easter. Per person **£8**

Natural Retreats Pistyll, LL53 6LR ☎01625 800494, ⓦnaturalretreats.com. The renovated buildings of a former farm now offer a luxury hideaway in one- to three-bed cottages. Rustic beams and stone walls, as well as modern rugs and natural fibres, soften the modern streamlined style, and the sea views from the front cottages are gorgeous. Minimum two nights in high season. **£199**

Penrallt Coastal Campsite Tudweiliog, 6 miles southeast of Morfa Nefyn, LL53 8BP ☎01758 770654,

ⓦpenrallt.co.uk. Tricky to find (the turn-off is a mile south of Tudweiliog), this is a back-to-basics site set back from the cliffs, with spacious pitches in fields. It also has wooden "pilgrim pods" that sleep up to four (own sleeping bags required; minimum two nights except for Coast Path hikers), plus direct access to the Coast Path. Facilities include firepits, a freezer and laundry. The *Lion Inn* in Tudweiliog is a 2-mile walk away. Closed Oct–Easter. Camping **£12**, pods for two **£35**

★**Tŷ Coch Inn** Porthdinllaen, LL53 6DB ☎01758 720498, ⓦtycoch.co.uk. Forget the overpriced bar meals – jacket spuds with prawns (£9.95), sandwiches, pasties. Come instead to grab a pint: sit outside on the sea wall with the sand between your toes and enjoy the mountain views. Perfect. June–Aug & bank hols Mon–Sat 11am–10pm, Sun 11am–5pm; rest of the year Mon–Thurs 11am–3pm, Fri & Sat 11am–3pm & 6–10pm, but it's worth calling to check.

The north coast and Anglesey

390 Holywell and around

392 Rhyl and around

393 St Asaph and around

395 Colwyn Bay and around

396 Llandudno

403 Conwy

408 Around Conwy

409 Bangor

414 Anglesey

BEAUMARIS CASTLE

The north coast and Anglesey

It's hard to pigeonhole Wales' north coast and its natural extension, Anglesey; they encompass both the geographical and social extremities of the country. At one end, in the northeast, are some fairly scruffy holiday resorts where the street signs are the only indication that you are in Wales. Yet head all the way west to Anglesey and you'll find yourself in rural villages where English is seldom spoken other than to visitors. Two major forces have shaped the region. One is the thirteenth-century English king Edward I, who defeated the Welsh princes with a series of impressive castles, built ever-deeper into Wales as his conquest progressed. The other is the arrival of the railway. In the nineteenth century, English mill-town factory workers came over the border by the trainload to take their holidays, leaving their legacy in a string of beach resorts along the northern coast.

Having consequently suffered from the rise of the budget package holiday, the **north coast** today is largely composed of rather down-at-heel resorts; a strip of caravan parks and amusement arcades that starts in Prestatyn, also the north end of the Offa's Dyke Path, and reaches its apotheosis in raucous **Rhyl**. Near-neighbour **Colwyn Bay** is smarter and quieter, but for serious culture you'd do best to head inland: to **Bodelwyddan** and its Victorian portrait gallery; **St Asaph**, home to Britain's smallest cathedral; or **Holywell**, a pilgrimage site of varied fortunes for thirteen hundred years.

The undoubted highlight in these parts is Victorian **Llandudno**. It was always the poshest beach resort around here, and after some drab years it has emerged once more to become the queen of the north Wales coast. With its truly splendid Victorian pier, handsome period architecture and good accommodation, it offers good, old-fashioned pleasures: come to promenade, perhaps to wet an ankle, and to eat and sleep well. Though no less attractive, **Conwy** is a different proposition. It may lack a beach – although it does have an inland surf break twenty minutes away in the form of the brilliant **Surf Snowdonia** attraction – but it packs into a lovely small town more sights than the rest of the coast put together, not least one of Edward's most mighty castles, and girdles the lot within 700-year-old town walls.

In terms of looks, Conwy is rivalled only by the postcard-perfect fortification in **Beaumaris**, across the **Menai Strait** on the island of **Anglesey**. The island, a rural backwater that ticks over at a delightfully slow pace, also abounds in good **beaches**. From the southwestern resorts of **Rhosneigr**, **Rhoscolyn** and **Trearddur Bay** – the favoured spots for swimming and watersports – through the dunes of **Newborough** to the quiet family resorts of the east coast, you're spoilt for choice. There's also superb sea-cliff scenery around **South Stack** (great for birdwatching) and, inland, a patchwork of rural communities dotted with burial chambers, standing stones and Wales' greatest concentration of **Neolithic remains**. To top it all, the island is also emerging as a serious **dining** destination.

Greenfield Valley Heritage Park stroll p.391
Pilgrimages and ritual bathing p.392
William Morgan and the first Welsh Bible p.394
Alice in Llandudno p.396

The Iron Ring p.405
Walks around Conwy p.406
Rural accommodation on Anglesey p.414
Spanning the Menai Strait p.419
From sea to seasoning p.420

Highlights

❶ Llandudno This lovely holiday spot is not only a splendid Victorian seaside resort, but also boasts the quiet sands of West Shore beach and, to top it all, breezy hilltop walks and sea views on the hummock of Great Orme. **See p.396**

❷ Conwy The pick of north Wales' small towns, with a picture-postcard medieval castle and a ring of ramparts enclosing a smart little centre. See p.403

❸ Surf Snowdonia Come surfing in the hills at the world's first man-made commerical point break – right here, in a tiny village in the Conwy Valley. **See p.409**

❹ Beaumaris The most picturesque castle in the region, a brightly coloured Georgian townscape, poetry-inspiring views and good places to eat and sleep. See p.415

❺ Newborough Warren She loves me, she loves me not: find out the truth in the well of the patron saint of lovers on Llanddwyn Island. If "not", you can console yourself with the spectacular views on the wild beach. **See p.421**

❻ Anglesey food Long the breadbasket of Wales, Anglesey has a growing number of interesting small restaurants focusing on great local produce. The *Marram Grass* in Newborough is one of the best. **See p.421**

❼ South Stack Wheeling sea birds, stunning sea cliffs, a picturesque lighthouse on a small island and great coastal walking. Magic. **See p.423**

HIGHLIGHTS ARE MARKED ON THE MAP ON P.390

By train The train links the coastal resorts all the way to Bangor, then across to Anglesey for the run to Holyhead.

By bus With the exception of National Express bus services from Manchester, Liverpool and other English cities to Bangor and Holyhead, bus travel is much more piecemeal, although services are fairly frequent and come listed in excellent timetable booklets available free at tourist offices.

By car The A55 dual carriageway allows you to drive from the Welsh border just south of Liverpool through Anglesey to Holyhead in little over an hour, bypassing all the coastal towns and skirting the northern reaches of Snowdonia.

Holywell and around

The slow route into north Wales diverts off the A55 dual carriageway and potters along the coast via a couple of modest sights at **HOLYWELL** (Treffynnon) – neither really worth an effort to visit but enjoyable if you're passing. It's a modest place of pilgrimage fancifully billed as "The Lourdes of Wales" (albeit without the tacky souvenir stalls selling Virgin Mary lighters), because of its **holy well** downhill from the town centre.

St Winefride's Well

Greenfield Rd, CH8 7PN • **Well** Daily: April–Sept 9am–5pm; Oct–March 10am–4pm • £1 • **Museum** April–Sept Wed, Sat & Sun noon–4pm • Free • ☎ 01352 713054, ⓦ saintwinefrideswell.com

Never mind that the Romans used the healing waters of **St Winefride's Well** to relieve rheumatism and gout. A seventh-century legend claims that the virtuous Winefride

THE NORTH COAST & ANGLESEY

> ### GREENFIELD VALLEY HERITAGE PARK STROLL
>
> St Winefride's Well and Basingwerk Abbey are just a mile apart, linked by a woodland trail along the track of an old pilgrims' train line. Paths weave past five mill ponds, a series of water races and the preserved remains of copper works and cotton mills, which once manufactured Queen Victoria's underwear, apparently. Together they form the **Greenfield Valley Heritage Park**. About 200yd down the Greenfield Road from the Well, take the footpath behind the factory then follow whichever paths take your fancy.

(Gwenfrewi in Welsh) was decapitated after resisting the advances of Prince Caradoc. The well is said to have sprung up where her head fell; when St Beuno, her uncle, placed her head beside the body, prayer and the waters revived her, setting her on track to serve as an abbess at Gwytherin Convent near Llanrwst.

Richard I and Henry V provided regal patronage, ensuring a steady flow of believers to what became one of the great shrines of Christendom – the pilgrimages became more clandestine after the Reformation, when the well became a focal point of resistance to Protestantism. A century and a half later, the Catholic king of England, James II, came here to pray for a son and heir.

Pilgrims spent the night praying in the Gothic **St Winefride's Chapel**, which encloses three sides of the well. Henry VII's mother, Margaret Beaufort, paid for the construction and earned herself a likeness among the roof bosses that depict the life of St Winefride in the ornate, Gothic fan-vaulted crypt that surrounds the well, their columns etched with graffiti dating from the 1500s.

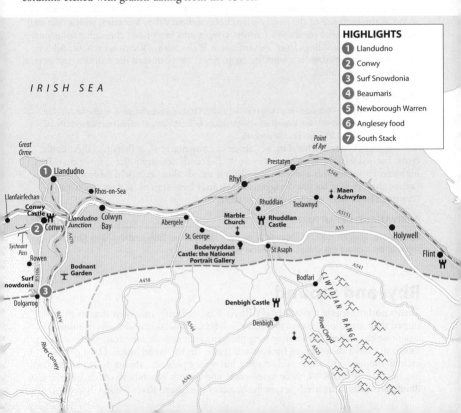

HIGHLIGHTS

1. Llandudno
2. Conwy
3. Surf Snowdonia
4. Beaumaris
5. Newborough Warren
6. Anglesey food
7. South Stack

PILGRIMAGES AND RITUAL BATHING

Pilgrimages to **St Winefride's Well** mainly focus on St Winefride's Day, the nearest Sunday to June 22, when more than five hundred pilgrims are led through the streets by the Bishop of Wrexham. The procession ends by the open side of the crypt, where a few dozen faithful wade three times through the waters of a calm pool in the hope of curing their ailments. Immersion isn't limited to the procession: anyone, whatever their beliefs, can take the **cure**, albeit in a shallow stone pool rather than the well itself (daily: April–Sept 9–10am & 4–4.45pm; Oct–March 10–11am & 3–3.30pm). You'll need to wear suitable attire and bring a towel. A word of warning: it's chilly, which might explain why summer tends to be known as "curing season".

The former custodian's house contains a small **museum** with painted banners, priests' vestments, the skeletal remains of Reformation martyrs (one of whose heads clearly ended on a spike as a warning to others) and a beautiful silver reliquary designed to display Holywell's relic – part of Winefride's thumb bone.

Basingwerk Abbey and Greenfield Valley Museum

Greenfield Valley, CH8 7GH • **Abbey** Daily 10am–4pm • Free; CADW • ☎ 01443 336000, ⓦ cadw.gov.wales/daysout/basingwerk-abbey • **Museum** Mid-March to Oct daily 10am–4.30pm • £6.70 • ☎ 01352 714172, ⓦ greenfieldvalley.com

Further downhill from the well stand the remains of **Basingwerk Abbey**. There's not much of it left – just vaulted slabs of stonework and a few domestic building foundations. Still, it was obviously a grand place for the Cistercian abbot and dozen or so monks who lived here.

A small visitor centre opposite the ruins contains historical material on the abbey and serves as the entrance to the family-friendly **Greenfield Valley Museum**, which tells the story of the industrial revolution (cotton, copper and brass here) through a collection of reconstructed buildings from around north Wales with a Victorian school. Adding to its appeal for children is a working farm, where you can feed the animals, and several adventure playgrounds.

Maen Achwyfan

Four miles west of Holywell • Open access • Free; CADW • ☎ 01443 336000, ⓦ cadw.gov.wales/daysout/maenachwyfancross • Take the A5026 almost 3 miles northwest from Holywell and turn right onto the A5151; after almost a mile take the third exit at the first roundabout and follow signs to Trelogan for a little over a mile

The impressive **Maen Achwyfan**, or "Stone of Lamentation", is Britain's tallest **Celtic cross**. Incised with interwoven latticework, the tenth-century pillar is more than 10ft high and crowned with a wheel cross. That it stands alone in a field far from a church (although near four barrows) suggests that it may have started its days as a pagan standing stone, later adapted for Christianity.

ARRIVAL AND DEPARTURE   HOLYWELL

By bus Buses along the coast call frequently at the bus station at the southern end of High St. They serve Flint (every 30min; 15min) and Rhyl (every 30min; 1hr).

Rhyl and around

There's nothing subtle about **RHYL** (Y Rhyl). Raw and fairly rundown after its clientele turned their attentions abroad for family holidays, this seaside resort offers a minor assault on the senses – a two-mile-long promenade of amusement arcades, fish and chip cafés and tourist shops selling buckets and spades for the broad beach. Don't get too excited, though – the sand's fairly scruffy, but on the plus side, there's decent **kitesurfing** just offshore. **RHUDDLAN**, three miles south, and essentially a suburb of Rhyl, is home to **Rhuddlan Castle**, attractively set on the banks of the Clwyd River (Afon Clywedog).

Rhuddlan Castle

Castle St, Rhuddlan, 3 miles south of Rhyl, LL18 5AD • April–Oct daily 10am–5pm • £4; CADW • ☎ 01745 590777, Ⓦ cadw.gov.wales
/daysout/rhuddlancastle

With Edward I's first castle – just beyond the English border in Flint – now nothing
more than a toothy shell, the impressive hollow ruin of **Rhuddlan Castle** far better
evokes the might of the early English fortifications in Wales. Constructed between
1277 and 1282, during the king's first phase of castle-building, it was designed both as
a garrison and royal residence, commanding a canalized section of the then strategic
river. **Gillot's Tower**, by the dock gate, provided protection for the supply ships, while
the concentric plan allowed archers on both outer and inner walls to fire
simultaneously. This innovation become irrelevant by 1648, when Parliamentary forces
took the castle during the Civil War and demolished it.

ARRIVAL AND INFORMATION

By train and bus The stations are next to each other, near
the intersection of the A548 (Russell/Wellington roads)
and Bodfor/Queen streets, which run to the sea.

Destinations by train Bangor (hourly; 34min); Holyhead
(hourly; 1hr 10min–1hr 30min); Llandudno Junction
(every 30min; 20min).

Destinations by bus Denbigh (Mon–Sat hourly, Sun 3;

RHYL AND AROUND

40min); Llandudno (Mon–Sat every 30min, Sun 6; 1hr
10min); Prestatyn (every 30min; 20min); Rhuddlan (Mon–
Sat every 30min, Sun 6; 10min); St Asaph (Mon–Sat hourly,
Sun 6; 25min).

Tourist office On the seafront at West Parade (Easter–
Sept daily 9.30am–4.30pm; Oct–Easter Mon–Fri
9.30am–4.30pm; ☎ 01745 355068, Ⓦ loverhyl.com).

ACTIVITIES

Marsh Tracks Marsh Rd, LL18 2AD ☎ 01745 353335,
Ⓦ marshtracks.co.uk. BMX riding is the mainstay here,
cycled on an Olympic-grade course, but this bike centre
also has a 0.8-mile road-race circuit and mountain-bike
trails in the surrounding countryside. Bike rental from £3/
session.

Pro Kitesurfing East Parade, LL18 3AQ ☎ 07926
943421, Ⓦ prokitesurfing.co.uk. Accredited kitesurfing
lessons either off Rhyl beach or nearby, depending on
conditions. One-day tasters £90, two-day beginner courses
£165. It also runs half-day paddleboarding sessions (£65).

ACCOMMODATION AND EATING

Barratt's Ty'n Rhyl, 167 Vale Rd, LL18 2PH ☎ 01745
344138, Ⓦ barrattsattynrhyl.co.uk. Rhyl's oldest house
provides traditional, Victorian-styled suite rooms plus the
smartest dining in town (open to non-guests, too). Expect
dishes such as local sea bass with garden chard and prawn
sauce on two-course menus that cost £35. Reservations

required. Tues–Sat 6.30–10pm, Sun noon–3pm. __£90__
Les & Rita's Fish Bar 28 Wellington Rd, LL18 1BN
☎ 01745 342315. Not just the best chippy in a resort
stuffed with them, but the best in north Wales according to
a regional newspaper. It's cheap, too: fish and chips, a slice,
peas and tea for just £5.20. Mon–Sat 11.30–6.30pm.

St Asaph and around

Because of its cathedral, diminutive **ST ASAPH**, six miles south of Rhyl, ranks as a
city. St Davids in Pembrokeshire may be a slightly less populous "city", but St Asaph
has the country's smallest **cathedral** – an edifice no bigger than many village
churches. There's little else to detain you in the town itself, but a couple of other
worthwhile sights lie in the surrounding area, including **Marble Church** and the
National Portrait Gallery.

St Asaph Cathedral

High St, LL17 0RD • Daily 9am–6.30pm • Free • Ⓦ stasaphcathedral.org.uk

Though dedicated to Asaph, its second bishop after St Kentigern (who founded the
church in 570), **St Asaph Cathedral** is often associated with **William Morgan** (see box,
p.394). From 1601 until his death in 1604, the creator of the Welsh Bible held the

> ## WILLIAM MORGAN AND THE FIRST WELSH BIBLE
>
> Until 1588 only English bibles had been used in Welsh churches, a fact that rankled Welsh-born preacher **William Morgan**, who insisted: "Religion, if it is not taught in the mother tongue, will lie hidden and unknown". This was the professed reason behind Elizabeth I's demand for a translation, though in truth her subjects' disaffection could be most conveniently controlled through the Church. Four clergymen took up the challenge, but it is Morgan who is remembered: working in Llanrhaeadr-ym-Mochnant, he got into such bitter squabbles with some parishoners (notably thwarting one local family's hopes of marrying their son to a wealthy heiress) that he needed an armed guard to get to his services and was said to preach with a pistol at his side.
>
> The eventual translation was so successful that the Privy Council decreed that a copy should be allocated to every Welsh church. Though it was soon replaced by a translation of the Authorized Version, Morgan's Bible differs little in style from the latest edition used in Welsh services today. More than just a basis for sermons, the **Welsh Bible** (Y Beibl) served to codify the language and set a standard for Welsh prose. Without it the language would probably have divided into several dialects or even followed its Brythonic cousin, Cornish, into history.

bishopric here and his work is commemorated by an octagonal monument in the churchyard. Morgan's grave beneath the presbytery has been unmarked since George Gilbert Scott's substantial restoration of the thirteenth-century structure in the 1870s. Around a thousand Morgan bibles were printed, of which only nineteen remain: one of them is displayed in the south transept along with Elizabeth I's 1549 copy of *The Book of Common Prayer*. There's also a collection of Psalters and prayer books, and in the north transept a sixteenth-century ivory Madonna said to have come from the Spanish Armada.

The church also contains a Welsh–Greek–Hebrew dictionary compiled by nineteenth-century polyglot Richard Robert Jones (usually known as **Dic Aberdaron**, after the fishing village where he was born). He lived more or less as a vagrant while acquiring command of fifteen languages (along with smatterings of another twenty) and is buried in the parish church at the bottom of the hill.

St Margaret's (Marble Church)

Bodelwyddan, off junction 25 of the A55, 2 miles west of St Asaph, LL18 5UR • No set times, but usually May–Sept daily 9am–6.30pm • Free

At Bodelwyddan, the slender 202ft limestone spire of **St Margaret's (Marble Church)** stands as a beacon over the flat coastal plain. The spire's finely worked Gothic tracery is its most impressive feature, and is continued inside where fourteen types of marble – Italian, Irish and Welsh – gave the church its name.

Bodelwyddan Castle: the National Portrait Gallery

Bodelwyddan, off junction 25 of the A55, 2 miles west of St Asaph, LL18 5YA • Generally April–Oct Tues–Thurs, Sat & Sun, plus daily in school hols 10.30am–4.30pm; Nov to mid-April Sat & Sun 10.30am–4pm, but check website or call for full opening times • £8.25 including audio tour and grounds; grounds only £6.05 • ☎ 01745 584060, ⓦ bodelwyddan-castle.co.uk

The most impressive sight in the region, **Bodelwyddan Castle** is essentially a nineteenth-century country mansion, its Victorian interiors re-created during restoration in the 1980s. It now houses one of three provincial outposts of the **National Portrait Gallery**, specializing in works contemporary with the castle. That said, much of the castle is occupied by a hotel chain: cue piped muzak, cafés and the inevitable giftshop. The landscaped **grounds** provide some escape, with a deer park, walled garden, maze, adventure playground and even a reconstructed World War I trench system – the originals were dug in the grounds to train troops for the Front.

The gallery

Most of the hundred paintings in the **gallery** are on the ground floor, approached through the "Watts Hall of Fame", a corridor lined with portraits of eminent Victorians by G.F. Watts. In the Dining Room, two portraits highlight the Pre-Raphaelite support for social reform: William Holman Hunt's portrayal of the vociferous opponent of slavery and capital punishment Stephen Lushington; and Ford Madox Brown's double portrait of Henry Farell, prime mover in the passing of the 1867 Reform Bill, and suffragette Millicent Garrett. Works by John Singer Sargent and Hubert von Herkamer also adorn the room, which, like the others, is furnished with pieces from the Victoria and Albert Museum in London.

More worthy Victorians line the library, which leads on to the Ladies' Drawing Room, with paintings of nineteenth-century society women. A grand staircase leads up to further examples of nineteenth-century portraiture.

ARRIVAL AND DEPARTURE	ST ASAPH AND AROUND

By bus St Asaph is on the #51 bus route from Rhyl to Denbigh, which also comes within a minute's walk of the Marble Church and Bodelwyddan Castle. All buses stop outside the cathedral.

Destinations Denbigh (every 30min; 15min); Rhuddlan (Mon–Sat hourly, Sun 5; 15min); and Rhyl (Mon–Sat every 30min, Sun 4; 25min).

7

ACCOMMODATION AND EATING

★**Kinmel Arms** St George, 4 miles west of St Asaph, LL22 9BP ☎ 01745 832207, ⓦ thekinmelarms.co.uk. A tastefully modernized historic inn in a pretty hamlet, offering fine Modern British dining without fuss: expect the likes of turbot with wasabi and romanesco or Menai mussels (mains £18–30). As good a reason to come are its four suites, an effortless blend of modernity and relaxed comfort. Tues–Sat noon–2.30pm & 6.30–11pm;

kitchen noon–2.30pm & 6.30–9.30pm. £135
★**Tan-yr-Onnen** Waen, 2 miles east, LL17 0DU ☎ 01745 583821, ⓦ northwalesbreaks.co.uk. Excellent rural, six-room B&B set among the green fields of the Vale of Clwyd, just off the Offa's Dyke Path. Rooms, all en suite, are comfortably stylish, finished in calming natural shades, with fluffy bathrobes as standard. £98

Colwyn Bay and around

With boats in the harbour and an architecturally intact Victorian main street, the merged towns of **COLWYN BAY** (Bae Colwyn) and **RHOS-ON-SEA**, twelve miles west of Rhyl, have marginally more charm than their eastern neighbours. There's not an amusement arcade in sight.

Harlequin Puppet Theatre

The Promenade, Rhos-on-Sea, LL28 4EP • School hols daily 3pm; 90min • £6 • ☎ 01492 548166, ⓦ puppetshow.info

One of the few remaining marionette acts in the British tradition stages shows in **Harlequin Puppet Theatre**. Britain's only dedicated marionette theatre, this cute little venue with muralled walls pitches its shows at young kids.

St Trillo's chapel

Marine Drive, Rhos Point, Rhos-on-Sea LL28 4HS • Generally Sun 11am (check the sign outside) • Free

Half a mile north of the Harlequin Puppet Theatre is the minuscule **St Trillo's chapel** – it has seating for just six worshippers, which means standing room only during services. More stone shed than religious building in appearance, the sixth-century chapel, reputedly the UK's smallest, stands above an ancient healing well. The story goes that it was from this spot that one Prince Madoc ap Owain Gwynedd embarked on a trip to America in 1170. No proof has been forthcoming of this New World adventure, three hundred years before Columbus made the journey, but that hasn't stopped a small town in Ontario being named in his honour.

ARRIVAL AND GETTING AROUND   COLWYN BAY AND AROUND

By train Trains stop in central Colwyn Bay, on Victoria Ave. Destinations Bangor (hourly; 22–34min); Llandudno Junction (every 30min; 5min); Rhyl (every 30min; 10min).
By bus Buses for Rhos-on-Sea stop on residential Rhos Rd, 1.5 miles northwest of Colwyn Bay train station.
Destinations Llandudno (every 10–20min; 15min); Rhyl

(every 10–20min; 45min).
By bike The nicest way to explore is on the Prestatyn to Rhos-on-Sea cycle path, which mostly follows the shoreline – you can rent bikes from West End Cycles, 121 Conwy Rd (Mon–Sat 9am–5.30pm; £15/half-day, £22/day; ☎01492 530269).

ACCOMMODATION AND EATING

Ellingham House 1 Woodland Park West, LL29 7DR ☎01492 533345, ⓦellinghamhouse.com. A considerable amount of care goes into the running of this elegant, traditional B&B. There are three vast rooms and two smaller upper-floor rooms, all furnished with antiques – one has a great view to the sea. **£85**
Pen-y-Bryn Pen-y-Bryn Rd; follow Kings Drive a mile inland, LL29 6DD ☎01492 533360, ⓦbrunningand price.co.uk/penybryn. Gastropub favourites such as steak and ale pie, interesting options including Sicilian fish stew (mains £12–18), changing regional beers and a relaxed but stylish atmosphere combine to create an award-winning

formula in this modern country pub with a large garden. It's uphill, behind town. Mon–Sat 11am–11pm, Sun 11am–10.30pm; kitchen Mon–Sat noon–9.30pm, Sun noon–9pm.
Plas Rhos 53 Cayley Promenade, LL28 4EP ☎01492 543698, ⓦplasrhos.co.uk. Sea views are part of the appeal at this smart five-star B&B, by the promenade; the largest, Victorian-inspired, bay-window room has the best vista (£110), but if your room is at the rear you get to enjoy the views from the terrace anyhow. Aside from the bay-window room, decor is crisp and modern. Closed Nov–Easter. **£85**

ENTERTAINMENT

Theatr Colwyn Abergele Rd, LL29 7RU ☎01492 577888, ⓦtheatrcolwyn.co.uk. Wales' oldest theatre and one of the UK's oldest cinemas (screening flicks since 1909)

has recently installed digital sound. Check the website for the schedule of films, gigs and shows.

Llandudno

Bill Bryson, writing in *Notes from a Small Island*, named **LLANDUDNO** his favourite British beach town, calling it "a fine and handsome place". And so it remains. At its core, this is one of Britain's finest examples of the genteel, purpose-built Victorian resort, and with the architectural bone-structure still in place – the grand hotels and smart townhouses, the good-looking shop facades and splendid pier – on a sunny day it offers quintessential seaside charm. Sandcastles on the beach and paddling holidaymakers; Llandudno is still a place of simple pleasures. In addition, in recent years a number of accommodation and restaurant launches has seen the town update what was threatening to become a rather tired chintz-and-doilies formula. Nowadays Llandudno is a supremely easy place in which to wander, to eat good food and to stay in comfort. Add to this two limestone hummocks – 680ft **Great Orme** and its southern cousin Little Orme, which hump up just west of the town – and **West Shore**, a strand

> ## ALICE IN LLANDUDNO
> On the tenuous grounds that Alice Liddell, the inspiration for Lewis Carroll's **Alice in Wonderland**, enjoyed her childhood holidays here, a walking trail has been created that takes in various town sights and Wonderland-related sculptures; there are 35 stops in all. The tourist office (p.400) sells maps (£2.99), or you can download the augmented reality app at ⓦalicecic.co.uk.

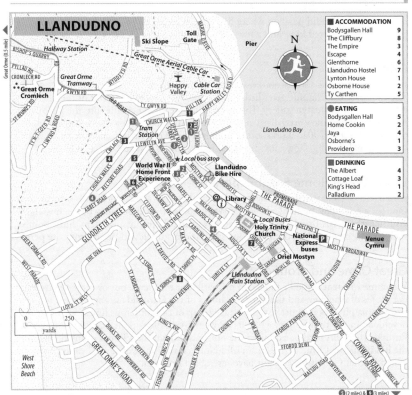

that, considering its location, comes surprisingly close to being a wild beach, and you basically have three holiday destinations in one.

Brief history

St Tudno built the monastic cell that gives Llandudno its name on **Great Orme** in the sixth century. When Victorian copper mines in the area seemed exhausted, local landowner Edward Mostyn exploited the craze for sea bathing, creating a resort for the upper-middle classes.

Within fifty years of its foundation in 1854, Llandudno had become synonymous with the Victorian ideal of a refined resort, drawing music stars such as opera singer Adelina Patti and Jules Rivière, a French conductor who sat in a gilded armchair facing the audience as he waved a bejewelled ivory baton. Mostyn Street was said to have some of the finest shops outside London, patronized by the likes of Napoléon III, Gladstone and Queen Elizabeth of Romania, who stayed here for five weeks in 1890 and reputedly gave the town its motto **Hardd, haran, hedd**, meaning "beautiful haven of peace".

The pier

North Parade, LL30 2LP • Daily: summer 9am–11pm; winter 9am–6pm • Free • ⓦ llandudnopier.com

Once the embodiment of Llandudno's ornate Victoriana, the **pier** remains a thing of joy. The longest in Wales at just under half a mile, it ticks all the requisite boxes: booths selling holiday essentials, from ice cream to buckets and spades, candy floss to shell ornaments; a splendid pavilion where brass bands once played, now home to coin-pusher games; excited kids; and a few old boys fishing for mackerel at the end.

Oriel Mostyn

12 Vaughan St, LL30 1AB • Tues–Sun 10am–4pm • Free • ☎ 01492 879201, ⓦ mostyn.org

The elaborate brick facade gives little clue to the raw, concrete interior of the refurbished **Oriel Mostyn** gallery. The revamp has breathed new life into the region's premier contemporary art gallery, named after Lady Mostyn, for whom it was originally built in 1901. Works, often from leading Welsh artists, supplemented by international touring shows, are displayed in five rooms. There's also a good shop.

World War II Home Front Experience

New St, LL30 2YF • Mid-March to Oct Mon–Sat 10am–4.30pm, Sun 10am–2pm • £3.50 • ☎ 01492 871032, ⓦ homefrontmuseum.co.uk

One for a rainy day, perhaps, the **World War II Home Front Experience** pays a nostalgic visit to early 1940s Britain, with re-created wartime shopfronts, wardens' huts, bomb shelters and the like all packed into one small room stuffed with items from the period.

Great Orme and around

You come to **Great Orme** (Y Gogarth) primarily for the views: out over the seascapes to the shores of Anglesey and the northern limits of the Carneddau range, where Snowdonia plunges into the sea. This huge lump of carboniferous limestone was developed in the Bronze Age, when its malachite-rich ore supplied copper throughout Europe. The Celts further exploited the ore, and though the Vikings didn't they gave the hill its name: Orme derives from Old Norse, meaning "worm" or "sea serpent", which is what Great Orme might have resembled from sea.

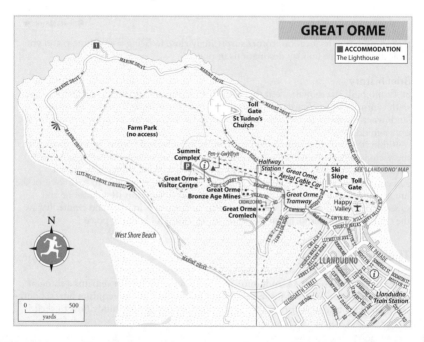

Walking aside, there are three ways to access the Orme – the **Marine Drive**, the **Great Orme Tramway** and the **cable car**. Once up there, you may be lucky enough to spot rare or endangered maritime botanical species – goldilocks aster, spotted cats-ear and spiked speedwell – or see fulmars wheel on updraughts. The feral **Kashmiri goats** that roam over the low mountain are easier to find; they are descendants of those given to Lord Mostyn as a gift by Queen Victoria.

Marine Drive

Free for walkers and cyclists; driving toll (£2.50) applies in summer (roughly 9am–8pm; winter 9am–4pm)

The easiest way to get a feel for the skirts of Great Orme, the four-mile **Marine Drive** circuit cuts into the rock high above the coast. The one-way loop starts near Llandudno's pier, has stops at various viewing points and a café at the tip. A summit side-road heads uphill a quarter of the way around.

Great Orme Tramway

Church Walks, LL30 2NB • Daily every 20min: late March & Oct 10am–5pm; April–Sept 10am–6pm • £6 single, £7.50 return • ☎ 01492 879306, ⓦ greatormetramway.co.uk.

The most atmospheric means of reaching Great Orme's summit is on the vintage **Great Orme Tramway**; the trams rattle along tracks one mile up to the top much as they have since 1902. Note that the journey is interrupted at the Halfway Station, where you change to a second tram.

Great Orme Aerial Cable Car

North Parade (Happy Valley Rd), LL30 2LP • Easter–Sept daily, roughly 10am–5pm, depending on the weather • £9 single, £9.50 return • ☎ 01492 877205

Near the base of the pier and close to the start of Marine Drive, the **Great Orme Aerial Cable Car** lifts people up to the summit – when it isn't too windy – in open four-seater cabins that glide above the formal gardens of **Happy Valley**.

Great Orme Country Park

Visitor centre LL30 2XF • Easter–Oct daily 10am–5.30pm • Free

However you arrive at Great Orme, all routes converge on the flat summit of the **Great Orme Country Park**, where there's a car park (small fee), gift shop and some uninspiring café/bars. There's also a **visitor centre** with display boards on the park's flora and fauna, including those goats; ask staff for advice about where you might find them. **Walks** are well signposted and easy to piece together using our map (see opposite): either loop around the walls of the farm park (2-mile loop; 1hr), or head down to **St Tudno's church** (1 mile return; 30min).

St Tudno's church

St Tudno's Rd, LL30 2XE • April–Oct daily 9am–5pm; Nov–March Wed, Sat & Sun 9am–5pm • Free

Small and pretty, **St Tudno's church**, once part of a substantial village, now stands isolated on the northern flank of Great Orme. The area's original church (after which Llandudno was named), it has kept some twelfth-century elements, despite later extensions and considerable restoration in the nineteenth century.

Great Orme Bronze Age Mines

Bishop's Quarry Rd, 430yd west of Halfway Station and 550yd east of visitor centre, LL30 2XG • Mid-March to Oct daily 10am–5pm • £7 • ☎ 01492 870447, ⓦ greatorememines.info

From the Great Orme Tramway's Halfway Station, it's a five-minute walk to the long-disused **Great Orme Bronze Age Mines**. The earliest workings were assumed to be Roman until excavations 200ft down in 1987 uncovered 4000-year-old animal bones that had been used as scrapers. This is one of the few sites in Britain where mineral veins were accompanied by dolomitization, a rock-softening process that enabled

7

copper to be extracted using the simple tools available in the Bronze Age, leading to Great Orme becoming the leading copper mine in Europe.

After an explanatory film, a **self-guided tour** explores some of the four miles of tunnels uncovered – enough to get a feel for the cramped working conditions. Topside, you can get an idea of how the ore was smelted to make tools.

Great Orme Cromlech

Cromlech Rd, off St Beuno's Rd, LL30 2NB, 300yd from Great Orme Tramway Halfway Station • Open access • Free

One of the most impressive remnants of the Orme's rich prehistory is the **Great Orme Cromlech** (Liety'r Filiast), a 5000-year-old Neolithic burial chamber in a field at the end of a residential road. It would have originally been covered by an earth mound.

West Shore Beach

LL30 2BG • Open access

West Shore Beach is the anithesis of Llandudno's main bay. Instead of promenaders and a pier, you have a long stretch of shingle, then sand, arcing south beneath Great Orme, all getting wilder the further you go. At low tide, the thin ribbon of pale sand expands into a vast spread; at high tide, **kitesurfers** tear across the bay. Sunsets are spectacular, conditions permitting.

ARRIVAL AND DEPARTURE LLANDUDNO

By train Direct services to Llandudno's train station arrive from Betws-y-Coed and Chester; for all other services change at Llandudno Junction, near Conwy.
Destinations Bangor (26 daily; 16–25min); Betws-y-Coed (4 daily; 45min); Blaenau Ffestiniog (6 daily; 1hr); Chester (roughly hourly; 1hr 10min); Holyhead (18 daily; 1hr 20min); Llandudno Junction (roughly every 30min; 10min).

By bus Local buses stop on either Mostyn St or Gloddaeth St opposite the *Palladium* pub, while National Express buses from Chester, Bangor and Pwllheli (bookings at the tourist office) stop at the Coach Park on Mostyn Broadway. Destinations Bangor (every 40min; 1hr); Betws-y-Coed (13 daily; 50min); Blaenau Ffestiniog (5 daily; 1hr 10min); Conwy (every 30min; 20min); Llanrwst (roughly every 30min; 35–50min); Rhyl (every 10min; 1hr 5min).

INFORMATION

Tourist office In the library, Mostyn St (Easter–Sept Mon–Sat 9am–4.30pm, Sun 9.30am–4pm, ☎01492 577577, ⍟visitllandudno.org.uk), the office is an excellent source of information on regional sights and has free maps

of Great Orme footpaths.
Internet Free access at the library on Mostyn St (Mon, Tues & Fri 9am–6pm, Wed 10am–5pm, Thurs 9am–7pm, Sat 9.30am–1pm).

GETTING AROUND

By bus Alpine runs an open-top double-decker bus (early May to Oct 10am–4pm hourly; £10 for 24hr; ☎0800 0432452) that loops between Llandudno and Conwy – it's useful for a day-trip.

By bike Llandudno Bike Hire, at Harmony House, St George's Place (☎07496 455188, ⍟llandudnobikehire. com), rents standard cycles (£15 for 7hr), including those for children and trailers, plus e-bikes (£15 for 2hr, £40 for 7hr).

ACCOMMODATION

Although Llandudno has several hundred **hotels**, you should book ahead in high summer, especially for bank holidays. Rates are often cheaper if you stay for two or more nights. St David's Rd, Deganwy Ave and Abbey Rd are your best options for inexpensive B&Bs. The nearest tent **camping** is at Conwy (see p.407).

LLANDUDNO

Bodysgallen Hall A470, 3 miles south, LL30 1RS ☎01492 584466, ⍟bodysgallen.com; map p.397. Sumptuous country accommodation – floral curtains, antique-filled rooms – in an award-winning National

Trust-owned manor-house hotel, set in 200 acres of parkland. Cottages in outbuildings are less grand and more homely than in the main building. There's a spa and two restaurants (see p.402). __£185__

★**The Cliffbury** 34 St David's Rd, LL30 2UH ☎01492

7

7

877224, ⓦ thecliffbury.co.uk; map p.397. Stylish wallpapers, sparkling bathrooms and dedicated hosts define this smart modern B&B on a quiet street, where six individually decorated rooms are regularly updated. The two bigger front suites (£80) come with DVD players. Breakfast ingredients are locally sourced where possible. Generally a two-night minimum stay. **£72**

The Empire Church Walks, LL30 2HE ⓣ 01492 860555, ⓦ empirehotel.co.uk; map p.397. This central, 54-room hotel, sensitively renovated to combine modern interior design with Victorian heritage, offers good facilities including a/c, swimming pools and a spa. The cheapest rooms face onto the inner courtyard. **£110**

Escape 48 Church Walks, LL30 2HL ⓣ 01492 877776, ⓦ escapebandb.co.uk; map p.397. One of the most celebrated B&Bs in north Wales, the *Escape* pioneered the boutique B&B experience in Llandudno. Its nine individually styled rooms are playful, offering clean-lined modernism, retro chic or feminine vintage style; book online to choose your favourite. Lovely hosts, and a guest lounge with honesty bar complete the package. **£110**

Glenthorne 2 York Rd, LL30 2EF ⓣ 01492 879591, ⓦ glenthorne-guesthousellandudno.co.uk; map p.397. Traditional, Welsh-speaking, seven-room guesthouse with great hosts who go the extra mile. It's a relaxing home from home; evening meals are available on request. Minimum two-night stay. **£70**

Llandudno Hostel 14 Charlton St, LL30 2AA ⓣ 01492 877430, ⓦ llandudnohostel.co.uk; map p.397. Family-run, friendly forty-bed hostel in the centre of town, with some twins and a family room. Sheets, towels and a continental breakfast are supplied, but there's no self-catering. It often gets full with school groups during term time, so call ahead. Dorms **£25**, twins **£60**

Lynton House 80 Church Walks, LL30 2HD ⓣ 01492 875009, ⓦ lyntonhousellandudno.co.uk; map p.397. Not only is this B&B an appealing base – the fourteen en suites (it's worth paying an extra £10 for a king-size) have pale neutral colour schemes and the owner is friendly – but the location, moments from the promenade, is excellent at the price. **£74**

★**Osborne House** 17 North Parade, LL30 2LP ⓣ 01492 860330, ⓦ osbornehouse.com; map p.397. Come to this seafront hotel for its spectacular Belle Epoque flamboyance – antique beds and marble bathrooms in six vast suites, all of them elegant rather than kitsch. Some rooms overlook the Promenade. There's a very good restaurant attached. **£155**

★**Ty Carthen** 12 Abbey Rd, LL30 2EA ⓣ 01492 875886, ⓦ tycarthenbandb.co.uk; map p.397. This Grade II-listed Georgian house on a quiet street provides an elegant, relaxing stay. The style is arty and distinctly Welsh: there's Welsh art on the walls and Welsh blankets in beautifully furnished guest bedrooms. Very nice hosts, too. Reservations recommended. Closed Dec. **£75**

GREAT ORME

The Lighthouse Marine Drive, LL30 2XD ⓣ 01492 876819, ⓦ lighthouse-llandudno.co.uk; map p.398. Though overpriced in terms of decor and facilities, this former lighthouse at the tip of Great Orme makes an eccentric, escapist stay. Seascapes come as standard – book the Lamp Room if you can – and the lounge is full of odd nautical knick-knacks. **£170**

EATING

As a major resort, Llandudno offers a good choice of restaurants. **Upper Mostyn St** has emerged as the foodie strip – it can be crowded at weekends. The town also has a couple of good **gastropubs** in the *Cottage Loaf* and *The Albert* (see opposite).

Bodysgallen Hall A470, 3 miles south, LL30 1RS ⓣ 01492 584466, ⓦ bodysgallen.com; map p.397. There's a modern bistro in the old coach house, *1620*, but really you're here for formal dining in the hall of a seventeenth-century manor (see p.400). Its Modern British dishes rank among the best in north Wales; expect the likes of slow-cooked local lamb with fennel pollen and smoked red pepper purée (£45 for two courses; £25.50 on Mon, when the atmosphere is more relaxed). It's a grand spot for afternoon tea, too (Mon–Sat 3.30–5.30pm, Sun 4–5.30pm; £24). Reservations and smart(ish) dress required. Daily 12.30–1.45pm & 7–9pm.

Home Cookin 139 Upper Mostyn St, LL30 2PE ⓣ 01492 876585, ⓦ homecookin-llandudno.co.uk; map p.397. A small modern bistro that's highly rated by locals because it does exactly what it says – light lunches, classics, bistro dishes (grilled salmon with a creamy tarragon Hollandaise sauce, say) and good veggie dishes such as sweet potato and spinach curry (£9.35) – all freshly cooked and at competitive prices. Daily 10.30am–9.30pm.

Jaya 36 Church Walks, LL30 2HN ⓣ 01492 818198, ⓦ jayarestaurant.co.uk; map p.397. You probably didn't come to Llandudno for a curry. However, this gets the nod from food critics for its short menu of authentic north Indian and Kenyan home cooking; there's no chicken tikka masala here. Mains £10.95–13.95. Thurs–Sat 6.30–9pm.

Osborne's 17 North Parade, LL30 2LP ⓣ 01492 860330, ⓦ osbournehouse.co.uk; map p.397. Opulent café and restaurant lit by chandeliers, with modern dishes the likes of slow-roast lamb or sea bass with garlic and crushed peas (£14.95). Come early for a cocktail. Lunch menus are lighter, and afternoon teas (Mon–Sat 3.30–5.30pm, Sun 4–5.30pm) splendid. Mon–Thurs & Sun 10.30am–9.30pm, Fri & Sat 10. 30am–10pm.

★**Providero** 112 Upper Mostyn St, LL30 2SW ☎01492 338220, ⓦ providero.co.uk; map p.397. A community-funded endeavour, launched in 2017, this buzzy, hip café,

with eclectic, industrial decor, epitomizes the new mood shaking Llandudno out of its Victorian schtick. Go for sharing platters and soups of the day with local artisan bread (£4.50), plus excellent coffee and tea. Mon–Thurs 8am–6pm, Fri 8am–9pm, Sat 9am–9pm, Sun 10am–4pm

DRINKING

The Albert 56 Madoc St, LL30 2TW ☎01492 877188, ⓦ albertllandudno.co.uk; map p.397. What looks like a standard-issue pub also provides good-value pub grub – blackboard specials range from local sausages and mash to home-made gnocchi with Mediterranean veg and sun-dried tomatoes (£11–15) – along with great Sun roasts and several fresh local ales. Daily 11.30am–10pm or later; kitchen noon–9pm.

★**Cottage Loaf** Market St, LL30 2SR ☎01492 870762, ⓦ the-cottageloaf.co.uk; map p.397. The best pub in town offers a slice of the country in the heart of Llandudno, all traditional beams and fireplaces in the front and a bright backroom decorated with nautical paintings and old maps. The modern British gastropub menu is the best in town (mains £12–17) and the cask

ales are local. Daily 11am–11pm; kitchen noon–9pm.

King's Head Old Rd, LL30 2NB ☎01492 877993, ⓦ kingsheadllandudno.co.uk; map p.397. Llandudno's oldest boozer – a snug cocoon beside the tram terminus – is a pleasant corner for a quiet pint. The menu serves substantial bar meals including home-made pies, fish and chips and pasta (mains £10–14). Mon–Thurs & Sun noon–11pm, Fri & Sat noon–midnight.

Palladium 7 Gloddaeth St, LL30 2DD ☎01492 863920, ⓦ jdwetherspoon; map p.397. It's a Wetherspoon pub, so expect uninspiring meals and discounted beer – but the building, an old theatre with its stalls and wonderful ceiling intact, is impressive. Daily 9am–midnight or later.

ENTERTAINMENT

Venue Cymru The Promenade, LL30 1BB ☎01492 872000, ⓦ venuecymru.co.uk; map p.397. North Wales' premier live entertainment centre, this modern 1500-seat

theatre lures a good range of touring companies and occasional international acts.

Conwy

CONWY, a highlight of the north coast, packs a lot into a small town. Its belt of town walls encloses not just a superb early medieval **castle** but some fascinating glimpses into the past of north Wales. Factor in its marvellous setting, abundant accommodation and flourishing restaurants and shopping, and you have the ideal base for a few days' exploring the Lower Conwy Valley and surrounding coast.

Its **setting** on the Conwy estuary, backed by a forested fold of Snowdonia, has proved irresistible to painters and photographers ever since Englishman Paul Sandby published his *Views of North Wales* in 1776. Nothing within Conwy's predominantly Victorian core is more than 200yd from the town walls, which makes it wonderfully easy to potter around. You can tick off the castle, march along the town ramparts and poke around Elizabethan townhouse **Plas Mawr** and **Britain's smallest house**, all in one busy day. But don't be surprised if you want to linger.

Brief history

For centuries the Conwy estuary provided a good living for the families who held mussel-gathering rights on the sands, while the Cistercian monastery of **Aberconwy**, established in 1172, attended to spiritual needs. A century later the monastery was moved eight miles upriver to Maenan, near Llanrwst, to make way for **Conwy Castle**, the strongest link in Edward I's chain of fortresses. During incursions along Wales' north coast, Edward I's Anglo-Norman ancestors never managed to establish a bridgehead west of the Conwy River. Accordingly, once over the river in 1283, Edward established another of his bastide towns, from which the Welsh were mostly excluded for well over a century.

Conwy Castle

Rose Hill St, LL32 8LD • Daily: March–June, Sept & Oct 9.30am–5pm; July & Aug 9.30am–6pm; Nov–March 10am–4pm • £8.95; joint ticket with Plas Mawr £10.95; CADW • ☎ 01492 592358, ⓦ cadw.gov.wales/daysout/conwycastle

Edward I chose a strategic knoll at the mouth of the Conwy River for the site of **Conwy Castle**, built in just five years by James of St George. Overlooked by a low hill, the castle appears less easily defensible than others along the coast, but James constructed eight massive towers in a rectangle around two wards separated by a drawbridge and portcullis, and added turrets atop the four eastern towers.

Bar a brief siege during the Welsh uprising of 1294, the castle saw little action until 1399, when Richard II stayed there on his return from Ireland. He was lured from safety by the Earl of Northumberland, Bolingbroke's vassal. Northumberland swore in the castle's chapel to grant Richard safe passage, but imprisoned him at Flint, enabling Bolingbroke to become Henry IV. From the fifteenth century, the castle fell into disuse, but was refortified for the Civil War. At the restoration of the monarchy in 1665, the castle was stripped of all its iron, wood and lead, and left as it is today.

The interior

Strolling along the ramparts, you can look down onto something unique among the Iron Ring fortresses, a roofless but largely intact **interior**. The outer ward's 130ft-long Great Hall and the King's Apartments are well preserved, but the only part of the castle to have kept its roof is the **Chapel Tower**, named for the small room built into the wall

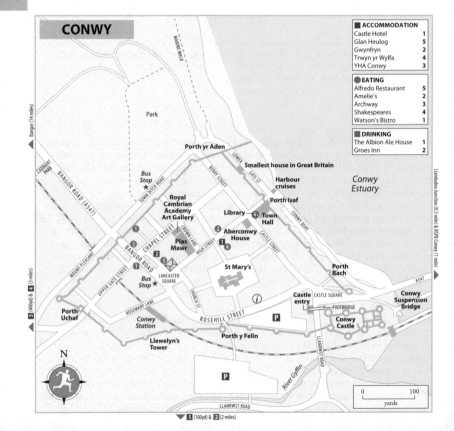

CONWY

ACCOMMODATION

Castle Hotel	1
Glan Heulog	5
Gwynfryn	2
Trwyn yr Wylfa	4
YHA Conwy	3

EATING

Alfredo Restaurant	5
Amelie's	2
Archway	3
Shakespeares	4
Watson's Bistro	1

DRINKING

The Albion Ale House	1
Groes Inn	2

THE IRON RING

Dotting the north Wales coast, a day's march from each other, Edward I's fearsome **Iron Ring** of castles represents Europe's most ambitious and concentrated medieval building project, designed to prevent the recurrence of two hugely expensive military campaigns (see p.431). After Edward's first successful campaign in 1277, he was able to pin down his adversary, **Llywelyn ap Gruffydd** ("the Last"), in Snowdonia and Anglesey, gaining space and time to build the now largely ruined castles at **Flint**, **Rhuddlan**, **Builth Wells** and **Aberystwyth**, and consolidate his grip by confiscating and upgrading several Welsh castles.

Although Llewellyn's second uprising (1282) also failed, Edward was determined not to have to fight a third time for the same land, and set about extending his Iron Ring in an immensely costly display of English might, which – together with the Treaty of Rhuddlan (1284) – effectively crushed Welsh resistance. **Harlech**, **Caernarfon** and **Conwy** are nearly contemporaneous, yet manifest a unique progression towards the later, highly evolved concentric design of **Beaumaris**. All these castles (and the town walls of Caernarfon and Conwy) were built by **James of St George d'Espéranche** – the master military architect of his age – whose work at Conwy, Caernarfon, Harlech and Beaumaris is now recognized with **UNESCO World Heritage Site** status.

Each castle was integrated with a **bastide town** – an idea borrowed from Gascony in France, where Edward I was duke – the town and castle being mutually reliant on each other for protection and trade. The bastides were always populated with English settlers, and the Welsh were only permitted to enter during the day, but not to trade and certainly not to carry arms. It wasn't until the eighteenth century that the Welsh would have towns they could truly call their own.

7

with a carved semicircular apse. The floor below holds a small exhibition on religious life. More appealing, perhaps, is the brilliant view from the **King's Tower**.

Conwy Suspension Bridge

Conwy, LL32 8LD · Mid-March to Oct daily 11am–5pm · Tollhouse £1; NT · ☎ 01492 573282, ⓦ nationaltrust.org.uk/conwy-suspension-bridge

Anchored to the castle walls as if it were a drawbridge, Thomas Telford's slender **Conwy Suspension Bridge** was actually part of an 1826 road improvement scheme. Contemporaneous with his Menai Strait bridge, it mimics the crenellations of the battlements above to compensate for spoiling the view of the castle immortalized by J.M.W. Turner. The bridge was used until 1958 and now serves as a footbridge linking the town to a **tollhouse**, furnished as it would have been in around 1900.

The town walls

The 30ft-high **town walls** branch out from the castle into a three-quarter-mile-long circuit around Conwy's core. Inaccessible from the castle they were designed to protect, the walls are punctuated by 21 evenly spaced horseshoe towers, as well as twelve latrines that bulge out from the wall-walk. Only half of the distance can be walked – the best section being from Porth Uchaf to Porth yr Aden, with great views over the town to the castle and estuary beyond.

Conwy Quay

Conwy's river and town walls meet beside the boats at **Conwy Quay**. It's a popular spot on sunny days, with kids dangling crabbing lines (buy yours, plus bait and a bucket, from Conwy Mussels beside the boatyard), adults sipping beers outside the *Liverpool Arms* and everyone eating locally made ice cream from *Parisella's* kiosk. This is also the embarkation point for regular **harbour cruises** (May–Sept every 30min; £6.50; ☎ 07917 343058). Wait for those aboard the *Princess Christine* – it's an open boat, so provides the best views.

Smallest house in Great Britain

Lower Gate St, LL32 8BE • Easter to mid-Oct daily 10am–5pm • £2 • ☎ 01492 573965, ⓦ thesmallesthouse.co.uk

The self-proclaimed **smallest house in Great Britain** is wedged between two terraces, one of them now demolished. The two tiny rooms combined are just 9ft high and 6ft wide, the door taking up a quarter of the frontage. Most people will have to duck to get in, a problem that vexed the last resident, a 6ft 3in-tall fisherman, until he left around 1900.

Aberconwy House

1 Castle St, LL32 8AY • March–June, Sept & Oct daily 11am–5pm; July & Aug daily 10am–5pm; Nov & Dec Sat & Sun noon–3pm • £3.40; NT • ☎ 01492 592246, ⓦ nationaltrust.org.uk/aberconwy-house

Timber-and-stone **Aberconwy House** is Conwy's sole surviving medieval building, dating from about 1300. Built for a wealthy merchant, it saw service as a bakery, antique shop, sea captain's house and temperance hotel – various incarnations which are re-created in rooms furnished with a collection of rural furniture on loan from the Museum of Wales. Visits start with an introductory film in the attic, and finish in the kitchen.

Plas Mawr

20 High St, LL32 8DE • April–Sept daily 9.30am–5pm; Oct Tues–Sun 9.30am–4pm • £6.50, joint ticket with castle £10.95; CADW • ☎ 01492 580167, ⓦ cadw.gov.wales/daysout/plasmawr

Conwy's grandest residence is the splendid **Plas Mawr**, or "great mansion", one of the best-preserved Elizabethan townhouses in Britain. It was built in a Dutch style for Robert Wynn of Gwydir Castle, a flamboyant character who was one of the first native Welsh to live in the town; he returned to the area after mixing at European courts. The main part of the house dates from 1576, with features such as the gatehouse added some ten years later to augment the grand effect. In the Great Hall, the plaster overmantel, repainted in its original colours, was designed to impress visitors with Wynn's noble credentials – especially his descent from the Princes of Gwynedd – and much of the superb plasterwork throughout relates to the Wynn dynasty. The exception is in the Great Chamber, presumably so as not to upstage visiting royalty. A self-guided tour – aided by an excellent recorded commentary – concludes with an exhibition about contemporaraneous attitudes to cleanliness that's compulsively gory.

Royal Cambrian Academy Art Gallery

Crown Lane, LL32 8AN • Tues–Sat 11am–5pm • Free • ☎ 01492 593413, ⓦ rcaconwy.org

The **Royal Cambrian Academy Art Gallery**, just behind Plas Mawr, is home to the Royal Cambrian Academy, a group aiming to foster art in Wales. At its best during the annual summer exhibition, the airy, well-lit galleries display work by the Academy members, almost all of them Welsh or working in Wales.

WALKS AROUND CONWY

Conwy Mountain (2 miles return; 1hr; 650ft ascent). One of Conwy's best short walks heads onto the gorse-, bracken- and heather-covered slopes of Conwy Mountain, and the 800ft Penmaenbach and Alltwen peaks behind, all giving fantastic views right along the coast. It starts at a small car park on Mountain Road, reached by following Cadnant Park off Bangor Road just outside the town walls.

Marine Walk (800yd return; 20min; flat). It is hard to beat a simple stroll along the Conwy Estuary. Start at the northern end of Conwy Quay and simply follow the path to Coed Bodlondeb, a woodland nature reserve where you might see nuthatches and jays.

RSPB Conwy

Off the A55, 1 mile east of Conwy, near Llandudno Junction, LL31 9XY • Daily 9.30am–5pm; free 1hr guided walks Sat 11am • £5, binocular rental £3 • ☎ 01492 584091, ⓦ rspb.org.uk/conwy

It's hard to imagine that what is now the **RSPB Conwy** wetland reserve was in the early 1990s a 3000-ton heap of silt dumped after the creation of the A55 Expressway tunnel. What you'll see depends on the season, but the star feathered species include black-tailed godwit, shelducks, lapwings and sedge warblers. You may also spot stoats, dragonflies and much more. The **lakes** are a tidal roost, so there's usually more birdlife when high tide forces birds off the adjacent estuary. The traffic noise near the visitor centre is another reason to rent a pair of binoculars and stroll along the boardwalks, spending quiet time in the hides; the longest two-mile trail provides great views. At least hang out in the café with its big windows overlooking the lake and reed beds, with telescopes trained on whatever is interesting that day – there's a great kids' playground just outside.

ARRIVAL AND DEPARTURE
CONWY

By train Llandudno Junction, less than a mile east across the river, serves as the main train station for services from Chester to Holyhead, as well as for trains heading south to Betws-y-Coed and Blaenau Ffestiniog. Only slow, regional services stop in Conwy itself (on request).
Destinations Bangor (10 daily; 20min); Holyhead (10 daily; 50min); Llandudno Junction (12 daily; 4min).
By bus Local buses stop either on Lancaster Square or outside the town walls on Town Ditch Rd. National Express

coaches go from Llandudno.
Destinations Bangor (every 15min; 40min); Betws-y-Coed (7 daily; 50min); Llandudno (every 30min; 15min); Rowen (4 daily; 13min).
By car There's no visitor on-street parking in central Conwy. There's a car park opposite the tourist office on Rosehill St (4hr for £4.50) and a cheaper long-stay option further south on Llanrwst Rd (8hr for £3.50).

INFORMATION AND GETTING AROUND

Tourist office Near the castle on Rosehill St (June–Aug Mon–Fri 9.30am–5.30pm, Sat & Sun 10am–5pm; Sept–May Mon–Fri 9.30am–5pm, Sat & Sun 10am–4pm; ☎ 01492 577566, ⓦ visitllandudno.org.uk).
Internet In the library, Castle St (Mon, Thurs & Fri

10am–5.30pm, Tues 10am–7pm, Sat 10am–1pm).
By bus Alpine runs an open-top double-decker bus service looping from Conwy to Llandudno and back (early May to Oct hourly 10am–4pm; £10 for 24hr; ☎ 0800 043 2452) – perfect for a day-trip.

ACCOMMODATION

In addition to the good options in and around town, a couple of places in the nearby village of **Rowen** make very viable alternatives (see p.408).

HOTEL AND GUESTHOUSES
Castle Hotel 5 High St, LL32 8DB ☎ 01492 582800, ⓦ castlewales.co.uk. A modernized central coaching inn that positively creaks with character. The 27 rooms have been renovated with sly flamboyance without abandoning the hotel's historic appeal. Free central parking for guests and a great restaurant (see p.408). Online booking yields cheaper rates. **£140**
Glan Heulog Llanrwst Rd, LL32 8LT ☎ 01492 593845, ⓦ conwy-bedandbreakfast.co.uk. Modern floral wallpapers, country charm and friendly owners make this one of Conwy's best small guesthouses; a Victorian house with six en suites (from £68), including family rooms, and one room with a private adjacent bathroom. It's 0.5 mile out on the B5106 Trefriw road. **£65**
★**Gwynfryn** 4 York Place, LL32 8AB ☎ 01492 576733, ⓦ gwynfrynbandb.co.uk. Two options in a central B&B: five eclectically furnished en suites in the main house, plus

slightly smaller and softly minimal rooms in the Vestry behind. All have a small fridge; those in the main house have DVD players and access to a film library. "Superiors" have more space, views and bathtubs (£88). **£78**

HOSTEL AND CAMPSITE
Trwyn yr Wylfa Conwy Old Rd, Penmaenmaw, 3 miles west, LL34 6SF ☎ 01492 650672, ⓦ tywcampingsite .co.uk. Sea views span the horizon below the gently sloping fields of this site – the name translates as "Watching Point". Modern facilities, rental tents and glamping options (minimum two nights, late May to Sept). Closed late Oct to Easter. Camping **£16**, rented tents **£45**, glamping **£60**
YHA Conwy Lark Hill, LL32 8AJ ☎ 0345 371 9732, ⓦ yha .org.uk/hostel/conwy. Spacious, recently refurbished hostel a 15min walk uphill from the centre. The purpose-built 1970s' block, with large windows, offers great views to the castle and inland down a valley, and the bright two- and

7

four-bunk rooms, twins and family rooms are all en suite. Good-value meals include an excellent £5 buffet breakfast, and it's licensed. Reservations recommended. Check-in in the afternoon only. Dorms **£21.99**, twins **£70**

EATING

Alfredo Restaurant Lancaster Square, LL32 8DA ☎01492 592381. It's a throwback to the 1970s decor-wise, but no one seems to care in this ever-popular Italian restaurant. A reliable spot for good-value pizza and pasta (£9–10), and respectable mains like steak in a creamy mushroom sauce (£17). Mon–Sat 6–10pm.

Amelie's 10 High St, LL32 8DB ☎01492 583142. A local institution, this lovely upstairs bistro offers home-made soups, light, fresh lunches – butternut squash with quinoa in a tomato and chilli sauce, perhaps, or salmon and spinach fishcakes (£11) – and coffee and home-made cake. Weekend evening meals have a French accent, with the likes of chicken cassoulet (£14). Tues–Thurs 11.30am–3pm & 6–9pm, Fri & Sat 10am–9pm.

Archway 12 Bangor Rd, LL32 8NH ☎01492 592458. Quality fish-and-chip restaurant for a cheap meal. Everything is cooked to order to eat in the modern café, which has a vintage industrial theme, or to take away – perfect for the quay on a summer evening. Mon–Thurs 11.30am–2pm &

4.30–8pm, Fri–Sun 11.30am–8.30pm.

Shakespeares Castle Hotel, 5 High St, LL32 8DB ☎01492 582800, ⊚castlewales.co.uk. Good hotel restaurant, using quality ingredients in seasonal dishes. Start with an aperitif then browse the Modern British menu: expect dishes like Conwy mussels in a white wine garlic and herb sauce (£12.95). The bar, *Dawson's*, offers cheaper dishes such as haddock and chorizo risotto for under £10. Daily: restaurant 6–11pm; bar noon–11pm.

★**Watson's Bistro** Chapel St, LL32 8BP ☎01492 596326, ⊚watsonsbistroconwy.co.uk. With a terrace beneath the town walls, this place offers the best eating in town, locals say – modern dishes like pan-roasted hake with spinach, shrimp and a herb glaze (£16.50). Local ingredients feature strongly and vegetarian options are excellent. Good-value two-/three-course lunch and early dinner menus (£13.50/£17.95). Wed, Thurs & Sun noon–2pm & 5.30–8.30pm, Fri & Sat noon–2pm & 5.30–9pm.

DRINKING

★**The Albion Ale House** Corner of Upper Gate St, LL32 8RF ☎01492 582484, ⊚albionalehouse.weebly.com. Four local breweries, including the excellent Conwy Brewery, joined forces to run this Grade II-listed pub. There's no muzak and no TVs, just eight ales on tap, bar snacks (including local pies), open fires and the charm of a wooden Art Nouveau interior that's as shiny as a conker. Mon–Thurs & Sun noon–11pm, Fri & Sat noon–midnight.

Groes Inn Tyn-y-Groes, 2 miles south on the B5106 to Llanrwst, LL32 8TN ☎01492 650545, ⊚groesinn.com. Good food and cask ales in a pub dating to 1573 – it's said to be the oldest licensed house in Wales. Mains like haddock and salmon fishcakes or ox cheek and mash cost £11–17. March–Oct Mon–Sat noon–11pm, Sun noon–10.30pm; Nov–Feb Tues–Sat noon–11pm, Sun noon–10.30pm; kitchen March–Oct daily noon–8pm; Nov–Feb Tues–Sun noon–8pm.

Around Conwy

There are many reasons to linger in Conwy, not least its surrounding attractions. Llandudno – a pleasing beachy counterpart to this medieval townscape – is a quick day-trip away (see p.396), while idyllic **Rowen** village, the unlikely **Surf Snowdonia** and the glorious formal **Bodnant Garden** are all within easy reach.

Rowen

Five miles south of Conwy on the eastern slopes of the Carneddau range, the tiny mountainside hamlet of **ROWEN** is one of the prettiest in the area, composed of a few cottages, a post office, a chapel and the excellent **Tŷ Gwyn** pub. The adjacent public telephone box contains leaflets of walks in the area. If you don't mind the drive into Conwy, *Tir y Coed* and the *YHA Rowen* hostel make good bases for the area.

ACCOMMODATION AND EATING   ROWEN

★**Tir y Coed** 300m east of village centre, LL32 8TP ☎01492 650219, ⊚tirycoed.com. This small hotel has

bags of style, whether in spacious doubles – some classic, some offering quietly modern glam – or the large Rowen

Suite (£185), yet it remains as relaxed as you'd hope of a small country five-star. The in-house restaurant is excellent. **£135**

★**Tŷ Gwyn** Rowen village centre, LL32 8YU ☏01492 650232. Life doesn't get much better than a sunny evening spent sitting outside this lovely village pub. There's a friendly atmosphere, honest home-made food – pub classics plus seafood gratin, fresh Llŷn peninsula lobster or roast lamb (mains £9–19) – and a pretty beer garden beside a stream. June–Sept Mon–Wed 4pm–midnight, Thurs–Sun noon–midnight; Oct–May Mon–Fri 4pm–midnight, Sat & Sun noon–midnight; kitchen June–Sept Mon–Wed 6–9pm; Thurs–Sun noon–2pm & 6–9pm; Oct–May Mon–Fri 6–9pm, Sat & Sun noon–2pm & 6–9pm.

YHA Rowen A mile up a very steep hill above the village, LL32 8YW ☏0345 371 9038, ⓦ yha.org.uk/hostel/rowen. Perhaps the ultimate retreat hereabouts – all silence and vast views across the Conwy Valley – in a former farmhouse on the flanks of the Carneddau range. Just ten beds, self-catering only. Reach it by turning right 200yd beyond the pub. Check-in after 5pm. Closed Oct–April. **£14.99**

Surf Snowdonia

Dolgarrog, 7 miles south of Conwy, LL32 8QE • Daily 10am–sunset • Freesurf from £40/hr, lessons from £45/hr (both beginners, includes equipment); Crash & Splash £25/hr (wetsuit rental £5) • ☏01492 353123, ⓦ surfsnowdonia.com • #19 bus from Conwy (roughly hourly; 20min)

Think Snowdonia, think mountains. Yet an audacious project has turned the lush Conwy Valley south of Rowen into an unlikely surfing destination – the world's first public surfing lagoon, **Surf Snowdonia**, was launched in 2016 on the site of a former aluminium smelting plant in the otherwise unremarkable village of Dolgarrog. Generated by a sort of underwater snowplough, the waves in the 1000ft-pool range from waist-high for beginners to head-high for advanced surfers. Equipment rental and lessons are available, and there's an aquatic adventure playground, Crash & Splash, and **accommodation** in camping pods (£70). Even if you're not into surfing, it's worth a visit simply to sit in the glass-walled **café** and watch the waves roar past.

Bodnant Garden and around

Tal-y-Cafn, off the A470, 8 miles south of Conwy, LL28 5RE • March to mid-Oct daily 10am–5pm (till 8pm Wed May–Aug); late Oct–Feb daily 10am–4pm • £12; NT • ☏01492 650460, ⓦ nationaltrust.org.uk/bodnant-garden • #25 bus from Llandudno and Llandudno Junction (Mon–Sat 5 daily; 25min)

During May and June, the 160ft laburnum tunnel blooms and rhododendrons are in flower all over the formal **Bodnant Garden**, one of the loveliest in Britain. Laid out in 1875 around Bodnant Hall (closed to the public) by its then owner, English industrialist Henry Pochin, the garden spreads over one hundred acres of the Conwy Valley, divided into an upper terraced garden and lower pinetum and wild garden. Shrubs and plants provide a blaze of colour throughout late spring and summer, but autumn is just as spectacular, with hydrangeas still in bloom and fruit trees shedding their leaves. Set aside half a day to fully appreciate the place.

EATING   **BODNANT GARDEN**

Bodnant Welsh Food Centre Tal-y-Cafn, off the A470, 9 miles south of Conwy, LL28 5RP ☏01492 651100, ⓦ bodnant-welshfood.co.uk. For foodies, one good reason to visit the Bodnant estate is the Bodnant Welsh Food Centre, a mile south of Bodnant Garden. It was opened in 2014 to showcase regional produce in a superb delicatessen – there's also an outlet of the National Beekeeping Centre of Wales here. It's an excellent option to stock up for a picnic or self-catering. March–Sept Mon–Sat 9.30am–5.30pm, Sun 10am–4.30pm.

Bangor

After a few days in mid-Wales or the mountains of Snowdonia, **BANGOR** hits you like a city. In fact, it's not big, but as the largest town in Gwynedd and home to **Bangor University**, which dominates the skyline, it passes for cosmopolitan in these parts. Aside from a couple of sights or perhaps a trip to the shops (don't get excited), there's little to detain you – Bangor only receives a trickle of summer visitors. In contrast to the largely English-speaking resorts on the north coast, Bangor is generally Welsh-speaking.

The cathedral

Cathedral Close, LL57 1RL · Mon–Thurs 10.30am–4.30pm, Fri & Sat 10.30am–1pm · Free

Christians have worshipped on this site since 530, when a nobleman established a church here within a "bangor" – a fence of poles and woven branches. That monastic cell developed into a **cathedral**; a hint of its ancient origins can be gleaned from the blocked-in window dating from the Norman rebuilding of 1071. The rest of the structure is the result of reconstructions after being sacked by King John (1211), Edward I (1277) and Owain Glyndŵr (1402), with heavy-handed touches by George Gilbert Scott in 1866.

The spacious interior houses the sixteenth-century wooden **Mostyn Christ**, depicted bound and seated on a rock. Look, too, for the arched tomb in the south transept said to contain the remains of Owain Gwynedd, although the story goes that after Gwynedd was posthumously excommunicated for incest with his first cousin, the Bishop of Bangor was asked to remove his body from the cathedral.

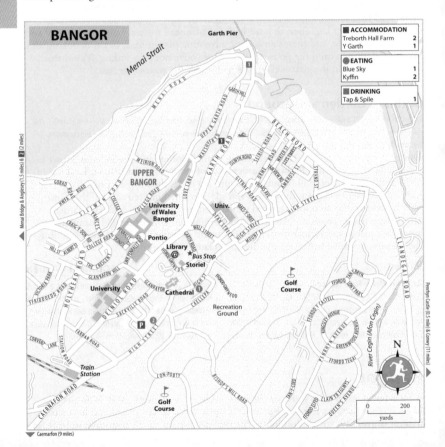

Storiel

Ffordd Gwynedd, LL57 1DT • Tues–Sat 11am–5pm • Free • ☎ 01248 353368

At **Storiel**, Gwnedd's regional museum and gallery, standard exhibits are enlivened by collections from Bangor Univsersity, including traditional costumes and an archeology room containing the most complete Roman sword found in Wales. Other rooms cover three hundred years of acquisitions, from a set of furniture from a moderately wealthy Criccieth farm to fine Italian pieces. There's also a small art gallery concentrating on Welsh contemporary works.

Garth Pier

Garth Rd, LL57 2SW • Mon–Fri 8.30am–dusk, Sat & Sun 10am–dusk • 50p (honesty box)

North of the centre, there's a fine view of Telford's bridge from Bangor's Victorian **Garth Pier**, which juts 1550ft into the Menai Strait – more than halfway across to Anglesey. Though it's a fifteen-minute walk from the town centre, it feels many miles removed – a good place to watch the world drift by.

7

Penrhyn Castle

Llandygai, off the A5, 2 miles east of central Bangor, LL57 4HN • House: March–Oct daily noon–5pm; gardens & Industrial Railway Museum: March–Oct 11am–5pm; Nov–Feb 11am–3pm • £11.80, gardens & Industrial Railway Museum only £7.90; NT • ☎ 01248 363219, ⓦ nationaltrust.org.uk/penrhyn-castle • Buses #5, #6, #67 and #75 run frequently from Bangor to Penrhyn's gates, from where it is a mile to the house

The awkward truth of **Penrhyn Castle**, a vast nineteenth-century neo-Norman fancy, built on the huge profits of a Welsh slate mine, is that it's testament to the gentry's exploitation of the rural Welsh. It also shows that the Victorians did nothing by halves – opulent doesn't begin to cover it.

The house was built by Richard Pennant, a Caribbean sugar plantation owner, slave trader and vehement anti-abolitionist. The first Baron Penrhyn, he built a port on the northeastern edge of Bangor to ship his Bethesda slate. But it was his self-aggrandizing great-great-nephew, George Dawkins, who inherited the 40,000-acre estate and transformed the neo-Gothic hall in the 1830s, encasing it within a Norman-style fortress with a five-storey keep. Leave time for the superb **gardens** – brilliant for children, with space to roam and trees to climb – and the excellent **café**.

The interior

Overblown it may be, but the **interior** decoration is undeniably impressive. Dawkins' architect, Thomas Hopper, even looked to Norman architecture for the furniture, but succumbed to mod cons for a central heating system which went through twenty tons of coal a month. Everything is on a massive scale, no more so than in the **Great Hall** and **Grand Staircase**. Upstairs, you'll see original William Morris wallpaper and drapes around the King's Bed – the Slate Bed was designed for Queen Victoria but she preferred a Hopper-designed four-poster in the **State Bedroom**. Away from the pomp you can visit the enormous **kitchens**; in peak season a costumed cook is usually bustling away.

A visit also takes in what was the country's largest private **painting collection**. In the two dining rooms there's a Gainsborough landscape, Canaletto's *The Thames at Westminster* and a Rembrandt portrait. During the Blitz of 1940, some 1800 masterpieces from London's National Gallery were sent here for safekeeping; apparently, the gallery's curators had second thoughts when Lord Penrhyn stumbled drunk among the canvases one evening. When he then demanded rental payments, prime minister Winston Churchill ordered the treasures to be moved to a former slate mine at Manod for the rest of the war.

Industrial Railway Museum

The castle's stable block houses the **Industrial Railway Museum**, packed with gleaming rolling stock that once hauled slate on the estate's quarry-to-port rail line. The star is the 1848 *Fire Queen*, a very early loco built for the Padarn Railway in Llanberis and retired in the 1880s.

ARRIVAL AND DEPARTURE   BANGOR

By train All trains on the north coast line between Chester and Holyhead stop at Bangor's train station on Station Rd, at the south end of Holyhead Rd.
Destinations Chester (roughly every 30min; 1hr 10min); Colwyn Bay (roughly hourly; 30min); Conwy (12 daily; 17min); Holyhead (22 daily; 30–40min); Llandudno Junction (roughly every 30min; 20min); Rhosneigr (9 daily;

25min).
By bus National Express and local buses stop in the centre of town on a short spur off Garth Rd.
Destinations Beaumaris (every 30min; 20–35min); Caernarfon (every 15min; 30min); Conwy (every 15min; 30min); Holyhead (hourly; 1hr 15min); Llanberis (hourly; 30–45min); Llandudno (every 15min; 1hr)

INFORMATION

Tourist information Limited tourist information is available from the Storiel (see p.411).
Internet Free access at the library, on Ffordd Gwynedd

(Mon, Tues, Thurs & Fri 9.30am–7pm, Wed & Sat 9.30am–1pm) and at the *Blue Sky* restaurant (see below).

ACCOMMODATION

The range of accommodation isn't huge and there's little reason to stop overnight. Most of the cheaper options are at the northern end of **Garth Road**, a 20min walk from the train station.

Treborth Hall Farm A487, 1.8 miles southwest of upper Bangor between the two Menai Strait bridges, LL57 2RX ☎01248 364104, ⓦtreborthleisure.co.uk. The nearest campsite to town is relaxed and well kept, partly enclosed by an old walled garden. Coin-operated showers. The #5 bus service passes the entrance. Closed Nov–March. **£13**

Y Garth Garth Rd, LL57 2RT ☎01248 362277, ⓦthegarthguesthouse.co.uk. Nothing to wow you, but probably the best value in the town centre, this decent B&B has ten rooms – en-suite doubles/twins and family options – and prides itself on its breakfast. "You won't eat till tea time", they promise. **£65**

EATING

★Blue Sky Rear of 236 High St, LL57 1PA (passage beside G Williams butcher) ☎01248 355444, ⓦblueskybangor.co.uk. Bangor's finest by a long shot and reason enough to stop at Bangor. The casual mood of the small room belies the superb food, mostly created from local and organic ingredients and often gluten-free. Come for breakfasts, sandwiches and sharing platters, plus daily soups and blackboard specials such as Welsh lamb meatballs with *fusilli* or mushroom rarebit; dishes £5–15. Occasional evening gigs and films; check

the website. Mon–Sat 9.30am–5.30pm; kitchen 9.30am–4pm.
Kyffin 129 High St, LL57 1NT ☎01248 355161. A sweet little vegetarian and vegan café serving tasty home-made lunches, often with Middle Eastern flavours such as spicy lentil lasagne at low prices, with gluten-free and non-dairy options; most plates are under £10. As appealing is a warm atmosphere that encourages you to linger. Mon–Sat 9.30am–5pm.

DRINKING

Tap & Spile Garth Rd, Upper Bangor, LL57 2SW ☎01248 370835. What appears outside to be a shabby boozer reveals itself within to be an airy pub that's as

welcoming as a ship's cabin, with lots of wood-lined corners to sit in. Beer-wise, it has north Wales craft ales on tap. Daily 11.30am–11pm or later.

ENTERTAINMENT

Pontio Deiniol Rd, LL57 2TQ ⓦpontio.co.uk. An "Arts and Innovation Centre" with a 450-seat theatre, outdoor amphitheatre and dining areas and bars, this

university-affiliated venue is northwest Wales' major performance hub, with comedy, theatre and cabaret, some in Welsh.

FROM TOP PENMON PRIORY (P.417); LLANFAIRPWLL RAILWAY STATION (P.419) >

Anglesey

The island of **Anglesey** (Ynys Môn) is a world apart. Its low green fields and farms are a far cry from the mountains of Snowdonia, and compared to its neighbour – hardly a region of whirlwind modernity itself – the pace of life is even slower. This is a place to amble along backroads, lingering over the sea views and superb coastal scenery, and to perhaps explore the many **restaurants** that have seen the island emerge as a foodie hot spot.

The gastronomy theme is the latest take on Anglesey's reputation as **Mam Cymru**, the "Mother of Wales", attesting to its former status as the country's breadbasket. In the twelfth century, Giraldus Cambrensis noted that "When crops have failed in other regions, this island, from its soil and its abundant produce, has been able to supply all Wales". Anglesey remains predominantly agricultural, with a landscape of small fields, stone walls and whitewashed houses. Linguistically and politically, it is solidly Welsh, with the language spoken as a matter of course. Most residents will at least understand the lines of one of Anglesey's most famous poets, Goronwy Owen, whose eulogy on his homeland translates as "All hail to Anglesey/The delight of all regions/Bountiful as a second Eden/Or an ancient paradise".

The main tourist town is **Beaumaris**, thanks to its beautiful setting and castle. Following the south coast clockwise you'll find a string of minor sights and lovely beaches on the way to **Holy Island** (Ynys Gybi); it barely deserves the name, in truth, since it's just a few yards off the northwest coast and connected by road and rail bridges. Come for the fine beaches at **Rhoscolyn** and **Trearddur Bay** – the sandy coves and rocky headlands here provide superb **sea kayaking** and there's good **kitesurfing** – or for the impressive sea-bird cliffs around **South Stack**. And if you really want to experience life in the slow lane, you could stroll around the whole lot in a fortnight or so on the 125-mile **Anglesey Coast Path**.

Brief history

The earliest people on Anglesey were Mesolithic hunters who arrived between 8000 and 4000 BC. Around 2500 BC, a new culture developed among the small farming communities, giving rise to the many henges and **stone circles** on the island – it has Wales' greatest concentration of pre-Christian sites. These communities held sway until the Celts swept across Europe in the seventh century BC, led by their priestly class, the druids. Anglesey – well positioned at the apex of Celtic sea traffic – became the most important druidic centre in Europe. The druids were so firmly established that Anglesey was the last place in Wales to fall to the Romans, in 61 AD.

RURAL ACCOMMODATION ON ANGLESEY

There are some excellent, moderately priced **B&Bs and farmhouses** buried in the Anglesey countryside. We list accommodation in Beaumaris (see p.418), Trearddur Bay (see p.424) and near Moelfre (see p.427); the following provide rural alternatives.

Llwydiarth Fawr B5111, 0.5 mile north of Llanerchymedd, LL71 8DF ☎01248 470321, ⊛llwydiarth-fawr.co.uk. A classy, award-winning B&B in a Georgian mansion, set among the hills of a working farm. Decor is traditional yet never cloyingly so. A self-catering cottage is also available for week-long stays (£750). A hugely relaxing, comfortable stay. **£90**

Tal-y-Foel Dwyran, Brynsiencyn, LL61 6LQ ☎01248 430977, ⊛tal-y-foel.co.uk. If views across the Menai Strait to Caernarfon appeal, this farmhouse B&B is your place. Though spacious, accommodation is simply furnished, and there's access to the horseriding school next door. **£85**

Tre-Ysgawen Hall Capel Coch, Llangefni, LL77 7UR ☎01248 750750, ⊛treysgawen-hall.co.uk. You're guaranteed a sumptuous stay in this grand Victorian mansion, set in acres of landscaped gardens. The focus is traditional – four-posters in the best rooms (£366), classic decor in standard doubles – while facilities include a spa and pool. **£216**

The vacuum left by the Romans' departure in the fifth century was soon filled by the greatest of all Welsh dynasties, the Princes of Gwynedd, who held court at **Aberffraw**. Under Rhodri Mawr, in the ninth century, their influence spread over most of Wales as he defeated the encroaching Vikings. Anglesey again fell to outsiders towards the end of the thirteenth century when Edward I defeated the Welsh princes, sealing the island's fate by forging the final link in his Iron Ring of castles at **Beaumaris**.

ARRIVAL AND GETTING AROUND ANGLESEY

By train The train line from Bangor crosses the Menai Strait, stopping at the station with the longest name in Europe – usually abbreviated to Llanfairpwll – before continuing to meet the ferries at Holyhead.

By bus Buses fill in the gaps left by trains – all services are detailed on the local government website ⓦ anglesey .gov.uk. One of the most useful is the #42, which links Bangor, Menai Bridge and Llanfairpwll before looping around the south coast to Aberffraw and then inland to Llangefni. The #62 bus from Bangor tracks the east coast from Red Wharf Bay to Cemaes Bay. Note that services are sketchy on Sun.

By bike Congratulations if you've come with a bike: Anglesey is crisscrossed by routes. Download maps from ⓦ visitanglesey.co.uk.

On foot The island is ringed by the 125-mile Anglesey Coastal Path (ⓦ angleseycoastalpath.com). Most people set aside twelve days for the complete circuit.

ACTIVITIES

B-Active@Rhoscolyn Outdoor Alternative, Rhoscolyn, LL65 2NQ ☎ 07833 424046, ⓦ b-active-rhoscolyn .co.uk. A small agency, based at the Outdoor Alternative campsite, which makes good use of the fabulous indented coast of southwest Holy Island. Its mainstay is sea kayaking, which includes wildlife watching – from £40 for a half-day – but there are also group coasteering trips.

Dive Anglesey 1 Church Terrace, Holyhead, LL65 2HP ☎ 01407 764545, ⓦ diveanglesey.co.uk. Rhoscolyn and the wreck of the 1880 steamship *Missouri* are two popular dive sites visited by this operator, with decades of experience. A one-day "Try Scuba" experience, including a sea dive costs £89.

Funsport 1 Beach Terrace, Rhosneiger, LL64 5QB ☎ 01407 810899, ⓦ www.funsportonline.co.uk. Right next to one of the best surfing, wind- and kitesurfing beaches on Anglesey, Funsport offers tuition (kitesurfing £25 for an hour's taster, or from £125 for a 5hr lesson) plus rental of surfboards, stand-up paddleboards and kayaks (from £10/hr or £45/day).

RibRide Porth Daniel Porth Daniel, Water St, Menai Bridge, LL59 5DE ☎ 0333 123 4303, ⓦ ribride.co.uk. Themed wildlife and scenic cruises on high-speed RIBs along the Menai Strait and Angelesy coast (from £24). It also rents out inflatable stand-up paddleboards.

Sea Kayaking Anglesey Porth Daniel, Water St, Menai Bridge, LL59 5DE ☎ 07973 172632, ⓦ seakayaking anglesey.co.uk. Weekend introductory courses for novices (£155) plus training courses in the Menai Strait and a full Anglesey circumnavigation for experienced paddlers; instructor Phill Clegg is the current record-holder for paddling around the UK in eighty days. Reservations essential.

Beaumaris and around

With its lovely setting on the Menai Strait, air of relaxed prosperity, handsome looks and plenty to see, **BEAUMARIS** (Biwmares) is the stuff of happy holidays writ large. Inevitably, that means modest crowds in summer, though no more so than in the Snowdonia resorts. Even then, evenings are magical – the **Menai Strait** stills to silver, nature holds its breath and a panorama of Snowdonian mountains fades into the dusk.

The original inhabitants were evicted by Edward I to make way for the construction of his new castle and bastide town, dubbed "beautiful marsh" in a ploy to attract English settlers. Today the place can seem like the small English outpost Edward intended, with a smart **Georgian terrace** (designed by Joseph Hansom, of cab fame) and more English accents than you'll have heard for a while. Many of their owners come by yacht, a faint echo of the eighteenth century when this was the largest port in Wales, with its own merchant ships. The Menai bridges and growth of Holyhead put paid to that.

While you can lose a happy half-day mooching around Beaumaris's giftshops and galleries, drinking in views across the Strait on the modest pier, the main attractions – the

castle, **court** and **jail** – each offer their own angle on Welsh history. For a jaunt, you could take a cruise out around **Puffin Island** or wander along the nearby coastline close to **Penmon Priory**.

Beaumaris Castle

Castle St, LL58 8AP • March–June, Sept & Oct daily 9.30am–5pm; July & Aug daily 9.30am–6pm; Nov–Feb Mon–Sat 10am–4pm, Sun 11am–4pm • £6.50; CADW • ☎ 01248 810361, ⓦ cadw.gov.wales/daysout/beaumaris-castle

The town's central feature is **Beaumaris Castle** which, with its water-filled moat and loop-holed ramparts, is the most picturesque of Edward's gargantuan fortresses. The castle was built in response to Madog ap Llywelyn's capture of Caernarfon in 1294, architect James of St George producing his finest and most highly evolved expression of concentric design. Whatever the intention of its build, it's a cracker of a castle: perfectly proportioned and less domineering than Caernarfon, Conwy or Harlech.

7

BEAUMARIS

0   50
yards

Chapel Tower

Gunner's Walk

Beaumaris Castle

Castle entrance

Queenot the Martyrs

Church Street

St Mary & St Nicholas

Steeple Lane

Beaumaris Gaol

Gaol Street

PROMENADE

● EATING
Pier House Bistro   2
Red Boat Ice
Cream Parlour   3
Ye Olde Bull's
Head Inn   1

Beaumaris Courthouse

Bus Stop

Castle Street

Rating Row

Little Lane

Bus Stop ★

Town Hall

Bulkeley Hotel

Pier

Puffin Island Cruises

The Front

Wall St

Baglan St

Alma Street

Margaret Street

Chapel Street

Gladys Lane

West End

New Street

Stanley St

Rosemary Lane

Bus Stop ★

Bus Stop ★

A545

■ ACCOMMODATION
Cleifiog   4
Kingsbridge Caravan
& Camping Park   1
Victoria Cottage   2
Ye Olde Bull's Head Inn   3

Located on flat land at the edge of town, the castle is approached over the moat and through Moorish-influenced staggered entries at the huge towers of the Gate Next the Sea and the South Gatehouse. The moat originally linked the castle to the sea (now well over 100yd away), with a shipping channel allowing boats of up to forty tons to tie up at the iron rings hammered into a protective spur of the outer defences, **Gunner's Walk**. Supplies could be brought in, including the corn that was fed into a mill.

When put to the test, the castle failed to withstand Owain Glyndŵr – who took it in 1403 and held it for two years – but during the Civil War, its Royalist defenders held out against General Mytton and 1500 Parliamentarian troops until 1646. After Charles II's accession, the castle was returned to the Bulkeley family, only to be left to fall into ruin before twentieth-century restoration returned some of its glory.

The battlements

Despite more than thirty years' work and plans for a lavish palace, the castle was never quite finished, leaving most of the inner ward empty, and the corbels and fireplaces unused. You can explore around half of the inner and outer **walls**, from which archers could fire simultaneously from the inner and outer defences. Then wander through miles of internal passages in the walls, finding your way to the first floor of the **Chapel Tower**, with a small lime-washed chapel.

Beaumaris Courthouse

Castle St, LL58 8AP • Easter–Sept Mon–Thurs, Sat & Sun 10.30am–5pm; Oct & half-terms Sat & Sun 10.30am–5pm • £5.25 • ☎ 01248 811691, ⓦ visitanglesey.co.uk

Beaumaris Castle overshadows the juridical instruments of English rule, the Jacobean **Beaumaris Courthouse**, which from 1614 until 1971 hosted the quarterly Assize Courts. These were traditionally held in English, giving a Welsh-speaking jury little chance to follow the proceedings, and defendants no chance against judges notorious for slapping severe penalties for relatively minor offences. Undoubtedly they would have sympathized with the sentiments embodied in **The Lawsuit**, a plaque in the main courtroom depicting two farmers pulling the horns and tail of a cow as a lawyer milks it. You can watch a DVD of a mock trial of a local man; ask, too, about the theatrical re-enactments of court cases, staged in high season (£6.50).

Beaumaris Gaol

Bunker's Hill, LL58 8EP • Easter–Sept Mon–Thurs, Sat & Sun 10.30am–5pm; Oct & half-terms Sat & Sun 10.30am–5pm • £7 • ☎ 01248 810921, ⓦ visitanglesey.co.uk

The obvious partner to the courthouse is **Beaumaris Gaol**, where many of the convicted wound up; many more local citizens were transported to the colonies. When it opened in 1829, this was considered a model prison, with running water and toilets in each cell, and an infirmary. Women prisoners did the cooking and were allowed to rock their babies' cradles in the nursery above by means of a pulley system. Advanced perhaps, but nonetheless this is a gloomy place: witness the windowless punishment cell, the stone-breaking yard and the treadmill water pump. The least fortunate inmates were marched along a first-floor walkway through a door in the outer wall to the gibbet, where they were publicly hanged. You're guided by an audio tour, which recounts various inmates' stories.

Penmon Priory

Penmon, 4 miles northeast of Beaumaris, LL58 8RW • Daily 10am–4pm • Free, but parking £3; CADW • ☎ 01443 336000, ⓦ cadw.gov .wales/daysout/penmonpriory

Penmon Priory's original wooden buildings were razed by the Danes in the tenth century. Their replacements, the twelfth-century church and the thirteenth-century south range of the cloister, are still standing, but only the **church** is in good repair and still used. The lime-washed nave houses an unusual Norman pillar-piscina – a font gouged from the plinth of a pre-Norman cross, still used for Sunday services – and the Penmon Cross, moved here to prevent Welsh weather scouring off any more of its plait and fret patterns. There's more patterned stonework in the south transept, approached through a magnificent chevron- and chequerboard-patterned arch.

The site was chosen for its proximity to the refreshing waters of **St Seiriol's Well**, which now feeds a pool and is reached by either the path behind the church, or another opposite a domed **dovecote**, built around 1600 to house one thousand pairs of birds.

Black Point and Puffin Island

The parking fee for Penmon Priory also covers you for the toll road that runs three-quarters of a mile beyond the dovecote to **Black Point**, the easternmost point of Anglesey. A short strait separates you from **Puffin Island**, known in Welsh as Ynys Seiriol, recalling Penmon's St Seiriol, whose original Augustine community was on the island. It is now home to nesting razorbills, guillemots and puffins, which were all at one time permissible food during Lent. Cruises leave from Beaumaris seafront.

ARRIVAL AND DEPARTURE BEAUMARIS

By bus Timetables for the #53, #57 and #58 services from Beaumaris to Penmon and Bangor are facing reduced services; visit ⓦ anglesey.gov.uk for up-to-date information. Currently buses arrive from Bangor (every 20–30min; 20–35min) and Menai Bridge (every 30min; 15min) and go to Penmon (13 daily; 15min).

By car The largest car park is by the Menai Strait, accessed from The Front (£3 for 12hr).

7

INFORMATION AND TOURS

Tourist information A desk in the foyer of the Town Hall on Castle St stocks leaflets and is sometimes staffed by volunteers.

Boat trips Seacoast Safaris (ⓦ seacoastsafaris.co.uk) and Starida Sea Services (ⓦ starida.co.uk) offer identical trips

down the Menai Strait (for history) and to Puffin Island (for wildlife); buy tickets (£9) from booths from the pier (Easter–Oct 4 daily; outside peak season you should be able to hop aboard the next trip). Starida Sea Services also runs fishing trips (£25/2hr, £40/4hr).

ACCOMMODATION

★**Cleifiog** Townsend, LL58 8BH ☎01248 811507, ⓦ cleifiogbandb.co.uk. A stay in one of the four rooms of this art-filled, Georgian B&B is the architectural equivalent of a hug. Best are the elegant front rooms, with beautiful antique panelling and views across the Menai Strait to Snowdonia. Factor in a lovely guest lounge and charming host and it's a struggle to leave. **£100**

Kingsbridge Caravan & Camping Park Llanfaes, 2 miles northeast, LL58 8LR ☎01248 490636, ⓦ kingsbridgecaravanpark.co.uk. Spacious, well-maintained campsite with pitches in flat fields, separate family areas, campervan hookups and four-berth static caravans for rent (one week minimum). Closed Nov–Feb. Camping **£24**, caravans **£64**

★**Victoria Cottage** Victoria Terrace, LL58 8DA

☎01248 810807, ⓦ victoriacottage.net. Built by Joseph Hansom, our favourite Beaumaris B&B is tucked behind the waterfront terrace. It offers sleigh beds in two spacious en-suite rooms and a family suite that occupies the entire top floor. Charm, great views and fine breakfasts come as standard. Note that the business was for sale at the time of going to press. **£95**

Ye Olde Bull's Head Inn 18 Castle St, LL58 8AP ☎01248 810329, ⓦ bullsheadinn.co.uk. The ancient coaching inn that has housed Dr Johnson and Charles Dickens still provides the best hotel accommodation in Beaumaris. Chic modern rooms are either in the main building, which benefits from original features like old beams, or across the road in *The Townhouse*, where some rooms are larger. All include an excellent breakfast. **£110**

EATING

Pier House Bistro The Front, LL58 8BS ☎01248 811055, ⓦ pierhousebistro.com. This café-bistro is the place to be on a sunny day – there are picture-postcard views across the Strait from the terrace. Menus pieced together from largely local ingredients list breakfasts, sandwiches and larger mains such as beef-brisket lasagne or fish and chips with gin-and-tonic batter (£12.95). Daily 9am–9pm.

Red Boat Ice Cream Parlour 34 Castle St, LL58 8BB ⓦ redboatgelato.com. Cheerful little café with an ever-changing selection of gelati and sorbets all freshly made on the premises, from standard vanilla to sea buckthorn – the owner trained at a prestigious Italian ice-cream academy.

There are also snacks: sandwiches, waffles, pizzas, panini and pancakes, all under £10. 10am–5pm.

Ye Olde Bull's Head Inn 18 Castle St, LL58 8AP ☎01248 810329, ⓦ bullsheadinn.co.uk. Beaumaris's top hotel hits the button for eating and drinking. *The Coach* brasserie has posh pub food – slow-cooked lamb or risotto of wild mushrooms and pine nuts, as well as fresh home-made burgers (mains average £13) – with courtyard seating in summer. Fine dining is offered in the *Loft* restaurant: expect seasonal Modern British dishes featuring island produce (three courses £47.50). The Coach: Mon–Sat noon–2pm & 6–9pm, Sun noon–3pm & 6–9pm; Loft: Wed & Thurs 7–9pm, Fri & Sat 6.30–9pm.

Menai Bridge

The gentrifying small town of **MENAI BRIDGE** (Porthaethwy) was created during the building of the first of the two bridges across the Menai Strait. The older of the two is a handsome structure, with a few private islands dotted in the strait to complete the view. Views aside, there's little to see unless you're an engineering nerd (see box opposite), but the **food scene** is good.

Oriel Tegfryn

Cadnant Rd, LL59 5EW • Mon–Sat 10am–5pm, Sun 11am–4.30pm • ☎01248 715128, ⓦ artwales.com

One of Wales' oldest galleries, launched in 1961 on the instigation of Sir Kyffin Williams, **Oriel Tegfryn** displays rotating exhibitions of painting, prints and sculpture in four small rooms. Alongside works by celebrated names such as Williams are pieces by less well known artists who are currently working in north Wales. Many are for sale.

SPANNING THE MENAI STRAIT

Two bridges – both engineering marvels of their time – span the **Menai Strait**, a fourteen-mile-long tidal race between Anglesey and the mainland that narrows to 200yd wide in places, accelerating the current to up to eight knots. The **best views** are from the Anglesey shore: make for the lay-by on the A5, a mile east of Llanfairpwll, for postcard images over the rocky mid-channel islets into the heartland of Snowdonia.

For centuries before the bridges were built drovers used the Strait's narrow stretches to herd Anglesey cattle to market. Travellers had to wait for low tide to cross Lafan Sands, northeast of Bangor, then find a boat to take them to Beaumaris, guided only by the sound of church bells in foggy weather. So it's not surprising that Irish MPs, needing transport to Westminster and a faster mail service, pushed for a fixed crossing.

The first permanent link, in 1826, was Telford's **Menai Suspension Bridge**, the world's first large iron suspension bridge, spanning 579ft between piers and 100ft above the water to allow high-masted sailing ships to pass. Almost everything about the project was novel, including the process of lifting the sixteen 23-ton chains into place, which required 150 men kept in time by a fife band. One man celebrated their achievement by running the length of the nine-inch-wide chain. In 1850, Robert Stephenson also made engineering history with his **Britannia Tubular Bridge**, which carried trains across the Strait in twin wrought-iron tubes. Severely damaged by fire in 1970, it exists now only as the limestone piers that support the road and rail bridges.

A small **community museum** on Mona Rd, 200yd from the Anglesey end of the bridge, has exhibits and screens a short film about the bridges (April–Oct Wed & Thurs 10am–5pm; £3; ☎01248 715046, ⓦmenaibridges.co.uk).

Church of St Tysilio

Church Island, LL59 • Mid-July to Aug daily; Sept to mid-July occasional Sun services • Free

Few places capture Menai Bridge's backwater appeal better than the fourteenth-century **Church of St Tysilio**. It occupies Church Island, where its patron saint founded his cell around 630 AD and which has lovely views along the Strait and to both bridges. Half a mile west of the centre (and bridge), it can be reached via a causeway off a waterside promenade named **Belgian Walk** (built by refugees during World War I).

ACCOMMODATION AND EATING MENAI BRIDGE

★**Chateau Rhianfa** Beaumaris Rd, LL59 9NS ☎01248 880090, ⓦchateaurhianfa.com. One for a splurge, this is a Grade II-listed Loire-style chateau beautifully located on the Menai Strait opposite the peaks of Snowdonia. Views and fairytale romance aside, it provides luxury accommodation – French country chic, or elegant suites if money is no object (£250) – plus a fine-dining restaurant. Sea views cost an extra £25. **£185**

Dylan's St George's Rd ☎01248 716714, ⓦdylans restaurant.co.uk. Come to this relaxed café-bar and restaurant for views – it's brilliantly situated above the Strait in an old timber yard and has two terraces over the

water – and seasonal dishes including Menai mussels, gourmet burgers and pizza (mains £10–19.95). Daily 11am–11pm.

Sosban and the Old Butchers Trinity House, 1 High St ☎01248 208131, ⓦsosbanandtheoldbutchers.com. This stripped-back butcher's shop – Sosban refers to chef Stephen Stevens' saucepan – is Anglesey's leading fine-dining address, offering farm-to-fork eating on Michelin-starred tasting menus (£65). There's no choice, but no pretentious attitude either. The catch? Getting in. Reserve months ahead. Thurs–Sat 7–11pm, Sat 12.30pm & 7–11pm.

Southwest Anglesey

When Robert Louis Stephenson wrote "to travel hopefully is a better thing than to arrive" he might have been thinking of **LLANFAIRPWLL**, the local name for the otherwise unremarkable village with the longest place name in Europe, **Llanfairpwll-gwyngyllgogerychwyrndrobwllllantysiliogogogoch**. (For obvious reasons, road signs prefer it as Llanfair Pwllgwyngyll.) "St Mary's church in the hollow of white hazel near a rapid whirlpool and the Church of St Tysilio near the red cave" is not even an authentic Welsh tongue twister. Rather, it's the fabrication of a Menai Bridge tailor in

---

FROM SEA TO SEASONING

With provenance being key in foodie circles, **Halen Môn**, which uses some of the country's purest sea water to produce its sea salt from the Menai Strait, is on a roll. Some of the world's top restaurants use it, and their smoked sea salt is an important ingredient in Barack Obama's favourite chocolates, apparently. The company explains the history, process and culture of salt-making on **tours** of its **Tŷ Halen** centre near Brynsiencyn, 5 miles west of Llanfair (10am–5pm: June–Aug 4 daily; Sept–May 3 daily; 50min; £6; ☏01248 430871, ⊕halenmon .com), which include tasting lessons. The stylish visitor centre also has a shop.

---

the 1880s. He added to the original first five syllables in an attempt to draw tourists – as indeed it has.

Take the obligatory photo of the famous name sign at the train station. Giggle at kitsch Welsh souvenirs in a vast tourist outlet on the station car park. Then push on. Beyond Llanfairpwll, Anglesey reverts to type: beautiful coast around the dunes of **Newborough Warren** and in the gorgeous beaches and coves surrounding the watersports capital of **Rhosneigr**. There's fascinating history, too, both ancient, in the burial sites of **Bryn Celli Ddu** and **Barclodiad y Gawres**, and more modern at **Plas Newydd** manor.

GETTING AROUND   SOUTHWEST ANGLESEY

By bus and train Without your own transport getting to this part of Anglesey is tricky. Trains to Holyhead stop at Rhosneigr; from Bangor there are 8 daily (25min). Otherwise, no bus loops around the southwest coast, so onward travel may require backtracking for another connection, usually from Llangefni. The #42 (Mon–Sat 11 daily, Sun 2) travels between Llangefni and Bangor via Newborough and Plas Newydd and Llanfairpwll.

Marquess of Anglesey's column
A5, 0.5 mile east of Llanfairpwll

You can hardly miss the bronze figure atop the 91ft-high Doric **Marquess of Anglesey's Column**. The apocryphal story has him declaring to Wellington, on having a leg blown off at Waterloo, "Begod, sir, there goes me leg", to which Wellington dryly replied, "Begod, sir, so it do". There hadn't been much love lost between them since the Marquess ran off with Wellington's sister-in-law some years previously. The 115 steps up to share the Marquess's view to Snowdonia have been closed for a while. Instead, go to see his replacement leg at Plas Newydd (see below).

Plas Newydd
A4080, 1.5 miles southwest of Llanfairpwll, LL61 6DQ • **House** Mid-Feb to early Nov daily 11am–4.30pm • £11 including gardens; NT • **Gardens** Early Nov–Easter 11am–3pm; Easter–early Nov daily 10.30am–5pm • £8.65; NT • ☏01248 715272 or ☏01248 714795, ⊕ nationaltrust.org.uk/plas-newydd-country-house-and-gardens

Plas Newydd has been the ancestral home of the marquesses of Anglesey since the eighteenth century. A house has stood here, overlooking the Menai Strait, since the sixteenth century, but it was the first marquess's huge profits from Anglesey's Parys Mountain and other ventures that paid for its transformation by James Wyatt and Joseph Potter into a Gothic mansion in the late eighteenth century.

The **Gothic Hall**, with its Potter-designed fan-vaulted ceiling, leads to the finest room in the house, the Music Room, originally the great hall, covered with oil paintings, including portraits of the first marquess and his wife. There's a transition to neoclassical in the Staircase Hall and a gallery lined with portraits of monarchs and family members; those of the sixth marquess and his sister are the work of Rex Whistler, who spent two years here in the 1930s.

Whistler's masterwork is a 58ft-long trompe l'oeil **mural** of a fantastical seascape towards the Snowdonia mountains and beyond. Portmeirion is there, as are the Round Tower from Windsor Castle and the steeple from St Martin-in-the-Fields in London.

Whistler himself appears as a gondolier and as a gardener in one of the two right-angled panels at either end. The **Cavalry Museum** beyond exhibits the world's first articulated leg, designed for the first marquess, who lost his at Waterloo.

Save time for the beautiful **gardens**, which were landscaped by Humphrey Repton in the early nineteenth century, and the lovely tiled **café** (open daily year-round) in the former milking parlour.

Bryn Celli Ddu

Signposted 0.5 mile north of the A4080, 2 miles southwest of Llanfairpwll, LL61 6EQ • Daily 10am–4pm • Free; CADW • ☎ 01443 336000, ⓦ cadw.gov.wales/daysout/bryn-celli-ddu-burial-chamber • The #42 bus passes within 0.5 mile; otherwise it's a 1hr walk from Llanfairpwll

Atmospheric **Bryn Celli Ddu**, the "Mound of the Dark Chamber", is one of Anglesey's most significant prehistoric features, built four thousand years ago on the site of a Neolithic henge. Archeological digs have shown it to be an extensive religious site, but all you can see today is a well-proportioned henge and stone circle, later built over to turn it into a passage grave beneath an earthen mound. The original entrance stone was whisked off to the National Museum in Cardiff, but a replica gives an idea of its carved spiral patterns. In the final chamber you'll find an impressive, smooth monolith beneath a far less impressive concrete beam.

Newborough Warren

Newborough • Open access, though seasonal toll road £4

The southwestern end of the Menai Strait is marked by Abermenai Point, a huge sand bar backed by the 600-acre **Newborough Warren**. Reached via the small town of Newborough (Niwbwrch), it's one of the most important dune systems in Britain, though the land has been forested in pines for decades, providing habitat for goldcrests, warblers and rare native red squirrels. Thick-horned **Soay sheep**, Britain's oldest native breed, are also common.

Llanddwyn Island

Park at Newborough Warren and you can pop over the dunes onto a long, wild beach with views across to Snowdonia. At its northern end is magical **Llanddwyn Island**, a glorious peninsula of rocky coves and sandy beaches. Here stands Twr Mawr (the Great Tower), built in 1800 to warn the ships in Caernarfon Bay; it was later supplanted by the disused lighthouse, built in 1873 in the style of an Anglesey windmill. There's also a row of restored sea pilot cottages and the ruined thirteenth-century **Church of St Dwynwen**, dedicated to the Welsh patron saint of lovers. In the fifth century, Dwynwen is said to have retreated to Llanddwyn to live as a hermit after a thwarted love affair with Welsh prince Maelon. The story states that an angel gave her a potion to heal her loss and turn Maelon into ice. She repented, Maelon thawed and in relief she asked that hopeful lovers who made a supplication to God in her name should receive divine assistance. Pilgrims anxious to know if they'd met their true love would peer into a shallow pool fed by a spring in rocks just north of the ruin. If sacred fish within stirred the water all was well. Certainly the location has heavenly scenery – even more so at sunset. You can also reach the beach from free forest car parks a mile north of Newborough – well-marked trails, none more than an hour or two's stroll, go through the trees to emerge at one of the most spectacular views in Wales.

EATING AND DRINKING   NEWBOROUGH

★**The Marram Grass** White Lodge caravan park, beside the roundabout on the A4080 link road, LL61 6RS ☎ 01248 440077, ⓦ themarramgrass.com. Who'd have guessed that a caravan-site shed could become a brilliant, snug restaurant? Beneath a tin roof, its young chefs craft create ambitious dishes from island ingredients – pan-roasted salt cod with Menai mussels, bouillabaisse and kale, for example. Highish prices (mains £14–22) guarantee the best ingredients and proper pay for serving staff. Reservations essential. Thurs–Sun 6–9pm.

Llangadwaladr church

Llangadwaladr, A4080, 4 miles northwest of Newborough, LL62 5LA • Often closed except Sun mornings • ☎ 01407 840282

The area around tiny **Llangadwaladr** – more a few scattered houses than a hamlet – was once the seat of the ruling dynasty of the Princes of Gwynedd, who from the seventh-century reign of Cadfan until Llywelyn ap Gruffydd's death in 1282 controlled northwest Wales, and often much of the rest of the country. Evidence lies in the thirteenth-century **Llangadwaladr church**, where a memorial plaque incorporated into an inside wall, carved in Latin in about 625, reads "Cadfan the King, wisest and most renowned of all kings".

Barclodiad y Gawres

South of Cable Bay beach • Visits to the interior of the burial chamber (April–Oct Sat, Sun & Bank Hol Mons noon–4pm) can be arranged in advance at Wayside Stores shop, 1 mile north in Llanfaelog • Free; CADW • Book visits at ☎ 01407 810153 , ⓦ cadw.gov.wales/daysout /barclodiad-burial-chamber

Cable Bay (Porth Trecastell) was the eastern terminus of the first telegraph cable to Ireland, though it is now better known for its good sandy beach. On the headland south of the beach, the heavily reconstructed remains of the 5000-year-old **Barclodiad y Gawres** (the Giantess's Apronful) burial chamber are more dramatic than Bryn Celli Ddu, with chevrons and zigzag patterns.

Rhosneigr

Not long ago **RHOSNEIGR**, a small-fry beach resort spread across several small bays, was just another peaceful Edwardian seaside town. While still justifiably popular with old-school holidaymakers, in recent years it has also been re-energized as Anglesey's **watersports** capital. It offers some of the best **windsurfing** and **kitesurfing** conditions in Wales, with both waves and flat water in winds from the north, through west to south, plus occasional surfing waves. Kitesurfing is best on the north beach, surfing on the southern Broach Beach. See our activities section (see p.415) if you feel like joining in.

EATING AND DRINKING   RHOSNEIGR

The Oyster Catcher 0.5 mile north on the A4080 link road, LL64 5JP ☎ 01407 812829, ⓦ oystercatcher anglesey.co.uk. New World beach cool meets Welsh wit – love the cute beach-hut booths on the upper deck – in a glass-walled place behind the sands. It's both an informal restaurant, serving the likes of Menai *moules* frites and chickpea and butternut squash tagine (mains average £14) and a design-led bar that's always buzzing in summer. Bar Mon–Fri noon–2.30pm & 6–11pm, Sat & Sun noon–11pm; restaurant Mon–Fri noon–2.30pm & 6–9pm, Sat & Sun noon–9pm (school hols daily noon–9pm).

Holy Island

At the western extremity of Anglesey is **HOLY ISLAND**, though as you cross a small inlet at Four Mile Bridge (via Valley) you'll barely notice you've moved from one island to another. While its focus, **Holyhead**, isn't worth a visit, there are some good sights nearby, particularly the birdlife at **South Stack** and the beach resorts of **Trearddur Bay** and **Rhoscolyn** further south.

Holyhead

Drab **HOLYHEAD** (Caergybi; pronounced in English as "holly-head") is Anglesey's largest town and the terminus for ferry routes to Ireland. Built on the site of a Roman fort and former hermitage of the sixth-century St Cybi, who put the "holy" into the name, it's really only of interest for ferry passengers. If you have time to kill you could visit the thirteenth-century **Church of St Cybi** beside the port (June–Sept Mon–Sat 11am–3pm; free) to see stained glass by Edward Burne-Jones and William Morris.

Holyhead Maritime Museum

Beach Rd, LL65 1YD • Mid-April to Oct daily 10am–4pm • £3.50 • ☎ 01407 769745, ⓦ holyheadmaritimemuseum.co.uk

Installed in Wales' oldest lifeboat station beside the Newry Beach seafront, the **Holyhead Maritime Museum** houses display cases of local maritime memorabilia: disasters and models of lifeboats plus information on the ferries that have plied the Ireland route over the centuries.

ARRIVAL AND DEPARTURE
HOLYHEAD

By train The train station, in the town centre, is linked by Arriva trains to north Wales and intercity Virgin trains as far as London.

Destinations Bangor (22 daily; 30–40min); Chester (23 daily; 1hr 30min–2hr); Conwy (11 daily; 1hr); Llandudno (18 daily; 1hr 20min); Llanfairpwll (9 daily; 30min); London (5 daily; 3hr 45min).

By bus Local and National Express bus stops are by the passenger ferry terminal.

Destinations Amlwch (Mon–Sat 7 daily; 50min); Bangor (Mon–Sat hourly; 1hr 15min); Cemaes (Mon–Sat 7 daily; 45min); Llanfairpwll (Mon–Sat hourly; 1hr); Llangefni (Mon–Sat hourly; 45min); Menai Bridge (Mon–Sat hourly; 1hr); Rhoscolyn (Mon–Sat 3 daily; 15min); Trearddur Bay (Mon–Sat 5 daily; 7–15min).

By ferry Ferries to and from Ireland are detailed in our Basics chapter (see p.27).

7

South Stack and around

By far the best reason to swing through Holyhead is to head out to **South Stack** (Ynys Lawd), two miles west of the town centre. It's a fantastic edge-of-world sort of place; a destination to watch sea birds, visit a dramatic lighthouse and, if you're keen, follow a path (45min) up **Holyhead Mountain** (Mynydd Twr; 700ft) to discover ancient history.

Ellin's Tower Seabird Centre

South Stack, LL65 1YH • **Tower** Easter–Sept daily 10am–5pm • **Visitor centre** Daily 10am–5pm • Free • ☎ 01407 762100, ⓦ rspb.org.uk/wales

Views of the cliffs around South Stack are best from the RSPB-run **Ellin's Tower Seabird Centre** on the cliff edges. During breeding season, from April until the end of July, binoculars and closed-circuit TV provide unrivalled opportunities to watch up to three thousand birds – razorbills, guillemots, puffins and peregrines – nesting on the sea cliffs beyond and wheeling outside the tower's windows. You'll find it just below the RSPB-run **South Stack Visitor Centre**, a café-cum-interpretive centre on the road.

South Stack Lighthouse

South Stack, LL65 1YH • Previously Easter–Sept Sat–Thurs 10.30am–5pm • £5.80

If the seabird centre teetering on cliffs seems precarious it's nothing compared to the pepper-pot **South Stack Lighthouse**, built in 1809. Visits had been suspended at the time of research; seek current information in the RSPB visitor centre (see above) where tickets were formerly issued. Even if it's not open for visits, it's worth taking the four hundred steps down to a suspension bridge across, once the keeper's only access, for close-up views of the cliffs and birds beneath. Good luck climbing back up again.

Cytiau'r Gwyddelod

Across the road from South Stack Visitor Centre • Open access • Free

Hoik over a style and you'll find the nineteen low rings that comprise the **Cytiau'r Gwyddelod** hut circles. A noticeboard explains the background of what was probably a late Neolithic or early Bronze Age settlement. There seem to have originally been fifty buildings, formed into eight distinct farmsteads separated by ploughed fields.

Caer y Twr

Open access • Free; CADW • ☎ 01443 336000, ⓦ cadw.gov.wales/daysout/caer-y-twr

Climb to the summit of Holyhead Mountain and you're rewarded with an asttonishing 360-degree panorama of sea, countryside and distant mountains. It's ringed by the remains of **Caer y Twr**, at seventeen acres one of the largest Iron Age hillforts in north Wales.

Seemingly, it was only used during times of war, as no signs of permanent occupation have been unearthed, just a 6ft-high dry-stone wall enclosure around the ruins of a Roman watchtower.

Trearddur Bay

If Anglesey can be said to have a smart beach resort, **TREARDDUR BAY** (Bae Trearddur) at the nipped-in waist of Holy Island's hourglass shape, is it. Chicer than its neighbour Rhoscolyn, with more of a village centre (albeit still grey pebbledash), it exists for a **beach** of heart-stopping beauty; a deeply indented bay with white sand beach and, beyond it, rocky coves. Sunsets can be magical.

ARRIVAL AND DEPARTURE   TREARDDUR BAY

The #23 **bus** serves Holyhead (Mon–Sat 5 daily; 7–15min).

ACCOMMODATION AND EATING

The Black Seal Ravenspoint Rd, LL65 2UP ☎01407 860008, ⓦtheblackseal.co.uk. Everything from pizzas and gourmet burgers to chili, crab and prawn linguine (£12.95) in an impressive, stylish bar-restaurant. Decor aside, the big attraction here is the location, right behind the beach – it's brilliant for a drink on the terrace, too. Daily 11am–11pm; kitchen Mon–Thurs noon–2.30pm & 5.30–9pm, Fri–Sun noon–9pm.

Blackthorn Farm 2 miles northwest, LL65 2LT ☎01407 765262, ⓦblackthornleisure.co.uk. A farm offering B&B in eight lovely rooms – homely, comfy, all en suite – plus a well-maintained campsite (closed Nov–Feb) with a good shower block. Camping/person **£12**, doubles **£72**

Trearddur Bay Hotel Behind the bay off Lon Isallt, LL65 2UN ☎01407 860301, ⓦtrearddurbayhotel .co.uk. Though perhaps a little tired, this is just what you need from a modern holiday hotel – a location moments behind the beach; breezy beach style, all pale blues and creams; and balconies overlooking the main bay in the best rooms (£229). **£169**

★**Ty Bae** Ravenspoint Rd, LL65 2YU ☎01407 860128, ⓦtybae.co.uk. New in 2017, this is a beautiful modern B&B, its crisp decor softened by driftwood-style headboards and vintage oars on the wall. Each of the three rooms – two doubles, one family option – have a balcony overlooking the beach plus a deep bath that could hold a hippo. **£145**

Rhoscolyn

The tiny seaside village of **RHOSCOLYN** scatters itself over the southern tip of Holy Island, barely knitted together with lanes. With a couple of exquisite beaches notched in a wild ragged coast, this is the ideal place to take a day or two out enjoying peace and quiet and a commune with nature. There's good coastal **walking**: a rewarding six-mile circuit starts on beautiful Borthwen Beach (car park £5 all day), heads south to Silver Beach, loops inland back into Rhoscolyn for a pint at *The White Eagle*, then proceeds west to craggy Porth Saint to track back along the coast. **Kayakers** also love the place, though you'll require your own equipment or need to join a tour (see p.415).

ARRIVAL AND DEPARTURE   RHOSCOLYN

The #23 **bus** runs here from Holyhead (Mon–Sat 3 daily; 15min).

EATING AND DRINKING

★**The White Eagle** Village centre, LL65 2NJ ☎01407 860267, ⓦwhite-eagle.co.uk. Excellent gastropub offering the best eating on Holy Island – try pan-seared hake with basil or braised ox cheek (mains £10–16) – and a selection of cask ales. The huge deck with long views of the indented coastline is a great spot for a pint or two. It's busy, and reservations are for large groups only. Pub & kitchen Mon–Sat noon–11pm, Sun noon–10.30pm.

Northern, eastern and inland Anglesey

The **northern and eastern sides of Anglesey** are quieter than the south and west; their settlements cluster behind sheltered coves that, with the odd rocky headland, form an appealing (if seldom dramatic) coastline. This is primarily family holiday country, albeit of a gentle bygone rural style – just a few caravan sites and not an amusement arcade for miles. Come to go rockpooling in **Porth Swtan** or to sit with a pint at low tide before the empty sands of **Red Wharf Bay**.

GETTING AROUND
NORTHERN, EASTERN AND INLAND ANGLESEY

By bike or on foot Towns are well spaced along (or just off) the A5025, making cycling between them, or walking the coastal path, an ideal way to get around.

By bus Relying on buses is possible, though somewhat frustrating. The #62 runs from Bangor to Amlwch via Red Wharf Bay and Moelfre (Mon–Sat every 30min), and on to Cemaes (Mon–Sat 4 daily).

Melin Llynnon

Llanddeusant, LL65 4AB • Easter–Sept Mon–Thurs, Sat & Sun 10.30am–5pm • £4 • ☎ 01407 730407

A few miles inland from the A5025, signposts tempt you towards **Melin Llynnon**, the only working, traditional windmill in Wales. At one time, around fifty mills on Anglesey ground away to feed north Wales; nowadays most are either rotting in fields or have been converted into barns and houses. Restored from dereliction, Melin Llynnon is now canvas-sailed and again producing flour; everything is wind-powered, even the hoists that lift the grain through trapdoors. Modern millers demonstrate the milling process and sell the results of their efforts from a good café.

This was originally the site of an Iron Age village, something recalled in the two 30ft-diameter, thatched **round houses** built here in 2007.

Porth Swtan

The highlight of the northwest coast is **PORTH SWTAN** (Church Bay), a gesture of a settlement gathered behind a deep half-moon of sand backed by low yellow cliffs dating from the pre-Cambrian era. Bring your shrimp net – there are rockpools at each end.

Swtan

Behind Porth Swtan, LL65 4EU • Easter & late May–Sept Tues–Sun noon–4pm • £5 • ☎ 01407 730186, ⓦ swtan.co.uk

Swtan, the only surviving thatched cottage on Anglesey, is now a community-run museum. A short film covers its restoration in 1999, and there's occasionally a fire burning in the inglenook fireplace in the tiny stone-flagged kitchen/dining room.

ACCOMMODATION AND EATING
PORTH SWTAN

★ **Black Bull** Llangaethlu, opposite Port Swtan turn-off on the A5025, LL65 4NL ☎ 01407 730718, ⓦ blacklionanglesey.com. One of Anglesey's many food highlights, this smart gastropub showcases the best regional ingredients: Anglesey fish and seafish; local veg and dairy bought direct from producers (or foraged); seasonal game. Expect well-crafted seasonal plates such as home-grown purple sprouting broccoli linguini with wild garlic pesto (£13.30) alongside classics like fish and chips. Reservations recommended. It also offers two smart en-suite rooms. Wed 5.30–8pm, Thurs noon–8pm, Fri & Sat noon–9pm, Sun noon–3pm. **£115**

★ **Wavecrest Café** Church Bay, LL65 4ET ☎ 01407 730650. A lovely little beach café with sea views from picnic tables on a grass bank. You come for owner Penny's home cooking: try the home-made baguettes or, best of all, a cheese and onion or fish pie (£5–9). Leave space for the best cream-and-strawberry-filled scones on the island. Cash only. Thurs–Sun 10am–5pm.

Cemaes

The harbourside village of **CEMAES** is wedged between several dozen **windfarm** towers and the bulk of the **Wylfa Nuclear Power Station** (decommissioned but still there). Nonetheless, Cemaes is a charming spot with one of the most attractive harbours on the north coast, occupied by the odd trawler and yachtie.

Llanbadrig Church

On the headland at the east side of Cemaes Bay, LL67 0LH • In theory May–Sept daily 9am–noon & 2–4pm • Free

Located on one of the island's most scenic headlands, the mainly fourteenth-century **Llanbadrig Church** is one of only two Welsh churches dedicated to St Patrick. Its origins date back to the fifth century, when Ireland's patron saint is supposed to have been shipwrecked. Having taken refuge in a cave below the site of the present church, they say he built a wooden chapel in thanks; the first Christian church in Wales. The current building was restored in the nineteenth century by Lord Stanley of Alderley, Bertrand Russell's grandfather, a Muslim who used Islamic geometric designs in the stained glass. Even if it's not open, the location is pure end-of-the-world magic. The current Dalai Lama visited and called it "the most peaceful spot on earth".

Amlwch and around

AMLWCH, five miles east of Cemaes, would be just another tiny fishing village were it not for the nearby **Parys Mountain** (Mynydd Parys; 482ft), once the world's largest source of **copper**. Neolithic and Roman miners were followed by industrial production in the eighteenth century, when Amlwch boomed. People noticed that the iron hulls of ships didn't corrode in the harbour's copper-laced waters, fuelling a demand for protective copper sheathing that boosted the market for Parys copper (and coined the term "copper-bottomed" to mean reliable). International competition virtually killed the mines in the early nineteenth century.

Copper Kingdom

Amlwch Port, LL68 9DB • Easter–Oct Tues–Sun 11am–5pm • £5.50 • ☎ 01407 830298, ⓦ copperkingdom.co.uk

On the wharf in the old copper bins, the **Copper Kingdom** museum explains how diminutive Amlwch became the copper capital of the world in the first half of the 1700s. Using interactive exhibits and touchscreen displays, it narrates the mine's history, covering the social side as much as the economic and allowing visitors to track the lives of miners, a "copper lady" and a mine assayer to see what the mine meant to each of them.

Sail Loft Visitor Centre

Amlwch Port, LL68 9DB • Easter & Whitsun–Oct Tues–Sun 11am–3pm • Free • ☎ 01407 832255, ⓦ copperkingdom.co.uk

The former sail loft at the end of the Amlwch's port houses the **Sail Loft Visitor Centre**, a community-run museum covering Amlwch's maritime past. Exhibits include model ships, sheet copper from HMS *Victory* (the caption dubiously claims Lord Nelson's victory was largely due to Amlwch copper) and artefacts from Anglesey shipwrecks.

Parys Mountain

Visit the ruined pumping mill on top of **Parys Mountain** by a path from the free car park on the B5111. A box at the car park has leaflets for the Industrial Heritage Trail that leads around Parys' ravaged moonscape, made all the more bizarre by the derelict remains, multicoloured rocks, coppery pools of water and patches of scrubby heather and gorse.

Moelfre and around

MOELFRE's branding as Anglesey's maritime village explains the number of anchors rusting around the village. It has a reputation for shipwrecks – they say the remains of the **Hindlea** can be seen at very low tides off a northern headland after it went down in October 1959, exactly a century after the 2700-ton **Royal Charter** foundered with the loss of four hundred lives and nearly £400,000-worth of gold – though that seems unlikely should you wander around the peaceful grey-pebbled cove on a sunny day. A little more than half a mile north of the centre, **Traeth Lligwy** is a lovely scimitar of white sand tailormade for summer picnics.

Din Lligwy Hut Group

One mile west of Moelfre, off the A5025, LL72 8NH • Open access • Free; CADW • ☎ 01443 336000, ⓦ cadw.gov.wales/daysout /dinlligwyhutgroup

The late Neolithic **Din Lligwy Hut Group** forms the centrepiece of a site spanning three thousand years of human occupation. A five-sided walled enclosure contains the foundations of several circular and rectangular buildings dated to the second and fourth centuries which, along with the hut group on Holy Island (see p.422), give the best indication of how people lived, rather than how they buried their dead. To the northeast of the main enclosure stands **Capel Lligwy**, a ruined twelfth-century church, and a short distance to the south is the **Lligwy Burial Chamber**, with a 28-ton capstone.

ACCOMMODATION   MOELFRE

Arlanfor Village centre, LL72 8HL ☎01248 410555, ⓦarlanfor.co.uk. Fantastic sea views are the big draw at this B&B, whether from the three homely, modern bedrooms or from a terrace. The continental breakfast is great, made from local, artisan produce. Minimum two-night stay. **£75**

Dafarn Rhos Camping Site Lligwy Beach, 1.5 mile

northwest of Moelfre, LL72 8NN ☎01248 410607, ⓦangleseycamping.co.uk. The downsides: portaloos in some fields and access gates that close at 9pm (though you can park outside and walk in to your tent). The upsides: gently sloping fields, sea views and, above all, direct access to the Lligwy beach just beneath. There's an adult-only field. Pitch price includes hook-up. Closed Oct–Easter. **£28**

Red Wharf Bay

A few miles south of Moelfre, **Red Wharf Bay** (Traeth Coch) forms a broad sweep of golden sand that never gets too crowded. Its scale is astonishing at low tide. Most people head for the northern side where facilities are concentrated.

ACCOMMODATION AND EATING   RED WHARF BAY

Anglesey Tipi and Yurt Holidays Cae'r Gaseg, Brynteg, 1 mile northwest, LL78 8JT ☎01248 853162, ⓦanglesey tipis.co.uk. A tranquil, natural retreat in five beautifully crafted yurts (sleeping two to five) – most of which come with a proper bed and have a woodburning stove or a chiminea – plus a tepee. Each is in its own grassy clearing in young woodland – magic for campfires at night. Minimum two nights; three nights on bank/school holidays. **£60**

The Boathouse Red Wharf Bay, LL75 8RJ ☎01248 852731. *The Boathouse* offers beach-shack chic inside and bay views from the garden terrace. A good choice for a home-made fish pie (£11) or steak-and-ale pies; fishcakes with lemon and lime aioli; platters; burgers and

sandwiches. It's always busy. Daily: Feb–Easter, Nov & Dec 10am–4pm; Easter–June, Sept & Oct 10am–7pm; July & Aug 9.30am–9pm.

Ship Inn Red Wharf Bay, LL75 8RJ ☎01248 852568, ⓦshipinnredwharfbay.co.uk. This traditional sailors' inn on the old wharf is one of the nicest spots for a pint (local, naturally) on Anglesey. It's all Toby jugs, ships' wheels and old beams in its two cosy rooms, with picnic tables beside the wharf for summer days. The food's decent, too: prawn sandwiches or full mains like sea bass with a fennel and black pepper crust (£15.95). Pub & kitchen Mon–Fri noon–2.30pm & 6–9pm, Sat & Sun noon–4.30pm & 5.30–9pm.

Llangefni

The main reason to head inland is to visit **LLANGEFNI**, Anglesey's low-key county town and the second largest on the island after Holyhead. A solid farming centre, it's a bastion of Welsh and is home to the **Oriel Ynys Môn** gallery.

Oriel Ynys Môn

Half a mile north of Llangefni on the B5111, LL77 7TQ • Daily 10.30am–5pm • Free • ☎01248 724444, ⓦorielynysmon.info

The combined museum and art gallery, **Oriel Ynys Môn**, provides an excellent overview of the island's turbulent history, from pre-Christian sites and the dynastic lines of the Princes of Gwynedd to exhibits about conservation, shipwrecks and the Welsh language. One corner is devoted to the life and works of **Charles Tunnicliffe** who spent thirty years from 1947 painting wildlife from his Shorelands home in Malltraeth, near Newborough Warren.

ARRIVAL AND DEPARTURE   LLANGEFNI

Llangefni is on the #4 **bus** route between Holyhead (hourly; 50min) and Bangor (hourly; 35min).

DYLAN THOMAS

Contexts

429 History

442 Modern Welsh nationalism

445 Natural history of Wales

451 Music in Wales

457 Film

459 Books

463 Welsh

History

Before the end of the last Ice Age around ten thousand years ago, Wales and the rest of Britain formed part of the greater European whole, while the early migrant inhabitants eked out a meagre existence on the tundra or a better one among the oak, beech and hazel forests in the warmer periods. Most lived in the southeast of Britain, but small groups foraged north and west, leaving 250,000-year-old evidence in the form of a human tooth in a cave near Denbigh in north Wales and a hand axe unearthed near Cardiff.

It wasn't until the early part of the **Upper Paleolithic age** that significant communities settled in Wales, those of the Gower peninsula interring the "Red Lady of Paviland" around 24,000 BC. This civilization remained on Europe's cultural fringe as the melting ice cut Britain off from mainland Europe around 5000 BC. Migrating Mesolithic peoples had already moved north from central Europe and were followed by **Neolithic colonists**, whose mastery of stone- and flint-working found its expression in more than 150 cromlechs (turf-covered chambered tombs) dotted around Wales, primarily Bryn Celli Ddu and Barclodiad y Gawres on Anglesey, and Pentre Ifan in Mynydd Preseli. Skilled in agriculture and animal husbandry, the Neolithic people also began to clear the lush forests, enclosing fields, constructing defensive ditches around their villages and mining for flint.

The earliest stone circles – more extensive meeting places than cromlechs – were built at this time. As the Neolithic period drifted into the **Bronze Age** around 2000 BC, with more sophisticated use of metals, social structures became better organized. The established aristocracy engaged in much tribal warfare, as suggested by large numbers of earthwork forts built during this period – the chief examples being at Holyhead Mountain on Anglesey and the Bulwarks at Chepstow.

The Celts

Celtic invaders spreading from their central European homeland settled in Wales in around 600 BC, imparting a great cultural influence. Familiar with Mediterranean civilization through trading routes, they introduced superior methods of metalworking, forging iron into weapons and coins. Gold was used for ornamental works – the first recognizable Welsh art – heavily influenced by the symbolic, patterned **La Tène** style still thought of as quintessentially Celtic.

The Celts are credited with introducing the basis of modern Welsh (see p.463). This highly developed language was emblematic of a sophisticated social hierarchy headed by **druids** (see box, p.430). Yet the Celts were unable to maintain an organized civic society to match that of their successors, the Romans.

250,000 BC	2000 BC	600 BC	78 AD
Earliest evidence of human existence in Wales.	Bronze Age settlers arrive from the Iberian peninsula.	Celts reach the British Isles bringing their ritual priests, the druids.	Roman conquest of Wales completed as Agricola kills druids of Anglesey.

THE DRUIDS

During Celtic times, the **druids** were a ritual priesthood with attendant poets, seers and warriors. Through a deep knowledge of ritual, legend and the mechanics of the heavens, the druids maintained their position between the people and a pantheon of more than four thousand gods. Most of these were variations of a handful of chief gods worshipped by the great British tribes: the Silures and Demetae in the south of Wales, the Cornovii in mid-Wales and the Ordovices and Deceangli in the north.

The Romans in Wales

Life in Wales, unlike that in most of England, was never fully **Romanized**, the region remaining under legionary control throughout its three-hundred-year occupation. **Julius Caesar** made cross-Channel incursions in 55 and 54 BC, kicking off a century-long but low-level infusion of Roman ideas that filtered across to Wales. After the full-scale invasion in 43 AD the Romans swept across southern England to the frontier of south Wales. Expansionism fomented anti-Roman feeling along the frontier between the lowland zone (southern and central England) and the highland zone (northern England, Scotland and Wales). Traditionally insular Welsh hill tribes united with their Brythonic cousins in northern England to oppose the Romans, who forced a wedge between them. The Roman historian **Tacitus** recorded the submission of the Deceangli near Chester, providing the oldest written mention of a Welsh land. The Romans sent an expeditionary force against the Silures and the toughest nut, the druid stronghold of Anglesey, but were kept at bay until around 75 AD, when legionary forts were built at Deva (Chester, England) and Isca Silurium (Caerleon).

By 78 AD, Wales was under Roman control, its chief **fortresses** at Deva, Isca Silurium and Segontium (Caernarfon) boasting all the trappings of imperial Roman life: bath houses, temples, mosaics and underfloor heating. Through three centuries of occupation, the Celtic people sustained an independent existence, though Roman elements filtered into the Celtic culture: agrarian practices improved, Christianity was partly adopted, the language adopted Latin words (pont for "bridge", ffenestr for "window") and the prevailing La Tène artistic style took on classical Roman elements.

The Roman Empire was already in decline when **Magnus Maximus** (Macsen Wledig) led a campaign to wrest control of the western empire from Emperor Gratian in 383 AD. Maximus' rule was short-lived but Wales was effectively free of direct Roman control by 390.

KING ARTHUR MUDDIES THE WATERS

The fourth and fifth centuries AD were marked by the establishment of the main dynastic kingdoms that were set to steer Wales through the next seven hundred years. The already sketchy history of this period was further muddied in 1136, when Geoffrey of Monmouth published his *History of the Kings of Britain*, portraying **King Arthur** as a feudal king with his court at Caerleon. Victorian Romantics embellished subsequent histories, making it practically impossible to extract much truth from this period.

80–100	Early 4th century	5th–6th century	c.589
Construction of Caerleon amphitheatre completes the trappings of Roman life.	Roman departure from Wales.	Age of Saints.	St David (Dewi Sant) dies after a life of miracles. He later becomes Wales' patron saint.

IRELAND INVADES WALES

In the fifth century, the **Irish** (Gwyddyl), who had a long tradition of migrating to the Llŷn and parts of mid-Wales, attacked the coast and formed distinct colonies, but were soon expelled from the north by **Cunedda Wledig**, the leader of a Brythonic tribe from near Edinburgh, who went on to found the royal house of Gwynedd, consolidating the Brythonic language and naming regions of his kingdom – the modern Ceredigion and Meirionydd – after his sons. In the southwest, the Irish influence was sustained; the kingdom of **Dyfed** shows clear Irish origins.

The age of the saints

Historical orthodoxy views the departure of literate Latin historians, skilled stonemasons and an all-powerful army as heralding the **Dark Ages**. In fact, a civic society probably flourished until a century later, when the collapse of trade routes was hastened by the dramatic spread of Islam around the Mediterranean, and Romanized society gave way to a structured form of **Celtic society**. For the next few centuries, **Teutonic barbarian tribes** struggled for supremacy in the post-Roman power vacuum in southern and eastern England but had little influence in Wales where Irish incursions took place against a background of increasing religious energy (see box above).

Between the fifth and the sixth centuries the **Celtic saints**, ascetic evangelical missionaries, spread the gospel around Ireland and western Britain, promoting the Middle Eastern eremitical tradition of living a reclusive life. Where their message took root, they founded simple churches within a consecrated enclosure, or llan, which often took the saint's name, hence Llanberis (St Peris), Llandeilo (St Teilo) and numerous others. In south Wales, **St David** (Dewi Sant) was the most popular (and subsequently Wales' patron saint), dying around 589 after a miracle-filled life, during which he established the religious community at St Davids, which had become a place of pilgrimage by the twelfth century.

The Welsh kingdoms

Towards the end of the sixth century the **Angles** and **Saxons** in eastern Britain began to entertain designs on the western lands. The inability of the independent western peoples to unify against this threat left the most powerful kingdom, Gwynedd, as the centre of cultural and political resistance. The weaker groups were unable to hold the invaders, and after the battle at Dyrham, near Gloucester in 577, the Britons in Cornwall were separated from those in Wales, who became similarly cut off from their northern kin in Cumbria after the battle of Chester in 616. In the meantime, and bonded by their resistance to the Saxons, the Welsh started to refer to themselves as **Cymry** (fellow-countrymen), rather than the Saxon term **"Welsh"**, which is generally thought to mean either foreigners or Romanized people.

The eighth-century construction of **Offa's Dyke** (Clawdd Offa) – a linear earthwork demarcating, rather than defending, the boundary between Wales and the kingdom of Mercia – gave the Welsh a firm eastern border and allowed them to concentrate on unifying the patchwork of kingdoms as their coasts were being harried by **Norse and Viking invaders**.

616	c.784	c.900–1050	1066
Battle of Chester – Wales isolated from rest of Britain.	The completion of Offa's Dyke physically separates England from Wales.	Hywel Dda largely reunifies Wales and codifies the Law of Wales.	Normans invade England and set up Lords Marcher to control the Welsh borderlands.

Rhodri Mawr (Rhodri the Great) killed the Viking leader off Anglesey, helping the country's rise towards statehood through his unification of most of Wales. By this stage, England had developed into a single powerful kingdom, and though the various branches of Rhodri's line went on to rule most of Wales down to the late thirteenth century, the princedoms were frequently forced to swear fealty to the English kings. Defensive problems were exacerbated by the practice of partible inheritance, which left each of Rhodri's sons with an equal part of Wales to control.

Rhodri Mawr's grandson **Hywel Dda** (Hywel the Good) largely reunified the country from southwest Wales. He added Powys and Gwynedd to his domain, but his most valuable legacy is his codification and promulgation of the medieval **Law of Wales** (see box above). After Hywel's death in 950, anarchy and internal turmoil reigned until his great-great-grandson, **Gruffydd ap Llywelyn**, seized power in Gwynedd in 1039. He unified all of Wales, taking the coronation of the weak English king, Edward the Confessor, as an opportunity to annex some of the Marches in Mercia. Edward's successor, Harold, wasn't having any of this and killed Gruffydd, heralding a new phase of political fragmentation.

The arrival of the Normans

In 1066, the **Normans** swept across the English Channel and stormed England. Though Wales was unable to present a unified opposition to the invaders, the Norman king, William, didn't attempt to conquer Wales. The **Domesday Book** – commissioned in 1085 to record land ownership as a framework for taxation – indicates that he only nibbled at parts of Powys and Gwynedd. Instead, he installed a huge retinue of barons, the **Lords Marcher**, along the border to bring as much Welsh territory under their own jurisdiction as possible. Despite generations of squabbling, the barons managed to hold onto their privileges until Henry VIII's Act of Union more than four hundred years later.

A lack of English commitment or resources allowed the Welsh to claw back their territory through years when distinctions between English, Normans and Welsh were beginning to blur, which helped form three stable political entities: Powys, Deheubarth and Gwynedd. The latter, led by **Owain Gwynedd** from his capital at Aberffraw on Anglesey, now extended beyond Offa's Dyke and progressively gained hegemony over the other two. Owain Gwynedd's grandson, Llywelyn ap Iorwerth (the Great), incorporated the weaker territories to the south into his kingdom and captured several Norman castles to reach the peak of the Welsh feudal pyramid. After tussling with England's King John, Llywelyn won a degree of Welsh autonomy, though this largely fell apart after his death.

1180–93	1188	1196–1240	1246–82
St Davids Cathedral built.	Archbishop Baldwin (accompanied by Giraldus Cambrensis) recruits for the Third Crusade.	Llywelyn ap Iorwerth (the Great) rules as Prince of Gwynedd and later most of Wales.	Llywelyn ap Gruffydd (the Last) intermittently rules large parts of Wales.

Edward I's conquest

Most of the work of regrouping Wales around one standard fell to Llywelyn the Great's grandson, **Llywelyn ap Gruffydd** (Llewellyn the Last). In the 1250s, he won control of Gwynedd, then pushed the English out of most of Wales. The English king Henry III was forced to ratify the **Treaty of Montgomery** in 1267, thereby recognizing Llywelyn as "Prince of Wales" in return for his homage. The English monarchy's war with the barons allowed Llywelyn time to politically consolidate his lands, which now stretched over all of modern Wales excepting Pembrokeshire and parts of the Marches.

The tables turned when **Edward I** succeeded Henry III and began a crusade to unify Britain. With effective use of sea power, Edward had little trouble forcing the already weakened Llywelyn back into Snowdonia. Peace was restored with the **Treaty of Aberconwy**, which deprived Llywelyn of almost all his land and stripped him of his financial tributes from the other Welsh princes, but left him with the hollow title of "Prince of Wales".

Edward now set about surrounding Llywelyn's land with castles at Aberystwyth, Builth Wells, Flint and Rhuddlan. After a relatively cordial four-year period, Llywelyn's brother Dafydd rose against Edward, inevitably dragging Llywelyn along with him. Edward didn't hesitate and swept through Gwynedd, crushing the revolt and laying the foundations for the remaining castles in his **Iron Ring**, those at Conwy, Caernarfon, Harlech and Beaumaris. Llywelyn, already battered by Edward's force, was captured and executed at Cilmeri in 1282.

Throughout the fourteenth century, famine and the Black Death plagued Wales. The Marcher Lords appropriated the lands of defaulting debtors, while royal officials clawed in all the income they could from towns around the castles. These factors and the pent-up resentment of the English sowed seeds of a rebellion led by the tyrannical but charismatic **Owain Glyndŵr** (see box, p.283).

The Tudors and the Act of Union

During the latter half of the fifteenth century, the succession to the English throne was contested in the **Wars of the Roses** between the houses of York (white rose) and Lancaster (red rose). Welsh allegiance lay broadly with the Lancastrians, who had the support of the ascendant north Welsh Tewdwr (or Tudor) family. Henry Tudor escaped from besieged Harlech Castle to Brittany when Yorkist Richard III took the English throne in 1471. Fourteen years later, Henry returned to Wales, defeating Richard at the

---

THE STATUTE OF RHUDDLAN

The **Statute of Rhuddlan** in 1284 set down the terms by which the English monarch was to rule Wales: much of it was given to the Marcher Lords who had helped Edward I, the rest was divided into administrative and legal districts similar to those in England. Though the treaty is often seen as a symbol of English subjugation, it respected much of Welsh law and provided a basis for civil rights and privileges. Many Welsh were content to accept and exploit Edward's rule for their own benefit. In 1294, however, a rebellion led by Madog ap Llywelyn gripped Wales and was only halted by Edward's swift and devastating response. Most of the privileges enshrined in the Statute of Rhuddlan were rescinded.

1270–1320	1277	1277–83	1284
Tintern Abbey built.	Llywelyn humiliated. Signs Treaty of Aberconwy at the end of the First War of Welsh Independence.	Edward I begins Aberystwyth, Flint, Rhuddlan, Caernarfon, Conwy and Harlech castles.	Statute of Rhuddlan signed by Edward I.

Battle of Bosworth Field, so becoming **Henry VII** and sealing the Lancastrian ascendancy.

For the most part Henry lived up to the high Welsh expectations, removing many of the restrictions on land ownership imposed at the start of **Owain Glyndŵr's uprising** against the Kingdom of England at the beginning of the fifteenth century (see p.283) and promoting many Welshmen to high office.

Just as Henry VIII's decision to convert his kingdom from Catholicism to Protestantism was borne more from his desire to divorce his first wife than from any religious conviction, it was his need for money which brought about the **Dissolution of the Monasteries** in 1536 – ultimately resulting in a more studied approach to religion and learning in general. Under the reign of Elizabeth I, Jesus College was founded in Oxford for Welsh scholars, and the Bible was translated into Welsh for the first time by a team led by Bishop **William Morgan** (see box, p.394). The Dissolution hastened the emergence of the Anglo-Welsh gentry, a group eager to claim a Welsh pedigree while promoting the English language and the legal system.

Act of Union

Wales had been largely controlled by the English monarch since the Statute of Rhuddlan in 1284 (see box, p.433), but sovereignty was finally fixed in Henry VIII's 1536 **Act of Union** (and a subsequent act of 1543). It's a misleading title, and one that was not used to describe the Act until the twentieth century, for it implies a level of equality between the two nations that did not exist. Unlike the Acts of 1707 and 1800 that brought Scotland and Ireland into the Union – and were the decisions of independent parliaments in Edinburgh, Dublin and London – the 1536 Act was a unilateral decision by Westminster, which had no Welsh representation. It decreed that English was to be the only language of the courts and other official bodies, effectively creating a two-tier Wales of English-speaking lords and masters and a Welsh-speaking proletariat. At the same time the Marches were replaced by shires (the equivalent of modern counties), the Welsh laws codified by Hywel Dda were avoided, and partible inheritance (equal among all offspring) gave way to primogeniture, the eldest son becoming the sole heir. This period set in stone the struggles and the injustices that are still playing out nearly five hundred years later.

The Civil War and the rise of Nonconformism

A direct descendant of the Tudors, **James I** came to the throne in 1603 to general popular approval in Wales. Many privileges granted to the Welsh during the Tudor reign came to an end, but the idea of common citizenship was retained, the Council of Wales remaining as a focus for Welsh nationalism. James, fearful of both Catholicism and the new threat of Puritanism – an extreme form of Protestantism – courted a staunchly Anglican Wales and curried the favour of Welsh ministers in the increasingly powerful Parliament. Though weak in Wales, **Puritanism** was gaining a foothold, especially in the Welsh borders, where William Wroth and Walter Cradock set up Wales' first dissenting church at Llanfaches in Monmouthshire in 1639.

The monarchy's relations with the Welsh were strained by **Charles I**, who was forced to levy heavy taxes and recruit troops, but the gentry were mostly loyal to the king at

1301	1400–12	1485	1536–38
Edward I revives title of "Prince of Wales" and bestows it on his son, Edward II.	Owain Glyndŵr's revolt ushers in a third War of Welsh Independence. Glyndŵr dies in hiding in 1416.	Henry VII ascends the throne after landing from exile at Pembroke and beating Richard III at Bosworth.	Henry VIII orders the Dissolution of the Monasteries.

the outbreak of the **Civil War**, which saw the Parliamentary forces install **Oliver Cromwell** as the leader of the **Commonwealth**. The Puritan support for Parliament didn't go unnoticed, and after Charles' execution, they were rewarded with the livings of numerous parishes and the roots of Puritan **Nonconformism** spread in Wales.

As Cromwell's regime became more oppressive, the Anglican majority welcomed the successful return of the exiled **Charles II**, and the monarchy was restored, thereby suppressing Nonconformity. The Baptists, Independents and Quakers who made up the bulk of Nonconformists continued to worship in secret until **James II** passed the **Toleration Act** in 1689. Despite finally allowing open worship, the act still banned the employment of dissenters in municipal government, a limitation which remained in force until 1828.

The rise of Methodism

The propagation of Nonconformism led to a welter of new religious books in Welsh in the late seventeenth century, but with most people still illiterate, religious observance remained an oral tradition. In 1699, the **Society for Promoting Christian Knowledge** established schools where the Bible, along with reading, writing and arithmetic, was taught in Welsh as well as English. This met with considerable success in middle-class anglicized towns, but failed to reach rural areas where children couldn't be spared from farm duties. The next big reformist push came in 1731, when **Griffith Jones** organized reading classes in the evenings and quieter winter season, so farmers and their families could attend. Within thirty years, half the Welsh population could read.

By the middle of the eighteenth century, a receptive and literate populace was ready for what became the **Methodist Revival**, driven by a strong belief in a resurgent Welsh nation. In contrast to the staid Anglican services, the Methodists held evangelical meetings. Meanwhile, improved schooling brought about a literary revolution, and Welsh re-established itself as the language for a vast body of literature.

In 1811, the Calvinist Methodists broke from the framework of Anglicanism. As the gentry remained with the Established Church, the chapel became the focus of social life, discouraging folk traditions considered incompatible with puritanical thrift and temperance. Political radicalism was also discouraged and since only property owners were eligible to vote, established dynasties were perpetuated.

The Industrial Revolution

Small-scale mining and smelting had taken place in Wales since the Bronze Age, but agriculture remained the mainstay of an economy centred on meat, wool and butter. The enormous rise in grain prices in the early nineteenth century forced Welsh farmers to diversify and adopt the more advanced English farming practices of crop rotation, fertilizing and stock breeding. Around the same time, acts of Parliament allowed previously common land to be "enclosed", the grazing rights often being assigned solely to the largest landowner in the district. Inevitably, this forced smallholders to migrate to the towns where ever more workers were required to mine the seams and stoke the furnaces, fuelling the **Industrial Revolution**. In the north, **John Wilkinson** started his ironworks at Bersham and developed a new method of boring cylinders for steam

1536–43	1588	1639	1646
Acts of Union unite Wales and England, conferring equal rights but with government conducted wholly in English.	The complete Bible is translated into Welsh for the first time, chiefly by William Morgan.	First Puritan congregation in Wales convened at Llanfaches, Gwent.	Harlech and Raglan besieged during the Civil War. Harlech, the last Royalist castle, falls in 1647.

RAIL, STEAM AND SPEED

Britain's greatest nineteenth-century **engineers** made their names in Wales: **Thomas Telford** built canal aqueducts and successfully spanned the Menai Strait with one of Britain's earliest suspension bridges (1826); **Isambard Kingdom Brunel** surveyed the Merthyr–Cardiff train line, then pushed his Great Western network almost to Fishguard; and **Robert Stephenson** speeded the passage of trains between London and Holyhead on Anglesey (1850) for the Irish ferry connection.

---

engines; in the south, foundries sprang up in the valleys around Merthyr Tydfil under English ironmasters. Gradually the under-educated, impoverished, chapel-going Welsh began to be governed by rich, church-going, English industrial barons.

Improved materials and working methods enabled the exploitation of deeper **coal seams**, particularly in the south Wales valleys, not just to supply the iron smelters but for domestic fuel and to power locomotives and steamships. South Wales' rural valleys were ripped apart and quiet hamlets turned into long rows of terraced houses snaking up the valley sides, roofed in north Wales slate. **Transportation** of huge quantities of coal and steel was crucial for continued economic expansion, initially on the roads and canals built in the early nineteenth century, then by train as the 1850s rail boom took hold.

In mining towns, working conditions were atrocious, with men and women toiling incredibly long hours in dangerous conditions; children as young as 6 worked alongside them, until this was outlawed by the Mines Act in 1842. Pay was low and often in a currency redeemable only at the poorly stocked, expensive company ("truck") shop. The **Anti-Truck Act** of 1831 improved matters, but a combination of rising population, fluctuating prices and growing need for political change brought calls for reform. The 1832 **Reform Bill** fell far short of the demands for universal suffrage by ballot and the removal of property requirement for voters. This swelled the ranks of the Reformist Chartist movement, and when a petition with more than a million signatures was rejected by Parliament, the **Chartist Riots** broke out in northern England and south Wales. In 1839, Newport was witness to a disastrous Chartist demonstration, the marchers walking straight into a trap laid by troops, who killed more than twenty men and captured their leader, **John Frost**. The movement continued in a weakened form for twenty years, buoyed by the **Rebecca Riots** in 1839–43, when guerrilla tactics put an end to tollgates on south Welsh turnpikes.

The second half of the nineteenth century

During the latter half of the nineteenth century the radical reformist movement slowly became entwined with religion, with the Nonconformists petitioning for **disestablishment** of the Church in Wales. Eventually, as a consequence of the 1867 Reform Act, industrial workers and small tenant farmers got the vote, giving a long-awaited strong working-class element to the electorate. The following year, **Henry Richard** was elected as Liberal MP for Merthyr Tydfil, becoming the first Welsh member of what soon became the dominant political force and bringing the ideas of Nonconformity – land reform, disestablishment and the preservation of the Welsh language – to Parliament for the first time.

1759	1782	1794	1839
Dowlais Ironworks started, followed by Merthyr Tydfil iron industry.	Beginning of north Wales slate industry with the opening of Pennant's Penrhyn slate quarry at Bethesda.	Cardiff to Merthyr canal completed.	Chartists uprising in Newport led by John Frost.

THE RISE IN WELSH CONSCIOUSNESS

Immigration to the coal fields from England in the mid- to late nineteenth century meant that English became the language of commerce and the route to advancement, Welsh being reserved for the home and chapel life of seventy percent of the population. Welsh was still being spoken in Nonconformist schools when, in 1846, they were inspected by three English barristers and seven Anglican assistants. The inspectors' report – known as **The Treason of the Blue Books** – declared the standards deplorable, largely because of the use of the Welsh tongue. The public defence of Welsh that ensued failed to prevent the introduction of the notorious "Welsh Not", effectively a ban on speaking Welsh in school.

As the nineteenth-century Romantic movement took hold throughout Britain, the London Welsh looked to their heritage. The ancient tales of *The Mabinogion* (the earliest prose works in Britain) were translated into English, the **Welsh Language Society** was founded in 1885, eisteddfodau (see box, p.452) were reintroduced as part of rural life and the ancient bardic order, the **Gorsedd**, was reinvented. But disestablishment remained the *cause célèbre* of Welsh nationalism. Perhaps the greatest advocate of both separatism and Welsh nationalism was **Michael D. Jones** (see box, p.322), who helped establish a Welsh homeland in **Patagonia**. By 1907 Wales had a national library at Aberystwyth, and twenty years later a national museum in Cardiff, which was now the largest city in Wales.

The 1872 Secret Ballot Act and 1884 Reform Act enfranchised farm labourers and further freed up the electoral system, although the Anglican Church was only disestablished in 1920. The Nonconformist Sunday Schools offered primary education for the masses, supplemented by a number of secondary schools, as well as Wales' first major tertiary establishment in Aberystwyth in 1872, followed by colleges at Cardiff (1883) and Bangor (1884). Until they were federated into the University of Wales in 1893, voluntary contributions garnered by Nonconformist chapels supported the colleges. The apotheosis of "Chapel power" came in 1881 with the passing of the Welsh Sunday Closing Act, enshrining Nonconformism's three basic tenets: observance of the Sabbath, sobriety and Welshness.

Industry and the rise of trade unionism

The rise in Welsh consciousness in the mid-nineteenth cetury (see box above) paralleled the rise in importance of the **trade unions**. The 1850s were a prosperous time in the Welsh coal fields, but by the end of the 1860s the Amalgamated Union of Miners was forced to call a strike (1869–71), which resulted in higher wages.

A second strike in 1875 failed and the miners' agent, **William Abraham (Mabon)**, ushered in the notorious "sliding scale", which fixed wage levels according to the selling price of coal. This brought considerable hardship to the Valleys, which became an insular world with strictly ordered social codes. Meanwhile, annual coal production doubled in twenty years. By 1913, 57 million tons were being extracted each year by a quarter of a million people. Similarly punitive pay schemes were implemented in the north Wales slate quarries where membership of **Undeb Chwarelwyr Gogledd Cymru** (the North Wales Quarrymen's Union) was all but outlawed by the slate barons. Things came to a head in 1900 when the workers at Lord Penrhyn's quarry at Bethesda started one of Britain's longest-ever industrial disputes, lasting three years.

1845–50	1872	1884	1900
Britannia Tubular Bridge built across the Menai Strait.	University College of Wales opens in Aberystwyth, followed by Cardiff (1883) and Bangor (1884).	Reform Act. Farm labourers and small tenant farmers get the vote for the first time.	Britain's first Labour MP, Kier Hardie, elected for Merthyr Tydfil.

From 1885, the vast majority of Welsh MPs were Liberals who helped end the sliding scale in 1902 and brought in an eight-hour day by 1908. The start of the twentieth century heralded the birth of a new political force when **Keir Hardie** became Britain's first Labour MP, for Merthyr Tydfil.

The world wars

World War I (1914–18) was a watershed for Welsh society. The Welsh identified with the plight of defenceless European nations and rallied to fight alongside the English and Scots. At home, the state increasingly intervened in people's lives: agriculture was controlled by the state, which rationed food, and industries, mines and railways were under public control. The need for Welsh food and coal boosted the economy and living standards rose dramatically. Many were proud to be led through the war by Welsh lawyer **David Lloyd George** (see p.442), who rose to the post of minister of munitions, then of war, becoming prime minister by 1916. By the time conscription was introduced, patriotic fervour had waned. Many miners, reluctant to be slaughtered in the trenches and resentful of massive wartime profits, welcomed the 1917 Bolshevik Revolution in Russia, and though Communism never really took hold, the socialist Labour Party benefitted from the postwar fallout.

Similar dramatic changes were taking place in **rural areas**, where Welsh farming was embracing new machinery and coming out of nearly a century of neglect. High wartime inflation of land prices and the fall in rents forced some landowners to sell off portions of major estates to their tenants in the so-called "green revolution".

After the postwar boom came the **Depression**. All of Wales' mining and primary production industries suffered, and unemployment reached 27 percent, worse than in England and Scotland. South Wales soon became the **Labour movement**'s stronghold in

---

PLAID CYMRU: THE EARLY YEARS

By 1925, as a new sense of nationalism was emerging in Wales, champions of Welsh autonomy formed **Plaid Genedlaethol Cymru** (the National Party of Wales), often known as Plaid. In September 1936, in one of the first modern separatist protests, its president **Saunders Lewis** joined two other Plaid members (the Rev. Lewis Valentine and D.J. Williams) and set fire to the construction hut of a new aerodrome being built on the Llŷn as part of Britain's build-up to the war. They immediately reported themselves to the nearest police station, attracting huge publicity in the process. Interest in the ensuing trial electrified Wales, causing howls of outrage when the government decided to divert it from sympathetic Caernarfon to the Old Bailey in London. Even recalcitrant nationalist Lloyd George was outspokenly critical of the English decision. The three men were duly imprisoned for nine months, becoming Plaid Cymru's first heroes. Lewis spent the rest of his life immersed in literary criticism, and developed into one of Wales' greatest modern writers.

Similar public displays and powerful nationalist rhetoric won over an intellectual majority, but the voting majority continued to fuel the Labour ascendancy in both local and national politics. Plaid Cymru were less enthusiastic about World War II, remaining neutral and expressing unease at the large number of English evacuees potentially weakening the fabric of Welsh communities. However, the war saw the formation of a Welsh elementary school in Aberystwyth and Undeb Cymru Fydd, a committee designed to defend the welfare of Wales.

1925	1926	1936	1951
Plaid Genedlaethol Cymru (Welsh National Party) formed.	Miners' strike and General Strike.	Saunders Lewis and nationalist colleagues burn building materials on the Llŷn.	Minister for Welsh Affairs appointed.

Britain. This was challenged by Lloyd George's newly resurgent Liberal Party, but his Westminster-centred politics were no longer trusted in Wales and Labour held firm, seeking to improve workers' conditions: the state of housing was still desperate, and health care and welfare services needed boosting. The Labour Party effectively became the hope that had previously been entrusted to the chapels, though nationalists were drawn to a new party, **Plaid Cymru** (see box opposite).

Some relief from the Depression came with re-armament in the lead-up to **World War II**, but by this stage vast numbers had migrated from south Wales to England, leaving the already insular communities banding together in self-reliant groups centred on local co-ops and welfare halls. The demands of the war saw unemployment all but disappear and the Welsh economy gradually restructured, with more people switching from extractive industries to light manufacturing, a process that continues today.

The postwar period

Any hopes for a greater national identity were dashed by the Attlee Labour government from 1945 to 1951, which nationalized transport and utilities with little regard for national boundaries. However, under the direction of Ebbw Vale MP, **Aneurin Bevan**, the postwar Labour government instituted the National Health Service, dramatically improving health care in Wales and the rest of Britain, and provided much-improved council housing.

The nationalized **coal industry**, now employing less than half the number of twenty years before, was still the most important employer at nationalization, but a gradual process of closing inefficient deep mines saw the number of pits drop from 212 in 1945 to 11 in 1989 – and none is working today. Sadly, the same commitment wasn't directed at cleaning up the scars of more than a century of mining until after 1966, when one of south Wales' most tragic accidents left a school and 116 children buried under a slag heap at **Aberfan** (see p.111).

The Labour Party remained in overwhelming control during the 1960s and 1970s, though the party's reluctance to address nationalist issues allowed Plaid Cymru to become a serious opposition for the first time. Attlee had thrown out the suggestion of a Welsh Secretary of State in 1946, and not until Plaid Cymru fielded numerous candidates in the 1959 election did the Labour manifesto promise a cabinet position for Wales.

The position of **Secretary of State for Wales** was finally created in 1964 by Harold Wilson's Labour government, who also created the **Welsh Development Agency** and moved the Royal Mint to Llantrisant in south Wales. With Plaid Cymru's appeal considered to be restricted to rural areas, Labour was shocked by the 1966 Carmarthen by-election, when **Gwynfor Evans** became the first Plaid MP. It wasn't until 1974 that Plaid also won in the constituencies of Caernarfon and Meirionydd, and suddenly the party was a threat, forcing Labour to address the question of **devolution** (see p.440).

Modern Wales

In 1978 Labour tabled the **Wales Act**, promising the country an elected assembly to act as a voice for Wales, but with no power to legislate or raise revenue. In the subsequent **referendum** in 1979, eighty percent of voters opposed the proposition, with even the

1955	1966	1967	1982
Cardiff declared capital of Wales.	Gwynfor Evans, first Plaid Cymru MP, elected for Carmarthen. Aberfan disaster kills 147.	Welsh Language Act passed. Limited recognition of Welsh as a formal, legal language.	Welsh-language TV channel S4C begins broadcasting.

nationalist stronghold of Gwynedd voting against it. That same year, the Conservative government under **Margaret Thatcher** came to power, winning an unprecedented 31 percent of Welsh votes. The referendum that year effectively sidelined the home-rule issue and Thatcher was able to implement her free-market policies. With 43 percent of the Welsh workforce as government employees, privatization had a dramatic impact. The number of jobs in the steel industry, manufacturing and construction all plummeted, doubling unemployment in five years. Despite this, the Conservatives increased their tally of MPs at the 1983 election, while Labour saw their lowest percentage since 1918.

The resulting breakdown of traditional Valley communities and successive anti-union measures failed to break the solidarity of south Welsh workers during the year-long **miners' strike** (1984–85). Meanwhile, the Welsh continued to turn away from the established religions and the chapel ceased to be the focal point of community life. Something like two-thirds of the country's six thousand chapels have since closed.

During the 1980s, support for Plaid Cymru shifted back to the rural areas, enthusiasm for the Welsh language increased and a steady decline in numbers of Welsh-speakers was reversed. New Welsh-only schools opened even in predominantly English-speaking areas, learners' classes sprouted everywhere and in 1982 S4C, the first **Welsh-language television channel**, began broadcasting (see box, p.443).

The National Assembly and devolution

When Tony Blair and "New" Labour won a huge majority in the general election of 1997, one of the central policy proposals was the **devolution** of some degree of power from London to a parliament in Scotland and a **National Assembly for Wales** – the first all-Wales tier of government for six hundred years. The proposal was endorsed by the Welsh people only by the most slender of margins – just six thousand people – in a referendum. The first of the four-yearly elections to the Assembly took place in 1999, when a huge swing to Plaid Cymru denied the Labour party its assumed overall majority. Labour has remained the largest party ever since, with the late **Rhodri Morgan**, who was a committed supporter of Welsh devolution, as First Minister for most of that time. **Carwyn Jones** took over as leader of Labour and First Minister in 2009, a position he still holds.

In 2006 the Government of Wales Act affirmed that the Queen would, for the first time, appoint Welsh ministers and sign Welsh orders in Council. As the Assembly moved into a snazzy new building on the waterfront of Cardiff Bay, the Welsh Government really began to enmesh itself into the fabric of Welsh life. In the National Assembly 2007 election, after more than eighty years in opposition, **Plaid** helped form the government, but in the 2011 elections, its support dropped dramatically and it recorded its worst showing at an assembly election (just eleven seats) – so low that the Conservatives became the major opposition.

The 2006 Government of Wales Act had made provision for a **referendum** on further **devolution** of powers, and in March 2011 a "Yes" vote finally allowed the Welsh Government to create primary legislation (ie "Welsh laws") without consulting Westminster. Almost two-thirds of voters supported the change, with Monmouthshire the only county to vote "No". In the 2015 general election, the Welsh Conservatives

1984–85	1992	1997	1999
Miners' strike.	Welsh Language Bill gives Welsh equal status with English in public bodies.	Referendum on Welsh Assembly. Only half the country votes, of whom 50.3 percent vote yes, a majority of just six thousand nationwide.	First Welsh Assembly elections. Assembly begins sitting. Wales hosts the Rugby World Cup.

made slight inroads into Labour, gaining three seats, while Plaid Cymru retained its three seats in Westminster. Meanwhile, in the National Assembly election of 2016, a partial revival by Plaid Cymru saw an increase in its number of seats to twelve and a return to its position as the official opposition to Labour.

Brexit and the future

In Britain's 2016 **"Brexit"** referendum, Wales voted to leave the EU by 52.5 percent to 47.5 percent, a figure that roughly mirrored the numbers in the UK as a whole. Given that Wales had long been one of the biggest beneficiaries of EU financial aid, this was one of the most startling aspects of the referendum result, and while the impact is yet to be fully played out, there is no doubt that the effects of departure from the EU are likely to be profound for the country. In the 2017 snap **general election**, Welsh Labour achieved its highest share of the vote since 1997, gaining three seats in the process. Conversely, the Conservatives fared poorly, losing three seats, while there was an additional seat for Plaid Cymru, taking its tally to four, its highest number since 2001.

Brexit aside, there are other serious issues facing Wales today: farming lurches along in a state of semi-paralysis, and poverty and ill health still dog many old working-class communities. Nevertheless, these are interesting times: even taking into account the uncertainty ahead there is the undeniable feeling that this small country is facing a brighter future than many would have dared predict even one generation ago. Recent years have seen a significant surge of national confidence and self-expression, particularly in the cultural and sporting arenas, while much hope is invested in a thriving **tourism** industry that is seeking to make the most out of Wales' wonderful natural resources.

2006	**2011**	**2016**
The new Welsh Assembly building (the Senedd) opens on St Davids Day. Government of Wales Act gains Royal Assent.	Wales emphatically votes for primary law-making powers.	Wales votes to leave the EU, along with the UK as a whole.

Modern Welsh nationalism

Plaid Cymru – the Welsh nationalist political party – was formed in 1925 (see box, p.438), but the political impetus that gave birth to the new movement had been bubbling for decades, if not centuries.

The Welsh identity had always been culturally rich, but was politically expressed only as part of the great Liberal tradition: in the dying years of the nineteenth century, 25 or 30 Welsh Liberal MPs often voted en bloc, making their voice heard. The fiery Welsh patriot **David Lloyd George** (1863–1945; prime minister 1916–22) had embodied many people's nationalist beliefs, although his espousal of greater independence for Wales came unstuck when, ever the expedient politician, he realized the potential difficulty of translating this ideal into hard votes in the industrialized, anglicized south of Wales. During Lloyd George's premiership, the Irish Free State was established, drawing inevitable comparisons with the Home Rule demands being less stridently articulated in Scotland and Wales. But the Liberal Party was in sharp decline, nowhere more markedly than in the industrialized Valleys, which had deserted them in favour of new socialist parties. With the urban slide of Liberalism, Welsh nationalism was gradually honed into the embryonic **Plaid Cymru**.

Postwar Wales

Prewar Liberal tradition was still strong in rural Wales, though by the 1951 election this had become just three parliamentary seats out of 36. The **Labour party** was now the establishment in Wales, winning an average of around sixty percent of votes in elections from 1945 to 1966. Two Welsh Labour MPs, Megan Lloyd George, daughter of the great Liberal premier, and S.O. Davies, spearheaded new parliamentary demands for greater Welsh independence, presenting a 1956 petition to parliament demanding a Welsh assembly. Massive popular protests against the continued flooding of Welsh valleys and villages to provide water for England shook the establishment.

The 1963 formation of the boisterous Cymdeithas yr Iaith Gymraeg – the **Welsh Language Society** – attracted a new youthful breed of cultural and linguistic nationalists. The ruling Conservatives offered the sop of nominating a part-time Welsh minister, confirming Cardiff as the capital and making the red dragon the official Welsh flag. Meanwhile, the Labour party formed a Welsh Council where Labour MPs, trade unionists and ordinary party members began to articulate the need for greater independence.

In the **general election of 1964**, the Labour party stood on a more nationalistic platform than ever before. As usual, they swept the board in Wales, and finally won throughout the UK as a whole. The post of **secretary of state for Wales**, backed by a separate Welsh Office, was created, although with fewer powers than the Scottish equivalent.

Plaid Cymru starts to win

Plaid Cymru scored its first hit when its president, Gwynfor Evans, won a by-election in Carmarthen in July 1966. In the heart of socialist south Wales, Plaid ran the Labour government astonishingly close in two by-elections – in Rhondda West (1967) and Caerphilly (1968) – and the party saw swings of over 25 percent to cut Labour majorities of more than twenty thousand to just a couple of thousand. It seemed that Plaid's time had come. Its traditional vote in the north and west was soaring and it appeared that the party had finally overcome its single-issue status around the Welsh language.

Despite amassing 176,000 votes (eleven percent of the poll in Wales) in the **1970 general election**, Plaid failed to take any new seats and even lost their place in Carmarthen.

Gwynfor Evans was returned in Carmarthen in 1974, but Plaid's earlier success in the industrialized south had evaporated, and they once again became a party of rural Wales.

The new Labour government now set up the **Wales Development Agency**, devolved the huge responsibilities of the Department of Trade and Industry in Wales to the Welsh Office in Cardiff, and even supported a referendum on devolution.

The 1979 referendum and beyond

On St David's Day 1979, the Welsh people made their feelings known, when a four-to-one majority rejected the devolution proposal. People feared being swamped by (toothless) bureaucracy, and a large number of the eighty percent of the country who did not speak Welsh feared that a Welsh assembly would be the preserve of a new "Taffia", a *Cymraeg* elite. Both north and south Walians worried about potential domination by the other.

The shock waves were great. Weeks later, the Labour government fell and **Margaret Thatcher**'s first Conservative administration was ushered in. Political nationalism seemed to have gone off the boil, and Plaid Cymru were back to just two MPs in the northwest. In the early 1980s Britain's manufacturing base collapsed and unemployment rose, particularly in south Wales, where mines and foundries closed. Welsh nationalism was suffering an identity crisis, typified by Plaid Cymru's controversial 1981 rewriting of its own constitution to fight for an avowedly "Welsh socialist state", causing some of its more conservative members to quit the party. Basing itself as a republican, left-wing party would, it was believed, bring greater fruit in the populated south.

In the 1980s, Plaid Cymru began to broaden its base with a firmly socialist, **internationalist outlook**. The party matured, developing serious policies on all aspects of Welsh life, from traditional rallying calls of language and media to sophisticated analyses of economic policy, the Welsh legal framework and the country's role in the European Union. But Welsh devolution ceased to be the preserve of Plaid Cymru alone. Both Labour and the Liberal Democrats evolved devolutionary strategies for Wales and Scotland. Even the ruling Conservatives devolved more decision-making out to the Welsh Office in Cardiff. This, ironically, strengthened the nationalist hand. Plaid and the other parties pointed out that a huge swath of government existed in Wales, not overseen by any all-Wales authority. The call for a Welsh assembly to oversee this vast array of public expenditure was consistently supported by huge majorities in opinion polls, and formed the basis of the Labour Party's manifesto for Wales throughout the 1990s.

Labour government and a new referendum

The **1997 general election** changed everything. The Conservatives were spectacularly swept from power, failing to keep any seats in Wales. Labour – or "New" Labour as the party was styled under Tony Blair – won hugely, denting any further Plaid progress.

Within six months of Blair's election, **referendums** took place in Wales and Scotland

S4C: A CHANNEL FOR WALES

Plaid President and former MP Gwynfor Evans was single-handedly responsible for the most high-profile activity of Welsh nationalism in the early 1980s. The Conservative party had fought the 1979 election on a manifesto that included a commitment to a Welsh-language TV channel. When plans for the new UK Channel 4 were drawn up, this promise had been dropped. Evans decided to fast until death, if necessary, as a peaceful protest. The huge publicity quickly forced the Thatcher government to make its first U-turn, and **Sianel Pedwar Cymru** (S4C) was born in 1982. Perhaps the Tories realized the political advantage of bringing Welsh nationalism into the legitimate fold, for the Welsh media industry dissipated many angry and impassioned arguments for national self-determination. Certainly, many of the most heartfelt radicals ended up in prominent positions within Wales' media.

> ### NATIONALISM AWAY FROM THE ASSEMBLY
>
> With Plaid Cymru having to play it as a sober democratic party, much of the more interesting aspects of Welsh nationalism are to be found away from party politics. Regular dust-ups over patronizing English attitudes still periodically ignite the media, while debates rage on about English in-migration and the purchase of second homes in the heartlands of the Welsh language and culture. In a journalistic atmosphere that has at times been decidedly febrile and ill-tempered, the first casualty has been proper debate, with everything reduced to hysterical soundbites. Out of this environment has come the pressure group **Cymuned** ("Community"; Ⓦcymuned.org), whose slogan "Dal dy dir!" ("Hold your ground!") is seen daubed all around Wales. Cymuned is slick, modern and thoughtful, and could well prove to be the intellectual driving force for modern Welsh nationalism, especially as Plaid Cymru continues to struggle.

on the devolution proposals. Scotland voted for its parliament; in Wales, the proposals barely scraped through. Although this was potentially the first piece of self-government for Wales in six hundred years, many nationalists felt that it fell far short of expectations and was not worth supporting. Plaid Cymru's own stance mirrored this ambivalence: initially unenthusiastic and only coming out for the Assembly in the latter stages of the campaign. Wales itself was split in half by the devolution vote. The border areas and Pembrokeshire, true to their historical anglicization, voted no, while Plaid's west coast strongholds and the "Old" Labour bastions of the industrial Valleys were just enthusiastic enough to swing the ballot.

The National Assembly for Wales and beyond

When it came to voting for the **Welsh Assembly**, Plaid Cymru achieved spectacular gains, taking Labour strongholds like Rhondda, Islwyn and Llanelli. The Plaid share of the vote, at nearly thirty percent, was enough to deny Labour – once the absolute party in Wales – an overall majority. So far, this has proven to be Plaid's high-water mark.

One of Plaid's main drawbacks in recent years had been confusion, and disillusion, over its leadership, particularly in the Assembly under the lacklustre Anglesey AM Ieuan Wyn Jones. In 2012, however, he stood down and the party elected a new (and the first female) leader, **Leanne Wood** who, thus far, has proved to be a steady rather than spectacular figurehead; the 2016 National Assembly elections saw Plaid Cymru gain just one seat more than they did in 2011.

Since the arrival of the Assembly, it's hard for even the most ardent of nationalists to argue that Wales' **system of government** is the most pressing issue facing the nation. With farming in crisis, one of the poorest standards of living in the UK and job opportunities limited, there are plenty of meatier matters to chew on. If the Assembly can be seen to make a difference to these issues, its reputation will soar. However, in the first decades of the 21st century, it's safe to say that the majority of Welsh people are fairly happy with things as they are. Despite the gradual decline in the number of Welsh-speakers – according to the 2011 census, nineteen percent of the population speak Welsh (though this is not much below the level in the 1970s) – the feeling of Welsh identity appears to be growing, with 66 percent of the population calling themselves Welsh.

Today the proliferation of great Welsh **music** (and in particular Welsh-language music) remains a source of enormous pride. The entrance of **football clubs** Swansea and Cardiff into the Premier League for the first time, in 2011 (Swansea have remained there ever since), has also led to a much greater profile for the country in general; the continued success of the Welsh **rugby** team, alongside the remarkable achievements of the national football team in getting to the semi-finals of the 2016 European Football Championship, has been a great fillip. With all this, Wales is more and more happily, and very easily, calling itself a nation. The question that still hangs in the air is simply this: to be a nation, does Wales really need to be a state?

Natural history of Wales

Whole bookshelves are devoted to Wales' landscapes, land use, flora and fauna. What follows is a general overview of the effects of geology, human activity and climate on the country's flora, fauna and land management. It must be remembered that while Wales is covered with a wide array of sites deemed to be of national or international importance (see box below), nowhere in the country is untouched. Almost every patch of "wilderness" is partially the product of human intervention, thoroughly mapped, mined and farmed. Nor is anywhere free from pollution: the conurbations of England are too close, power stations and factories dot the countryside, and the sea is in a poor state. That said, several clean-air-loving lichen species – found in few other places in Britain – abound in Wales. The country also supports 1100 of Britain's 1600 native plants, with ferns and other moisture-loving species particularly well represented.

Geology

Wales' mountain ranges often provide the best insight into the country's **geological history**. Between 600 and 400 million years ago, **Snowdonia** was twice submerged for long periods in some primordial ocean where molten rock from undersea volcanoes cooled to form igneous intrusions in the sedimentary ocean-floor layers. Snowdon, Cadair Idris and the Aran and Arenig mountains are the product of these volcanoes, with fossils close to the summit of Snowdon supporting the theory of its formation on the sea floor.

After Silurian rocks had been laid down, immense lateral pressures forced the layers into concertina-like parallel folds with the sedimentary particles being rearranged at right angles to the pressure, giving today's vertically splitting sheets of **slate**, the classic metamorphosed product of these forces. The folded strata that rose above the sea bore no resemblance to today's mountains; the cliff face of Lliwedd on Snowdon shows that the summit was at the bottom of one of these great folds between two much higher mountains.

In the very recent geological past, from 80,000 to 10,000 years ago, these mountains were shaped by the latest series of **Ice Ages**, with glaciers scouring out hemispherical cirques divided by angular ridges, then scraping down the valleys, gouging them into U-shapes, with waterfalls plunging down their sides.

WALES' PROTECTED AREAS

National parks The country's three national parks – Snowdonia, the Brecon Beacons and the Pembrokeshire Coast – comprise almost twenty percent of Wales. All are outstanding, though they do contain towns, accommodation and even industry.

Areas of Outstanding Natural Beauty (AONB) The Anglesey coast, the Llŷn coast, the Clwydian Range and Dee Valley, the Gower peninsula and the Wye Valley (partly in England) collectively encompass two percent of Wales.

National Nature Reserves (NNR) Wales has 72 NNRs, smaller areas (from a few acres to large chunks of the Cambrian Mountains) with specific habitats such as lowland bogs, sweeping sand dunes or ancient woodlands. They're widely promoted, usually posted with information boards and threaded with easy, well-signed walking trails.

Sites of Special Scientific Interest (SSSI) Generally small areas singled out for special protection. Most of Wales' one thousand SSSIs are on private land with no right of access.

THE ROCKS OF WALES

Geologists puzzled over the forces that shaped the Welsh landscape for centuries before early nineteenth-century geologist **Adam Sedgwick** and his collaborator (and later rival) **Roderick Murchison** began to unravel their secrets. They explained the source of the shattered, contorted and eroded rocks that form the ancient peaks of Snowdonia and gave the rock types names associated with the land where their discoveries took place. Anglesey, the Llŷn and Pembrokeshire all have older **pre-Cambrian** rocks, while those around St Davids are some of the most ancient in the world.

The **Silurian** period (400–440 million years ago) is named after the ancient south Welsh tribe, the Silures, while the Celtic Ordovices who occupied mid- and north Wales gave their name to the **Ordovician** period (440–500 million years ago), and the **Cambrian** period (500–600 million years ago) is named after the Roman name for Wales.

Snowdonia is linked by the long chain of the **Cambrian mountains** to the dramatic north-facing scarp slope of the **Brecon Beacons**, south Wales' distinctive east–west range at the head of the south Wales coal field. Erosion of the ancient rocks that once covered what is now northern Britain washed down great river systems, depositing beds of old red sandstone from 350 million to 400 million years ago. These **Devonian** rocks lay in a shallow sea where the molluscs and corals decayed to form limestone, which in turn was overlaid by more sediment forming millstone grit. Subsequent layers of shale and sandstone were interleaved with decayed vegetable matter, forming a band known as **coal measures**, from which the mines once extracted their wealth. The whole lot has since been tilted up in the north, giving a north-to-south sequence that runs over a steep sandstone ridge (the Brecon Beacons), then down a gentle sandstone dip-slope arriving at the pearl-grey limestone band where any rivers tend to dive underground into **swallow holes**. They reappear as you reach the gritstone, often tumbling over waterfalls into the coal valleys.

Land settlement and usage

During the last interglacial period, Wales was warm enough to support hippos and lions, but **humans**, pressed for space by the expanding ice sheets, killed them off, leaving bears and boars, which in turn were dispatched by human persecution.

After the last ice sheet drew back from Wales around ten thousand years ago, the few plant species which had survived on the ice-free peaks were in a strong position to colonize, producing an open **grassland** community. Over several thousand years, **forests** of birch, juniper and hazel became mixed deciduous woodland with oak, elm and some pine, and in wetter areas damp-loving alder and birch.

Early settlement

The Neolithic tribes began to settle on the upland areas, using their flint axes to clear the forests. The discovery of bronze and later iron hastened the process, especially since wood charcoal was required for **smelting** iron ore. And so began the spiralling devastation of Wales' native woodlands. As the domestication of sheep and goats put paid to any natural regeneration of saplings, more land became available for arable farming. Thin, acidic mountain soils and a damp climate made **oats** – fodder for cattle and horses – about the only viable cereal crop, except in Anglesey which, by the time the Romans arrived in the first century AD, was already recognized as Wales' most important **wheat**-growing land. Meanwhile, some of the last beaver lodges in Britain dammed the Teifi in the twelfth century, while half a millennium later, wolves disappeared from the land.

Cattle droving and the textile industry

Until the sixteenth century, Cistercian monasteries kept extensive lands, cleared woods and developed sheep and cattle farms which subsequently became part of the great estates which still take up large tracts of Wales. By contrast, the less privileged were still smallholders living simple lives. In the 1770s the travel writer Thomas Pennant noted in his *Tours in Wales* that the ordinary people's houses on the Llŷn were "very mean, made with clay, thatched and destitute of chimneys". The poor state of housing had much to do with the right to build (Tŷunnos) on common land with common materials.

In the eighteenth century, **droving** reached its peak. Welsh black cattle, fattened on Anglesey or the Cambrian coast, were driven to market in England, avoiding the valley-floor toll roads by taking highland routes that can still be traced. Nights were spent with the cattle corralled in a halfpenny field (so called because this was the nightly rate per animal) next to a lonely homestead heralded by three Scots pines, which operated as an inn. It was a hard journey for men and cattle, but tougher still for the geese, whose webbed feet were toughened for the long walk with tar and sand.

At home, women ground the wheat, aided by mills driven by fast-flowing streams which later provided power for textile mills, especially around Ruthin, Denbigh, Newtown, Llandeilo and along the Teifi Valley. The Cistercians had laid the foundations of the **textile industry** for both wool and flannel, but it had generally remained in the cottages, with nearly every smallholding keeping a spinning wheel next to their harp.

Towards the Industrial Revolution
The next major shift in land use came with a wave of **enclosure acts** from 1760 to 1820, which effectively removed smallholders from upland common pasture and granted the land to holders of already large estates. The people were deprived of their livelihood, and access to open country was denied.

The mountain building processes discussed above have left a broad spectrum of minerals under Wales. **Copper** had been mined since the Bronze Age and the Romans dabbled in **gold** extraction, but mining became big business in the latter half of the eighteenth century with the extraction of **slate** (see box, p.365) in north Wales and **coal** (see box, p.105) in the south.

Forests
Until five thousand years ago, birch, juniper, hazel, oak and elm covered the mountainsides, but devastating forest clearances and a wetter climate have left only a few pockets of native woodland in the valleys. A far greater area is smothered in gloomy forests of planted **conifers** (predominantly sitka spruce), which are too shaded and acidic for wild flowers and are forbidding to most birds.

Pengelli Forest in Pembrokeshire represents one of Wales' largest blocks of ancient woodland, comprising **midland hawthorn** and **sessile oak**, the dominant tree in ancient Welsh forests. Parts of the Severn and lower Wye valleys are well wooded, as is the Teifi Valley, where oak, ash and sycamore predominate. You can still occasionally see evidence of **coppicing** – an important and ancient practice common a century ago – where trees are cut close to the base to produce numerous shoots harvested later as small-diameter timbers. Under the canopy, **bluebells** and **wood sorrel** are common, and in the autumn look out for the dozens of species of **mushroom**, especially the delicious but elusive **chanterelle**, found mainly under beech trees.

Open moorland and mountains
Grazing makes forest regeneration impossible, as animals munch on fresh seedlings. It may look like only grass survives, but open **moorlands** are also home to **arctic alpines**, which cling to small pockets of soil among the high crags and gullies of Snowdonia and the Brecon Beacons (their southernmost limit in Britain). Their range hasn't changed since they were discovered by seventeenth-century botanists such as Thomas Johnson and Welshman Edward Lhuyd, who found *Lloydia serotina*, a glacial relic more

popularly known as the **Snowdon lily**, actually a spiderwort that looks not unlike a small off-white tulip. In Britain, it is found only around Snowdon and then only rarely seen between late May and early June, when it blooms.

Cwm Idwal in the Ogwen Valley is a great place to spot some of the more common species, in particular the handsome **purple saxifrage**, whose tightly clustered flowers often push through the late winter snows, later followed by the starry and mossy saxifrages and spongy pink pads of **moss campion**. The star-shaped yellow flowers of **tormentil** are typical of high grassy slopes, and you may also find **mountain avens**, distinguished by its glossy oak-like leaves, and, when it blooms in June, by its eight white petals. From June to October, purple heads of **wild thyme** cover the ground, providing food for a small beetle unique to Snowdonia.

Poor acid soils on the igneous uplands foster the growth of lime-shy bracken, bilberry and purple **heather** which combine with decayed **sphagnum moss** in wetter areas to form peat bogs. These support the **bog asphodel**, which produces its brilliant yellow spikes in late summer, often in company with the **spotted orchid** and less frequently the tiny **bog orchid**. Insectivorous plants such as **butterwort** and **sundew** both gain nutrients that their poor surroundings cannot provide by digesting insects trapped on the sticky hairs of their leaves.

Rivers, estuaries and wetlands

Wales' rivers spawn estuarine "meadows", which in summer are carpeted with bright violet **sea lavender** and mauve **sea aster**. An unusual coastal feature is the dam-formed string of **Bosherston Lakes**, south of Pembroke, where the fresh water supports rafts of **white-water lilies**. Further west, the Pembrokeshire coast is a blaze of colour in early summer, with white-flowered **scurvy grass** and **sea campion**, yellow **kidney vetch** and **celandine**, and blue **spring squill**. **Bluebells** and **red campion** cloak Pembrokeshire's islands, while the majority of species mentioned can be found in abundance in Newborough on Anglesey.

Fauna

Dipper and **kingfishers** flourish along the streams in Wales' ancient oak **woodlands**. On sheltered water you might also find shelduck, Canada geese and three species of swan. **Conifer forests** are the realm of elusive **pine martens**, who find a readily available diet of small rodents. Both pine martens and the more common **polecats** are found in wild corners throughout Wales. **Foxes** are widespread, along with **brown hares**, **stoats** and **weasels**. **Rabbits** seem to be everywhere, and the North American **grey squirrel** has all but dislodged the native red squirrel from its habitat.

Thanks to its protected status, the elusive **badger** is increasingly common. However, and despite years of vigorous opposition, in 2017 the Welsh government revealed plans for an official culling programme to combat the spread of TB in cattle – whether this goes ahead, though, remains to be seen.

With Welsh red dragons dying out along with King Arthur, much smaller lizards and two species of snake are all that remain of Wales' **reptiles**. The venomous, triangular-headed **adder** is sometimes spotted sunning itself on dry south-facing rocks, but, except in

---

TOP 5 WILDLIFE VIEWING SPOTS

Bwlch Nant yr Arian Rheidol Valley. Red kites. See p.277
Newborough Warren Anglesey. Red squirrels, soay sheep. See p.421
Ramsey Island Pembrokeshire. Sea birds and dolphins. See p.184
Skomer, Skokholm and Grassholm Pembrokeshire. Sea birds. See p.176
South Stack, Holyhead. Sea birds. See p.423

RED KITE RECOVERY

Like many other raptors, fork-tailed **red kites** were traditionally persecuted by gamekeepers and suffered from the use of pesticides, which caused thinning of eggshells. Before the banning of DDT in the 1960s Welsh red kite numbers were down to a handful of breeding pairs, mostly in the Elan Valley. But with careful management numbers have been on the increase for years and there are now estimated to be more than eight hundred breeding pairs. Their once narrow range has expanded as far south as Pembrokeshire, and they are now even seen far across the border into parts of England.

Though best observed in their natural environment hunting or simply wheeling on thermals, for a real spectacle, head to one of the **feeding sites**: Bwlch Nant yr Arian, near Aberystwyth (see p.277); the Red Kite Feeding Centre in Llanddeusant in the Brecon Beacons (see p.201); or Gigrin Farm, near Rhayader (see p.230).

early spring when it is roused from hibernation, it frequently slithers away unnoticed. The harmless **grass snake** prefers a wetter environment and is equally shy. Easily mistaken for a snake, the **slowworm** is actually a legless lizard and is common throughout Wales, as are **toads** and frogs – though the rare **natterjack toad** is only found in a few locations.

Much of the Welsh **high country** is grazed, both by farmed sheep and (in Snowdonia) by **goats** which are descended from domesticated escapees. Generally welcomed by farmers, they forage on the precipitous ledges, thereby discouraging sheep from grazing ventures beyond their capabilities. On the Carneddau on Snowdonia and on the Brecon Beacons you might also see shy herds of feral **ponies**. The high country also supports a substantial number of **red kites** (see box above) and large populations of **kestrels**, usually seen hovering motionless before plummeting onto an unsuspecting mouse or vole. Golden-brown **buzzards** gently wheel on the thermals on the lookout for prey which can be as big as a rabbit. Buzzards and peregrine falcons are as happy picking at carrion, but have to compete with sinister black **ravens** that inhabit the highest ridges and display their crazy acrobatics, often banding together to mob the bigger birds.

Acidic **heather uplands** provide habitats for **grouse**, whose laboured flight is in complete contrast to the darting zigzag of its neighbour, the **snipe**. On softer grassland, expect to find the **ring ouzel**, a blackbird with a white cravat, and the **golden plover**, a bird still common, but being threatened, like many others, by the spread of conifer forests.

Wales' clean, fast-flowing **rivers** make ideal conditions for the **brown trout**, a fish managed for sport throughout the country. **Salmon** are less common, found mainly in the Wye (where it is important as game fish) and the Usk. Along with **roach**, **perch** and other coarse fish, the depths of Bala Lake (Llyn Tegid) claim the unique silver-white **gwyniad**, an Ice Age relic not dissimilar to a small herring, said never to take a lure. **Otters** almost became extinct in Wales some years back, but a concerted effort on the part of the Otter Haven Project has seen their numbers climbing in the Teifi and some of the rivers in Montgomeryshire, though they are seldom seen.

The mud flats and saltings of Wales' **estuaries** provide rich pickings for wintering waders. The **Dee estuary**, on the northern border with England, plays host to Europe's largest concentration of **pintail** as well as **oystercatchers**, **knot**, **dunlin**, **redshank** and many others. Numerous terns replace them in the summer months. Commercially viable beds of **cockles** still exist on the north coast of the Gower and families still own rights to musselling the sands of the Conwy estuary.

The long Welsh **coast** is thick with **sea birds**, thanks partly to the profusion of islands and its position on the main north–south migratory route. The islands off the Pembrokeshire coast are incomparable for sea-bird colonies, the granite pinnacle of **Grassholm**, eight miles offshore, hosting the world's third-largest Atlantic gannet colony with forty thousand. Nearby, **Skokholm** and **Skomer** between them support 3500 pairs of **storm petrels** and an internationally significant population of 150,000 pairs of the mainly nocturnal **Manx shearwater**, which spend their winter off the coast of South America. Burrows vacated by rabbits on the islands also provide nests for puffins, while **razorbills**, **guillemots** and **kittiwakes** nest on the cliffs. Since the eradication of the rats that previously deterred burrow-nesting birds, Manx shearwaters are also now colonizing nearby **Ramsey Island**. In the north, make for **Ynys Enlli** (Bardsey Island) off the Llŷn coast, and the wonderful **South Stack Cliffs** on Anglesey which, especially from May to July, are alive with breeding guillemots, razorbills and puffins.

In the water, dolphins can often be seen: the coast of mid-Wales, particularly around New Quay, is notable for **bottlenose dolphins**. The same territory has also seen occasional visits by **leatherback turtles**, particularly in late summer. Perhaps global warming is attracting new species to Wales just as it threatens others.

Ecology and the future

With smokestack industries now largely absent from Wales, and the **Valleys** mostly devoid of working coal mines, nature is struggling to claw its way back. A verdure inconceivable forty years ago now cloaks the hillsides, and already the industrial remains are being cherished as cultural heritage; as much a valid part of the "natural" landscape as the mountain backdrops. If you need convincing, climb up to the disused slate workings behind Blaenau Ffestiniog or walk the old ironworks tramways around Blaenavon.

In other areas, much remains to be done to restore the ecological balance. The increasing commercialization of farming has led not just to the damaging application of pesticides and excessive use of nitrogen-rich fertilizers, but to the wholesale removal of **hedgerows** and **dry-stone walls**, ideal habitats for numerous species of flora and fauna. Conservation groups promote the skills needed to lay hedges and build dry-stone walls, but for every success, another chunk of farmland is paved over with a new bypass, or a meadow is turned over to **conifers**, which are clear-felled every thirty years or so.

The largest forest owner, **Natural Resources Wales** (ⓦ naturalresources.wales), is keen to shake off its monoculture image and is bordering its forests with a mix of broad-leaved trees and conifers of different ages. As an extended public relations exercise it also welcomes mountain bikers in some forests. Far from being areas where nature is allowed to take its course, the **national parks** can be their own worst enemies, attracting thousands of people a day. Some attempt is being made to control the effects of tourism through path management and the promotion of public transport, but this is more than outweighed by the increasingly aggressive promotion of these regions. Paradoxically, and for all the wrong reasons, **military zones** – Mynydd Eppynt and most of the Castlemartin peninsula, for example – have become wildlife havens away from the worst effects of human intervention.

Environmental groups are also keeping a weather eye on offshore **oil** and **gas** exploration off the west Wales coast, while in south Wales there has been considerable resistance to developments in Milford Haven where, since 2009, huge liquefied natural gas-carrying ships from Qatar have been offloading their cargo and feeding it into Britain's gas network.

COUNTRYSIDE AND WILDLIFE ORGANIZATIONS

Campaign for the Protection of Rural Wales ⓦ cprw.org.uk.

Friends of the Earth: Cymru ⓦ foe.cymru.

Llanelli Wetland Centre ⓦ wwt.org.uk/wetland-centres/llanelli.

Natural Resources Wales ⓦ naturalresourceswales.gov.uk.

Royal Society for the Protection of Birds (RSPB) ⓦ rspb.org.uk/wales.

Wildlife Trust of South and West Wales ⓦ welshwildlife.org.

Music in Wales

Dylan Thomas' observation that "We are a musical nation" is as relevant as ever. Despite the near-obliteration of the mining industry, male voice choirs (see box, p.116) remain a feature of Welsh life, with many choirs opening their practice sessions to the public. But Welsh music extends far beyond the dwindling chapels into the country's village halls, clubs, festival sites and pubs. In quieter venues, harp players repay their musical debt to ancestors who accompanied the ancient bards (traditional poets and storytellers), while modern folk music draws directly from the broader Celtic musical tradition.

Welsh-language rock musicians have traded commercial success for unabashed **nationalism**, spanning styles from punk to hip-hop. Some bands sing in both English and Welsh, and there is a fast-growing scene in English-language Welsh rock, building on the success of outfits like the Manic Street Preachers. These days, Wales continues to punch above its weight, churning out a phenomenal amount of good music for a country its size.

Folk

The Welsh **gwerin** has a much wider meaning than its English counterpart "folk". At a Welsh *gŵyl werin* (folk festival), you're as likely to encounter the local rock band as the local dance team – with the entire community turning out, too.

Welsh folk song has always remained close to the heart of popular culture, conveying political messages and social protest. After centuries of political and religious suppression, traditional Welsh music and dance have fought back from near extinction. Unlike their Celtic cousins in Ireland, Scotland and Brittany, many folk musicians in Wales have learnt their tunes from books and manuscripts rather than from older generations of players.

As you travel around, scan posters for the word **twmpath** – the equivalent of a barn dance or ceilidh, and used when Welsh dances are the theme of the night. Calling (dance instructions) could be in Welsh or English, depending on where you are in the country. *A Noson Lawen*, literally "a happy night", usually offers a harpist, perhaps some dancers and a repertoire of Welsh standards.

History

The **bardic** and **eisteddfod** traditions have played a key role in Welsh culture. Often the bard, who held an elevated position in Welsh society, was the non-performing composer, employing a harpist and a *datgeiniad*, whose role was to declaim the bard's words. The first eisteddfod (see box, p.452) appears to have been held in Cardigan in 1176, with contests between bards and poets and between harpers, pipers and *crwth*-players (see p.452). Henry Vlll's **Act of Union** in 1536 was designed to anglicize the country by stamping out Welsh culture and language, and the eisteddfod tradition degenerated over the next two centuries.

In the eighteenth and nineteenth centuries, the rise of **Nonconformist religion**, with its abhorrence of music, merry-making and dancing, further hammered Welsh traditions. **Edward Jones**, *Bardd y Brenin* (Bard to the King), observed sorrowfully in the 1780s that Wales, which used to be one of the happiest of countries, "has now become one of the dullest". Folk music only gained some sort of respectability when London-based Welsh people, swept along in a romantic enthusiasm for all things Celtic, revived it at the end of the eighteenth century.

In the heartland of the Welsh language around mid- and northwest Wales, folk music can be heard in many of the same **venues** that stage rock events. The language is

EISTEDDFODAU

The National Eisteddfod Society was formed in the 1860s, and today, three major week-long competitive events are held every year: the **Llangollen International Eisteddfod** (Ⓦ international-eisteddfod.co.uk) in July; the **National Eisteddfod** (Ⓦ eisteddfod.org.uk) in the first week of August; and the **Urdd National Eisteddfod** (Ⓦ urdd.cymru), a huge youth festival, at the end of May. The National and the Urdd alternate between venues each year.

The competitions' rules have meant that eisteddfodau have helped formalize Welsh culture. Such parameter-defining is naturally alien to the free evolution of traditional song and music, but eisteddfodau have played a major role in keeping traditional music, song and dance at the heart of national expression.

considered more important than musical categories, and the folk club concept is alien to Welsh speakers, who never saw the need to segregate music that was a natural part of their cultural life. Folk clubs are found in the anglicized areas and only a few of them feature Welsh music.

The harp

Historically the most important instrument in the folk repertoire, the **harp** has been played in Wales since at least the eleventh century, although no instruments survive from the period before the 1700s. The only surviving ancient music is the manuscript of **Robert ap Huw**, written about 1614 in a strange tablature that has intrigued music scholars: five scales were used, but no one has yet defined satisfactorily how they should sound.

The simple early harps were superseded in the seventeenth century by the rich-sounding **triple harp**, with its complicated arrangement of two parallel rows of strings sounding the same note, with a row of accidentals between them. The nineteenth-century swing towards classical concert music saw the invasion of the large **chromatic pedal harps** that dominate today, but the triple, always regarded as the traditional Welsh harp, was kept alive by gypsy musicians who preferred to play something portable. One Welsh harp performance that's well worth catching is the **Cerdd Dant**, where the harpist leads with one tune, accompanying soloists and groups take a counter-tune, and they all end up together on the final note. Wales even has a royal harpist, a position reinstated in 2000 after almost a century and currently held by Anne Denholm from Carmarthen.

In recent years craftsmen have re-created the *crwth* (a stringed instrument which may have been either plucked or bowed), the *pibgorn* (a reed instrument with a cow's horn for a bell) and the *pibacwd* (a primitive Welsh bagpipe), championed by masters such as Ceri Rhys Matthews.

Folk musicians

The country's foremost triple harpist, **Robin Huw Bowen**, has revived interest in the instrument with appearances throughout Europe and North America, and also makes unpublished manuscripts of Welsh dance music widely available through his publishing company. The lineage of north Wales triple harpist **Llio Rhydderch** stretches back centuries. For a more contemporary take on the instrument, poet/musician **Twm Morys** (son of writer Jan Morris) blends modern Welsh and Breton influences.

One of Wales' best-known harpists is **Elinor Bennett**, who has accompanied some of Wales' biggest rock acts. Her daughter-in-law, **Catrin Finch**, is even more famous: the country's (if not Britain's) foremost harpist, she was the Official Harpist to the Prince of Wales between 2000 and 2004. Her wonderful collaborative album, *Clychau Dibon*, with Senegalese kora player Seckou Keita, won the Songlines Music Award for best cross-cultural album of 2014; *Tides*, released in 2016, is a mesmerizing collection of self-composed songs that also features Finch on piano.

In a similar vein, listen out for Welsh-language poet **Gwyneth Glyn** – whose gorgeous, album *Tro* (meaning "Turn"; 2017), also featuring Seckou Keita, is sung largely in her native tongue – and young blues-folk harp songwriter **Georgia Ruth Williams**, whose two albums to date, *Week of Pines* and *Fossil Scale*, are sublime.

The father of Welsh folk, politician/songwriter **Dafydd Iwan**, remains as hugely popular and prolific as ever with charismatic performances and powerful albums such as 2007's *Man Gwyn* (featuring songs about the early Welsh emigration to Patagonia and North America). Songwriter **Meic Stevens** (often referred to as the "Welsh Bob Dylan") straddles folk and acoustic rock; if you get the chance to see him live, grab it. Singer/harpist **Siân James**, from mid-Wales, has found fame for her spine-tingling voice and exquisite tunes. Other female pacesetters include the Cardiff-born veteran singer **Heather Jones**, and the soulful **Julie Murphy**, born in Essex but now a fluent Welsh-speaker and part of Welsh cultural ambassadors, **Fernhill**.

Terrific young bands include **Mabon**, a high-energy five-piece led by Celtic accordionist Jamie Smith, **Elin and the Tribalites** and **Calan**, who mix Welsh and Irish traditions with a contemporary edge. All regularly play high-profile festivals.

English-language Welsh pop

The historic lack of **international pop artists** to emerge from Wales – long blamed on the music-industry dominance of London-based labels and media – has changed utterly in the last couple of decades, at least for English-language groups. It started with the Manic Street Preachers in the early 1990s, who spawned an unprecedented interest in contemporary Welsh rock. London A&R reps descended on Cardiff and Newport in search of the next big thing, accelerating the careers of bands like the Super Furry Animals, Catatonia and the Stereophonics.

The early years

The most enduring name in English-language Welsh pop is **Tom Jones**, a 1960s sex symbol now in his late 70s and still pulling in crowds around the world. Similarly, Cardiff-born singer **Shirley Bassey** has carved out a hugely successful career since the mid-1950s, particularly with the immortal theme song to the 1964 James Bond film *Goldfinger*, and, in 1972, *Diamonds Are Forever*; her most recent crowning glory, however, came in 2007 when, aged 70, she played to a rapturous Glastonbury crowd.

Cardiff musician-turned-record-producer **Dave Edmunds**, whose first band Love Sculpture scored a UK hit in 1968, has had his hands on many a hit record since then – both as a producer and a solo performer – during the 1970s and 1980s. Classically trained pianist **John Cale** went to America in 1963 and found fame alongside Lou Reed with the **Velvet Underground**, one of the most influential avant-garde rock bands of the 1960s. Following his departure from the band, he worked as a producer and collaborator, working with the likes of Nick Drake and Brian Eno. In addition, he has recorded numerous solo records, his latest offerings being the enjoyably odd *Shifty Adventures in Nookie Wood* (2012) and *M:FANS* (2016), which features reworkings of several songs from his earlier album *Music for a New Society*.

As in much of Britain, the 1980s mainstream music scene in Wales was generally pretty dire. Welsh rock music was personified by Rhyl's rabble-rousing rock fundamentalists **The Alarm**, fronted by Mike Peters, while Swansea's husky-toned rocker **Bonnie Tyler** was still building on the huge commercial success begun in the late 1970s. Possibly the most surprising Welsh success story of the 1980s was **Shakin' Stevens**, who had a string of massive, nostalgia-driven hits evoking the sounds of the 1950s.

The Welsh renaissance

It all changed in the 1990s following the emergence of south Wales rock nihilists the **Manic Street Preachers**. The band's first two albums merely set the scene for the industrial art-rock masterpiece that was *The Holy Bible* (1994), a record as thrilling and as visceral as any produced in the 1990s, and one that still resonates today. The 1995 disappearance,

GIGS AND FESTIVALS

Wales has dozens of venues – typically pubs and social clubs – where you can catch great live folk music, the best of which we have listed here, along with a rundown of the country's best folk-music festivals.

VENUES

The following venues are listed approximately from south to north.

Newport Folk Club Newport Fugitives Athletic Club, High Cross Rd, Rogerstone, Gwent, NP10 9AE ☎01633 897923, ⓦnewportfolkclub.co.uk. Sessions Thurs at 8.45pm plus two acoustic sessions a month and occasional other gigs.

Llantrisant Folk Club Pontyclun Athletic Club, Castan Rd, Pontyclun ☎01443 226892, ⓦfolk. wales. International guest list and local sessions centred on Welsh tunes. Wed at 8.30pm.

Barry Folk Club Glenbrook Inn, Coldbrook Rd East, Barry, CF63 2NP ☎01446 402822, ⓦfacebook.com/Barryfolkclub. All are welcome to perform. Second Tues of the month at 8pm.

Pembrokeshire Folk Royal Oak, Fishguard, SA65 9HA ☎07934 418186, ⓦpembrokeshire-folk-music.co.uk. Tues at 8pm.

Pontardawe Valley Folk Club Glais Rugby Football Club, 609 Birchgrove Rd, Glais, near Swansea, SA7 9EN ☎01792 425231, ⓦpontardawefolkclub.co.uk. Mainstay of the Welsh folk scene, good for anything from very traditional stuff to modern folk-rock. First and third Fri of the month.

Llangollen Folk Club Sun Inn, 49 Regent St, Llangollen, LL20 8HN ☎01978 860233. Cheerful session and open mic. Wed at 8.30pm.

Conwy Folk Club Conwy Comrades Sport and Social Club, 8 Church St, Conwy, LL32 8AF ☎01492 877324, ⓦconwyfolkclub.org.uk. Mon at 8pm.

FESTIVALS

The following events are listed in chronological order.

Cwlwm Celtaidd Porthcawl, early March; ⓦcwlwmceltaidd.org. Fantastic, increasingly high-profile Celtic festival of pan-Celtic music and partying over a long weekend.

Cadi Ha Holywell, first weekend May. Small traditional dance event.

Tredegar House Festival Newport, Monmouthshire, mid-May; ⓦtredegarhousefestival.org.uk. A laidback and enjoyable long weekend at the National Trust-owned country house, good for session players and dancers. See p.91

Fishguard Folk Festival Late May; ⓦpembrokeshire-folk-music.co.uk. Small, traditional event with a good spread of international performers and plenty of busking.

Gower Folk Festival Gower peninsula, mid-June; ⓦgowerfolkfestival.co.uk. Varied and high-quality line-up in beautiful surroundings. The festival wasn't held in 2017, so check the website for developments.

Gŵyl Ifan Cardiff, mid-June; ⓦgwylifan.org. Wales' biggest and most spectacular folk-dance festival, with hundreds of dancers giving displays throughout the city centre.

Sesiwn Fawr ("Big Session") Dolgellau, mid-July; ⓦsesiwnfawr.cymru. This major festival returns to its Celtic roots with a week of gigs held in various venues. See box, p.295

Gwyl Pontardawe Festival Pontardawe, mid-Aug; ⓦen.gb.facebook.com/GwylPontardaweFestival. One of Britain's flagship folk events, with an ambitious line-up of international performers.

Green Man Crickhowell, mid-Aug; ⓦgreenman.net. Wales' largest music festival, this fantastic three-day happening in the Brecon Beacons offers everything – including folk, new folk and Americana. See box, p.214

FOLK MUSIC RESOURCES

Cob Records ⓦcobrecords.com. Extensive mail-order business.

Cwmni Fflach ⓦfflach.co.uk. Great label, with indie, rock, pop, folk and choral releases.

Cymdeithas Genedlaethol Ddawns Werin Cymru (Welsh National Folk Dance Society) ⓦdawnsio.com/en. A useful source of events information with access to heaps of CDs, DVDs and dance pamphlets.

Sain ⓦsainwales.com. The major Welsh recording company.

St Fagans National History Museum Near Cardiff ⓦmuseum.wales/stfagans. A vibrant museum (see p.77) and a vital centre for research and collecting work.

Tŷ Siamas Dolgellau ⓦtysiamas.com. The National Centre for Welsh Folk Music.

and presumed suicide, of fractured, anorexic guitarist Richey Edwards remains the band's defining moment, but they returned as a three-piece a year later, displacing their bedsit rock/punk for the anthemic *Everything Must Go* (1996), their most successful album to date, which also features their most famous song, the rousing *A Design for Life*. Their follow-up album, *This Is My Truth, Tell Me Yours* (1998), continued their progress to megastardom, though it took several patchy records before they discovered a return to form with the blistering *Journal for Plague Lovers*, the album featuring lyrics left to the band by Edwards. Their fine output has continued in recent years with the gorgeous, largely acoustic *Rewind the Film* (2013) and the heavy rock blast of *Futurology* (2014).

The now legendary Welsh bands compilation album *Dial M for Merthyr* (1995) showcased the Manics alongside many who subsequently became huge, all united by a tendency towards clever, zeitgeist lyrics and Welsh loquaciousness. Most exciting among them were the **Super Furry Animals**, whose fusion of Seventies psychedelia with new millennium clubland quirkiness and techno-geekery created a niche all of their own. Their ten albums to date range from poignant ballads to thumping raw rock, proving them to be masters of many genres and true innovators; their all-Welsh-language album *Mwng* (2000) became the best-selling work ever in Welsh; for a thoroughgoing overview of this band's output, grab a copy of their compilation album *Zoom! The Best of 1995–2016*. Save for the odd gig, the band remain on sabbatical at present, though a couple of members have undertaken solo projects, not least the prolific frontman, **Gruff Rhys**, whose two most recent releases, *Hotel Shampoo* (2011) and *American Interior* (2014), are typically off-kilter affairs, the latter a combined album/film project. Check out, too, Rhys' side-project, Neon Neon, and their two releases to date, *Stainless Style* (2008) and *Praxis Makes Perfect* (2013). Meanwhile, the Super Furries' keyboard player **Cian Ciaran** has also released two albums, the latest being the excellent *They Are Nothing Without Us* in 2013.

In a similar vein, indie-psych band **Gorky's Zygotic Mynci** were responsible for a handful of marvellously quirky records, such as the folksy *Barafundle* (1997) and the gorgeous *The Blue Trees* (2000), before splitting in 2006. Lead singer **Euro Childs** has gone on to carve out a solo career, with albums like *Situation Comedy* (2013), a piano-pop delight.

A more mainstream sound came from the likes of now-defunct **Catatonia**, whose Welsh-accented frontwoman **Cerys Matthews** was responsible for some wonderful lyrics; the most memorable of these feature on their best-selling album *International Velvet* (1998), whose title track contains the chorus "every day, when I wake up, I thank the Lord I'm Welsh" – still something of an unofficial national anthem. Yet another lead singer turned solo artist, Matthews' subsequent output has ranged from US-inspired country/folk to an album of traditional Welsh songs, *Hullabaloo* (2013). Another of the big 1990s Welsh bands was Valleys outfit the **Stereophonics**, whose distinctive sound was shaped around singer Kelly Jones' rasping voice. They are still recording, and regulars on the festival circuit; the 1997 debut *Word Gets Around* remains their best record to date.

The new millennium

While the likes of the Manics and the SFA continue to produce exciting records, there has been a new generation of bands whose influence has come more from the thrashier elements of post-millennial American rock. South Wales has been a particularly fertile breeding ground for this angst-ridden wall of noise, producing some of the genre's most celebrated protagonists, notably Bridgend rockers **Funeral for a Friend** (who disbanded in 2016) and **Bullet for My Valentine**. Spearheading the charge from north Wales are **The Joy Formidable**, a powerful, guitar-heavy trio whose 2013 album *Wolf's Law*, and its 2016 follow-up, *Hitch*, are ferocious, anthemic works. Another north Wales outfit are **Catfish and the Bottlemen** from Llandudno, whose two releases to date, *The Balcony* (2014) and *The Ride* (2016), are hugely enjoyable slices of unpretentious rock.

More offbeat is psych-folk singer **Cate Le Bon**, who first came to prominence providing guest vocals on albums by Neon Neon and the Manic Street Preachers. Another artist who sings in both English and Welsh, she's now a bona fide star in her

> **ESSENTIAL LISTENING**
> **Catatonia & Cerys Matthews** *Way Beyond Blue* and *Hullabaloo*
> **Cate le Bon** *Crab Day*
> **Gorky's Zygotic Mynci & Euro Childs** *The Blue Trees* and *Situation Comedy*
> **Manic Street Preachers** *The Holy Bible* and *Journal for Plague Lovers*
> **Super Furry Animals** *Rings around the World* and *Radiator*

own right; seek out the slightly bonkers but utterly charming *Mug Museum* (2013), which she followed up with the equally beguiling *Crab Day* in 2016.

There's a thriving **dance music** scene, too, in all its fragmented glory. Tongue-in-cheek Newport rappers **Goldie Lookin' Chain** had a mammoth following for a while in the early 2000s. Rural west Wales is the base for dub gurus **Zion Train**, doing spliffed-up remakes of classic new wave tracks. Big beatz'n'breaks come from Cardiff's **Phantom Beats**. **Vandal** is a local hero in the dance music realm, as is James Hannam who operates as **Culprit One**.

Welsh-language rock

While English-language Welsh bands have usually enjoyed success by making their nationality an irrelevance, Welsh-language bands have highlighted their strong national identity, fostering a unique, self-propagating Welsh-language rock scene. Boundaries are now increasingly blurred: many bands choose to sing in both Welsh and English, simply because it's the way most of their members use both languages. Indeed, established English-language artists like the Super Furry Animals' frontman **Gruff Rhys** has raised the profile of Welsh-language music to new heights. But this is only a recent phenomenon and remains largely outside the mainstream.

The roots of this thriving, youthful and innovative scene owe much to the punk explosion of 1976 which kicked over many of rock's statues, partly thanks to the anarchic fervour of London bands like The Clash and the Sex Pistols, but also by virtue of its strong DIY ethic. The home-grown Welsh-language pop scene consolidated when in 1983 Caernarfon punk band **Anhrefn** (Disorder) set up **Recordiau Anhrefn**, churning out what it called "dodgy compilations of up-and-coming left-field weirdo Welsh bands". Throughout the 1980s, any band that couldn't get some sort of record deal would simply press their own vinyl and sell their records at gigs. From this era, perhaps the most enduring legacy is the band **Datblygu**, most often described as a Welsh version of spectacularly misanthropic The Fall. Meanwhile North Walians **Llwybr Llaethog** (Milky Way) were ploughing their anti-establishment furrow.

Such DIY efforts were boosted by Radio One DJ **John Peel** – to many, the standard-bearer for underground pop in the UK. Peel became aware of the growing number of Welsh-language bands and began playing their records on air and inviting them in for sessions. This introduced Welsh music to a Europe-wide audience and proved an important catalyst to new Welsh bands. By the 1990s, Welsh-language pop music had established a solid infrastructure of bands, labels and venues that continues to this day. One of the most prolific, eclectic and innovative of these labels is **Ankstmusik**, releasing Welsh-language pop of varied styles, best seen in wonderful compilation albums, including *S4C Makes Me Want To Smoke Crack* (1995). On the same label, former Tystion rapper Gruff Meredith has metamorphosed to great acclaim into **MC Mabon**.

Other major promoters of Welsh-language pop are the Caernarfon-based **Crai Records**, a subsidiary of the more folk-oriented **Sain Records** and the **Fflach** label in Aberteifi (Cardigan), and their subsidiary **Rasp** for dancier artistes and projects. The grassroots Welsh **gig circuit** is also healthy, with a lively local pub and club scene. University student unions also regularly put on Welsh bands. Welsh-language pop bands can also be found at the **National Eisteddfod** (see box, p.452), and at local bars and clubs.

Film

Wales' wonderful scenery has formed the backdrop to many a film – from low-budget local efforts to *Lawrence of Arabia* and even Bollywood blockbusters. However, few of the big movies have Welsh themes, and those that do have tended to be at the budget end of the spectrum, often playing on a slightly whimsical view of the country. There's no doubting, though, that Wales has produced some of Britain's finest actors over the years, not least Richard Burton and Sir Anthony Hopkins; of the modern crop, A-listers include the likes of Christian Bale, Rhys Ifans, Ioan Gruffudd, Matthew Rhys and Michael Sheen. While such stellar names haven't necessarily helped the domestic industry, the Film Agency for Wales was established in 2006 with a charter "to ensure that the economic, cultural and educational aspects of film are effectively represented in Wales, the UK and the world".

This commitment to a viable and sustainable Welsh film industry was further boosted in 2014 when the famous **Pinewood Studios** opened a studio in Cardiff. BBC Wales is also now very prominent down in Cardiff Bay, thanks to the hugely impressive Roath Lock **Drama Village**, where several of the BBC's flagship programmes are filmed, most notably *Doctor Who* (its spin-off, *Torchwood*, was also filmed here) and *Casualty*. Location-seekers should check out ⊛doctorwholocations.net and ⊛visitwales.com/things-to-do/attractions/tv-film-locations.

American Interior (2014). Super Furry Animals frontman, Gruff Rhys, traverses the continent in this spontaneous movie in which he retraces the steps of his eighteenth-century relative, the explorer John Evans.

The Edge of Love (2008). Jealousy threads through this fairly limp exploration of the relationships between Dylan Thomas (Matthew Rhys), his wife (Sienna Miller) and his childhood sweetheart (Keira Knightley). Partly filmed in Thomas's old haunts on the Cambrian coast around New Quay.

First Knight (1995). Sean Connery stars as King Arthur, with Richard Gere as Sir Lancelot, in this patchy action film filmed largely in Snowdonia.

Happy Now (2001). Distinctly oddball thriller, filmed in and around Barmouth, which becomes the mysterious Welsh seaside town Pen-y-Wig.

Hedd Wyn (1992). First Oscar-nominated Welsh-language film, about the north Wales poet who went off to fight in World War I and never returned.

House of America (1997). Dark and depressing tale of secrets and yearning in a family stuck on a mouldering farm in west Wales.

How Green was my Valley (1941). None of it was filmed in Wales, but this Oscar-winning version of the classic Welsh book came to define the world image of Wales for generations.

Human Traffic (1999). Feelgood E-culture film, with a superb performance from John Simm, as well as a star cameo by the late Welsh drug-trafficking guru Howard Marks; great soundtrack, too. Filmed in Cardiff.

Inn of the Sixth Happiness (1958). Snowdonia puts in a fine performance as northern China in this Ingrid Bergman-led classic tale of self-discovery.

King Arthur (2004). Big-screen epic, with huge battles and a rather less sensational account of the "real" king of the Britons than had gone before. Ioan Gruffudd shines as Sir Lancelot.

Kyun! Ho Gaya Na Pyaar (2004). Translating as "It has happened – love", this is a big-budget Bollywood production, with former Miss World, Aishwarya Rai, as the love interest. Large sections were filmed in mid-Wales and Snowdonia.

On the Black Hill (1987). Hauntingly beautiful adaptation of the downbeat Bruce Chatwin novel about twin brothers growing up in the Black Mountains.

Patagonia (2011). Romantic road movie starring Matthew Rhys with parallel stories following both a Cardiff couple visiting Welsh Patagonia and two Patagonians travelling through Wales. Not entirely successful, but sumptuously shot.

Pride (2014). Delightful film recalling the true story of how a group of gay and lesbian activists decided to raise money for the families of miners in a Welsh village during the 1984 miners' strike.

The Prisoner (1971). Big-screen version of the enigmatic cult TV series, both of which were filmed largely at the fantastical village of Portmeirion.

Sleep Furiously (2008). This tender documentary tells about the slow decline of Trefeurig, the tiny Ceredigion farming village where the director, Gideon Koppel, grew up after his parents sought refuge from Nazi Germany there.

Solomon a Gaenor (1998). Filmed in both Welsh and English versions, this Oscar-nominated weepie is a *Romeo and Juliet* tale set in the Valleys in Edwardian times.

Submarine (2011). Richard Ayoade's quirky, funny and warm-hearted coming-of-age drama is set in 1980s Swansea. Wonderfully offbeat.

Tiger Bay (1959). Cardiff Bay provides a suitably gritty backdrop to this engrossing British crime drama, starring John and Hayley Mills, the latter starring in her film debut.

Twin Town (1997). Entertaining drug-fuelled romp set in Swansea that introduced Rhys Ifans to the world; he stars here with his brother, Llyr.

Under Milk Wood (1972). Phantasmagoric take on the classic Dylan Thomas "play for voices", with an all-star cast including Richard Burton and Elizabeth Taylor. Filmed partly in Fishguard.

Very Annie Mary (2001). Offbeat tale of love and singing in the Valleys, with Ioan Gruffudd and Matthew Rhys camping it up to the nines as the only gays in the village.

Books

Some of the books listed here are published by small local presses, and you're unlikely to find them in bookshops outside Wales, though most can be ordered online. The Welsh Books Council website (⦿gwales.com) sells a huge selection, and you'll often be able to pick up rare and out-of-print titles by scouring the many independent or secondhand bookshops in Wales – Hay-on-Wye, of course, being particularly good for the latter.

For information on readings and literary events, check the **Literature Wales** site (⦿literaturewales.org); **The New Welsh Review** (⦿newwelshreview.com) is an excellent resource for all the latest book releases. Welsh **fiction** is undergoing something of a renaissance; names to watch include English-language writers such as Trezza Azzopardi, Kitti Harri, Rachel Tresize and Dannie Abse, and Welsh-language authors including Tony Bianchi, Gwyn Jenkins, Ceri Wyn Jones and Alan Llwyd. A good place to start for fans of fiction is *Rarebit, New Welsh Fiction*, an anthology of short stories.

TRAVEL AND IMPRESSIONS

★**George Borrow** *Wild Wales*. Highly entertaining and easy-to-read account of the author's walking tour of Wales in 1854.

Giraldus Cambrensis (Gerald of Wales) *The Journey Through Wales* and *The Description of Wales*. Learned ruminations and unreserved opinions form the basis of two witty and frank books in one volume, written in Latin by the quarter-Welsh clergyman after his 1188 tour around Wales recruiting for the Third Crusade. *The Journey* "through our rough, remote and inaccessible countryside" contains anecdotes and ecclesiastical point-scoring, while *The Description* covers rural life.

★**John Davies and Marian Delyth** *Wales in 100 Places*. Sumptuous coffee-table book packed with gorgeous illustrations accompanied by extensive and illuminating accounts of each place, including many unexpected and unfamiliar locations. Great for dipping into.

★**Gwynfor Evans** *Eternal Wales* (published as *Cymru o Hud* in Welsh). With magnificently moody photography by Marian Delyth, this is a passionate and erudite tour de force through some of Wales' lesser-known corners.

Peter Finch *Real Cardiff, Real Cardiff Two* and *Real Cardiff Three*. Compelling ambles around the Welsh capital, full of oddball nuggets and with a terrific sense of context and place.

Jon Gower and Jeremy Moore *Wales at Water's Edge*. Beautifully produced coffee-table book documenting – both in words and visuals – the wonderful Welsh coastline, published to coincide with the opening of the Wales Coast Path in 2012.

Jeremy Moore and Nigel Jenkins *Wales, The Lie of the Land*. A gorgeous, glossy tome that combines the luscious photography of Jeremy Moore and the musings of poet Nigel Jenkins. Spirited, passionate and a fine souvenir of contemporary Wales.

★**Jan Morris** *Wales: Epic Views of a Small Country*. Prolific half-Welsh travel writer Jan Morris immerses herself in the country that she evidently loves. Highly partisan and fiercely nationalistic, the book combs over the origins of the Welsh character and describes the people and places of Wales with precision and affection.

H.V. Morton *In Search of Wales*. Learned, lively and typically enthusiastic snapshots of Welsh life in the early 1930s. A companion volume to his *In Search of England*.

★**Mike Parker** *Neighbours from Hell?* English émigré Parker holds few punches as he rips into English attitudes to Wales, the Welsh and all things Cymric. A hugely entertaining romp through history, politics, the nature of Welsh tourism, sex and the royal family. No less enlightening, or revealing, is Parker's *The Greasy Poll*, which documents his experience standing as a candidate for Plaid Cymru in the 2015 general election – the title says it all.

★**Jim Perrin** *Snowdon, The Story of a Welsh Mountain*. Dense, riveting and highly personal account of the iconic mountain, placed within the wider context of the region's history, language and folklore. Great footnotes, too. In *Hills of Wales*, the author travels the length and breadth of the country offering revealing insights into how this magical landscape has been shaped.

Pamela Petro *Travels in an Old Tongue*. An American woman comes to Wales to study, is bewitched by the place, attempts to learn Welsh and then sets off on a global pursuit of Welsh enclaves and speakers from Japan to Norway, Germany and Patagonia. Funny, informative and extremely perceptive about the language and its wider cultural significance.

Peter Sager *Wales*. A passionate and fabulously detailed four-hundred-page celebratory essay on Wales, and especially its people, by a German convert to the cause of all things Welsh.

Meic Stephens *A Most Peculiar People: Quotations About Wales and the Welsh*. Varied volume of quotations going back to the century before Christ and up to 2000. A superb portrait of the nation, with all of its frustrating idiosyncrasies and endearing foibles.

HISTORY, SOCIETY, ART AND CULTURE

Jane Aaron et al (eds) *Our Sisters' Land: The Changing Identities of Women in Wales*. A series of challenging and well-written essays that delve deep into male-dominated Welsh society, from the home to the political system. Includes personal testimonies and some startling facts about just how entrenched bigotry still is within much of the Welsh establishment.

Richard Booth *My Kingdom of Books*. Typically bullish autobiography by the man who made Hay-on-Wye the world's biggest secondhand bookshop. Some interesting stuff on his tussles with authority and his semi-serious declaration of Hay as an independent country.

Janet Davies *The Welsh Language*. Very readable history and assessment of one of Europe's oldest living languages. Packed full of maps showing the demographic and geographic spread of Welsh over the ages.

★**John Davies** *A History of Wales*. Exhaustive run through Welsh history and culture from the earliest inhabitants to the 21st century. Clearly written and very readable, but at seven hundred pages, it's hardly concise.

Gwynfor Evans *Land of My Fathers* and *For the Sake of Wales*. Plaid Cymru's late elder statesman first produced the former tome in Welsh, translating it into English for publication forty years ago. It's a thorough and polemical history of the country. The latter work, his autobiography, covers Welsh political and social life from World War II to the National Assembly. Hugely readable and inspirational.

Geoffrey of Monmouth *History of the Kings of Britain*. First published in 1136, this is the basis of almost all Arthurian legend. Writers throughout Europe and beyond used Geoffrey's unreliable history as the basis of a complex corpus of myth.

Jon Gower *The Story of Wales*. Gower's book is a spin-off from the television series – he's a former BBC Wales Arts and Media correspondent – but it's no worse for that; concise and well structured, the coverage of the country's recent history is particularly lucid.

★**Ron Jones and Joe Lovejoy** *The Auschwitz Goalkeeper: A Prisoner of War's True Story*. Written with the football correspondent of *The Guardian* newspaper, this is Welshman Jones' extraordinary account of his incarceration in Auschwitz following his capture in North Africa; the aftermath of Auschwitz is no less gruelling, including the infamous death marches.

Alan Llwyd *Cymru Ddu/Black Wales: A History*. A long and insightful look at the history of multiracial Wales in both Welsh and English.

Peter Lord *The Visual Culture of Wales*. Lavishly produced and beautifully illustrated three-volume overview of the art and architecture of Wales, from the early industrial society to the present day.

★**Gaynor Madgwick** *Aberfan*. Written by a survivor of the disaster (in which both her brother and sister died), this is, inevitably, a powerful and moving account of the horror of October 21, 1966, and the fight thereafter to seek justice for the victims.

Elizabeth Mavor *The Ladies of Llangollen*. The best of the books on Wales' most celebrated lesbian couple traces the ladies' inauspicious beginnings in Ireland, their spectacular elopement and the way that their Llangollen home, Plas Newydd, became a place of pilgrimage for dozens of influential eighteenth-century visitors.

Owen Sheers *Calon*. Written by the Welsh Rugby Union's poet in residence, this is not only a riveting account of one year spent with the national team, but also goes to the heart of what rugby means to the Welsh. Check out, too, his non-fiction narrative, *The Dust Diaries*, set in Zimbabwe.

LITERATURE

Enid Blyton *Five Get Into a Fix*. In this, the seventeenth of Blyton's timeless series of kids' adventure novels, Julian, Dick, Anne, George and Timmy the dog unearth secret passageways to rescue an old woman from a sinister tower in the snowy Welsh mountains. Vintage "Famous Five".

Bruce Chatwin *On the Black Hill*. This entertaining and finely wrought novel follows the Jones twins' eighty-year tenure of a farm on the mid-Wales border with England. Chatwin casts his sharp eye for detail over both the minutiae of nature and the universal human condition, providing a gentle angle on Welsh-English antipathy.

★**Alexander Cordell** *The Fire People*. Set against the backdrop of the Merthyr Tydfil riots of 1831, this is a feisty fictionalization of the life and unjust death of Dic Penderen, the "first Welsh Martyr of the working class". The same author's *Rape of the Fair Country*, *Hosts of Rebecca* and *Song of the Earth* form a dramatic historical trilogy in the bestseller tradition, partly set in the cottages on the site of the Blaenavon ironworks during the lead-up to the Chartist Riots. *This Sweet and Bitter Earth* immortalizes Blaenau Ffestiniog in a lusty slate epic.

Lewis Davies *Work, Sex and Rugby*. Perennially popular novel that tells you all you need to know (and much you don't) about Valleys men.

Richard John Evans *Entertainment*. Scabrous roller-coaster ride through Rhondda living and loving, guaranteed to offend and cause maximum hilarity.

Thomas Firbank *I Bought a Mountain*. One of the few popular books set in north Wales, in which Anglo-Canadian Firbank spins an autobiographical yarn about his purchase of most of the Glyder range and subsequent life as a Snowdonian sheep farmer during the 1930s.

Iris Gower *Copper Kingdom; Proud Mary; Spinners' Wharf; Black Gold; Fiddler's Ferry; The Oyster Catchers* – the list goes on. Romantic novels by Wales' most popular author, who died in 2010, mostly set in and around Swansea and the Gower (from which she took her pen name).

★**Niall Griffiths** *Grits; Sheepshagger; Kelly + Victor; Stump; Wreckage; Runt*. Arguably the best dissector of darkness, drugs, camaraderie and hopelessness in modern Britain, Griffiths has penned a panoply of novels set between Aberystwyth and Liverpool, all suffused with a metaphysical sense of culture and landscape.

Emyr Humphreys *The Gift of a Daughter*. The mood and landscape of Anglesey are beautifully evoked by perhaps the greatest living Welsh novelist. His final publication, a collection of short stories called *The Woman at the Window*, was completed when he was in his nineties.

Siân James *Not Singing Exactly*. Dazzling and diverse short-story collection from one of Wales' premier romantic novelists. In *The Sky over Wales*, she recalls her childhood days in the 1930s in a series of charming vignettes.

★**Cynan Jones** *The Long Dry*. Set in coastal west Wales over the course of one hot summer's day, this is an engaging tale of one farmer's struggle with life on the land. The rural theme is continued to even more thrilling effect in *The Dig*, a tense short story which explores the fate of a recently widowed farmer and his relationship with a badger-baiter.

Glyn Jones *The Island of Apples*. Set in south Wales and Carmarthen in the early years of the twentieth century, this is an artful portrayal of a sensitive Valleys youth's enthralment with the glamour of the district's new arrival.

Gwyn and Thomas Jones (trans) *The Mabinogion*. The classic of Welsh mythology. These eleven orally developed heroic tales were finally transcribed into *The White Book of Rhydderch* (around 1300–25) and *The Red Book of Hergest* (1375–1425). Originally translated by Lady Charlotte Guest between 1838 and 1849 at the beginning of the Celtic revival.

Lewis Jones *Cwmardy*. Perennially popular socialist novel, written in 1937 and portraying life in a Rhondda Valley mining community in the early years of the twentieth century. Followed by its sequel, *We Live*.

Tia Jones *The Moss Gatherers*. Two rural communities either side of the Irish Sea provide the backdrop to this atmospheric story of family intrigue and betrayal.

Richard Llewellyn *How Green Was My Valley; Up into the Singing Mountain; Down Where the Moon is Small* and

---

TOP 5 WELSH READS

Alexander Cordell *The Fire People* opposite
Jan Morris *Wales: Epic Views of a Small Country* p.459
Mike Parker *Neighbours from Hell?* p.459
Caradoc Pritchard *One Moonlit Night* below
R.S. Thomas *Selected Poems* p.462

Green; Green My Valley Now. Vital tetralogy in eloquent and passionate prose, following the life of Huw Morgan from his youth in a south Wales mining valley through emigration to the Welsh community in Patagonia and back to 1970s Wales. A bestseller during World War II and still the finest introduction to the vast canon of "valleys novels", *How Green Was My Valley* captured a longing for a simple, if tough, life, steering clear of cloying sentimentality.

★**Caradoc Pritchard** *One Moonlit Night*. Dense, swirling tale of a young boy's emotional and sexual awakenings in an isolated north Wales village. Full-blooded Welsh prose at its most charged.

Malcolm Pryce *Aberystwyth Mon Amour*. Surprise bestseller in the shape of this furious, funny black comedy set in an Aberystwyth overlaid with film-noir surrealism and dastardly plot twists. Follow-ups *Last Tango in Aberystwyth*, *The Unbearable Lightness of Being in Aberystwyth* and *Don't Cry for me Aberystwyth* are just as entertaining.

Kate Roberts *The Living Sleep* and *Feet in Chains*, among others. Penned by the pre-eminent Welsh-language writer of the twentieth century, these two novels, available in English translation, tell tales of life in a north Wales slate village.

★**Dylan Thomas** *Collected Stories*. All of Thomas' classic prose pieces: *Quite Early One Morning*, which metamorphosed into *Under Milk Wood*; the magical *A Child's Christmas in Wales*; and the compulsive, crackling autobiography *Portrait of the Artist as a Young Dog*. In all of Thomas' works, the language still burns bright.

★**Dylan Thomas** *Under Milk Wood*. Thomas' most popular play tells the story of a microcosmic Welsh seaside town (modelled on New Quay) over a 24-hour period. Ideally, obtain a recorded version of the play to absorb its rich poetry (or, as Thomas himself described it, "prose with blood pressure").

Alice Thomas Ellis (ed) *Wales – An Anthology*. A beautiful book, combining poetry, folklore and prose stories rooted in places throughout Wales. All subjects, from rugby and mountain-climbing to contemporary descriptions of major events, are included in an enjoyably eclectic mixture of styles. Excellent introduction to Welsh writing.

Rachel Trezise *In and Out of the Goldfish Bowl*. Firmly established as one Wales' brightest authors, Rachel Trezise's unsparing account of one girl's life growing up in the

Rhondda is a great read. Her latest offering, *Cosmic Latte*, is a fine collection of short stories, featuring an array of wonderfully disparate characters.

★**Charlotte Williams** *Sugar and Slate*. Humorous and unstintingly honest memoir of mixed identity: the author is the daughter of a black Guyanese father who grew up in a Welsh-speaking community.

John Williams *The Cardiff Trilogy*. Omnibus of Williams' contemporary low-life Cardiff crime writing containing: *Five Pubs, Two Bars and a Nightclub*, a very funny short-story collection that inspired the E-culture hit film *Human Traffic*; *Cardiff Dead*, a full-length novel that packs in the Welsh cultural references effortlessly and to great effect; and *Temperance Town*, a novella in the same vein.

Raymond Williams *Border Country*. This 1960 novel perfectly captures the sense of change overwhelming rural Welsh life in that era. A timeless classic.

POETRY

★**Dannie Abse** *Welsh Retrospective* and *Arcadia, One Mile*. Two superb collections from one of Wales' most prolific twentieth-century poets (who died in 2014), showing his huge range of intellectual interests and warm, beguiling writing style. His final work, *Speak, Old Parrot* (2013), reflects on his Jewish upbringing, among other subjects.

John Barnie *The City* and *The Confirmation*. One of Wales' best contemporary writers, notable mainly for his combination of poetry and prose styles, narration and description. Evocative tales of wartime childhood and stifling parenting, leading to a poignant search for love.

Gillian Clarke *Collected Poems*. A good introduction to the nature-inspired and homely poetry of one of Wales' leading contemporary writers and the current National Poet. Her latest work, *Ice*, is a delightful set of poems on a distinctly wintery theme.

Dafydd Johnston *Iolo Goch: Poems*. All of the surviving poems of Owain Glyndŵr's court bard are shown in translation and context. A fascinating insight into courtly medieval Wales at a time of great national resurgence.

Gwyneth Lewis *Keeping Mum*. Wales' first-ever National Poet shows her verbal power and dexterity with this 2003 collection, especially when combing over the irregularities of bilingual existence.

Robert Minhinnick *Selected Poems*. Overview of the early career of one of Wales' finest poets: best when picking over his English-speaking south Walian youth in rich, impassioned imagery.

Meic Stephens (ed) *New Companion to the Literature of Wales*. A customarily thorough volume of Welsh prose, spanning the centuries from the folk tales of *The Mabinogion* to modern-day writings.

Dylan Thomas *Collected Poems*. Though Thomas is renowned for his dense and difficult poems, look out for lighter works which resound with perfect metre and precise structure. Classics include *Do Not Go Gentle Into That Good Night*, a passionate, touching elegy to his dying father.

★**R.S. Thomas** *Selected Poems*. Thomas wrote poetry that tugs at issues such as religion (he was an Anglican priest), Wales ("brittle with relics") and family. His passion shines throughout this title, probably the best overview of his prolific work.

★**Harri Webb (ed Meic Stephens)** *Collected Poems*. Fine collection of 350 works by a modern-day patriot and poet of biting satire and eloquent expression.

WILDLIFE AND THE ENVIRONMENT

Douglas Botting *Wild Britain: A Traveller's Guide*. Not much use for species identification but plenty of information on access to the best sites and what to expect when you get there. Excellent photos.

Collins Field Guides Series of thorough, pocket-sized identification guides. Topics include insects, butterflies, wild flowers, mushrooms and toadstools, birds, mammals, reptiles and fossils.

★**William Condry and Jeremy Moore** *Heart of the Country*. Jeremy Moore's gorgeous photography is the perfect accompaniment to the late William Condry's "Country Diary" entries from *The Guardian*.

David Saunders *Where to Watch Birds in Wales*. Enthusiasts' guide to Wales' prime birding locations, along with a bird-spotting calendar and a list of English/Welsh scientific bird names. Not an identification guide.

OUTDOOR PURSUITS

Cicerone Guides *The Wales Coast Path*; *Offa's Dyke Path*; *Walking on the Brecon Beacons*; *Mountain Walking in Snowdonia*; *Scrambles in Snowdonia*; and others. Clearly written pocket guides on most of the country's long-distance walks as well as the best aspects of Welsh mountain activities.

Ordnance Survey National Trail Guides *Offa's Dyke North*; *Offa's Dyke South*; *Glyndŵr's Way*; *Pembrokeshire Coast Path*. Large paperback editions full of instructive descriptions and additional side-walks.

★**Carl Rogers** *Mountain and Hill Walking in Snowdonia*. Superb pocket hikers' guide in two volumes, the first covering Snowdon and its environs, the second detailing southern Snowdonia. Beautifully produced, with great photos, detailed colour maps and info on the best parking spots and some of the easier scrambles.

Welsh

The Welsh language, Cymraeg, is spoken widely throughout the country and as a first language in many parts of the west and north. Its survival and resurgence is remarkable considering that the heart of English culture and its language – the most expansionist the world has ever seen – lies right next door.

Brief history

The Welsh language can be traced back to the sixth century. Celtic inscriptions on stones, a section of written Welsh in the eighth-century **Lichfield Gospels**, the tenth-century codified laws of Hywel Dda in neat Welsh prose, and the twelfth- and thirteenth-century **Mabinogion** folk tales (believed to have been collated from earlier Welsh writings) show that Welsh was a thriving language for centuries. Moreover, the early language is still identifiable and easily comprehensible for any modern-day Welsh-speaker. English domination since the Norman era has been mirrored in the fate of the Welsh tongue. The Norman lords were implanted in castles throughout Wales to subjugate the natives, with official business conducted in their native French.

Real linguistic warfare came with the 1536 **Act of Union** (see p.434), which legitimized the growing practice of imposing English lords and churchmen on the restless, but effectively cowed, Welsh. It is likely that the language would have died out, but William Morgan's 1588 **translation of the Bible** into Welsh brought Welsh into the everyday public arena, ultimately ensuring its survival. Certainly, new and Nonconformist religious movements from the seventeenth century onwards embraced the language.

In the first half of the nineteenth century, more than ninety percent of the country's population spoke Welsh, with English dominant in pockets of Pembrokeshire and along the English border. But as the **Industrial Revolution** progressed, mine owners and capitalists from England came into the rapidly urbanizing southeastern corner of Wales, substantially diluting the language.

In 1854, **George Borrow** undertook his marathon tour of Wales and noted the state of the native tongue throughout. As a natural linguist, he had mastered Welsh and fired questions at people he encountered as to their proficiency in both Welsh and English. The picture he paints is of poorer people tending to be monolingual Welsh-speakers, wealthier people and those near the border bilingual.

Discouragement of Welsh continued in many guises, most notably in it being forbidden in schools in the latter half of the nineteenth and early twentieth centuries. Anyone caught speaking the language had to wear a "**Welsh Not**", a piece of wood on a leather strap that would only be passed on if someone else was heard using Welsh. At the end of the school day, the child still wearing the Welsh Not was soundly beaten. It is hardly surprising that use of the language plummeted.

THE CELTIC LANGUAGE FAMILY

The original Celtic tongue was spoken over a wide area, gradually dividing into two forms which, although there are occasional similarities, have little in common. Goidelic (or Q-Celtic) is now spoken in the Isle of Man, Ireland and Scotland; **Brythonic** (P-Celtic) is spoken in Wales, Cornwall (where it is barely hanging on) and Brittany in France.

THE FALL AND RISE OF CYMRAEG

According to the first British census of 1851, 90 percent of Welsh people spoke the **Welsh language**. Every decade thereafter the figures dipped quite spectacularly – 49.9 percent in 1901, 37.1 percent in 1921, 28.9 percent in 1951 and 18.9 percent in 1981. Then, in 1991 and again in 2001, the percentage of Welsh-speakers rose slightly. The proportion still hovered around the one-fifth mark but the most marked increase was among the lower age groups, those most able to ensure its future.

From the sharp decline of the mid-twentieth century, it's a dramatic turnabout and testament to bold policies, particularly in education and mass media. National TV and radio stations broadcast in Welsh; road signs are written in both Welsh and English; official publications, many tourist brochures and even restaurant menus are bilingual; Welsh-medium schools are everywhere; books in Welsh are published at a growing rate; and magazines, newspapers and websites in the old language are mushrooming.

WHERE WELSH IS SPOKEN

According to a 2016 survey, twenty percent of the population speak Welsh, but the spread is far from even, with a far lower percentage of speakers in the populous and anglicized regions of Gwent and around Cardiff; that said, this is one of the few areas where the language is actually growing in popularity. Although it is unusual to hear Welsh regularly in the border counties, it is commonly understood throughout most of West Glamorgan, Carmarthenshire, the northern half of Pembrokeshire and around Cardigan Bay. The northwestern corner of the country, centred on Snowdonia, Anglesey and the Llŷn, is the real stronghold of the language, reflected in these areas' steadfast political affiliation to nationalism.

The politics of the language

Welsh has survived thanks to those who campaigned to save it, principally the eisteddfod revivalists of the eighteenth century and the political movements of the twentieth century. The formation of **Plaid Cymru**, the Welsh National Party, in 1925 (see box, p.438) was largely around the issue of language, as indeed its politics have been ever since.

Concerns about the language reached their peak with the 1962 radio broadcast *Tynged yr iaith* (The Fate of the Language) by the Plaid founder member, Saunders Lewis. This became a rallying cry that resulted in the formation of Cymdeithas yr Iaith Gymraeg, the **Welsh Language Society**, the following year. One of the highest-profile early campaigns was the daubing of monoglot English road signs with their Welsh translations. Nearly all signs are now officially in both languages. A 1967 Welsh Language Act allowed many forms of officialdom to be conducted in either language, stating that Welsh, for the first time in more than four hundred years, had "equal validity" with English.

Welsh medium education also blossomed, with bilingual teaching in all primary schools and for at least a year in secondary schools. In traditionally Welsh-speaking areas students got five years of Welsh, and since 2000 all Welsh schools much teach the language to students up to the age of 16. Today, increasing numbers of schools across the land teach all subjects in the Welsh language; early objections from some non-Welsh-speaking parents that their children were being "forced" to learn a "dead" language have largely abated. Welsh-language university courses are also becoming more popular, so, for pretty much the first time in Wales' history, it is possible to be educated in Welsh from nursery to degree level.

The other modern cornerstone for developing Welsh has been **broadcast media**. The BBC Welsh-language Radio Cymru began in the late 1970s, to be joined – after a considerable battle – by the S4C TV station in 1982. Together, they have sponsored and programmed popular Welsh learners' programmes and given the old language greater space than it has ever enjoyed before. Welsh-language classes are now offered right across the country, as well as in language centres across Britain and universities in Europe and North America.

The situation today

The Welsh language is both one of Wales' key strengths and its key drawbacks in the quest for some sort of **national emancipation**. There is still suspicion towards the Welsh-speaking "elite" who are seen to control the media and local government in the country. Welsh nationalism is so defined by the language that Plaid Cymru has nearly always had great difficulty in appealing to those who speak only English, particularly in the urban southeast. Nonetheless, the Welsh language continues to flourish. The **Welsh Language Board** was formed in 1994, and with the arrival of the **National Assembly** in 1999, with around half of its members proficient in Welsh, the language has gained a number of firm footholds in official life. In 2010 the Welsh Assembly unanimously passed the **Welsh Language Measure**, which puts Welsh on equal footing with English, though some contend it still doesn't make Welsh an official language in all cases. Still, its other provisions should ensure that Welsh continues to flourish. Increasingly, Wales is developing as a model **bilingual** entity, in which there is room for both languages to thrive together.

Speaking Welsh

Although Welsh words, place names in particular, can appear bewilderingly incomprehensible, the **rules** of the language are far more strictly adhered to than in English. Thus, mastering the basic constructions and breaking words down into their constituent parts means that **pronunciation** need not be anywhere near as difficult as first imagined.

The Welsh alphabet and pronunciation

The Welsh **alphabet** is similar to the English, though there are no letters j, k, v, x and z – except in occasional words appropriated from other languages.

As well as the five English **vowels**, Welsh has y and w. Most vowels have two sounds, long and short: a is long as in car, short as in fat; e long as in there, short as in pet; i long as in sea, short as an tin; o long as in more, short as in dog; u roughly like a Welsh i; w long as in soon, short as in look; y long as in sea and short as in bun or pin. A circumflex over any vowel lengthens its sound. **Adjoining vowels** are generally pronounced as the two separate sounds, with the stress generally on the first.

Welsh **consonants** are pronounced in similar ways to English, except c and g are always hard as in cat and gut (never soft as in nice or rage), and f is always pronounced as v as in vine. Additional consonants are ch, pronounced as in German or as in loch, dd, pronounced as a hard th as in those, ff and ph as a soft f as in five, and si as in shoe. The Welsh consonant that causes most problems is ll, featured in many place names such as Llangollen. This has no direct parallel in English, although the tl sound in Bentley comes close. The proper way to pronounce it is to place the tongue firmly behind the top row of teeth and breathe through it without consciously making a voiced sound.

Some Welsh words also **mutate**, where a word affects the beginning of a following

---

RESOURCES FOR LEARNING WELSH

Acen ☎ 029 2030 0800, ⊛ acen.co.uk. Cardiff-based, S4C-originated company providing a multimedia Welsh course, a Welsh-learners' magazine and copious numbers of useful contacts.

Cymdeithas Madog (Welsh Studies Institute in North America) ⊛ madog.org. Runs an annual week-long residential language course in the US or Canada, plus a directory of resources.

Cymdeithas yr Iaith (Welsh Language Society)

☎ 01970 624501, ⊛ cymdeithas.org. Campaigning and political organization dedicated to improving the status of the Welsh language.

Nant Gwrtheyrn ☎ 01758 750334, ⊛ nant gwrtheyrn.org. Residential national language centre on the coast of the Llŷn (see p.50).

National Language Unit of Wales ☎ 029 2026 5000, ⊛ wjec.co.uk/nlu. Provides a comprehensive guide to Welsh teaching provision.

one, principally to ease pronunciation. Prepositions commonly mutate the following word, turning an initial B into F or M, an initial C into G or Ngh, a D into Dd or N, F into B or M, G into Ngh or the initial letter being dropped altogether, Ll into L, M into F, P into B, Mh or Ph, T into Th, D or Nh. Thus, "in Cardiff (Caerdydd)" is "y**ng Ngh**aerdydd" (note that the "yn" also mutates to ease pronunciation) and "from Bangor" is "o **F**angor". Mutated words are extremely common in the component parts of place names.

WELSH VOCABULARY

aber	mouth of a river; confluence of two rivers	Cymraeg	Welsh
		Cymreictod	Welshness
afon	river	Cymru	Wales
Alban	Scotland	Cymry	the Welsh people
amgeuddfa	museum	da	good
ap (ab)	son of	de	south
ar Agor	open	Dewi Sant	Saint David
ar Gau	closed	dim	no (as an instruction), nothing
ar Werth	for sale		
araf	slow	din or dinas	fort
bach	small, lesser	diolch	thank you
bara	bread	diwedd	end
bore da	good morning	dros	over
bore	morning	du	black
bron	slope of a hill	dŵr	water
bryn	hill	dydd	day
bwlch	mountain pass	dyffryn	vale
bwrdd	table	dyn (-ion)	man (men)
bws	bus	eglwys	church
cadair	stronghold, chair	eisteddfod	festival
caer	fort	esgair	ridge
cân	song	fach	small, lesser
canol	centre	fawr	big, greater
cant	hundred	fferm	farm
capel	chapel	ffordd	road
carreg	stone	fforest	forest
cartref	home	gardd	garden
castell	castle	glas	blue
cenedlaethol	national	glyn	valley
clun	meadow	gwesty	hotel
clwyd	gate, perch	gwyn	white
coch	red	hafod	temporary summer-house
coed	forest, woodland		
craig	rock	hanner	half
crannog	artificial island on a lake	heddiw	today
crefft	craft	heddlu	police
croeso	welcome	hen	old
croglen	rood screen	heol	road
cromlech	literally "curved stone", generally used to refer to megalithic burial chambers	hiraeth	longing, yearning
		hwyl	spirit
		isaf	lower
		iaith	language
Cwm	valley	llan	sacred enclosure, early church
Cyhoeddus	public		
Cymdeithas	society	llety	lodging place, b&b

Lloegr	England	pen	head, top (as of a valley)
llwybr	path	pentre(f)	village
llyfr	book	Plaid Cymru	the Party of Wales
llyn	lake	plas	hall, mansion
llys	place, court	pont	bridge
maen	stone	porth	port, gateway
maes	field	rhiw	hill
marchnad	market	Saesneg	English language
mawr	big, greater	Sais	Englishman
melin	mill	sant	saint
menyw	woman	Senedd	Parliament
merthyr	burial place of saint	shwmae	hello
milltir	mile	siop	shop
moel	bare or rounded mountain	sir	county, shire
môr	sea	stryd	street
morfa	coastal marsh	sut ydych chi? (formal) or sut ywt ti? (informal)	how are you?
mynydd	mountain	swyddfa	office
nant	valley, stream	swyddfa'r post	post office
neuadd	hall	tafarn	pub
newydd	new	traeth	beach
nofio	to swim	tref	town
nos da	good night	twr	tower
noswaith dda	good evening	tŷ	house
os gwelwch chi'n dda	please	uchaf	uppermost, highest
p'nhawn da	good afternoon	y, yr or 'r	the
pant	vale	ynys	island
parc	park	ysbyty	hospital
pêl-droed	football	ysgol	school

WELSH NUMBERS

1	un	20	dau-ddeg
2	dau (fem. dwy)	21	dau-ddeg-un
3	tri (fem. tair)	22	dau-ddeg-dau
4	pedwar (fem. pedair)	30	tri-deg
5	pump	40	pedwar-deg
6	chwech	50	pum-deg
7	saith	60	chwe-deg
8	wyth	70	saith-deg
9	naw	80	wyth-deg
10	deg	90	naw-deg
11	un-deg-un	100	cant
12	un-deg-dau	200	dau gant
13	un-deg-tri	1000	mil

Small print and index

469 Small print

470 About the authors

471 Index

479 Map symbols

A ROUGH GUIDE TO ROUGH GUIDES

Published in 1982, the first Rough Guide – to Greece – was a student scheme that became a publishing phenomenon. Mark Ellingham, a recent graduate in English from Bristol University, had been travelling in Greece the previous summer and couldn't find the right guidebook. With a small group of friends he wrote his own guide, combining a contemporary, journalistic style with a thoroughly practical approach to travellers' needs.

The immediate success of the book spawned a series that rapidly covered dozens of destinations. And, in addition to impecunious backpackers, Rough Guides soon acquired a much broader readership that relished the guides' wit and inquisitiveness as much as their enthusiastic, critical approach and value-for-money ethos. These days, Rough Guides include recommendations from budget to luxury and cover more than 120 destinations around the globe, from Amsterdam to Zanzibar, all regularly updated by our team of roaming writers.

Browse all our latest guides, read inspirational features and book your trip at **roughguides.com**.

Rough Guide credits

Editor: Samantha Cook
Layout: Pradeep Thapliyal
Cartography: Rajesh Chhibber
Picture editor: Aude Vauconsant
Proofreader: Ruth Blackmore
Managing editor: Edward Aves, Mani Ramaswamy
Assistant editor: Payal Sharotri

Production: Jimmy Lao
Cover photo research: Phoebe Lowndes
Editorial assistant: Aimee White
Senior DTP coordinator: Dan May
Programme manager: Gareth Lowe
Publishing director: Georgina Dee

Publishing information

This ninth edition published March 2018 by
Rough Guides Ltd,
80 Strand, London WC2R 0RL
11, Community Centre, Panchsheel Park,
New Delhi 110017, India
Distributed by Penguin Random House
Penguin Books Ltd, 80 Strand, London WC2R 0RL
Penguin Group (USA), 345 Hudson Street, NY 10014, USA
Penguin Group (Australia), 250 Camberwell Road,
Camberwell, Victoria 3124, Australia
Penguin Group (NZ), 67 Apollo Drive, Mairangi Bay,
Auckland 1310, New Zealand
Penguin Group (South Africa), Block D, Rosebank Office
Park, 181 Jan Smuts Avenue, Parktown North, Gauteng,
South Africa 2193
Rough Guides is represented in Canada by DK Canada, 320
Front Street West, Suite 1400, Toronto, Ontario M5V 3B6
Printed in Singapore
© Rough Guides
Maps © Rough Guides
Contains Ordnance Survey data © Crown copyright and
database rights 2016

480pp includes index
A catalogue record for this book is available from the
British Library
ISBN: 978-0-24130-637-6
The publishers and authors have done their best to
ensure the accuracy and currency of all the information
in **The Rough Guide to Wales**, however, they can accept
no responsibility for any loss, injury, or inconvenience
sustained by any traveller as a result of information or
advice contained in the guide.
1 3 5 7 9 8 6 4 2

Help us update

We've gone to a lot of effort to ensure that the ninth
edition of **The Rough Guide to Wales** is accurate and up-
to-date. However, things change – places get "discovered",
opening hours are notoriously fickle, restaurants and
rooms raise prices or lower standards. If you feel we've got
it wrong or left something out, we'd like to know, and if
you can remember the address, the price, the hours, the
phone number, so much the better.

Please send your comments with the subject line
"Rough Guide Wales Update" to mail@uk.roughguides
.com. We'll credit all contributions and send a copy of the
next edition (or any other Rough Guide if you prefer) for
the very best emails.

ABOUT THE AUTHORS

Tim Burford studied languages at Oxford University and worked briefly in publishing. In 1991 he began writing hiking guides to east-central Europe and then Latin America. Somewhat randomly, he also works on the Rough Guides to Romania and Alaska, and leads hiking groups in Europe's mountains. He lives in Cambridge, loves train travel in Europe and flies as rarely as possible.

Norm Longley Having spent most of his life writing Rough Guides to countries in eastern Europe and the Balkans, Norm has now turned his hand to the UK, having researched guides to Scotland, Ireland and Wales. He lives in Bath and can occasionally be seen erecting marquees on the Rec.

James Stewart (@itsjamesstewart) is a freelance journalist who has covered Wales for the *Sunday Times*, *Telegraph* and *Guardian* newspapers among others. He is the author of more than fifteen guidebooks, and has written about Wales in the *Rough Guide to Camping* and *The Best Places to Stay in Britain on a Budget*.

Acknowledgements

Tim Burford Thanks to Norm, James and all at Castell Rough Guides (especially for putting up with my technical incompetence). Also Freddie, Robbie and Katy, Jane Harris at Visit Wales, Emma Bowen at *Twr y Felin*, David Shiel at Loggerheads, Sarah Beynon at The Bug Farm and Gavin and Christopher at *Manorhaus*.

Norm Longley Thanks to Sam for her first-rate editing and inordinate patience (again), in the process of updating this book. Very special thanks to Jane Harris, whose assistance throughout has been nothing short of spectacular. Thanks are also due to Tom Watts in London; Jo Nugent in Abergavenny; Corum Champion and Hugh Murray in Porthcawl; Gareth Jones and Allison Cadoret at the Vale of Rheidol railway; my colleagues Tim and James; and Nick and Jo for the caravan in Aberdovey. Most importantly, thank you to Christian, Anna, Luka and Patrick.

Photo credits

All photos © Rough Guides, except the following:
(Key: t-top; c-centre; b-bottom; l-left; r-right)

1 Robert Harding Picture Library: Billy Stock
2 Robert Harding Picture Library: Billy Stock
7 Alamy Stock Photo: The Photolibrary Wales (t). **Getty Images:** Steve Coleman (b)
8 Corbis: Peter Lewis/LOOP IMAGES
9 Robert Harding Picture Library: Billy Stock
10 Getty Images: Redferns/C Brandon/Contributor
11 Alamy Stock Photo: James Osmond (b). **Getty Images:** AWL Images (t)
12 Alamy Stock Photo: Jon Arnold Images Ltd
13 123RF.com: chrisga (t). **AWL Images:** Gavin Hellier (b)
14 Alamy Stock Photo: The Red House Image Library (cr). **Surf Snowdonia:** (t)
15 Alamy Stock Photo: Nick Fell (t). **Corbis:** Aaron Black (b)
16 4Corners: Chris Warren (t). **SuperStock:** NaturePL (b)
17 Alamy Stock Photo: Stephen Saks Photography (tr). **Corbis:** Skyscan/Corbis (br). **Getty Images:** Travel Ink (tl)
18 Alamy Stock Photo: Jon Arnold Images Ltd (b)
19 Alamy Stock Photo: Chris Howes/Wild Places Photography (tr); Dorset Media Service (b); Mick Sharp (tl)
20 Alamy Stock Photo: Andrew Lloyd (cl); Christopher Nicholson (t). **Getty Images:** Photolibrary/Maremagnum (cr)
21 Robert Harding Picture Library: David Noton (t)

55 Alamy Stock Photo: Martin Wilcox
134–135 Alamy Stock Photo: CW Images
147 Alamy Stock Photo: pronature (b)
194–195 Corbis: David Cheshire/LOOP IMAGES
197 4Corners: Justin Foulkes
213 Alamy Stock Photo: Chris Howes/Wild Places Photography (b); The Photolibrary Wales (t)
231 Corbis: Colin McPherson (b). **Dreamstime .com:** David Pickles (t)
253 Getty Images: Gallo Images
269 Corbis: Chris Warren (b)
289 123RF.com: Valery Egorov (b). **Alamy Stock Photo:** Ian Dagnall (t)
302–303 Getty Images: Latitudestock
319 Corbis: Jim Richardson (b)
330–331 Alamy Stock Photo: Andy Teasdale
333 Corbis: John Warburton-Lee Photography
351 Ffestiniog & Welsh Highland Railways: (b)
367 Alamy Stock Photo: Dave Porter
386–387 SuperStock: age fotostock/Funkystock
389 iStockphoto.com: Nicholas E Jones
413 AWL Images: Alan Copson (b). **Corbis:** Peter Watson/LOOP IMAGES (t)
428 Getty Images: Francis Reiss/Picture Post

Cover: *Fishing boats at Llyn Nantlle* **Kris Williams**

Index

Maps are marked in grey

A

Abbeycwmhir 233
Aber Bach.....................................187
Aber Mawr 187
Aberaeron 263
Abercastle 186
Abercynon 111
Aberdare 112
Aberdaron................... 380–382
Aberdaugleddau 171
Aberdovey....................................287
Aberdulais 119
Aberdulais Tinworks 119
Aberdyfi 287
Abereiddi......................................186
Aberfan...111
Abergavenny 18, 215–219
Abervagenny 215
Abergavenny Food Festival ...218
Aberglaslyn Gorge 362
Aberglasney 21, 146
Abergwaun 187–189
Abergwesyn Pass.......................226
Abergynolwyn 290
Aberhonddu 204–209
Abermaw......................................296
Abersoch 379
Abertawe..................... 119–125
Aberteifi 255–258
Abertillery 106
Aberystwyth 271–276
Aberystwyth 272
accommodation................31–34
Act of Union 434
Afan Forest Park 117
Afon Tryweryn 323
alternative Wales 45
Amlwch 426
Angle..170
Anglesey..................... 414–427
Anglesey, The north coast and
.... 390
Antur Stiniog Bike Park 366
Arberth 155–157
Ardudwy 298–301
Arthur, King 93, 133, 144,
285, 326, 356, 383, 430
Arthur's Stone............................133

B

B&Bs 32
Bae Colwyn 395

Bae Trearddur.............................424
Bala.............................. 321–323
Bala Lake Railway 322
Bangor 409–412
Bangor 410
banks...49
Barafundle Bay..........................169
Barclodiad y Gawres.................422
Bardsey Island...........................382
Barmouth 296
Barri 96
Barry 96
Basingwerk Abbey 392
Bassey, Shirley............................453
bastide towns 405
Beacons Way 199
Beaumaris 415–418
Beaumaris 416
Beaumaris Castle 416
Beddarthur...................................193
Beddgelert 361–364
Bedwellty House.........................109
beer 36
Bersham Ironworks....................309
Betws-y-Coed 338–343
Betws-y-Coed 339
birdwatching...............................382
Biwmares 415–418
Black Mountain 201
Black Mountains 219–221
Black Point 417
Black Rock Sands.......................372
Blaenau Ffestiniog
.... 364–369
Blaenavon 18, 104–106
Blorenge 220
Bodelwyddan Castle 394
Bodnant Garden 409
books 459–462
Booth, Richard 221
Borth 280
Borth-y-Gest 369, 372
Bosherston Lily Ponds 169
Braich-y-Pwll 382
Brandy Cove 129
breakfast 35
Brechfa Forest............................145
Brecon.......................... 204–209
Brecon................................... 205
Brecon Beacons and Powys
.... 198
Brecon Beacons National Park
.... 21, 199–224
Brecon Beacons National Park
.... 200

Brecon Beacons National Park
Visitor Centre...........................201
Brecon Mountain Railway 209
Bridgend.......................................116
Britannia Bridge 419
Broad Haven (St Bride's Bay) ... 177
Broadhaven South 169
Bryn Celli Ddu.............................421
Bryngarw Country Park...........117
Bryntail lead mine 238
Builth Wells 227
Bullslaughter...............................170
bunkhouses 33
buses around Wales...................29
buses to Wales............................26
Butetown......................................109
Bwlch Nant yr Arian..................277
Bwlch Pen Barras.......................325
Bywyd Gwyllt Glaslyn Wildlife
....372

C

Cable Bay....................................422
Cadair Idris 13, 281, 291
Cadair Idris, Around 285
CADW 46
Caer y Twr...................................423
Caerdydd............................57–76
Caerfai Bay 182
Caerffili 107
Caerfyrddin................... 141–144
Caergybi.......................................422
Caeriw..157
Caerleon 92–94
Caernarfon 357–361
Caernarfon 358
Caernarfon Castle.....................357
Caerphilly 107
Caerphilly Castle 108
Caerwent 87
cafés 35
Caldey Island 162
Caldicot Castle 86
Cambrensis, Giraldus 376
Cambrian coast 254
camping...33
canoeing......................................211
Capel-y-ffin 221
Capel Bangor 277
Capel Curig 345
Capel Garmon Burial Chamber
....339

Capel Salem.....................299
car rental..............................31
caravanning......................33
CARDIFF.................16, 57–76
Cardiff.............................. 58
Cardiff Bay........................ 66
Cardiff and southeast Wales
....56
Central Cardiff................. 61
  accommodation..........................70
  airport...69
  Alexandra Gardens....................63
  arrival...69
  Bute Park....................................63
  Butetown....................................68
  Cardiff Bay.................................65
  Cardiff Bay Barrage...................67
  Cardiff Castle..............................62
  Cardiff International White Water
 67
  Cardiff Market............................60
  Cardiff Story...............................60
  Castle Arcade.............................60
  Cathays Park..............................63
  City Hall......................................63
  city transport.............................69
  Civic Centre................................63
  clubs...74
  Coal Exchange Building..............68
  comedy..74
  Craft in the Bay.........................68
  drinking......................................73
  eating..71
  farmers' markets.......................72
  High Street Arcade....................60
  history...57
  Llandaff Cathedral....................68
  Morgan Arcade...........................60
  Mount Stuart Square.................68
  music venues..............................74
  National Museum.......................64
  nightlife......................................74
  Norwegian Church.....................67
  Old Library..................................60
  Pierhead, the.............................66
  Pontcanna Fields.......................63
  Principality Stadium..................60
  Senedd, the................................67
  Sophia Gardens.........................63
  sport..76
  St David's Centre.......................60
  theatre..74
  Tiger Bay.....................................65
  tourist information.....................69
  tours..69
  Wales Millennium Centre..........65
  Welsh Institute of Sport............63
  Wetland Centre..........................67
Cardigan...................... 255–258
Cardigan 256
Cardigan Island Coastal
  Farm Park..................................257
Carew..................................157
Carmarthen................. 141–144
Carmarthen 142
Carn Ingli.........................190

Carn Llidi.............................184
Carn Menyn........................193
Carneddau mountains............347
Carreg Cennan Castle 15, 148
Carreg Coetan Arthur 190
Carreg Samson...................186
Carregwastad Point..............187
Cas-Gwent.....................78–80
Casnewydd-ar-Wysg 88–92
Castell-y-Bere...................290
Castell Coch 76
Castell Dinas Brân...............315
Castell Henllys....................192
Castell Newydd Emlyn............266
Castlemartin Ranges...............170
Caswell Bay........................129
cattle droving 446
Cefn Bryn............................132
Cefn Coed Colliery Museum..119
Cei Newydd................. 260–262
cellphones............................49
Celts..................................429
Cemaes................................425
Cenarth...............................265
Central Snowdonia 336
Centre for Alternative
  Technology 284
Ceredigion Coast Path............257
Chapel Bay Fort...................171
Charles, Thomas..................322
Chartists, the 90
cheese................................107
Chepstow 78–80
Chepstow 78
Chepstow Castle...................79
Cheriton.............................133
China Works Museum.............109
Chirk 310–312
Chirk Castle........................310
Church Bay.........................425
Cilgerran Castle............... 265
Civil War............................434
Claerwen reservoir................232
Cleddau Bridge 168
climate..................................47
Clwydian Range...................325
Clynnog Fawr.......................384
Clywedog Valley 308
Clywedog Valley 309
coal industry, in Wales............105
coasteering 43
Cob, the..................369, 372
Coed-y-Brenin....................293
Coed Llandegla....................327
Coity Castle........................117
Colby Woodland Garden 158
Colwyn Bay.........................395
Conwy 13, 403–409
Conwy 404
Conwy Castle......................404

Conwy Falls..........................340
Conwy Gorge........................342
Conwy Mountain...................406
Corn Du...............................204
Corris..................................284
Corris Railway......................285
Cors Caron..........................270
Cors Dyfi.............................281
Cors Fochno.........................279
Corwen................................320
costs.....................................46
Court Cupboard Craft Gallery
....217
Cowbridge 101
Craig-y-nos Castle 203
Craig Goch...........................233
Craig y Deryn.......................290
credit cards...........................49
Criccieth.............................376
Criccieth Castle....................376
Crickhowell 212–215
crime....................................46
Crucywel....................... 212–215
Crychan Forest.....................226
Culver Hole.........................130
currency...............................48
Cwm-yr-Eglwys....................191
Cwm Afan............................117
Cwm Gwaun.........................192
Cwm Idwal..........................347
Cwm Nantcol.......................299
Cwm Rheidol Reservoir.........277
Cwmcarn Forest...................107
Cwmtydu..............................262
Cwmyoy...............................220
Cwn Cau.............................291
cycling..................................42
Cydweli...............................141
Cymdeithas yr Iaith..............442
Cymer..................................117
Cymer Abbey.......................293
Cymraeg...............................464
Cynon Valley.......................109
Cytiau'r Gwyddelod................423

D

Dale....................................174
Dan-yr-ogof Showcaves...........203
Dee Valley 302–323
Dee Valley............................. 306
Dee Valley Way....................315
Deer Park, the.....................175
Denbigh...............................328
Denbigh Castle....................328
Devil's Bridge......................278
Devil's Quoit.......................170
Dewstow Gardens.................. 86

dialling codes................................49
Din Lligwy Hut Group.............426
Dinal Oleu...................................296
Dinbych-y-Pysgod 160–164
Dinbych.......................................328
Dinefwr Castle...........................148
Dinorwig Power Station.........352
Dinorwig Slate Quarries.........350
disabled travellers.....................50
Doc Penfro..................................167
Dolaucothi Gold Mines 150
Dolbadarn Castle.......................350
Dolforwyn Castle.......................243
Dolgellau...................... 293–296
Dolgellau........................... 293
Dolgoch..226
Dolgoch Falls..............................290
dolphin-watching......................261
Dolwyddelan Castle 366
Dr Beynon's Bug Farm..............183
Dre-fach Felindre......................266
drink...35
driving around Wales.................30
driving to Wales...........................26
druids...430
Druidston Haven 178
Dunraven Bay 99
Dyffryn Ardudwy Burial
   Chamber..................................298
Dyffryn Gardens...........................96
Dyfi Furnace...............................280
Dylan Thomas Boathouse 153
Dylife...239
Dysynni Valley.............. 290–292

E

eating...................................34–36
ecology..450
eisteddfodau..............38, 312, 452
Elan Valley...................................232
Electric Mountain 352
electricity......................................47
Eliseg's Pillar.............................316
Ellin's Tower Seabird Centre...423
emergencies.................................47
entry charges..............................46
entry requirements....................25
Epynt Way....................................226
Erddig Hall..................................309
events...38

F

fact file...6
Fairbourne...................................292
Fairbourne Railway...................292
Fairy Glen....................................339
Fall of the Fuller.......................202
Fall of Snow................................202
fat biking.....................................100
fauna...448
ferries to Wales............................27
Festival No. 6..............................373
festivals...38
Ffestiniog Railway 15, 370
Fforest Fawr................................202
film..457
Finch, Catrin...............................452
Fishguard 187–189
fishing...341
Flat Holm 95
flights to Wales............................25
Flimston......................................170
Foel Cwmcerwyn.......................193
Foel Fenlli...................................325
Foeldrygarn.................................193
folk music 451–453
food..................................... 34–36
football...44
forests...447
Freshwater West........................170

G

Garn Fawr.....................................187
Garreg Ddu reservoir 233
Garw Valley.................................117
gastropubs.....................................35
Gateholm Island........................175
Gelert's Grave.............................362
geocaching..................................294
geology...445
Gerald of Wales.........................376
Gerddi Penlan-Uchaf..............192
Gigrin Farm Nature Reserve...230
Gigrin Farm Red Kite Feeding
   Station 230
gin..36
Glasbury.......................................211
Glaslyn...239
Glyder Fach.................................347
Glyder Fawr................................348
Glyderau mountains.................347
Glyn Ceiriog................................310
Glyncorrwg Ponds.....................117
Glyndŵr, Owain............. 283, 433
Glyndŵr's Way............................235
Glyntawe......................................203
Golden Road, the.......................193
golf..100
Goodwick......................................187
gorge walking.............................317
Gospel Pass.................................221
Gower.....................13, 126–133

Gower 127
Grassholm....................................177
Great Orme..................................398
Great Orme........................ 398
Great Orme Country Park.......399
Great Orme Tramway...............399
Green Bridge of Wales 170
Greenfield Valley Heritage Park
  391
Greenfield Valley Museum 392
GreenWood Forest Park..........360
Gregynog Hall............................241
Grosmont Castle..........................85
Gruffydd ap Llywelyn..............432
Grwyne Fawr...............................219
guesthouses..................................32
Gwaun Valley..............................192
Gwbert..257
Gwely a Brecwast.......................32
Gwenffrwd-Dinas Nature
   Reserve....................................150
Gwili Railway..............................143
Gwydir Castle.............................343
Gŵyr............................. 126–133

H

Hafren Forest..............................238
Harlech 300
Harlech 300
Haverfordwest.............................172
Hay-on-Wye 21, 221–224
Hay-on-Wye........................ 222
Hay Bluff.....................................220
Hay Festival.................................223
health...47
Hell's Mouth 379
history................... 429–441
hitchhiking....................................31
Holy Island 422–424
Holyhead......................................422
Holyhead Mountain 423
Holywell...................... 390–393
horseriding 201, 210, 341
Horseshoe Falls (Brecon
   Beacons)..................................203
Horseshoe Falls (Llangollen) ... 316
hostels 33
hotels 32
Huntsman's Leap.......................170
Hwlffordd.....................................172

I

Idwal Cottage.............................347
Inigo Jones Slateworks............360

insurance 47
International Eisteddfod,
    Llangollen 312
internet 48
Iron Ring, the 16, 405
itineraries 22

J

Jones, Mary 322
Jones, Michael D. 322
Jones, Tom 453
Jubilee Tower 325

K

kayaking 44, 174, 181, 249,
    317, 345, 379, 415
Kidwelly 141
King Arthur 93, 133, 144, 285,
    326, 356, 383, 430
kiteboarding 43, 177
Knighton 235

L

Ladies of Llangollen 314
Lady Falls 203
Lake Vyrnwy 248
Lampeter 267
Lampeter 267
Lamphey 168
Landsker Borderlands 155
Langland Bay 128
language 463–467
"Last Invasion of Britain" 187
Laugharne 153–155
Laugharne 153
Lavernock Point 95
Lawrenny 157
LGBT Wales 48
lift-sharing 31
Little England Beyond Wales
    156
Little Haven 177
Llanandras 233
Llanarmon Dyffryn Ceiriog 310
Llanbadarn Fawr 274
Llanbadrig Church 425
Llanbedr (Brecon Beacons) 214
Llanbedr (Gwynedd) 298
Llanbedr Pont Steffan 267
Llanbedrog 378
Llanberis 349–355

Llanberis 349
Llanberis Lake Railway 350
Llanberis Pass 356
Llanberis Path 354
Llancaiach Fawr 111
Llanddeusant 201
Llanddwyn Island 421
Llandeilo 146
Llandovery 149–152
Llandrindod Wells 227–229
Llandrindod Wells 228
Llandudno 21, 396–403
Llandudno 397
Llandyfai 168
Llanegryn 290
Llanelli 139–141
Llanelli Wetland Centre 140
Llanerchaeron 264
Llanerch vineyard 98
Llanfair Caereinion 244
Llanfairpwll 419
Llanfairpwllgwyngyll
    gogerychwyrndrob
    wllllantysiliogogogoch 419
Llanfihangel-y-Pennant 291
Llanfihangel Crucorney 219
Llanfyllin 246
Llanfyllin Workhouse 246
Llangadwaladr church 422
Llangar 320
Llangedwyn 248
Llangefni 427
Llangelynin 291
Llangennith 132
Llangollen 312–318
Llangollen 313
Llangollen, Ladies of 314
Llangollen Canal 316
Llangollen History Trail 315
Llangollen International
    Eisteddfod 312
Llangollen Railway 314
Llangorse 210
Llangrannog 259
Llangynog 248
Llangynwyd 117
Llanidloes 237–239
Llanidloes 238
Llanmadoc 133
Llanrhaeadr-ym-Mochnant 247
Llanrhian 186
Llanrhidian 133
Llanrwst 343
Llansteffan 152
Llanthony 220
Llanthony Monastery 221
Llanthony Priory 220
Llantwit Major 98
Llanwnda 187
Llanwrtyd Wells 15, 224–226

Llanwyddyn 248
Llanymddyfri 149–152
Llanymynech 248
Llanystumdwy 376
Llechwedd Slate Caverns 365
Lloyd George, David 376,
    438, 442
Llugwy Valley 342
Llwynypia 116
Llyn Brianne 150
Llyn Celyn 321
Llyn Clywedog reservoir 238
Llyn Cwm Bychan 298
Llyn Efyrnwy 248
Llyn Idwal 348
Llyn Nantlle 363
Llyn Ogwen 347
Llŷn peninsula 18, 375–385
Llŷn, Snowdonia and the
    334
Llyn Tegid 321
Llynfi Valley 117
Llywelyn ap Gruffydd
    ("the Last") 433
Loggerheads Country Park 324
long-distance paths 41
Lower Gushing Falls 203
Lower White Meadow Fall 202

M

Machynlleth 282–287
Machynlleth 282
Madocks, William Alexander
    369
Maen Achwyfaen 392
Maen Llia 202
Maenorbŷr 164
Maesteg 117
magazines 37
Magic of Life Butterfly House
    277
mail 49
male voice choirs 18, 116
Manic Street Preachers 453
Manorbier 164
maps 48
Marble Church 394
Margam 118
Mari Llwyd 117
Marine Walk 406
Marloes 175
Marloes Sands 175
Martin's Haven 175
Matthews, Cerys 455
Mawddach estuary 292
Mawddach Trail 15, 294
media 36

Melin Llynnon.............................425
Menai Bridge.............................418
Menai Strait 419
Menai Suspension Bridge 316
Merlin..144
Merrion.......................................170
Merthyr Tydfil................ 112–114
Mewslade Bay...........................131
Milford Haven 171
Mill Bay......................................174
mine exploring........ 286, 341
Minera Lead Mines 309
miners' strike.............................440
Miners' Track.............................354
Minffordd Path 291
mobile phones 49
Mochras.....................................298
Moel Famau.................................325
Moel Hebog................................362
Moel Siabod 345
Moelfre.......................................426
Mold..324
money...48
money-changing........................49
Monmouth.....................82–84
Montgomery 242–244
Montgomeryshire........ 236–249
moorland.....................................447
Morfa Bychan.............................372
Morfa Dyffryn nature reserve
....298
Morfa Nefyn 383
Morgan, William.........................394
mountain biking........21, 42, 278,
286, 293, 327, 340, 352, 366
Moylegrove.................................191
Mumbles.......................................126
music.......................10, 451–456
Musselwick Sands 175
Mwmbwls.....................................126
Mwnt...259
Mynach Falls...............................279
Mynydd Ddu 201
Mynydd Epynt 226
Mynydd Mawr.............................382
Mynydd Moel..............................291
Mynydd Preseli............. 189–193
Mynydd Twr................................423
Mynydd y Gelli...........................116
Myrddin.......................................144

N

Nant Ffrancon..............................347
Nant Gwrtheyrn.........................384
Nant Mill.....................................309
Nantgarw....................................109
Nantlle Valley 363

Narberth...................... 155–157
National Assembly 440, 444
National Botanic Garden 145
National Library of Wales.........273
National Portrait Gallery 394
National Slate Museum.............350
National Trust............................46
National White Water Centre
....323
National Wool Museum............266
nationalism, Welsh
.... 442–444
natural history............. 445–450
Nefyn..383
Nevern 191
New Quay 260–262
New Quay 260
New Quay Honey Farm 261
New Radnor.................................235
New Tregedar..............................108
Newborough...............................421
Newborough Warren 421
Newcastle Emlyn 266
Newgale......................................178
Newport (Monmouthshire)
....................................88–92
Newport (Monmouthshire)
.... 89
Newport (Pembrokeshire)
.... 189–191
newspapers 36
Newton House...........................148
Newtown 240–242
Niwbwrch.....................................421
Nolton Haven.............................178
Nonconformism.........................434
Normans 432
North Berwyn Way.....................315
north coast and Anglesey, The
.... 390
Nyfer estuary..............................190

O

Offa's Dyke 237
Ogwen Falls................................348
Ogwen Valley 347
Ogwr Valley................................116
Old Beaupre Castle 102
Old Radnor.................................235
opening hours............................49
Ordnance Survey......................48
Oriel Plas Glyn-y-Weddw........378
Oriel Ynys Môn 427
Osprey Project...........................281
outdoor activities 39–45
Owen, Daniel.............................324
Owen, Robert.............................240

Oxwich 129
Oystermouth Castle..................126

P

Padarn Country Park 350
Palmerston, Lord.......................164
Parc Glynllifon...........................360
Parc le Breos 129
parking 30
Parkmill 129
Parrog 190
Partrishow 219
Parys Mountain 426
Paviland Cave.............................131
pay and display parking 30
Pembroke 165
Pembroke Castle.......................166
Pembroke Dock..........................167
Pembrokeshire Coast Path...... 16,
159
Pembrokeshire National Park
....159
Pen Caer....................................186
Pen y Fan 204
Pen-y-Garreg.............................233
Pen-y-Pass 356
Penarth..95
Penarth Fawr 377
Penbryn......................................259
Penderyn Welsh Whisky
Distillery..................................203
Penfro 165
Penmachno 340
Penmon Priory...........................417
Pennant Melangell....................248
Pennard Castle 129
Penrhyn Castle..........................411
Pentre Ifan.................................192
Pentwyn reservoir 209
Penygadair 291
pharmacies 47
phones 49
Picton Castle..............................173
Pig Track.....................................354
Pilleth 230
Pistyll 383
Pistyll Rhaeadr...........................247
Plaid Cymru 438, 442–444
Plâs Brodanw 374
Plas Mawr 406
Plas Newydd (Anglesey) 420
Plas Newydd (Llangollen).......314
Plas Tan y Bwlch.......................368
Plas y Brenin mountain centre
....345
Plas yn Rhiw 381
Plynlimon...................................238

police 46
Pont-y-Pair Falls 338
Pontarfynach 278
Pontcysyllte Aqueduct 317
Pontfaen 192
Pontneddfechan 202
Pontrhydyfen 118
Pontrhydygroes 279
Pontsticill reservoir 209
Pontypool and Blaenavon
   Railway 105
Pontypridd 110
Pony Path 294
pony trekking 44
pop music 453–456
Port Eynon 130
Port Talbot 118
Porth 116
Porth-yr-ogof 202
Porth Ceiriad 379
Porth Clais 184
Porth Neigwl 379
Porth Oer 382
Porth Swtan 425
Porth Trecastell 422
Porth y Swnt 380
Porthaethwy 418
Porthcawl 100
Porthdinllaen 383
Porthgain 186
Porthmadog 369–373
Porthmadog 370
Porthmelgan 184
Portmeirion 16, 373–375
post 49
Powis Castle 244
Powys, Brecon Beacons and
   198
Precipice Walk 294
prehistoric Wales 8
Preseli mountains 189–193
Presteigne 233
Principality Stadium 21, 60
Prisoner, The 373
public holidays 49
pubs 35
Puffin Island 417
Pumlumon Fawr 238
Punch Bowl, the 278
Pwllcochran 187
Pwlldu Bay 129
Pwllgwaelod 191
Pwllheli 378

Q

Quarry Hospital 352

R

radio 37
Radnor Forest 235
rafting 44, 67, 317, 323
Raglan Castle 88
rainfall 47
Ramsey Island 184
Range East 170
Rebecca Riots 230
red kites 449
Red Wharf Bay 427
restaurants 35
retreats 45
Reynoldston 132
Rhaeder Gwy 230
Rhaeadr Ogwen 348
Rhayader 230
Rheidol Cycle Trail 277
Rhinog Fach 299
Rhinog Fawr 299
Rhinogs 299
Rhondda Fach 116
Rhondda Fawr 116
Rhondda Heritage Park 114
Rhondda Valley 114–116
Rhos-on-Sea 395
Rhoscolyn 424
Rhosili 131
Rhosneigr 422
Rhossili 131
Rhuddlan Castle 393
Rhuthun 326–328
Rhyd-y-Benwch 238
Rhyd Ddu Track 355
Rhyl 392
Rhymney Valley 108
Rhys, Gruff 456
rock climbing 41, 181, 317,
   345, 352, 356
Romans in Wales 430
Rosebush 193
Rowen 408
Royal Mint Experience, the ... 101
Royal Welsh Show 227
RSPB Conwy 407
rugby 21, 44
Rug Chapel 320
running trails 294
Ruthin 326–328

S

S4C 443
sailing 379
St Ann's Head 174
St Asaph 393–395

St Bride's Bay 174–185
St Bride's Haven 175
St Davids 179–182
St Davids 179
St Davids Cathedral 15, 179
St Davids Head 184
St Davids peninsula 182–185
St Davids peninsula 183
St Fagans Castle 77
St Fagans National History
   Museum 77
St Florence 165
St Govan's chapel 169
St Justinian's 184
St Lythan Long Cairn 96
St Non's Bay 184
St Winefride's Well 390, 392
Saundersfoot 158
Scolton Manor 172
scrambling 41, 347, 352
Segontium Roman Fort 359
self-catering 34
Senghenydd 109
Sesiwn Fawr 295
Sgwd Clun-Gwyn 202
Sgwd Ddwli Isaf 203
Sgwd Ddwli Uchaf 203
Sgwd Gwladus 203
Sgwd Isaf Clun-Gwyn 202
Sgwd y Bedol 203
Sgwd y Pannwr 202
Sgwd yr Eira 202
Shell Island 298
shopping 50
Silver Mountain Experience ... 278
Sirhowy Valley 108
Skenfrith Castle 85
Skirrid 220
Skokholm 176
Skomer 176
slate industry 365
Snowdon 16, 355–357
Snowdon Horseshoe 354
Snowdon Mountain Railway
   349
Snowdon Ranger Path 355
Snowdon Sherpa buses 337
Snowdonia 332–375
Snowdonia and the Llŷn
   334
Snowdonia, Central 336
Snowdonia National Park 335
Soar-y-Mynydd 227
soccer 44
Solva 178
South Stack 423
southeast Wales, Cardiff and ...
   56
Southgate 129
Southwest Wales 138

sport..39–45
Stackpole Head............................169
Stackpole Quay...........................169
stand-up paddleboarding........43
Statute of Rhuddlan.................433
steam railways..............................30
Strata Florida Abbey................270
Strumble Head.............................186
student cards................................46
studying in Wales.........................50
Sugar Loaf....................................220
Super Furry Animals..................455
Surf Snowdonia..................15, 409
surfing 43, 100, 130, 170,
181, 379, 409
Swallow Falls...............................340
SWANSEA 119–125
Swansea.................................. 120
accommodation...............................124
arrival..123
Brangwyn Hall....................................123
Castle Square......................................121
Cwmdonkin Park..............................123
departure...123
drinking...124
Dylan Thomas' birthplace............123
Dylan Thomas Centre....................122
Dylan Thomas Theatre...................125
eating...124
Egypt Centre.......................................123
entertainment....................................125
festivals...125
getting around...................................124
Glynn Vivian Art Gallery...............121
Guildhall..123
history..121
Maritime Quarter..............................122
market...121
National Waterfront Museum
....122
nightlife...125
Swansea Indoor Market................121
Swansea Museum.............................122
Taliesin Arts Centre.........................125
University..123
swimming 43
Sycarth..248
Sygun Copper Mine..................362

T

Table Mountain............................212
Taff Trail...206
Taff Valley......................................109
Talacharn....................... 153–155
Talgarth...211
Talley..150
Talybont-on-Usk.........................209
Talybont reservoir......................209
Talyllyn Railway...........................288
Talyllyn Valley............... 288–290
tearooms...35

Teifi Marshes Nature Reserve
....256
Teifi Pools.....................................232
Teifi Valley 264–270
Teifi Valley Railway....................266
television...37
Telford, Thomas..........................316
temperature...................................47
Tenby 160–164
Tenby 161
Thomas, Dylan........119, 122, 123,
153, 154, 261
Thomas, R. S. 381
Thorn Island.................................171
Three Castles.................................84
Three Chimneys..........................175
Three Cliffs Bay...........................129
Three Peaks Yacht Race...........297
Thurba Head.................................131
time..50
Tinkinswood Long Cairn............96
Tintern...81
Tintern Abbey................................81
tipping...50
Tongwynlais...................................76
Tonypandy....................................116
Torrent Walk.................................294
tour operators...............................27
tourist offices................................50
Traeth Coch.................................427
Traeth Llanbedrog.....................379
Traethmawr...................................190
trains around Wales.....................28
trains to Wales..............................26
transport 27–31
travel agents...................................27
travel costs.....................................46
travellers with disabilities.........50
Tre'r Ceiri.......................................384
Trearddur Bay..............................424
Tredegar..109
Tredegar House.............................91
Tref-y-clawdd................................235
Trefaldwyn 242–244
Treffynnon.....................................390
Trefriw..344
Tregaron...268
Trehafod..114
Tremadog.......................................371
Treorchy...116
Tresaith...259
Tretower...212
Tryfan.....................................16, 346
Tryweryn River.............................323
Tunnicliffe, Charles....................427
Twll Du..348
Tŷ Hyll...340
Tŷ Mawr Wybrnant.....................340
Tyddewi 179–182
Tyn-y-ddôl.....................................291

Tywi Valley 144–152
Tywyn..288

U

Upper Gushing Falls.................203
Usk...87
Usk Valley 209–215

V

Vale of Clwyd............... 323–329
Vale of Edeyrnion......................320
Vale of Ewyas...............................219
Vale of Ffestiniog.......................368
Vale of Glamorgan.........94–102
Vale of Neath...............................119
Vale of Rheidol 276–279
Vale of Rheidol Railway...........276
Vale of Ystwyth...........................279
Valle Crucis Abbey.....................316
Valleys, the.............18, 102–119
Valleys, the 103
visas..25
Visit Wales......................................50
Vortigern's Valley.......................384

W

Wales..5
Wales Coast Path.............80, 257
walking...40
Water-Break-Its-Neck Waterfall
....235
Watkin Path..................................355
weather..47
Welsh Highland Heritage
Railway.....................................371
Welsh Highland Railway........360,
363, 371
Welsh language 463–467
Welsh Language and Heritage
Centre..384
Welsh Language Society........442
Welsh Wildlife Centre..............257
Welshpool 244–246
Welshpool 245
Welshpool and Llanfair Railway
....244
Weobley Castle............................133
West Dale Bay..............................174
Whimble, the................................235
whiskey...36
Whistling Sands..........................382

White Castle 85
White Meadow Fall 202
Whitesands Bay 184
Widg 187
wi-fi 48
Williams-Ellis, Clough 373
Wilson, Richard 324
windsurfing 43, 174, 422
wine 36
World's End 309
Worms Head 131
Wrecsam 306–310
Wrexham 306–310
Wrexham 308
Wye Valley 18, 77–86
Wye Valley Walk 80
Wylfa Nuclear Power Station
.... 425

Y

Y Bala 321–323
Y Bont Faen 101
Y Drenewydd 240–242
Y Fenni 215–219
Y Gelli 221–224
Y Rhyl 392
Y Trallwng 244–246
Y Waun 310–312
Ynys-hir Nature Reserve 281
Ynys Enlli 382
Ynyslas Nature Reserve 280
Ynys Lawd 423
Ynys Meicel 187
Ynys Môn 414–427
Ynys Pyr 162
Ynys y Barri 96

youth cards 46
youth hostels 33
Yr Eifl 384
Yr Wyddfa 355
Yr Wyddgrug 324
Ysgyryd Fawr 220
Ystradfellte 202
Ystwyth Trail 277

Z

zip wires 18
ZipWorld Bounce Below 366
ZipWorld Caverns 366
ZipWorld Titan 366
ZipWorld Velocity 348

Map symbols

The symbols below are used on maps throughout the book

▬▬ - -	International boundary	★	Bus stop		Whisky distillery	⌒	Arch
▬ ▬ ▬	Chapter boundary	✈	International airport	🐘	Zoo	⌁	Mountains
	Motorway	✚	Hospital		Golf course	⌣	Swamp
	Major road	🅿	Parking		Swimming pool		Abbey
	Minor road	⛫	Fortress		Bridge	⬭	Stadium
	Pedestrian road	♦	Point of interest	▲	Mountain peak	‡	Church (regional)
▭▭▭▭	Steps	∴	Ruins		Viewpoint		Building
▬ ▬ ▬	Footpath	🏛	Stately home	↑	Wind farm		Market
▬▬▬	Railway	�	Castle		Country park		Church
▬▬▬	Tourist railway	♥	Museum		Waterfall		Christian cemetery
▬ ▬	Ferry route	⚘	Gardens		Cave		Park
▬▬▬	Wall	@	Internet access	☒	Gate		Beach
●- - -●	Cable car	ⓘ	Information centre	≈	Pass		Pedestrianized area
	Gorge	✉	Post office		Surf beach		
▥	Archeological site		Nature reserve		Birdwatching		

Listings key

■ Accommodation

● Eating

■ Drinking/nightlife

● Shopping